File: Downtown New Paltz, NY

FROZEN

TIME

A Novel By:

Journalist Correspondent

GARY L. KONIZ

For Tony, Jenny, Henry, and Waldo

A Revealing Insight Into The Enduring Works
Of World Class Novelist Anthony Robinson
And Other Matters Of The Heart
As Life Proceeds Upon Us
In Its Solemn Procession of Days

"Trial By Trial"

Fond Memories

WITH MY LOVE

Photos of New Paltz, NY, The Shawangunk, and Others, are
Courtesy of Internet Public Domain ... Photos of The Author and
Wife Kathleen were taken by Jennifer Stetler - Sears Photo Studio

Frozen Time
by Gary L. Koniz
Copyright © September 5, 2011
ISBN 978-1-105-36456-3
Labor Day Edition – The Final Order
All Rights Reserved

Published by Createspace, Inc.
by arrangement with the author Gary Koniz

ISBN-13: 978-1722840754
ISBN-10: 1722840757

Createspace Publishing
4900 Lacross Road
North Charleston, SC 29496

Photo of Tony as a young man with Robert Frost
Bread Loaf Writers' Conference, 1960

ROAD LESS TRAVELED

Two roads diverged in a yellow wood
And sorry I could not travel both
And be one traveler, long I stood
And looked down one as far as I could
To where it bent in the undergrowth

Then took the other as just as fair
And having perhaps the better claim
Because it was grassy and wanted wear
Though as for that, the passing there
Had worn them really about the same

And both that morning equally lay
In leaves no step had trodden black
Oh, I kept the first for another day!
Yet, knowing how way leads onto way
I doubted if I should ever come back

I shall be telling this with a sigh
Somewhere ages and ages hence
Two roads diverged in a wood
And I took the one less traveled by
And that has made all the difference

Robert Lee Frost
(March 26, 1874 – January 29, 1963)

Published in 1916 in the collection *Mountain Interval*
as, "The Road Not Taken"

Come In

As I came to the edge of the woods,
Thrush music–hark!
Now if it was dusk outside,
Inside it was dark.

Too dark in the woods for a bird
By sleight of wing
To better its perch for the night,
Though it still could sing.

The last of the light of the sun
That had died in the west
Still lived for one song more
In a thrush's breast.

Far in the pillared dark
Thrush music went–
Almost like a call to come in
To the dark and lament.
But no, I was out for stars;
I would not come in.
I meant not even if asked;
And I hadn't been.

Robert Frost

The Darkling Thrush

By English Poet Thomas Hardy 1840–1928

I leant upon a coppice gate
When Frost was spectre-grey,
And Winter's dregs made desolate
The weakening eye of day.
The tangled bine-stems scored the sky
Like strings of broken lyres,
And all mankind that haunted nigh
Had sought their household fires.

The land's sharp features seemed to be
The Century's corpse outleant,
His crypt the cloudy canopy,
The wind his death-lament.
The ancient pulse of germ and birth
Was shrunken hard and dry,
And every spirit upon earth
Seemed fervourless as I.

At once a voice arose among
The bleak twigs overhead
In a full-hearted evensong
Of joy illimited;
An aged thrush, frail, gaunt, and small,
In blast-beruffled plume,
Had chosen thus to fling his soul
Upon the growing gloom.

So little cause for carolings
Of such ecstatic sound
Was written on terrestrial things
Afar or nigh around,
That I could think there trembled through
His happy good-night air
Some blessed Hope, whereof he knew
And I was unaware.

Albert Einstein saw no distinction
between science and religiousness.

Albert Einstein saw no distinction between science and
religiousness. It was all encapsulated in one sublime vision.
"The most beautiful thing we can experience," he tells us, "is the
mysterious." In Einstein's view, the religious feeling of the
scientist "takes the form of a rapturous amazement at the harmony
of natural law, which reveals an intelligence of such superiority
that, compared with it, all the systematic thinking and acting of
human beings is an utterly insignificant reflection."

THE FINAL ORDER

I dream of a different social order for the world,

other than "Dog Eat Dog," as the saying goes.

Something kindly and obvious of its intent, to

achieve dignity to the Toil of Humanity in their

efforts to survive. And survive they must, each

and everyone, for it is the nature of things.

Let us therefore, begin a new era together

then of that regard, and forthrightly create

a just and humane society, In Name To God,

that may emulate the Ideals of Paradise.

YHWH

Iron Bridge Over The Wallkill River At New Paltz
Heading West Toward The Mountain

The Shawangunks

Mohonk Tower

"Sky Top"

Women Who Are Used To Using Hard Drugs
Never Do Make Good Wives

And always to say about the past, that it all, and all of it
together, exists in the mind and occurs to be remembered at the
same time simultaneously of its influences to reflect on, every
part of it that has already happened. But as to why that any
particular episode of the past may appear, or arise, to surface from
the realm of one's subconscious at any particular time, is
anyone's guess, that all of sudden happens to surface to be made
aware of themselves and inevitably to judgments over.

Which is always different then to observe and to judge the past
in a totally objective way from the vantage point in perspective of
the present a long time into the future, of the events and
impressions of things that happened a then a long time ago, that
still exist and linger on in the mind for good or bad as memory.
In that, such memories and their recollections, as feelings and
attitudes that imbue the mind, are always clouded over from the
subjective perceptions of the present awareness through the
passage of time and with advanced impressions and attitudes and
judgments of life that have been aborbed and assimilated through
the passage of time into one's stream of consciousness to exist as
all one thing, as instinct, in the continuum of time to the present.

These perceptions of the past then in one possitive sense
become more intelligently perceived in their analysis and less
emotionally troubling with oneself about, less contentious as to
say, of the negative aspects of it, to be thought of creatively with
fresh new eyes of appraisal in the self-judgments we make upon
ourselves, or to perhaps in the negative way become completely
the opposite of effect of the influence of the future time upon the
past in the nature of truama in the mind's total absorption and
complete abandonment to emotional distress. And of what it the
nature of the paradox of Heaven and Hell to be wrought on Man's
Self, and of what is the Nature of God to conceive.

So that, past events, as individually and uniquely experienced,
are always viewed and judged from among the vast entanglements

of insights and judgmental impressions of everything else in the grand total of one's life, and combined over with the pressures of the super-ego of humanity's common history, in experience; which are never viewed with the same eye as when they first occurred, but which are looked back upon with serious hindsight, to influence the present and to create the future from, of the hindsight of the past upon life being carried-on into the present.

And with some memories to become less painful to think-on, and with others even to seem irrelevant with time, and perhaps some to become more poingant of their experience for their importance of knowledge gained or for the elation of their nostalgia; of the thoughts and feelings one has about the distant things of time that have been mined over and gleaned through.

And indeed with some thoughts in painful memories of events to occur, to be traumatized over them, and as the mind dredges them around in its eddies as a preoccupation in its facination with self-torture, to recall and relive horrible and horrifying events of the past over and over again through the years to be burned by their morbid and repetive self-torture into the everlasting consciousness, as memory repeatedly remembered compounds itself and becomes the dominant and total theme of one's life's expression, and to become an indelible neurosis left on a besieged memory of conscioiusness to be forced to endure.

But with most memories, of their impressions, are to be felt of well thought-out subjective analyses of the events to be reflected on with the words, "I wish I knew then what I know now;" and for what memories of God that the Angels Of Heaven always make excuses for one's behavior over, to ease the course and the destiny of anyone's burden of guilt over, of what and how that we now look over and view the past by in different ways of intent and meaning.

But mostly it is with thoughts, to be "thought out" and exhausted, for good or bad, in somewhat of a detached way, now over and done with, that cannot ever be done over, and that can never be changed, and that cannot ever be over and done with completely as far as memory is concerned, intelligently perceived, to be completely forgotten, to relive with delight, or to torment one's self to death with, in the meanng of madness and to suicide, about them. To what that we can kill the body over, but not the Soul about.

The Soul will survive, to be doomed to conscious thought without the ability of action, to act in any way to correct its misdeeds and who therefore in its attempts to justify and to sooth its condition of self-torment, sets about upon the Earth in madness condemned in its anguish to torment the living for the motive of jealousy of their goodly nature and to create companionships of evil by the temptations they present, to do the evil as they did. And to what then is the nature of the Devil and of Hell.

And so it is, to what end et al in fate, for good or for bad in the real nuture of the memories we gather and collect, and all too Frozen In Time in our collective memories about, of what we do, or don't do, that we all die alone with, the memories of our lives, as that is what life becomes in the long and the short of it.

We live our lives looking-out from the inside, as Plato said, like being in a dark cave, peering out throught the windows of our eyes from a mind encased in a Bonehouse of Flesh and Blood that holds our entire nature, of individual mental, and emotional, reasoning, and fantasy, and our memories of events, as was made for us to be that way by The Creator of All Things, Who made Us All to be in His Image and Likeness, to be Human, and just another Humanto be thought about in that way, to exist in the relentless Ant Hills of Life, indiscernable from all the rest of all the other Ants, except as differenct species, but individually indiscernable when looking down upon the whole of it; called Humanity, whom we all are and individually, and insignificant in that way in the sense of each one's being individually Created of The Creation that is all comprised of The Heavenly Father's Aspect of Being aspired to as Personae of Being, Of The Diety.

And As The Diety Itself, and being The Diety Itself, Whom we are either doomed, or embraced, as it is, to live with The Diety in a constant thought stream To Itself, and to Abide With Him, Who we have no choice in being, and Who is forever to remain unnamed and personally undefined; as to being a Person, Place, or Thing, but of Whom we like to speak fondly of and reverently of as The Father Almighty in Heaven, for the gesture of obeisance or sympathy, to be kind towards, Who We Are Also to be an everlasting and an integral part of, referred to in the Man Sense of the Ego Setting of the Impersonal Creation, which we have all inherited from the Nothingness of Timeless and Space, To Exist, and never knowing how or why, pivoting on a point of deep mystery that even The Creator Divine Himself does not know.

And importantly to comprehend that we are The Diety too, abiding to be a part of individually, to have nothing to do with Its Creation of us, spoken of impersonally, of The Creation that was made for us to live in, but not personally created for, expressed in that way, and like God, Who did not create Himself, but Who discovered Himself to exist, alone in the vast and timeless darkness of the eternal night, To Have To Make The Best Of.

And so it is, to be hovering on that great point in manifestor, as that we too, and all alone, do discover at some point in time, in a Great Awakening Of The Spirit, like The Creator, that we do exist, and perplexed by it all, to live out our lives and to die alone.

And from such portals of our eyes, from out of the depths of the inner sanctum of our Bonehouse, to look out upon the world, alone; alone with our thoughts, and alone with God Who is always there, and with no one else there with us … except or perhaps to have a clutter of tormenting or helpful Spirits and Angels for good or bad abiding with us, to confound the idea of being alone and of who we are, God or Man, depending on one's particular predilection to entertain such Spirits in the mind's indulging social awareness to be bothered with such nonsense. To be describe as "The Inner Dialogue," or Talking With Oneself.

And to say that we do not know the mind at all, or that some of us do. And as well to add, that we all have secrets to keep, some personal, and some involving others, not to tell, or maybe to tell, depending on how we feel about the secret on any particular day and the need for us to tell it for a particular reason, to regret later about there telling, or maybe not, to feel relief from, like having the catharsis of a private confessional or a public confession. And what does it all matter then anyway … about such secrets, if only to die alone with them.

****

So to what idea, of purging some disturbing secrets and for the thought of sharing the important knowledge of other profounder ones, that I have been harboring the notion these many years now culminating in decades about, to set down of what constitutes the memories of my life upon the earth, my life, in those terms of personal interest, to share with humanity.

To what starting point in revealing that I had a thought the other day, a memory, that emerged intact from the dark recess of a forgotten record repressed, that I viewed differently from the origin of being lived as if I were looking at the past, in the present, as all one thing and as if it were being re-lived again in the present, as a real feeling to experience, like a companion spirit that emerged as a fantasy imagination of the mind and real almost to the sight and touch and awareness of the mind, almost, like being inside of a dream that I had awakened in, and thereby existed in, and knowing it to be a dream, intact, to re-live the memory of the past, as if I were viewing it as an iceberg that had been in a suspended animation and the great part of it submerged in the subconscious as a citadel of Frozen Time.

That becond me further into its analysis transfixed for the longest period of the forgotten things; important things of knowledge, repressed things, things abandoned, things longed for, things never to be again, and things sought after and clung to to be relived, to be redeemed, and so importantly, to be redeemable, to be able to live with oneself again about them, those memories, floating along in the eternal infindubulum of past, present, and future time, in the vast and eternal time in the Eternal Now that it always upon us and not measured out in days and nights but moment to moment from the infinite beginning of time to its indefinite conclusion, that the moment is always passing through, in that feeling of it, without beginning, and without end in sight.

And so you see that you cannot die in your mind's eye, to yourself be true, for eternity cannot endure a flaw. That the memory would always be a part of me of, in such an eternity of thought to dwell in , and to dwell upon, and to be with God, The Creator, in that vast and total condition of time.

And that I viewed with a curiosity as if in a detachement from a distance, like an iceberg in its grandiose state of solitude, as a container of many things of the time past, time present, and time eternal, adrift in a real and unseen sea, of frozen things, tortured with grating in straining unresolution against each other, of ice caked shrieking minds, encased in their own isolations of memory, as the only existent thing unto themselves, isolated in their lonely solitude of life unable to be whole without the embrace and the presence of The Creator to hold to, and to the real embrace and companionship of a mate or a friend to be with in the eternity of time as it is ongoing; and for the companionship and society of other human beings in the fellowship of belief in the Eternal Now that governs over the judgment of things and guides our actions for us not to be frivolous with the life we have about, which we are being driven to endure and forced to live out, frozen in our individual and lonely solitude until we melt, with its memories of lost loves, and the lost opportunites, and the disappointments of life, and with the reassurances of life's successes and the great knowledge of life's valuable experiences, and the valuing of all of that up to what happiness we can glean from it all until we melt into the heart of it and disolve bit by bit and disappear back into the Great Eternal Being Of The Creator from whence we came, and God a mystery to Himself, Herself, Itself, as well, Who did not Create Himself, but only to become aware of His tormented existence in isolated and eternal solitude to contemplate the condition of His Own Creation, to be conscious and alone in the infinite darkness with Himself.

Can you imagine?

And also, as we are individually and together that way, a great mystery to our own selves, not knowing from where or how that we came to be in existence, and only knowing that we are, to be forgotten, to flow along in the murky suspense of the cold and impersonal slate gray eddies in the waters of The Creator Mind Substance and all embracing that we come to fathom the solemn doom of a certain conclusion, that no life is really significant, and

is really in the end and all along, and all at the same time, all only
One and the Same Thing all along, being God, The Creator,
Ourselves with it, being Man and Woman and the Inanimate and
The Creator God Ourselves, of All Things Great and Small, in All
His and Hers and Its Great and Magnificent Many Manifestations
to experience what goes on in the nature of life, and always within
the confines of a tortured juxtapostions to itself, in its battles
waged for good and evil, pleasure and pain, joy and suffering,
comfort and hardship, rest and toil, and all else of the duality of
life of what about life is that life is all about in the absolute
meaning of, and meaning, that It Cannot Be Denied of what it is,
The Life that The Creator God Created of His Own Imagining, To
Be, that we are prisoners to in real life, the life that we were each
born to experience with absolutely No Choice In The Matter, the
greater concern, and the same as God is the prisoner of His Own
Awareness, with no way to escape its unending destiny unfolding
in the eternal moment of decisions to make the best of, or not, and
for any mistakes that The Creator Made, or Makes, to make the
best of, as The Creator Self is forced to endure in eternity, as well
is not His Way for it, that we ourselves find ourselves to be
crippled by also. This is the end of that sermon and the beginning
of our story together about life as we find it to discover, and only
later on, and after many seeming mistakes, to discover how to do
it right.

✳✳✳✳✳✳✳✳✳✳✳

And so it happened one day, that and on such a particular
occasion of the memory in me that happened in a moment of The
Eternal Now, as the memory of it occurred to arise in my thought,
that began in the pre-dawn darkness on the cold gray morning of
a forlorn and dismal overcast day in the early Spring in the later
part of the month of March in 1978, in the Northern latitude of the
Hudson Valley Region of New York State and after a solid week
of the heavy Spring rains had been falling daily.
    That it was on such a melancolly day, as the memory of it lives
in me to be told, that I found the nature of my internal conviction

to survive. And who can decribe such a mood of such a melancolliness from where it arises and why; or why too that certain memories choose a certain time to arise from the depths of the subconscious and while others may remain dormant in the forgotten silence of memory; as who can fathom why that the memory of something becomes conscious of itself again with a muted gasp and a pang that catches in the heart, and sometimes with a muffled cry of desperation in the attempt to supress it, of what occurred of the past, attempting to surpress itself from beinb remembered, to be called to the conscious fore by God perahps, of the memory system with no way to escape from it in the stream of time to be remembered and to be wholly grasped as being real again, to be conjured in the fantasy of remembrance as come to life again to be thought of and experienced, and by a certain understanding of its predetermined fate, in the meaning that there is no way that we can escape the recorded memory of the life we live, to be haunted by.

Of which day that occurred to be recalled then, as I will tell you of, tha I will remember forever and for the remainder of my days upon the Earth assuredly, as a turning point, and always as a source of inspiration to look back upon through-out the days, of my life, and although painfully felt with a wince as every occasion of its recorded memory in me.

As I found myself marking time by that day of reckoning, in my passage through each of the day's of my life, of its successes, and of its failures, to hing upon, and of its failures to guide myself upwards into heaven by particularly; that I would never have had the opportunity to do if that particular day in my life had turned out differently. But I especially mark the happy things of life, by that day, that it was, that day, the turning point to; which, if the event of that particular day had turned out the other way on that day, that those happy things to me were never to have happened, if the thoughts of ending the life I had that I had entertained on that day were to have convinced me to their final course in my destiny, of the things that never were to have been, to find myself awakening to that day in the upstairs back room of Tony's house, the old parsonage house on Historic Huguenot Street in the

Village of New Paltz, NY, in the room that he always referred to as, "Mary's Room," and as so called by Tony as the room where Mary had killed herself with a shotgun in, two years earlier.

I had gone to college and graduated with a Bachelor of Arts from the nearby SUNY University and remained on there to study the craft of literature and creative writing with Professor Anthony Robinson,who was himself a renouned novelist, like his father, Henry Morton Robinson, who wrote The Cardinal, Water Of Life, and other great books, and to whom I became the grateful understudy of, to both of them, through my friend Tony, to my being personally tutored and home schooled by him to polish off my education, as he phrased it, and as who had been my teacher of Creative Writing and American Literature at the State University of New York at New Paltz that was situated on a gentle hill in stately enclave above the Village of New Paltz and overlooking the great majestic panorama of The Shawangunkg Mountain Range.

I was still attending graduate studies there at that University, auditing a few courses, and signed up for and taking several others, with select teachers of mine, centerering on Music, the study of the piano, Fine Arts, sketching and oil painting on canvass, Law, American History, and Creative Writing; and which was also a reason to be living there in Tony's house, to be close to the school, but not the only reason.

I felt close to Tony too also in a paternal way, and there was also a love relationship that had begun to develop there between myself and Tony's then at that time seventeen year old daughter Jenny, that was not yet fully developed but which kept me on there at the home in interest to be close to her, and a breath of life in me that she was, and as well for the sake of Tony's fourteen year old son, Henry, who I was very fond of, as he was taken by me too as well, and to whom that I had become a personal companion to. Henry was deeply troubled still from the death of his mother, whom he had found dead and torn apart in the chest from the shotgun blast, with blood everywhere, that he discovered when he came home from school in the afternoon, while Tony was at the Univerity teaching.

I also had a place there in Tony' house where I could keep my beloved pet Sophie, to have a big yard to run around in, and people to look after her, and love her, and care for her, if I happened to be away, and who was a one year old female Irish Setter and a hyper active chore of a hand full that way in requiring my constant attention. To what dog that I was to devote thirteen years of my life too, in necessity to provide a suitable habitat for her to be happy with, until she died of old age set in.

It was also convenient to my social and psychological Anthopoligical Research on the street, as a Study of The Street Culture and the Hippy Culture in the afermath of the Vietnam War. And which I had undertaken as a Graduate School Project for a former female teacher of mine, Ms. Suzan Valenti, "to get to know my own back-yard before taking on the world," in the words of Ralph Waldo Emerson, and to learn about the environs of the artistic and intellectual community that I was exploring being exposed to, in part as a pastime, and also to a higher plane to promote and inspire the philosophy of a religion, that was inspired in me by the writings of the great metaphysical shaman philosopher, Carlos Castaneda, about The Impeccable Will, and the propagation of desire of caring regard for the earth and the life it bore and for one human being to another, as human beings, that is called, "All Things" by The Yaki Indians; a Faith To Live By, of Respect, Reverence, and Cherishment, for "All Things" Living and Sentient, to include The Inanimate by that statement. And of what religion that I had become an astute and devoted follower of.

Castaneda's first three books — _The Teachings of Don Juan: A Yaqui Way of Knowledge_; _A Separate Reality_; and _Journey to Ixtlan_ — were written while Castaneda was an <u>anthropology</u> student at the <u>University of California, Los Angeles</u> (UCLA). He wrote these books as his research log describing his apprenticeship with a traditional "Man of Knowledge" identified as don Juan Matus, a Yaqui Indian from northern Mexico. Castaneda was awarded his <u>bachelor's</u> and <u>doctoral degrees</u> based on the work described in these books.

In 1974 his fourth book, Tales of Power, was published. This book ended with Castaneda leaping from a cliff into an abyss, and signaled the end of his apprenticeship under the tutelage of Matus. Castaneda continued to be popular with the reading public with subsequent publications.

In his books, Castaneda narrates in first person the events leading to and following after his meeting Matus, a Yaqui "Man of Knowledge", in 1960. Castaneda's experiences with Matus inspired the works for which he is known. He also says the sorcerer bequeathed him the position of *nagual*, or leader of a party of seers. He also used the term "nagual" to signify that part of perception which is in the realm of the unknown yet still reachable by man, implying that, for his party of seers, Don Juan was a connection in some way to that unknown. Castaneda often referred to this unknown realm as nonordinary reality, which indicated that this realm was indeed a reality, but radically different from the ordinary reality experienced by human beings.

But it was to the study of and to learn of The Creator first hand, that had become my true Post Graduate Project, to devote my life and my talents and all my entergies as a dedicated and scholarly man to learn about The Creator, and to make friends with God, which I succeeded in doing, in the real way of being formally married to HIM, and HE to me. Who I had given everything up, of all my ambitions after worldly treasures to pursue, to be with, and that had become my sole purpose in life up to that point at that time, To Be In Compatible Harmony With.

And also, truth be known, and to the reason for my being an intimate companion to my Professor friend and colleague to have taken up with resdence there at the house where he lived, was also to be close to Jenny, Professor Robinson's now seventeen old daughter, who I secretly was in love with, and who was still measuring her life out in half years eager to grow up in those days, and who I had fallen madly in love with, for the sweet and genuine and caring person that she was, as a case in fact, and the long dreamed of girl from my youth who I cared for dearly, the girl that I had always dreamed of having when I was a young man myself back in the day and involved then in a military way with my life with the romantic side and its longings put on hold.

I also as well had an involved and personal relationship with Tony's then fourteen year old son Henry, that I stayed on there in those years for whose behalf of companionship, who needed me, for the reasons that he did, and who I was quite fond of and cared for deeply, as I would my own son, or younger brother, as the case is, in the inbetween years of such things, who had lost his mother in that tragic way he did, and who had grown attached to me in a mothering and nurturing sort of way.

I had been staying there now at Tony's house for nearly a year then at that point, since the later part of May in 1977 when Tony had asked me to help him out with a landscape renovation project in exchange for room and board ... and his professional company, which I eagerly accepted and appreciated, like Plato who was the student of Socrates, one learning from the other, and many the nights that we spent philosophizing and discussing the essences of the life about us.

It was now Wednesday in the third week of March of 1978 and Jenny was home for the week on her Spring Break from her Ivy League Prep School named, Oakwood, over across the river in Poughkeepsie. And on that particular night I had elected to spend sleeping out on the sofa that lay up against the far wall beneath the lacy curtained side window in the room called Mary's Room. Which was the room that Mary had killed herself in. I had no desire to sleep in the bed, and so as not to disturb the already made bed in that room that was never slept in by anybody except for the occasional guests to come through.

I had gone in there after spending the night watching T.V. in the upstairs T.V. room with Tony's children at a little past 10:00 p.m., and after saying goodnight to them, who that I was more or less and had become an alternate parent figure to, and something of a mothering figure to them both in that way; Jenny, and Henry, who were now going off to bed in their separate rooms, Henry's directly across from the T.V. room, and Jenny's on the same side, one door down from the bathroom and opposite Mary's room. I had been watching television shows with them for a couple of hours, Jenny and I sitting on the couch togather, with Henry stretched out in the big recliner, and together with our two dogs.

Socrates

My dog Sophie, who nuzzled her chin on my lap with me on the couch, and with the Robinson family dog, Tony's dog, named Waldo, on the floor at our feet, between Henry and myself.

Waldo was a skittish four year old medium size male brown and white Cocker Spaniel, who could be a bit growly at times, depending on his moods, and who I didn't bother to pet, exept at certain times when he seemed to want me to, for that reason; and all of us together that way, in a family way of intimate and closely bonded familiar companionship, sharing the enjoyment of the television shows until just after ten o'clock. Tomorrow was a school day for them.

The T.V. room was one of the two big rooms upstairs on the left side of the house and the one that faced out on to Hugeunot Street, and which was adjacent to Mary's room down the hall. It was furnished with a big sofa up against the street side window and with an easy chair to sit in directly to the left side of it. The T.V. sat directly across from the sofa, and Tony's gun rack with its assortmet of hunting rifles and shotguns sat against the opposite wall on a big chest of drawers, next to what was the door for the closet. Against the side wall of the room, in the corner, was a green wingbacked chair next to a nightstand with a lamp.

It was a Wednesday night mid-week night, and Tony wasn't at home. He didn't have classes to teach until late in the afternoon on Thursdays, and had gone out after dinner that night to socialize and out looking for ladies to be with in the bars in town, either to P&G's or to The North Light, as were his favorites, and who wouldn't be back in until late that night, around one or so, as we would expect.

Usually I slept in the basement apartment, with its own separate entrance, bathroom and shower, and kitchen. And sometimes I slept there in the t.v. room on the really cold winter nights because it was quite warmer there than it was in the basement apartment and more comfortable to sleep in the T.V. room than in the cold and clammy damp basement, which Tony deliberately kept the temperature low down there in the basement to save on his heating bill.

But on that particular night, and as Jenny had been quite often complaining of late, about feeling like wanting to do a swan dive off the cliffs on the mountain to be with her mother who she missed terribly, I had opted to sleep on the couch in Mary's room, with Sophie, my faithful female red Irish Setter, lying at my feet on the rug, as a seance experiment, as I related with to Jenny, to see if her mother's spirit was there, and to know if my powers of extrasensory perception could detect her presence.

Before I went to turn-in however, I took the dog's downstairs and let them out the back door to relieve their bladders so they could rest comfortably with the long night's sleep ahead. I always had a policy of not giving them any water after their evening feeding at 6:00 so that the nights could be spent sleeping and not be interrupted by insistent dogs wanting to go out at awkward times of the night to interrupt your sleep for and then having to wait on the dogs to return. I stepped outside onto the pack deck and lit a cigarette while I waited for them to come back. It was dark and clammy damp out with a windy chill portending of more rain, after nearly a week of on and off rainy spells. Sophie came back right away, but Waldo ran off chasing something and it was some time before he returned, panting and eager to get back inside.

I gave Waldo a friendly pat on his back on his return to bond and reinforce an affection with him, and heard Sophie growl at me in jealously and nudge her nose into my leg. After I let them back in, Waldo went into Tony's bathroom in the hallway between the Kitchen area and Tony's master bedroom, and began lapping water from the toilet.

"Waldo," I scolded, "you stop that!" and went into Tony's bathroom, just as Waldo had finished lapping getting his drink. He bolted past me and off into Tony's bedroom to lie on the bed. I closed the toilet bowl lid, which was supposed to be kept down and went back into the kitchen. I turned the thermostat in the hallway next to the kitchen door down to 65, and shut the lights in the kitchen off, except to leave the small night-light on over the back counter for Tony to see by when he came in, and went back upstairs.

The house was still fairly warm. I didn't bother to undress, and slept in my jeans and tee shirt, as I was accustomed to sleeping in, with just a good and substantial comforting blanket over me for warmth, and using the sofa cushion for a pillow. I gave Sophie the small comforter throw that was on the couch to nose up under if she got cold in the night.

Out of sensitivity for the dead I said a silent prayer of intention to The Heavenly Father asking with my heart and not with words for the understanding to these matters concerning the affairs of Mary the departed, and with a certain element of sympathy, as I had told Jenny about earlier in the evening, to be able to heal the wound of a broken heart, too broken to be mended, I breathed softly and slowly in and out to silence my mind and to make it receptive to the any other thoughts around me, if indeed, to see if Mary's spirit would come to visit me in the night and to learn her secret, if she would reveal it to me, as to why she had committed such a terrible act, and to help heal her heart if I could, and out of hallowed deference to her, for respect to her memory, as who was Tony's beloved wife, Mary Chica, and the mother of Jenny and Henry.

I had been startled wide awake at precisely three a.m. that night, according to the time in the luminous dials of the alarm clock on the bureau that was along the back wall of the room adjacent to the T.V. room, as I was sleeping East to West with my head on the far Western end of the sofa and could see its dials of the clock without stirring in the dimly perceptible light, that I had the alarm set to for five a.m. to get up by to get ready for work.

I was filled with a feeling of bristling fear and dread in me, like the kind of hair raising fright one gets in being snarled at by a dog that one can't see in the dark of night, and that one has to pass by, that makes your hair stand on end. I found myself lying there in that fearful state of mind breathing deeply to myself in and out listening to the heaviness of the silence of the house pressing on my ears.

The sound of the big grandfather clock was ticking solemnly as it always did in an air of seriousness downstairs in the foyer, and there was the sound of Sophie's sleeping steady breathing, that they were the only sounds in the house. Then I was filled with the thought as if someone were sitting at the foot of the couch telling it to me, of a certain sense of realness to it, and with the thought, I seemed to feel an imperceptible tug on the blanket and a touch pressing against my calf needing sympathy.

"What is point of living at all," the thought said, "if all you can do is sin and be punished by God to go straight to hell for and to burn forever there in hell in the end, for what life of sin that you had nothing to with making, and never wanted to have the decisions to be made about, to commit sins that were forbidden by God and nigh-on impossible not to commit, life being what it is to have to endure in the name of living, for God to have made the rules of sins over, and not to not have consulted with us over, and to our not even having to be evil to be going to hell, just not in accordance with His Rules in judgment, as if it is our nature to be that way, as it is our nature to sin, that involve us with things as our dispositions and circumstances of our life compel us to do in the moment to be lived, that we have to abide by in the way of God's Law to, or go to hell for a lot of rules made up about and over what people can and cannot do with their own lives to live out.

What kind of life is that to bear, and what kind of God is it that to be involved with, Who would create such an existence of life with its many snares and trappings, and so called pitfalls, to torment the pittied souls who fall into His trap of sins of the flesh, and for the other sins that mortal flesh is err to; of jealousy and revenge, power and avarice, envy, cruelty, and anger, laziness, drunkenness, drug addictions, and gluttony; and to delight in the torment of His Captive Humanity either way, like a spider drooling over its meal, in our inablity to resist the temptations, not to sin, and to their inevitability of sinning, then to delight in their banishment from the joyous Kingdom of God's Heaven, and to whatever it is that souls do there, to go straight to hell and to burn there in excruciating pain for all eternity for God's sake of glowering over His Prize Condemnation of Sadistic Cruelty for the Pleasure as His Pastime in the end.

Better not to have such a life, now to end such a life with rational foresight and to take it from God, by doing away with yourself, by your own hand, to cheat God of His siniser victory over you, by force, so as to cheat God of His miserable and cursed sadism, that you do by dying bravely by your own hand rather than to take a chance on the living life out to its finality, to finally, and in the end, to be sent straight to hell for it, for having bravely lived it out."

And with that the thought ended as abruptly as it had begun in my mind and my mind was left silenced again to the sound of the ticking of the grandfather clock in the foyer downstairs, with the lingering in the afterthought of what was put to me that night; but that left me with one final parting remark further.

"The idea of Heaven and Hell is an abstract fabrication of unkind expectations. They don't exist as they are thought of literally expressed to be real by the living consciousness to be what they intend. What matters here is if you are happy with the extent of your existence, or not, and which you cannot escape from at all, that existence, or that happiness … or not, by killing your human form. But that's not what you have to come to terms with. What you really want is to find out is … what is beyond the veil of life and death, in store for you. That is what you really want to know… Isn't it? To hasten it along … or not. To be … or not to be. To be here or there in the afterlife. To go on living… or to find out what happens to you after you die. Isn't that the paradox of the mystery that you are trying to solve? That you are tired of waiting around for, to kill yourself to find out?"

I lay there, still startled wide awake by the parting thought until it was near five a.m. and got up. My usual time for awakening was 5:30. The house seemed unusually warm for the night, which Tony always instructed be kept at cool sixty-five degrees to save on the heating bill, and which I had personally set to that degree before going up to bed. Or perhaps that I had become a little flushed.

As I stood up and shut the alarm off, Sophie immediately jumped to her feet, shook herself from head to tail jangling her dog tags and wimpered a greeting. I stroked and patted her affectionately on her head as she nuzzled up against my leg. I folded up my banket neatly, folded Sophie's trow, and put them both together on the sofa at the Eastern end with the cushion on the Western end, or the end towards the back of the house that faced the mountain, as was my discipline of neatness to do. I put on my shirt, buttoning up to the neck for warmth but not bothering to tuck it in yet. Sophie was at my heals waiting impatiently to go out.

When I opened the door to the room that was situated on the side of and at the top of the stairs landing to the left from the front of the house facing the back, I saw that both doors to Jenny's and to Henry's room were open slightly. Jenny was sound asleep in her bed breathing lightly, in and out. I listened there to the comforting sounds Jenny's breathing for a while and thinking of her there in her bed dreaming her thoughts going on in her head, and then went down the hallway to Henry's door and listened there for a while to his breathing, also comforted by his Being, as a presene in my world, and alone with his young boy's dreams, and the home that he would wake up to, being nurtured and watched over, in part, by myself, and finally came back to the top of the carpeted stairs and went quietly down to the kitchen and turned the light on.

In the absolute stillness and quietness of these early morning times, it was always a preoccupation of mine to try and move about without making any noise, or to be making as little noise as possible, in part in deference to the other sleeping members of the household, not to disturen and awaken them, and also as an exercise in ability to be able to do that. All movements were conducted slowly and carefull. Everything made a noise, but the challenge in question not to make any being, how much. Sophie and Waldo were another matter.

I opened the back door softly and let Sophie out. Waldo, on hearing this, came bounding with the sound of four feet scurrying along out of Tony's room and down the hardwood floor from the master bedroom down the hall. Waldo brushed past me without so much as a friendly greeting and a pet from my hand wanting to go out too and banging the door with his body as he did.

I let Waldo out and closed the door back up. It was a damp cold morning in the mid-fourties as would guess. While I waiting for the dogs to returen in the meantime I went and used the toilet in the bathroom in the hallway to Tony's room, not flushing the toilet down when I had finished, so as not to wake him up, and to save on the water bill as was Tony's command, that would all be flushed down at once in the morning, of the toilet paper and urine, when Tony got up. Everyone's bowel movement got fushed down immediately. When I finished, I closed the lid back down so that Waldo wouldn't drink from it. Waldo drank indiscriminately from that toilet, if anyone left the lid up, whether there was urine to be flushed down in it or not.

I went then and fixed a big pot of coffee for myself and for Tony. Jenny didn't care much for coffee and Henry was still too young to have aquired a liking to it. While I was waiting for the coffee to drip through the liner, I picked up the literary book to read, that Tony had left on the shelf of the china hutch that was positioned in the kitchen table eating area against the dining room wall.

The book was Ernest Hemminway's story "Across The River And Into The Trees," published in 1950, and which was one of the novels that Tony taught periodically in his American Literature classes. It was a tale set in Venice in the aftermath of WWII, and is about a middled aged and meloncholy American War Commander named Richard Cantwell, who was a 50 year old Colonel in the U.S. Army Infantry, in failing health with a heart condition, who lost his entire Regiment to the German Army in the battle for France and was left with a horrible wound in his right hand, that split his palm between his third and forth fingers all the way up almost to his wrist. And who finds love, however brief and fleeting, with young Italian Countess, named Renata, who is more than half his age at the very moment when his life was becoming a hardship to him and beyond hope. I was nearing the middle of it, and feeling a noble kindship with the author, reading it page by page in my off hours. As it always pleased me to be reading something and to have the expanse of time stretching out ahead of me and planned out of a story to finish, that was always something productive to have in progress.

The title, "Across The River And Into The Trees," was taken from General Stonewall Jackson's memoirs from the Civil War; in which, after being mortally wounded in battle, said to his Aid … "Order A.P. Hill to prepare for action. No, no, let us cross over the river and rest under the shade of the trees." Which became the symbol of a resting place to await their death for men who know they are about to die.

I sat back in one of the four spacious comfortable table chairs situated around the heavy round oak kitchen table, chosing as I always did, and which was my place at the supper table, the chair by the back window at the far end of the kitchen closest to the back of the house; and propped the book up on a stack of four ceramic coasters at a good angel to read while I was having my morning coffee and eating breakfast.

None of the windows in the downstairs part of Tony's house, except for his bedroom down the hall, had curtains. In all, it gave me a stark and eerie impression, to have no curtains at all on any of the windows, and with a wide open feeling about the whole downstairs of the house, with the whole world being able to watch the comings and the goings-on there. There were two windows there in the kitchen table area at right angles to each other, one facing the side yard and the other the back of the house, that reflected in the pitch darkness outside like mirrors showing the image of myself and the interior of the kitchen area; which you knew that people from the outside could look in on.

I lit up a cigarett from my pack of Winstons, taking in a big drag of the smoke and let it out in the solemn silence of the house at that hour, hearing my own breath as I did, and began to read. The silence in the house, especially in the early morning hours, was deep and contemplative, and made especially ponderous and captivating with the steady ticking of the big grandfather clock that was in the downstairs hallway by the stairs.

Sophie and Waldo came bounding back up onto the back deck porch with much heralded bravado and scratched insistently at the kitchen door. I got up and opened it for them to the sounds of their their labored and excited panting and let them in, careful not to pat Waldo too affectionately in front of Sophie this time, but I did a manage to get in a little pet, in attempting to bond with the dog, stroking his back with my hand as he barreled past me.

Returning into the kitchen I went to the pantry against the far wall, and grabed the big bag of dog food from the bottom of it, and poured them both a big bowl of dry dog food to eat, and with a little water, not a lot, but enough water, to wash the dog food down with. Then I sat back down in my chair to watch them eat. I did like to watch the dogs eat. It was such a basic and comforting feeling I had to be able to provide for them and to watch them in their eager satisfied enjoyment of their meal, and to know that I was creating such fundamental happiness in them, to what activity that they devoted their entire and consuming spirit in the moment to, savoring every chomp with their teeth; that made me feel proud and masterful as their provider, to delight in their dependency to my hand and to their loyalty to me in that way, that satisfied and fulfilled a basic human need in me to be needed and useful and in control of their destiny, that instilled such reciprocating devotion in them, and at least with Sophie. Waldo's loyalty lay elsewhere with Tony.

While they ate I made myself up a bowl of bran flakes cereal with cold milk, as that was my daily ritual tribute to the cows and the other liveshock animals for their sake not to eat them in the morning meal; and only to eat a token agrarian grain breakfast in deference to the beloved amianls who were daily being killed, slaughtered for our sake to survive. I ate the hearty good tasting cereal down and tipped the bowl back to my lips to finish off the milk and the last of the good tasting little bits of the cereal with the good feeling in positive affirmation to my Karma. So, we all became finished and satified in our primal morning hunger together, me and the dogs.

Waldo finished his bowl of dog food and lapped a little at the water I gave them and without a gesture of gratitude or affection went back into Tony's bedroom without acknowledging me. Waldo lived in his own world. Sophie finished her bowl, lapped a little at the water, and nosed around the bowels knowing all the while that there was nothing left to eat there, but she nosed around, looking from one bowl to the other disenchanted fashion none-the-less, as if I were going to give her some more for her pouting. I finish my coffee, read a page more in the book until I got to a placed to leave it comfortably went to the sink and washed off the dish and the coffee cup, and then went down into the basement apartment with Sophie to shave, shower, and get dressed and ready for the day.

I didn't make a lunch on that particular day, although sometimes I did, depending on the food supply available, and on the morning in looking in on it from the open refrigerator door, that looked pretty meager in the cold cut department, and which I decided against out of deference to Tony and the children who would need what remained for their own lunch meet of what was there to have and I wanted them to have enough of to make their own lunches with for both today or tomorrow, or that perhaps Tony, on seeing that supplies were running low, would stop in at "Jack's Prim Meats" on Main Street next to P&G's Bar in New Paltz after his classes that day to pick up some more fresh cold cuts from his friend Jack as he often was fond of doing.

Friday was Jenny's and my night to do the family shopping for the week together at ShopRite as Tony gave us the assignment and the money to do and furnished us with the list personally made out by him to go by. It was always a fun time to go food shopping with Jenny after Friday's supper, who took it all so personally and formally to be shopping for her family, with me.

I could always get a sandwich to take with me from The Hobo Deli when I stopped by on my way to the Bus Depot when I didn't have a lunch to take with me, or today I figured I would get Walter, who I had acquired as a "Runner" at my C.E.T.A. job over in Poughkeepsie, as I often did, to run and get me a sandwich for lunch. Walter, was a white haired middle-aged homeless derelict in baggy trousers, worn out shoes, a tattered trench coat and scarf, who had approached me, and asking others on the staff as he entered the room looking for "the supervisor" at the beginning of my work there with C.E.T.A. to inquire if I would "hire" him "to go for" coffee in the mornings. I felt for him and asked him how much he wanted for the job and he said, "two dollars, plus coffee and a hard roll for himself," and I said all right it's a deal.

Walter always came most every morning during the workweek after that in a heart warming way looked forward to by everyone as a bright spot of optimistic expectation on the face of Walter who was always eager to be of use and most appreciative for the fulfillment of his position with the office staff and took his expected place in the world of things with regal bearing. He went around to each of us and took the orders from everyone who wanted coffee and a roll, collecting the money as he went. It was his "rice-bowl," or his "place in the world," as the saying went; light, light no sugar, black, black with two sugars, and so on, with everybody personalized in their choices. He left each time and was back in twenty minutes each time faithfully as agreed with everyone's change, keeping the tally in his head, and brought the coffees back to us in a light cardboard box with the logo of The Acropolis on it from the Greek Deli Restaurant around the corner and up the street from where our make-shift office was located, with individually wrapped buttered hard rolls or bagels and cream cheese, depending on the order. Everyone always looked forward to the office Coffee Break. Office life on our project was relaxed and informal.

By the time I finished with the morning ritual to get over with; starting with going to the bathroom; and which I always did like to have a good thorough expursion with to eliminate all the bad noxious gas and uncomfortable feeling of having to go during the work day, but that on that particular morning which was not cooperating with me about. I finally gave up on the idea of sitting there wasting time trying to go and went about shaving, showering, brushing my teeth, and with the other morning getting myself ready chores. It was now nearly a quarter after six.

The bus for Poughkeepsie that was across the Hudson River and fifeen miles away, left the downtown New Paltz Bus Depot at 7:05 a.m.. That gave me a good fourty-five minutes in liesurely walk to get uptown and have a coffee before walking to the Bus Station. Once in Poughkeepise, which was a fourty minute ride with stops along the way, it was a twenty minute walk to the building where I had to report to for daily work with the C.E.T.A. Program at eight o'clock.

The house was still quite. No one upstairs stirring yet, and Tony would be asleep for a good while. No telling what time he had gotten in, probably around one a.m. or so. Jenny and Henry wouldn't be up for a few minutes yet, as was their time, to get ready for school.

My job as a C.E.T.A. worker, was located in the makeshift office for what purpose, that was temporarily set up and located in an abandoned building appropriated by the public works department, and which was a good fast walk not far from the bus drop. I was at the time The Project Development Team Supervisor, in charge of seven employees and our mission of developing and creating a thousand or so new temporary jobs with not-for-profit agencies, to be utilized in the place of regular employment, by the poor and the economically displaced population of Dutchess County, NY under President Jimmy Carter's make work program named C.E.T.A., that stood for the Comprehensive Employment and Training Act. It was a good job as I happened to get by applying for it using my parents address near Vassar College in Poughkeepsie, and where I stayed periodically when the trip back and forth from the Robinson Family home became too oppressive, and back again, missing them, Tony, and Henry, and Jenny, and for the matter, and their missing me also, love being a two way street.

I happened to be on foot at the time in those days because I was stranded there in the Town and bent on experiencing the sensation of being left on foot with no personal transportation available, as I had often wanted to do in a real way as a social science project while I was in a cosmotolital frame of mind mood that year, of what it felt like being a pedestrian, and like so many people to be dependent on the public transportation, and the transportation and kind friendship of others, and foot power, to get me where I needed to go. That at other times became a chore and burden, not having my own car, and with a feeling of being out-of-class, as I wasn't used to it, but for what matter in concern right then that served my ego in a nice way of being intrepid to do it, be on foot a lot. I always had a car available to me though when I needed one, that was my fathers '71 Chevy at my parents home in Poughkeepsie, that I could borrow, and that he didn't use very much, being in a car pool to get to this own job; and with my own car, the '69 Mustang that I used to have, having broken down and bit the dust, with myself, and just out college with all my savings exhausted and with not being able to find any union construction work in those times in which the construction industry as a whole was suffering from a recession, being unable to fix it up and to keep it going on the road, as to the reasons for my indigent and dependent circumstance, with being noble.

But I wouldn't be there to work on that day and although I didn't quite know it at the time when I said goodby to Sophie with a kiss on her sweet head, and left her at the house, exiting through my basement doorway, that was an old heavy oak door with a rustic iron handle, closing it tighly behind me. It was six thirty a.m. and I was dressed in my daily work clothes of dark blue sports jacket, neatly pressed black slacks, a white shirt and traditional blue and white striped tie, with my trench coat and scarf buttoned to my kneck for warmth. I stepped out into the predawn morning darkness chilly cold carrying my black satchel that my father had given me for Christmas that year, on my daily walk into the Village that was nearly three quarters of a mile or so distance away to catch the 7:05 bus at the Bus Station on Main Street over across the river to Poughkeepsie, which took me fifteen minutes to walk.

As I shut the door to my basement apartment, Sophie whimpered a little in her way of being disappointed at not being included in the process of going out. I had left the upstairs door at the end of the stairway to first floor open so that Sophie could go up and down the stairs and be let out if she needed to go outdoors when the rest of the family woke up.

"You stay, Sophie," I said to her in a soft command tone through the door and she was quite. She would probably go lie down on the bed, although I always scolded her not to. But she never liked the basement floor to lie on, even though it had a nice rug.

I took in a deep breath of the morning air and let it back out through my nostrils. There was an early Spring Robin singing close by, up quite early in the morning, as was their way, and who was pontificating profusely, in their multi-tonal Robin language that they converse in, from under the eave of the roof on the upstairs window ledge of the garage/garret. I had learned of the Robins telepathy transference last spring from my friend Maureen Riley, who was herself a psychic and who lived on the second floor of The Riverboat rooming house, as it was named, while I was sleeping in the hallway outside her door one night and on into the hours of day break when the Robin's thought came to me, and knew what the Robin was saying. It was "The Morning Greeting" that the Robins say to each other as they awaken to one another in their respective territories.

That goes:

"I admire you. I admire you indeed. Indeed I do. He'll say it again. I admire you. I respect you. I respect you indeed. Indeed I do. He'll say it again. I respect you."

I repeated each of the sayings in my mind-thought to the Robin, and as the Robin said them to me, and who was all too eager and delighted to assist me in finishing the phrases, particularly when it came time to say, "He'll say it again… I admire you, I respect you."

And there were other nuances to their psychic conversations, which came with the mind image-thought of the Robin People full red breasted and confident in the bearing of their demeanor as they hopped around, at that time of day, saying to each other, "I admire you indeed. I respect you." One of their thoughts was, if any humans were listening in to say, "We eat worms, don't make fun;" and which the Robin thought-said on that occasion to me then. "I'm not making fun," I thought back.

And otherwise that he took no delight to have any interlocution with humans at any other time of day other than at first light. Other times of the day were busy with other chores, such as feeding, finding a mate, and keeping up with the flock, which they worry over, during their annual migration through an area on their way north for the summer and as such who don't have time for idle chit chat with passerby humans, other than at the proscribed time of daybreak. Robins arrive in New York State from their southern nesting grounds in late March of every year when the average temperature reaches 37 degrees, and not because they can't endure the cold, but because of their food supply becomes available, which is earthworms in the spring, and then later on to feed on their fruit diet when in season. Robins sing when they arrive on their breeding territories. Sometimes robins even sing in winter flocks, due to surging hormones as the breeding season approaches. However, in the majority of cases, robins really do wait to sing until they have reached their territory.

I said good day in my mind-thought to the Robin in Tony's garage and went on my way up the street to town. "And good day to you," the Robin said as I departed.

When I got to the Main Street in the Village, walking down to the old Huguenot Settlement Stone Houses and then left out to Route 32 and on that way into Town, I noticed that the traffic was stopped by a road block at the bridge over the Wallkill River. And looking on in the hastening break of the gray dawn in the grim overcast and damp twilight of that morning, I saw that overnight the ice jam, which had been holding the water back upriver, had broken at the low falls area of the river half a mile to the South upstream and that the entire area of the river basin, known as The Flats, was a lake flooded with big chunks of ice floating solemnly by in the slow moving current. The Eastern bank of the river rose sharply and was always out of reach of the yearly Spring flooding, and which could occur, depending on the amount and duration of the rain, at other times of the year as well.

I turned left, and crossed over Chestnet Street, as Route 32 was named, and which indeed had a large overlooming Chestnut Tree on the Eastern corner of Main and Route 32, across from the Municipal Parking lot, and before it was cut down later on that year, in the name of progress, to widen the road and put in a modern side walk. After crossing the street I went up the four steps to the Hobo Deli, which was then open at six a.m.. It was a pleasant feeling reaching the front walkway with its bright and friendly welcoming florescent lights streaming out from the big plate glass windows upon the sidewalk and out into the street, in contrasting comfort to the lonely feeling of the isolated darkness.

I went inside and made myself a meduim size cup a coffee to go from the open coffee pot on one of the two burners marked Regular, with the other marked as Decaf; both of which that the local street mafia was fond of "dropping" liquid Lygersic Acid in as a come on to their street business, and otherwise to be making Monkey Business on the local straight people. I mixed in a little dairy creamer to the coffee, light, no sugar, as I preferred it, and went to the counter where Ralph the proprietor waited on me and paid for the coffee and bought a fresh pack of Winston Cigaretts in the box. I then went out and stood at the top of the stoop on the walkway at the Deli, sipping on my coffee and smoking a cigarett, with my black bag against the overhead awning post, waiting for the time to pass before I had to go up to the bus station several blocks up the street to catch the 7:05 to Poughkeepsie.

To know Richard Rizzi was an experience to be reckoned with beyond any other I had ever known in my time because Richard was totally counter culture and beyond everything that I had known beforehand and who had been secretively introduced to me by my school chum and best friend of that time, Timothy Shoh in the early August of the summer of 1976 when I was in town one day looking for my lost wife Doreen who had just run-off and abandoned me, and secretively in the meaning as if Richard would know something about her disappearance; which if he did, and upon my mention of it to him, he never revealed it. Richard wasn't someone who you could pry into or ask certain questions of. Richard was who he was, a Supernatural Presence and an extremely talented Spiritual Medium who knew he possessed the power of life and death over people.

Timothy Shoh, was himself an inveterate drug user, and like Doreen my wife who was that way also, of life in the fast lane, and as that was the way of everyone in those days of The Vietnam War and its aftermath, except for myself, the returned from the

war Combat Veteran on Tactical Task Force Mission on the street
to quell the Drug War, that I truly rue the day I ever became
intimate friends with, and rue the day that way with Richard also,
to know then, and to become involved intimately with, and in, the
Drug World, to use, and to deal in, and to traffic in, the illegal
contraband of drugs, and involved in their life or death war world;
which cut across my grain fundamentally and was alien and
antithetical to me to be involved with.   And as Timothy would
say at times, to know in your heart that is wasn't right, of what
was, and wasn't, right.

His resume, which appeared in The Cadmium Text Series, a
reading series for innovative writing in and around the Hudson
Valley, written about himself as of Jan 16, 2009 reads:
"A doorway partially open, may one come in? "
Richard Rizzi was born on New Year's Eve 1936, in the
backroom of a pool hall in Brooklyn, NY to an unwed factory
worker named, Vera, and the gangster Duke Rizzi. After serving
in the United States Army in occupied Germany, he returned to
the United States in the 1950's to pursue his career in Jazz as a
tenor and alto saxophone player and settled in New York City
where he began a life long pursuit of study and exploration of
music, poetry, visual, and performance art. He has been the
founder or co-founder of numerous poetry reading series, benefits
for the arts and artistic groups, including the Hudson Valley
Poetry Society and the poetry performance group Outist Living in
America. Over the last 40 years, he has periodically combined
this eclectic mix of art forms to create several public live
performance pieces being realized in both theater and nature.

From 1947 to the present he studied the arts and literature and
wrote poetry. Since the 1960's Rizzi has traveled extensively to
study visual and poetic arts, including trips to Spain to study
Garcia Lorca; to Switzerland to study Paul Klee; to Amsterdam
for Van Gogh, and to Japan were he studied Zen Shiatsu with the
late Master, Masanaga and Master Yuho. He has traveled the
world extensively in pursuit of artistic knowledge.

Between travels Rizzi is a life-long resident of New Paltz, NY
where he spends much of his time fostering the work of younger

artist in his community with the same enthusiasm, dedication and curiosity that he brings daily to his own work. For the past seven years he has traveled back and forth between the U.S. and Denmark, performing with Trio CHROCH, a word/sound experimental improvisational ensemble. In addition to writing poetry, Richard has spent the last 30 years as a Performance and Multi Media Artist.

Richard is most famous though for his resurgence of the progressive academics of **The New School**, based to spontaneous teaching and education without walls or structure of curriculum within the artistic and literary community of The State University of New York at New Paltz. **The New School** began in 1933 as the University in Exile, an emergency rescue program for threatened scholars in Europe. The school is renowned for its avant-garde teaching of a variety of disciplines, social sciences, liberal arts, humanities, architecture, fine arts, design, music, drama, finance, psychology and public policy – and functioning as an International Think Tank and World Policy Institute.

Richard's middle name was Ambrosio, and in the sense of the past tense of being thought about now in the past, and that perhaps still is his middle name as of the last known mention of him in 2010 as being still alive and with us. It was Richard after whom that Michael Corleone's nephew and godson in the movie The Godfather Part II was named after, Richard Ambrosio Rizzi, in the Christening Scene in tribute, on the day that Michael Corleone was Taking Care Of and Settling All Family Business.

And although stated in that way of, "perhaps still is," to wonder if he is still alive and at the age of 75, and like is idol Salvador Dali, who quoted the phrase, "Life Begins At 75," to have wind in his sails yet to produce the great works of Zen Art and Dada Poetry and Theater.

Dada (English pronunciation: /ˈdɑːdɑː/) or **Dadaism** is a cultural movement that began in Zurich, Switzerland, during World War I and peaked from 1916 to 1922. The movement primarily involved visual arts, literature-poetry, art manifestoes, art theory—theatre, and graphic design, and concentrated its anti-war politics through a rejection of the prevailing standards in art through <u>anti-art</u> cultural works. Its purpose was to ridicule what its participants considered to be the meaninglessness of the modern world. In addition to being anti-war, dada was also anti-bourgeois and anarchist in nature. Dada activities included public gatherings, politics, demonstrations, and publication of art/literary journals; passionate coverage of art, and culture were topics often discussed in a variety of media.

And for the very fine Saxophone instrument that he played, to admire him greatly about; that he is capable of greatness; and in all that Richard has the profound and talented gifts of life for.

Richard has always cared for us and blessed us with his appreciation for life and with his sophistication and respectful regard for everyone.

I did read about the review of his poetry reading in Kingston, NY in 2009 when he was listed then as being seventy-three years old, and another mention of him also a year later at a poetry reading in Woodstock, NY, that was visually recorded and made available live on YouTube.

And other than that, regretfully, that I have lost track of him in these past fifteen or so years since I had seen him last, as I really do love him in my heart for the fine character of the man that he is, and now approaching our senior years together, to live on with the knowledge of one another's presence upon the planet, and not so much in the declining sense of decrepitude of our age being limited in scope, but vibrant and alive about to bear fruit with. And put in perspective with everything there is to know about, knowing more now about it than we did then back a long time ago in time when we didn't know as much, to have made the mistakes with it, the life we had, that we did, and if we did at all, make any mistakes, and to what that even now that we don't know everything about what it is we are doing here, and still learning the lessons the hard way.

And maybe they weren't mistakes after all, only to be viewed differently, as learning experiences in The New School, The School Of Life, taught and learned from one another in the streets, in just the way that things happened and went down back then. And I hope that he is still alive at this date in time since my last seeing him in 1996. It would be sad to think that he isn't and of the world without him.

It was in that year of 1996, in June, when I had come back home from my new life in Buffalo, NY to visit with everyone, that I had seen Richard last and learned from his grieving heart that his only daughter had committed suicide in Denmark, for whatever reason that she did, as she seemed happy enough when I had met her several ten years before, when Richard had brought her back home from his travels abroad in Denmark, to visit his former wife there who he had married and had a daughter and son with while Richard was in the Army stationed over in Post War Germany, for her to meet everyone and see what his life as the Godfather and admired artist and poet of an intellectual community was like. She had been a very beautiful and very sweet charming shy girl, when she had come to New Paltz for a visit that year, to commiserate with Richard over.

I got to know Richard quite well over the period of twenty years that I was to remain on the street there in New Paltz, NY, as the son of "The Duke," who was the boss of the local regional Organized Italian Crime Family Syndicate, who had, and connected to the New York City Mob, himself taken over the Mid-Hudson Valley Region of New York State, and particularly The City of Poughkeepsie, Highland, and New Paltz area, with its heavy and predominantly Italian Immigrant Population, (and particularly New Paltz, NY, which was a rich and prosperous tourist town and with its lucrative to the underground activities of the bars, drugs, prostitution, and pornography.)

And who, as to say of Richie's father, The Duke, who wasn't that visible or involved with us at all on the street level to be regarded as a Godfather, as the meaning of a God Father's protection and support and loyalty for the people is conveyed; which made The Duke's son Richie the visible Godfather to everyone. And he was. We didn't think of his father in any way as being "The Godfather," as we didn't really know him there where he lived in Highland, NY, which was ten miles South of New Paltz, who was not visible to us, and who rarely ever visited in the Bar Zone and University Town of New Paltz where Richie lived. But Richard was always visible.

Richard always said to anyone who was new to the street, and who had said it to myself upon meeting him, that other people of the Town only resided here in the Village Of New Paltz, but I live here. New Paltz is my home. I know everyone and everything that goes on. And it was his town. Richard knew and daily spent time with everyone; all the shopkeepers and the other residents from the surrounding, and the street people; of which I was an anomaly, not quite anyone who could be pinned down and put up a label on.

And to what sacred function to him, of shepherding everyone in a godfatherly way, that he always sincerely endeavored by, of that function entrusted to him by his birthright, to help everyone survive the streets, who needed his help; by turning tricks, in the meaning of prostitution, either way of the male or female variety to turning tricks, or by hooking up drug deals, being a contact person, or a drug runner to pick up and deliver the drugs, or by dealing the drugs in a cottage industry fashion of selling the drugs out of your own rented room or apartment, or by making pornography videos or pictures for the magazines, anything that a person needed to do, in the terms of what was considered to be the underworld, to get by in the day to day. And which, after all, to the people who needed to survive, it meant that, survival, in those terms of solidarity and loyalty to the code.

And which was, the underworld, as it is discussed to exist, more real to each of those participating in it, and more rewarding emotionally to be involved in, than the Real Straight World itself, in the underground's sympathetic bonding and need in mutual reinforcing dependency for each other; that the Real World, with its ruthless care-less about anyone attitude, wasn't about to help anyone survive in the gut sense, and to bond in the necessity of life and death to one another. And which was all conveyed in a knowing look between the eyes, that didn't have to say anything to know that someone was on the same side as yourself, and that existed as a conspiracy between everyone connected to itself and with the underground economy, to know in the certain knowledge of "the look" that they were an organization together, and that each person in that organization meant something to each and every other person in it, and to everyone else on perceiving it to witness in admiration for the closeness of the underground society. And so that to what that the mafia world cared about the people who were involved with itself, who were in it, as a family, in a real sense in contrast to the indifference of society, and which went beyond the societal sense of people being paid to be friendly to you.

And what Richie always said about his Town was that, "other people may reside here, and come and go, but I live here and run the town, and nobody stays on around here for very long without my permission." And in another way of phrasing the matter of Richard's meaning, was, as he was always fond of saying, "As 'we' move in, 'they,' move out." And in another way, in his referring about the local police, "They don't like me because I do Monkey Business." Monkey Business meant Drug Warfare and particularly with the LSD, which came in a liquid form as well as Blotter Acid in those days, and which was the Italian Mafia's, weapon of choice. Or which could be anything of any type of a drug or drug chemical, or poison, to be mixed with a person's food or beverage, particularly with alcohol and involving with the police in the enforcement of the D.W.I. Law. To what that no one could complain about to the police or to the medical authorities without getting "run down" with psychiatric involvement, and forced treatment with deadly pharmacy, which was, "the technically legal element" of the drug warfare occurring against The American Population, and the reason that I was there on The Street to intervene.

The Italian Mafia, as we knew it, was involved with the human vices of the seamy side of life, and as to why that it was called The Underworld, that preyed on the soft underbelly and weakness of the middle and upper classes; for sex, drugs, alcohol, gambling, politics gerrymandering controlling the property assessments and tax revenues, and other types of economic extortion, and all things corrupt, as the depraved and infantile purblind immigrants from Italy conveyed, who by brute force of deception and foul play had begun to take over the territories they implanted themselves in, and using The Underworld as a means to survive, (coined in the phrase, "that even my own wife and sons and daughters are forced to prostitute themselves and make pornography;") and to the utter undermine and desecration of The American United States by forming themselves, like the Jewish Underworld Mafia, into a Warfaring Underground to subvert, exploit, abuse, suppress, and take over the indigenous and law abiding innocent population and territory of the American Citizenry by making the indigenous population slaves to drug addiction, and pornography, and easily susceptible to the black-hand tactics of blackmail and scandal, for extortion and to do the bidding of foul play directly; and to essentially, of the indigenous American Population in tow that way, to do their bidding of foul play against their own loved ones, and particularly, and like The Black Mafia in such regard, by involving and making use of the White Females in the Heroin Addiction and by blackmail to the ultimate subversion of the White Males of their own households by putting drugs and poisons into the food and beverages; in aiding the overthrow of The United States; which could be overthrown by Attrition, (as in surreptitious murders,) Politics, (by criminal gerrymandering,) and by Inter-Racial Assimilation into the Dark Race, (Through the entrapping means of Drug Addiction,) without seeming to be.

The Italian Mafia was of that automaton mentality that constituted The Underworld, and The Underground Economy, and of Criminal Drug Trafficking what "had fed" The Drug War of The Hippie Draft Resistance and The Civil Rights Movement, "Revolution," of the very lucrative heavy narcotics, Heroin and Hashish directly from Afghanistan, cocaine and marijuana, LSD, and Drug Chemicals, Trade, as to the extent of the Drugs Trafficking, and which also involved Street Prostitution and Smut Pornography, connected blatantly with the Hollywood Movie Industry, and Big Business, with their vampire-esque Snuff Movie Thrill Killings pastime, (that everyone involved had to be initiate into to prove their loyalty,) South of The Border Way, (tongue-in-cheek, that all the young porno stars had to commit, of

these torture sex murders, in order to prove themselves trustworthy as an initiation, in the meaning in mafia logic of; "if they
were guilty of murder too, then they wouldn't be prone to squeal
on anyone else.") Prostitution, Corrupt Money Extortion, and
Mafia Gerrymandering, of foul play involving Drug Warfare and
Black Hand Coercion Tactics, of Mafia Politics, were always on
the table, and to the stated election of the public elected officials
supervising overhead of the population and thereunto to their
having control of the Taxation Coffers, and overall installations of
their own Mafia Installed Police Departments to enforce the ways
and the dictates of the mafia as their own policies, and to silence
the complainers to it, by foul-play outright, or by psychiatric
intake to forced treatment with disabling chemicals. Who were
now being called, "The New Regime." The New Regime had
taken power.

    And in total as an organization that way to be thought of, as
came to be known as, "The New Regime," that was to be
described of as, a Mafia Empire, to what no one could complain
about being abused or bumped-off by The Mafia, without
complaining directly "into" the hydra of The Mafia itself, and as
to of what the public was up against, to the idea of the "Mafia
Draft," impressments of, " better to join and try and stay alive
than to resist and die." Which I was up against, and which we all
paid allegiance to in one degree to another, and not just to the
Italian, Jewish, Black, and Police Mafias, to include for Local and
The New York State Police, and The D.E.A.; to what that many
men did die over trying to make a stand against, and myself
included that way in the way when I did, as they did me in for my
reporting of the situation to the F.B.I. and to the New York State
Police many years into the future who betrayed me; in 1982, and
again in 1886 as I was struggling then to intervene in behalf of a
beleaguered and complaining citizenry left at the mercy of the
mob; and in which I was then set-up by the Italian Mafia Police
and the New York State Police in their tow, by means of the foul-
play tactic of physical assault to be removed to psychiatric
custody on suspense of being a deranged killer from Vietnam, and
to psychiatric disposal with a Thorazine needle without any Court

Processing on either account, and tantamount to a chemical lobotomy, that I was extremely fortunate, and only by my sheer wits and charm in the good graces of my captors, to have survived by getting the Cocaine Antidote in time, mixed in with my orange juice, on both occasions, which neutralized the deadly effects of the Thorazine Chemical, and as was administered to me by someone close to me, my sister Peggy, who knew those things about the Cocaine from her Hippie Days and which she knew to be the Antidote to the Catastrophic Sedation Death, and as you do now know it too.

And so I toughed it out, while others gave their wives and sweethearts to it, and their own very souls, in their efforts to stay alive, and who abandoned their own lives and their self respect in their subjugation to it, that no self respecting American would ever by able to live with themselves in their heart with wholly submitting to, and better off to die trying to defend America against than to submit and loose one's manhood, and the nation, spoken in a man's terms, as to point out concerning the involvement and the roll of the women, and the Women's War Mafia and their part in the whole of the truth of the deadly sadistic arrangement that they played.

I had only seen The Duke three times. Once in September of 1977, when Richie, who never owned or operated a car to my knowledge, had asked me for the special favor of a ride, as he frequently did on many occasions, this time to see his father in Highland who he looked in on. Richie was having a scheduled Poetry Reading and had wanted to court his father's admiration at the time to see if he would come to the event.

Richie had preceded me up the stairs to his father's apartment that was located in a two story building over the family Jewelry Store Front on Main Street, that was operated by Richie's Uncle Vinnie, who we also looked in on and said hello to, with Richard introducing me, before going upstairs to see his father, and who Richie introduced me to as, "my good friend, Gary."

When we went up the stairs, which went at two flights around the back corner of the Jewelry Store, Richie had opened the door to the apartment and had stepped back to the side with his arm holding the door open to let me peer past around him to see his father, The Duke, lying sound asleep, angelic-like, on the sofa. He was lying on his right side with his head facing out to the living room with a light blue blanket pulled up to his neck. He looked beautiful and serene lying there.

"He's been up playing cards all night," Richie had said in a soft voice. "Let's not disturb him."

And with that, indicating one last loving look at his father, Richie closed the door behind us and we left, tip-toeing quietly back down the stairs. We made one last stop in to see Uncle Vinnie for Richie to say that his father was asleep and just to tell him when he woke up that he came to see him.

The second time I saw The Duke was in the fall of the past year, in October, and getting closet to the time when I had help Richie put together a Poetry Reading of his very fine superb analytical Poetry for the assembly of students, SUNY faculty, and the entire Literary Society of New Paltz - Woodstock, NY, who were sponsoring the event at the Dance Theater on Front Street in New Paltz, and a week before which that The Duke had been in The Deli House Restaurant sitting with Richie at one of the four chair tables against the wall, when I had stopped in early in the evening around seven o'clock, and this was a week before the scheduled event was to take place. Richie had introduced me to his father personally that night, who glared at me politely, not cracking a smile to his lips, in mistrust, I felt, and nodded. I had ordered a coffee from Willie, who ran the twenty-four hour operation of The Hebrew National Deli House, while his brother John worked the day shift. And who both worked twelve-hour days seven workdays a week, with hired help on from time to time. The menu at the Deli House was entitled, "The Stash Story," and featured Hebrew National Hotdogs, Knishes, various types of Salads, Bagels and Lox, Bagels and Cream Cheese, Sandwiches, Chili, Soups, and other tasty dishes.

On the back wall of the Deli House, where the narrow hallway for the doors to the men's and lady's rooms was, were pictures of local Italian Celebrities. There was Alvin, the partially crippled New Paltz Street Sweeper who was in the Sicilian Village Scene

seen white washing a wall in The God Father Part I, and Modesto
Cuomo, related to Mario Cuomo who was then the Governor of
New York State, who was in, and had a small part in the Wedding
Scene with Marlon Brando in The Godfather Part I. It was
Modesto who through the sandwiches to Sonny with the line
"Cabbagoal," which is the Italian American slang for Capicola, a
type of spicy ham sandwich. And there was the elegant photo of
Richie, lighting up, and "toking" on, (in the jargon of the reefer
trade "taking a drag from,") a thickly rolled joint of "Marijuana
Weed;" for all, including The Police, look at and to marvel over.

And if I can describe the stage to you that way, on that
particular morning, just beginning to get light, with The Flats
flooded and barely visible in the gray twilight of morning, cold
and forlorn, the temperature at the First National Bank clock
down the street reading forty one degrees Fahrenheit, when
Richie rounded the corner of Main Street and Route 208 walking
with his head down and with his hands in his jacket pockets and
stopped in front of The Chez Joey Italian Restaurant to look up
and over across the street at me and started across the street
toward me.

He was coming from his room that was located on the first
floor of the rooming house just around the corner next to The
Bacchus Bar, which he shared with his lovely companion girl
friend Rebecca Howells who worked as a waitress at The Cosmos
Restaurant up the street, and his brown Dachshund dog who was
getting old as a dogs life is, and who he had rescued from the
pound and named Lady.

Richie was heading somewhere I thought, either up to the Deli
House, or to the Cosmos, having just smoked his morning joint of
reefer, to sit for an hour or two for coffee talking shop and telling
stories with the other café sitters who came into town to hang out
or to do business with or get a hand out from Richie.

Richard was ten years older than myself, and forty one then at
the time, and a Capricorn, and was a strikingly handsome man,
with dark wavy hair but which he kept cut rather close at the time,
and although that he had different looks through the years, of hair
length and with a beard off and again. There was a charismatic

blood vessel burst and coloring in the white of his lower left eye. He was tall, roughly six foot one, with strong and powerful muscular build, and who carried himself well, as a man does who knows he has power.

He was clean-shaven on that particular morning, and although that his looks could vary on a daily basis, depending on what kind of drugs he was using, the amount of sleep he was getting, and what his state of mental health was, and who was often on bizarre and esoteric episodes, some of them dark and moody, and other often frivolous and quite carefree. He had many aliases, so named about himself, by himself, to event his personalities. One of which was, "Doctor Dot." So named for his penchant for using LSD, who no one could be around him and get close to without "doing," as Richie described it, of "getting dropped on," in his term for it called "Monkey Business," or Drug Warfare going on, which Richie called, "Dada."

Another nickname he had coined for himself, was "The Wizard," so named because his Segregationist Attitude of Protecting the White Females from the Black Heroin, Prostitution, and Pornography of The White Slavery Trade. And also that, for what the term Wizard was used for was that for the price of drug connection, or a packet of even a line a Cocaine he could get anyone who was addicted to the drug, and dependent to his supply, that Richard could get anyone to do just about any thing he asked, and who could arrange all kinds of things going on behind the scenes.

Such was the power of being the Drug Boss, and to what power that everyone lived in the limbo shadow land of boogie men, in total fear of being wacked, as the familiar mafia term for being killed was coined, or imprisoned for a long time, depending on whose toes, the street mafia's, or the mafia's police department, that one happened to step on.

For what expression that the men all had a way of deferring to Richie in tribute for who he was, and not that he didn't have the great respect of regard of everyone for who he actually was, who was a very kind, and generous, and sensitive and extremely intelligent man, and a friend to all the people and to the shop keepers in The Village, in his own right, and who everyone loved instinctively, and on his own merits won.

But who was also "not just anybody" on his own, to be shown tribute and respected for, for the sake of the case that he was the vested and agreed upon primogeniture of a common destiny, being the son of The Duke and the heir apparent to The Thrown; and which was, the way of deference in tribute that the men used with Richie, to pretend to look fearful and drop a coin or other object from their pants pocket, and then stop, in feint of a gesture of genuflection, to pick it up, as a bow, whenever Richie appeared. And which I always loved to play up to him with doing also, dropping a penny to the ground then, and then picking it up as Richie came across the street to me.

If Richie liked you he would drop a coin back and stoop to pick it up when he was before you, which he did with me.

"Hey Richie," I said, "did you see The Flats are flooded with cakes of ice floating in the current. I've been watching it."

Richie turned to look without acknowledging the flood. He smelled of the sweet scent of freshly smoked Reefer.

"How are you, Gary? he asked peering into my eyes. "Are you going off to work?"

"I'm fine, doctor," I said. "And you? How are you this fine morning?" I asked, peering back into Richard's eyes. He seemed alert and wide-awake.

"I'm good," Richie said in a friendly chipper way.

"I was going off to work on the 7:05," I said back, "but there's something else I need to do. I'm thinking seriously of taking the day off. I feel in my gut that I need to be somewhere else."

"You don't look happy."

"I'm not really, there's something troubling me. I'm not cut out for a suit job and it's starting to disturb me in the way of not being happy with it. I'm more of an earthy kind of fellow, you know, hands on out in the day kind of physical work. But for now it's a needed job, that I was lucky to get, and something of the fulfillment of my college career to have to wear a suit to the job for a while."

"I know the feeling of needing to be free of those constricting business clothes," Richie replied. "Look at you. You look miserable." Richard lived on government checks from a military disability he suffered when a five-ton truck backed over his left foot. "You need to be on government checks live me." Then to me in a more serious and bragging overtone way he said, "We're in serious trouble here, are you in or out." Which was code spoken in the Greek for, 'there's something in the wind,' meaning, "something has come in."

Richie was an experienced organizer and a brilliant warrior leader who always made the extra effort to include everyone, everyone, in the special feeling of being needed and wanted, which made him popular and always looked to by people for reinforcement.

"I'm always in," Richie, I said, "you know that."

"See me later on then," he said, "when you get back from wherever it is that you are going today."

And with that I was sucked in and swept along.

"If I get back," I said. "I have to go and talk to Aba."

"Where are you going?" Richie asked showing a grimace with his clenched teeth.

"Up there," I said, pointing out towards Millbrook Mountain far out on the South End of the Shawangunk range. "I'm in the mood for a good long hike."

"Ha!" Richie replied, on a reflective note of concern. "You're going out there." He thought a moment and then told me a story, fingering the lapel of my trench coat in his fingers as he did, standing too close in to me, in my zone. It made me feel a little ridiculous and uncomfortable but I didn't move and let him talk into my face in his endearing way of heavy Brooklyn New York accent.

"I once knew a man who fell two stories off a ladder on a construction job he was working, and who landed in some bushes and miraculously survived without any serious injury to himself. And do you know what he did? After gathering his wits about him, he picked up his hammer and tool bag and went and got his lunch bucket, and then went home and made mad love to his wife.

You should do that instead of going out there. Take my advice."
Then he thought another moment and said. "You know you could
make a good living here with us if you would just let me set you
up with a nice franchise. You could get a quiet place outside of
Town and have a good life. That would make you a power."

"And what? Turn 'the stones' into bread," I replied, on a play
on the words, 'getting stoned on marijuana.' "It's not really in my
nature to do that. You were born into that world, Richie, but it's
entirely alien and a bit frightening for me to conceive of because I
wouldn't know my way around about in it as you do, who have all
the power over it. No offense, though intended. I appreciate your
offer, as always. I will stop by later when I can. I promise."

I was in a manner of saying a doctor to Richie also, and
Richie's head shrink, because I listened to him, and for a certain
way of saying, as he was my shrink too in his way of knowing
things and with his own unique perspective on things to inform
me about, and which was the reason that I phrased in that manner
of hopeful commitment to Richie, as Richie needed to talk with
me, to read me his poetry or just to converse, and as I needed to
talk with him as well, and who was a good and patient listener in
his own right, on different subjects of life to gain an appreciation
and analysis of.

And to what talk that I would listen to him patiently for hours
and hours on end; and, as he would listen to me respectfully and
with concerned and genuine interest, as was his charismatic way
in approach with everyone, in his room, or in the cafes, or just
standing or sitting out on the stoops of the street. And when we
were together in his room, alone together, or in the company of
Rebecca Howells, his fiancé, or in a group with other friends
gathered around in conversation, that I would patiently look at his
artwork, read his poetry back aloud to him, and listened to him
read his poetry, and listened to him play his instrument, the
saxophone.

"Good stuff?" I asked.

"Ha!" Richie stated, rolling his eyes upwards, "We are indeed
very fortunate to have scored something good this time. Have
you seen anything Kenny Lightfoot?"

"Not since the day before yesterday in the Cosmos. He should be around though. He said he is doing a block job for a house and needs a ride to work every day. So he should be out on the street sometime soon to wait for his ride."

"Tell him that I need to see him if you do, o.k.?"

"I will do that," I said.

And which was my job of sorts on the street, or my 'bowl of rice,' as the saying went, in Richie's eyes of me with the Company Drug Smuggling and Trafficking Business, and for the privilege of being there to be allowed, 'to hang out on the street,' with everyone, to be expected, 'to put the word out,' about what was going down. And which was an important post to have, and among other posts such as being a "Scare Crow," or as a "Heavy Strong Arm" to stand around and intimidate people and causing them to think carefully about their "dealings" going down on the street. And which I filled the rolls of quite nicely, whose place was to stand around and to look stern and quietly intimidate people into falling into and towing the mafia line.

Everyone in some way, who stayed around on the street, worked for "The Company," or paid tribute and allegiance to it, even to keeping silent, and most importantly, to keeping silent, in that way. And as the chain of command went, no one knew from one level to another who the others were to be named. Those involved with the smuggling and most dangerous end, were never known to the middlemen, and who were never known to the street dealers. No one ever asked where anything came from, or who was involved in getting it there. Only curious narcs asked those kinds of questions and who were either short lived or to whom certain mishaps befell, to those of them, the suspected narc types, who weren't on the Company Payroll to look the other way. It was such a massive thing, The Business.

It also had to be understood that there was always just so much product to sell to only so many customers, in that meaning, to what that any outside rival suppliers were discouraged from competing against by Richard, and who, after being informed of this, would put the word on them to the Italian Mafia Police in tow, to have the rivals arrested and eliminated by the local police, their drugs confiscated and then given over to Richard to redistribute and deal back out on the street. It was a lucrative cutthroat business in the downtown area belonging to Richard alone, with the warning, all others stay away.

"Where are you off to?" I asked.

"The Deli House. I have a poem I woke up with running around in my head, since around midnight and I want to get it down on a napkin before I forget it. I write a lot of poems out on napkins."

The Chief of Police, Charles Bagdonowicz drove by coming back up the hill from the river where they had been setting up barricades, and heading no doubt for the Police Station on Plattekill Avenue for the change of shifts. I waved to him, and Richie also turned and waved. Charlie waved back and smiled at us, a good sign.

"I remembered your great poem, 'The Bone House' poem, I woke up thinking about it this morning, Richie. It was on my mind when I woke up. I always loved the line, 'I live in a Bone House.' To me it had a special place at the heart of everything, to live in a Bone House. You have a fabulous gift of intellect." Then remembering something from the recent past that I had wanted to tell him, I blurted it out. "Richie, I am sorry about that one night, you remember, it was a while ago, when I was alone in the room with Rebecca and you came back and got upset with her and with me about my being there. Well, I am sorry about that, that it happened. I only went there and knocked on the door to see you and Rebecca said that you would be right back and to come in if I wanted to and wait for you. Then she asked me if I wanted to smoke a joint with her, and I did, which was the reason that I wanted to see you. And which she then told me that she thought it had been laced with a tranquillizer, which put me right off to sleep. So that 's what it looked like when you came back.

"I had the wrong idea," Richard said. "Thanks for telling me."

Richard began to recite his poem, which he named Angel Birds to me in an animated way, standing very close and gesturing over each phrase of it with his arms and fingers, his lips hurling little drops of spit, his eyes wild with a look of fervor.

Angel Birds

A doorway partially open
May one come in?
Revenge left a memory
Taking refuge in bad weather and some noise
It was only thunder
It is no longer necessary
Dust is everywhere from the whole idea
It is no longer necessary
earth and snow
Inheritance in the noise
That is naturally silent
Tuning to a firing squad
And through a secret dimension heard
The sound of a bullet hitting a human heart

No one dies in a traffic jam
You are officially talking to
A colored lady who worships
Large toes and painted nails
Having a conversation with a firing squad
At the bottom of a garbage can
Remove the error with a pair of scissors

We are all the honored guests
We freeze in mid-air real close to the eyelid
No one dies in a traffic jam
Demented crumbs from an old nightfall
Please remove your shoes and socks
Consume what you can
Starving smile like a Hindu
Taking refuge in the bottom of a garbage can Begging
Put back the cover
Put back the cover
Freeze in mid-air
Real close to the eyelid

No pity from blind frozen smoke
We are all the honored guests
We are all

Predestined to be dust
Lift the corpse over your head
No bird can forgive this excuse
Satan falling out of a limousine
Dead frozen smoke
Revenge of a drowned fly
In the dark waiting on a plate
for a ripe piece of fruit
It's a struggle Misbehaving wind
The propositions change when the eyelids close
Necessary intimacy no pity for the dead frozen smoke
Maintenance needed on a southern cloud
Every prisoner needs a rat resistant room
Wait for the dark
No bird can forgive this excuse
No pity for the dead
We are all the honored guests

We are all

The Honored Guests

He lingered on the last reverberation of the word, "Guests."
"I did good," Richie said, "didn't I."
"You did real good, Richie. That's a very lovely, thoughtful, and moving piece of work. Truly I do admire you, indeed I do," I said, imitating the Robin. I respect you, indeed I do."
"I respect you too, Richie said, "Indeed I do. I hope you go an fall off a cliff and die today." Said in Richard's style of wizardry, using reverse psychology to make people, instinctively inclined to reject advice, to do the opposite of what you want them to do.
"You don't mean that, Richie. I know you don't."
"I know I don't," he said, emphasizing the I, " but you do,"

Richie concluded, peeing closely at me and looking at me into my right eye with his blood discolored and hypnotic left eye. "Ha! Just look at you. You have the obsessed hollow look of a suicidal killer written in your eyes. I spent a year one time doing nothing but staring at the wall in my room with the same look in my eyes as you have now. Are you still over there with the Professor."

"Private duty," I said. "He has a Moss Mafia issue with his daughter, and the boy Henry is not doing well. Their mother committed suicide last year and he discovered the body."

Old Location Of "The Hebrew National Deli House"
No Longer In Business – Is In The Far Left Corner

"I'm only here to put an end to the Heroin Trafficking on the earth, Richie, as God has Commanded, and To Defend America,

and To Save the White Race from Inter-Racial Extermination ...
The wheat from the tears and the sheep from the goats."

"So am I," Richard said. "So are we all. But we just can't go
about making enemies of those people and targets out of
ourselves. In our business you can't afford to have any. Be
careful with it."

"We're hard pressed not to," I said. "They want our souls for
the price of the drugs they deal. How can anyone deal with
them?"

I purposely didn't say, 'how can you,' deal with them, because
I knew better, although I implied it with the tone of my remark.

"Be careful with it," Richard said. "Young girls are hard to get
rid of. They smell so good, and they're sweet and very eager.
But in the end they prove hard to handle and are full of danger.

"Try not breathing until you get across the street to the Deli
House," I said to him, "that will demonstrate to yourself how
powerful you are. I bet you'll take a breath before you get there."

"I bet I will too," Richard said.

And with that he turned and sauntered off across the street.

And that was what my particular style of Private Practice
Therapy amounted to; being mindful of people, taking an interest
in what they were saying, asking and making them answer
questions about themselves, provoking them to think, and very
importantly remembering what they have told you to be able to
refer to their advise and exert knowledge, or to the details of just
plain conversation, on different topics to be able to bring the
topics up at another time of a meeting to continue the friendship
in conversational relationship with interest, once and a great while
interjecting something about yourself to make a point or for them
to ponder and reflect on.

Richard had a great gift for that, which I was learning from in
my study of him. And with whom, as who was ten years older
than myself and a great deal more sophisticated in matters of the
street that I was only the apprentice to, that I had a rather
awkward, and although warm hearted relationship with. I always
liked and appreciated to follow the rule of the older brother in
these matters, that whoever was the senior always had the power

and the grace of ascendancy to be deferred to and respected, that was akin to the term rank in some way, but which went down as custom, to respect one's elders, no matter how elder.

Detective Brad Birchel drove by in his unmarked prowl car on his way to look at the flooded Flats and waved to me. I waved back to him. Brad a handsome man in his mid-thirties then, and straightforwardly very professional in a mind-your-own-business-way in his police demeanor; who I personally was fond of, and as I was too with The Chief and with several others of the New Paltz Police Force. I watched him pass and drive on down to the river and lapsed again into my reverie on the nature of friendship and attentiveness, and of my thoughts that day that I would carry with me to the mountain to be alone with The Father.

There were several other too who had that fine trait of attentive listening and involved conversation, who I respected and looked up to as examples of what life was like when not encumbered with one's own ego, to be able to get out of one's self with and explore the worlds of others around you.

My great school friend and chess mate Timothy Shoh was like that, and who that I learned the technique of patient listening from first. Best to listen to what other had to say, than to try and dominate the social setting with one's own hot air of conversation.

And of course there was Tony, the novelist Anthony Robinson, and our great college Creative Writing Professor who had the superb gift of making people feel cared for and important.

And there also was my dear friend Arnold Moodnick, who everyone called "Marky," but who I called Arnold in a more serious and less familiar manner in my endeared and respected regard for him, that seemed more of the right way to be for our relationship. And who was, Arnold Moodnick, the Jewish War Commander and who was coincidentally ten years my senior and the same age and rank as Richard Rizzi on another plane of action in the Jewish Mafia, akin to the godfather, and allied with the gangster Duke Rizzi and to his son Richard together as Murder Incorporated. It was all that serious of a dealings with everyone, on the plane of life and death with many people looking at prison time and needing a bond of trust and loyalty to get them through the day, that was not to be betrayed, and there it was, and to what that Arnold was one of the enforcers to, and myself too included to be as one of the enforcers because of my friendship and close proximity to Richard and with Arnold, and which opened all the doors there were to open to me within the Organization.

And who, as to say of Arnold, was quite an attractive man, large of bone and stature and very charismatic in his friendly and great manly way, with his deep baritone voice and slow moving walk, and who always seemed very interested and very attentive in courting me in a manly way in our meetings and dealings and of a genuinely inquiring intent of knowing me, as I was with him that way, to inquire after his boyhood and parenting and his love-life, in his regard of his relationship with him, and he with me, and as I was frequently with him hanging out together in a boy-hood like and mutually likeable eager way of our friendship, the way of common trust and intent of intellect to be real friends and genuine colleagues of an knowledge forming way, both of us endeavoring the forming the tight bond together of a long-lasting relationship. And who may be dead by now as I have not heard from him these many, many years now, since about the last time that I saw Richard, sometime in those years around 1996 when I last was ever in New Paltz, NY.

It was from Arnold whom I learned everything of the ever-ongoing Jewish Plot; of, there are Good Jews and Bad Jews way of meaning, "Inch By Inch," to take over their own Territory from the Americans here in the United States. And for what purposes that he needed everyone who he associated with to side with him and to justify with the Jews about, and who would spend hours talking to everyone of his inner-sanctum persuading them with tales of the horrors of Jewish Persecution through the centuries in justifying their need for war actions to carve out, in meaning of conducting clandestine warfare, a place and territory for themselves among their host nations, and to one day coalesce all their Jewish National Organizations into The New Promised Land of Zion, with the indication being at the present time here in America; the Good Jew and the Bad Jews, and all on the same side of Zion and The Promised Land, with the Good Jews doing nothing about the Bad Jews involved in the process, and murder of the indigenous population under siege in the Take Over.

To what that everyone had to agree with them, or to be classified as the Enemy, and regarded to be the Enemy, in the meaning by the local Jewish Army, and in the meaning of the intimidation of foul play, and like the tactics of the Italian Mafia that way, by the local Jewish Military in Bad Mafia Terms.

And it was from Arnold "Marky" that I learned of Jewish "Angel Dust War," (and which was like the LSD War being waged by the Italian Mafia in a Jewish sense in those years of 1978 well into the early 1980;s,) which was the chemical Phencylidine, (PCP,) that the Jewish Mob surreptitiously administered to the food and beverage supplies on an ongoing and methodical basis, the effects of what were symptoms significantly more dangerous than other categories of hallucinogens that mimic schizophrenia such as delusions, hallucinations, paranoia and disordered thinking, that made people feel like they were coming out of the skins and crazy with hallucinating notions of violent tendencies, that had everyone running around trying to find a sedation "Quell" to its effects, not know where they were coming from, in a sadistic torment on the part of the Jews involved with it, who knew very well what was happening and who were always eager to supply the narcotics and tranquillizers to alleviate the homicidal irritation of the PCP, or to point the way to psychiatric intake where the victim would be lobotomized with pharmacy chemicals such as Thorazine and Haldol. And to what that no one could complain with being handed over to psychiatric by the authorities and disposed of; which Arnold constantly referred to as "The Angel Movie." That was being done on a relentless and methodical and quite surreptitious manner, by the current trend of the Zionist Jews, to drive the local innocent indigenous Gentile Population away to make room for the new incoming influx of Jewish National Émigré replacements from Europe and other parts of the World in their grand design to take over America, to share with The Italian Fascists.

View From The Gay Nineties Bistro On Main Street

A local Jewish Warlord Pornographer also may have had designs to kill me once, either myself or someone who I was with, some several years later in the future from that present date of 1978, to be tortured to death in one of their Pornographic Video Thrill Killing Snuff Movies that were being made behind the scenes back then, with their victims, so I've been told, being tied to a bed and cut into little pieces as a part of the Jewish population disposal pogrom, and independent of the Italian Mafia Porno Snuff Mafia network that way, by functioning in a similar manner of reciprocity in sinister intent, as an Active Arm of the

Combined Jewish-Italian, Black Makimbo War Operation, that
was on that night's occasion headed by the Jewish Movie
Producer Allen Epstein, now deceased, (or at least of many years
back ago, as advertised to be deceased, who as we all know only
takes a crooked mafia coroner and a crooked undertaker to
arrange for a person to appear deceased and for the payment of an
insurance policy premium ahead of time, and to allow persons to
disappear into the criminal underground.)

And who, as to say, Allen, lived out in the vicinity of
Rosendale, NY along a deserted back road, and had invited me to
his house one night, and along with Arnold and my friend and
Arnold's side-kick Joey St. George, and Ray Bremzer, who was
just recently released from a prison in upstate New York for
manslaughter after serving twenty years, and who Arnold was
looking after and taking care of in giving him a place to stay and
some work to do about the property there at Arnold's old two
story white farm house in Modina, NY, nearby the Village of
New Paltz about five or so miles distance to the Southeast.

Allen's house was crowded with people when we got there
driving up in Joey's old delivery van with myself sitting behind
Joey and Ray in the other back seat at around eight-thirty p.m.
and got out to go inside.

We were greeted at the door by Allen who was a medium
height man with pimply face in his mid-forty's, who was dressed
oddly that night for the occasion in a purple and white sacrificial
robe, or so I got the impression of, with his hair slicked back, and
who offered everyone glasses of wine with little tabs of acid,
LSD, adhering to their edges, which Allen called "Treats" after he
saw me scrutinizing the one edged over the side of my glass,
which he referred to as, "Mellow Blotter," and which I tactfully
disposed of on the floor while he wasn't looking letting it drop by
the side of my pant leg.

All in all it was a nice home, tastefully furnished with nice
curtains at the windows, and traditional style furniture and with a
combined kitchen-living room open room peaking to a high
vaulted ceiling and with the living room separated from the
kitchen by an island counter with chairs on the living room side of

it to the left, and with steps ascending to a railed hallway on the second floor opening onto two doors. There was a dining room table set up with places for eight at the far end of the room opposite the front door. On the far wall to the side where the dining room table was there was a door leading to another back part of the house.

There were about twenty or so people there, counting myself, Arnold, Joey, and Ray, with a few people, acquaintances that I knew from Town. Kurt Grimes was also there, who I knew from the street and from his dealings with Ernie Shaw, the psychiatrist sculptor who had been involved with Mary Robinson and with Jenny shortly before Mary's apparent suicide with a shotgun.

About a half hour into the evening of listening to conversations and mingling my way around taking in the atmosphere, Ray Bremzer who came up to me and tipped me off to something going on. He said, "Did you ever meet a group of people who seem very friendly, but who really aren't? I'm not getting a good vibe here at all."

"I know that topic," I said. "It's called the Double Bind."

"Well," he said, "I have the uneasy feeling here that this is more of an 'All Of A Sudden' group thing, than a slow burn, like everyone who at first seems normal and friendly all of sudden turning into Vampires and overpower you, and in the sense that these people would all be in the blood movies, the gang of them, and who know each other that way, and perhaps that you would be the only one present who hasn't been initiated into their blood thing yet. Or, perhaps it's me they are about to gang up on, or maybe you, and I'm the initiate to watch. I've been around."

"I see," I said. "Well in that case, that explains what Joey was saying the other night when he said that he overheard, 'That I Was Being Groomed For Something.' Why don't we just step outside and smoke a joint and see what they do. We'll have more room to maneuver out there."

And which was what we did, motioning to Joey and to Arnold Moodnick with an uplifted nod of our heads and our eyes to join us. We were outside for about fifteen minutes when Allen appeared at the doorway and stepped out onto the front porch being followed by several of his entourage of guests. And who, Allen, kept nervously pacing back and forth on the porch in his ridiculous costume with his hair slicked back trying to gather his courage and at the doorway finally coming to a stop saying and gesturing by crossing and separating his arms in the signal of denunciation over and over again,

"Can't Do It! Can't Do It!"

And with that he went back inside with his gathered entourage behind him and closed the door.

"Good thing," I said to Ray, "I knew in my heart and in my gut that he couldn't go through with it out here one on one. Thank you for the warning. I will always have your back too."

"It may have been me they wanted," Ray said, "Thanks for having my back. My God, they care nothing for friendship, These People. Certain things, like trust and friendship are sacred." Which was meant more for Arnold's and Joey's ears that for mine. And I felt it too; as to what they were going to do if indeed either Ray or myself become the targeted victim.

"I've got a shotgun in Joey's van if we need it," Arnold said.

We stood around for a bit until the strong effects from the marijuana wore off and not wanting to appear to be intimidated, but standing down whatever that was that had confronted us until it was apparent that had stood them down, then we left together going back to Arnold's for the night. I was again in the back seat behind Joey with Ray, and with Arnold and Joey up front, as we had come, and talking about different things on the road other than what had just happened, while Joey was solemnly driving us on in silence, taking in the headlights cutting into the darkness ahead heavy with thought.

And though that nothing was ever really said about the incident; but that things were never right again and the same with my private practice in the way that it had been, with Joey and with Arnold, in the way and meaning of trust and to be able to enjoy their company again in that close feeling. That in the years to follow formed the basis for my secret Alliances with Law Enforcement and my ongoing Intelligence Reports that I would periodically file with them, on the nature of these mafias to expose them for the dire threat to the Nation that they really are, and to prepare the nation to defend themselves about what I was being exposed to. And for the time, I made my way as everyone did in the mafia on the street, knowing who you couldn't trust, and not really knowing who you could trust, and living and alive on the strength of one's own personal power holding on in the day to day of it.

It wasn't long after that incident that we heard Allen Epstein had died of a bad heart, congenital heart failure, as it was put out.

And all of this and many other intrigues that lay ahead of me in time, and as time is measured among the living, in my future, were held in the fate for my decisions and actions that lay in store for me on that day, as I watched Richie's back until he had crossed the street and walked into The Deli House with its bright window light emanating out into the road. It was Richie's world. And for all its great danger and troubling allure involved with it, I found I liked Richie very much. He was a down to earth kind of guy who dealt evenly with you. And importantly, he was deep thinker, and real, and not a pasteboard kind of person of superficial manners. When he asked, "How are you?" he validated your existence and meant it.

Drugs though were not the only world that Richie had been born into. He was also born into the world of Gay Pornography, at the very young age of puberty, and as all the young mafia males of the area, and others who could be seduced and recruited, were taking in by and trained by the elder homosexuals at that early age and raised to adopt and to accept Homosexuality and Pornography in general, as a normal course of life, and as a part of the Italian Heritage in America. And for what background that he had become and was aggressively and outspokenly homosexual, in his way of compensating, and although that he always conveyed to be a heterosexual kind of guy and lived with a woman as well. But he would often have men to his side to have sex with him too as a normal course of events.

He was however, a moral person with a conscience and easily put in his place if you didn't care for such things. And he was introspective in a soul-searching way, honest in his dealings, and fair and square with everyone and expecting everyone to be square with him as well. All the shopkeepers and street people knew and respected him. He was a Vegetarian and outspokenly in defense of the suffering of the poor animals to be slaughtered, and he studied Zen, with its philosophy of mindfulness, justness, and fairness, which made him a decent Godfather to everyone. And that was not a position that anyone else could occupy, as no one had and possessed in a personal way of power, the depth of field that Richard did have.

One of the rules he had was don't cheat on your wife, or don't have two women, which was a rule that Richard always kept everyone honest about, and for the two important reasons, the first being for the undeniable moral integrity of the matter, and the second being, that one can't afford to make enemies in our business, as he always put it to you, possessively, as if you couldn't say no.

And then I knew what the treasure in the field had to do with, and why that it would be kept secret. The treasure is the joy of good deeds in your own heart that loses its value if it is bragged about.

'Again, the kingdom of heaven is like a treasure hidden in the field, which a man discovers and hides, and because of his joy, he goes and sells everything he has, and buys the field.' Matthew 13:44.

[The treasure in the field is the secret wisdom enjoyed of a good and honest life, full of charitable works and kindness towards others. And the greatest joy is to instill the sense and the meaning of joy in others, and where in the heart is the Kingdom of God, and with the meaning of being "hidden" to possess the silent respect and solemn admiration of the society in which we live, in the noble spirit of the soul of personal relations that we are disinclined to brag about, and which turns us ill-will if we do. And for which reason that we keep our feelings about ourselves hidden, deep in our soul, where we each live and breath the air of our neighbors, in the real setting of reality, of how that we perceive and experience it, that is apart and distinct from one's public presentation. Blessed is he who knows the way.]

And always, if you have two women, you would wind up with none. The society didn't like cheaters and it didn't like men with two women. That would open the door for the society to try and take both women away from you with their drugs and other means of porno star persuasion. And otherwise, that they respected your relationship with your wife or sweetheart if you were sincere and faithful to her and they left you alone or looked after things to protect you in that regard, and respected you as a strong member of the community. And in turn they asked that you respect their relationship; that in Richard's case was the love of his life, Rebecca. It was Richard's Zen approach to life to be faithful and loyal in love.

'So will it be at the end of the world;' I thought, 'the angels will go out and separate the bad from among the righteous, And they will throw them, [the bad] into the furnace of fire; there shall be weeping and gnashing of teeth.' Matthew 13: 49-50.

So there is a hell. The prophecy of hell-fire is real.

Lip, Lung, and Tongue, is a Mafia Term used in the meaning of the word "Craft" or otherwise spelled out to be, "Witch Craft," knowingly applied, and that is in the knowledge of the effects of the use of the drugs directly, of the drug residue thereby being on the lips and tongue, to induce the effect of the drugs, or chemicals, on other people, and in the lung way of the intent, to infect the air surrounding the person using the drug to affect, like second hand tobacco, or marijuana smoke, to affect those in close proximity with in contact effect of the drug, and with Heroin that way of inducing an hypnotic affect, and with Cocaine inducing a hyper invigorated state in their unknowing victims, in for instance; or which can be cross referenced of the drugs' effects from kissing or sharing a beverage with the saliva of the drugs present, or to just plain grinding them up and dropping the drugs in food and beverages, called Spike Warfare, on unsuspecting people through mafia waitresses, cooks, and otherwise kitchen help, and having to do with home life too, and atmosphere; and what are the methods used to take Drug Prisoners.

To what intrigues that No One Was Safe from the effects of. And which, depending on the drug being used, to take a person prisoner, would make the person given the drugs 'addicted' to the person, or to the place, that they came into contact with who administered the drug to them, or the contact high of the drug, as to the way it went.

Steve, the proprietor of The Gay Nineties Restaurant, who was in his mid-thirties, opened the door at precisely seven o'clock and let in several customers who had just arrived and had been standing outside waiting for the restaurant to open. Doctor Price Charlson, a Professor of Philosophy at the University, and who my close friend of the street James Bosciano stayed with, and who always let me stay over at the house when I needed a place to sleep, came walking across the street dressed in his traditional suit and tie and overcoat buttoned to the neck against the morning air. He nodded his usual formal greeting to me, and to Steve, and hurried inside to take his place at the counter for his leisurely daily breakfast before heading up the hill to the College and to his office for his morning classes.

Having let all the customers in Steve briefly stepped outside onto the sidewalk and looked up and down the street. I nodded a greeting good morning to him and he nodded back his reply.

"Ed may be a little late getting in this morning," I said to him pointing out toward the flooded Flats, and knowing he was looking for Ed. Ed was an old man and our mutual friend Ed Brandes with long white hair, who dressed eccentrically, and who walked the four miles into Town each day, or was picked up by friends along the way, from his wooded estate where he lived in an old ramshackle two story red house out by the mountain on Warwarsing road. And who Steve out of the kindness of his heart had provided the job to, of sweeping up the sidewalk and shoveling the snow, in the front of the restaurant in exchange for a hardy breakfast and a few dollars which Ed religiously put in the bank to save for his yearly taxes.

Steve was a man of few words and not much for small talk. He looked out at the Flats, nodded his head one last time to me, and then went back inside closing the door behind him.

I turned and went inside The Hobo Deli with its two tiers of stacked shelves in the center of the floor and the walls lined with

expensive cans and other dry goods, and with its two coolers
filled with rapidly consumed sodas and beers of every description.
The deli counter was along the back wall with its cold cut meets
and delicious dishes of egg and potato and macaroni and other
kinds of inviting salads all made up. The worker Doris, a nice
college girl and the proprietor Edgar, a man in his early fifties,
were busy behind the deli counter. I asked for change for the
phone from Doris and she gave it to me. I nodded and smiled
affectionately to Edgar, who smiled and nodded back to me, and
then I called my friend Timothy Shoh from the payphone by the
door on the right side of the store.

I had gotten the job for Timmy with The Dutchess County
C.E.T.A. Program as he was so desperate for work after finishing
his school studies, and to being a friend to him in my position of
being able to hire my own staff, by using my parents address to
list him, and myself, as a local Dutchess County residents there,
and which technically and theoretically we were, if I was, and he
was therefore to, by virtue of my intimate and close friend who
stayed overnight at the house on many occasions through the
many years of our friendship over time. And to what that sending
him a few letters addressed to that address did the job as proof of
residency.

I told Timmy to make my excuses to everyone, of the six
others plus Timmy of my C.E.T.A. Project Development Staff,
and who were operating out of a building without any phone
lines, and to apologize for my not feeling well, and if he would
please pay Walter for me for running for coffee and that I would
pay him back.

To what Timmy said he would hold the fort in my absence,
and that he would give Walter his money for running for coffee,
and wanted to know if I would like a ride there over to
Poughkeepsie in the morning. I said I would give him a call that
night to confirm, but that most likely it would not be a bad idea
and would appreciate having a ride over and not having to take
the bus very much.

Timmy's girl friend whose name was Carla Chico who he
lived with at University Apartments drove Timmy across the

Hudson River each day, as Timmy had not car, and would often, to save me having to take the bus, come by to pick me up at Tony's house.

And with that, I hung up the phone and began to walk down to the green iron bridge on Route 299 that crossed over The Wallkill River. At the entrance to the bridge the road crew had set up barricades with the sign with flashing yellow lights, ROAD CLOSED. I crossed over the bridge to the other side and stood on the roadway just before the flooding waters sweeping past with their chunks of ice, some of them quite large, looking out toward the mountain.

Bridge Across The Wallkill and The Flooded Flats

The air smelled musty of the river, a dank fishy aroma, that was not however unpleasant. I took in a deep lung fulls of it and let it back out slowly through my nostrils, praying to God The Father to guide me along in a sense of the way. Then I fell into a deep trance, bracing myself for what I was about to do, the step taken and from what that there was no turning back. And Oh, the finality of certain thoughts that could never be returned from, that was in the moment.

I took another deep breath of the dank river air and stepped out into the ice-cold water that would forever be frozen in my memory. No turning back now I thought as the icy water sloshed into my shoes and pressed against my legs in the current. I kept moving, holding my brief case and with it papers inside to my chest with both arms, fetal fashion for a time, and then with one arm and then another as they became weary. It was not too far though across the Flats and I was soon out of the wet and onto dry land one again, soaked and freezing from the waste down.

The Shawangunks, (pronounced SHON-gums), stretch 50 miles from the New Jersey border at Port Jervis northeast to Rosendale, NY in a series of parallel rolling ridges. Dramatic white quartz vertical escarpments line the southeast face of the ridge, while the backsides gently slope northwestward, sinking into fertile river valleys.

Geologically, they are part of the Appalachian Mountain chain that passes through the Hudson Valley creating the dramatic Hudson Highlands.

The Shawangunk ridge top is an ecosystem of pitch pine barrens, dwarf pine plains, quartz conglomerate cliffs, slab rock and virgin hemlock forests and is rich in wildlife, deer and porcupines, and home to many rare and endangered species, providing habitats for spotted salamander, migratory birds, black bear, bobcat, fox, fisher and over 200 species of nesting birds. Rare and endangered species found along the ridge include clustered sedge, broom crowberry, timber rattlesnake, hyssop skullcap, Carolina cranesbill, and mountain spleenwort, and which was also home to the peregrine falcons, which were settled there by naturalists in recent years, and that now nest on cliffs in the ridge where they are making a tenuous recovery.

I looked out to Millbrook Mountain as it was named, to the Southeast, were I was about to go, which was the last big and magnificently majestic quartz conglomerate cliff to the Southeast on the Range.

At The Intersection of Route 44-55 and 299
With The Mountain General Store and Bill's Garage
The Near Trapps Ridgeline Is In The Background

The English name, Shawangunk, derives from the Dutch *Scha-wan-gunk,* the closest European transcription from the colonial deed record of the Munsee Lenape, Schawankunk (German orthography).

Lenape linguist Raymond Whritenour reports that *schawan* is an inanimate intransitive verb meaning "it is smoky air" or "there is smoky air". Its noun-like participle is *schawank,* meaning, "that which is smoky air". Adding the locative suffix gives us *schawangunk* "in the smoky air".

Whritenour has suggested that the name derives from the burning of a Munsee fort by the Dutch at the eastern base of the ridge in 1663 (a massacre ending the Second Esopus War), where it spread quickly across the basin on land deeds and patents after the war. Historian Marc B. Fried writes: "It is conceivable that this was...the Indians' own proper name for their village [and fort] and that the name was appropriated for use in subsequent land dealings because of the proximity of the...tracts to the former Indian village.... The second possibility is that the name simply came into existence in connection with the Bruyn [purchase of Jan., 1682, the first appearance of the name in documentary record], as a phrase invented by the Indians to describe some feature of the landscape."

However, Fried also notes that the name's swift spread in the deed record suggest it was in use as a proper name before the Bruyn purchase. Shawangunk appears nowhere in reference to the fort itself in the extensive, translated Dutch record of the Second Esopus War. Shawangunk became associated with the ridge in the 18th century.

European colonists began to truncate Shawangunk, pronounced /ˈʃɑːwəŋɡʌŋk/, into "Shongum" /ˈʃɑːn.ɡʌm/ *SHAHN-gum*. Shongum was mistakenly identified as the Munsee pronunciation by the Reverend Charles Scott writing on Shawangunk's etymology for the Ulster County Historical Society in 1861. The error has been reinforced in ethnographic sources and ridge literature, and by historians, librarians, and ridge educators for more than 140 years.

Both "Shawangunk" and "Shongum" are popular usages among locals native to the region. The "Gunks" is also a widely used endearment and which may have originated among rock climbers.

The Geography of the Shawangunk Ridge is the northern end of a long ridge within the Appalachian Mountains that begins in Virginia, where it is called North Mountain, continues through Pennsylvania as Blue Mountain, becomes known as the Kittatinny Mountains after it crosses the Delaware Water Gap into New Jersey and becomes the Shawangunks at the New York state line. These mountains mark the western and northern edge of the Great Appalachian Valley.

The ridge is widest (7.5 miles/12 kilometers) near the northern end, narrow in the middle (1.25 miles/under 2 kilometers) with a maximum elevation of 2,289 feet (698 m) near Lake Maratanza on the Shawangunk Ridge. The Ridge rises above a broad, high plain which stretches to the Hudson River to the east. On the west the low foot-hills of the Appalachian Mountains mingle with a low flat made by the Rondout Creek and Sandburgh Creek, the Basher Kill and various small kills as well as the Neversink River and Delaware River at the southern end. These adjacent valleys are underlain by relatively weak sedimentary rock (e.g., sandstone, shale, limestone).

The Geology of the ridge is primarily underlain by Shawangunk Conglomerate, a hard, silica-cemented conglomerate of white quartz pebbles and sandstone that directly overlies the Martinsburg Shale, a thick turbidite sequence of dark gray shale and greywacke sandstone. The Martinsburg Shale was deposited in a deep ocean during the Ordovician (470 million years ago). The Shawangunk Conglomerate was deposited over the Martinsburg Shale in thick braided rivers during the Silurian (about 420 million years ago); both sequences of sedimentary rock were subsequently deformed and uplifted during the Permian (about 270 million years ago).

As a result of this deformation, strata within the ridge are involved in a northward plunging series of asymmetric folds (e.g., anticlines and synclines) that dip gently towards the west. These same folds, involving strata that overlie the Shawangunk Conglomerate, are exposed north of Shawangunk Ridge in the Rosendale natural cement region, where they can be directly examined in abandoned cement mines. Strata along the eastern margin of Shawangunk Ridge are truncated by erosion, resulting in the prominent cliffs characteristic of Shawangunk Ridge. The Shawangunk Conglomerate is very hard and resistant to weathering; whereas the underlying shale erodes relatively easily. Thus, the quartz conglomerate forms cliffs and talus slopes, particularly along the eastern margin of the ridge.

The entire ridge was glaciated during the last (Wisconsin) glaciation, which scoured the ridges, left pockets of till, and dumped talus (blocks of rock) off the east side of the ridge. On top of the ridge, the soils are generally thin, highly acidic, low in nutrients, and droughty, but in depressions and other areas where water is trapped by the bedrock or till, there are interspersed lakes and wetland areas. Soils on top of shale are thicker, less acidic, and more fertile. Topography on the top of the northern Shawangunks is irregular due to a series of faults that form secondary plateaus and escarpments.

There is an unusual diversity of vegetation on the ridge, containing species typically found north of this region alongside species typically found to the south or restricted to the Coastal

Plain. This results in an unusual area where many regionally rare
plants are found at or near the limits of their ranges. Other rare
species found in the area are those adapted to the harsh conditions
on the ridge. Upland communities include <u>chestnut oak</u> and
mixed-oak forest, <u>pine barrens</u> including dwarf pine ridges,
<u>hemlock</u>-northern hardwood forest, and cliff and talus slope and
cave communities. Wetlands include small lakes and streams,
<u>bogs</u>, <u>pitch pine</u>-<u>blueberry</u> <u>peat</u> swamps, an inland <u>Atlantic white
cypress</u> swamp, <u>red maple</u> swamps, acidic seeps, calcareous
seeps, and a few emergent marshes.

   My home and life with my lovely wife Doreen had been at that
base of Millbrook Mountain on McKinstry Road in the Town of
Gardiner, NY; where we had lived in a nice modern ranch style
single story yellow house in that year of our marriage in 1976.
And it was there that my climbing friend Michael Migliori, who
lived in the neighboring farm house on McKinstry Road that he
rented and shared with his girlfriend Caroline and with another
couple, and I, on the day of Good Thursday of Easter Week that
was late in April of that year, on The Feast of The Last Supper,
camped out at the very top of Millbrook Mountain, after scaling
the sheer cliff on a perilous climb. Doreen had dropped us off at a
spot along the mountain road to begin the hike to the cliff, that
had taken us all morning of arduous toil scrambling up and down
through the great bolder field just to get to the base of Millbrook
Mountain to begin the climb, which took us nearly another three
hours, taking our time, to complete, on a route up treacherous
loose rock that we had never climbed before, and that had never
been climbed to our knowledge or at least that was never reported
about, and which we would never remember, of the exact route,
how we climbed there to report about it ourselves.
   And which we did climb, both of us spent in sheer exhaustion
from the dramatic effort, reaching the summit, at approximately
four in the late afternoon, and after hauling up our knapsacks and
gear with our sleeping bags and jackets for the night chill, one
pitch at a time on a separate rope, and made a light bivouac camp
at a nice grassy spot at he very edge of the three hundred foot

precipice there at the top of Millbrook, and ate a dinner meal of
wine and cheese and bread. And real manly adventure it all was.

Then as we watched the sliver of the full moon appeared on
the Eastern Horizon and began its slow ascent into the sky. It had
been a brilliant full moon that night in a crystal clear sky full of
bright stars, and the brightest of stars shone there on the mountain
without any of the interference of the city lights.

And as it rose, the enchanted full moon that night, we both
became, Michael and I, in the spell of the moon's display of light
that shown in the sky and that reflected in the lakes far down in
the valley, for us to witness, and to marvel at the idea of there
being such things as a Star and the Earth and a Moon to exist, and
to be reflected in the pools of water, for us to bear witness to, and
for the fact of ourselves being alive, for out own existence, that
we became profoundly aware of the incredible thing of our
existing, of our being alive, in the here and now of eternal time, to
witness the moon and the universe stretching out before us into
the limitless unknown, into the infinity of the darkness beyond.

And so that we both fell down on our knees, right there to that
spot, and verbally Acknowledged and Gave Thanks to The
Creator for the life we had, that we each promised to do good
with and to do all we could to help The Creator make the world a
better place in The Creator's design for it. And it was on that
night that we both became intimate with The Creator in the
meaning of being touched with His Personal Friendship and
Grace and knew The Existence of God, The Father, Who made
the Universe, and the Sun and the Moon, and the Earth, and us, in
the Image of Himself, to view and witness it all. And it was all
quite startling in its revealing nature in the awakening of some
inner strength and determination within us both to somehow
embark on a new course with our approach to the life we had in
common, not so in any way to due with preaching, but with The
Great and Vast Knowledge of a purpose to live life out in the
hallowed terms of appreciating our existence, and not for the sake
of doing anything or accomplishing anything, but to respect and
appreciate just being alive to bear witness to the creation and to
delight in its character, akin to reverence, and awaiting the next

revelations of the oncoming mystery in anticipation. All of life had meaning in phenomenon. And then it became clear that we were living out our part in God's Great Dream of Creation. And to which dream that we were awakened in our minds to then.

It was warm that night and the night air was very still. We were able to sit out comfortably and were both filled with a wonderment of being alive. And which became a special place to us, that particular place, for the feat we had accomplished to be there, and for the special grace of The Creator to have bestowed the inner knowledge of existence to us there, which became a place of power and source of inspiration, to be able to reflect upon and to draw strength from in all of our days.

And it was to that place where I was going to on this particular day, with the knowledge of Mary Robinson's death by her own hand weighing forlornly on the venture and motivating it along.

In the morning, after a long night of lying awake unable to sleep in the wonder of the setting around us, that seemed all too real, and perhaps to myself dozing off and on lying at the very edge of the great cliff and holding on to a bush fearful that I would roll over the cliff in my sleep, we did finally awaken and stretch our limbs, and ate a meal of Gorp, as it was called, or trail mix consisting of mixed nuts, sunflower seeds, raisins, chocolate chip morsels, and other good things, chex cereal, and cinnamon.

We made a rock altar in a little alcove and piled small stones, the largest to the smallest, seven high, upon one another there, as was the custom throughout the Gunks for the climbers to mark their climbs in that way, then we broke camp, donned our knapsacks and started to make our way out of the forest.

Michael had been hiking first and spotted a deep several feet away as he rounded a bend in the rocks and motioned for me to be still and approach carefully. We watched the deer, a nice stag buck with several points to his antlers, for a long while, as it grazed on the grass, and then for some reason who sensed our presence, snorted, and bounded away through the brush.

As we continued walking, Michael happened to look back and shouted, "Look!" pointing to the fire raging up behind us.

Billowing up behind us was a terrifying ugly black cloud of smoke, high as the sky, coming from a forest fire burning out of control and raging just a short distance away behind the trees as we could see the sparks flying up behind us. We began to pick up our pace to running jog, in attempt to fly to try and outrun the fire, as we continued making our way along the well worn path over the top of the mountain the distance of three mile from Millbrook to get to the highway 44-55 at the Near Trapps on the Mohonk Preserve, and then down to the Mountain General Store at the intersection of 44-55 and 299 to where we had made arrangement to call Doreen from to come and pick us up.

The Flooded Flats On A Bleak March Day
View Of The Shawangunk Cliffs Is In The Background

The forest fire was not our doing as we had lit no campfire, but which may have been started by careless campers somewhere else nearby, as we had seen a group of men on the way up through the mountain forest on the way to the boulder field. And which was of unknown origin, and always did remain so, how it got started.

By the time we arrived back at our home on McKinstry Road, we watched as aircraft were already at work dumping water and chemicals on the fire to put it out; which was accomplished by one p.m. on that day, Good Friday, of the year 1976.

And all of this I thought about as I crossed the flood and stepped onto the dry shoulder of the roadway, suit and all, and still carrying my black brief case intact, from the icy water.

And that was it. I crossed over the great flood, which never got over three feet deep as far as my upper thigh area at any time, with the caked ice in the flow of the flood across the road bumping into my legs. And finally I stood on dry ground again where the land began to rise at the intersection of 299 and Libertyville Road. I was dripping wet from thighs down and my legs were numb from the cold. I began my long walk up the gradual rise of the highlands toward the mountain in a brisk way to keep the circulation going until I reached my final destination. After that it wouldn't matter, I was thinking, but I needed to get there. At four miles out I passed Ed's place, which was a ramshackle two story yellow house with a basement apartment, if you could call it that, where his boarder at the time, Donna, stayed. Ed was nowhere to be seen. Donna, who was young troubled girl from the streets who Ed had taken in, was home, as I could see her light on in the basement window, but I didn't stop to socialize. On I went in a fierce determination, beginning now the gradual ascent of the foothill up the mountain.

At the intersection of 299, that I had been walking on, and Route 44-55 that ran on this side of the Hudson River from Highland, NY, all the way over to the other side of the mountain, and at the base of The Shawangunk Mountains, I paused briefly to survey the lay of the land, and the ponderous sheer cliff, known as The Near Trapps, straight ahead, with the Mountain General Store directly in front of me, the Texaco Garage and Filling Station

directly to the right of the General Store, and the Mountain
Brauhaus Restarant to my immediate left.

I wasn't far away now from my point of entrance into the great
wilderness and the trail to Millbrook Mountain that ran along the
ridgeline. It was only another mile, around Hair Pin Turn, and
The Trapps Cliffs to the Iron Bridge across the highway where the
trail began along the ridge of the Near Trapps began to Millbrook
Mountain.

And then I was in the forest and walking fast out on the trail
trying to keep my legs and feet from freezing, they were already
starting to grow numb and though the temperature of the air was
tolerable, but the long time of my immersion in the water had
chilled my legs and feet to the bone, and in spite of my fast paced
walk out to the mountain thus far had not managed to warm them
much.

And out along the trail I went, carrying my brief case. There
were still patches of snow on the ground. Along the way and close
to the end of my journey as I approached the familiar landmarks
indicating my proximity to the face of Millbrook Mountain, I
began to walk very fast, almost approaching a jog, when the
outreaching branches of a prickly brush, snagged my stocking cap
off my head and nearly tore the pocket off my trench coat. But I
was close now and did not stop. And finally I came to I, to the
place where Michael and I had been, and I saw the little stone
altar we had built to commemorate the climb still in its place
where we had made it in the alcove of the rock as we had
fashioned it nearly two years ago in 1976.

I stood for a moment looking at it, not touching it, to leave it in
tact exactly as we had fashioned it, and then set my brief case
down there in the rocks, and took off my wet street shoes and
socks, tucked the socks neatly into the shoes, and walked straight-
ways, not wasting any time, to the very edge of the cliff and
planted my feet deliberately with my toes stuck over the edge, and
I looked down at the rocks below.

It was only a decision to be made, by my mind in me to make
it, to take the step off the cliff into oblivion, to find out what lay
beyond this life.

"Who will save the World if you leave it now," the voice of
The Creator said to me. "Who will defend Me. Who will defend
The Faith? Who will be my companion on the earth."

And that was all that was said. The Thought-Voice of The
Creator was silent, and with it, that silence, there loomed a
perilous decision.

I stood there for the longest moment longer, looking down, and
only needing to take a step from which there would never be a
return to consider. To stand there was the moment I had lived for,
to ask the question whether I truly desired to live or not.

It seemed a waste to have invested all those years in training to
be a soldier, and a pilot, and to graduate Summa Cum Laude from
College. I especially I thought of my dog Sophie, who would
miss me and wonder where I had gone, and of my family, and of
Tony and Henry and Jenny, and all of my friends and how they
would feel to learn the news of my death. And I thought then of
all that I had accomplished in my life at great and monumental
effort, to myself, of all the hard and devoted work that I had put in
to it, my life up to that time. And I thought about what The
Father had said to me about the World and about the necessity of
reforming it in the spiritual work needing to be done, not only by
myself, but by humanity, that lay ahead, and about I would feel,
without earthly form in the spirit world, to having taken my own
life prematurely, and never being able again to affect any changes
to the betterment of my spiritual destiny and for God's Earth itself
and for the behalf God's Children, the generations of people to
live on it. There was no other thought in my head and my heart
was pounding, to take the step and end it all in one fateful
moment. Only I knew that in my heart I didn't really want to.

And then I turned away from the great precipice of the abyss,
with great relief and with the alarm of reprehension racing in my
head for the close call of a moment's decision, and I walked back
to where my shoes and brief case were staged, and put my shoes
back on again. I picked up my briefcase and without looking back
again to the edge of the cliff, I left the area. On the way back
across the mountain I retrieved my stocking cap that I saw, to my

great relief, a touch of familiarity with the old life that was still in existence, still dangling from the branch that had snagged it.

I retraced my steps out to the highway and down the mountain, and to the long walk back to town, and out across the flooded flats again, this time, and by this time it was late in the afternoon, with a County Truck and County Workmen with high hipped boots wading out on flooded roadway steering the big chunks of ice along across the roadway with polls. And I was quite a sight to see walking determinedly past them thigh deep in the current of the fast water with my suit and trench coat and brief case.

I wasn't much in a hurry and ambled slowly across, my feet and legs grown used to the chill. The overcast sky had broken with big low hanging puffy clouds drifting by. The sun was out intermittently and the afternoon air was bit warmer now.

When I got to the Wallkill Bridge and the Village I could see that the temperature by the Bank Clock was fifty-three. I did not want to go into the Village, but turned left on to Huguenot Street, which ran parallel to the river and headed home the mile distance to the Robinson House. Where, as I approached, I saw Jenny dressed in her dungarees and sweater out walking with the dogs, Sophie and Waldo, along the road just in the front of the house.

I called to her, and she turned and saw me, beautiful Jenny with her eager to please warm and wonderful winning smile, smiling at me. Sophie came running up to me all excited, as she usually got when ever she first saw me upon my return whenever I was away, and tried to jump up on me and put her front paws on my pants and coat, which she nearly succeeded in doing, but I held her down firmly, and as I always did in trying to train her, with not much success at it, not to jump, with command words.

"Stay down, Sophie. Stay down!" which she finally did stay down. And it felt good to be alive. All was well with the world.

Waldo was Tony's dog and didn't show much enthusiasm for me, but I called him over anyway and gave him a nice friendly affectionate pet on the back of his neck and head, before he went off locked into his own world to sniff something. Sophie growled a little for my petting of Waldo and stayed by my side for a moment until I reassured her of my affection for her by petting her back and head for a long time. And then she ran off to play with Waldo who was on the scent of something out by the garage.

"What happened to you?" Jenny asked, seeing that my coat pocket was ripped and that I was still dripping wet from the thighs down, from my pants and part of my trench coat, from my walk back across the Flats, "and why aren't you at work?"

"I took the day off and went up to the mountain to commit suicide, something to do with your mother last night."

"Well, I am glad you didn't. You look a wreck," Jenny said, "I take it the séance didn't go too well. Come in the house."

We went in the house together through the back door and stood by the island in the kitchen. I set my brief case down on the chair by the phone near the doorway to the living room hallway.

"Dad is going to be away tonight," Jenny was eager to report. "He has a date for dinner … with Heather. Good for him. And, Henry is staying over night with a friend. They have a basketball game at the school. So there's just going to be the two of us for dinner." "I'm making spaghetti. I'll probably ruin it."

"How can you ruin spaghetti," I said. "You put the sauce in a pan and on the stove to simmer while you're waiting for the water to boil. Then you break the spaghetti in half, put it in the pot, cook it until it's al dente, and put out some bread and butter. We'll have ice water with it. It'll be fine. What could go wrong?"

"You need a good hot soaking bath," she said. "That's what you need. Why don't you go upstairs and run the tub and I'll go down to your room and get you some dry things out to put on. What in God's name happened to you?"

"I woke up with the empty feeling that I didn't want to live anymore and went out to mountain to talk with God about it."

"You walked across the flooded Flats?"

"I walked through the flood along on the road. It was only three feet deep at the deepest part, and then hiked up to the top of the mountain past Hairpin Turn to the Iron Bridge and then out along the woodland trail across the mountain as far as Millbrook Mountain to my sacred place, and there I stood at the edge of the cliff in my bear feet with my toes curled over the edge of it, to see if I could bring myself to take the step and hurl myself over the cliff and commit suicide like your mother, a step away.

I stood there for the greatest while, knowing that would be it forever. But I decided after thinking it over that I really wanted to live. It's a hard thing to do to take your own life."

"I'm glad you want to live," Jenny said. "I want to live too. There's so much to live for isn't there? I am happier now than I have been in the longest time, since mom died. I'll go get you some nice clean warm clothes and bring them upstairs to you." Then she touched my right arm. "Why, you're chilled to the bone," she said.

And then in scrutiny, handling the torn pocket of my trench coat with her fingers and helping me to get it off around my shoulders, she said, "I'll mend that coat for you later on tonight. And all those clothes you have on need a good washing, even your sport coat. You can't go into work looking like that. We'll have to send your sport coat, trench coat, and slacks to the dry cleaners. They smell like the river."

"You're a fine girl, Jenny. Thanks for being my friend."

"Thanks for being mine," Jenny replied. "It's nice being friends, and we are more than that, aren't we?"

She took a step towards me a little and I took her left hand in my right hand and pulled her in to me and I hugged her close in to my pounding heart for the longest time that seemed like eternity. I could feel her own heart racing as she pressed hard against me in my arms, breathless, her own arms holding me fast against her in return and her head pressed tightly into my chest.

At long last Jenny raised her face to me and with her eyes in that certain way of a look invited and urged me to kiss her, and I wanted to then, and so I did, and felt the soul of her surrender.

I went upstairs to the bathroom with Sophie following me, took off all my clothes and left them in a pile in the middle of the floor, started the warm bath water going in the tub, and sat down on the toilet to move my bowels what I couldn't do that morning, and was still sitting there when Jenny came through the door with my clothes. She set the clean clothes down on the chair in the corner, checked on the bathwater, and left to go back down stairs.

"Mafia hypothesis"

Brood parasitism is an awkward term to describe an interaction between two species in which, as in predator-prey relationships, one species gains at the expense of the other. Brood parasites "prey" upon parental care, and the victimized species usually have reduced breeding success, partly because of the additional cost of caring for alien eggs and young, and partly because of the behavior of both adult and young brood parasites which may directly and adversely affect the survival of the victim's own eggs or young.

There are two avian species that have been speculated to portray this mafia-like behavior, the brown-headed cowbird of North America, *Molothrus ater*, and the Great Spotted Cuckoo of Europe, *Clamator glandarius*. The Great Spotted Cuckoo lays the majority of its eggs in the nests of the European Magpie, *Pica pica*. It has been observed that the Great Spotted Cuckoo repeatedly visits the nests that it has parasitised, a precondition for the Mafia hypothesis.

The Common Cuckoo presents an interesting case in which the species as a whole parasitizes a wide variety of hosts, but individual females specialize in a single species. Genes regulating egg coloration appear to be passed down exclusively along the maternal line, allowing females to lay mimetic eggs in the nest of the species they specialize in. Females are thought to imprint upon the host species which raised them, and subsequently only parasitize nests of that species. Male Common Cuckoos will fertilize females of all lines, maintaining sufficient gene flow among the different maternal lines.

The mechanisms of host selection by female cuckoos are somewhat unclear, though several hypotheses have been suggested in attempt to explain the choice. These include genetic inheritance of host preference, host imprinting on young birds, returning to place of birth and subsequently choosing a host randomly ("natal philopatry"), choice based on preferred nest site (nest-site hypothesis), and choice based on preferred habitat (habitat-selection hypothesis). Of these hypotheses the nest-site selection and habitat selection have been most supported by experimental analysis.

Among specialist avian brood parasites, mimetic eggs are a nearly universal adaptation. There is even some evidence that the generalist Brown-headed Cowbird may have evolved an egg coloration mimicking a number of their hosts.

Most avian brood parasites will remove a host egg when they lay one of their own in a nest. Depending upon the species, this can happen either in the same visit to the host nest or in a separate visit before or after the parasitism. This both prevents the host species from realizing their nest has been parasitized and reduces competition for the parasitic nestling once it hatches.

A Shiny Cowbird chick being fed by a Rufous-collared Sparrow

Most avian brood parasites have very short egg incubation periods and rapid nestling growth. This gives the parasitic nestling a head start on growth over its nestmates, allowing it to outcompete them. In cases where the host nestlings are significantly smaller than the parasite nestling, the host nestlings will often starve to death. Some brood parasites will eliminate all their nestmates shortly after hatching, either by ejecting them from the nest or killing them with sharp mandible hooks which fall off after a few days.

It has often been a question why the majority of the hosts of brood parasites care for the nestlings of their parasites. Not only do these brood parasites usually differ significantly in size and appearance, but it is highly probable that they reduce the reproductive success of their hosts. So what possible benefits are gained from providing this parental care? Through studies in an attempt to answer this question evolved the "Mafia hypothesis". This hypothesis revolves around host manipulations induced by behaviors of the brood parasite. Upon the detection and rejection of a brood parasite's egg, the host's nest is depredated upon, its nest destroyed and nestlings injured or killed. This threatening response is indirectly enhancing selective pressures favoring aggressive parasite behavior that may result in positive feedback between Mafia-like parasite and compliant host behaviors.

Numbers: Chapter 32:20 And Moses said to them, If you will do this thing and arm yourselves before the Lord for war, 21: And will go all of you armed across the Jordan before the Lord, to war, until he has destroyed his enemies from before his presence, 22: And the land is subdued before the Lord; then after that you shall return and be guiltless before the Lord and before Israel; and this land shall be your possession before the Lord.

Numbers: Chapter 33:50 And the Lord said to Moses in the plains of Moab by the Jordan near Jericho,

51 Speak to the children of Israel and say to them, When you cross the Jordan into the land of Canaan; [To destroy nations from before you who are greater and mightier than you are, to bring you in, to give you their land for an inheritance,]

52 Then you shall destroy all the inhabitants of the land from before you and destroy all their idols and destroy all their molten images and demolish all their high places;

53 And you shall possess the land and dwell therein; for I have given you the land to possess it.

54 And you shall divide the land by lot for an inheritance among your families; and to the large families you shall give a large inheritance, and to the small families you shall give a small inheritance; every man's inheritance shall be in the place where his lot falls; according to the tribes of their fathers they shall inherit.

55 But if you will not destroy the inhabitants of the land from before you, then it shall come to pass, that those who are left of them shall be splinters in your eyes, and spears in your sides, and shall trouble you in the land wherein you dwell.

56 And as I thought to do to them, I shall do to you.

William Shakespeare

The Chandos portrait, artist and authenticity unconfirmed. National Portrait Gallery, London.

Born Baptised 26 April 1564 (birth date unknown) Stratford-upon-Avon, Warwickshire, England

Died 23 April 1616 (aged 52) Stratford-upon-Avon, Warwickshire, England

Occupation Playwright, poet, actor Literary movement English Renaissance theatre

In *The Merchant of Venice*, Shylock is a <u>Jewish</u> <u>moneylender</u> who lends money to his <u>Christian</u> rival, <u>Antonio</u>, setting the <u>security</u> at a pound of Antonio's flesh. When a <u>bankrupt</u> Antonio defaults on the loan, Shylock demands the pound of flesh, as he dislikes Antonio because Antonio used to loan money without charging any interest and thus made Shylock lose business. Meanwhile, Shylock's daughter, Jessica, elopes with Antonio's friend Lorenzo and becomes a Christian, further fuelling Shylock's rage. She also takes money and jewels from Shylock.

During Shakespeare's day, <u>money lending</u> was a very common occupation among Jews. This was due to Christians staying out of the profession due to their belief at that time that <u>usury</u> is a sin and the fact that it was one of the few professions available to Jews in medieval Europe, who were prohibited by law from most professions. Jessica, Shylock's daughter did not adhere to these beliefs and left Shylock for a Christian man.

The play is frequently staged today, but is potentially troubling to modern audiences due to its central themes, which can easily appear <u>anti-Semitic</u>. Critics today still continue to argue over the play's stance on anti-Semitism.

The character's name has become a <u>synonym</u> for <u>loan shark,</u> and as a <u>verb</u> to *shylock* means to <u>lend money</u> at exorbitant <u>rates</u>. In addition, the phrase "pound of flesh" has also entered the <u>lexicon</u> as <u>slang</u> for a particularly onerous obligation.

English society in the <u>Elizabethan</u> era has been described as anti-Semitic. <u>English Jews</u> were <u>expelled</u> in the <u>Middle Ages</u> and were not permitted to return until the rule of <u>Oliver Cromwell</u>. Jews were often presented on the Elizabethan stage in hideous caricature, with hooked noses and bright red wigs, and were usually depicted as avaricious <u>usurers</u>; characterized as evil, deceptive, and greedy

During the 17th century in Venice and in some other places, Jews were required to wear a red hat at all times in public to make sure that they were easily identified. If they did not comply with this rule they could face the death penalty. Jews also had to live in a ghetto protected by Christians, supposedly for their own safety. The Jews were expected to pay their guards.

OTHELLO

ACT I, SCENE 2, 62-81

More Challenging Contextual Questions

William Shakespeare

BRABANTIO

O thou foul thief, where hast thou stow'd my daughter?
[Desdemona]
Damn'd as thou art, thou hast enchanted her;
For I'll refer me to all things of sense,
If she in chains of magic were not bound,
Whether a maid so tender, fair and happy,
So opposite to marriage that she shunned
The wealthy curled darlings of our nation,
Would ever have, to incur a general mock,
Run from her guardage to the sooty bosom
Of such a thing as thou, to fear, not to delight.
Judge me the world, if 'tis not gross in sense
That thou hast practised on her with foul charms,
Abused her delicate youth with drugs or minerals
That weaken motion: I'll have't disputed on;
'Tis probable and palpable to thinking.
I therefore apprehend and do attach thee
For an abuser of the world, a practiser
Of arts inhibited and out of warrant.
Lay hold upon him: if he do resist,
Subdue him at his peril.

****

It was in the late summer of our discontent in the year of 1977 that Tony and I had sat outside on the deck talking after supper one evening.

Tony, who we of the immediate family consisting of myself, and Jenny and Henry Robinson, named affectionately "Big T," was born in 1931 and was precisely fifteen years my senior. Therefore we were at an ackward age to one another with nothing in common socially and for that reason had trouble with one anther being friends, as the meaning of friendship is concerned, and although we were friends, but not in the way as familiar buddies would be, and he had been and was the English Professor and my teacher of Creative Writing and American Literature at The SUNY University at New Paltz, NY, and all that that entailed in the way of dominance over me and with my obeisant respected courtship of his favor in looking up to him as a superior personage and intellect to myself, that prevented us from engaging one another on equal footing.

And for the fact too that he had been an Officer in the Navy and I had been an Inlisted Man in the Army that set us apart in the sophisticted class world of brinksmanship. And he was too more of an upper class person to me also, having the great house and the rather large estate to reside in, and although however he came by his wealth that wasn't mine to have the good fortune of inheriting.

He was too young to be my father figure, and to old to be my brother, and although we were brothers of a fashion in kindred spirit of our genuine affection for one another and for the penetrating and incisive philosophical side of life that were at all time fond of pursuing with each other, but we were never really close that way either. There was something always distant inbetween. But he was pleasant company to be around and I found with a little forceful persuasion of insistance that I could bully him around a bit and play at him in a prodful manner in making more of an even game of it. But in the end, and afte all

was said and done, I made him my teacher as a permanent
relationship and looked up to him for that.

But that wasn't quite right either, and which I felt particularly
in a keen way, for that elusive sense of a relationship to pin down,
as we sat together talking that evening on the back deck of Tony's
house. But I liked him greatly as person and admired his
personality and sentive nature and struggled to hold my own as
we two sat there talking coming to terms with the idea of being
intimate friends and remembered a quote from The Bible of John
Chapter 14 Verse 2 which I uttered aloud.

"In my Father's house are many rooms…"

And which I spoke in appreciation for the nice quarters that I
had been provided with then by Tony. And then, sensing I had an
opening to speak and to make a point to him, I asked,

"What do you suppose Jesus meant when he says in the
Chapter and Verse of St. John's Gospel, John 14:6,"

'I am the way and the truth and the life; no man comes to my
Father except by me.'

"And when at the earlier verse in the Gospel of John, John
6:44-46, He says,"

'No man can come to me unless the Father who sent me draw
him; and I will raise him up on the last day.

For it is written in the prophet, They shall all be taught by
God. Everyone therefore who learns from Him will come to me.

No man can see the Father except him who is from God; he
can see the Father.'

"Is that a paradox?"

"It seems to me we are at Their mercy either way all along,"
Tony replied, "whether it is a paradox or not. The can't get to be
with The Father unless you are good, in the nature of Jesus, and
you can't be good, and that is to say, to have the compelling
nature to be good, unless The Father moves you to you in the
spirit, in the sense of befriending you … no man gets to me unless
The Father moves him. And which all comes down to fate then,
as we are born, and to the parents we are born to, and to the
society that we are born into, and depending to the friends be
meet and make along the way, which helps us out if things are

good and go well, and of course there is always The Other Way of
error and evil to have befallen anyone, poor devils, as they say.

Photo of Tony by Norbert Heermann - Woodstock, NY, 1960

Tony had four religious paradigms to serve as virtuous models
of wisdom and reasonableness and several maxims of sound
advise to follow of his ways or formulas on how to live life
successfully, that he was always fond of telling his students about
and which have stuck in my mind ever since, and as I am sure, as
they have stuck in the minds as well in being imprinted on
everyone in Tony's Church, who he has every come into contact
with, of his way in undertaking of the responsibility of taking an
interest in and in caring about everybody, as a Modern Secular
Religion of Practicing Sincerity, Caring, and Concerned
Attentiveness, clean and to the point, to whom Tony was the

viruous ideal and well expressed demonstrated master of, and the professing inspiration to, to always look up to him about.

The first paradigm was this: "That it was never good enough, nor ever rested easy in the mind of anyone, to leave unfinished business of a conflict behind, being recorded as permanent memeory to call anything at the conclusion of to be at the end of it. Because it never "is finished" and needs to be "brought back" at some future date in time to achieve a final anc conclusive resolution to, to be analyzed in a colder and less empassioned light of day.

The feeling being, that in order to achieve a final and lasting catharsis, as a purging of emotions, over any event in conflict which has occurred needing resolution, whether it be in literature or in life itself to resolve, that it always has loose ends to care of and is never really over about. And for what reason that you have to eventually return to to achieve a successful finish to it, by bringing the main characters back into focus together again to see how things have worked out for them in order to feel completed and satisfied with the outcome of the matter to be settled, being finally put to rest.

And which, of the experience of true catharsis achieved, was the only way that anyone, whether it be a reader to a story, or of the participant to a real life drama of an event, could ever feel whole in their minds and hearts be at an end of what it was that was troubling between them and completed in a satisfied sense of ultimately achieving a resolved experience."

The second maxim was, "to always be impeccably ruthless and honest with yourself in the introspection of your dealings with yourself and with others, to be completely truthfull and ethical, and to correct whatever it was that is in error, by that way of self-examination, to prevent the past from building up a repression of self-loathing inside of a person and haunting them with ill memories that negatively affect on the present. Which judgment was to be stringently guarded for one's own safety and good."

The third was, "to never wear your heart out on your sleeve for everyone to see and gawk at."

And the fourth was, (and which Tony was always fond of using as a direct quote from Ralph Waldo Emmerson's famous work, "Self Reliance," in his college course of American Literature:)

"Get to know your own back yard first before you set out to conquer the world."

All of which have their place here, and along with a fifth and sixth maxim. The fifth that was perhaps one reserved for Tony's household, stated in the tone of, "Who ate that nice piece of Roast Beef that I was saving for my lunch this afternoon?" And which was,

"Never eat the last of anything."

That has several other meanings besides its literal one depending to one's level of sophistication and their interpretation of the intent of the phrase.

And the sixth, as Tony was always fond of telling at every occasion, which was, what Tony called, John Wayne's Law, reputedly told by the famous actor in one of his famous films.

"Don't disappoint them," (and in the meaning of the people who admire and respect and look up to you, and to whom it is bestowed upon you to lead an example to,) "Lie a little if you have to. And always lie if they are going to kill you for it, telling the truth. What would be the point in that, of your being a Boy Scout for the truth, if they were going to do that?"

And there were always promised secrets to keep and sworn oaths of allegiance which no power of the interrogative could breach.

But the paradigm that made the most impression with me as I remember Tony for his heart in it of poignancy, and for the sincerity of his heart in compassion that he had in relating it, was actually a parable of the story that he told me one summer Friday evening, relaxing at weeks end, in the latter part of the month of May of 1977, and just two weeks after I had begun my Summer project there with Tony to landscape and grade the land in the back of his estate.

It was just beginning to be Summer and not yet in the doldrums of the hot days, and quite a pleasant Summer Evening after supper that we were spending together in shared bonding conversation of intimacy sitting out on Tony's weathered cast iron deck chairs, with our two dogs, my dog Sophie, my red Irish Setter, who was just over a year old and who was my constant companion in the days, and Tony's dog Waldo, a brown and white Cocker Spaniel who was then at that time around eight years old, lying beside our respective chairs.

Our feet were both propped up on the railing of his impressive large deck that he had recently had built onto the backside of his house, complete with an outdoor shower, au natural, earlier in the year. We were drinking rye whiskey and soda water cocktails in the twilight of the evening looking out onto the great expanse of the darkening hulk of the ridge of the Shawangunk Mountain Range over which the retreating sun had just set, and upon which that the beacon light in Mohonk Tower had just come warmly on, that was a symbol of unity to the people of the Wallkill River Valley to focus on no matter where they were, and which seems especially comforting on that particular night as we sat out there talking.

With the encroaching dark, the great bullfrogs in the Ox Bow began to croak back and forth, and the Ox Box came alive with the higher shrilling sounds of other smaller frogs. It was also the cyclical seven-year revival of The Locusts, and who, lodged in the trees, began their shrill mesmerizing methodical evening discussions with the Surroundings, bdddddddd, bdddddddd, of the Kadydids. There was the smell of the wetlands on the slight breeze stirring in from the direction of the Ox Box in the air, and all around seemed well and soothing of the Surrounding.

But as looked over at Tony, he was grimacing his jowls and there was something in his vacant bearing and in the plant of his eyes which had a distracted and vacant look in indication that a preoccupation was occurring; of which I suspected that there was something profoundly wrong that was troubling him that he plodded along in the coming out with it in his half stammering way of getting something across, and with a melancholy tone of the point of the story that he was about to tell me, and as I could detect from to his eyes of the seriousness to him as he was telling it.

And which was the story he told me that night about a Swami who upon seeing a Scorpion foundering just off shore in the water struggling for its life, went into the water to attempt its rescue and tried to lift the Scorpion out with his hands cupped and put is safely on to the bank. But the Scorpion stung his hand and he had to drop it in recoiling.

The Swami then collected himself and tried once more. But the second time the Swami tried the Scorpion stung him again, and he had to drop it again back into the water. He tried a third time, and this time he was able to place the Scorpion on the bank of the water and the Scorpion scurried off.

Nursing his swollen poisoned fingers at the fate of the Scorpion's sting, a gathering of onlookers inquired.

"Swami, why have you risked your own life to save the worthless life of a Scorpion? Is not your life more valuable and worth more than the life of the Scorpion who can do no good upon the earth for anyone."

To what the Swami replied.

"It is the nature of the Scorpion in defensive reaction to sting its presumed adversaries. It is the nature of a Swami to be kind, and understanding, and patient, and importantly helpful and caring to other creatures of God who are in need whenever he may be needed of assistance, and as to say, that such action is always to be kept within sound judgment of good reason.

I am not about to throw my life away for no good reason. But as I judged it, I know that I am not going to die from these bee-sting like bites of the Scorpion and even though painful to endure, but the scorpion I am sure is quite happy to be rescued from its fate of drowning and happy to be alive and that is my reward for me in Heaven in the thought of being proud of myself for rescuing him.

Were it not for me it would most certainly have met its fate, and a handsome male scorpion he is. And that is my reward for helping it, to know in my heart that that I did the right thing and assisted that poor foundering creature, as we ourselves in our vicarious empathy would be most grateful and appreciative for such assistance to be rendered to us by someone in our time of need. For such memories of good works and intentions will always sustain us throughout our lives and into eternity in our times of strife and provide us with the confidence to lead others by in the important struggles of life."

But that and despite its honorable intentions all in all about the parable, and as I knew what Tony was trying to impugn by it about the Negro Race of Mankind in general, that was something that struck me as being a little cowardly at its base of intentions, and appeasing to hateful and irrational enemy to insult our intelligence by concerning the assuaging of their aggressions upon us of the Negro Race as for at Tony was trying to imply, "of the helping hand offered, though bitten back repeatedly."

And I told him so.

"I like the story of the wise householder, who seeing that a vine was gaining access to the top branches of his favorite shade tree in the back yard, took measures of precaution and severed the vine at its base with a pair of pruning clippers. To forgive the insults of their outright warring aggressions and to put up with the forced assimilation of our White Females to addict them to drug and to carry them off to marry with them, our women, and create the Race of Mulattoes over and beyond our abilities combined to defend ourselves from such relentless and subversive onslaught, and to annihilate The White Race in that manner of assimilation eventually, and by violence also, to become extinct forever from off the Face of the Earth in the name of their Mulatto Religion of Islam.

That has nothing to do with The Black African Race of Mankind at all, this concept of Islam, but what is a warring of The Mixed Births against both parents, White and Black, from which mixing that their tortured egos en masse cannot escape, and for what reason that there is no feasible way that anything we say or do can appease them to, because it is in their blood, and in their genes, to be both White and Black at the same time, and to experience rejection, and thus to their hatred of us, and their Black Parent for creating them. To what that we can never expect for them to accept their fate in that manner for the sake of a speculation that eventually that one day they will be healed by our kindness and on their way to a serene an blissful lives by our show of patience with them, that is sheer madness on our part.

They are friendly to us up to a point of our appeasement to their demands. But try and call them Negroes and tell them that they can't marry with our White Women and see what happens.

Who, in Truth, were The Moors of Ancient Times, and the Moors of 14th Century Spain who The Defensive Crusades under Emperor Charlemagne vanquished, and only to come here to America under the guise of slavery.

And who existed long before then into the millenniums since they were created by man's folly of miscegenation, as they always have been, the anomaly of nature, who having been rejected and Racially Alienated by The White Race for those millenniums for their accidental mis-creation of birth, that the Mixed Race of Mulatto Offsprings of The Negro and The Caucasian Races have waged relentless wars of aggressions, that was never going to be healed by kindness in appeasement of their hatred of retaliation against The White Race, particularly against The White Men, and taking the White Women in prize to assimilate with, that is to say, to mate with, as is their nature, and to use the White Women then, as prostitute bate, called "Negro Bloods" of "Bitches" to do their bidding as household assassins, in the Drug Warfare Poison Method of Food and Beverage Sabotage, of the White Males, to kill us off.

And as to say of The White Men in their path, who are either forced into the acceptance of their Inter-Racial Assimilation, through cowardice, or by virtue of the White Males being addicted to the drugs and dependent to Moors Drug Supply or Heroin and Cocaine, to do their bidding against the remainder of the other White Males for, or be killed, and who are in that end, killed anyway.

And who, speaking of The Americanized Mulatto Moors, you will never reach, not in a million years, by kindness, to change their ways, not by understanding, nor by tolerance, termed as mealy mouthed appeasement. The only way to reach them is to teach them submission and acceptance of their fate at the hands of God Who ordered their annihilation in the ancient Holy Land, and discipline them in that regard to their proper places in our White Society, and which is to maintain sexual apartheid, subordinated to the will of innate Self-Preservation and Protection of The White Race From All Harm and Extinction.

The Book of Revelations 21:1-3, states it right," I said.

"And I saw an angle come down from heaven, having the key of the bottomless pit and a great chain in his hand. And he seized the dragon, that old serpent, which is the Tempter and Satan, who deceived the whole world, and bound him a thousand years. And cast him into the bottomless pit and shut him up and set a seal over him, that he should no more deceive the nations until the thousand years should be past; after that he will be loosed for a short time.

What we are experiencing here is, 'for the short time' that he is to be loosed right now," I concluded. "And which ties into another Bible Quote, of the Final Days of Reckoning as I am paraphrasing:

That: No miracle will be shown to an Idolatrous generation, and the hand of The Creator will be stayed from The Final Judgment until all the people of the earth have borne witness, so that all may judge for themselves of the nature of forming a conclusion to act upon in their common defense. And the dead will lie in the streets for three days."

And all of which diatribe that I justified to Tony on the theme of mutual self-preservation and defense from and against irrational forces, that I ended on the note that just because The Negroes residing here to us, and representing a certain minority of our entire White European population, was a made the victims of a prejudice and persecution, and for the reasons that they were of preventing their drug trafficking and mission of inter-racial procreation with The White Women from infecting the rest of The White Race, (that needed to be redressed without saying as it goes,) but for what that there was no excuse available that way for us The American People all to quake in boots and to surrender our women and out beloved Country to the Negroes and to all other types of foreigners along with the idea of Equal Rights, for us to roll over and die en masse for sympathy of the mistreated or otherwise Minorities, who only need to be more formally included into the mainstream of the culture in ethical standard and contingent to certain conditions of non-violence and other forms of aggressions, as named, against us being met. And although that Tolerance is a prideful aspect of our culture, Nobles Oblige, that it could, at point of order to be realized, the idea of Tolerance, be stretched too far out, in the Liberal Meaning, for our own good in common sense, and that it was time to know when to put our foots down collectively to state whose Country it is and what our Standards are to be.

All of what Tony acquiesced to without commenting, tensing his jowls and grinding his teeth and looking at me intently with his stark blue eyes as I talked.

Tony lived in a great old majestic slate gray house, that was built in the early 1930's in that grand style of elegant architecture, and which used to be the former Parsonage to The United Methodist Church that was situated just a short way up the street from him. The house had two stories, with four bedroom and a bathroom on the second floor, and on the first floor was Tony's bedroom, built on as an addition shortly after he had moved in ten years earlier, and a half bath off the hallway that connected it to the main parts of the house, the living room, formal dining room, kitchen dining area and kitchen, and that was actually three stories counting the raised basement that Tony had converted into an apartment composed of a kitchen area, a bedroom, and a bathroom in the basement part, and that entered to down a series of stone steps.

Separate from the house, at the far end of a gravel driveway was a one car garage, also painted slate gray, with a loft Writer's Garret on the second story, that was always Tony's idea of Earnest Hemmingway's Garret when he lived in Key West, FL with his second wife Pauline, and which he gave to me to live in, and to write in, while I was there working on the estate.

The house with its Garret Garage, and which I shared with a homeless friend from off the street named Lloyd Barzell, who I had hired on to help me with the work on Tony's estate, was situated on a nice parcel of land, roughly just over an acre and a half to manage, overlooking an old Oxbow swamp area of the wayward Wallkill River that had once been the river bed itself, that at one time in far distant past during the yearly Spring floods that inundated the river valley, that had been by-passed, by the river's cousing in a staighening out shortcut of the river's miandering serpentine way, with the roaring cutting of the Springs thaw and heavy rains cutting a new bed through in a different location in its course to its now current position.

Further out from the backyard was the view from behind his house of the cliffs of Bontecou's Crag, named the Lost City, as that section of the Cliffs was named, and to the Mohonk Cliff line itself, now darkened by the setting sun, onto which that the imperious Mohonk Tower was built overlooking the Wallkill Valley on one side and of the Resort of Lake Mohonk Hotel that lay behind the cliffs on the other.

"Childe Roland to The Dark Tower came," I said at the sight of the light in the tower coming on, paraphrasing Robert Browning's poem of 1855."

"The dying sunset kindled through a cleft: the hills, like giants at a hunting, lay ... I saw them and I knew them all. And yet duantless the slug-horn to my leps I set, and blew, 'Childe Roland to the Dark Tower came.'"

Tony had been in a pensive mood that night.

"Tell me, Gary, what do you suppose that Jesus meant when he said, 'Let the dead bury their dead?' 'Let the dead bury their dead.' That's an odd thing to say."

"It means what it does," I said. "It's from the Gospel of Luke. The other part to it is, and I paraphrase, 'but you go and preach the word of God ... No man who puts his hand on the plough and looks back is fit for the kingdom of God.' It has something to do with their being dead spiritually, and what does it mean to be spiritually awakened?"

"I like the part about Separating The Sheep from The Goats," Tony said.

"Yes, from the Gospel of Matthew, Matthew 25:31-33, I know it well."

"When the Son of man comes in his glory, and all his holy angels with him, then he will sit upon the throne of his glory. And all nations will gather before him; and he will separate them one from another, just as a shepherd separates the sheep from the goats; And he will set the sheep at his right and the goats at his left."

Tony's lot was quite as impressive a piece of land and handsome backyard as anyone could have on Huegenot Street along the street of the old stone house of the early French Huegenot Settlers who settled there in 1678 and which was called the Historic District of New Paltz.

Tony then told me the story of how he had hired the old Negro Carpenter Oscar Moss, and a good and decent friendly well mannered man and a neighbor of sorts who lived a few miles further out of Town down the road from Tony on Old Kingston Road, to built the back deck for him, and toward whom that Tony had felt generous and kindly to him to have hired him, to provide Oscar with some work, and to set an example in the community of reaching out to the hiring the Negroes, and to help heal up the wounds of prejudice of the past by befriending them in solidarity that Tony had felt proud to do.

Oscar had come with his son Ricky as his helper, and which took the two of them a little over month from start to finish to complete the deck. And in the meantime, with Ricky putting Mulatto moves on Jenny, as was their entitled right to do, and demanding the right to go with the White Women, and a feather in their cap to capture the White Girls away from the White Households, as the story was told.

Tony informed me that he suspected about his daughter, Jenny,

"It's Jenny," he blurted out, "I think she might have become a little 'Jaded,'" stating this in a cryptic way of meaning and clenching the jowls of his teeth together as he did until the muscles in his cheeks bulged.

That apparently had transpired from Jenny's daily contact with Ricky Moss, as Oscar's helper back then; and about which matter that I suspect was the reason that he had told me a Parable as he did, intending to refer to of our acceptance in understanding and tolerance of the tumult that the Black, or Negro Community, was raging on the White Man in the streets, and in making use of The White Man's Women by making them slaves to the addiction to Heroin and Cocaine and by threats of coercion, to attack their own men, husbands, fathers, brothers, boyfriends, and acquaintances, of their murderous rampaging and threats of murder mayhem in intimidation in their hold over the White Race and demanding our surrender to their retaliation for their ancestors having been made slaves of at one point in time in their history, so they claim, more so of a Moorish plot to infiltrate and overtake The White Race. And which claim was being used as such to explain and exonerate them for the state of their present hatreds of prejudice against them by the White Race, and for what logic that the White Race was supposed to accept and embrace their being attacked and their own demise, as prophesied.

"O thou foul thief, where hast thou stow'd my daughter?" I said, mimicking Desdemona' attraction to the Moor, in Shakespeare's, Othello. "Damn'd as thou art, thou hast enchanted her; Of such a thing as thou, to fear, not to delight. Judge me the world, if 'tis not gross in sense That thou hast practised on her with foul charms, Abused her delicate youth with drugs or minerals."

"Mary killed herself in that bedroom right up there," Tony had said, gesturing with a wave of his arm at the bedroom on the back left side of the house.

It was earlier in the previous year in 1976 that Tony's wife Mary was found dead of an apparent suicide from the second blast from Tony's Remington Twelve Gauge Shotgun, the first of which, as Tony explained, was fired into the ceiling of the bedroom, and the second into Mary's heart. My wife Doreen and I had attended her funeral, Closed Casket, in Woodstock, NY in February.

"For some reason she tested the weapon out before she did the job. They kill themselves for the reason to get back at and to hurt other people, believe it or not. It was Henry who found her when he came home after school. Poor fellow."

Henry had gone upstairs after supper and after helping me and Jenny with the chores of cleaning the table and doing the dishes, to do his homework. Jenny was in the kitchen baking.

Lloyd came back from Town and said hello to Tony, who he addressed as Mr. Robinson, and to me. Sophie and Waldo had both barked in alarm and jumped to their feet and bolted down the steps to greet Lloyd who on hearing his footsteps crunching on the gravel drive, and who address them both also and petted them before climbing the ladder to the second floor Garret to his space there on the far side of the open Garret loft that was partially separated by a partition from my space that faced onto the back deck. Tony and I watched as the kerosene lamp came on with its magical glow of hominess emanating through the open window of the Garret.

Jenny came to the back door.

"Does anybody want any chocolate cake," she announced. "I made it myself just now from scratch."

"I'd love a piece," Tony said.

"I'd love some too," I said also.

And she was back out in short while with two big pieces of cake on white china with two forks and two napkins. The pieces looked rich and chocolatety good with lots of gooey chocolate icing.

"Wow," I exclaimed in exaggerated glee, "what a wonderful treat. Thank you so much Jenny."

"You are welcome," she said to me. "I hope you like it."

She handed me my piece, and then gave Tony his.

"Thank you, Jenny," he said. "You're my pride and joy."

She nuzzled close up to him and he put his right arm around her waist, holding the cake and napkin and fork with his other hand. He rubbed her back a bit and she kissed his forehead.

She was by far the loveliest and most attractive young girl I had ever seen, a real beauty. She was just seventeen then, and in the height of her feminine bloom, with a lovely young figure, lustrous shoulder length jet black hair, deep and ponderous brown eyes that penetrated you and took you captive into her soul when they looked at you with her big wide smile in attraction, and a wide smile showing perfect teeth that made you feel welcome with its sincerity and eagerness to be loved not to be disappointed.

And who I was embarrassed to look at for fear of gulping and overly gawking at her charming beauty, and who I was deeply appreciative to for any conversation with her to give me an excuse to focus on her without attracting undue attention to my doing so.

She was barefoot that evening with inward pointing big toes dressed in faded denim frayed cut-off shorts and a cool white short sleeve summer blouse open down two buttons from the neck. And she put her hand on my shoulder as she left Tony's side to go back inside the house, sliding it down my back as she went.

"The cake is delicious, Jenny," I had said to her, turning around in my chair to watch her go back inside the house with her long shoulder length black hair swaying a little as she open the screen door to do so. "Still nice and warm from the oven."

"I baked it especially for you and dad," she said, turning and standing in the doorway, and then as an after thought, "and for Henry, which reminds me to bring him up a piece. He's been begging me for days to bake a cake."

And with that she was gone, leaving an empty spot in the night.

"Maybe we are all already dead and living out our karma in a Limbo State of Purgatory in the Infindibulum of God's Mind, which is a dream and could be anything at any time only to imagine it, until we get it right enough to enter into the lasting peace of The Kingdom of Heaven," I surmised, referring to Tony's earlier remark, "about letting the dead bury their dead."

"Maybe so," Tony said politely, distractedly.

"But even then," I said, "being in Heaven doesn't really change anything about what it is that have to do in the terms of strife and toil. We're not going to heaven just to lie around all day long and do nothing. I know that. That's not really what being in Heaven is meant, is it?"

"I would say not," Tony said.

"I'm going into town for a bit to walk the streets," I said.

"Stay a bit before you go," Tony said. "Let's have a toke on the pipe together."

He reached into his left pants pocket and took out his marijuana pipe.

"This is the last of my stash," he said pressing down on the Marijuana Bud firmly which was already in the bowl and puffing and murmuring as he lit the pipe with his Bic lighter. He got the bowl glowing good and bright and inhaled a big lungful of the pungent smoke holding it in and grunting with his breath as he did.

He held it in for a long time and then exhaled it, letting it out slowly, and passed the pipe secretively, although there was not any need to, palming it in his hand over to me as he let the smoke back out slightly and took another breath to keep some of it still in his lungs.

Tony liked to smoke Marijuana in the evenings especially and to ruminate in that state of illuminated effulgence on the great essentials of life, in which Mind and Matter merged under its Saintly Influence to become One with The Creator for a time.

He liked being in the conspiracy of it all, as did I, and as that I too was taken-over by the idea, that had to do with the secret society of close and intimate friendships that were not to be found anywhere for any other motives, of people liking and needing to be together to be close with God, that was the secret society of the Ganja Church known only to the initiates that was the joy of great solidarity among the people, to see and to greet one another and to be together. If you possessed the Ganja you had all the friends in the world courting you, at least in these parts of the world, rendered to be an Art Colony and of the various motives of the diversity of humanity who inhabited the region to make it that way.

I took a hit and passed the pipe in the same secretive manner that it was given to me back to Tony. I didn't take a big hit but left some of it for Tony for later on which was the polite thing to do as Pipe Politics goes, to always defer to the master of the house, and don't take the last of anything. To do so was an unspoken onus.

"The Father wants His Religion and His Church back," I said to Tony after we had sat a long while absorbed in our own thoughts to ponder. "He wants it as it was in the beginning before Jesus with just Himself at the center of its devotion; which The Father Intends of His Sacred Church In Name of a Religion After His Heart To Be Proud Of, to be named affectionately to be, The Church of The Heavenly Father."

And with that I began to expostulate on the subject to Tony, who sat back and listened with serious intention. I know not how or where the power came of the inspiration to move me so eloquently but became entranced with its profundity and let it flow out of me feeling delighted with my power of reasoning as the thoughts came into me and arranged themselves in dictation to be discussed professionally to the esteemed Professor.

"To what purpose, and about Jesus," I continued, "Who has been, in a sense, and throughout the history of Christianity, "Placed Before," The Father; in The Religion of Christianity, (and in a manner of strictly speaking, that as well is in violation also of The Father's Covenant TO Us, In Commandment; Not To Have Any Other Gods Before Me!) that we argue, that the format of our Christianity needs to be restructured in deference with The Father's Wishes, In Fulfillment With The Father's Need To Be Central, In Dominant Focus Of Our Thoughts In Worship Among Us, politely phrased that way, in reverence to Jesus. Who is in no way being removed from The Church Hierarchy Of Consecration, but Only Being Subordinated To The Father, As The Dominant Force Among Christians. Currently To Whom, (in meaning of Jesus,) That Reflections And Prayers Are Centrally Directed To In Bypass Of The Father. That, Jesus Himself In His Heart Wills To Occur. And Who Himself, has always professed that in The Bible, that He, Jesus, Was Always The Servant Of The Father In Heaven, and Could Do Nothing Without The Father's Will In Direction To Guide Him.

For it is written in The Bible, as Jesus said, that: "No man gets to The Father except through me, but no man gets to me except that The Father moves him." In our need for The Father, and in our need for Jesus, (in meaning that, We Need To Be Holy And Perfect In The Father's Sight, As Jesus Instructed Us How, IN Order To Be At Peace Within Ourselves, And So To Be Able To Live In The Presence Of The Father.

That Jesus, Our Human Counterpart And Intercessor, Has Taught To Us, And Who Is Our Companion In Spirit Always!) And Who Is Always In Need To Be Included In Our Religious Worship And Service, but not furthermore in being, "Central" To It. For as Jesus said, "Why do you call me good, there is no one good except The Father, and I can do nothing unless The Father Works In Me." And It Is To The Father First Who We Must Look To, To Move Us In Spirit To Be Christ-Like! And So To Follow Jesus In The Direction Of Proper Faith.

And not to be taking anything away from The Great Work, and The Sacrifice of Our Lord And Savior, Jesus, either. Who died on The Cross at Calvary, for The Sake of The Sins of Our Humanity, and in painful agony that way, as was His Predestined and "Inevitable" Fate To Do, Who Is Deserving Of Our Great Esteem In Respect.

But it is, that we are all too painfully reminded of His Death, in the ceaseless and repeated reminding of It, at each Celebration of The Mass and with every visit to The Church, in gaze upon the horrifying and cruel display of The Central Crucifix, in huge scale, (which dominates the foreground of nearly every Church in Roman Catholicism.)

And as well, who as parishioners of the congregation, are surrounded "in the walls of the sides of The Churches," at all times, in every Catholic Church, by "The Twelve Stations of The Cross," depicting the sorrowful scenes in agony leading to The Crucifixion Of Jesus.

And with each year passing of our collective mourning of the event, as we are reminded of, with The Ritual at Easter, and of Holy Week, of when Our Lord "Chose" The Apostle Judas "To Betray Him," at The Last Supper, from among The Twelve Apostles.

And it was The Apostle Judas whom The Lord chose, from among The Twelve Apostles, (who each in turn asked of The Lord, "Is It I?") and who were All Ordained Priests, including Judas, and as such, Who Were Given The Power Over Unclean Spirits, TO Cast Them Out and To Heal Every Kind Of Disease and Sickness. And Who Were Each And All, Holy Consecrated Men, Incapable Of Human Error! To Make A Point.

And the names of The Twelve Apostles are these: The first of them Simon, who is called Peter, and Andrew his brother; James the son of Zebedee, and John his brother; Philip and Bartholomew, Thomas, and Matthew the tax collector, James the son of Alphaeus and Lebbaeus surnamed Thaddaeus; Simon the Zealot and Judas of Iscariot, who was chosen to betray him.

And, of The Apostle Judas, who, after The Lord Chosen Him! (by dipping bread with His hand with Judas into a wine bowl in ceremony of blood,) and who was The Apostle who Jesus Loved The Most. Who said then to Jesus: "Master, perhaps it is I?" To what that Jesus replies to him: "You say that." Who then ran out into the night in sheer agony To Betray his Master Jesus. Who was then crucified.

And of poor Judas, who became despondent over the tragedy, after he had learned that Jesus had been convicted, who went then to The Temple to confront The High Priests and Elders Of The People, and said: "I have sinned because I have betrayed innocent blood," and threw the thirty pieces of sliver that he had received in payment To Betray Jesus onto The Temple Floor and departed, to be found hanged. Which The Bible states was a Suicide.

To what that The High Priests in the temple remarked over the event of Judas hurling The Thirty Pieces Of Silver onto The Temple Floor:

"Then what was spoken by the prophet was fulfilled, namely, I took the thirty pieces of silver, the costly price which was bargained with the children of Israel, and I gave them for the potter's field, {a cemetery for strangers bought with The Price Of Blood, and which is called The Field Of Blood,} as The Lord commanded me, because it was not lawful to be put into the house of offerings, because it is the price of blood."

In discussing The Element "Of Prophesy Needing To Be Fulfilled!" concerning Judas, and to "The Exact Amount Specified."

Who we collectively take pity and mourn for also in reflection to the event, Of Easter! And who, regarding Judas, that The Church, and indeed That All Humanity, has traditionally made into a "Scapegoat," for all that is weak and deceptive and sinister about Humanity, (as if The Fact Of Jesus' Crucifixion would not have occurred at all were in not for The Betrayal By Judas,) in not viewing, or of not choosing to view, the incident of The Betrayal Correctly, in presuming that the words of Jesus, Who said, "one of you is to betray Me," were meant to convey The Lord's Ability TO Read Minds, instead of choosing to look at it correctly as, A Command Of The Lord, that, "One Of You Is TO Betray Me." Which takes meaning in another, and tragic, light then, which is one of a double ritual suicide.

So stating to The Event Of The Crucifixion Of Our Lord, (speaking reverently for "The Victim," of Judas Iscariot, who Jesus spoke to in these terse words before he was singled out by The Ceremony Of Blood, To Perform The Ritual Function Of Betrayal, Who said: "The Son of Man is going just as it was written, woe to the man by whose hand The Son of Man is betrayed. It would be better for that man never to have been born.") As was The Instruction To Judas, To Die With Him!

And which in a sense alters our conception of The Teachings Of The Lord for this wording to be taken in a vindictive and revengeful way. As it is in direct contradiction to The Great Gospel Of Divine Love And Forgiveness, As Jesus Taught.

Who Professed To, The Doctrine Of Genuine Love And Caring For Our Fellow Human Beings At All Times:

Do unto others, as you would like them to do unto you.

Forgive thy neighbor's transgressions against you.

Turn the other cheek.

And love thy enemy, for hatred and enmity are always theirs.

And concerning the final words of Jesus on the cross, "Father forgive them for they know not what they do.

That is all completely 'Out Of Character,' for Jesus to have made such remarks to Judas, don't you agree?"

"I do agree," Tony remarked, taking up his beautiful carved and darkly stained Meerschaum Pipe from the deck table and packing full of tobacco from the pouch on the deck table, putting the pouch back on the table and then lighting the pipe with his Bic lighter exaggerated puffs as I continued. Puff ... puff ...

"Jesus was not speaking then in an embittered and vindictive nature, in seemingly to be putting a curse unto poor Judas, but meant in a totally different meaning of intent. He was instructing Judas to expect bad things to happen with Him in that way concerning The Betrayal he was to perform. That is the only way of such a remark by The Lord to be taken, in keeping to The Lord's manner, in example, of perfect intention."

And again Tony said, "I agree."

"And concerning the idea of Jesus "Instructing" His Apostles regarding The Crucifixion, (in further argument of Its planned destiny,) that Jesus as well said to His remaining Apostles on The Mount Of Olives later on that night, following His Command To Judas, (and to where that Judas knew exactly where to lead The Roman Soldiers in arresting Jesus coincidentally, in indication that "The Betrayal" was indeed planned out in advance,) saying to them, who of the other eleven Apostles gathered there, "All of you will deny me this night; for it is written, I will smite the shepherd, and the sheep of his flock will be scattered. But after I am risen, I will be in Galilee before you."

Which Cannot Be Construed In Any Other Meaning But That Jesus Had Planned The Event Of His Crucifixion To The Last Detail, To Fulfill The Scripture.

Which we need to drastically altar the setting of The Church's Imagery about, both literally, and psychologically, for The Sake Of The Faith, and for The Sake Of Humanity, to free Judas Iscariot from the eternal curse of being The Betrayer of Christ.

We ought not be going To Church, "To Mourn!" and To Reflect On Inane Logic of Tortured and Morbid Crucifixion, In Psychological Torment any further. And especially concerning The Little Children of the matter, who have to contemplate these

Church Teachings and Events that are beyond their scope in
dimension of intelligence To Correctly Perceive In Reasoning
For. That has "A Deadening Effect!" On The Young, and what
'Scars Them Emotionally In Trauma,' Inversely Of The Conduct
In Intent! Of Religion, Which Should 'Uplift' and 'Inspire.'

That in all, as has an adverse effect on everyone
psychologically and emotionally. And what makes The Church a,
'Death Oriented,' and, 'Futilistic,' and, 'Somber Place!' to visit.
And that is always visited in hushed and solemn reflection.
Instead of The Church Itself being a Vital and an Enlightening
and Spiritually Uplifting Happy Place To Visit, and To Pay Our
Respects To The Father In Tribute.

And of what is not a Healthy and a Happy Place either, for The
Spirit of Lord Jesus To Be Present To, Psychologically, either, to
have to be in reminded reflection all the time, 'In Spiritual
Trauma!' of that painful day in agony of the day when He was
publicly condemned and nailed to The Cross and Died. Jesus was
a man and with emotions the same as we.

And of what Diabolic Cross, In Direct Image of The Work of
Satan, As Horrifying As Anything Imaginable, that has become
The Symbol of All Christianity Itself And That Does Not Having
Anything Whatsoever To Do With The Worship of The Father! in
a clean, wholesome and healthy way, in Proper Conduct of The
Religion. To Get The Point Across!

And Which Death of Jesus Was Not At All Inevitable! for
Jesus, as It Was His Appointed Predestined Sacrifice! to reflect
on, of its outright truth. Which was a death that Jesus, 'Could
Have Easily Avoided!' by choosing, to surrender himself over to
High Priests, (as He was bent on ritual suicide, To Prove He
Could Resurrect Himself From The Dead!) or as was his choice to
leave the area, or that He could have always simply vanished,
(Reality Being The Ethereal State Of The Father's Mind, Which
Was The Point Proved By The Miracles That Jesus Worked In
The Father's Name, which Jesus could easily have relied on To
Disappear! In the same meaning as when He Was Transfigured
Into Pure White Energy, and when He Rose From The Dead, and

when He Ascended Into Heaven!) and spared Judas of his cruel fate of as well.

And although that The Catholic Church reminds us at each Mass, that it was, 'a death that He, Jesus, freely accepted.' But It Was! A Human Sacrifice, after all, To What That The Current Orientation Of The Church Worships.

To what that Jesus boasted of: 'that if you destroyed this Temple, {meaning His Body,} that I Will Rebuild It Again In Three Days,' By Resurrecting Himself. Which He Did. And for what is the reason Why He Was Crucified, Not By Pontius Pilot, (who was The Roman Governor,) but at the behest of The High Priests, out of envy, in instigation of The Jewish People to choose Jesus, (and instead of the condemned murder Bar-Abba who was offered in the place of Jesus,) because Jesus had boasted that He could Resurrect Himself, and not for anything else that Jesus had done that He was crucified, for He was Blameless and a Righteous Man.

But Strictly Speaking For The Case, which represents, The Hideousness of The Crucifixion Of Jesus As The Central Symbol Of The Christian Religion, that is quite difficult for us as strong reasoning adults as it is, to be forced to contemplate, in the manner of Its constant presentation in remorse, but what is present to All The Little Children as well, in display of the cruel meanness of Humanity for all time as well, (And Central To The Church's Teachings,) and TO The Little Ones, who have to endure and suffer Its vicarious torment emotionally, In Trauma Psychologically, as to the regard of, "The Cross," with its apparent 'Human Sacrifice,' implied, (that is always 'Dominating' To The Altars, and especially of The Catholic Church, in large display of, 'Jesus Nailed To The Cross,' to reflect on,) that we need to change The Presentation of The Church about, and especially for the sake of The Holy Innocent Children. That Has Always Been Urgently Required! not to scar any of them emotionally on any further!

Which is to become straightforwardly, and concerning The Ritual of The Mass In Worship, devoted more centrally and dedicated, (in a certain starkness of simple format, with clean white linens in display, devoid of The Blood of The Crucifixion in reminder altogether,) 'To The Father. (Who Is The Ultimate Object Of! And The Center Of! All Of Our Thought And Devotion, In Peace! Religiously Invoked.)

And of the new format of The Church, which is to have an absence Of All Graven Images In Statuary altogether, centrally featured to the main setting in the place of Worship, on display in format. And what is to manifest a certain "Starkness," about it, having nothing expensively gaudy or lavishly ornate to display in The House Of Worship, To The Father."

"Party the house, was the paradigm rule to apply here." I murmured to my self under my breath grateful to have completed my dissertation, and grateful I was to have such a fine place.

"Gary," Tony said in his stumbling way after we had settled back into the evening after along and reflective silence, "I don't usually reveal my inner side of myself to anyone, but I do want you to know that I am very grateful to you that you are here, for having come to live here with us. Since Mary died I have slowly been going a little crazy for some mature company and friendly companionship to be with and to have intelligent conversation with. I have missed that so much. Mary and I were close friends that way. And what with having to raise the kids all by myself, with Mary gone from us. It's good too that you can be here to watch over things while I am away. I worry all the time about leaving Jenny and Henry alone here when I need to go out at night. And I need to go out a lot, missing the female companionship to be with as I do. It's been a long while."

"I'm grateful to be here with you, Tony. There are things in life that you can't learn from books or from formal education that have to do with the way we feel and the strategies we need to adopt to get along with everything that there is to content for in this life. Which day-to-day discourse with a fellow colleague seems to be the only way to accomplish such a feat of magic, to talk about the inner things of life that need to be talked about but never are. We live such reserved and guarded existences, don't we? It seems that no one ever goes much beyond the mundane routines of their dreary daily existences and all blocked up with inhibitions to communicate what they really feel. That if they only did, it would free them from the inner torment of themselves. And so, in that regard, I am grateful to have you to converse with in these times. You have no idea what it means to me."

The Cliffs to Sky Top Tower at Mohonk
that Tony and I and the rest of his Class of 1974
Climbed together on a fine early June day

Downtown New Paltz Facing West
From The Intersection Of Church Street

View Of Shops Along North Chestnut Street

"I never met a man I loved more than you, Tony," I replied.
"And I am grateful to be here with you and to share in your lovely
home, to be a part of your family and for the nice outdoors work
to do of transforming your yard.

Tony looked out into the darkness of the swamp and was
silent, inward looking in his eyes. I watched him for a long
moment and then wanted to change the topic away from the
awkwardness of personal conversation nature.

The kerosene lamplight went out in the upstairs garret loft
above the garage. Lloyd was turning in to sleep for the night. It
was getting close to nine-thirty.

"I always wondered," I said to Tony, startling him back from a
writer's rumination, or the thought of a woman, the consequence
of living in the world of one's imagination, and who looked up
and over at me with half attention, "what Jesus meant when He
said; 'The Kingdom of Heaven is like a man who finds a treasure
hidden in a field, which he re-hides and then goes and sells all
that he has and buys the field.' Why would anyone want to hide
the treasure of Heaven? Wouldn't he want to share it, the
knowledge of Heaven, with everyone?"

"I have no idea at all what that passage means." Tony replied,
grinding his teeth and clenching his jowls together and I knew he
wasn't totally focusing on my query, but he managed to go on
with an answer gathering his wits about it in his stumbling
hesitant way of talking that was so endearing.

"I have often wondered myself what that means, and like so
many other mysterious phrasings of the gospels. Why would
anyone indeed want to re-hide the treasure of Heaven?" Tony
was quiet again for a time, looking out into the darkness of the
night and listening to the night sounds. It was, his mansion
house, a wonderfully secluded place to live, and I could
appreciate his need to share it, and the thoughts what go with it,
with someone who could also appreciate it, and I felt close to him
in a bond of friendship in that moment akin to family. "Tell me
about Doreen," he asked. "Why did you two break up? If you

don't mind my asking? You always seemed like a happy and together couple."

"I don't mind," I replied. "I know it's not important to you, but in the way that it is important to me, it's a story which I have never told to anyone, and I would like to tell you, if not just for the fun of it. Which begins like this ... You can tell me your story too some time if you want but this is my story in a nutshell.

My first steady girl friend's name in High School was Roseanne Smith. She had bad cavities on her upper front teeth and her mother Ellie Smith, who worked as cleaning woman, could not afford to get fixed for her at the dentist, and whose husband, who the kids called 'Old Bird' was a drunken laborer and had left poor Ellie Smith to bring up their six children in a three bedroom rented house; whose names were, beginning with the oldest down; Mora, Charlie, Andy, (who died while Roseanne and I were dating, found dead in his car of a Heroin overdose,) Micky, Roseanne, and Eileen. I mention this only because we pledged our hearts to each other forever, Roseanne and I, only to fall out of love a year and a half later when I enlisted in the Army for a three year tour of duty and went overseas to Vietnam. That was realistically too much to ask a young girl to wait around for. And so we fell out of touch with one another. I had a longing for her in my heart a lot while I was away, but it was something I knew I had to let go of.

When I got home after returning from the War, I saw Roseanne, who was the first person I wanted to see. Her front teeth were patched up, sort of, with off-color porcelain fillings on both sides of her two front teeth that were too white for the rest of her teeth, but I was relieved that she at last looked presentable. Poor dear.

She broke the news to me then that night that she wanted to tell me in person and not by letter that was going to marry someone else whose name was Danny Gaspero who was the son of the owner of Gaspero's Bakery in Poughkeepsie, which was a prosperous business. And so that was the end of that. Before I shipped overseas to Okinawa and then on to Vietnam, I used to hitchhike home from Fort Bragg, NC, which was six hundred miles, and later on all the way from Fort Stewart, GA, which was a thousand, on the weekends just to see her. That's how crazy in love I had been with her. But the war and the long years apart had taken their toll on either side of our romance.

Roseanne said her younger sister Eileen wanted to go out with me, if that would help, but it didn't. You can't pledge your heart to someone and then go out with her sister and make like it never happened between you. What were all those endearing words and vows we had exchanged with one another. I did though go out with her sister Eileen for a few dates while I was home on leave after Vietnam, but I felt foolish and knew it just didn't feel right in my heart to do that. You just can't switch love around with the emotions in your heart like that, not if and after you pledged your heart.

After I had gotten out of the military for a while I began dating a girl named Carol Walen, who was two years younger than me and coincidentally who had gone out with my younger brother Ronnie, who was three years younger than me. I was Carol that my brother had been sitting with to greet me when my parents had brought me home from Kennedy Airport after my arrival back in the States from Vietnam. That was two days before Christmas in 1966. She was a real beautiful girl.

However, my brother Ronnie had subsequently gotten another girl pregnant and married her, an Italian girl named Terry Migliori, (and always pronounced in Italian 'Miori' with the gl silent,) who was the sister of my brother's best friend Michael Migliori, who Doreen and I moved out neighboring to on Mckinstry Road, in Gardiner, NY, later on in time when we live there in 1976, and who later on, that I would climb the cliffs of the Shawangunk Mountain with. I was the best man at my brother Ronnie's wedding.

So he had left poor Carol all alone, who had been in love with him, and so too that Carol had grown involved and attached to my family, and particularly my mother, and who my father had grown fond of, in an emotional way. It happened that I had seen Carol out at a nightclub one night. She had a bad drinking habit I need to say, and was quite sloshed, and as one thing leads to another falling all over me out drinking we went out together out to the parking lot and began making out in my car later on in the evening.

It was then all of a sudden that she confides to me that my brother Ronnie had broken her virginity. Which was quite a revelation to lodge in the back of my mind, but a girl in hand to a young man was what it was. Enough said. I knew that wasn't right, but I was lonely too and love starved at the time and in need of that soothing female intimacy at the time.

It is one of The Creator's Commandments in Leviticus: 18-16, not have sexual relations with your brother's wife. That goes like this: 'You shall not approach your brother's wife; it is your brother's nakedness.' But try as I would I couldn't shake Carol. She kept dogging me. She would show up at my apartment, almost every Friday night like clockwork at around 10:30, always sloppy drunk, and want to go to bed and spend the night with me and what became a habit with her. I was renting a second floor apartment with my friend Dick Frahm, who we all called Big Dick, while I was working for the Operating Engineers Union, and going to flight school then at the time at Sky Acres Airport in Billings, NY. He was a good friend and weight lifting buddy of mine. I was always tired from the workweek on Friday nights and wanted to rest, sometimes having to work on Saturdays, but Carol kept coming over drunk to stay the night and became a regular fixture. Saturday morning would turn into all day and Saturday night into Sunday.

Needless to say, things never did work out, although, Carol courted me for several years and finally talked me into marrying her, which I did. But my brother Ronnie was always in the picture, if you know what I mean. He always had that secret intimacy of sexual knowledge of her that way between them, that I could pick up on whenever they were together, and even though that we tried to act grown up in our attitude about the situation, our real and genuine feelings always got between us, and I think to this day that there exists a major rift over the issue. I always felt in my mind's eye that there was something between them then and all the time and still.

And so we were married, Carol Walen, my first wife and I, in 1970 on March 7th, on the day of the total Solar Eclipse, and the wedding was timed to come out of the church at exactly the precise moment of the eclipse. And we all watch as the sky was darkened upon our nuptials, that was quite an event and a very ominous sign in the heaven, and that proved to be prophetically real concerning our marriage that ended precisely two years later after a rocky start and a stormy conclusion that went like this.

It seems that poor Carol had several personalities, one of which was a loving caring wife, that other was wounded bird with a broken wing that needed my sympathy, and the third was a tyrant that absolutely hated me, and who yelled and hurled obscenities at me at regular intervals like clockwork, and who revealed herself all to two weeks on best behavior into out marriage.

Later on that year in the fall of 1970 I began my return to school at Dutchess Community College to complete my life long dream and calling from God to get a college degree. And it was there in that fall semester of 1970 that I met my present wife Kathy Mabee in Professor Muller's Chemistry Class, and who I fell in love with in relief from the tyrant woman I had married and began on a make shift dating arrangement of Friday nights out with the boys shooting pool or whenever and whatever excuse I could come up with and could get away with to get around and out from under my marital duties to date Kathy, and who I fell more deeply involved with, if not in love with, even to the point of meeting her parents and becoming a member of her household in that regard. That became an absurdity.

When I finally had to tell Carol that I wanted a divorce it was the hardest thing in the world to do. Carol freaked out needless to say.

Kathy and I dated through college and set the date for our own wedding in 1975 in the summer after graduation. And that was when I met Doreen in the Old Main Building on campus who happened to be sitting in on Professor Harry Stonebeck's class on William Faulkner that I was enrolled in and just finish up with right in that time just before graduation. Later on I just happened to see her out at P&G's, and though I didn't plan it, of anticipate it being that way, I wound up picking her up and spending the night with her in my apartment at Colonial Arms in the Village where I had been living with my roommate Lou Vilardo who worked at Barnaby's as a Bartender.

I needed to break up with Kathy, and although I was in love with her, and she with me, because her parents knew nothing about my being a married man, while I had been dating Kathy and eating dinners in their home with them. And so the deception, if it were ever to be revealed, and it would be because we were planning to bet married in the Catholic Church and could not without a formal Annulment from the Catholic Religion, which I didn't have. We had a Civil Annulment, but not the one that Kathy and I needed to be married formally in the Catholic Religion. And so I was in a deep bind about that and needed to bail. To tell Kathy's parents of the deception, and to this day that has not been ever revealed, would have been too much to handle. And so Doreen played a convenient roll that was of breaking us up; which was a very painful thing to do.

You can see that, can't you, Tony?"

"It's a horrible thing isn't it," Tony replied, "to have to tell someone you are going with another and to break their heart. It breaks your own heart too, to have to do it."

"Well, in any way, that was it. I left my one true love and never did settle in very good with Doreen because of it. You know, something is always there about it nagging on in the back of your mind that won't let you go on. And do Doreen and I finally split after being married for all of six months. We had gotten married by the Justice of the Peace, Judge Stokes, who lived down the road from us when we lived on Mckinstry Road in Gardiner.

And I say all of this, because, in the end, who are all those people who we pledged our hearts and our lives to in the end, and who are all interchangeable, like spare parts. I'm sure you feel that way too. We take wives as we find them to suit us in the moment that is being lived. And depending to if we get along with any of them or not is another matter. They ought to have a Lemon Law in regard to marriages, to be able to free us up from defective products. It's all too quixotic in the pursuit of ideals. There are no ideals when it comes to marriage, are their?"

"There are if you know what it is you're after and you have two people who are willing to participate maturely in the outcome of the event, the event being, to live together for life. It's a major undertaking in commitment that's bigger than the sex you have with your partner. And there you are, out after another partner to have sex with and saying the same out clichés out of your mouth and calling it love. Only to find out that it's another person whose as complicated as you are on the inside, and maybe more so."

"I always like to end the story about what happened to Doreen and to my brother Ronnie, and to Michael, and to everybody out there at the Hippy Drug Farm and an arm of The Italian Mafia and the leading edge of the deluge of drugs coming into the area which were used to subvert the population and topple the war effort in Vietnam, and although that it made everyone involved with it conspiratorial criminals and traitors to the American People as a consequence, with the quote from Leviticus: 19:16. You shall not accuse your own people; neither shall you stand upon the blood of your neighbor. I am the Lord. But it never does feel right to gossip about the faults of others does it, regardless of how noble the motives."

"No it doesn't," Tony stated. "It never does. The Bible always tells it right. And that is, if and when we can ever figure it out what it means; which isn't always that apparent."

"It's apparent enough where it is important," I replied. "As far as I am concerned there are only three major Commandments in The Bible to be concerned with; two from The Heavenly Father Himself. One concerning the proper diet in sensibility for Mankind, and the other the admonition against the use of The Poppy Flower Seed Ball, Opium/Heroin, and the one from Jesus for us to be perfect like our Father in Heaven is perfect.

And of what paramount idea of achieving, "Perfection," that is the prime motivator and Commandment of our Lord and Savior, Jesus Christ, as He relates about it to us in the verse of The New Testament of Holy Christian Faith Bible of, Matthew: 5:48:

"Therefore you are to be perfect, as your Father In Heaven Is Perfect."

Of which verse is according to the established teaching of The Catholic Church, IS NEVER TAUGHT! by the entire structure of present Christianity, in grave issue of Reasoning! For It Is "The Key Note!" To All of Human Existence Taught In The Holy Bible, "To Be Perfect," in all of our Thoughts, Words, and Deeds, and to bear forth with an Immaculate Will upon The Blessed Earth in our approach to The Way Of Life.

That and as well concerns the conduct of our human earthly affairs in The Perfection of Holiness, as concerns the orientation that behooves us all in the understanding of The Creator's Intent, of what The Kingdom Of Heaven is like, to be observant and mindful of THE CREATOR'S FIRST COMMANDMENT, that is also Never Taught by The Christian Churches either, of The Faith of The Old Testament of Genesis: 1:29:

"And God said, Behold, I have given you every herb yielding seed, which is upon the face of all the earth, and every tree which bears fruit yielding seed; to you it shall be for food."

Some contemplative monks like Lloyd and myself chose to labor in the elements of the out-of-doors each day in harmony to the sun and the moon and the stars, close to the sensations of the earth.

The miraculous exists in the dream of life, to realize the nature of the dream for your self in awakening to its reality, and to know in the heart of The Creator that you are a part of the dream taking place and a part of everything there is to be at one with God about.

And do let us always be mindful of the great teachings of The Lord and Savior to his disciples and to us, as it is conveyed to us by Matthew in his Gospel, Matthew: 18-20:

18 Truly I say to you, whatever you bind on earth will be bound in heaven, and whatever you released on earth will be released in heaven.

19 Again I say to you that if two of you are worthy on earth, anything that they would ask will be done for them by my Father in heaven.

20 For wherever two or three are gathered in my name, I am
     there among them.
And of John: 13-15.

13: And whatever you ask in my name I will do it for you, so
that the Father may be glorified through his Son.

14: If you ask me in my name, I will do it.

15: If you love me, keep my commandments."

Also, "and in "Stillness" there I AM also;" and in all things
Still, to beckon us into the hallowed silence of the empty mind at
rest, wherein dwells the thought of The Creator ... and Peace.

"Gary that was lovely. You have certainly given me a great
deal to think about. I am going in now to turn in. You should
turn in too, get some rest for tomorrow."

"I'm still going to go into Town and walk around a bit, see
what's going on, maybe something will turn up. You have a good
night. And thanks always for the inspiration."

"The Pleasure is all mine," Tony said.

And with that Tony got up with Waldo jumping up abruptly to
his heels and went back inside the house. He held the door open
for Waldo and then went in. I listened to the screen door while it
opened and closed and then sat alone with the silence of the night
air for long while.

What blessed peace ... In my Father's Kingdom there are
many rooms.

****

As I remember, it has been many years gone by, over twenty
now in fond nostalgia of recollection by my calculation, from the
last time that I had physically actually seen Tony, as I was out
walking along the highway on Route 32 just on the outskirts of
The Village of New Paltz, NY heading East towards The Village
of Rosendale, one day in the early Saturday morning air around
9:30 a.m. in the late of the summer month of August, 1989.

The sound of flies were buzzing around something they were
feeding on in the scruffs of grass along the side of the road. I

didn't look closely to see what it was. And the traffic along the road was making whooshing sounds as the vehicles drove past that I was half paying attention to out of the side of my left eye not to get hit.

I was in a quiet and contemplative mood, fully awake, and with a great deal of enthusiasm for the day's adventure after the good night's sleep I had had sleeping over at my friend Eric's room. It was the beginning of a bright sunny day with the Sun full-up just over the tops of the trees in a cloudless morning sky and already starting to get hot and heavy in the humid morning air and the heat was already shimmering skyward off the pavement of the shoulder of Route 32.

I had been walking and hitch-hiking a ride out to The Village of Rosendale, that day that Tony crossed my path again, literally, almost absentmindedly bumping into me, or pretending to, as I was in the process of hitching a ride with my thumb out walking backwards when Tony appeared at my right shoulder having crossed the street right ahead of me while my back was turned.

I had not seen anything of him before then for quite a while and was startled to see him. He was with one of his distinguised looking Collegue friends who displayed a polite disinterest in me. They were both in their mid-50s then and apparently out for a walk and judging from the direction they had just come from, from Tony's home in the neighborhood across the street, and apparently headed for The Stewart Convenient Store, as it seemed.

I had just spent the night in Town with my friend Eric Iverson; with him, and with four other fellow companions of mine and two women, Bart Kruas and his wife Ellen Ganzer, John Martin and his brother Keven, a lovely street girl named Fellipe,, and Jay Lipshitz, all of us together, along with myself, making eight of us, sleeping on the floor of Eric's small room in Fred's Rooming House at 13 Church Street that was just off Main Street in the Village.

Some of us slept on foam mats, that were stored in the closet along with the spare blankets, and which Eric reverently got out each evening and passed out to anyone in the Gang who was staying and with the comforted feeling of someone caring enough to lay a blanket over you and tuck you in at night.

Others, including myself, preferred sleeping on the bare rug floor.

I liked the feel of the hard floor as a discipline in obeisance to toughening of my body in my ascetic practice of mendicancy. The room had been turned into a Club House for The Gang, as Eric likes to describe us as, "his gang," on the second floor of Fred's rooming house on Church Street.

Fred lived on the fist floor with his wife with rules of No Double Occupancy to be mindful of the noise and the water consumption about.

I was sleeping next to John Martin on one side of me, and next to Flip, (an endearing nickname for Felippe that was her true name, and who had cozied up to my side in the night with her groin leg snuggled close over my bottom inner thigh.) I had awakened from my slumber to find her that way and didn't want to move to awaken her even though I felt the need and had to get up to use the bathroom soon but not wanting to disturb the moment in dilemma. Finally I did get up carefully without disturbing her at all, still sound asleep, and left the room.

When I returned it was now just beginning to get light with the gray dim twilight of the morning coming in through the open window, and with the stark reality that the place of refuge of the night would soon be at an end. The hardest part about being a Hobbo Difter was in having to vacate the premisis of wherever it is that you are sleeping and have taken refuge at for the night and to have to head back about on to the steet, or highway, again. Mornings weren't good times to be a lonely wanderer, and they were psychologically the hardest meanest part of being a Hobo to endure.

It was a calm quiet morning with just the sound of period traffick stopping and going for the light at the intersection of Route 299 and Highway 32 behind the rooming house. I layed quietly back down again for a few more moments of blessed rest.

John Martin and and Bart on the other side of the room were snoring lightly.

Eric and Kevin had both gone out to do their Bar Mob Jobs when John came in from closing P&Gs Bar at 3:30 a.m., and who had brought back a six pack of Budweiser with him in from the bar for the gang with the instructions to save him two beers for the morning.

John, and who would now sleep until late in the afternoon, and who was now out cold, never moved at any time in the way he slept from the time he had laid down until he got up and was now lying on his side curled up in a fetal position in the same position he had gone to sleep in.

It seemed to be a rituail of the gang for everyone to lie perfectly still and not to move. And for the fact that no one, and I would say the same for everyone in gang, moved at all from the positions that they took when they started out sleeping until they woke up, or if they moved at all, would just to get up to go to the bathroom, and to do what that occassionally someone would get up and step carefully over the bodies lying on the floor to do out to use the bathroom and return to take their place on the floor, or to smoke a cigarette and drink down a beer if anyone felt like it at odd intervals of the long night, and go back to sleep and other than that everyone in Eric's Gang always kept perfectly still. They all, and the women in the gang too, each slept like stones. People would be awake or sleeping at any time, or talking quitely, which made no difference to whoever was resting. Sleep our way, was deep and sound, or we were just awake and lying there listening to what else was going ton, to rest.

I found in trying to sleep like like that, without moving, and as I picked it up from admiring John, and then Ellie, who never moved either, at first, that it just took the getting over of the initial aches in my body position that soon past into a numbness and that I had gotten quite used to the idea of doing it too, not moving at all for the long duration of my rest from the position I took when starting out, which was most generally to lay on my left side with one of my arms streched out in front of me to the side and one positioned, my right arm, on the top of my thigh, and to lay that way in that position perfectly still without moving.

After a time, and for anyone who would care to try it, the idea
of sleeping perfectly still, you can feel the spirits in your body
swirling around in your extremities trying to get a finger or an
arm of leg to twitch. I found I was able to contain the feeling and
the restlessness all bottled up inside me soon subsided into a
numb acceptance of the motionless prison I had confined them to,
and became somewhat subdued and docile to the notion of having
something to do, remaining motionless, and with a feeling of
accomplishment of not succumbing to the temptation, To Move,
and which the tormented and restless spirits inhabiting my body
craved to do, to toss and turn, and that you could feel swirling
there inside of you, but which was being denied to them. It
seemed to be a ritual of their way of sleeping of the street people,
that I took to, that for me took some getting used to and to
suppress the craving to be restless and to disturb the others around
me. And it became more serious of a pastime too, not to move,
that anyone can try it for themselves, to lie still in their
extremities and then begin to feel the motion in other sensitive
parts of the anatomy with the need to quell your tongue from
moving, that wants to dart around your mouth, and next to stop
your eyes from darting around. Tonge Lies Flat, was the motto.
Jowl and Facial Muscles are relaxed. Eye Balls become fixed and
motionless, and do not dart around, (the eye balls are the most
difficult.) Your breath comes slowly then in and out of your nose.
The spirits are contained. You can fall asleep or not to, for you
are a rest and remain that way in mastery over yourself.

And too, when you were crashing out, as the phrase went, and
that is to say imposing on someone else's turf intruding for a
night's rest, you wanted to be as unobtusive and as pleasant to be
with as possible. The last thing you wanted to do was to disturb
your host as their quest and to become an unwelcome guest and
not be invited back because of it.

Ten minutes or so went by, and it was starting to get ligher
outside. Bart got up to use the bathroom and when he returned
chose to sit up awake for awhile sitting with his back to the wall
in the corner or the room by the window to smoke a cigarete and
letting the smoke curl and drift out the window quickly with the

breeze. He popped open one of the six pack of beers that John had brought back and began drinking it down. The other beers still left were keeping cool in the window.

Ellen was sound asleep, or seemed to be, and looked very pretty in the twighlight with her relaxed and angelic-like composure of slumber. Ellen always slept very still like a stone. She was lovely and angelic to watch, sleeping there.

An hour later in the morning we each left very early, as it got to be on toward 6:30 a.m. or so, to one by one tip toe down the stairs and open and shut the outer door to the street without making a sound. Fred liked us and was a friend to all the street people he took in, but no one wished to rub his nose in his kindness with our indescretions.

To have a place to sleep for the night, out of the elements was a God Send that no one wanted to spoil, by running up his water bill for showers and by flushing the toilet to often. Eric always kept a plastic one gallon milk bottle in the closet to pee in, and that was a necessity in rooming house anyway, with other people being in the bathroom when you had to go. Eric always dumped the pee bottle and flushed the toilet down once in the morning after everyone had left. The rest of the time all was quite. Sometimes in the late of the afternoon when no one was around, you could sneek in a quick shower, no more than to get wet, soap up, and rinse off. But that wasn't to be counted on everyday.

Most times I stayed out on Ed Brandes land out by the mountain and slept in Jay Lipshitz's old abandoned school bus which was cast off and rusting out there.

Ed lived out on Wawarsing Road along Route 299 and right across from the Psychiatrist Iron Welding Sculptor Doctor Ernie Shaw, who lived at the end of a long dirt road that wandered in a ways to his Modern Ranch Style House back in the woods and which was lined along the way with an impressive collection of Ernie's Art Work that stood at frequent intervals like totems.

Ernie was the son of a favorite and beloved by all Jewish Professor friend of mine who taught English Literature at The SUNY, named, Sam Shaw, and was kind of an avante guard loner who, with his longish and unkempt hair in the artist's style of the day, kept to himself on his land, doing his iron welding work and coming into town on occasion to have breakfast and coffee at The Gay Ninetees Café, who I would happen to see there. Who about that Professor Shaw remarked to me one day that he was happy to see his son Ernie finally making an honest living, and whatever that meant about the wording of the comment to be implied.

I had helped Ernie move a piece of Iron Sculture one time several years prior, (and who I wanted to check out anyway because of what happened to Mary and that somehow involved Jenny with regards to Ernie, as I heard from Jenny who told me about it that she and her mother used to go to visit Ernie together,) when a friend of mine then, when he had been a friend of mine, by the name of Kurt Grimes who used to work for Ernie part time as a helper had asked me to go along with him to move the Piece of Art to a new location to a University Library in Massachesettes. Which Ernie paid by check for, inviting me into his Ranch House to write me the check. It was a nice home, nothing out of the ordinary.

Kurt on the other hand was an imposter, who posed as a low level Street Dealer, but who in actuality turned out to be involved with The Poughkeepsie Police Mafia Drug Trafficking on the New Paltz side of the Hudson River, and who I caught Red Handed one night out high-lifing, finely dressed, and seated with another man at the bar at The Southern Dutchess Country Club in Beacon, NY, when I was out making my appointed rounds down that way, and to see my old friend William H. Ashburn, who was then around 1986 when I caught Kurt out that night, at that time the Chief of Police of The Beacon Police Department, that is also named Heroin City.

Chief Ashburn, who is since then now retired, and who I grew up together with until the age of thirteen as a child, and whose own father had died and who my father as raised as his own, and who I often slept with in the same bed when we where little children, and who was my confidant and advisor to the Military Operation I was involved in, was always very accomodating to me, and in his wary of "not trusting the locals," in the meaning of Local Law Enforcement, with any information of Pornography or

Drug Trafficking and Foul Play, as they were, as Chief Ashburn put it, "The New Regmine," and that being The Black/Italian and The Jewish Drug/Porno Mafias in power and Democratically Gerrymandered to their own Political Machinery, with only their own Political Mafia People allowed to run for the available Public Offices, including The Judiciary, and who therefore were able and allowed to establish their own Police Mafia Departments on American Soil with impugnity.

My proplem was, as things turned out for the worst that Kurt had "made me," and that is to say, had "seen me" too, and knew also that I was not who I was not pretending to be. And so that an intrigue developed between us that involved me with foul play on the Poughkeepsie Street where I lived on arriving home from work one night some months later, and none of which I remember happening, in which I was hit in the face and on the back of my head, knocked unconscious, and assualted on both legs with a stun gun and subsequently on "coming to" some hours later to find myself on a gurney in St. Francis Hospital and on my way to be locked up in the psychiatric ward of Hudson River State Hospistal for the insane to be injected with a crippling substance called Navane, to look and feel the part.

Heroin does funny things to time. If people snort it up their nose and stand or sit around talking in a long winded way to anyone, they will most likely induce a vacant time-lapse, or black-out condition in their intended victim for a period of time depending on the strenght and duration of their exposure to the drug, and otherwise that would cause people to "nod," and that is very deadly especially around the use of alcohol. Kurt was playful that way. And that is why that the vicinity of New Paltz, NY, and the environs of the Wallkill River Valley is called Black Out Valley by those who know the score, and for the old Herion Mafia who had established itself there, fellow Draculas, and past down throught the generations for the past hundreds years or longer.

And for the same way of understanding of, "funny things with time," that Heroin was also used as a "knock-out" drug. And which was the reason that in the treachery of The Italian Mafia in the movie The God Father that they could knock-out the movie director in the scene and put the severed head of his favorit horse under the covers without him knowing to discover on his awakening the morning.

And such was the nature of the Drug War in the streets of our Nation that we were defending America over.

With The Italian Mafia taking over the local Territory to Dominate the population for the sadistic sport of it and with a conspired to local gerrymandering to take over everyone politially, economically, of the "we move in, you move out," variety, and of the take over of local police departments.

And with the Jewish Mob, of a similar vein, in the name of a Zionist Movement, having their own designs of taking over territory simultaneously, and having the territory exclusively to themselves known as "The Catskills" to the West and South of The Italians. And who were, like the Italians, using Corrupt Economic Warfare, and Drugs and Chemicals in sabotage upon the innocent residing population to get the job done, of making pyshciatrics out of the people with the idea of drug sabotage in a prearranged plot upon the nation of The American People, for what eventually would be the greater glory of Israel and conquest outright of The United States, like Palestine, to be under the stated Jewish Flag, of the Jewish Mafia, "Murder Incorporated."

And of what warfaring front to speak of, who are not anything like the bearded effeminate Jewish Rabbis that the media of Jewish Propaganda films being put out to show of their being persecuted for their faith, but of those types of Jews who fly the false flag under the banner of The Jewish Faith Rabiis of treachery and betrayal as Mafia Counterparts are conceived of with "guns at the door" in the middle of the night, to overrrun and to conquer The United States, as a People and as a Faith together, like the original conquest of The Holy Land, as you now see them also conspriring to do to The United States.

And their being different, as to The Jewish State Ambitions, than the Italian Mafia representing The Italian People; whose main desire, as to state for The Italian Mafia, is to subjugate and to dominate the indigenous population, to exact tribute and levy taxes, in their Roman Tradition of conquest, and to enslave and to terrify and to plunder, and to rape the women, and the young boys and men, in that regard.

And with The Black Mafia fighting their own band of hatred and torment to the White American Nation of The United States in plot to overrun and to assimilate by conversion to mulattoism, to the ultimate annihilation of The White Race and to slaughter with the use and the means of Drugs and Chemicals, to mate with The White Race and take us over, for The United States to become like the Sub Continent of India in outlook.

That White America was not taking the proper stance in their precautions to defend themselves against.

And to what all was my thought as I had signaled to Bart sitting on the floor to pass me one the beers left to cool in the window, which he did, and which I temporarily set down on the floor while I placed my blanket carefully over Flip and tucking her in lovingly in the early chill to keep her snuggly warm. Nothing feels better to a gang member than to have someone care for you enough to put a blanket over top of you, as I discovered the feeling in having it done to me.

I then picked the can of beer back up and stuffed it into my front pants pocket to keep it concealed, and left Eric's room to go outside.

It felt good, as it always did, to step outside and greet the beginning of a brand new day in the fresh air of morning. It was 6:45 by the clock at the First National Bank down the street as I rounded the corner of Church Street onto Main.

In the mornings I liked to think of the Earth orbiting a Star in the Heaven of Stars to think on, and to marvell at the life around me and how that it all came to exist out of the darkenss of nothing, and to ask the question of The Creator Divine how I was to fit in with the scheme of things, as I proceeded on in the fresh air of the morning and with the songs and chatter of the birds in the trees. It was indeed a fine morning.

The pidgeon flock that perched above the street on the roof of the Building that housed The Deli House took off all at once, circled the building and then fly West out to the Flats to feed.

Main Street and Church Street Facing North
Fred's Rooming House is on the left by the parked car

Church Street was a little short side street that ran diagonally and parallel to Route 32 North, off of the Main Street to North Front Street; with a used appliance store, Fred's Rooming House, and other shops, The Jewish Synogogue, and some white painted two story old homes with apartments bordering its tranquil and off the beaten track sides.

Main Street on the other hand was, and except for the early morning times, always noisey and bustling with people at any other time of the day or night. It was a properous and busy three block area, with early 1930s red brick two and three story architecture, that held shops and business of various sorts, apartments, thirteen Bars and seven Restaurants and Café's, or Bistros as some of them were called, and that served the State University population, situated further up on the low hill overlooking the Village, Tourists from all parts of The United States and the World who flocked there, local residents of the area, townies, as the people who lived in the rooming houses were called, and street people like myself, and other visitors. The street was always lined with persons "hanging out," sitting on stoops or standing idly about. Loitering was the stock and trade of the Village, and people from all walks of life would come from all over just to stand there or sit there on the street. You couldn't figure anyone to be who they portrayed themselves to be on the street that way. Many lived successful lives in other part of the territory who would come there to hand around for the bars and the nightlife, and for the girls, or for other sexual motives, or for the drugs, and many for the drugs, or for the counter culture flaire and adventure of it. New Paltz was a big drug and porno whore town as it always had been and more so even since the Hippie Revolution took place there and took over the SUNY Campus the The Village beginning in the late 1960's and on through the '70's, remaining as a drug conclave stronghold into the current era of its history, that had made it into the Drug Capital and Drug Mecca of The Word that it had now become, and besides of the area being a tourist attraction of and in itself to start with.

The air had a nice and refreshing early morning in late summer coolness to it that seemed very exhilerating as I took my first steps out onto the street and took up with a position briefly in the alley, where no one could see, to drink my breakfast beer down. It was still chilled and felt good going down. I finished it quickly prefering not to linger there in the alley and risk the open container violatino with the local police. I hid the can where I could find it later on when I would collect all the empty cans and return them for the nickle each they were worth in New York State to buy more beer with. I lit up a Winston cigaratte from the hard pack in my jeans pocket, took nice deep drag and let it out, and then went and stood on the stoop in front of The Hobbo Deli to wait for friends to come along, either to go into the Hobo Deli or into the Gay Nineties Cafe that was situated on the corner of Main and Church Streets, and watched waiting for any persons of interest, and that is to say, friends and aquaintances of mine, who I could hit up on for the coffee, beer, and cigarette money that I needed to get through the day.

Bart and Ellie came down the street together a short while later. Bart went into The Gay Nineties and while Ellen waited mulling around in front, followed by Jay Lipshitz who went into the Gay Nineties Cafe. Bart came back out and went off down the street to the laundromat in the Municipal Parking Lot by the Post Office to use the bathroom. The laundromat was unattended and we all went in there discretely to use the Restroom when we needed to. There was also a bathroom in the Mobile Station there, but you had to be a customer or know the cashier to get the key. And that was available too, at times.

Bart was a good-looking fellow, rather tall, with sandy brown hair and with a persuasive and insistent personality that was useful for panhandling on the street.

I had a light beard kept close in those days and was dressed in my standard live-in-my-clothes summer fair, of dungarees, sturdy work boots, heavy socks, a green stort sleeve T shirt, and carrying a hooded pull over jacket that I was never without for the chill of the night air, draped over my right shoulder, and was two days out so far without a change of underwear and that I would have to visit my camp out at Ed's soon to remedy.

We all slept and lived in our clothes, and our clothes, were like the outer fur of an animal is to them, to us. Once in a while we did laundry. I always had a light carry bag, or a pack, with a change of clothes and several changes of underwear. And which I kept in the abandoned school bus out at my friend Ed Brandes at that time, who lived out by the Mountain on Wawarsing Road.

Ellen was aways so lovely to gaze upon in her demure way of innocent and inviting seduction, that captivated the eyes and imaginations of male onlookers, myself being no exception. She was dressed that morning, looking very demure, in soft gray denim long pants, a slightly wrinkled short sleeve white cotton blouse with a floral arrangement on the collar, white socks, and tan petite looking soft canvas tennis shoes.

I had enough small change for coffee, $.70, and went into The Hobbo Deli, which opened up each day at 6:00 a.m., and made up a medium size cup, light no sugar, for Ellie and I to share, who was pacing fidgitively when I came back out needing her morning caffeine fix, which she took eagerly from me for her first sip and held on to. I let her drink the coffee down until she offered it back to me, took another sip and gave it back to her, and stood there on the stoop watching the traffick go by sharing the rest of the coffee with Ellen as we passed the cup back and forth until it was gone, and who stood next to me, slightly touching me at my left side, down on the sidewalk in front of the Deli.

Then we waited there like that, close standing close together in the cool air of the morning and mulling around waiting for Bart to come back for a half an hour and watching the people come by to trying our luck panhandling. Asking for a quarter from certain persons for the laundromat was easy and which delighted Ellen to be successful at. She rummaged around in the trash can in the ally by the Deli and found half a cream cheese bagel, left carefully by a sainted early morning patron being kind to the hungry Street People, lying very neatly wrapped on the top of the paper trash in the can in the ally.

"Look," she said, "a nice half a bagel."

Photo of Ellen Ganzer
As She Looked On Her 30th Birthday in 1991

She offered me a bite but I shook my head no.

"You enjoy it," I said, "I'm holding out for beer money,"

"Gary, I'm so depressed," Ellen said.

I looked at her with compassion, almost wanting to touch her then to resolve her mental pain, but I didn't.

Instead I said, "Have a few beers, that's what I do. Maybe we can come up with some money."

Bart finally came back from down the street showing us some small change, looking to be about $.50, in his hand, and went into the Nineties.

The Police Chief, Charles Bagdonowitz, went by in his Patrol Car and I waved to him as he passed heading up the Main Street to the Police Station. He had waved in his usually friendly way. We were friends and who I addressed as Charlie whenever we happened to meet. Charlie had hired me, earlier in the Spring of that year of 1977, as I had interviewed with him, as to why I was on the street in looking for my wife Doreen who had run off, and provided him my background credentials and references, and that is in the sense of being hired, given me the position of running the street. Exactly what that meant was a gray area.

Chief Bagdonowitz was retiring at the end of September though, and it was time for me to move on then as well. It was after all a private surveillance job in a wide open drug town with crooked police and dangerous criminals to rub elbows with and be wary of, that had already burned me bad on several occassions in the past through the years in trying to steer a safe course through, that was like a mine field to know one's way around about, and which wasn't always easy, even with the guidance and cover of personal protection of the Chief. I was off-sides of the law living on the street and the new people coming into power when the Chief left and wouldn't know my history to be mindful of me over.

Jay came out with a cup of coffee to go. I hit Jay up for thirty cents, which was all he had, and that was our start on the beer money we needed. In a little while Joey St. George approached heading into the Nineties. I signaled to Joey and asked him for a

dollar which he gave me. That made $1.30 we had now. Only
$.59 to go before we could get a six pack of Shlitz Beer, the
cheapest, and catch a buzz to start out the day. A good buzz to
start the day with always made you more aggressive and thereby
more successful with the day's hunting.

   Ellen was a beautiful and demure young girl, with wispy long
blond hair that hung neatly cut seveal inches below her shoulders.
She had blue eyes, a lovely trim figure and firm full breasts. And
at five foot three she weighed all of 108 pounds. I could pick her
up off the ground and lift her all the way over my head, which I
did indeed become fond of doing as time evolved on between us.
And who had captured my heart from the start, finding her to be
irrisitable and impossible not to look at longingly, and what made
me go weak in the knees to look at her for the first time, for those
who know the feeling.

   The only other girl to ever do that to me was Jenny. But that
was a long time ago and Jenny was separated irritrievably from
me now. Ellen reminded me a great deal of Jenny in girlish
playfuy spirit and was the same age as Jenny, in 1989, which
would make Jenny 28 then also.

Elting Memorial Library
Ellie's Morning Reading Bench in The Village

Ellen was also a slightly challenged girl who seemed to suffer from autism. She seemed lost, totally self abosbed in the mind of her own world, and unawares that there was anyone else in need of her attention for her to relate to. Or maybe she was a Narc pretending to be that way, which I always thought she was in the days of who knew who anybody was. She seemed in her coy erotic way of being self absorbed, unigue in her own existence, exotic in another meaning, having the endearing and overly sexy mentality and disposition of a spoiled two year old innocent child, looking eagerly about for the comfort of companionship and love, and frowning if it wasn't' provided. Who anyone would only be all to eager to help with the supplying of such happiness, the way a mother looks to her child in wanting her child to be happy, and worried as to what to do to make things better when she wasn't.

She talked a nonsensical psychobabble endearingly all day long of things that ordinarily to ordinary people would not constitute conversation. But I made sense of her, and little by little began to draw her out and to establish a rapport with what goes on there in her mind, where Ellen lived, and from where the window of eyes look gazingly out from.

That morning in particular she going on about how she could feel her her ovulation beginning to start, and how heavy her period flows were since she had been put on her Medication at the hospital, or whether approaching thirty soon, of whether I thought that her titties were starting to sag, and wanting me to look at them, or how bad her gas had smelled to everyone the night before, and other sublime discourse of that nature, such as getting a lawyer to change her name to Ellie Malancamp.

But she was fun and pleasant to be with and I related to her on her level of no stress conversation that only needed to be listened to and not interrelated with any intent of serious intelligent conversation.

She had been a troubled girl as a teenager, a run away from home, and out alone on the streets at the tender age of sixteen, and had she found herself pregnant then with a Mulatto baby at the age of seventeen, which she had and gave up for adoption, who she named Gregory and had never seen since.

On the down side, she did have a mecurical and sometimes violent temperment that often got her into trouble on an ongoing level of crisis. Ellen was a troubled girl who I found myself taking care of more and more as time went by, and who I was making progress with as she attached herself to me and to my way interest and attentiveness to her in her forceful Transference, and by Transference I mean in the meaning of her taking full and irretractible possession of me.

One of my most loving and endearing memories of Ellie, and there were many of them, occurred one night when we had been out together all night in the Bacchus Bar; panhandling money, drinking swill beer left on the tables by departing patrons and unnoticed in the crowed bar room, and hustling drinks shooting pool for draft beers in the pool and pin ball back part of the Bar Restaurant area that continued further on after that to a narrow hallway where the restrooms were located with doors for the ladies and gentlement on the left, and then out into a back door.

It was a Friday night in the crowded Bacchus Bar, that also served as a Restaurant for the dinner crowd, and which was owned and managed by my friend Steve, who also owned and managed the Gay Nintees Café on Main Street, was located on Route 32 not far down from the corner of Main Street in the Village and right next to the Chez Joey Italian Pizza and Sub Restaurant that my friend Jerry Nuesbaum was the owner of and which occupied the intersection catty-corner of Main Street and Route 32 that was rebuilt after the fire in 1978.

The Bacchus had a long Bar along the entire extent, about fifty feet, of its Southern wall on the left side, with booth tabled on the right, that led down to the pool table and pin ball machines, and a stairway on the right close to the entrance that went upstairs to where there were more table and the restruarant kitchen, which served up a basic bohemian fair of steaks, pork, ribs, pasta, and an assortment of vegetarian dishes.

It was the very dead of winter in early February of 1991. A foot of snow lay deep on the ground. The streets had just recently been plowed over again that morning, and some of the sidewalks were still blocked with snow and crusted over. It was dreadfully cold night out.

I had a nice muscular build and was about one hundred and eighty pounds in those days at five foot ten and half inches tall with a light beard, as I always had whenever I was living out on the street, with every day shaving being to difficult, and which I kept neat and trimmed up with frequent visits to my friend Bob the Barber who owned the Barbershop next to P&G's.

I met Ellie on happenstance, as was generally with case with her showing up on the street, as I was standing in front of the Hobo Deli pandhandling for beer money when she happened to come by. I was delighted to see her as I always was and my heart lept out a little in my chest, as it always did, whenever I had the opportunity of a possibiliy to be with her. I had asked her that night what she was doing and when she shrugged her shoulders I knew that she was mine for the evening. I suggested we go over to The Bacchus and we went there, grateful to be holed up inside the warm Bar with a friendly bartender who we both knew, who paid us no mind. And other than that I had no place lined up to go with her for the night except to walk the four miles out of Town to Ed's, and as a last ditch resort to crash the rest of the night sitting up or trying to catch some sleep on the cold cement floor in the launry room at the Huguenot Apartments; which at least, was a warm place to offer her and which we frequently did use, when there wasn't a vacant apartment left open for us to stay in.

It got late as such evenings of quite desperation always do. The Bar patrons by ones and twos left and dwidled out the door until we were the only ones there and finally had to leave ourselves as the Bar tender, whose name was Pat was already beginning to clean up and was gettnig ready to close for the night.

"Last Call!" he shouted facetiously in a loud voice wiping a wet rag around the bar top, knowing we were the last ones in the bar and that we had no money. He was secretly in love with Ellie too and was deferring to us to pass a few minutes of time with him alone there in the bar with him just to be clsoe to her.

Ellie downed the remains of a pitcher of beer left on one of the tables by pouring it into an empty glass and I ordered a dollar draft from Pat and tipped him a dollar to cheer him up from my take for the night, which I counted, and after paying the barman, still left for coffee and beers in the morning, seven dollars. Being kind to the waitresses and barpeople was something I was fond of doing, when I had it. I always did like to reciprocate for our entry into the world of bar hustling. Ellie of course and as always was the main attraction. I always enjoyed that she was loved by a lot of men, and women too. She lived in her own world. When she wanted to be with me, she would be, and then she would leave out all of a sudden and I wouldn't see her again for days at a time, and then again, she would be, and we'd take up again where we left off. What she did in the time she was away I never asked.

When we exited the Bacchus Bar we walked the short distance North on Route 32 to the corner where the highway intersected Route 299 that was Main Street in the Village. The clock at the First Nation Bank down the street going towards the mountain read 1:30 p.m. and the temperature was 6 degrees Farenheit.

"Let's go out an walk the roads all night," Ellie said, pulling me along by the arm in the frosty air, air so cold it took your breath away. "Come on. It will be fun. I don't feel like sitting up in the laundry room tonight."

She pulled me by the arm, as was her silent way of insisting on doing things she wanted to do and and to go in the direction she wanted to go in, which was to cross the road and turn left at the light on Main Street and to head down the hill to Iron Bridge that spanned across the Walkill River. Which we did, walking in the road down the right side of Main Street past the First National Bank and on down to the river, which was easier footing in the roadway as not all parts of the sidewalk were clear.

The snow crunched under our feet. The sky was clear and the stars were out. There was a crescent moon getting ready to set a near quarter of the way up from the Western Horizon. There was no wind and the air was still and cold and heavy to breath and our slow and labored breathing left its vapor trails in the air.

I didn't say a word as we went down the hill past the Bank to the Bridge. We were high from drinking in the Bar and were still retaining its warmth and putting out plenty of body heat and were impervious to the temperature at that point. We were both bundled up and dressed warm for the part of being out-of-doors. I had on my heavy hooded overcoat, a wool stocking cap, scarf, heavy thermal underwear, top and bottom, a heavy long sleeve shirt, a thick pair of dungarees, and two pairs of socks, and a nice pair of winter gloves, although Ellie was dressed a bit too girlish in her way. She too had a heavy hooded overcoat, scarf, wool mittens, and woolen stocking cap, and a good pair of boots, but she was inadequately dressed for the iron cold of near sub-zero temperatures without long underwear, top and bottom, double socks, and a warmer pair of gloves.

I had commented to her earlier about it what she was wearing and wondering if she was going to be warm enough later on, and I knew that she wasn't planning at that time on being out all night, and living in the cold, enduring the cold, as I was and had gotten used to doing, frequently, to be prepared for.

If I hadn't met up with Ellie earlier on that night I was prepared to walk the four miles out to Ed's near the Mountain where I had a standing place to sleep in a plastic room that Ed had made up special for me and provided with plenty of warm blankets, seven in all for the Winter Bivouac out on the porch of Ed's house. I paid him a little money, thirty dollars, each month for the privilege having a 'residence' to call home, and in case anyone challenged me for being a vagrant.

The walkway on the Bridge was not shoveled and the snow was deep on the walkway from the plows having been past. But it had been fairly well trammeled down by previous foot travel during the day and so we used the walkway to linger close to the rail on the North side of the bridge and look down over at the frozen river. The river was eerie in its stoic frozen silence. It was a solemn time of night to be there in the cold frozen space of time.

Ellie pulled on my coat to get my attention, and when I looked, produced from her coat pocket with her right hand a good sized 'joint' of marijuana nicely rolled and a bottle of Heineken Beer with the cap partially uncapped and stuck back on, which Ellie bit off with her front teeth and spit out over the rail into the snow on the river ice. A gift from the bartender Pat no doubt, or from some other friend of Ellie's, or hopeful friend of Ellie's as those things went, one favor leading to another later on.

"This should hold us for the night," Ellie said.

"I should say so. I do believe you love me, Ellie. Do you?" Ellie smiled. "Let's fire it up."

Ellie struck a match without comment and drew in the first toke. We smoked it down to the roach and shared on the beer sipping slowly on it until it was gone. Ellie hid the beer bottle in a iron notch on the bridge where it would be safe until we could come back to get when we were out collecting bottles and cans for the five cents New York State deposit on each of them that was always good for those days early in the mornings when we had no money and there was nobody with any money around to panhandle off of.

"Let's save the roach," I said. "Put it back in your cigarette pack and we can smoke it in the morning with our beers for the 'hair of the dog.' Here, look at all the money I collected."

And I showed her, pulling five crumpled bills out my front pants pocket one by one as I had stuffed them in there, minus the dollar that I had given Pat for the last call draft beer to humor him and the dollar I had left him for his tip. I smoothed them out one by one straightening them with my fingers and neatly refolded them and put them back into my pocket again.

"Not a bad haul," I stated, "all in all considering we drank and shot pool for free all night besides."

"I've got a little money too," Ellie said. "We'll have plenty for breakfast at the 90's and beers later."

"Sounds good to me," I said.

Ellie dropped the roach into the cellophane wrapper of her cigarette pack and we each smoked a cigarette from her pack of

Winston's enjoying the 'buzz' from the marijuana and the beer
and the tobacco and lingered there on the bridge.

After a time Ellie said, "let's go," and tugged on my sleeve
again. And we were off. The Shawangunk Mountains were in
the distance a long way off seeming very cold and lonely and
inhospitable. Want to walk out to my place at Ed's?" I asked.

"Naw ... I don't feel like walking all the way out there. Let's
walk out along Springtown for awhile and be close to the River."

"Sounds good to me," I said. "Let's do that."

We walked down to where Mountain Rest Road broke off to
the right from Route 299, not far from the bridge, and turned right
on to Mountain Rest and then on a bit further to where
Springtown Road broke away from Mountain Rest and turned
right onto it.

We walked briskly on in silence, the cold making us step fast.
Away from the lights of The Village, the cold and lonely Stars
were out in clear force, silent sentinels of places we would never
be. Orion, The Big Dipper, and Cassiopeia, the Big W, were
clearly visible. I took them in, in reflective silence, and let Ellie
lead the way. The crescent moon in the sky about to set was
shedding an eerie light of pale luminescence on the snow. The air
was deadly still and cold. I stopped to take a leak by the side of
the road and so did Ellie, squatting down and making a puddle in
the crusted snow. We walked on a mile or so past Floyd
Patterson's Home and Training Camp, and on a bit further when
Ellie turned right abruptly and walked off into a snow covered
field heading toward the River which wasn't far off the roadway
at that point. I followed her in.

The virgin snow was deep, nearly a foot and a half where the
wind had drifted it unimpeded over the flood plain, and it was
difficult going. Finally she stopped. The frozen River was close
by. She waited for me to come up to her and then when I arrived
to stand next to her she pulled me down with her into the snow
and we lay there together on our backs looking up at the stars and
the eternity beyond feeling comfortable with the heat was still in
our bodies from the exertion of the hike. In a minute I closed my

eyes. It felt good to lie there in the snow beside Ellie. She was a dear and trusted companion in the night.

We laid there for a long time and I don't know for how long or whether I slept or not, I must have, to find that Ellie was kneeling beside me and pushing insistently on my arm in a state of forceful alarm as I could tell. The warmth from the Bar and from the high we were on and from the exertion of the trek out there, had left me. I tried to get up to stand but found that I could not feel my legs to stand on and had to guess about where they were in relation to the rest of my body. My teeth were chattering and my upper body, the part I could feel, was wracked with convulsive shudders. Brrrrr … I knew the deadly hypothermia had set in on us and I hoped not too late to do something about.

"Oh … Ellie," I said. "I think we are in serious trouble now if we don't get moving."

"I can't feel my legs," Ellie said, enunciating through the chatter of her teeth, with her upper limbs were shuddering.

"I can't either. Come on let's try and run for it to see if we can't get some circulation going. Do you think you can run? I can carry you if I need to."

"I can run," Ellie said.

I started to shuffle along in the snow in a light jog, not feeling the ground beneath me but trusting on instinct just to get some movement and blood circulation going.

"Come-on, Ellie, come on, you do the same," I said, turning around on the run and shuffling my feet in place to encourage her. " Get your legs moving."

"I can't feel my legs," she complained again in her whiney tone.

"You don't need to feel your legs. I can't feel my legs either. Your legs are down there beneath you holding you up. You just have to trust that they are there and to get them moving. Move your arms about like I am doing as well. That will help get the blood flowing again. We need to hurry now."

She began to jog in the snow, a slow shuffle just like me. In no time we were back on the roadway again and heading back into the Village. I could see the glow of the lights not too far off in the distance and that gave me hope. We were then about a mile and a half out.

"Keep running," I said. " Beat on your legs and rub them a bit. We'll be there when we get there in a bit. In the meantime we need to stay alive. We'll die out here tonight if we don't take action. There's no one out here to save us but ourselves."

And if there ever was a night for a car to come by that we could flag, but tonight was that night. No miracle ride came by. Finally after a time I could feel the circulation returning a little to my extremities.

"I can feel my legs a bit now," I said to Ellie. "How about you?"

"I can feel mine a little."

"Slap your legs some more and tense your arms and stomach muscles like I'm doing to generate some heat." I showed her on the run how to do the isotonic muscle compression exercise. "Come on, keep tensing up, and let's pick up the pace now."

We began to run faster, not all out, but at a good clip now. Ellie too. I was pleasantly surprised to see Ellie running along with me keeping pace, carrying her own weight and dedicated to the seriousness of our needing to survive.

Finally after what seemed an agonizing eternity of uncertainty we made the turn back onto Mountain Rest, not far then on to Route 299, and finally we were at the bridge, still jogging on in.

We ran up the hill in a slow gate to the Bank. The clock read 4:30 a.m., and the temperature was five below. The crescent moon was just above the cliff line on the Shawangunks ready to set.

"No wonder we almost froze to death. The temperature has dropped nearly ten degrees since two o'clock. I dropped really fast and it must have been even colder down in the valley by the river. Lucky we are to still be alive. If an Angel hadn't awakened you we'd be dead by now."

"Maybe we are dead," Ellie replied. "Maybe we died together out there tonight and our spirits have left our bodies and come back to Town. Maybe that's the end of our suffering."

"Maybe you are right," I said. "But right now let's see if we can't get into The Riverboat."

"An Angel didn't awaken me," Ellie said. "I was watching over you while you were sleeping. You passed out and then I couldn't wake you when it came time to go. I kept trying and trying to shake you awake for the longest time and finally you did. Thank God."

"Bless you dear heart, Ellie," I said. "Thank you for standing by me. You saved my life. I owe you."

"Now you really do," Ellie said.

The Riverboat, also called The Heart Break Hotel, was a three-story rooming house at 16 Main Street that was located right across the street from the Bank. I had lived there for a while briefly with Julia years before, before she blew-me-away with her lesbian potions, and I knew many of people who lived there now. It was a favorite rooming house for street vendors, or police authorized marijuana dealers, the girls from town to have a place to bring their johns after the bars closed, musicians, and artists, and other aficionados of the Town to have a place to 'party' in when they were there. The hallways were positioned in the shape of a square rectangle with the stairway on the right side going up. The stairs and all the hallways were thickly carpeted to muffle the sounds of foot traffic. All the rooms and saloons, which were like efficiency apartments comprised of two rooms combined, faced out and had windows. The bathrooms, two on each floor, occupied the inner core of the building and had no windows.

A mutual friend Eric Iverson lived there now on the third floor in the room on the right side of the building facing the street. His room was dark now at that hour, but as long as I knew someone I knew we were safe in going there, and especially tonight in the urgency of survival. The only other place open at that hour was the bus station and the police station or the laundry room at the Huguenot as a very last resort. I jogged across the street with Ellie behind me and up the short steps to the front porch of The Riverboat. Ellie ran up ahead of me anxious to get in doors.

"The door's locked," Ellie said trying the door handle.

"No it's not," I said, and yanked hard on the door, which opened. "I know that door well I said. There's a knack to it. Let's be quiet now, okay? Shhhh ..."

"Okay, shhhhh ..." Ellie replied.

The heat from the building overpowered me. It was always a nice friendly well-heated building in the winters. We tiptoed up the stairs quietly to the third floor. I put my index finger to my lips and motioned to her to follow me as we got there and we went into the big bathroom together at the top of the stairs and closed the door and locked it behind us from the inside. The third floor, and high above the bustle of the street, was sanctuary. And I felt a relief as I reached it with Ellie.

The third floor bathroom, on the stairs side, and opposite the side that our friend Eric roomed at, and as I remember it well that night as the life-saving haven that it was, was a large bathroom with a sink against the far wall, a toilet on the left side of the sink, a shower on the right side, and there was a straight back chair in the corner of the wall by door on the left, to sit on for viewing, or for dressing, however it figured in. It had a white linoleum floor and yellow walls with a white ceiling. The shower curtain was a single strip of light pliant plastic with a floral design. In the middle of the room on the floor was a medium size dark blue throw rug that was about an eight by twelve rectangular piece.

"We're safe now," I remarked to Ellie. " No one will be up at this hour, and if someone does have to use the toilet, there's another bathroom around the corner that they could use, or one downstairs. No one is going to press the issue so let's relax."

"Okay," Ellie said. And she smiled and poked me playfully in the stomach.

And otherwise that no one would really question us anyway. The type of people who lived in The Riverboat were wise to the ways of the street and wise to the ways of minding their own business, as they would respect and appreciate having their own business minded, and everyone knew to be respectful of others in silent regard. And what besides that no one, at least on the third floor, ever got up before three p.m., except to go the bathroom, in 'sleeping off,' to use an industry term, the effects of whatever it happened to be that they were 'partying with the night before.'

"We're safe for now," I said, "for a time at least. Let's take off all our clothes and get into the nice hot shower as quickly as we can and get warmed up."

We both took off our clothes and left them in two piles against the far wall. Ellie looked really pretty naked. She was five foot three and weighted all of a hundred and nineteen pounds soaking wet. She had two very nice well-developed breasts with lovely well-formed nipples that were perked up now from the cold, and she had a nice lovely to look at vagina mound area with a light cropping of golden pubic hairs. Her legs were firm and shapely and her buttocks were nice and firm in a muscular way. She was busying herself with bobby pins in her mouth in a totally famine way trying to pin her hair up so it wouldn't get wet in the shower.

"You get the shower going," Ellie said. "I need to use the toilet. I have got to go really bad. I've been having to go for a long time." And as she looked around, exclaimed. "There's no toilet paper."

"Everybody brings their own in around here, but I have some clean napkins that I got from the Bacchus Bar for just such an occasion in my coat pocket. Here, I'll get them for you."

I went to my coat and got the napkins out. Ellie had already sat down on the toilet and was letting her tummy gas out in a rush and was passing her stool as I handed them to her. I heard the stool plop into the water beneath her and Ellie heaved a little sigh in satisfaction of a successful evacuation. I saw it floating there in the water and watched the steam of her urine coming out hard and the sound of it hitting the water. She urinated for a long time.

"Boy, did I ever really have to go. I hope I didn't smell things up too bad for you." She stuck her finger into her anus and held it up to my nose. Her excrement had an earthy intoxicating aroma.

"You smell good to me, Ellie. "I like the way you smell," I said standing close to her. "I love everything about you."

I peered between her legs into the toilet bowl and watched her stool floating there again in the water and massaged her tummy softly, as my own mother used to do to me, and stroked the crease of her vagina where her clitoris was which seemed to sooth her.

"There, there, do you feel better now dear?" as my mother used to say. "I'll get the shower warmed up for us."

I went and turned the hot water on, and then the cold, and waited for it to adjust to the right temperature.

The shower on the third floor, as I was frequently fond of using at the odd times when it wouldn't be overly conspicuous, and being a street-person in the know about such things, was a nice strong hot shower, one of the finest around anywhere and The Riverboat always had plenty of hot water for its guests which was a feature of it that I really liked. I had to urinate really bad.

I turned the knobs to the shower until I got the temperature just right feeling the hot strength of the shower with my fingers in wonderful anticipation of the moment I would enter, and when the temperature was just right I did. I stood under the hot water totally relaxed and let the urine flow out of me into the drain. I heard the toilet flush as Ellie was finished with her poddy. In a moment she opened the shower curtail and slipped in behind me.

"Come here," Ellie, I said grabbing her by the waist. "You go first, get under the hot water and warm yourself up."

"I don't want to get me hair all wet," she said. "It'll take me forever to get it dry. And there is nothing worse then wet hair out in the cold. It'll be wet all day if I do. I've no way to dry it."

"Don't worry," I said. "If you're careful you won't get it wet. Just get your body and your legs in. The water feels really good."

Ellie backed in under the water and got her back wet a little and then she turned around right under the strong stream of hot water with her head held back and let the water wash over her breasts and stomach. I could tell she was luxuriating in the feel of it. I got in close behind her and knelt in the tub and fumbled underneath her buttocks and between her legs for the stopper.

"Let's put the stopper in and fill the tub up a bit so we can sit down in it."

I fixed the stopper and the hot water began to fill the tub.

Kneeling, I could feel the firm cheeks of her buttocks against my face and chest and I pulled her in close around the waist and felt upwards for her breasts to fondle them in the streaming water. Then I began to massage her legs from behind, each one, rubbing them briskly, one at a time, up and down, a little at a time, up to her crotch and down again to her feet, massaging her toes, and back again repeating the process to get her circulation going.

Someone in a godsend had left a bar of soap in the holder. I held the bar in my hand and soaped up into crotch and around her pretty blond pubic hairs and washed up into her vagina running my thumb up into her and feeling the protrusion around her cervix. I soap up around her anus good and run my thumb up into it beyond her sphincter into the soft fleshes pouch of her large intestine and rested there in her secret place feeling a place that no one else knew of Ellie but me, and ran my thumb in and out of her a few times to clean her out good. Then felt for her clitoris and stroked it gently up and down feeling it engorge with blood with my touch and elongate in preparation for orgasm as I did. I left her organism alone for now, not wanting to spoil her moment and stood up and washed her back and her underarms and soaped up her breasts.

"Here, you kneel down in the water behind me and let me get under the hot stream for a bit."

Ellie got behind me kneeling in the water that was now nearly half way up in the tub. Five minutes in the shower had already gone by and I wanted to be quick about it so as not to use up all the hot water to be polite and spoil my welcome. Ellie took the bar of soap from me and washed up my groin, feeling my penis with her fingers and my scrotum holding both my testicles in her hand, and ran her thumb up into my anus and knew me there, as I had done to her, resting there inside me as I had done, feeling the inside of me, moving in me briskly in and out of it a few times. I knew that she felt my stool ready to come out up in there.

"Somebody has to go to the bathroom too," Ellie laughed.

"I know I do," I stated. "It can wait until late though."

Then she washed my legs and messaged them briskly, as I had done to hers, up and down, and then up my back and scrubbed under my arm pits and reached around my waist in a hug and

my head to go back down still further some more into her anus again, which I did and lingered in her hole there enjoying it with my tongue for the longest time while Ellie pulled on me, on my left leg to come over top of her face, which I did, and felt her pull my buttocks down on top of her face to where she could kiss it and lick the underside of my penis and scrotum and kiss my own anus and delve deeply into it with her own tongue; all of which made my penis rock hard and getting ready now to enter her.

She licked on my testicles some more and I had to take my cues from my own inner urges of male timing in those matters to break her off from me from doing that so as not to overly excite me too soon. I raised myself slightly from off her and turned back around, kissed her long and fully on the mouth, with my tongue swirling inside her mouth and her tongue swirling inside mine, and assumed the position, with her on her back, to enter her.

But before I did that, to enter her and take possession of her being, and on my knees facing her, I bent over and licked her clitoris some more and down to her vagina and into her anus one last time, as deep as I could go with my tongue, lifting her hind end up as I did to do that, and then I turned and penetrated her. Ellie gasped as my hard penis entered going inside her. I went all the way in, as far as it would go, and then I rested insider her there for a bit, letting the urge to let myself go subside, and then, in my knowing way of those things, moving a little when I need to, to keep my penis hard, I started to move on her again, slowly massaging against her clitoris with my body at the end of my penis. Then I rested some more. It was wonderful for her, I knew, and for me as well, just to be inside of her, and I knew she was in no hurry, as I was certainly not, to finish, for it to be over.

I heard a door open and close nearby not far down the hallway and soft footsteps. Someone tried the door and finding it locked, went away around to the bathroom on the other side and all was quiet once more.

I began to move on Ellie again, this time with more manly vigor. I reach around with my right hand in back of her leg and pulled it forward, resting on my weight on my left elbow, so that there was a nice position opening her vagina wide for me to work on her. And I did now, as my urgings to ejaculate ebbed and would come up again, and then ebbed again as I frequently rested until my penis became numb to the forceful movements and I could go at it with full force and vigor; which I began to do until dear Ellie collapsed back into herself and began to shudder and I knew she was having her orgasm. I went really hard making a slapping sound with my testicles and hips against her buttocks until she became limp and still, and then I rested inside of her, until she pushed me off. I had not ejaculated in her, and really had no intention to. But I knew she had gotten what she needed.

"Do you want me to suck you off?" she asked.

"Naw," I said. "I'll save it for later." I stood up. "I'm getting nervous about being in here too long. Let's wind things up before we wear out our welcome."

The toilet flushed in the other bathroom around the corner and there were once again the soft footsteps in the hall and the sound of a door closing.

"Did I do you good?" I asked her. Ellie smiled. "Let's get dressed." I knew that I had.

Ordinarily I would have washed my penis off, but there was no washcloth to use and I did not want to have to use my thermal shirt, which I needed to dry clean before I put it back on. And besides, Ellie had a good vagina smell about her, so I just put my underpants back on and my long undergarment over them and my dungarees and heavy shirt, put on my boots and tied my laces.

When Ellie was dressed, we picked up our coats and accessories, gloves, scarves, and stocking caps, and I opened the door cautiously and peered around into the hallway. There was nobody there. All was quiet. I motioned for Ellie to be silent and we walked around the corner, and out of harms way from our trespassing in the bathroom, to Eric's room at the far end of the hall. I knocked softly on the door.

"Who's there," I heard Eric say sleepily, "friend or foe?"

"Two friends," I said in as quiet a voice as I could muster and still maintain some air of masculine authority. "It's Ellie and me. Can we come in? It's freezing cold out there."

Eric opened the door and let us in. I looked out the window at the clock on the bank. It was five o'clock and still five below. Eric climbed back into bed under the covers.

"There's a couple of blankets over there in the corner and a mat. Make yourself to home." The room was nice and warm.

"Thank you dear Eric," I said, not wanting to play on the supplicating angle too long with him, and after all, that we were indeed members of his gang and which gave us a sense of entitlement to barge in on him on demand and be there in his company, weather, and in the meaning of Eric's mercurial temperament, permitting.

"You are a life saver, Eric," I said to him. It's deadly cold out there. We almost died out there tonight." Eric feigned to be half asleep. I turned to Ellie. "Why don't you take the mat Ellie? I prefer the hard floor for my back myself."

Ellie went over to the corner and got the mat, that was just a strip of foam rubber that Eric kept for guests to sleep over on, and one of the blankets from the corner and spread the mat out to lie next to Eric as he was situated against the far wall in the room.

Eric's room was a nice size, fifteen wide by twenty feet long. It had a closet to hang stuff in, and a window that looked out onto Main Street where one could sit and watch the comings and goings of the traffic to while away the days and nights.

Eric was a very charismatic fellow who genuinely cared for people, particularly those whom he had chosen to be members of his personal gang. His job in the Village that he did for the money to keep himself alive and occupying a room in Town was to clean the Bars out at night after they closed and get them ready for the next day's business. In that regard he had just come back in from sweeping and mopping Adrian's Bar and Grill, just up the street, which he did with his girl friend Janet, who liked Cocaine.

In the terms of his reputation in the Art Colony, he was a local artist of some renown as a focus of personal identification, an oil painter, and who always had a painting going on that he worked on when he could get stoned and drunk enough to enjoy his pastime of playing with the paint. He liked to paint and drink and get high and stand around talking with his comrades through the days. There was an easel in the far corner of the room where Ellie had gotten the mat and the blankets from with a painting started on it and partially described in charcoal of a naked lady seated provocatively looking very demure and seductive with an okra colored sheet draped over her right shoulder and with a well-formed breast and length of inner thigh revealed.

He was also a musician of sorts and liked to play the guitar and lead the gang along in song, which we all sang with him out of tune. There was a string acoustic guitar standing in the corner of the room behind the easel. Several recent painting of his also hung around the room on the walls, some mountain scenes, local street scenes, a surreal piece of a barren dreamscape in burnt rust and umber, and an amber lantern hanging in the darkness.

Eric was a fine good looking man in his late thirties or early forties as I was, and of average medium height and slight of build. He looked something of what John Lennon of the Beatles would look like if he were still alive, and whom I always thought was the ghost of John Lennon.

It was a no mind to me where Ellie slept or who she slept with. If she wanted to sleep next to Eric to keep him company in the night, it was her way of ingratiating herself of a warm place to stay in an otherwise hostile world. And I understood those things, to share her graciously with Eric about. She was not my wife, although she was a wife to me. And she was still married to Bart, and although that they seemed to be broken up for now. Ellie kept talking it up about getting a divorce. And she was a gang wife to us all in another regard, who would spend time with and be with everyone of us in a sexual way, depending on who was around in the day-to-day of it, and who had any money to blow on beer and pot and foot and other things, and what in particular that anyone wanted to do, that we all looked on as interchangeable about, and always off about our own pursuits in time anyway to be bogged down with a female in tow. And so we each were delighted in her being with the other gang members when she was, or whoever she was with, and as we were thought of in that way too, about being left alone with her, by everyone about each of ourselves being out privately with her, and more or less not to form any attachment about. When we were with her, we were, and when we weren't, we weren't.

Ellie could be tedious and difficult too to be with, and was often violently mercurial, sometimes hysterically so. Out of the blue she would hold off and sock you in the face or start screaming nonsensically and with people having to get the police involved to quiet her down.

And who incidentally, in speaking reverently of the police, all loved her too. She had that kind of effect on people.

And so it was a symbiotic kind of thing of who would get down and take care of her when she became that way. Myself, I preferred to leave her cold for a few days whenever she didn't behave right with me. I did have my limits. But sometimes too, whenever I needed her, like tonight, that I mean, I really needed her; I did become and could become quite possessive over her.

I took care of her head in psychological way, in the meaning of satisfying her sexual needs, as well as her emotional needs to be cared for, whereas the other men in certain regard only wanted her to get themselves off and to drop here then they were done with her, only to leave her wandering the streets in search of me to care for her. And I did care for her. I cared affectionately for her well-being.

I took the other blanket as Ellie handed it over to me and taking off my boots made a pillow out of my coat to lay down on the hard wood floor next to the radiator by the window and hung my thermal shirt over he radiator to dry. It was toasty warm, almost too warm. Eric had opened the window a little already with the heat. Ellie slept in her clothes as I did. We would all three of us sleep like stones, never moving from the positions we assumed when we started out. It was a tactic of ours to sleep without moving so as not to disturb anyone and to cause any annoyances with restless behavior. Hangovers, and those sleeping them off, needed to be soothed with the sign posted: 'Do Not Disturb.'

"Anybody got any pot?" Eric asked mumbling from his slumber.

"Ellie does," I replied. "We had a good size roach left over from before. We couldn't finish it."

"That's good," Eric said. "I'll have that to look forward to when we wake up, which maybe soon. I'm not really too sleepy right now. The '90's will be opening up in a little while and we need to get beer at the Hobo. Has anybody got money for beer?"

"We've got some money," Ellie replied.

"Then we are safe here," Eric said.

Beer money and Refer were the medium of exchange in these parts, good Wampum in Native American Indian terminology that could get a man, or a woman, almost anything they needed. Eric was already planning to make a day partying out of it I could tell.

"Hey Eric," I said. "While you're awake I want to run a song by you. It's a song that Lenny from The New York Café taught to me, called: Five Below. It came to me in a different version of it tonight when Ellie and I almost froze to death down by the River."

"We almost died together tonight," Ellie interjected seriously.

For her to say thank you to Eric for taking us in I knew was beyond her grasp to do, so I did, with a tone expressing our grateful appreciation at being taken in.

"Thank you so much for taking us in, Eric."

"It's nothing," Eric said. "I am glad you are both here and alive with me. Now, what's the song, how's it go?"

"It's a Concerto in C Minor that came to me tonight as Ellie and I were freezing to death. The chords, as Lenny taught them to me were for a blues rhythm song that he composed to go like this:

C Minor, G Minor, repeats, C Minor, G Minor, then A Flat Major, B Flat Major, C Minor, F Minor, E Flat, G, C, D, B Minor, E Minor, and then C Minor again.

But I changed the tempo and the beat around to make it a grand concerto, as occurred to me when Ellie and I were freezing to death, that starts out in a frantic desperation that comes into terms with our fragile mortality on a planet in outer space. It begins in a frenzy to start then goes on very methodical and determined to survive and telling the story of that determination heading toward the end that never does resolve, it just keeps going, like a caravan, until you get tired of playing it, if you ever do. It's a hypnotic rhythm.

"I can't wait to try it," Eric said. "Let's get some sleep right now though. I'm drifting off. Pleasant dreams."

"Pleasant dreams," Ellie said.

"Let us thank God that we are safe this night," I said.

I asked Eric for toilet paper and a washcloth and went quietly down the hall to use the bathroom to use the toilet and wash up. When I returned I lay down on the floor grateful to be there and closed my eyes. The next thing I knew it was after ten in the morning and the street outside was alive with movement and traffic sounds. Eric had already been out to the Hobo Deli and had just returned with nice big 32 Ounce bottle of Papst Blue Ribbon Beer in a paper bag and three paper coffee cups to drink it with. Ellie was still asleep, or so she appeared, her face seeming angelic like lying there. She had not moved from the position she had laid herself down with. Eric cracked open the beer with his opener, poured a cup full for the two of us and we began the day.

To everything there is a season, and a time for every purpose under the sun; A time to be born and a time to die; a time to plant and a time to pluck up that which is planted; A time to kill and a time to heal; a time to tear down and a time build up; A time to weep and a time to laugh; a time to mourn and a time to dance; A time to cast away stones and a time to gather stones together; a time to embrace and a time to refrain from embracing; A time to loose and a time to seek; a time to tie up and a time to untie; A time to rend and a time to sew; a time to keep silent and a time to speak; A time to love and a time to hate; a time for war and a time for peace. What profit has the worker in his labor? I have seen the toil which the Lord has given to the sons of men to be engaged therewith. He has made everything beautiful in its time; also he has made the world dear to man's heart, so that no man can find out the works which the Lord has done from the beginning to the end ... Ecclesiastes: Chapter 3 Verses 1 – 11

To my everlasting mourning I learned from my friend Betty
Hassell, who was an elderly heavy set colored lady who operated
a social sitting parlor in her upstairs apartment on the corner of
Main and North Chestnut Street next to The Mobile Station, that
was open to visits from the street mafia at all hours of the day or
night, where we could get in off the street to drink and smoke
refer and hang out; and who I had met a good while ago at the
introduction of my street friend Chuck McGill who introduced me
to Betty; who called me on the phone at my apartment in Buffalo
one day in the early summer of 1993 with the terrible news of the
tragedy that Ellie had been found dead from a shotgun blast in her
room where she lived on Front Street.

I had been away from Ellie and from New Paltz for several
months then at the time having returned to my home with my
nurse friend Kathleen and to my work as a Journalist in Buffalo,
NY. And of what had been, "A Tale Of Two Cities," out of the
Charles Dickens novel, with two entirely different life styles
being lived. It was then mid-June.

The police called it a suicide, but I felt and suspected that it
couldn't have been.

There was no way in my mind that Ellen would ever have in
her possession, or be able to get a Shotgun on her own, and also
that she was and had been a hard nosed needle drug addict, with
needle track Mulatto Trouble in the form of Oscar and Rickie

Moss (and Rickie especially who was the White Slavery Captain with his prominent seat in P&Gs Bar that everyone cowtowed to,) and all a part of the Big Black Voodoo Heroin Pornography and White Slavery Prostitution Mafia that prevailed in the Newburg Poughkeepsie, New Paltz, Kingston, NY areas, and who then used the White Women that they enslaved as weapons against their White Male Rivals, to drug and poison their food and beverages, and along with The Italian and Jewish Mafias of the warfaring tactics that way, who were the suppliers of drugs to the downtown area of New Paltz, and Police Protected.

Oscar was away in Prison at the time when Ellie was murdered, where we had put him, by organizing and informing on him, for Cat Burglary Charges which sent him up for eight years, in retaliation for his White Slavery messing around business the way he was with Ellen and with the other White Girls he tortured with drugs and needles and forceful intimidation as he, and the other Mulatto Pimps with their whore lines around the Village, did, to put an end to.

Ricky Moss, Oscar's older brother, and Oscar's father, Oscar Sr., who all lived out at the end of Old Kingston Road, and reputed to be the local Black Mafia Heroin Drop for the surrounding area, and Police Protected, and as that the Herion Supply for the local area, came through, and was delivered to, and kept in, Black Hands, to prevent unwarrented investigation, as White People would not be inclined to come sniffing around. Ricky had found out what we had done to Oscar, because I had let it slip to Oscar's father and told him what we had done to set Oscar up to have him arrested and why we did it to get him off of Ellen as a warning to all the Negro Molesters, to stop what they were doing to the White Girls.

But and which apparently such understanding was lost on them, and that was the reason, I suspect, for them to murder Ellen in retaliation, to what the local police who investigated Ellen's death called it a suicide. And to in that way, that I have always felt unsettled with Ellen's death in thinking myself to blame for it, in not thinking of the possible ways that they would seek their revenge, their stock in trade, The Black Hand, to get even for it.

My position here is always that of a surviving Vietnam Veteran in Task Force Attachment to the local Police Department involved to the intervention and cessation of The Drug War, and Volunteers all like fighting a forest fire, and for the protection and survival of our beleaguered Nation in approach.

What you need to understand about The Drug War, and about the concept of Mafia Pornography coinciding to it, that is being allowed and even encourage to flourish here on both accounts; is that it involves us, the citizenry, in a Real War, attacking us with the condition of Drug Warfare, at close range involving our "Loved Ones" and "Family Members," and to the Physical and

Mental Maladies that such a Warfare induces, and for the
Psychiatric Intake of the population of that regard, to be finished
off by, legally to their demise with Lethal Psychiatric Style
Pharmacy while the Legal Authorities motivate the Afflicted
Population into its Intake and "Look-On." That, for the sake of
our lives and the lives of our loved ones at stake, that needs to be
intervened to properly and in a life saving timely way that we, as
civilians, are unable to intervene to ourselves on our own to
defend our lives about. And who therefore have to complain
directly to the authorities, who in certain instances may be
themselves involved with the criminal conspiracy.

And not only do we have to contend with the issue of Drugs
and Pornography in their raw motives of viciousness of foul play
occurring to us, but also which involves certain Ethnic and Racial
Motives For War using the corruptions and addictions of Drugs
and Pornography as a War Machine against the innocent
population, "to whittle us down," inch by inch, in a sustained and
dramatically forcible Attack taking place at a glacier speed in
slow motion over centuries, and against the larger mass of an
unsuspecting host population in objective to defeat it by being
systematically replacing it and which goes on barely perceptibly.
That involves "The Intake" and "Initiation" of the population into
the use of Hard Drugs and Pornography, (to what they have to
prove "Their Loyalty To," by murdering a family member or
friend, or loved one, by Drug Warfare, to obtain their drug supply,
and otherwise to be blackmailed and coerced in extortion to the
behest of their Drug Suppliers to do their bidding, whatever that
may be, (as to indicate as to whoever is supplying their addicting
drugs to someone, having The Power over the craving of their
addictions, to involve them with The Active Warfare Arm of their
Enemy Aggressions.

And on the topic of The Pornography Mafia that once they
have anyone in their grip, (and they begin very young with the
homosexuals on the young boys beginning at the age of puberty,
and with the young girls too that way who their addict mothers
initiate into child pornography,) to what that they become "The
Property" of the Pornography Ring for all time to come after that

and from what they can never escape from. So that, The Pornography Ring, (and who all know who each other are to themselves, but not so the "outsiders" to,) can essentially "gang-up" on anybody and do them in with foul play, and that is especially sinister and lethal to the households; the parents, relatives, and the siblings, involved with these individuals, to able to "Hit" with Drugs and Chemicals and Poisons, for the sake of the Ethnic or Racial Motives of the advancing Army. And that is particularly heart-felt regarding the plight of the young girls who are inducted and who become the prisoners of a Pornography Mafia when it comes time for them to fall in love and get married, who then have to "bump-off" their boyfriends or husbands at the behest.

And let us here have The Reasoning Right about The Miscegenation of the Black Heroin Mafia and concerning their sense of Inter-Racial Marriage being used as a means to Wage War By Assimilation of The White Race to create The Race of Mulattoes in The Islamic Design of Conquest, by coercive means of forcible aggressions against the White Females, involving their entrapment to the use of Heroin and Cocaine, and other means of White Slavery Prostitution, to attack the White Males by with Drugs and Poisons.

These Forces Against Us, and as we have described them, need to be intervened to, and not for The Authorities In Charge to continue to eliminate us by Psychiatric Intake.

It was very stange with Ellen. That became for me in the years that followed the spark of a romance that was lit then, a Tale of Two Cities. She was married to Bart, and I know that he meant something endearingly to her as her husband, but Ellen had a lot of husbands, who Bart was only one of, and her ackowledged official one.

I was destined to become one Ellen's husbands too and as I was also destined to leave for my new post location in Buffalo, in late September of that year of 1989, that Ellen began writing to me when I arrive there in Buffalo and beginning shortly after I arrived and that really put a jam into my new found and formally developing relationship with my now wife Kathleen then. And who I explained to Kathy that Ellen was the wife of a friend of mine, which she was, for Ellen to be sending me post cards and envelopes with her art work and poetry, but which never did sit right with Kathy about it.

The strange point was, that it all of Ellen's correspondences, which she wrote to me in the Fall of 1989, had the wrong street address and no zip code on the letters she mailed me, just my name, the wrong address, which was a smudged attempt at the right one, Kenvale Road, instead of Kenville Road, and Buffalo, NY; that somehow and quite mysteriously wound up in my mail box, each of them, week after week, delivered.

In a million years you could not get a letter delivered with even one number of the zip code out of line if you tried, and I have on several occassions gotten letters mis-zip-coded returned, stamped, improper zip code return to sender. And I know that I was never that famous to warrant such postal service, like Santa Claus, North Pole, with no Zip Code.

And so I returned to New Paltz one day when Kathy and I came to see my mother in Poughkeepsie, NY at Thanksgiving time and I went over to New Paltz alone in the morning after my arrival to see what the trouble was there with Ellen, and only to find myself getting set to be arrested for a trumpt up charge of walking into a bar to find the waitress telling me to get out and who called the police to charge me with trespassing, that Kathy didn't have the money to bail me out for and had to return to Buffalo alone about. And that was the beginning of another period of tense estrangement between Kathleen and I not getting along.

And which went on, of other false arrested, after that first incident of false arrest was resolved; which I plead guilty to, "Time Served," to get out of having to come back to court in another month, and only then to be postponed to another later Court Date, as Court Dates went without an attorney. But there was yet more trouble still to come; that other bar maids and waitresses in the cafes, and clerks in the stores, each in their own way connected with the White Slavery Whore Line, would charge me with trespassing, or that some person on the street would complain that I said something out of line to them, and would press the charge on me for harassment. To the point where I found myself being in the area awaiting Court Processing more that I was, or could be, at home with Kathy in Buffalo. And, when being there at my home, in having to return to New Paltz in a month or two for a set Court Date, that I found returning to keep, only to find the matter postponed, that I began to run into Ellen more and more during those intervals and myself attracted to her then in wanting to return there to Ellen about and to spend time with.

I would take her out on long excursion walks along the roads in the Wallkill Valley and on the back roads of the Shawangunk Mountains. And we would sleep together under six blankets in the winters camping quite often in the bus near the mountain where I had a place on Ed Brandes' land off of Route 299 on Wawarsing Road.

Ellen was a homeless waif of the streets and a wild animal of prey like myself. We worked the roads and panhandled together, used the public restrooms, or the great out-of-doors, for toilets, slept in the basements of Apartment Buildings, and in vacant apartments left unlocked, slept and showered with friends, and went our separate ways when we needed to. Ellen would always need to leave after a few nights camping out at Ed's, to get a shower somewhere and fresh clothes, only to see each other again on the street and resume our courtship of one another whenever it was that we would.

That quite frankly about it, I found myself needing her, and I ended up spending three more winters and two summers there with Ellen, (and while things were still unsettled between Kathleen about my settling down, and about a job and finances and the serious business ahead of getting married.) Off and on, back and forth, from Buffalo to New Paltz I went, until the day I got the word that Ellen was found dead.

Ellen had another male friend who took care of her by the name of Scott Rama, (who liked for people to call him "Pastor.") And who was every bit a Pastor and Reverend in the sense of looking after his Street Flock, to include for Ellen and myself.

And he took very good care of Ellen in giving her a place to live in his small sail boat that he had parked beneath the big Elm Tree behind his ground floor apartment next to the Mobile Station in the rear of an Apartment House at 9 North Chestnut Street in the Village. Who, Scott, after learning of the news of Ellen's tragic ending, was found dead floating face down in a lake along the Highway 44/55 in Modina, with his mutt dog Sadie howling for him alongside the roadway from the bank.

Ellen was a really dramatically beautiful girl, who I always felt was the real life Incarnation of Artemis, goddess of the moon and the natural environment, of chaste and proper behavior, and the lady of wild things; who is the daughter of Zeus and Leto and the twin sister of Apollo, full of life, as Ellen depicts her, and with a longing in enthusiasm for something ineffable, to be described as a delight in the feeling of being loved and cared for and accepted in a family member to come and go as she pleased and to feel secure in the company of friends to come back to.

She was always a loving and caring girl to those who were fond of her, the lonely men in need of a companion that she cared for on a regular basis. Everybody in their turn truly loved her for the sweet innocent girl that she was. And most of the days she was a peaceful icon of meditative virtue who would walk around The Village by herself with her wonderful smile greeting the people who she would meet, or she sit quietly reading a book on the Village Bench in perched in front of the Library on Main Street, or she would have a table to herself in the warmth of the early morning sunlight coming in through the big window of the Gay Nineties in one of the booths overlooking the side-walk and the street, always reading a book over coffee and looking up and out smiling at the people as they passed, as they caught her eye, and waiting for someone to come by to be with her and buy her breakfast.

But she had a mercurial temper too, a rage that too often got her into trouble as she would fly unpredictably into a vile temper, of the other side of Ellie, of verbal assault and physically punishing attacks on her intended target for things that only Ellie understood the reason why for in her logic; of being abandoned, overlooked, mistreated, or cheated out of something. For what reasons that she was too often removed forcefully by the police, who loved her by the way, at infrequent intervals and had to be taken away to the Psychiatric Facility at Hudson River in Poughkeepsie for brief periods and put on Strong Tranquilizers to quell her rage.

The Tranquilizers that they forced her to be on, with names like Navane, Prolixin, and Lithium, disturbed her anatomy terribly and caused her to be listless and lethargic in a suicidal depression and often in an agitate state as well from the effect and side effects of the forced medications she was on, and that also caused her to lactate abnormally, and with very heavy menstruation, that she quickly over-road, or to antidote, by drinking alcohol, smoking marijuana, and doing cocaine, or "shooting dirty cocaine, as the Mulattoes had her doing with tracks all up both arms, as soon as she was "back out" on the street, and hence which was a need that brought her into susceptible contact with the dirty business of the local Mulatto White Slavery Prostitution Trade, who knew "what she needed" to take advantage of her by. And by what tactics of the Negro Mulattoes that the White Females were literally held as prisoners to, and to be threatened, or to have their loved ones threatened, with physical violence and mayhem if they, The White Females, did not do what the Mulatto Pimps demanded and when they demanded, and with whom, that in turn perpetuated the cycle of her vicious behavior.

And which was, truth be known, the reason for such violent outbursts of temper in the first place, to try and get away from the clutches of, for prostitution, or from the murder behests, of the Mulatto Pimp, if even for a short time.

And there were many females too around and about the town, just like Ellen, who would start to scream in the night and have to be taken away to the asylum to be put on Strong Tranquilizers and destroyed by modern psychiatry, that sedates and subdues the symptoms of the condition instead of addressing the root causes of the behavior, which was the sexual and depraved and murderous aggressions of the evil Mulatto Drug Lord, of Pornography and Prostitution White Slavery Mafia, being backed by and supported and reinforced by the corrupted Police, who supplied the drugs and participated in the prostitution and who would do nothing about the situation.

Ellen became then and was in that regard the symbol and the rally figure of Joan of Arc and The Crusades to the White Men, and who initiated the local chapter of The Society For The Preservation Of The White Race to The Village of New Paltz, NY, in retaliation for what the Colored were doing to the White Girls in those precarious years, over the issue of the Mulattos being allowed to Deal Drugs to the White Females, and being supplied to them by the Local and NYS Police, and the Drug Heroin included, and protected by the police to enslave the White Woman and to make Drug Chemical Warfare Assassins out of them by means of coercion to go out and to maim and to destroy, and to murder the White Males in such fashion by sabotaging their food and beverages as an inside job by the White Females being the ones who prepared the meals of the household of that nature, by such nefarious warfare. And victim after victim of the White Males would succumb with no intervention of support from the local law enforcement to have to combat the Mulatto White Slavery Whore Line on their own and through our own means of intervention and retaliation and at our own risk of peril for doing.

But what were the men to do? A man of any honor and sense of worth in self respect, could not be forced to watch his lady, or a female loved one, being tormented by a Mulatto Oppressor, to drug addiction, insufferable blackmail, and black-hand coercion to foul play at their behest, to injure and to murder outright their own loved ones with drugs and chemicals, and turning our White Women into hysterical Witches in an era of Witchcraft. With some of the White Women succumbing to insanity that way, and others taking up with the stand, as having a Mulatto Buck to hide in the closet for them and to wait on them hand and foot, for the opportunity to murder-off a White Man, that the White Women in such a position, would take up with being stone cold killers of The White Males themselves as a means of compensating for their lack of internal fortitude in their fear and inability to say no to the Black Oppressor.

And as for the local Police, who do nothing, and who claim it is the Constitutional Right of the Black Race to make the Race of Mulattoes with the White Women, that the blood of all the White Males slain is on their hands, to the point where all is madness.

Bart was the one who would visit her in the asylum and who kept her company in her days there, and it was for that reason and for the love of him that she had married him. She was Bart's wife and she was a wife to him in that sense, in her way of being a wife, and he was a good husband to her.

She was a good person in her heart, who was always loved by those who knew her, and I wish her well in the afterlife in that regard and for her happiness in eternity. I did love her very much, and still do in Spirit and her Spirit is always with me hovering close by in the air, to know she is missed.

We took many wonderful walks on the mountain together, Ellen and I, and shared our days together through all of the seasons of the year for two years, even in the winters, sleeping the nights in makeshift shelters with only our blankets and our body heat to sustain us.

Ellen was always a very spirited girl with me, who delighted in the elements and who was content, as I was, just to be together in the days, sleeping where we could out of the rain and the cold and foraging for food where we could find it. Such days that will never come again in this life to recall. She would come and go with me and it was always delight again to see her whenever I did. We spent the long winter nights huddled together for warmth under the many blankets I kept out at Ed's Place by the mountain, sleeping out in the abandoned bus that Jay Lipshits had left parked out there. With three blankets down on the bottom and four on top and with our body heat for warmth, it was quite cozy. Often on late nights in town we would sleep down in the Laundromat of the Huguenot Apartments, or in one of the vacant apartments that were left unlocked, if one was available, and some nights we just walked the roads after the bars closed until it was daylight. Ellen was always a good panhandler for cigarette money, or for beer, or for something to eat. And she always loved to go hitching rides with me. Those days are sadly missed.

Artemis

. . . .

Tony and his friend were heavily engrossed in some ponderous weight of discussion, walking and talking quite seriously, as they crossed the highway, and had crossed the road right ahead of me as I was backing up facing the traffic hitching a ride, before Tony happened to notice me, almost colliding head on into me by accident, and I think on playfully on purpose, before he acknowledged me.

Tony was a strikingly handsome man, with perfectly formed impressive rows of very white teeth that he showed off with his ever present gregarious smile. His hazel green eyes had genuine sinserity to them, and he had a strong classic English Viking cut to his face and jowl. He innately possessed the kind of enviable geniology of good looks that made other men study his features and admire him enough to be jealous of. And I suspect that he knew it and that as was the reason for his ever-apparent and aloof smugness.

This day he was puffing on his traditional brown pipe and had on a pair of blue plaid shorts and a color coordinated blue knit polo shirt tucked in neatly at the waist with a belt cinched tight and with a nice manly buckle and wearing a pair of brown loafers with no socks. Apparently he and his friend were headed on their way to the Stewart's Store on the side of the road where we were on, and a popular meeting place, for people to sit and greet other people in the mornings as an intellectual gathering spot to sit and read the papers and chat with arrivals for the coffee hour.

I had helped Tony with the project to clear the land in his backyard one year many years in the past, in the Summer of 1977, and which he had recruited me to do, after I had arrived at his door one day with a girl friend from camping date that had gotten rained out on the Mountain at the Minnewaska Camp Grounds where I had just been hired as an Attendent to work for the Phillips family.

I had begun my work part time there on the mountain, off and on, as a Park Ranger and Mountain Rock Climbing Guide for the

tourists for the Phillips Family, Ken Phillips and his son Ken Jr.,
then, the early in the summer of 1977, after school had finished
for the year, and a job to have while I was laid off from my
regular construction work with The Operating Engineers Union.

The girl, , and I had stayed there with Tony, as his guest for
several days. She was some girl I had met at Low Falls the day
before, who appeared to me walking naked down the stream, and
who's name I forgot, but who I think whose name was Gail, and
whose sister Mona worked as a waitress in the The Village Nook
on the corner of Route 32 and Route 299, and who a few weeks
later left New Paltz to go to her home in Hyde Park, NY.

And perhaps I had brought her there for Tony to meet and
perhaps date at some time. I felt sorry for him in his lonely way,
and as I could relate to, being quite lonely and sad about it myself.

We had stayed at Tony's for a few days, at his insistance until
the weather cleared. I woke up one night and find our bed in the
basement apartment there in Tony's house empty and discovered
the girl sleeping on the couch in the living room of the upstairs.
She said I had been snoring and maybe I was. But always tickled
to think that I may been able to do Tony a favor.

In the morning we had breakfast, which Tony graciously
prepared and then departed to return to the camp grounds, only to
find that my tent which I pitched at my campsite on the top to the
cliffs overlooking Low Falls had been stolen.

It was several days later after that Tony had approached
me on the street one day and asked me if I wanted to come and
stay with him at his home and help him with the project to clear
the land in his back yard for the summer.

I said, "yes."

It was a big sweeping extent of downward sloping land that he
wanted cleared, that dropped fairly quickly maybe ten or fifteen
feet as I recall from the lawn and back deck of his house and then
leveled off more or less for a nice recreation area as it got closer
to the Ox Bow. Tony said I could hire someone if I needed to,
and I said that I had just the right friend in mind. And so I
recruited my dear friend Lloyd Barzel, called Benjamin off the
street to help me, who was one on my followers, as to say,

hangers-on, and who I created a home and position with the Robinson household for the project. Which had been a massive tangle of brush and dense underbrush to start with, that we cut down and burned all the brush and pulled up all the roots to the brush and undergrowth and raked and graded the land and put up a nice golf driving range recreation area with a big canvass tarp which we strung across a long pole that we had lashed to two trees to stop the balls for Tony to practice his swing on.

That project had lasted us all that Summer, and that was the memory of our history together that flashed before my mind on this encounter, and among other things of memories about our falling-out over Tony's young daugher Jenny, who had fallen madly in love with me, and I with her also, the truth be known, that Tony had broken us up over.

"How are you, Gary," Tony had said to me in his stumbling paternal way of concern and aloof disinterest as he sometimes expressed to me. I could always be playful with him, and sometimes had been in the past, but he seemed to prefer me to be a devout disciple of his, and I always felt in my heart to heal him by being that. He could have other friends nad acquaintences to joke around with and poke fun at each other. And maybe too, in such a Transference, of him looking to me for loyal support, and by my being that, that I became a condescended to type of person to him to be overlorded around to make himself feel more masterful. Such a reaction seemed to be a trend in my clients who I trief to help by reinforcing their egos, and thus the Transference to occur over it, and to the inverse formulation of a Master-Slave reaction instead of being grateful and apprectiative to me.

Lower Main Street Looking East From The Municipal Parking Lot

"Look, Tony," I had said, "they've made a Homeless Veteran out of me." And I meant it for real with and air of apology in my tone for my present state of being for not being a successful and financially properous student yet. But also with a certain lingering meaning of pride for the adventure in it of the life I was living then, of not being anybody important, or of having anything enduring works of literature yet under my belt to feel self-worthy of, or of having anything financially to my name, (and like a great house like Tony had to call his own;) but with pride unto myself for my ability to survive it all, the life I was leading on the mountain out living in the wilds, and surviving each day on the street, and with the very different people from those who I was accustomed to be with, that I was surviving it with. And although that it was very far away from where I needed to be psychologially, or truly in my heart ever wanted to be, that I felt it was the right place in my heart for me to be at this particular time of my lilfe, in my way of relating to Tony and his guest in their world of being successful writers and College Professors.

"That's wonderful!" Tony had exclaimed. "I can't wait to see what you are going to have to write about it."

"I can't wait either," I replied, "if I ever can get out of this place to write about it, and if they'll let me write any of it;" which conveyed hidden concerns of meanings. "I have a piece written out longhand, called, "Exit," a whole notebook full. But I will probably do like Samuel Clemmens and leave instructions to wait a hundred years after my death to publish it.

Tony's didn't introduce me to his friend and I didn't offer to introduce myself to him either, who seemed a bit too distant and reserved and judgmental in a stand-offish way, or maybe it was I who was just projecting that.

I had asked Tony for $5.00 in parting as I remember; which I desperately needed for cigarettes and beer, "the hair of the dog," but which he didn't give me as he didn't have it to give me so he had said. And I had given him my blue Yankee Baseball Cap, with a big White Y and Yankee Emblem on the front, as a parting gesture to remember me by, forcing the hat onto his head, the brim of the hat already starting to show a band of sweat from the damp from the sweat off my brow, but it smelled pleasant enough of my unwashed hair and slept in stale sweat.

"I would autograph it for you, Tony, but I don't have a pen with me," I said sportingly.

"I will treasure it always and wear it proudly," Tony had said, as I stuck the cap on his head, which he re-adjusted brushing back the thinning part of his red hair on the top of his head as he did, and I noticed his hair just starting in with long stands of graying age as he did. We were getting older.

As he put the ball cap on his head, I look Tony aside leading him by the elbow a short respectful distance away and out of ear shot from his friend who I didn't look back on to see what he was doing.

"I need to tell you, Tony," I said, talking sideways to him so as not to seem intimidating with what I had to relate to him to look him in the eye, "we never settled up with that bad Ricky Moss business. I saw Jenny going by on Main Street the other day. I was sitting in the alley next to the Hobbo Deli, and she didn't see me, but Ricky came running down the street from P&Gs calling after her. He finally caught up with her at the Liquor Store, as I looked around the corner to see, and she talked intimately with him for a while. She seemed nervous. He thinks of her still as one of his "Bitches."

You know we had that bad business back along while ago when I was living at the house, and got "Hit" with a Qaalude in my coffee in the Cosmos Diner by Mary Anne, one of Ricky's Bitches from the old days.

And I saw Jenny a while ago, back in early July at Split Rock walking naked with The Sicilian Porno Boss from P&Gs. The same fellow that Doreen had been with the night that I picked her up at P&Gs back in 1975, to date him. And who had told Doreen at the time, to go with me. Something ominous in those words, don't you think? Jenny came right up to me with this man and stood there, naked like that, of all the insensitive nerve, without thinking and broke my heart. I didn't stay around. I wouldn't say there is any love lost now between us.

I just wanted you to be aware of it. You didn't hire me back then just to do your yard work, did you? You really hired me to be Jenny's body guard, to watch over the place, and her, during the days while you were away.

"I'm so sorry that all happened to you, Gary," Tony replied. "I really am. You know I didn't mean anything by the remark I made the day you were "Hit." I was bragging on you to the street gathering and didn't think, was all. I'll take care of Jenny with those other matters."

"Sometimes far away from here is the best place to be, is were they need to go. I had to send Kathy away too," I stated, "and that's the reason she is in Buffalo, NY right now, living close by to her brother. A wise cop friend of mine once told me that. There really is no "legal" way to protect them from those Mulatto preyers. You can't put a twenty-four hour guard on them, or arrest people without a charge, or take matters into your own hands without risking major trouble. Or, in other words in another way of stating, that … a rolling stone gathers no Moss."

The incident that I had referred to about the "Hit" with Tony had occurred on a fine Saturday morning in the late August of the year 1977 when I had come to live with Tony and to help take care of his family. It was around 10:00 o'clock and I was on my way up to The Campgrounds where I worked at Minnewaska Park as a Park Ranger to report for duty there at 11:00 a.m. and to start out on the day selling weekend tickets for admission to the Low Falls Swimming Hole as it was called.

I had been at my parent's house in Poughkeepsie with my dog Sophie in the car, as my brother Stanley had come home from Colorado and I had been spending some time with him. I had parked my car, which was a 1969 light brown Ford Station Wagon at the time, in the little municipal parking lot behind the Deli House Restaurant and with Sophie left in the car to wait for me went into the Cosmos Dinner up the street for coffee. I would have gone into the Deli House but it was cramped for space and seemed too crowded for my mood at the moment for me to be taking up a whole table, and with paying breakfast customers turning away at the door, just to drink a cup of coffee. John, who was the proprietor, was a friend of mine that way.

The Cosmos, and where I had the position as "The Greeter" in helping to build the business up for Peter and his wife Anna the Greek Proprietors, who had felt sorry for initially as their restaurant had virtually no business that I decided to go their for my daily coffee and attract people to come there as a meeting place, and since when, and for over a year now that I had been going there and doing that, it was never empty.

This day I sat down at the counter and ordered a cup of coffee from the Maryanne, one of the two waitresses on duty, the other one was named Rebecca, and who was my friend Richard Rizzi's girl friend at the time. Maryanne had brought it to me, and drank it sipping on it gingerly waiting for it to cool and smoking a cigarette, and then pushed the cup across to the far side of the counter to order a refill.

While Maryanne was getting me the refill I had left the counter and went into the bathroom and came back out to find, and to what seemed rather odd, that the saucer to my cup was on top of my cup covering it. Rebecca, who was Richard Rizzi's girl friend at the time, came by me warning me quietly talking out of the side of her mouth in her high pitched feminine tone as she past by from the behind the counter in front of me, not to leave my cup unguarded around here.

I drank the refill down, not thinking anything really about what Rebecca had said, and thought perhaps that it did taste a little funny, but drank it anyway, not knowing any better of it, left a good tip for the waitress, as I always did, picked up the tab, paid for the coffees at the register, and left the Cosmos.

I walked the half a block to the driveway for the Municipal Parking Lot that ran just to the side of and up from The Deli House, and as I rounded the corner, I felt my legs begin to buckle out from underneath me. I would take two steps forward and three steps falling backward. Finally I made it to the little park behind the parking area and collapsed on the grass there.

I couldn't move. I was there for a good while like that when Harold Hudson Channer happened to come by, my good friend, and saw I was in bad shape. He tried to talk to me but I couldn't respond to him with any degree of coherency. Harold left and a few minutes past and then it seemed like the whole town had come to see what was happening. Tony and Jenny came and The New Paltz Rescue Squad came.

The Rescue Squad was trying to determine by questioning me what was wrong but I couldn't respond to them.

Jenny was trying to comfort me.

Tony then, at that time, addressed the members of The Rescue Squad who were trying to get me onto the stretcher to move me, and told them in a loud and commanding voice,

"I'd be careful with this man, if I were you, and clear all that gear you have there away, I've seen this man in action."

Which immediately go me into trouble as being a potentially violent Vietnam Veteran who the military had "Programmed To Kill." To what that the Rescue Team then made up a needle injection of a Strong Tranquillizer for me, and on top of what I was already "Hit" with, which made me void and release my urine to wet my pants in disgrace. I pounded my head into the ground and screamed bloody murder, as it was going down, but it was too late to stop it and I went into a coma.

At the Saint Francis Hospital to where I was taken, I lay on a gurney for a long time until I awakened, to find the Psychiatrist Friend of SUNY Professor Dr. Rudolf Kossman, Dr. Stephen Dobo, looking me over. Rudolf had brought me to see Stephen for the depression I was in after Doreen had dumped me. They had me listed as a Violent Combat Veteran who had just possibly O.D.' on Heroin and put me into the Psychiatric Ward. Stephen Dobo was no help for what ailed me, but he did get me out after two day of being there, and after filing a written request for discharge, and waiting the mandatory three days waiting period for Voluntary Admissions was over which I was forced to sign for.

It had taken me five days of missed work to get out of there. And when I did I was badly shaken, damaged, by the Medications, Strong Tranquillizers that the Doctor Dobo had put me on, "as a precaution."

And this was all because Tony had opened his mouth to say what he did about me. And which as all over an incident of my showing Tony a Judo Move I had learned in the Military with Lloyd Barzell, the fellow I had hired on to help me with the renovation project there at Tony's, who I flipped to the ground one day in a mock demonstration of tactic combat as he lunged at me in a mock fight pretending he had a knife. And to what that Tony was referring to when he stated, "I've seen this man in action," and to give everyone the impression like he had ever seen me really being violent toward anyone, which was a misnomer.

And from what labeling as being a potential violent Veteran that I was not only "Damaged" about, Mentally, Physically, and Emotionally, at The V.A. Hospital two years later where I had gone to be rescued from the condition of Joblessness and Homelessness, and only to find myself being disabled by their brand of Forced Treatment I then incurred there with Strong

Tranquillizers, which everyone had to be on to remain there, and having "done nothing wrong" at all to deserve such treatment to begin with, and with being "the victim" thereof; but for what and over that I also acquired a "Psychiatric History" because of it as well. And which spelled the death knell for anyone in the New Regime Order of Fascist America, to be labeled with a Psychiatric History, to thereafter and at any time by chemically Lobotomized and as all The Vietnam Veterans in America were, over 1,000,000 in toll, with Thorazine, and that had the effect on many of them, over 68,000, to death by suicide in that manner of Thorazine Treatment, and in more numbers by suicide than were killed outright I the war.

And which would occur for any incarceration for anything, that they would demand someone's personal psychiatric history about, and to Forced Treatment at any time thereafter for any incident of involving the Veterans with psychiatric.

That it was far better to be a Homeless Veteran Hobo and live in the woods about, rather than to run afoul of the government or to ask the government for any help, both of which ended in the same place by some obscene and sinister plot of the imagination.

And to what all that I had written Tony some years ago prior to explain about. And which was the reason now that Tony had apologized to me for the misunderstanding.

Maryanne, one of the Town's Bitches on the White Slavery Whore Line, was living in the Colonial Apartments at the time with a Black Porno Heroin Mobster named Marcela Sing who had just recently come in from Detroit and who was setting up a Black Pornography Gang, and giving out "Thick Identifying Finger Rings" to those whom he had recruited.

Maryanne then had "Hit" me again in the Cosmos, two days after I was released from the Psychiatric Ward there at St. Francis Hospital in Poughkeepsie, NY, saying the words, "Back to Back," to me as she wrote me out my check for the cup of coffee and refill that I had and slid it over across the counter at me.

I had gone back there to The Cosmos for spite and for stubborn pride not to be given in to paranoia, as that was the diagnoses that

the doctor's had given me at the hospital for telling them that I
had been drugged.

I paid for the coffees, left no tip for Maryanne, and walked out
of the restaurant feeling different effects from the "Hit' I had
before starting to come on, but not as catastrophic in the sedation
passing out sense. It was a strong dose of something, perhaps
Liquid Acid, LDS, or PCP this time, and that after half and hour
the effects of what I was starting to feel building up inside of me.
Motions of things around me were leaving long trails in my
vision.

I was no stranger to being "Hit" with it though as nobody
could live in the Village without being Sabotaged, or "Hit" with
LSD, the Italian Mafia's and the Black Mafia's Drug Warfare
Clandestine Weapon of Choice to what no body could rationally
complain about being "Hit" with. Because, "if" they, they were
automatically whisked away to psychiatric for their own
protection and destroyed with Haldol or Thorazine Treatment.

As I walked down Main Street toward the river and thinking to
get out of town and walk off the "Hit" out on the road, I heard a
loud voice calling out from behind and perhaps from the doorway
of P&G's. It sounded like Kurt Grimes, although I did not turn
around to look. It was shouted in a taunting way."

"Don't complain!"

And I knew it too. You became a "tainted" victim, and a
psychiatric in the eyes of the local police for complaining. Being
"Hit" with Acid or with any drug for what matter, was the same in
the eyes of the law as outright doing the drug of your own
volition. There was truly no difference. The effects of the drug
did not differentiate whether someone had taken it themselves or
was sabotaged with it. It was all the same. What you couldn't get
out of being was a certified legal psychiatric with a psychiatric
history trail leading you always back to return.

It was therefore better not to say anything and to suffer the
"Hits" going on in silence. Worse than the LSD, was the PCP
Angel Dust, that a favorite around the bars to spike the drinks
with which induced a agitated violence in its victims and that
compounded the problem with a criminal record history, in

addition to the psychiatric one, of aggressive behavior, and in all required lethal pharmacy treatment.

I vowed right then that that was the last time I was going to knowingly be "Hit" again by that woman, and who had to brag about it in her arrogance of invincibility, in the air of a "can't be touched" attitude, or by anyone else for that matter without my taking care of matters personally myself doing something about it personally.

Down the street, at The Mobile Station, I ran into John Rahls, the drug dealing resident Narc who lived on North Front Street, who was filling the gas tank on his old 1976 red Ford Tow Truck that he used to make his legitimate undercover living with, towing old junk cars to the Wrecking Yard. I had begun to growl like a bear from the over-effects of the Acid. John saw I was in distress and offered to give me a ride out to the Aqueduct, the water supply for New York City that ran parallel to and at the base of the Shawangunks from the Esopus Reservoir in The Catskills; which I gratefully took him up on to walk-off the "Hit" on the mountain and also to put the word out to him about Maryanne.

"It's the season of The Witch," John had said. "Let's be careful with the women."

He dropped me off on Mountain Rest Road on the way up the mountain towards the Mohonk Hotel Resort and where the New York City Aqueduct intersected Mountain Rest Road at the base of the rise of land. John reached into the ashtray on his dash and picked out several good-sized potent high grade marijuana roaches, from his ashtray that were confiscated from drug busts, and passed them in a secretive conspiratorial way to me, and although there was no one watching us.

"These will take the edge off," he said.

And with that I thanked John, said "I'll see you later," and got out of the tow truck and began my walk along the Aqueduct, praying to The Father the whole time that I would return safely later on.

I walked the length of the Aqueduct until it reached Duck Pond, that was a turning point intersecting with the trail that would lead up to the Mohonk Resort and to points to the South along the ridge line beneath the cliffs. I walked up to that point where the trail divides and proceeded out along the cliff line to Route 44-55, a distance in toll of eleven miles, and then another five back in to Town. It was the next morning around first light when I got back there into the Village. I was out of cigarettes. I sat down on the concrete stoop by the ally steps beside the Hobo Deli with an eye on the street waiting for someone to come by.

And in toll about the incident that I put "the word out" to the people on the street to beware of Maryanne for what she did, and to Pete and Anna Chikalis the Greek Proprietors there at the Cosmos, and to people of a different sort who were involved with The Klan, and with an ax to grind against all Mulattoized White Men Hating Dyke Women and Mulatto Bitches, called Black Widows, or Negro Bloods, and to my several Police Office friends, including Chief Bagdonowicz, about her to be aware of.

And who, as to Chief Bagdonowicz in concern, as well had inquired of me what had happened; which I told him about, and also that was the reason for his "taking me on," as an Independent Investigator concerning the ongoing crisis there of the Drug Warfare raging as a forest fire to be brought under control by and all means available in the use of manpower in and around The Bar Zone of New Paltz.

I told him about the mulatto war, and about Ricky Moss and Jenny and about Maryanne, and about Jenny trying to drug me too two days before the first "Hit" in the Cosmos. I had caught, or thought I did, Jenny at the island counter in the kitchen of the Robinson house, trying to stir something up with her finger in it.

It was glass of ice tea she was making up for me. But she was clumsy with the powder and nervous about it, and tried to stir too hurriedly and the powder spilled as I was coming in the kitchen door from the porch deck, and she handed it to me in a funny way of saying, "I made you some ice tea," that made me suspicious, and I passed on drinking it.

"No thank you I said," turning her down curtly, thinking... you too, Jenny. And such was the nature of the paranoia they induced.

Or maybe it was only a sugar substitute that she was mixing in

that I startled her at doing. I learned not to look too close at things in those days and to spare and keep and repair a friendship that might otherwise be lost forever to an unpardonable sin.

It was easy to be paranoid. The trick was not to be, but to also be prudent and wise. Such things as Drug Warfare are true. But you can't openly concede to the mistrust of it, otherwise you are done for. It's an important lesson here to be learned about life. And which is, to be smarter that they are about it.

MaryAnne mysteriously disappeared shortly after the second Hit Warfare Incident, fired from her job as Waitress at the Cosmos by Pete and Anna, and the word was put out several weeks later that she had left town, and along with that Detroit mobster Sing and her mulatto baby named Jasmine, and neither of whom was never seen again in those parts.

Some street friends of mine, Brother John The Monk, as he was called, Ed Brandes, and James Monte, had gotten my dog Sophie who was wandering around confused in the little Municipal Park and brought her back to Tony's home on a rope after I was taken away by The Rescue Squad in the ambulance. I was always very grateful to them for doing that, as Tony had told me about later after I had returned there from the hospital, and Tony had cared for her like his own dog until I was released mid-week of the incident to thank him for.

My brother Stanley had to come over from Poughkeepsie to get the car, my father's red '71 Chevy that I had borrowed and brought it back home for me.

And with that, I turned and began to resume my journey. And that was the last time I had seen Tony on that road in August of the year 1989. It was the year after my father had died, as I remember it.

And as to what journey, that I patterned myself and my life's endeavors after our Lord and Savior Jesus, in His work unto The Heavenly Father upon The Earth, and to Whom that I had also devoted and dedicated my own life to shortly after completing my formal college work in application to my life's meaning in a certain way of phrasing it. To what point is life without a

purpose to shape it and to convey its importance out, to live?

And perhaps that was a huge mistake in the meaning of my personal sanity at issue, having: "to give all that I owned to the poor and to come and follow Jesus on His path to salvation." That destroyed my relationship with The Superego framework of my Surroundings in the Middle Class World in expectations of me, that people began to look down on me about, and that somehow was to contribute to the foundations of achieving the Peace of The Father on Earth, and if only to convince me that poverty was not the way to do it, having learned that lesson then, the Hard Way.

I was at lose ends with my life for a lot of reasons then, mostly to do with the Kathleen needing a stable and prosperous man to many with, and in being at odds with her parents over me and my ways of life then, and with the alienations and homeless and joblessness associated with being a Vietnam Veteran of the ear of the aftermath of The Vietnam War, in which the civilian population regarded the Veterans as being brain damaged from Agent Organge, as the propanda against us was being put out, and programmed to kill, about our former combat killer status, and as the truth of it was that we were indeed killers, just as the public feared us to be, to be forced into the forests in living arrangements en-masse committing suicide from the social rejection in the aftermath the War, with war being what it is, The Act of Killing People; and lots of them in the meaning of mass slaughter on the battlefield, that I was on my way to Rosendale to deal with, to see if either of my two trusted friends of mine Paul Sullivan, whose nickname in the Gang was Dutch, or Jim Frazier, who we called Jimbo, were at home to take me in for the day or a few days; and in failing that, to then wander up to the top of the hill past St. Peter's Catholic Church in Rosendale to see if my Undercover Narcotics Trooper friend John Rahl, who posed as a drug dealer supplier to the other Narc Dealers in the area, was home.

John lived in the renovated old red barn that he had bought and along with the old Railroad Bridge that crossed over the Roundout Creek and local highway below to the other side of the mountain pass to the old cement Quarry. I had helped John out a lot in the renovation of his barn, and always had a welcome there, and that was how I had gotten to see his display of seized contraband merchandise, that he used to lure unsuspecting drug dealers into his web of intrigue with, that John made a point of "trusting" me with the knowledge of. And with trust in that knowledge to mean, "that I knew too much."

They were, the three of them, Jimbo, Paul, and John, three of my closest and dearest friends of the era, and just a few of the many fine friends and acquintences I had made and encorproted to my elaborate hobo route as I liked to call it, that was actually a Private Psychology Practice based on my need to survive with my ordeal and on other people's need of company, and of someone to work with, and/or someone to party with, as a form of medicinal therapy, to have some fun with in their lives.

And at least in consolation to me, and that bit about having "fun," that I was helping them to feel better for the moment with their lives, and myself included in that breath, and to tell their life stories and their troubles to, and mine to them also as the case went, misery loving company, to who I was always an avid and interested listener and attentive healer for, and adept at making concerned and meaningful consoling conversation with the troubled souls of my flock, that was literally my stock in trade.

And I suppose that most of the men bonded with me for that reason in a real way of genuine friendship, in the Gang Club Houses that were formed around my practice, (that had been going on now for roughly thirteen years in the field by that time, in their being in the need of my listening and practicing attention to them, and perhaps too of some of them of being of the homosexual male sexual orientation of persuasion, (that I didn't practice,) although I sympathized with them in their common human plight on guarded ground.

I never like to use the word, "Gay," in describing the homosexual motive because I thought it ruined a perfectly good word, and never quite figured out how the term got to be a popular coloquialism, as to how it got started. I didn't like the used of the condscending term of "Queer," either in the insulting sense. And the word homosexual seemed to stuffy and text book about to use, for what it was, the practice of homosexuality.

Most of the men I knew though didn't outwardly display such things, and those who ever did on occasion found in me a guarded and distant defensive reaction to any such advances that I did my best to discourage from the outset of any relationhips and to skirt around their hints and asides and to never look at any of their Girlie Magazines laying around that signaled a come-on, as I could see them coming from a distance and to begin to set my own guarded and defensive standards down about such conduct of matters on the table for them to recognize and aspire to not being.

And which a great many did. And with relief to me for my own ends of survival also, because I found that if any of them ever did summon up the courage to make the proposition to me, and to declare their queer intentions with me, and found themselves rejected, as they were destined to be, that they were then too embarrassed to continue on with the relationship that I had taken the time to build up with them after that, and I found myself loosing a potentially good and decent friend and to the idea of my surviving off the relationship that was ended; which most of the time none of the men ever broached the subject with me.

And so that I found myself befriending the men guardedly in a respectful manner, as they were genuine friends to me all along, and with treating the idea of male bonding as a sacred thing to be loftily weighed and measured and for the gift of life that it was, real fond friendship between men, and real in the intimate sense of needed companionship as it is spelled out for in its refined ways of meaning, counting my friends and numbering them in the night, touching each one of them and cherishing them with my thoughts, as people do think of their bank accounts, in the need of savings in the same thought of fond friendships that are set upon to dwell in the hearts between men, as strong brothers of a close-knit family are regarded, and set upon the earth in the business of the days having a common purpose to achieve the satisfacion in meaning of being highly thought of and well regarded, in the solemn and long passing of the procession of the days, whether being for work or play, being juxtaposed to a lonely isolation, that is something on the plane of the intimacy that men and women share together, but in the terms of manliness, being man-to-man, among men.

Not all of men were that way of the sickness of peverted homosexuality, and those who were its outspoken advocates found out their places about it among those who weren't. It seemed that the sickness of homosexuality has taken over the entire area, and was becoming more and more out in the open about it.

This perverse sickness comes from a lack of understanding into our Divine Nature and to the male addictions to their own sticky orgasms acquired, without proper counsel in those matters, from puberty, one after the other in the days, and to their filthy habit of jerking themselves off on the toilet bowl and sticking carrots up their rectums after their bowel movements and then licking off and sucking on the the fecal matter on the carrots in Gay Fantasy while they achieved their sensual orgasms of pleasure, if you would call it that, as a pastime; as to what that their perverted Homosexuality consisted of, and literally. To what that they are never happy with themselves about, and to say, who don't like themselves afterwards for their conduct and who are always sick at heart and even to the point of self-loathing and suicide for their crude perversity, that continues on and on every three days, or more frequently, in its cycle of abandon, and the spawn of wars to it in its effort to annihilate itself and to burn in hell, cursing God, and blaspheming the life that God has provided, for their lack and want of ability in abondon to control themselves.

Let us perceive it and call it for what it is that men do with each other, as they call, "Gay Pride," and "Gay Solidarity," with themselves, that is as an utterly depraved condition for the men to fornicate with their partners in the rectum, can you imagine? and then to suck-off the fecal matter there on the phalluses to get their depraved sexual playmates off to climax in their mouths.

And perhaps that the words of The Holy Bible written long ago state for the matter most appropriately:

Leviticus 20:13 "If a man lies with a male as he lies with a woman, both of them have committed an abomination; they shall be put to death, their blood shall be upon them."

And over time, which pastime with their fantacies of anal and genital fixations in entertaining themselves in the mind with such thoughts attached to their orgasms that would turn to runimation of mental fantasy around their orgasms to the arousal of the sickness of homosexuality with other men in their fantasies of imagination, and then with groups of men, as participants together acting out their mind's fantacies with their depraved desires for other forms of perverted erotisicm to heighten the sensations of their organasm, and to the cult of Sado-Masachism, of needing to receive and to inflict pain, and in these times of Gay Pornography to the exercise of cruel and sadistic Torture Snuff Movie Thrill Killing Homosexual Ritual Eroticisms for pastime, for the pleasure of it, like Vampires, in conspiratorial preying over the population who become their hapless victims, as a group, and who are prone to engage in the tactics of Drug Poison Warfare to Out Their Foes, who are known to each other, but not so the public who are being "Set Up" who they are.

And such has been and is the bane of men everywhere and the curse of all generations passed on from one generation to the next generation, and from father to son, in its igorance, as the older men indoctrinate the younger ones into the shamefull practice of abhorent homosexuality, and from such memories of shame as no one can escape, and that can't be made right by their massing together as a group, or together as a political movement, to dominate the society. And who cannot escape from such internal shame in their efforts for acceptance and to their banding together as a Movement for reinforcement, to that endeavor, to make themselves seem decent and respectable, which they can never achieve.

And so it needs to be stated to these people, To Give It Up! the awful habit of their homosexuality, like any other bad habit of addiction, and to become real men again in their own eyes.

Those desiring true inner peace of mind, and I would speak sensibly to everyone that way, therefore, needed to break the spell of this ill-fated cycle, and with it to achieve the strength and inner serenity of fulfilling a useful and purposeful orientation in life beginning in the control over one's body, and with the control over one's body to become infused with the sanity needed to stop with their eternal Self-Loathing and the Self- Flagellating guilt of remorse over their ill-fated conduct that is caused by the improper use of the sex organ, that such relentless depravity induces, who would do well to practice the discipline of self control, (and that is, a real discipline, as the meaning of the word stands,) and with it to extinguish in a real way the tendencies to masterbte as a daily exercise in addiction to their orgasm, the crux of the matter. And with that all the urges of their homosexuality will go away and we too can all call them men in our own eyes, and in God's Eyes, more importantly, again.

This practice of Self-Discipline which I have come to cherish as a foundation to my inner-self of peace and self reliance of thought, I professed to as a Volition, in the meaning that it is more pleasant for me to be that way of Self-Control, in the powerful mastery over the physical body, than to be of the other persuasion, and I say, persuasions then, in the plural, the phallus that way being root of all evil, as we are all aware; and however that the Wet Dreams never do leave us alone, do they. And always in the night while we are sleeping, the Inubus and/or the Sucubus will come to sit on our chests and causes us to have Wet Dreams, in which all the gooey mess of our stored up semen comes out and lays smelling the way of pungent semen in your underwear.

The Sucubus, and that is the presence of a female spirit demon in the dream, to induce the Wet Dream Orgasm, and being somewhat pleasant, is one thing; but the Incubus is an hermaphrodite who has the desire to suck his own penis. Which arises and comes from the ancient source of The Creator Himself in throwback to the time in Hell when He was all alone in the eternal darkness and became an Hermaphrodite in the only way of expressing his sexaul nature, of relating sexually to and with himself, and what has left our human nature scarred in its propensity of depraved condition and plagued with an imagination of that way of sexuality that The Creator Himself had with himself and is responsible for.

Ah, but there's the rub, because there can never be any real peace with it, if The Creator has an Error To Be Castigated For and to be looked down upon by anyone of us who does not profess to have the errror, and with being guiltless and blameless in their own minds over it, and condescending to God, and to The Fallen Angels for their flaw, if everyone does not take a little piece of the sin into and for their own way and Exonerate The Creator of the Error. OTHERWISE, The Creator will never be able to be with us on the plane of perfect acceptance in understanding as our God, in such a troubled way. And who will always then be reclusive to us.

We therefore, need to accept Him, and everyone else of the Fallen Nature along with God, as being that way of being victims of a freak of nature, to be overcome.

It is in The Overcoming that the strenght of Perfect Mastery of the matter can be achieved, that is the important thing here to digest; and not that anyone was, or is, ever in that way of being a Depraved Homosexual, or a Depraved Lesbian in the Female version, (and let us reason and call it for what it is,) as hopeless souls banding together in a Rights Movement, to make what is not properly normal, normal, which it can never be. And to to the outright disillusionment of our age, the age we live in. And I say this with all sincerity to reform the ways of humanity, and perhaps our Creator, the truth be known.

The trouble then being that way, of Self-Disciplined Nature, when one is sleeping as the guest of anyone, and for what reason that Wet Dreams are most annoying, that a change of garments is required, and that no such change of garments is available.

And which for that reason that there were a few quiant female acquintances who I had joined forces with, over the matter, Street Women of the Night as the drift goes, who psyhogicaly bonded with me of that nature for companionship, and to supply them with libation when they were down and out to get them High and started on their way for the day, or night, depending, and for protection, who I was commonly known as a Jack to, (a Jack being someone who acted as their "Old Man" and the one they came to when they were through with their Johnny's and when a

Johnny got to possessive and wanted to marry them and things of
that nature, who a prostitute (by and other name,) could go to and
who would scare away the other men that they had acquired from
coming around.

A Street Jack usually carried a big knife on his belt, as a ward
away, but I never did, (as I found it was not really in my nature to
display such a weapon.) I would just be there, big and bad
enough in my rough and woodsy smelly way, and who wouldn't
care in getting his clothes scuffed up in a fight to the death, who
could always count on having a place to go to when I needed a
place to crash for a while, or on a cold and dreary night, and when
the timing was right for one of the girl's to need me for company
in the night, and otherwise that they would give me the sign of
being busy. They were all Gang Wives too in that way, being
with whoever they happned to be with, and needing the comfort
of and the company of another gang member at the moment, and
otherwise that everyone was interchangable with the Gang
Women depending on who was around on the street and who the
girl wanted to be with.

The local Rastafarians of The Zionist Coptic Religion used
Marijauna as their Sacrament and were always eagerly looking for
converts and disciples to swell their ranks and any excuse to Rasta
and Jam and to beat on their drums and offer their Marijuana as
incense intoxication to everyone who showed up at their door and
although that you never needed to smoke any of their Ganja to be
among them and imbibe their Raggae Spirit.

Each drum had a different sound depending on how it was
constructed, and each drum had different tones within its surface
to hit on. Each player was given a note or a series of notes to
strike in a continuous rhythm, to what sound that all would lend
an orchestra of drums to, to provide the lead player with the
opportunity to "Rift" off the top. And the Drum Concerts they
did would last for hours.

And who were always a part of my route, as I admired the way
that they treated and related to all the people of God's Earth in
respect and with regard to their individual needs to belong and to
feel of being a part of a group in being cared for as fellow

disciples of a community of fellowship that did not discriminate, but which welcomed each individual person as a fellow human being. And all of which was attributed to the influence of the Ganja.

Revelation Chapter 22:2 "In the midst of the great street of the city, and on either side of the river, was the tree of life, which bore twelve kinds of fruits, and each month it yielded one of its fruits; and the leaves of the tree were for the healing of the peoples."

The leaves of The Tree of Life in the midst of the Great City are the leaves of the Cannabis Bush, and the yielding of the Twelve Fruits one for each month of the year are the delights of each month of the year to savor.

And there were all other sorts of motives for my practice, with religious or philosophical conversational zealots, and fellow writers, poets, song writers, and those dedicated to music, needing peerage and disciples to profer their views upon who would gladly open their doors. And some, and mostly all, who just liked to have an excuse to "Party," or "To Get High" as the meaning was expressed. New Paltz, and the surrounging environs that way, that used to be a "Hippie Draft War Town" during the Vietnam War, that smoked marijuana openly as a sign of solidarity and protest, and still was after all a wide open, "Drug Town," with LSD being the weaopon of choice, a "Party Town,", and "Gay Community," a, "University Town," and "Tourist Town," a "Wild Bar Town," featuring live band music prevailing in many of the bars throughout the Village, a "Mafia Porno Town," and a, "Fine Arts Colony" of culture also for the refined residents of the area and the tourists to "nose around" about, to get used to.

And besides being established as a Writer, that my extended studies there in the College Town of New Paltz, NY, and connected with associated with The University on the hill there, were Music, as I had advanced degree studies in the piano, and in the Fine Arts, and had also established myself as a Painter in those years.

And in other ways that I worked in the field of Mental Health, that is not as menacing concept as it intends in its sinister applications and misuse.

Genuine concerns and meaningful contributions to Sound Mental Health is something that we all need to work on, like Dental Hygiene, that no one can do without, and what we cant' begin to teach to the young children to begin the practice and the discipline of too soon enough, about what to do, (involving a systematic discipline of learning; To Think Correctly, and To Behave Correctly,) to foster, and to strengthen, and to preserve good Mental Health, (and concerning the motivating reasons for preserving it, good mental health;) by the practice of industrious diligent work ethic, and good manners, and proper conduct, and to the sense of responsibility in all things, dedicated to the creation of harmony in the mind' one breath at a time; and to be trained as well defensively for on how to prevent bad situations that would bring about a deteriorating state of emotional well-being occurring, and as best that we can manage that way of prevention in the face the negative forces in play among us in the world, to act upon us in ways we can't control; and to concern with the biological malfunctions and diseases such as Syphilis and Alzheimer's, to deal with.

I was and still am a Faith Based Psychologist, trained in Psychotherapy during my employment as a Therapy Aid formally at the Hudson River Psychiatric Facility during the time frame of 1979-1980, in Gestalt Therapy also of the era and while attending Graduate Studies ongoing at the SUNY University at New Paltz, (as to say of the sense of perception to the things around us of The Surroundings, and of the ability and the openness to communicate freely as to the attitudes and the perceptions that we feel, in order to develop a required Fellowship with Everyone, and Everything, in a practical sense of nurturing the world around us, and to a discipleship of healing;) and in that meaning of being based in Faith to The Creator in appreciation to life, engendered to a strong sense of morality and propriety in correctness in foundation in thought, word, and deed, and to the formulation of successful relationships, not just with our fellow human beings but as well

All Things Sentient of The Creation, including The Inanimate
Objects, and to be fully cognizant of the play of The Spirit World
on and influencing the affairs of Human Beings. To what living
appropriately we should have no fear of.)

I also had extensive Para-Medical, Para-Legal Mental Hygiene
Law, and Pharmacology Training, having interned directly there
at the Mental Institution of Hudson River Psychiatric and
graduated as a Therapy Aid during the Winter and Spring of
1981, and was trained and thoroughly astute in the ways of
Psychiatry regarding the perceptions of injury and disease, and as
well with being a Medical Nutrition Specialist, in the assessment
of proper diet, and to do with other negative aspects of life; such
as; Joblessness, Homelessness, Drug Addictions, Alcoholism, and
Hypoglycemia, (or Low Blood Sugar,) having a profound bearing
on the ways that people think, and behave, and react, in the affairs
of sound Mental Hygiene.

To what inducing mental illness conditions in all that the
Medical Practice does not need to be administering Strong
Tranquillizers at every turn to Treat and to Heal People.

And in all, of my route, which I undertook of my Private
Practice and as a Circuit Preacher would in such regard to look
after his "flock" in concern for their well-being, spanned the four
counties of; Dutchess, Ulster, (which housed The University and
The Village of New Paltz, NY and environs,) Orange, and
Sullivan Counties. And of all the people that I managed to know
by that time, that if I counted them up on my fingers would
number in the hundreds, and who took care of me in the ways
they did at time, as I took care of them in the ways I did, which I
called my Church.

And Who, concerning Jesus, that I modeled my own campaign
to, and at the exact same age as He was when he began His public
career, as I began mine at the same age of thirty years old. Who
had twelve Apostles to help reform the way of man upon the
earth, to what mission that I had recruited for myself well over
several dozen Disciples to to help me with mine.

They were, and all writers and artists, musicians, teachers and
preachers, in their own right, and myself more inclined to be their

disciples as they were disciples of mine. But who were hand-
picked by me to represent The Work of The Lord, and the Work
of The Undercover Operation, and combined as a group into a
penetrating Force To Be Reckoned With to the common purpose
of Defending America from the ruin of an evil enemy.

And who were, of the many to be counted; my dear friends,
Kenny Hasbruck, (nicknamed Lightfoot,) Richard Martinolich,
(Conga Richie,) Paul Schubert, Joey St. George, Arnold
Moodnick (Marky,) Richard Rizzie (who was the son of the
Italian Mafia Boss and local Godfather,) Glen River (a local film
producer,) Eric Iverson, Buzzy Gardiner, Jim Frazier, (Jimbo,)
Mike Deluca, Michael Malcom Mitchel, David Weitz, Arthur
Kutchner, David Munn, Harvey Phillips, Paul Sullivan (Dutch,)
Ed Peters, Paul Tobin and his young son Toby, Bart Kraus,
(Ellen's husband,) Ed Brandes, John Carey, James Monte,
Modesto Cuomo, (who played a small part in the movie, The God
Father,) John McKenna (Brother John The Monk,) James
(Jimmy) Boseano, Chuck McGill, John (Cosmic Jack) Edwards,
Marc Reisner, (the photographer,) Tony Robinson, (who was the
charismatic founder of our Church,) Timothy Shoh and Michael
Mulvihill, (my close friends and college classmates,) Dewit
Clinton, (Rich Rizzi's friend,) Steven Bell, (the D.E.A. Agent in
residence,) John Rahl, (the Undercover NYS Police Narcotics
Officer in residence,) Andy Easton, (tragic suicide victim of
Hudson River Psychiatric,) Terry Connoly, Mike Catlit, Jeffrey
Spangler, Michael Horowitz, the brothers, John, Kevin, and
Dennis Martin, Donald Bellinger, Terry Reily, Jerry Neusbaum,
(who owned The Chez Joey Italian Restaurant on Main Street,)
Norman Stone and his cousin Bruce Peterson, John Vett (the
Mayor's son,) Jon Ross, (my famous mountain climbing friend,)
Michael Migliori, (another climbing friend of mine,) Dick
Williams, (the proprietor of Rock and Snow Climbing Store in
downtown New Paltz,) Peter and Anna Chikalis from the Cosmos
Restaurant, Manny Lipton and his wife Freeta, (proprietors of
Manny's Book Store next to P&Gs,) Charles, (Chuck,) McGill,
(my steet companion,) Ron Thompson, (The Head Ranger at
Minnewaka Park also a dear friend,) Shamus (the Boss,) Scotty

(who married Lighfoot's fiance Annie,) and many, many others
known to me casually only by their first names to whom I
appologize to, and who would go by the names of; Willie, (who
lived on the street in his bus,) Bob the Barber, Robert the
Hairdresser, Lenny the proprietor of The New York Café, (where
I worked,) Stormy the daytime bartender at P&G's, Willie and his
brother John from The Deli House, Steve the proprietor of The
Gay Nineties, as the list goes on in memory. Who were a valient
and imposing Vigilante Street Force Militia to be reckoned with.

And who, in all, were a tight band of men dedicated, beyond
themselves, to a solitary purpose, To Serve The Creator, and to
preserve and to serve and to protect and to defend the integrity
and the standards, as The Creator Instructs Us, of The Nation of
The United States of America, and to the Preservation of the
White Race, as The Creator has Ordained, and to the Sovereign
Preservation of The Government of The United States to be held
securely in the American European Hands of The Founding
Fathers in International Agreement, and in pledge to defend the
Security of American Sovereign Soil and the Sovereign Soil of
The Native Indigenous American Indians, In Those Terms, Under
God, The Creator, Dedicated in our position to the Human Rights
of The American Constitution, and for Humane Treatment in the
fellowship with all men in brotherhood on the Earth, For All.

That is the way the wording of such a unified position should
be, and that should have been worded that way at the outset of
The Civil Rights War Aggression all along in Just and Sound
Reasoning of the Sovereignty Issue in Acknowledegment, that
was now left up to the Private Militias of the American Public To
Defend, and for us not to have to have Surrendered The United
States To It in the first place. In the meaning of its being forced
upon us, of The Civil Rights Movement of Hostile Take-Over on
their Militant Terms of, "Push Come To Shove," in stated
Aggressions upon us, and undermining us with the peril of their
Drugs and Perversely Immoral Conditions of Pornography and
Prostitution, inducing the perverted tendencies of Homosexuality
and Lesbianism and to the destruction of the American Moral
Standard, to get away with it, Attacking The Soul of White Man's

America and of the fabric of The United States itself, as the case stood to be earnestly defended about.

And to the regard of the Civil Rights Era of the 1960s; to state that we respect the efforts in regard to securing the Rights of Humanity in our United States of America, and as a very necessary in defense of our nation's Civil Rights Policy against the Racial Crimes of Hatred, Prejudice, Bias, and Discrimination. However to add that cuts both ways in Reverse Discrimination, as to the concept of what this is about, and which concerns The Civil Rights of The White Population as well to the issue of The Civil Rights of The Black People needing to be defended against the evilness and ways of bigotry and prejudice. And what is the object of this discussion here to follow.

To indicate to you that your attitude of failing to concern yourself with both sides of the indictment, is not only short changing The White Race from the intervention of Just Due Process under law, but is also fueling the hatred upon us on the part of the Black Race in instigation to their attitude of justification for their ways of aggressions against us; that is not being very intelligently conducted and put forth regarding your concern to us in the state of an undeclared Civil War has existed here in this country on both sides between the Whites and the Blacks, (and as to say of The Negro African American Race that lives among us, and their Mulatto Offspring,) and regarding their prevailing use and addictions to the deadly Narcotic Heroin, and other Drugs in general, Drugs Trafficking, and to the Ultimate Weaponry of Drug-Chemical-Poison Warfare Sabotage Assault with Drugs as their Weapons against The White Race occurring and ongoing; (which can't be complained of for the reason of the Psychiatric Intake involved with the complaint, and that can't be proved, and which therefore cannot be Legally Intervened With.) And of what therefore that is being left unchallenged by the lawful Authorities here in their abandoning of the hapless White American Citizenry to this form of torture and demise, and left up to the hands of Self-Help Vigilantism, organized White Militias, and the defensive barricade of The Klu Klux Klan, to remedy, for our own Government's failure to intervene to the bloodless Drug/Poison Massacre of The White Race occurring.

The other orientation concerning the Civil War occurring, besides the Drug Use and Trafficking, and the associated Drug/Chemical/Poison Warfare, to be dealt with at this time has to do with the issues of; the White Women's War against their White Male counterparts, in direct alliance with The Negro Mulatto Race, involving the issue of Miscegenation, and to their use of The White Females by means of Black/Colored Heroin Aggression, (taking prisoners of the White Females through Heroin Addiction, and by other means of Fear Coercion, such as Black/Mulatto Gang bullying, (that begins at a young age in Grade School,) of the White Women, and to the threats of Foul Play and the Killing of their Loved Ones if they don't cooperate, that is known as White Slavery,) to be used as tools in the Extermination of the White Males; in the Mulatto Islamic Plot to Assimilate the White Race by Inter-Racial Procreation, and to what that the White Female is a Prize Captive and a Household Assassin to the Conduct of Drug Poison Warfare, to the ill-health, insanity, and deaths of the White Males, to Carry-Out, as a prevailing ideology of the Black/Mulatto Race, also known also as Islam; that has been ongoing for a very long time into centuries and millennia, to be recognized about, and as to what are the reasons behind the conflict between the Races to exist, to the point.

And emphatically here to re-emphasize to you of The Civil Rights Division of The F.B.I., that as we have been after now for some time to guarantee and ensure the safety of the entire White population at the hand of the Drug Warfare occurring and resulting Psychiatric Intake without Due Process of Law to then be legally Force Treated with deadly Chemicals, for you to take steps to remedy the atrocity that is occurring, and not against the Black People of this Nation, (or the Colored People as the case concerning the Nation's Mulatto Population, being both Black and White and confused and confounded in their lineage, to be able to reckon with,) but to the warfare against The White Race, (and for the motives that you are siding with, of their "getting even" with us for their alleged conditions of ill treatment during their Era of Slavery here in the United States.

We needed the Authorities to be mindful in our behalf of The White Race where justice needs to be rendered, and not for you to continue-on to be profiling the beleaguered White Race, who face extinction, (by Inter-Procreation and Drug Warfare Sabotage Intrigues,) as intolerant bigoted racists, (and which has nothing to do with Racism,) for settling our own affairs of survival, (where no justice exists to intervene for us in our behalf of survival,) of the White Race being Murdered-Off and Whittled Away piecemeal fashion by Drug Chemical Warfare, and/or to be Rendered into Psychiatric Custody for its effects, or for the complaining about it, (to be murdered there in that legal setting with lethal Pharmacy Brand Chemicals;) and in all that is being conspired with and committed by the coercion of the Females of The White Race in Clandestine Collusion to their Heroin Suppliers of the Negro/Mulatto Race; who are for the reasoning of their untenable aggressions, in violation of their terms of the Social Contract of their living arrangement with the White People, being sided with by the Government of The United States.

"The Society For The Preservation Of The White Race," is just that; "An Organization Set-Up To Defend and Preserve The White Race From Extinction." That is not to be viewed as a Racist Organization, but as an Racial Alliance to Defend and Preserve Our Interests and to Prevent Our Extinction as a Race of Humanity from perishing off the Earth by the foul play aggressions of Drug Poison Warfare, and through Miscegenation, and in valid reasoning of necessity; in preventing their use of The White Females in tow of The Black/Mulatto White Slavery Heroin and Prostitution Mafias, from doing us in.

All of whom, of these men, had cultivated "followings" of their own, and who were Commanders in their own right, and as to the reason that I chose them, because it would all, the movement we were organizing, get "big" and grow national and international very fast, and our combined agendas would create a new world to live in.

And who together as well along with many, many, other close male friends, who at any one time I could count on and along with the original disciples that I had picked and chosen, to do "the work," of the Lord with, that who in general would always display good faith and good intentions to everyone they met in the course of their days, in building up the base of our Religion of Practical Applied Sociology in caring for the needs of others, and in sharing the burdens of others, and the burdens of State Matters in obligatino, that we each and all alike referred to as, "The New School," which was about the studying and the learning of the

John Rahls' Railroad Bridge over The Rondout Creek
Looking down on it from the top of Look-Out Mountain
On A Bleak and Forlorn Winter's Day In Rosendale, NY
John's Red Barn is to the left out of the picture

adaptations of the ways to get along in the world and to learn to live together as people and as an integrated society as a whole, with the others around us.

And they each and all liked my company for the reasons that I like theirs'. They did in my version of an applied psychology practice and were always helping other's out with a polite meal, a cigarette, a cup of coffee, and maybe some day work together, that I could count on for a night's lodging or two now and then, or for a few days of work, or a few hours now and again, and maybe a few dollars to spare, or more, for the road on parting.

I was always fairly good at Panhandling, having graduated from Panhandling School, Summa Cum Laude, in knowing how to touch the people up for money, and someday's were better than other about it.

Mostly though the streets were barren and forlornly desolate, and you always had to keep moving and not stand around in any one place for too long.

"Party the House," was the rule of the day that way, as the day's went, and always with a basic instinct to survive off the fat of the land, as an animal would approach the days ongoing before itself, having nothing for the morning and always having to start out empty with a growing and ravenous hunger afresh looking for food, and for a warm and comfortable and safe place to sleep at night. And in my case also, as was, for the Adventure of it that I craved, that simulated combat and stimulated me in its sensuous uncertainty of daily survival at odds with the hostility of the world the way it really was, and dangerous full of unseen perils to comfront and defeat, as was the way it went.

Not that I cared much for any of it, but libation served its purpose of opening doors, and only in the necessity of shared intimacy with the habit of others in passing the time. I had my Epiphany about such matters of addictions and preferred the clean fresh air of the out-of-doors keeping mostly to myself, to give them all up, one fine day, and on the day I did, each one, and entirely, and to live a straight and productive life afterwards, with my wife, and to produce good and sober works in the world, that I needed to be clear headed to accomplish, the truth of it know, that I became enlightened to by the Grace of God, The Great Father Almighty, to achieve in the end.

But the outright lure of being a Vagabond held me in its spell right then and there, and it was right just then at that time, that I was exploring that particular, and other realms of reality about, (call it as a writer's curiosity to know these things, and I do now, being Full Blooded to them,) and not to lure anyone on into bad habits needing to be given up, but which always is there in the back of my mind, of my nature that way, that was not all that unpleasant, but only dissatisfying in the strick sense of feeling one's responsibility in life ebbing away that only being a Hobbo can bring out in a man, that I just might become a Highway Man again, and if the circumstances, God Forbid, were ever right again for me to be that way, which in itself was an addiction to its adventure of day-by-day survival.)

The first Golden Rule for survival as a Hobo Scavenger on the road, was to "Party The House," that is a lesson in how to Party Politely and Expediently so as never to be turned away, that consisted of the principles to never to ask for any of it, or to turn any of it down when offered, as that was their "Head" to have someone To Party With. It spoiled things if you turned it down, and it spoiled things if you asked for anything. Althought it was always polite to ask encouragingly after the libations to bring matters along which one had to play by ear, in reading the intuitive moods of one's clients as to whether or not it would be taken the wrong way, and as it was never your motive to show up at someone's door and ask for anything as your motive for being there. Your motive for being there was always to see your old friend and to be with that person, and always to wait for in invitation at their insistence for anything else, and never to take too much of whatever it was, to size up what they need for their own consumption to be satisfied with, the way it went, but never to be discouraging or displeased by anything anyone did either.

The second Golden Rule of the road was to always try and reciprocate whenever it was possible to do so, to come bearing gifts, and to repay all "Mafia Debts," of a dollar, or whatever they were, for what you borrowed and promised to repay at a certain time. There was never any interest to a Mafia Debt in our way of the meaning, which was lent to a friend in need in the idea of being a friend, and of having a friend, and which wasn't loaned out in the idea of loan sharking, but a dollar borrowed needed to be repayed with a dollar and at the time when you promised to repay it, or to say you were sorry if you couldn't pay and to make other arrangements when circumstances intervened and you could't pay, and to state when you would next be able to.

A third and unspoken Rule was, and as each Club House had a Boss and company of his own other than yourself to discuss, to never rival the possessiveness of the Boss's affection with his men over, of his Transference with you, in the meaning of needing you for emotional verification and support, and that is like a wife in such regard to be respected and who one does not wish ever to rival with another, by taking up a separate, and to say affectionate, relationship with any of the Boss's men to make him envious to have a jealous reaction over.

And so that it was in that way with Tony and I, of our friendship and relationship having been spoiled by my involvement with his daughter Jenny that I always felt very deeply bad about.

And all of this that I had a profound keeness of awareness in, and in remembering Tony then at that time, as I had walked away from him on that day. And in also with the feeling one day of wanting to make it up to him for "falling in love with" and for going out with his young teenage daughter Jenny, some of what was behind his back for a while, not very long, but enough to be angry over, before I told him one day, that was a month or so after I had been living there, about our affair, (and that it was like the relationships of; Sonny and Cher Bonno, and Elvis and Presilla Presley, and Prince Charles and Lady Diana, in reference, of the age difference, and of the relative times of the beginning of their courtships being fifteen and at a much earlier age not be naïve with, that began in the teenage years of women,) and like Jenny and I having fallen madly in love together in the Summer of 1977.

I was just past 31 at the time, and Jenny was just 17, and I was in my prime of my life in those days, recoiling from a painful separation from my second wife Doreen who I had met and picked up in P&G's Bar one night two years before and married

in a Civil Ceremony by Judge Stokes, the Justice of the Peace in
Gardiner, NY, in April of 1976. And who was always a good
woman to be friends with, as so many women are, but not so to be
married to in the closed in day-in day-out possessive sense of
finality to the outcome of the female's multiple-personalities to
contend for, with their migrane headaches and foul moods at
times, to bless their hearts about, as long as don't become abusive
and berating, and especially of the drug related kind of abuse.
Love is after all a two-sided coin, and always amazed at how it
can turn about not so easily into hate, but it does, and can,
awaiting a harsh word or an unfaithful act, the turn of a head, the
look of an eye.

****

If we studied the Women for an hundred years and determined
that they are what they are, and that way to be thought of, it
would be enough said. But in the end we no longer longed for
them in the captivated way that we did before we knew them well
in the days of our innocence and naiveté, before we started out to
study them of necessity to survive.

There were also at the time certain internal longings that I had,
or desires, besides the relentless desires for women and wanting
to mate with each of them that I saw, and for the relentless
wanderlust that I had for adventure in my blood, and besides of
my desire to wander the valleys and the mountain roads and to
return to my primal roots in the forest, and for a certain discussion
of life to delve briefly into the off-beat nature of things going on
unseen in the upstairs parlor rooms and flats of the gang club
houses in the Village of New Paltz, NY, and to partake in the
private goings-on behind in those places behind closed doors of
the secret life that those people led who were shoulder to shoulder
in camaraderie on the street, and to learn what made them that
way, the way they are, when people lived dependent to one
another's trust and loyalty, on-the-street, that lay closed and
mystery to outsiders peering on, like myself, that involved the
drug culture the mysterious world of the woman of the night.

And perhaps it was in my blood from the start to be curious that way, something of an inborn nature reverting to a past and former life in incarnation to relive over again until I got it right, and not quite ready for the formal and starched shirt straight business world of the expectations of my college training, in wanting to cut-loose a bit before I died and to learn what it was that made other people happy the way they were, and about their mystic of drugs to learn, that they treated so off-handedly and smugly and secretly together closely conspiratorial about, as to what exactly the drugs were to them that made them so closely bonded, and what they did to your body and to your mind to experience for myself, that made those people want to take up with that sort of thing, as I found myself in a curious way wanting to experiment with, just for my own knowledge about the nature of these drugs, to be a man about, to cut loose for a time and explore.

And to what, in the midst of all this curiosity going on, that I was after all at the time in the midst of the real Drug War going on, that had been going on the whole time that I was in college since the late 1960's of The Vietnam War, and during which that the drugs were being openly flaunted as an expression of Social Rebellion and Defiance with The Government of The United States, that in all which I had been an outsider to.

To what formal beginning in the world that I had just finished with College, graduating Summa Cum Laude in a straight A sort of way of diligence and intelligence and was at loose ends with my life, uncertain about my job prospects, and attending Graduate School at the State University at New Paltz, NY in the meantime until my mind got settled. That it was on the final day of my William Faulkner Class with Professor Harry Stonebeck in the late of May of the year 1995, that a woman named Doreen entered my world and changed my life around forever, some ways, and many ways, for the better, and other ways for the not-so-good, but which were in all always a lesson to be learned from, of the experiences that I gained from her, that proved invaluable to me in the end for the work that I needed to be doing, which as it turned out to be later on in the year and concerning my work on

The Race War and in Defense of America to become an Undercover Narcotics Authority with the Drug Enforcement Administration in that regard; and which evened things out in the end, my experiences with Doreen and the drugs she bore, to be able to provide me a background for in the meaning that I had no regrets and harbored no ill-will towards her in the aftermath of our relationship.

And this was in the middle of various romantic entanglements when I met her, on the rocks with my breakup from Pauline, who I fell in love with and who broke my heart in breaking up with me, being pregnant at the time, and her choice of remaining married with another man, her husband, to be with; and engaged to Kathleen, who herself had just graduated college six months later than me the Winter the before, and who had been Student Teaching for her degree at a school in Monroe, NY, who had set up an engagement plan with me to get married and who was now in the process of setting a date, as we had been going on together then for a number of years.

Kathleen was in love with me, as I was with her, and who had been the reason for the breakup with my first wife Carol, over Kathleen, who I met my Freshman year in College, but with whom that I was not really ready to be married to, who was looking to settle down with me and have children, and I too with her, just not at that time of hastily rushing into things so soon after our mutual graduating from college, to just get married without experiencing certain other things of travel and adventure, and to pursue my literary craft, that life had to offer.

Who I was to break-off the engagement with to leave for Doreen, that was a very painful and doubt ridden thing to do and that troubled me deeply in the heart, before I broke it off with Doreen in my own heart a year later over my love for Kathleen in pang of regret over having jumped her for Doreen, and over Doreen's relapse in use of Hard Drugs, Heroin and Cocaine, and in my desire not to be around her in that manner any more, and that had already been taken prisoner by her in such regard and that had caused me enough grief that way already to last a life time, that I didn't wish to linger on with.

And that was after the affair with my college friend Mrs. Pauline Brower broke off, and before Jenny came along and happened into my life, and before Julia Gerstmann, who was a Lesbian Porn Star, unknown to me at the outset of our brief and stormy entanglement of relationship, and who was besides a Negro Blood assassin having a drug alliance with certain mulattoes of the local Mulatto White Slavery Ring, in the meaning of luring in White boyfriends to her bedside and doing their "Hit Work" of Drug Poison Sabotage for them at their behest in taking out the White Males who she had in tow. And although, how had found me sleeping in the third floor hallway outside her door in the dead of winter and freezing cold outside to take me into her room and provide me shelter and a place to stay, and another classic Double-Bind setting of friendship and murder.

And who was like Typhoid Mary in that regard and a real and accomplished Feminist Assassin of White Males, who took me in and did me in that way in a grand style of Poison Drug Sabotage with LSD while on an Outward Bound Hitchhiking Adventure Excursion with her, that she had wanted me to take her on, and in setting me up for the kill, in the late of March of 1982, with a backpacks and tents, to hitchhike with her to Steve Gaskin's Hippie Farm in Tennessee, but which once out on the road and spying her entourage of Black Mulatto Bucks going by in a car who were tailing us, that I redirected our course from Steve Gaskins' Farm to take to her to my Uncle John Carter's Farm in Shorter Alabama, where I could handle the situation better, so I thought.

And which is another story of some detail to relate altogether, or how she had drugged me and the whole Carter Household with LSD and Rat Poison and dumped me there at my Uncle's farm to rent a car and drive back to New York State on her own, and that left me sick on the road to hitchhike back home alone, only to collapsed on the road after standing on a ramp to Interstate 85 for twelve hours, with my legs beginning to buckle and darkness closing in, to be taken by the local law to a psychiatric facility in Columbia, South Carolina, "for observation," and being a Carpetbagger from the North, and a Brain Damaged Vietnam

Veteran "Programmed To Kill," besides, with no Health
Insurance, to be maimed there at G. Werber Brian Psychiatric
Hospital with Strong Tranquilizers called Loxitane and Cogentin.

And that was before the tragedy of Ellen Ganzer, my dear
friend and sweetheart companion of the times, who was
murdered, or who committed suicide with a shotgun, which we'll
never know and which the local police however labeled as a
suicide. And all of whom, and long with several lesser briefer
romantic affairs, constituted the involvement with women in my
life in those days, before I settled down and finally married, and
took to steady routine work in a living arrangement with my one
true love Kathleen, who came had come in her mercy to rescue
me from it all, and to whose life and happiness that I am now
totally devoted. And what could be a more Fairy Tale and
endearing of an ending to it all.

"Qui peut tourner à l'amour," or, "Who can turn down love,"
in the French Translation that I was never any good at.

Charmi Neely, was a very pretty petite and charming long red
haired girl, who I fell madly in love with. She was slightly older
than myself, who had a hard life having been raised in an
orphanage called Greer School in Millbrook, NY, and who I met
in my senior year of college. She was always my favorite girl
friend, and fond intimate traveling companion. We traveled to
Mexico together with after our graduation from SUNY in 1974,
with a stressed emphasis on the word, friend, who I was intimate
with, but not in a possessive way, and nor she with me, and we
were always close friends in each other's hearts to one another
and took in each other's other love relationships to heart as our
own.

I was with Charmi that I had the profound Revelation of
Solipsism, about the Divine Nature of being God Ourselves.

Doreen's full maiden name was Doreen Dedrick, and who was
truly a remarkable and wonderful caring woman, who I met when
she was just twenty-eight years old and I was twenty-nine, under
her married name as Doreen Tigert.

Doreen's father was a musician name was **Lyle "Rusty" Dedrick** of Summitville, NY, and whom I thoroughly enjoyed meeting and being a part of his family during our brief romance, and who sadly passed away at home on December 25, 2009. His obituary reads as follows. He was the son of the late George and Edith Dedrick, and was born in Delevan, NY on July 12, 1918. With a career spanning over seven decades. Rusty made a unique contribution to the world of Jazz. As a trumpeter, solo brilliance was his hallmark, in addition to his creativity as an arranger and composer. Rusty studied at Fredonia College and was tutored by composers Paul Ceston and Stefan Wolpe. He played with several prominent "Big Bands" including Dick Stabile, the Red Norvo/Mildred Bailey Orchestra, Ray McKinley, and the Claude Thornhill Orchestra. Rusty had a long career in the New York City Jazz music field. His credits include writing and/or playing with Don Elliot, Urbie Green, Maxine Sullivan, Lee Wiley, Lionel Hampton and others, as well as radio and television work with Arthur Godfrey, Ed Sullivan, Sid Ceasar, and more. At the same time, Rusty was recording his own LP's. In 1971, Rusty joined the faculty of the Manhattan School of Music as Director of Jazz Studies. As a pioneer in Jazz Education, his jazz band charts for the education field received acclaim for their creativity and accessibility by musicians of all ages. Throughout his jazz education career, Rusty continued to arrange and play, and in 1996 he was the musical director of the prestigious Smithsonian Institute American Songbook Series tribute to Fats Waller and Andy Razaf. Rusty completed the writing, arranging and recording of Music of America in 2007, which was a decade long project. Survivors include his wife, best friend, and soul mate of 64 years: Patricia Dedrick at home; his daughters: Doreen Dedrick and her husband Mark Lonergan of New York City, and Karin Dedrick and her husband George Piskoz of Kingston, NY; his son: Jeff Dedrick and wife Gail Dedrick of New York City; a sister: Ruth Taber of Belfast, NY; as well as many nieces and nephews. Rusty will be remembered for his love of family, nature, the New York Yankees, music and more than words can express. He was a gentle soul who left this world all too soon.

And however about Doreen, whoever she had been married to, or what her life was like before I met her, I never found out. And which taught me a great lesson of life not to sleep with, and take up with, and marry with a stranger lady who one doesn't really know.

Doreen was in truth of fact, and as she turned out to be, and who she often made mention of it to me, the lovely Reincarnation of Lilith.

Lilith had been the dominant male-hating mythical first wife of Adam before Eve, and who was made of the same soil and at the same time as Adam had been; and who, as his first wife had refused to be "on the bottom position of their lovemaking," and subordinated in other ways to him and had run off to pursue her own and independent destiny in the world.

Doreen always looked at me in the way of admiration for the powers of my manhood, and with what was a big term in use in the day, in penis envy, and with a certain well-felt hatred for the fact of my being a man, and although admiringly, which she never let me forget. But she did teach me openly and frankly about womanhood, and as the Feminist Julia Gerstman also did, of what it was like to be a woman, with specific instructions to me on where exactly that the Clitoris of a woman was located at in the Vagina, and which they thought of as being like a little penis, and how to stroke it, or lick it, or make love to it with your big male penis, to get her off to her quivering climax. And which was all that she lived for; that, and destroying her male partners, rivals.

And of what female instruction also included the ongoing detailed illuminating discussions about other matters psychological pertaining to a woman; of what it felt like to be in the body of a woman directly, and to look out onto the world from the eyes of a woman, and about how to regard and respect a woman from a woman's point of view. To always say, "Thank you," and be appreciative for the meals she cooks, and for the other chores around the domestic scene of doing housework, to

© Beth Hansen-www.wyrdhaven.com

Lilith

help with, and for cleaning up and doing the dishes afterwards of the meals, and for the shopping she does, to be appreciative about.

And although that I found myself in love with her, for her charming and ego reinforcing ways, to add, that she was always a little "Too Fast" for me, in that certain meaning of her sophisticate and refined use of Marijuana, and her container full of Pills of varying descriptions, uppers and downers, such as Valiums and whatnot, and the occasional Hard Drugs, Cocaine, and sometimes with Heroin mixed in, which Doreen called a Speedball.

To what in all that I was in truth totally ignorant of at the outset of in my relatively long relationship with her that lasted all of a year and a half, but which I was all to tragically to learn from her about first hand, being taken and held by her as her Drug Prisoner, which was her way of relating with me in a dominating way.

Doreen had lived at the time I met her on the eleventh floor of a high-rise apartment building on 208 West 23rd Street in New York City and taught English at a High School in Suffern, NY. She was of all time to that date, my favorite kind of woman. She was the daughter of Musician Lyle "Rusty" Dedrick, who who played the trumpet and composed music and who was at the time of our first meeting The Director of Jazz Studies at The Manhattan School of Music, very intelligent and in a sophisticated way of meaning quite well bred, independent very and cultured, a school teacher, an oil painter, a horse woman who owned her own jumping horse, a White Gelding, named Ashes, a great gourmet cook, and an outdoors tomboy kind of girl, who was brave and cautiously fearless, like me, with a lot of guts, who I could take out rock climbing in the Gunks with me, on dangerous climbs up on the big sheer cliffs together, and also who I would take spelunking down into dark and dangerous rock fishers on the backside of the mountain. And we grew together that way of adventure with a strong bond of trust between us that was meant for just the two of us.

She was all the things that I had always wanted in a woman, and I did cherish her for a time as my counterpart and companion,

to be with me; and not that all the rest of the women in my life
before then and to follow were not wonderful persons in their own
right to be with, but Doreen was a special talented and wonderful
girl to be with, a kindred spirit, who was particularly interested in
me and my career as a writer, and who helped me with my work,
and always full of charm and grace, and we did things together I
never thought about doing until I met her, traveling back and forth
to her apartment on the weekends in New York City, and taking
in the sights and the museums and concerts, and traveling
together, touring The United States and Mexico, and before she
decided to move in together with me in an apartment at Colonial
Arms in New Paltz, that began our formal relationship as a couple
that way. And which was in July of 1975 that we moved in
together, after moving all of her furniture out of her apartment in
New York and subletting it to her brother Jeffrey.

And it happened one late afternoon, on a Friday, that I met her
at the end of a long Spring Semester, in the days when college
didn't wind up until late in the month of May, that it was in the
latter part of the month of May in 1975 that I set eyes on her that
day while I was sitting in the second floor classroom of the Old
English Building listening to Professor Harry Stonebeck's
concluding lecture on Faulkner, and which Doreen that day had
been sitting in on. She had just driven up from Suffern, NY, as
she told me later on, from her teaching job, as it turned out, to see
Harry, who she had studied with previously and with whom that
she now had a personal tutorial relationship with. She was
however not one of his students then at the time and I had never
seen her before that day. She was however keenly interested in
Faulkner, and intent on and interested in, as well, with Professor
Harry Stonebeck himself, as I could observe from her eyes, that
she had a way of skewing up endearingly to study him
admiringly, who was in his mid-forties, tall and suavely
handsome with light brown hair falling just over his ears and
behind his neck to the collar of his shirt in the fashion of the
modern avant-garde professor, and with very warm and friendly
brown eyes that invited you into his world of thought, who also
played the guitar and sang, and in all a real popular fellow.

As it was late in the day, the afternoon setting sun had been coming in over the ridge line of the Shawangunk Mountains in the background as seen through the big second floor class room windows that were sectioned in three part across the far outside wall of the building, and was casting a shining beam on Doreen's wispy blond shoulder length hair who was sitting cross legged on the seat at the desk in the front corner of the room by the windows, studying Harry, dressed in dark blue slacks and an off-white knit pull-over blouse that highlighted the very attractive curves and figure of her breasts.

She was five foot four inches with a slender well-toned muscular build as the fashionable girls have as I could judge from the tone of her arms, shoulders, and trapezoid muscles, with a very cute piggish sort of nose and a smooth oval face with a few freckles around her nose and on her cheeks, that I found myself attracted to, and hard to take my eyes off of, and with being polite about in avoiding overly doing, not wanting to appear to be staring, but inexplicably returning to nonetheless, one of those unexplainable things of how love at first sight happens to people, smitten.

I don't know then what possessed me, as the class was winding down and in the final moments that I found myself drawn to somehow attract her attention to me, and to what purpose that I had wadded up a small bit of loose leaf paper, as I remember, aiming the trajectory, and arced it gracefully across the room at her from where I was seated at one of the desks by the door in the crowded classroom, and without disturbing Professor Stonebeck behind his back while he was busy making notes about the upcoming final exam at the blackboard, to land softly in her in her lap with it and to watch her lift her eyes to mine as it did.

She looked down at the small wad of paper in her lap again and then over across the room at me with her eyes, and our eyes met there for a brief interval of time, and she smiled at me before she turned away to focus in her intent way of skewing her eyes on Professor Stonebeck who was concluding his notes and turning back around to face the class. I had smiled in return, but not quickly enough, as I could tell, for her to see. I hadn't giving it another thought at the time and that was all there was to it then.

The class was over. The students were gathering up their papers and books preparing to leave, and she was preoccupied with waiting to see Harry. I left the building then without saying anything to her and without further acknowledgement not looking back, and not even thinking that I would ever see her again. But I did. And little did I know that it would change my life forever.

As it happened that particular night, on the last night of classes, that a group of us had planned to meet for an end of the semester socializing out with some friends down at a local bar named P&G's on the corner of Main and North Front Street in the Village, that I happened to arrive at an hour or so later in the evening to go into, and having gone home to my apartment at Colonial Arms a short distance from Town first to clean up and change my clothes.

To the left as you opened the door to P&G's was the long bar with its bar stools, and the room divided by a partition, and with a big room with tables for drinking on the other side of it. My heart thumped as I saw her again there as I looked around the bar and at the tables to see who was there. She was seated with some other people, another man, who she appeared to be sitting with, and two other girls and a guy at one of the big black stained bench tables with people's initials carved into it by the big picture window that looked out over the Main Street of The Village from the Bar. I had walked over to her right away to her table, kind of muscling my way emboldened in not wanting to pass on the opportunity to speak with her, and remembering her smile from before, asked her directly, since I was going up to the bar, if I could buy her a drink.

She seemed hesitant, and looked across the table at the other man who was a dark complexioned kind of fellow who looked to be Sicilian in origin with a heavy five o'clock shadow coming in, closely cropped black hair, close beady eyes, who looked to be in his early thirties, as I could tell, who instinctively I didn't like, and who I could feel from the vibe between her and him that she wasn't quite into being with.

"I could use a drink," she said to him, not to me, "do you mind?"

"Go with him," the man stated, not unpleasant sounding as if indifferently giving her the instruction to be with me and not him, but who otherwise could not disguise a miffed and huffy tone. He got up and left to go to the bar and stand around with some other men there on a pretext of interest to look up at the sports program on T.V. and keeping his back turned away from her the whole time. It should have been the tip-off, never to trust a girl who is sitting with another man who tells her who to go with, but it wasn't a tip-off to me then, as I was still quite naïve and full of myself, and as yet a babe-in-the-woods in those quarters.

"What do you want to drink?" I asked.

"Scotch and water will do me just good," she had replied. "It's been a long day."

I went to the bar and ordered a bottle of Budweiser Beer for myself, and the Scotch for her, not even knowing her name yet. When I returned with the drinks, I introduced myself.

"I'm Gary," I said. "I couldn't take my eyes off you in Professor Stonebeck's class.

"My name is Doreen," she replied with a warm smile. "The feeling's mutual."

And that was the beginning of it. When we finished our drinks I asked her if she wanted to come up to my place for a few drinks and she said, "Yes." She followed me home with her car a short time later and ended up spending the night. We partied all that night sleeping late into the morning together and partied all the next day on Saturday. On Sunday morning after fixing Western Omelets for us she left and drove back to the City, and the following weekend on Friday night she was back knocking at my door again.

It was a marriage that lasted for all of four months before Post Traumatic Stress in the from of a relentless and black suicidal depression, a God aweful weariness and revulsion with the human side of life that set in in earnest upon me, remorse of combat, guilt, and sorrow for the world and its humanity that could

engender the horror of relentless wars, combined with latent
combat fatigue in the need for prolonged periods of sleep to rest,
and a desire to be on the mountain with God and a part of the
Earth in another way in ways other than what civilization had to
describe for me to do, that put a wall up between us, myself and
Doreen, that left me off the deep end, and with Doreen suffering a
tragic relapse of her earlier drug addictions as a result,
succumbing to her previous heroin and concaine drug habits and
related porno troubles, that had left her suicidal of her own to deal
with, to run off with a Heroin Supplier Jon Ross, who lived out in
Rifton, NY, overlooking the horse farm there, and who, as to say
Jon, that I had seen red handed one day with the kingpin of the
porno mafia who owned The Highland Art Cinema, in Highland,
NY; who Jon said he was picking apples with, and didn't know I
knew the Porno Boss from another source and having been told
who that man was.

Jon had been mine and Michael Migliori's rock climbing
buddy and guide on the big cliffs in the Shawangunks, and who
was also my school chum from a graduate course at the
University what we had been taking together, as to how we had
met, (and independent of his being a Herion addict and drug
supplier, specializing in exotics, as to how, and at the age of
thirty-one then, in 1976, that he made his primary living,) and as
far as friendship goes, and not too far, which he abandoned me for
to take up with and to be with my drug addicted wife Doreen.
And why I ever wound up with and married her I will never
know. Which I do know, but it still begs the question.

And that somehow in that time frame that I had ended up being
doused with every conceivable drug known to man by unknown
assailants in conspiracy and left to crash and burn, while Doreen
mocked and bragged about it, telling me to be ware of, "The
Double Bind," where people smile at you and pretend to be your
friend, while all the while scheming to do you in, that is also calle
a Paranoid Paradox, just because you suspect that people are out
to poison you, doesn't necessarily mean that they aren't.

Which was done by dousing you each day with Cocaine and
Heroin, Quaaludes, and LSD, and Gaslighing you into a neurotic

depression, to make me think I was going crazy, before they ran off together to snort their Heroin Powder and make porno movies, and to the idea of "Offing Me," in the way of Women's and Gay Men's Porno War Version, (which is the torture of The Double Bind, that being to make your suppers and tend to your clothes while they smile in your face and administer the poison to your lips to watch you suffer in a sad sickness of drug sabotage;) that was the The Feminist Drug Warfare Version of sabotaging the wine glass and the dinner plates of their male counterparts, in having the ultimate power over them to destroy them, like the female Preying Mantis who devours her lover's head after he makes love to her.

And who, the two of them, my friend Jon and my wife Doreen, abandoned me for near dead, crashing out from the drugs, weeping hysterically in the midst of a nervous breakdown in September of that year of 1976, "Blown Away," as the saying goes, that took me nearly six months of being nursed back to health by my mother and father, as I had to repair home to recover from. And although that it wasn't Jon but Doreen's Black Drug Supplier who did the poisoning job, which Doreen did the same thing to Jon about as he confided to me later, that Doreen ditched Jon, and left him for dead like she had done to me, and left him for "another White man" who like the rest was at the fate of the mulatto drug supplier to Doreen all along, as I found out, whose name was Roy Green, now dead.

And that left poor Jon abandoned, though unlike me who was naïve, back then, as to what exactly had happened to me, that Jon and being experienced in those wasy and wisely knew how to antidote the effects of the Herion and Cocaine and LSD and other Drugs that I had also been hit with, and as a "babe in the woods" as I was then, concerning the wiles of the deadly drug warfare going on of the White females and to the psychiatric effects of the idea of Drug Warfare, that was called, "Craft," and in, "Witch Craft," which I became very quickly educated and experienced expert with, self-educated about, in the year before Jenny and I had become involved.

For what knowledge in all, about the drugs, and about the effects of the drugs, that I was always ever after grateful to Doreen over for providing me with, that most people never know about.

But she was, and still is too, a love in my life, to care for. That I did, and who I still do, care for. In time we'll see how it all turns out. She was after all intimate with me, and needed me for her longing of emotion, of a need in her, that I took care of, once.

Jenny and I had been thrust together by fate in my being taken in by Tony to live in his home and to help take care of his family, as a family member to fill the voit after his wife's Mary's suicide, or so it was labelled, and who provided me with a place to sleep in the Writer's Garret up above the garage, (that I shared with my friend Lloyd Barzell, who was homeles waif of the streets himself, who was a friends of mine also who I was fond of and took care of emotionally and who I had had to opportunity to make work for on Tony's estate to provide him with room and board to help me with the renovation project, and the grounds, and to do some landscape property renovation for him for the long hot summer. Together we put in an excellent Vegetable Garden for Tony that won him first place in the Huguenot Historical District Street Society Garden Contest for that year of 1977.

And in a manner of being thrust at me by Tony's circumstances himself, to say that he found himself to be overwhelmed with the chores and the responsibilities of managing a family, and needed me for companionship and as a nanny to take care of and to look after his two children, Jenny and Henry, who were seventeen and fourteen at the time. Who I had became a mother figure to in moving into Tony's house with him that summer, after the tragic death, of Tony's wife Mary.

Mary, who was a Psychologist and had become involved with a Jewish Psychiatrist by the name of Ernie Shaw who worked as an avante guard welding scultor and who had a house out in the woods in the foothills of The Shawangunks below the Gunks cliff line, and who had become involved with Mary somehow and according to Jenny, with Jenny too in that relationshp; that for some unknown reason that way and during that time, (and while Tony had moved out of his home to take an apartment on Main Street in the Village during their period of estrangement,) that Mary Robinson, and the mother of Jenny and Henry, had killed herself as it was stated by shooting herself in the heart with Tony's shotgun, and a profound tragedy in all of their lives to occur, for it was Henry who found the body. And who, Mary, had died a year and a half earlier in February of 1976, before I came to live there and who I replaced in a way of companionship to meals and other family driving chores of transportation to functions and to school and other activities to attend to during my stay with Tony and his family beginning in the Summer of 1977 that lasted intimately on and off and for nearly two years, and as I had other things to do as well; in which during this time that I had many excursions and field trips and sports activities with young Henry.

Henry was a fine young man. We traveled at one time all the down the Eastern Seaboard together in Tony's car on a sighseeing adventure trip, together with my dog Sophie, all the way to Virginia Beach and back on a Discover America Excursion, and we took another trip together to The Hamptons on Long Island, NY, to meet with Tony and Jenny who had gone ahead to stay with relatives at a rented beach house there.

I had taken an interest in Tony's daughter Jenny to heart in my sympathy for her over her tragic sorrow for her lost mother, who had become mopey and lethargic, and over what that she bonded with me and became attached and emotionally dependent with me in Transference, in the meaning that I began to validate her existence in a positive way and away from the desperation of her outward expression of despondent depression that hung over her in a pall of melancholy over her sorrow for the death of her mother. And with Henry too, who felt a tragic sorrow also, in bonding with me, both of whom who were in mourning.

I took both Henry and Jenny along with me and always together with my faithful red Irish Setter "Sophie" and spent large amounts of time with each of them each week, separately, or together, on my Outward Bound Wilderness Program where I

worked on the Mountain with The Phillips Family on
Minnewaska Land, and where I always had free access and use of
the vast land there along on the trails on many excursions hikiing,
taking in the magnificent scenery, and rock climbing in the
Shawangunks, in the manner of the Native Indian Trails with the
Wind in The Tall Pines and the trees and rocks for companions.

All of what that Jenny loved especically and that was a special
and consecrated hallowed time for Jenny, and for myself to be
with her, in the spell of the rocks of the magnificent mountain air
was all that Jenny needed to revive her, and in being alone
together there on the mountain, which we claimed for our own
territory there and with the felt presence in the wind and in the
play of the clouds on the distant Catskill Mountains, of The
Algonquin Indian God named, The Manitou, "The Giver Of
Gifts," Who was always with us out along on our walks, and who
married us in the leave there in the late Summer, and then it was
on into the Autum and the Fall, and into the Winter of 1977, and
on into the following Spring and Summer, as our love for one
another grew hiking along the trails to Awosting Falls, and to
Lake Awosting itself, and to even swim across together one day,
and back, with my dog Sophie swimming along too, on
Minnewaska Land, were I worked as a Park Ranger on patrol and
the "Ticket Taker," and on many occasions especially to visit a
place called Low Falls, that cascaded down the mountainside of
The Peterskill Creek, as it was named, that was a famous secluded
Nudie Swimming Hole, clothing optional, below the
Campgrounds and the bottom of the abandoned Ski Runs on the
Minnewaska Private Park in the Shawangunk Mountains with a
lovely cascading water fall where Jenny loved to sunbathe and to
swim in the icey cold mountain water of in the hot afternoons of
the summer days. And in all regards that Jenny was Biblical Eve
reincanate to me that The Creartor had provided to my lonliness.

Such therapy did magical wonders for Jenny, as she had
become happy and vivacious again, and it was good for young
Henry too.

Which went on for a time of a good long while that I took care
of Jenny in a very special and serious way of intimate bonding
with her.

That Tony himself had put me up to, in a manner of speaking,
broaching the subject to me one evening in the mid-Summer-time
just as it was getting to be dusk, and just before supper was being
served, as we were working on the dinner together each to our
separate tasks, while I was putting out the plates, silverware,
napkins and setting the table and he was finishing up with the
supper of pot roast, mashed potatoes, string beans, and gravey,
that Tony paused to stop what he was doing and say to my face
very seriously:

"I think Jenny is in love with you, Gary," Tony had said,
"You could be her teacher. I think she's a bit Jaded, as I told you,
and I'm afraid that she's going to prove to be too much for the
both of us."

And that's the way that Tony had put it too me, to what
comment that I did not reply.

But, who was I but a mere man weak in the knees already with
Jenny's demure and captivating charms to turn away the offering
of such a proposal of eager and aggressive young love, and much
as I did my best to deny my feelings. But I was with her all the
time, morning, noon, and night, with Tony and I having drinks,
and all of us watching T.V. together, or playing games like
Monopoly, and Scrabble, or just sitting out on the back deck with
Tony talking about philosophy and other things. Jenny was
always there always around.

And we were always being put together by Tony in that way of
playing Match Maker for the past month since I had arrived at his
home. to be asked to help with the household chores of having to
take Jenny once a week with the car to go food shopping for the
week at Shop Rite on Friday nights each week, or to take Jenny
here and there to where she had to go.

And I needed to be with Henry too, who was a very bright lad
with a high I.Q. and good conversational skills, and who was very
personable to be around, who I enjoyed being with too very much
especially. We played golf and baseball catch regularly together,

and took walks down the road past the old stone houses into Town, and who was included in being taken places and looked after and cared for each day by me.

But as it happened I knew I had fallen for Jenny, in the same way as Tony loved her. I knew it too, as I felt it in my heart, in a fierce devotion of possession to the idea of being loved by her.

But ever in our hearts and minds with Jenny and with myself especially as I knew that our relationship was always predicated to the unexpressed arrangement on the certain terms of the knowing of our needing to part our ways eventually at Summer's end; which turned into next year, and on into the next, with Tony, after a lengthy period of denial with the arrangement of the affair, and not wanting us to be married, not being happy any longer with the agreement. And who in turn was torn up in his own heart about it too, over the propect of our breaking-up, who finally initiated the break-up one day. And I myself knowing it wasn't going to work out either with Jenny and had to be broken off.

Tony eventually took up a strong hand and forced Jenny, under threat of losing him, and who Jenny was by that time deeply enamoured with me, and for me too with her, enamoured, to have go our separate ways, "for the good of Gary and yourself," Tony had told her. That one day we just broke it off about and never looked back.

It was very hard on us to accept that judgment, but that it was always expected and I respected Tony for the noble truth of the exercise of his keen discernment of decision in the matter in knowing when to break it off with Jenny, that Jenny had to go away to college and to be a young girl like the other girls, and not be a married lady to such a worldly man as me at such a young age, and to a much older man, who would grow too old ahead of her before her time. And as I knew it too, that I always kept my word with Tony about it to respect his decision, always!!

"Perhaps in our old age we will see each other one more time, and hold each other for a long time in each other's arms once more before we die," I had said to her.

To what her reply to me was,

"I hope we can," Jenny had said, "I'd like that very much."

To what that I always intended for her to keep her promise to.

And so Jenny went off to college and then went off to join the Navy, and I went off my ways of whatever it was that I was doing, and I never saw much of her again after that, or if there was a time or two in the earlier stages of the painful parting in separation that we chanced to come upon one other at the college, or on the street in passing, as lovers abandoned in the storm of their lives, as lovers, do in torn emotions on chancing to behold each other, but only then of a few brief moments snatched from time, to say our breathless and fertive "hi's" to one another with with somewhat averted eyes, not wanting to dwell too long on the forbidden delight of looking at one's love.

And of these things that way that I had wanted to tell him at our parting then twenty years ago, and perhaps to say that I was sorry about what happened, as things never did work out and really sit well with us since then over the matter, that was over, but not really, that I would never say anything about at all of the sentiments that I had, there on our last meeting together on the Highway to Rosendale, NY then.

But as I walked away, in my heart I knew I knew it wasn't over, that there would always be the memory of Jenny, and of Tony, and Henry, and Tony's Springer Spaniel dog Waldo. And I suppose in hoping that their memories of me as well were fondly regarded.

I had waited there in New Paltz and on The Mountain, and hung around there waiting for Jenny to return to me long enough, if that was my reason for being there so long. It was never really over with Jenny in my own heart, really over. And perhaps it was with her heart really over, and maybe she never really loved me at all in the way I loved her, which hit me hard in the heart, because I had to let her go, but my own heart was still there hanging on with her, something of the spirit kind of love that souls feel for one another, like God's Love, that doesn't need to be physically together to feel the warm of its sentiment of being thought of and cared for.

School and my Graduate Studies were definitely over, having run their course in enthusiasm for prolonged studies. My father had died of a brain tumor the year before in October of 1988, and my own dog Sophie had just died, after thirteen years with me of being my companion, that year in June of 1989 out on the farm where I had been keeping her at my friend Michael Migliori's home, where Doreen and I used to live on McKinstry Road in Gardiner, NY.

And who about Doreen, before I married her, had gone with me in the late of October, 1975, to Bayonne, NJ, while I was Sworn In to The Drug Enforcement Agency's mission, after passing my Federal Civil Service Exam in September of 1975 on Military Preference, and the year that we surrendered Vietnam to the Communists, (and with The United States, being lost to a similar Communist Drug Insurgency labeled Fascism.) All returned Vietnam Veterans who passed the Federal Civil Service Exam were giving Special Operations Preference Credentials as Military Advisors with The D.E.A..

I was getting old and tired out with my Secret Service Black-Ops Mole Operation of Low Level Undercover Work that had involved me in the madness of the Drug War that I was wholly unprepared to deal with, involved on The Secret Mission to resolve the Drug War and to bring the Civil Rights Race War to its knees, and that also involving other Ethnic Denomination Wars of their kind related to Fascism and Zionism, that for me had run its course. And as far as I was concerned of having to cover it on the street, that was becoming for me, dramatically too dangerous and too close for comfort, and that had left me with many uncomfortable and unresolvable compomises with the law, which had induced in me a kind of split personality type of a growing fultility of self-worth and kindling up a dark depression in questioning the reasons for my being out there in the field, that I was so proud of and that was so prized to master at the start of the ability to live-out on the street, and only to be left abandoned there on the lonely and forlorn streets of New Paltz, NY, ship wrecked and maroon there, all those years gone by in the first place.

And they were lonely and forlorn streets in the late of nights and in the desperate times of morning when no of any company

one was around, and with no place to call home to be able to
return to and to be a part of and with people scurring away as you
approached not wanting to be hit-on for money. Begging
weakens ones spirits.

And such that I was the scheduling to depart the area for
Buffalo , NY, about and regarding in a few weeks time to be able
then to begin to write-up and to file with the appropriate
authorities my professional reports about the Drug War and Race
War Matters. And as I was then yearning to do, in my attempt to
save America from the unseen perils of the clandestine warfare
going on, that had left the average American Citizen in the naïve
peril of being attacked with drugs and chemicals, and being
subverted on other levels economic and political, with having No
Defense to their own lives and the lives of the dear loved one to
protect, that required my presnese on and to the upper level
Military Supervisors, and with The D.E.A., and to The New York
State Police, to whom I reported to in Buffalo, NY, for direct
involvement of intervention; which was provided.

And, as Kathleen had gone ahead of me to secure a place for
us, and herself with being mollested by a negro pimp on The
White Slavery Whore Line, named Alexis Jason Fredericks the
III, who I had turned into the F.B.I., and who somehow had
locked into Kathy to try and intimidate and coerce her, and who I
had beaten to a pulp for in the middle of Main Street in front of
P&G.s Bar, as that story went, who she needed to be far away
from, to establish our residency there in Buffalo, and to where
that I also was destined to follow to begin my long involvement
of formal Military Duty and to do press relations work there for
our then New York State Federal Senators Moynihan and
D'Amato, and Congressman Jack Quinn, and other legislators of
running a Propaganda Mill reporting the actual facts about what
was the going on and the truth about the Drug War and Racial and
Ethnic War news with the Editor of The Buffalo News there,
Murry Light.

Where I was going to go and attempt to live a normal and
happy life with my eventual true love and now cherished wife and
faithful companion, then fiance, Kathleen Mabee, (as was all well

planned out in advance by the Hand Of God, and ultimately not to
be, at least not right then.)

I had smelled the Black Man on her sheets one time. You
don't mistake an odor like that. The next day, returning at an
unexpected time, I had them cornered. But when I put my key in
the lock and open the door, it opened to the latch with a thud.

"Go away," Kathy had said in a panick stricken tone. "I don't
want to see you right now. Just go away."

But I knew the reaon she wouldn't let me in and called out ot
her, "I'm not going away." And with that I position myself across
the hallway from her apartment in the launtry roon and laid seige
to the moor inside. Kathy called the police.

When a solitary policeman arrived, he looked me over,
scrutinized the situation and knocked on the door to Kathleen's
apartment. To what inquiry she opened the door partially to
speak with him. He spoke with her a moment and then turned to
me and told me to leave quitely and not to make any trouble. He
knew what the story was. And so did I. It was going to come to
blood shed and I knew it too.

"Let's spare the poor girl a heart ache and leave things as they
are," he said. "Some things you just need to let go. It won't be
worth the trouble."

He offered me a ride out of there, and I accepted, telling him
the story of White Slavery.

"What you need to understand, is, that we need our wives and
sweethearts. We need them for the women they are and we need
them for the things that they do for us like keeping house and
cooking our meals and going for the groceries. You claim that the
black devils have the right under your terms of law to get
involvement with our White Women for however reasons that
they do, but you know the score, by hooking them on Cocaine and
Heroin and other drugs, and who can then coerse our women to
murder us off and make us mentally ill with drug warfare and
poinsons. While you all stand around and watch it go down. And
you know too that our women get involved with pornography and
a worse scenario equally as deadly. Take our side," I said.

"I'll see what we can do with this one," the policeman replied.

Main Street Rosendale, NY
Paul's Apartment is on the second floor
third building from the right

Town Hall and Police Station
directly across from Paul's Apartment
on Main Street in Rosendale, NY

<u>HUNGER MAGAZINE</u>

FOXHOLES

RICHARD RIZZI

I FOXHOLES (the last dancer to get it)

around the edge of mirrors
(mirror thought to be time space)
and self becomes the text
I am planting the remains of Rizzi
it is a perfect mistake
no weather in literature
my politics as a criminal in hiding; I saw nothing
but from the viewpoint of a lunatic
I saw everything before it happened
we all have a target
to steal the minds of the 21st century

the great dog left in the gutter bleeding knowledge
into the sewer and the faithful artist
running down the streets
screaming Oh my body is sold too cheap,
my vision was mistaken for the head of the Messiah
(no name can be mentioned until twilight)

II   FOXHOLES (the last dreamer to get it)

if a war began in your soup, say on a dull Sunday
and the whole world refused to believe that your end
could make a difference to a system
that chews generations of people
and the problems of love are only small matters
when things are done for, let's say,
a revolution without cause.
I salute and then destroy
bring me all your naked money fast for a better world
of course we could even make believe
that there is still ways in and out of windows
for jumping away from the struggle of existence
in a new suit and a new hat and a new life

III FOXHOLES (the last talker in the nude to get it)

my lover turns the night into her cries
I die in the idea of blood
wash my naked face away from the dust
your voice haunts the sick mind of your danger
I am wounded and lost in some building
I smell from your music, sung low and long,
and when it ends the beautiful bystander will buy
our remains to eat as a cake before the day is over

****

For Immediate Release

Volume II, Number 6

June 1, 2002

Richard Rizzi

three poems

Cheap Hotel Rooms

danger at the border of her cunt
I was occupied with the knowledge in her eyes
the corner of my mouth erased the jungle in the window
I located the atmosphere to climb out my body
I found a photo of everyone who ever lived
multiplying the weather and the color of her lipstick
I could escape what's in my mind
the shade of her love made me illegal
I crossed the light unnoticed
my eyelids got heavy like a revolving door in a bad dream
I began to suspect my heart was wanted for firing ballistic
missiles

I was picking up momentum from the ghost eating the town
she told something about dark cherries
and her breath cut me angles to another world
she agreed that falling into the sea with a disguise would create an
absence
every time I looked up at the sky she let me touch her
echoes of words moving away
the perfect torn curtain stained with blood

Peninsula To Her Mouth

I entered the jewel surrounded with skulls
then came night that lasted four hundred wars
sitting at the next table turning green her bones were talking loud
she burnt down Florence
wrapped herself with fishes
she requested my eyes to sample some blood
the only obstacle was an insect on my tongue that spoke Latin
we looked at the menu to locate the dead
the future was wrong
leaving the room in a cloud
I sent for my country but the moon made an error
I stood watch as winter ate my words
terrible born flower rope the sea under my hair
my face is gone yellow
resistance to dust
I touched her breasts to remain in my body
alabaster stairs and a bushel of peaches
Napoleon fell out of my pocket
the wooden chair was empty in the mind
the demon gave orders
and everybody wept in Tangiers
nothing can stop the dark petals
and there is Mozart pissing in the fountain
the crystal laughter live as wind
suicide the day
trace the broken city then pretend

10-11-01

The Blind Hero Laughs Goodbye

the stone snow without question gave the enemy wings
someone we know will open their wounds to the sun
the luxury of death is forgiven
it bleeds the cruel song to get born again
the small mountain is sinking in my teeth
anything in my eyes could be eaten
suffocate your condition with guns brutal blazing
I want you to listen to the filthy cruel altar
my shadow leaves in the gutter
my judgment of summer
flat empty tongues milk the dark darker
dirty jewels
the journey to my breast rubbed the earthquake clean
the torture drips gold into my heart
and down in the eyelids of fish
my bones unbutton the mouth of god
you got to flower the victory with skin
your arms suddenly are ancient warriors
the image of the parrot talks back
and starts a war in the mirror
falls asleep in your womb
loves the pain of defeat
bad world under the fingernail
weep the ugly bird to crime

THE LOTUS EATERS

Alfred, Lord Tennyson
(1809-1892)

"Courage!" he said, and pointed toward the land,
"This mounting wave will roll us shoreward soon."
In the afternoon they came unto a land
In which it seemed always afternoon.
All round the coast the languid air did swoon,
Breathing like one that hath a weary dream.
Full-faced above the valley stood the moon;
And like a downward smoke, the slender stream
Along the cliff to fall and pause and fall did seem.

A land of streams! some, like a downward smoke,
Slow-dropping veils of thinnest lawn, did go;
And some thro' wavering lights and shadows broke,
Rolling a slumbrous sheet of foam below.
They saw the gleaming river seaward flow
From the inner land: far off, three mountain-tops,
Three silent pinnacles of aged snow,
Stood sunset-flush'd: and, dew'd with showery drops,
Up-clomb the shadowy pine above the woven copse.

The charmed sunset linger'd low adown
In the red West: thro' mountain clefts the dale
Was seen far inland, and the yellow down
Border'd with palm, and many a winding vale
And meadow, set with slender galingale;
A land where all things always seem'd the same!
And round about the keel with faces pale,
Dark faces pale against that rosy flame,
The mild-eyed melancholy Lotos-eaters came.

Branches they bore of that enchanted stem,
Laden with flower and fruit, whereof they gave
To each, but whoso did receive of them,
And taste, to him the gushing of the wave
Far far away did seem to mourn and rave
On alien shores; and if his fellow spake,
His voice was thin, as voices from the grave;
And deep-asleep he seem'd, yet all awake,
And music in his ears his beating heart did make.

They sat them down upon the yellow sand,
Between the sun and moon upon the shore;
And sweet it was to dream of Fatherland,
Of child, and wife, and slave; but evermore
Most weary seem'd the sea, weary the oar,
Weary the wandering fields of barren foam.
Then some one said, "We will return no more";
And all at once they sang, "Our island home
Is far beyond the wave; we will no longer roam."

Odysseus tells his mariners to have courage, assuring them that they will soon reach the shore of their home. In the afternoon, they reach a land "in which it seemed always afternoon" because of the languid and peaceful atmosphere. The mariners sight this "land of streams" with its gleaming river flowing to the sea, its three snow-capped mountaintops, and its shadowy pine growing in the vale.

Metaphysics is a branch of <u>philosophy</u> concerned with explaining the fundamental nature of <u>being</u> and the <u>world</u>, although the term is not easily defined. Traditionally, metaphysics attempts to answer two basic questions in the broadest possible terms: "What *is there*?" "What is it ... *like*?"

A person who studies metaphysics would be called either a *metaphysicist* or a *metaphysician*. The metaphysician attempts to clarify the fundamental notions by which people understand the world, including existence, the definition of object, property, space, time, causality, and possibility. A central branch of metaphysics is ontology, the investigation into the basic categories of being and how they relate to each other.

Prior to the modern history of science, scientific questions were addressed as a part of metaphysics known as natural philosophy. The term *science* itself meant "knowledge" of, originating from epistemology. The scientific method, however, transformed natural philosophy into an empirical activity deriving from experiment unlike the rest of philosophy. By the end of the 18th century, it had begun to be called "science" to distinguish it from philosophy. Thereafter, metaphysics denoted philosophical enquiry of a non-empirical character into the nature of existence

****

And now it was twenty years later and I was missing my old friend and former English Professor Creative Writing Teacher, Anthony Robinson, a great deal, who was called Tony by his students, and which was the best class I ever had as a class and together with a fine group of other eager and attentive students who we all bonded with closely together, as a kind of therapy group, and with Tony as our mentor and fellowship guide, who was a great psycologist writer himself, to become very close knit with as a group.

I had been missing my dear friend for a long time, when one day out of the blue that thought occurred to me to look him up on the internet to see if, being an established author, that he had a web site, and to my great glee he did, and that I had been wanting to read his books for a long time which I was delighted to find there also.

I knew that we were like Vincent Van Gough and Paul Gaugain in that era long ago when I lived in the Writer's Garrett at Tony's home, in the loneliness that writers feel in the longing for their own kind to be with and relate to, and lo and behold,

there he was to my great joy in delight. "Eureka!" I exclaimed
out load as the web site emerged.

And that was the beginning of it, the psychogogial drama of
the merging of our souls as I had longed for. I read there eagerly
and with deep nostaligia, Tony's biography from the internet as
he had chosen the cautious words of it to be revealed.

Anthony Robinson
A Brief Biography
http://www.tadrichards.com/arobinson/bio.html

Anthony Robinson, the youngest of Gertrude and Henry
Morton Robinson's three children, grew up on Maverick Road in

Woodstock, New York. The Robinsons' neighbors were the painters, sculptors, and musicians who lived and worked in the Maverick Art Colony. Young Tony Robinson wandered freely in the Colony in the years prior to World War II, making many friends, among them the man who founded the Colony in 1905, Hervey White.

Tony caddied at the Woodstock Golf Course and fished in the nearby Ashokan Reservoir, hunted and trapped in the fall and winter. At twelve he had his own trapline, checking his sets each morning before school, dreaming that one of his muskrat pelts would take first prize in the annual Sears & Roebuck Best Pelt Competition. His career ambition, in that period of his life, was to be a forest ranger.

His father, in no way critical of his son's activities or dreams, nonetheless thought that Tony would benefit by going away to school. Henry Morton Robinson (who would gain fame with his 1950 best-selling novel The Cardinal and A Skeleton Key to Finnegan's Wake with Joseph Campbell) enrolled his son at Phillips Academy, Andover, wanting him to have a top education and get to meet boys outside of rural Ulster County.

For the most part, Tony's four years at Andover weren't happy ones.. The school was too big, too removed from the life he had known, and he felt lost from the start. He kept his unhappiness to himself and began to write. A story about his beagle killed by a car, "My Finnegan," appeared in Hounds and Hunting in 1949. It was his first published work.

His college years were more rewarding. Several of Tony's professors at Columbia, notably Mark Van Doren and George Nobbe, influenced him greatly, encouraging him to pursue a career in writing. Tony joined Alpha Delta Phi, founded as a literary society in 1832, and on weekly "lit night" at the fraternity often read his stories to the assembled brothers. One story, "A String of Pearls," won first prize in the 1952 Alpha Delta Phi national literary competition.

Military service was compulsory at the time, and after graduating from Columbia in 1953 Tony earned his commission at OCS in Newport, R.I., serving on the USS Owen, a WWII

destroyer, in the final days of the Korean War. A story he wrote
aboard ship, "The Farlow Express," was published in Prairie
Schooner and was later included in Best American Short Stories
of 1957.

After the service, Robinson returned to his home on Maverick
Road and began his first novel, A Departure From the Rules. It
saddened him that the Art Colony, which he had so loved as a
boy, no longer existed; the artists' houses and cabins were empty,
falling into ruin. Only the summer concerts, in the Maverick
Concert Hall, had survived. In 1957 Robinson married Mary
Chika in New York City and entered graduate school. The couple
took an apartment in the Chelsea area of Manhattan, where Mary
worked as an executive secretary while Robinson attended classes
at Columbia and finished his novel. A Departure From the Rules
came out in 1960 and the couple left New York and moved into
the smaller of the two houses on the family property on Maverick
Road. A daughter, Jennifer, came along in 1960 and then a son,
Henry, two years later. In 1963 Robinson's second novel, The
Easy Way, was published. It seemed like a dream to him that he
was supporting his family on his writing.

The dream ended when his next novel, Forty Thousand
Brothers, about a major strike that crippled New York City, was
turned down. Taking his master's degree in American Literature
and two novels to SUNY New Paltz, twenty-five miles from the
Maverick, he applied for a job and was taken on as an instructor
of English in 1964. Robinson took the job seriously, loved
teaching, but refused to let teaching stand in the way of writing.
In 1969 a third novel, Home Again, Home Again, was published.
The following year, as an associate professor, he went with his
family to Paris in an exchange program and taught literature and
writing at the University of Paris at Vincennes. Back home in the
spring of '71, the Robinsons, largely at the urging of Mary, left
the Maverick and moved into a historic house on Huguenot Street
in New Paltz. It was a breaking away from the old, a new start.
Tragically, Mary died in 1976.

Two further novels came out while Anthony Robinson was on
the New Paltz faculty, The Whole Truth in 1990 and The

Member-Guest in 1991. He then began the novel that was burning inside of him, a story based on Mary's death called The Professor's Wife, but it wouldn't surrender to the writer's hand, and after ten years and several versions he set it aside.

In 1998, Tony married Tatiana Padwa of Woodstock, a childhood friend and an accomplished artist. They live in New Paltz, play golf at the local course, write and paint respectively, and occasionally visit with their children and grandchildren in Woodstock, Summerville, S.C., and the Coast.

Anthony Robinson plans a work about growing up in the Maverick Art Colony. When asked if it would be a memoir, he said no. He was a novelist.

****

I saw the books he had written listed there in the order of his having written them. They were; A Departure From The Rules, The Easy Way, Home Again, Home Again, The Whole Truth, and The Member Guest, as they were listed there.

The order form stated, allow five to ten days for delivery. And so I order, "Home Again, Home Again," that I had started to read at one time, but had lost the book someone, (and which I had borrowed to read from an English Profession colleague Jack Crawford, from his Office shelf, never to return,) and to what I had been longing to read, and began checking on faithfully since the fifth day following the order for its arrival.

As I checked on the mail on Friday, a full week after I had sent in my order, I stopping by the Office area of our Apartment Complex where the mailboxes for the all the apartments were located, and lined up along two opposing walls of an airy roofed over outdoor corridor, at around 3:30 p.m. after work, to find that Tony's book had arrived. I hefted the weight of it fondly as I took it out of the mailbox.

I was delighted to find at long last that the long awaited book, entitled, Home Again, Home Again, written by my dear friend and admired College Creative Writing Teacher Anthony Robinson had finally arrived in my mail box UPS Media Mail, that I had ordered and had shipped over the internet from a book dealer, Abebooks, Bank of Books, in Ventura, California.

When I got home, I went anxiously into my Study, with its two book cases full of the trophies of books read, spare room twin bed, a large trunk for storage, two chests of maple wood dresser drawers, and where four Oil Painting painted by my wife Kathy's mother Jean hung on the wall as impressive contemplative works of art, and where my writing desk and computer and copier were, and representing my inner mind bastion of professionalism, to carefully open up the package to see the book.

And I admired it instantly for its significance of importance to me, holding it up to the light to look it over, and with its dust cover, still in good condition as advertised, and for the handsome photograph of my dear friend Tony on the back, who was in his early years and extremely good looking man, that I looked at fondly and wincing with nostalgia from the memories of many wonderful occasions spent with him during the intimate days of our being a family together, and before the turmoil over Jenny had torn us apart, that had taken place in the past.

And of which photograph of him that was taken on a particular day, some time a long time ago in time as life goes, of Tony leaning on the door-frame of rustic looking writer's dwelling with his right wrist raised above his head. That I could tell from intuition was his family home in Woodstock, NY, and although that only the door-frame and the upper portion of Tony's handsome face and rugged body was visible in the photograph dressed in a heavy blue denim fall type over shirt and looking introspectively off into the distance, his eyes fixed at some dream, or vision, of his creativity in progress, that I could tell was his home in the often talked about and referred to Maverick Art Colony where he had lived as a child, and in his later early years as a writer.

It was a truly great moment to have captured on film I thought as I carefully opened the work and began to examine the monumental effort of literature before me, that had come to me, and which I had been longing to have a copy of ever since I had lost, or that had been misplaced in the shuffle of chaotic moves at the time of my school years and never to be found, although looked for, the one I originally had, that was on loan to me from Professor Jack Crawford with whom I had been sharing an office with during my Teaching Assistantship at the SUNY New Paltz University that one Spring Semester in 1976, and from whom I had borrowed to look at. And since then, one thing or another had led me to this date, but always vowing to one day finally read it, the great book, which had now arrived.

And there it was in my hands at last, "Home Again, Home Again," a novel by Anthony Robinson. On the dust cover was pasted on a sticker that read, Oxnard Public Library, Oxnard, CA and a bar code and some numbers. I opened the book and saw that the dust cover was taped on with scotch tape, and on the red inner page of the hard back was stamped, Oxnard Public Library. I turned the page and on the other side of the red page was pasted the write up for the book… "When a large electronics firm wants to buy the land of an old art colony" … And on the next page, the title of the book, Home Again, Home Again, and on the reverse side were a list of other novels written by Anthony Robinson, at that time in history to date, which was the publishing year of 1969, and to which that, Home Again, Home Again, was the third in success of two other novels that Tony had written up to that time in his life, "A Departure from the Rules," and "The Easy Way." And on the next page were two more stamps of the Oxnard Public Library, one stating, Discarded By Oxnard Public Library, 251 South A Street, Oxnard, California 93030, and the name of the publisher, William Morrow and Company, Inc., New York, 1969. And the Inscription, for Leonard Wallace Robinson, and the quotation from Hamlet: "He was a man, take him for all in all, I shall not look upon his like again."

That I mention in all and in wondering who Leonard Wallace Robinson was to you, in such detail of interest, only because it is the history of a book, not of any book off the shelf, but Tony's book, his third novel, a novel that "he" wrote as a man on the earth in time.

And following that, the initial feeling of the book and look
over, I put the book aside, not reading anything of it because I
didn't want to spoil the moment of my first in depth encounter
with it in a too hurried way of a look, and as my wife was
working her evening shift as a nurse at a local hospital on that
day, I took a shower, put on my pajamas, and went into the
bedroom to take my nap, I settled into bed, with a blanket cover
over me, like I did every day after work for two hours until 6:00
p.m. or so, as my work, that of being the Greenskeeper at a local
Golf Country Club, started each day, at 6:00: and with alternating
every other weekend to have to wake up to, that I found that a
good two hour nap after work set me up just right for a lingering
evening with my wife until around 10:30 or so, and otherwise to
what that I would be falling off to sleep.

And as I drifted off to sleep, counting my Zen Breaths to ten,
as I always do for the peace and relaxation of the inner tranquility
of mind in it, and thinking of the surrounding air as I did,
breathing it in and out in the counting of breaths, and thinking of
The Creator also, as I always do, and as the companion to me that
He became; that I eventually fell off to sleep to be pressed upon
with a strange clairvoyance, that was like a vision to be able to
gaze into with my mind's eye, of the book in its home amid the
thousands and racks of books, that had to do with the dark wood
brown colors of the desks and wooden book frames of book's
home among the other stacks and rows of books in the library
where he it been. And there was a man standing there among the
books as well, who was indiscernible. And which vision persisted
for the whole two hours of my sleep, or near sleep, lying there in
a state of trans-like rapport, so for me to discover, that the book,
and being an inanimate object, had a soul of deep thought to abide
with, and a memory, and who now belonged in my safe keeping,
not to be lost like the last copy I had, to me. And with that I
wrote him this letter over the internet remembering him and our
days together on the earth at that time.

Photo Resembling Myself In Those Years Circa 1988
Alone On Main Street On A Desolate Winter's Morning
Standing In The Doorway of the Old Gay Nineties

Tony's and my Favorite Bar called P&G's
Pat and Georges "The Corner Stone" of New Paltz
Life Is As It Is In Party Town USA

****

Fri, 6 Feb 2009 17:18

Dear Tony:

I never met a man that I loved more than you, Tony, for some reason, and your memory lingers and is always there with me in guiding spirit and in inspiration. I'm so glad you have found happiness at last with your Tatiana. She seems a lovely and devoted lady, and a mystical artistic painter too besides. Perhaps we live our lives through the eyes of other people sometimes. I always liked it there on Huguenot Street with you, and I thank you for sharing your life with me for the period of time that you did to admire you over and if I ever could have a life like yours to live.

Let me know if you can help me out with an Agent reference for my books. I sent you one of the books, The Orders Of The Day, a while ago to The English Department to forward to you to look over, as you were honorably mentioned in it. If you didn't get it, please let me know, I'll send a copy directly to you with your invitation. I've been in the deep mystery of faith and lingered with the earth, and perhaps for too long, in the gray dawns of too many mornings looking on from the cold at other at people's cozy homes with a light on in the window. And it got me to where I am, grateful for the home I have, and grateful to have a home. Thank you always.

Gary

From: robinsoa@newpaltz.edu
To: gary.koniz@hotmail.com
Subject: Hey, there
Date: Sun, 8 Feb 2009 10:08:42 –0500

Anthony and his wife, Tatiana, New Paltz, NY, 1999
Photo by Tony Robinson's sister, Robin Raymond.

Hi, Gary,

   What a nice surprise to hear from you! The last time I saw
you, you gave me the cap off your head. And I remember the
guitar you gave me and the stopwatch. What lovely symbols,
each and every one. I knew you'd continue to write. I've been
writing also but I have to tell you I can't get an agent myself to
handle my work. All they want is sure-fire stuff, quality doesn't
count. Anything that will make money for them. The whole
American economy (world economy) is in a very dark place, and
I don't have much faith that my new novel will ever ``see the light
of day. What might be best for you would be to check out some

small, independent presses, try to establish a relationship with someone; that could work. Or pick up a copy of a book with agents' names in it. I'm disappointed but not depressed, because I feel lucky to have the time and place to do what I love doing, and that is writing. The artist almost invites defeat because he's an artist but he's also the luckiest person in the world because he's independent and free. Your Orders Of The Day never reached me but and I would love to have a copy; it certainly is great title, I'll say that right now. Jenny is in Oregon, no kids but she's with a great guy; they have their own rehab center. She's a great woman, wonderfully strong and determined. Henry lives in S.C., two sweet children and a lovely wife; right now he's working for Golfweek magazine. Their son, Jack, is seven and already hits drive 150 yards; and what a swing! I remember those times we played and then had breakfast afterward. A lot of great times, Gary. Tania and I have a very fine marriage; we knew each other as kids in Woodstock. I'm happy you have a home and are happy with the home you have. Carry on. Yours,

Tony

Sun, 8 Feb 2009 19:30

Dear Tony,

How nice and good of you to write me, Tony. I certainly did enjoy seeing your email there in my junk mail box. Good thing I checked it out to see what it was. It was flagged as unknown sender, mark safe or unsafe. So I marked it as safe and it went to my inbox where I opened it. I was thinking just today of you by the way, and wondering if you'd write me, and wondering also about what my relationship to you is. And as I thought, it came to me that I am one of your disciples, and grateful to be, with you being the great and gifted "sage," that you were destined by birthright to be, (as was the word your Tania used in my mind,) who en-massed and inspired us all in the formative years of

scholarly nurturing, and that we all did, each and all, admire and
love and respect you and the work you did for us, each and every
one in our behalf. I will always remember your proverb, "It takes
courage to hit a good golf shot," and indeed it does, trusting
that all the moving parts will come together as they are planned
to, at the right moment to square off the club face and to send the
ball towards its intended target.

I'm glad you have a fine marriage, Tony. I too am happy.
Kathy and I, (who I know you have met on numerous occasions,)
were married in 1998 and have been living here in Jacksonville,
(and loving it in the warm climate, and although missing the
North at times,) since 2000. I've taken up to working on a golf
course, Tony. And what a wonderful job it is, out in the days and
the elements, starting in the early dark of the morning, (at 6:00
a.m.) to watch the sunrises and with the sounds of all the birds
just waking up. I work with a great group of men, "Forty
Thousand Brothers," strong, and enjoy all the days. And
especially since I get to play golf for free and hit balls whenever I
want. I usually though play once a week on Sunday's, (or every
two weeks as it goes, so as to get to spend time with Kathy, which
I found is the essential ingredient to a happy home life,) with my
buddies who get to play for a reduced price with me. But the job
is physically demanding and when I get home, (at 3:30 in the
afternoon,) I usually take a nap for two hours and revive a bit
until I feel refreshed and then begin my literary work whatever
that might be until well into the evening. Kathy works as a nurse
and in the evenings part time from 3:00 to 8:00 p.m.. So there's
plenty of extra time for me to write. I did enjoy looking over
your website. I was very impressed with it, and am planning
shortly to begin ordering and reading your books, as I have
always wanted to do. I am going to start with "Home Again,
Home Again," and then "A Departure From The Rules." They are
priced nice. Tony, I will send you out a copy of the book, The
Orders Of The Day," which I hope you will read for the pleasure
of reading it, and too that I think you will find the final chapter in
it, entitled, "Half Mast," about a Labor Revolution in the form of
a National Strike Ultimatum to occur here in defense of our

American Work Ethic being pirated and destroyed by corporate greed and foreign intrigues, which I thought you might be able to use in inspiration to revive, "Forty Thousand Brothers," in a modern theme. You might also wish to consider self-publishing as I have been doing with Lulu.com.

Thanks again, Tony, for your friendship. It sure feels good to have a friend in time, as we measure our days out upon the earth, a real friend to abide the passage with, as we slip away profoundly, doesn't it though. It's different than having a wife, to have a real friend in manly ways to share our thought with. Writers are like that as they look forward to their readers, and their readers often fall in love with the authors they admire, for the shock of recognition they find in the psychological exchange of the written pages. I too am a man like you. I intend to stay strong until the end. Your Friend,

Gary

Home Again, Home Again

William Morrow, New York, 1969

When a large electronics firm wants to buy the land of an old art colony where Roland Gray has lived since birth, he wages a valiant fight against company executives and local politicians who would turn the colony into an industrial park.
But the struggle is not only Roland's. His extremely attractive wife is leading an isolated austere existence with her writer-husband. When Phoebe meets the firm's general manager she sees in him all that her own marriage lacks: excitement, travel, elegance. Severely divided, she at last goes over to Robert Herter. Their affair is passionate and fatal.

Home Again, Home Again portrays the encroachment of suburbia on rural America, the commercialism of our age, the self-estrangement plaguing men and women in today's desperate society. But it remains the tender, tragic, human story of a man—an individualist—endeavoring to survive in a changing world.

Wed, 18 Feb 2009 19:30

Hi Tony,

Just writing to let you know that I ordered your book, "Home Again, Home Again," today from Abe Booksellers in Ventura, CA. "Dust Jacket in good condition." How (what's the word?) "reverenced" and "treasured" it all is, the love of good books, something really special to be "passed on" to the bookseller to be of benefit to someone else of interest, "dust jacket in good condition". I'm glad Jenny and Henry are both happy. I think of them fondly in memory, and along with you and TD, and Heather, and the little family we had together at one time in the summer of '77 when life was a method drama and primal screen therapy was all the rage for angst, and angst enough we had to last a life time, it seems now drawing to a lingering close in nostalgia. I gave up drinking and everything else considered bad ten years ago, (called an "epiphany,") and only sip on warm tea in the days and practice Zen Meditation, (the good stuff,) really works, deep breathing and the focus of the mind on the sensations of being present in the moment, nice and quite and still there in the mind, you hear the thoughts of God and everything, and almost don't want to have to leave it to continue on with what you need to do. You should be getting my book "The Orders Of The Day" in about now. And I do thank you, Tony, for everything. Your friendship means something. And like you always taught me, "don't wear your heart our on your sleeve all the time," but sometimes you can, if your heart is in the right place.

Yours, Gary

· · · · · · · · · · ·

A long time ago, over thirty years gone by now, when I graduated from college with a B.A. in English/Creative Writing, I set out with the ambition, (and as everyone has an ambition to accomplish something useful and worthwhile in purpose to their lives,) with that idea of "Repairing The World." That to me, was, and has been, the driving goal in my life to this very day to accomplish. And no easy task in statement to master, as you can surmise, that has taken me down many roads of self-study to accomplish; such as, history, politics, social science, sociology, psychology, psychiatry, anthropology, legal studies, law enforcement, the religions of the world, the economy, the environment, and with business and labor affairs. And what has involved me with many political offices, and with newspapers, television and radio shows over the years in richness of working experience, and that I pursue relentlessly, to let you know a bit about my motivations.

I am hoping for a major career impact with my writing in syndication to the nation's leading newspapers in coverage to The Positive Elements of our Social Responsibility, and what with as well to have a close working relationship of involvement with our current government leaders, at any time in the politics of transition that way, as a constant in the capacity of Monitoring

Correctness and Propriety, (and to that important function in the developing of news interests on vital issues of the hour as they surface to discuss.)

And in my own right to relate that I need to work steadily on the political-social dramas of our times as they present themselves in the day to day as the years evolve in spontaneity to be challenged or accorded to, in order to achieve an impact on the crucial issues of times needing to be resolved and to the idea of managing the government.

The Native American Indian agenda of Sovereignty Affirmation needs to be fulfilled in the promise of time to them in this country, in restitution for the blatant overrun and confiscations of their lands which occurred in the name to the establishment of our nation; which is of paramount importance to the success and vitality of The United States in spirit to resolve unto them, and along with their other issue, to the restoration of their dignity as indigenous sovereign, to be acknowledged for by The American Nation.

2.   Secondly, that the Nation's reasoning on Labor and the overall Economy needs to be repaired. Our Country needs Full Employment, and by Fiat Monetary Issue Resolution if and, and as, required. And there is absolutely no good reason at all for the government to go on with the attitude that Labor needs to work "solely" off The Supply and Demand concept of The Federal Minimum Wage as the only wage law in The Nation to exist. Which is blatantly the robbery of services for the vast majority of hard working and dedicated people across our land, as a concept to endure. Every category of work needs to have a Prevailing Wage set by formal legislation to the Government's General Schedule (GS) Pay Scale, which will force Private Employers to pay workers comparably for their training, occupational skills, and education beginning at the bottom of the food chain, (GS-1,) with The Cost Of Living Wage. This will also greatly improve things on the Industrial/Business side of the economy by increasing "The Purchasing Power" of the consumers, thus

generating the much-needed increase in production and employment.

3.   Thirdly, that a National Universal Health Care plan, based to an IRS Payroll Deduction formula in national enrollment base needs to be expeditiously implemented, and with immediate benefit of support to those currently without adequate or with no Health Coverage, (that involves a great percentage of the population;) which such a plan is designed to benefit. And to counteract those of the elitist economic camp of mentality who feel, "that they work hard to pay for their Health Care and don't intend to subsidize everyone else," who need to be told that the vast majority of The Nation's Rank and File Workers cannot afford to buy adequate Health Insurance, and that The IRS Deduction formula reaches out to provide for everyone, rich and poor alike, as well in fairness to all.

4.   And fourthly, that I would like to be able to finish up my ongoing business with The Federal Government, (going on now for over thirty years,) involving The War On Drugs, which would involve effective countermeasures for The Elimination of The Drug and Pornography Mafias that feed off the economic blight of the nation, and to related Violent Crimes and Robberies in our streets, by coordinating Local and Federal Law Enforcement with the Intervention of Military Units, (that is a point of law to be exacted for from The Federal Legislature,) to effectively remove the drugs from our population, and from our neighborhoods and schools. And in conjunction to The Drug War that we need the understanding with our Government, that our Nation's Combat Veterans are not to be left to waste and die at the hands of an irrational and irresponsible, and to a certain way of looking at the subject, corrupt, pre-meditated, and traitorous in the destructive sense, psychiatric industry; predisposed, not to healing, but to a hostile "pogrom-like," purging in mentality, bent on "disposing" of our returned home Combat Veterans, whose reward for their patriotic sacrifice and gallant service to our country has been, and is being, repaid with psychiatric treachery and devastation. So let

us handle the job at hand promptly together, and not to linger on any longer in the mind set to being ignored, and in making excuses of it being someone else's job to handle, on the part of the government that is constantly changing hands to us, to do so. This a crisis matter, and has been a crisis matter since the aftermath of The Vietnam War, of what concerned The Psychiatric Devastation and Massacre of The Vietnam Veterans, continuing on as yet to be rectified.

And which is the follow up to the Veterans Case, as we have been pursuing now for several decades with the "Authorities" of the Veterans Administration, the Military Association of America, all Local, State, and Federal Agencies of Law Enforcement, and with the Media to arouse public awareness and directed involvement to put an end to the psychiatric massacre of our returning home from combat Veterans and proud heroes to us all; that I need to finish up here on what we started working on many years ago, and with great suffering and loss of life involved with the toll for our government's inaction.

And it is all for the sake of money that the jobs we need to do, and which can only be done most effectively in non-political determination and strategy in point of policy, don't get done. And I mean, in the sense that they don't get done, to the loosing of our American Nation, (of the American People as we are described about in the meaning of Sovereign, before the era of Civil Rights, of the WWII generations,) for the aggressions of the many ways of wars now upon us; of corrupt, irrational, and immoral ideologies and for the allowing of distinctly foreign peoples to arrive here each day to take our place, in being overrun, that we need to correct for. Which you, and everyone else of our American Nation under God, can judge for yourself as to the direction it is going if I can get some help from you with finances to communicate with the powers to set things right again for America. We've been complaining of the injustices occurring for too many years now without anyone to assist us, to need a kind hand of finances with the project.

And besides that I have many other important issues in crisis to "Try" in the public press and to assist the Nation in resolving of such matters to the best of my abilities, (and as is my inner volition of convictions to do besides,) and which cannot under any circumstances get done without somebody, such as myself of concerned involvement, to do what it takes to make what needs to occur "happen" in our destiny, and to make things become a reality, in the technical meaning of "making" the news; which in no means as well can occur without a benefactor, (in the appeal to you,) to finance my endeavors. To what I am very hopeful you will consider me for my sincerity as a worthy candidate.

* We need "to save America now" at this crucial time in our history together from the forces of error and chaos that threaten us, in the opportunity of present action to do so. And which will involve me with supervisors everywhere on all of the upper levels of management, in private businesses, and with respected government leaders and agency heads in objectives. In what settings that I am well polished and experienced with from my prior work history, and as much a follower to every one of them in the overall to their objective as they would be to me in our mutual necessity to survive at what it correct.

Every leader, who expects to get things accomplished, also knows how to be a good follower to others when the need arises to them who are in the urgent crises of their own endeavors to have their wishes in supervision carried out; and as those leaders are good and decisive supervisors in their own right to those who they need to supervise and to command. You say what you want done, in example, and it gets done as you expect by those subordinated under you. But when you go out into other realms of expertise that lie beyond your own powers of dominion, you know when to be a "good follower" too. The mechanic says "don't start the engine until I tell you," and so you do as you are told and wait. And there are situations where the necessity of "seconding a motion" is crucial to the leadership involved to follow along with in providing "reinforcing support," to a worthy idea, and not just for the sake of getting things accomplished, but for the intention also of "making other people successful" at what they are doing, and from which we derive great personal and emotional satisfaction ourselves from doing; to what everyone as supervisors in their own way knows how "to follow along" about and to appreciate.

I am not the type of journalist to "talk at problems," but one that "inter-involves" myself with "the politics" of getting things done; (and as I know to respect for the egos concerned of the many superior positions to be dealt with;) to add that you need the jobs, as I have earmarked for, done in your own behalf as well, as you live in the country too.

There is nothing more important to us, as we of The American Nation are defined, than to proceed forward now in the crisis of our nation in disrepair in first priority to reform the ethics of our Economy with maturity as a civilized society to have a well regulated and fair-minded economy and not to continue on at each other's throats in laissez faire commercialism under the banner of Free Enterprise as to the outcome of who is going to be allowed to survive based to an Un-Christian concept of greed and power domination over others, to the unfair treatment of our fellow man as we know it to be occurring in shameful example presently being displayed of man's inhumanity to man by our Nation in disgrace to its former honor as Christian Faith Based Economy upholding to our American Tradition of Integrity and Fair-Minded Work Ethic involving the Nation's Honor. And to our ways thusly of a democratic capitalist society upon which our Free Enterprise System of Government is predicated, that is now in the shambles of the inverse relationship to its stated objectives of sustaining the people and our government through their tax association to it, of their being allowed to be exploited and profiteered off-of and ruined by the greed and the lust for power of elitist corruption.

And of what elitist corruption waging Economic War to us, who we are indeed in the need of at this time to correct and to hold in the check and balance of public outrage, (and as our very lives and survival depends to it,) and suffering as we are with a crisis in leadership here in our America allowing to the erosion of our Middle Class of recent years and going back in time along ways to the allowing of our economy to being systematically plundered; that we need to order challenged effectively, that we so now hereby, and as a collective body, to take charge of (presented as a blood oath,) for the establishing of appropriate legislative action, that we would like to initiate at this time.

The necessary legislation to save our economy; by legally providing for a Fair Standard of Wages and appropriate Health and Dental Care Benefits to the population, promoting the furtherance of Consumer Purchasing Power to keep our industries, businesses, and government services and infrastructure alive and prospering, and sparing our domestic industries and business from unfair competition, is entitled "The Fair Wage and Benefits Act," of 2009; which is to call for, in the immediate sense of Affirmative Action, to be passed by the Congress and signed into law by The President, of a Prevailing Wage Legislation to be established (and replacing the current Federal and State Minimum Wage Laws,) for all categories of employment, of benefit to all the people, based to The Federal Government's General Schedule (GS) Wage Rates in formal ethical standard; and for what is also to stipulate for a National Health Care Plan to be drafted based to a graduated IRS Payroll Deduction to provide affordable Health Coverage to the working class in expansion of Medicare to be made immediately available for every taxpayer in the United States on emergency basis, be they citizen or otherwise. And that is also to stipulate for the mandated oversight of a Congressional Price Regulatory Commission to monitor The Cost of Living, in order to curb inflation and to prevent the gouging theft of our Free Market Staples to the Economy. And which is also to call for stern Balance of Trade Agreements and Tariff Regulations with Foreign Powers. These matters in the terms of National Economic Reform are non-negotiable.

And on this note to note, (and as that we all do need to be supportive of a single leader in our need for unity,) that it is reassuring to know that we do not stand alone with these objectives here, and that we do have a strong National Sponsor in direct leadership to us overseeing to our needs for urgent action in the regard of our National Security and Economic Survival, who has been notably outspoken in this regard is the discerning leadership and keen judgment to the critique and evaluations of our Nation's problems confronting us, that of CNN's Anchor and Managing Editor, and 2012 Independent Presidential Candidate, Lou Dobbs', whose intellect, character, and leadership on his nightly television show, continues to lift our nation now with a clear vision. And who, in his thoroughly detailed book, (published in 2006) entitled "War On The Middle Class" has provided us with the critical investigative groundwork and astutely compiles analysis of data involved with the destruction of our American Economy that has now become a society owned by corporations and a political system dominated by corporate and special interests, and directed by elites who are hostile to our government of the people and to the consent of the governed, in and by their total corporate ownership of our political system in disregard of the public interest and to the preservation of our traditional national values; of independence, equality, personal freedom, the common good. Which previously were the causes for our traditional institutions that are now being destroyed.

Our Federal Government has become dysfunctional and no longer serves the needs of the people, and has become a slave to the special interests of unfettered capitalism and the campaign contributions of corporate lobbyists and special interest groups, and in relegating America to an unfair Balance of Free Trade Agreements, Off-Shoring of our production facilities, and the Outsourcing of jobs to overseas cheap labor markets, that has created an erosion of jobs and pay, health care, and education in this Nation, and to an economic system based upon Cheap Labor and Profiteering off of The Cost Essentials.

To make matters worse, the American Middle Class in their struggle to survive has replaced their previously legitimate wage earning Purchasing Power with Credit Card Spending for the Cost Essentials, that caused massive cases of bankruptcy and to what that the Federal Government, in creating The Bankruptcy Abuse and Consumer Protection Act of 2005, has sided with and to the

enabling of the Credit Industry to be further gouging out of our
Economy and making it impossible for the American Middle
Class to ever recover from their contracts of debt to the Nation's
ultimate collapse.

Our Middle Class core of Work Ethic, is for the preservation
of traditional values, based to the prevailing creed that every
citizen is important to the greater good, that is being undermined
now by; Corporatism, Consumerism, Ethnocentric
Multiculturalism, (and meaning that our Traditional American
Middle Class Structure is being permanently replaced by Third
World foreign speaking cheap labor,) and is now having to work
longer hours at reduced pay with fewer benefits, and to uncertain
job prospects and insecure financial futures, and is being forced to
accept and to endure a severely reduced standard of living in
national ennui and a numb and passive acceptance of the status
quo.

Individual rights and responsibilities have always been the
core of America. But we have allowed the elites to subvert the
principles of free market and a democratic society in detriment to
the preservation of our political system, which we have suffered
in silence for too long and must now face up to the challenges to
modify before it becomes too late.

A collective understanding of the needs and desires of the
entire country is needed here in state of alarm. The politically
powerful and wealthy, dedicated to attaining power and money,
and in their arrogant indifference and abuse of power, have over-
topped us now to dominate our society, our economy, and our
government, and are depriving the Middle Class, (as it is
presently defined for in economic terms to be the Middle Class,
with a mean at $46,000, and with $20,000 being poverty level for
a family of four, and with an impoverish Working Poor Lower
Class below that making up the bottom 20% of the Nation's
struggling economy,) who are being deprived of economic
opportunity, fair wages, their rightful voice and representation in
government by Class Discrimination, the discrimination being the
property ownership, higher education, occupational prestige,
income, and wealth, of the Upper Class criteria of class mobility

that is now being relegated into a "Two Class Society" of the
Very Rich and the Very Poor, and being subverted by a Class War
that is being condoned and aided to by a Congress that is bought
and paid for by the lobbying and campaign contributions of
Corporate and Special Interests; with roll back on estate taxes,
higher taxes on labor, tougher bankruptcy laws, lower taxes on
capital, and bought and paid for members of both parties. The
United States has become inversely culturally, socially, and
economically diverse, that has generated a new type of upper
class Big Business Establishment, with big compensation
packages, restricted stock options, and a share of global market;
while workers' pay stagnates. The reality of what is that the
American Middle Class is caught in a Class War, and to the idea
being, that if every person does not have the same opportunities.

Our Big American Corporations, (and for all of America's
Private Employers to be mindful of;) need to be reminded that
they have Civic and Community Responsibilities; and that we are
being challenged by values of greed and callowness (lacking
mature adult sophistication.) Our Corporations and Employers
need to be giving something back to the United States in return
for the benefits they are receiving. Many U.S. Corporations in
today's corrupt economic climate, have become Multinationals
and are creating a corporate tax problem of paying lower taxes
with their Off-Shoring and Outsourcing, and operating in the
absence of environmental and labor protection laws as in the
United States, and in the absence of health care and retirement
plan cuts, as they are being currently allowed to get away with it
by their lobby activities with the Congress.

To remind everyone that our government leadership has
created a destruction of Unregulated Capitalism in excessive
management incomes in and by their brand of class warfare,
allowed for by the benign neglect of the American People, in their
allowing for the migration of our manufacturing jobs lost overseas
and outsourced to foreign labor markets, and to the influx, (in
broken border arrangement with our current flock of politicians
on Capital Hill,) of plentiful cheap labor, and due to the Political
corruption in Washington, bent on Pork, (or federal monies

prioritized, as earmarked, for their private concerns of special interests,) who sponsor their political campaigns and their careers.

Health care has now become too expensive for many families, and many companies are opting to drop coverage, and while the Federal Government has provided 10 billion in subsidies to business end of insurance companies, that non of which has been passed down to the consumer in the form of lower rates. In 1991 – 80% of all companies provided health insurance, but with out of control payments for health care and treatment in the past five years, company premiums for family coverage have increased 73%, while inflation has increased 14%, and wages increased 15%, with the cost of $10,880 per year per employee being passed on in family coverage for employers to have to pay out.

In an attempt to make a real difference for the working men and women of our Country, and in statement that the country's elites need Congressional Oversight and can no longer continue to line their own pockets, and that big business is tired of paying for Health Insurance while doctors salaries and hospital services fees skyrocket, and while the Pharmaceutical Companies lobbying is passed on to insurance costs, and all the while in the collusion between government agencies and corporate America, the FDA, and the National Institute of Health, NIH, to ensure that overpriced, unsafe, and deadly drugs will remain on the U.S. market, and while Malpractice Insurance Fees are encouraged to remain high by the lobby of the Trial Lawyers Association, and while Big business backs illegal immigration which provides cheap labor and creates a labor force with negligible expenses such as Health Care in having to be provided for; the Middle Class is being forced to compete with the lowest cost labor in the world, and which is being invited for and sponsored by The Federal Government's Pro Amnesty – Guest Worker Program.

Illegal immigration also invites diseases. Tuberculosis, leprosy, chagas disease, and malaria, have been reported on the rise concerning the Open boarder advocates The economic, social, and environmental impact of illegal immigration is also affecting the high school drop out rate, and creating lower real wages overall and job insecurity. Third World Immigration, Illegal or

Otherwise, sends their incomes back to their own countries and does not spend it in The United States to propitiate the survival of our economy.

The foundation of our prosperity is our free enterprise democracy; however, if any part deems itself to be preeminent in our political economy the national interest suffers. The pharmaceutical industry has two lobbyists for every member of Congress. PACs, Political Action Committees, don't' have the same restrictions for campaign donations which are stipulated for by the Ethics In Government Act of 1978. Wages are stagnating. Energy and health care costs are rising, and high credit card interest rates are gouging out the purchasing power of our Nation's consumers causing the economy to collapse.

The downward pressure on wages is really hurting most employees – more than cheaper consumer goods are helping them. Free trade is destroying America's manufacturing base and middle class jobs. The National Interest is paramount. The well-being of our fellow Americans is the first duty of all of us as citizens to protect.

American industry cannot compete against the cheapest manufacturing environments in the world. America has suffered the loss of 3 million manufacturing jobs since 2000 and is dependent on the rest of the world for cars, computers, electronics, clothing, and food. 96% of our clothing is imported – FAA lacks oversight of outside contractors – back-office accounting and software programming outsourced. It is not true that increased pay and benefits for our work force will make consumer goods too expensive to purchase. The problem is the exorbitant salaries and compensation benefits paid to corporate elites.

The direct cost of globalization is that we have exchanged self-sufficiency for dependency, to our energy supply, our military sufficiency, and our domestic food supply; and there is no reciprocity in our trade relationships. Trade barriers and high tariffs are used against us while we reduce our tariffs and restrictions; in 1951, which were at 15%, in 1979 5.7%, and today under 3% average U.S. Tariffs. Our Corporations have been cutting competition and merging and consolidating with other industries in other countries, with lost jobs to workers in India, Romania, China, the Philippines, and other cheap labor markets, and outsourcing our financial and technology services industries, reducing our competitiveness, productivity, and efficiency, to cheap labor, lost jobs, and to jobs that pay less. And all the while that Corporate America is enjoying the best of times. Corporate taxes are the lowest in 100 years, and while profits have risen, corporate responsibility to employees and communities have become non-existent. When companies "pull out" to Offshore Overseas, the lost jobs leave communities with diminishing local economy and cut the tax base that supports public education, government services, and infrastructure; and the costs of outsourcing are worsening.

We as citizens share a common objection and offense to the way this country is being run, to give away our manufacturing jobs, while we suffer; higher property taxes, less disposable income, and less of a tax base to support our infrastructure and government services. Every single effort counts – angry voters without jobs are not inclined to vote for the status quo. We need to recognize the damages inherent in outsourcing and the pressures of illegal immigration on schools, jails, health care, and housing.

We need to change the fundamental flaws in the way this country is being run, and Take Back America! Every workingman and woman in this country must fight back against the powerful political, economic, and social conditions that threaten our way of life. No one will give us our country back, not without a fight. You must work to change a social order that is in disrepair, a body politic that is fractured, and a government that is dysfunctional. And we must begin with reforming ourselves as individuals, a good start.

We need to Secure our Borders and stand by the enforcement of HR – 98, the Illegal Alien Bill, that mandates for fines and jail time for employers who violate immigration laws. We need to raise the basic minimum wage to a living wage, (GS1), and to improve the overall standard of living with appropriate wages by the application of General Schedule Wage Rates. We need all shipping containers inspected for Drugs, Weaponry, and Illegal Aliens. We need our Trade Agreements with other Nations to be reciprocal. And we need to safeguard of our Sovereignty and Security. Our politicians must begin to represent our public interest, in reforming what has become a culture of corruption.

We are a nation desperate for leadership in our time. We need and require a strong and binding contract between working men and women and business, and between the people and their government who are left without real and legitimate representation.

That to secure these Rights, in the words and actions of The 2nd Continental Congress – July 4, 1776 – Declaration of Independence, "in every stage of these oppressions, We have petitioned for redress in the most humble of terms of justice and consanguinity [blood relationship] with the firm reliance of the protection of Divine Providence."

The Orders of The Day

From:
Anthony Robinson (robinsoa@newpaltz.edu)
Sent: Fri 2/27/09 12:18 PM
To: gary.koniz@hotmail.com

Hi, Gary,

I got your book with its splendid title and was very happy to have it. It's such a tremendous outpouring of the soul, wildly creative and honest. I especially liked the parts about Nam and all that happened there and in other lands. Now I know where you learned your skills in operating heavy machinery! The book is very much you, from word one to the end. Your poem to

Tim Shoh! How wonderful to see that name again and to read your words about you and him when you were such dear friends. I knew you both then and knew the depth of your friendship. I often think of Timmy Shoh. All very real stuff in your book, Gary. Your voice and spirit come fully across. And it's handsomely put together too. Tell me a little about Lulu. Will they print a number of copies at one time and distribute, or is it "print on demand"? Your life sounds great. Lloyd has visited me a number of times through the years, always memorable. What's your specialty on the course? And what's the name of it? Are you playing at all? Take care.

Tony

Fri 2/27/09 19:30 PM

Dear-heart Tony,

What a nice letter you wrote me, and so magnificently and thoughtfully worded. It's really all about friendship between men, isn't it, real manly friendship for those fortunate enough to have found such a relationship and who have the aptitude to appreciate for the life giving depth in the enjoyment of it. And I have always admired your approach to it, the nature of manly bonding, and for the keen regard in respect that you have for it, and always evaluating, and weighing, and judging for the outcome of events to and all actions affecting it, as to say, of what would be right and that wouldn't, and to being seriously involved with the process.

I remembered that one time that we moved "Bud's" property line back to its rightful place that one summer day, and you took the picture of me squatting there and holding "the line" after the surveyors had marked it. And I remember that I felt bad for the poor dog, who now had no shade for his dog house to lie in, in the heat of the summer days, where he had been beneath the shade of the tall pine trees at the very edge of your property, and Bud made

up a lean-to for the dog with his boat turned on its side to keep
some shade him. And I remember afterwards that Lloyd and I
picked you up and tossed you back and forth in our arms to
celebrate your decisive victory over the audacity of the
"encroachment," something's needing to be settled in manliness
to preserve a friendship, something's being given and something's
taken back. And in the end I felt that Bud was satisfied that the
right thing had been done, and even though, in the end of all ends
that what difference would it have made, in friendship, if the dog
had been allowed to stay where he was, but it wasn't my land to
say.

   I forgot to mention Sophie and Waldo, and Lloyd, in my last
letter of the fond memories of our family life together that I have
of that summer when "the workers" as you called us, as to say
which consisted of me and Lloyd, were there and we lived for
room and board and five dollars a week for the renovation of the
land and slept in the rustic garret over the garage and took our
showers au natural when no one was watching in the outdoor
shower you had made behind the back porch, (and which I
perceived a connection to in the opening pages of your wonderful
book, Home Again, Home Again, that I am eagerly wanting to
talk to you about, if I can "put it down" for a length of time to do
so.) What a charmed life to have had such a grand time.

   You can access Lulu.com yourself, Tony, and sign up for you
to have your books printed. It doesn't cost you anything for the
sign up part and they will print out any number of books that you
want in bulk and ship them off to any destinations you want. To
me it was a modern miracle to have discovered such a publishing
mechanism, and I have been publishing and sending out my books
to everyone, hundreds of people. Better to be read than to be rich
in that way, and why be so egocentric about it, to expect others to
buy your work just because you publish it, better to give them a
copy out of respect and as a token of friendship, but I could use
the money too to further my work, and sometimes it works out
that way. Just the other day I got a notice on my email that
someone had bought a copy. The money you make from sales
that way goes into a Paypal Account which you can transfer into

your own bank account. I am most appreciative and humbled and grateful to you for reading me and for your kind words.

As far as my work on the Golf Course goes, I am the Greenskeeper there at a course called DeerCreek Country Club, to what that you and Tatiana are always invited as my guest to play there, if you would like to come down and take-in that fine March or April weather here in Jacksonville. You could stay with myself and Kathy, or get your own place down the road close by at the Embassy Suites for a reasonable rate, but you are always welcome here for a golf holiday. I play most every other week, (I need to be with Kathy too, to take her shopping and do the things she likes to do on her days off.) I'm playing well, although I could be better, and I am always trying to improve my swing, (old bad habits die hard being programmed into the motor memory to do much with.) They just keep coming back.

That's a lot for now. I'll write you more about your book soon. It just arrived yesterday has quite a history with me, this particular book, that I have been wanting to read for thirty years. And believe me, I am so impressed with you as a writer. What a way you have with it, so sensitive and so attentive to detail ... that begins trout fishing in Maverick Creek in Ulmer County and with the development with their guzzling 220 foot wells draining the old 90 foot well on Roland's property and with Phoebe liking to take her outdoor showers and to dry off naked in the backyard sunlight. Can't put it down.

In the meantime, here is a sample of what I have been working on, not great novel writing like you, but dramatic enough ...

In reply to my inquiries of Psychiatric Revue to the former Secretary of Veterans Affairs Doctor James B. Peake concerning the conduct of care and treatment for our returning home from combat American Veterans, present and past, as it relates to the harmful and damaging effects of Anti-Psychotic Medications, and for the easing of the prevailing Stigma associated to the Diagnosis and Treatment of Mental Disorders; to its being legally clarified;

particularly as to what constitutes a Legal Diagnosis and
concerning a person's Right To Refuse Treatment, and with
appropriate protection of Legal Counsel to be provided for by The
Veterans Administration, as to The Rights of our Veterans to be
covered under the Ninth and Fourteenth Amendments by Legal
Due Process in the event of their being Psychiatrically Accused,
and to their Safeguard of Beneficial Treatment:

I was personally, and expressing for the behalf of the entirety
of the remaining Veterans of The Vietnam War Organization,
(68,000 of whom have committed suicide, of the over 1,000,000
of whom who were made into psychiatrics, in their own eyes, and
in the eyes of society,) and for all Veterans, as a body of men
collectively, very impressed with his detailed and clarifying letter
in heartfelt sincerity for the burden of his position relating to his
duties of responsibility in care to the lives, and livelihoods, and
families involved, of our Veterans at issue for the present status of
care and treatment of; Post Traumatic Stress Disorder (PTSD),
Traumatic Brain Injury (TBI), Major Depression, types of Mental
Disorders such as Schizophrenia and Bipolar Illness, Mood and
Anxiety Disorders, and for other forms of Stress Related
Conditions as they manifest in the Addictive Disorders of
Substance Abuse; to thank you for your personal time and
assistance in assurances to us that our Veterans will be receiving
the very best Health Care possible throughout our Nation's
Veterans Administration Health Care Facilities, and as you stated
for so nobly for in your own words in closing to us, to: "Be
assured that VA health care providers share your concerns about
the stigma that has been associated with mental disorders and the
importance of eliminating that stigma. Also be assured that VA
providers take every care to prescribe only those medications that
are necessary for improvement of the patient and only for so long
as those medications are needed."

We do know the very difficult position that The Veterans
Administration faces with these issues, the hardest part being to
try and change the current errors involving psychiatric stemming
from the past which the government doesn't want to admit to
having errors with, (in face saving and involving litigation,) and

so which continue on about themselves in that vein of being made excuses for remaining uncorrected. But it occurs to me that we are suffering here to our end from a misunderstanding of the terms in our purpose of objectives in not being able to get through to an appropriate response from The Veterans Administration about.

This is a very old case concerning the destructive treatment of our Veterans with Anti-Psychotic Drugs, and for the removal, or easing of, the tortured stigma associated with the idea of being Mental Ill. Everyone knows that the genuine issue of insanity does exist in the society, of those who portray irrational and oftentimes violent behavior to be severely dealt with; and of necessity, who are therefore deemed to be that way by the Courts and placed in the protective custody of the State confined to Mental Asylums. And which involves also of those as well, who are mentally defective, mentally deficient, brain damaged, and retarded, to be cared for by the State, under the wording of Parens Patriae, or Wards of the State. As into what generalized setting, termed "Mental Health," in the eyes of society, and in terms of their own Self-Esteem, are placed the precious lives of our Veterans who have survived mortal combat in the service of their country, in the supreme offering of their lives, to return here with Service Connected and Combat Stress Related Emotional Problems and Disorders to be treated for and assisted to recover from, and only to their being placed in with and along side of these truly mentally ill, mentally defective persons, who then that the public presumes our Veterans to be, and to our Veterans then being treated as presumed to be insane, who are otherwise normal and only needing temporary assistance to recover, and to their being undifferentiated by treatment with the Neuroleptic, Anti-Psychotic, Strong Tranquillizers, and to their utter ruination.

And with that being said, the problem is and still remains; that there is more to this issue of Mental Health Psychiatric, (on the corrupt and dirty maniacal business side of the Medical Pharmaceutical Psychiatric Industry, (that has a Captive Market in which a person perversely has NO Rights whatsoever over their Diagnosis, Commitment, and Treatment to occur under the heading of Mental Hygiene Law, and having also to do with social fears, biases, and ignorance,) some of it involving the VA to correct, and some of it lying beyond the scope of The VA in the civilian sector pertaining for the Courts, local Mental Health Centers, local Hospitals, and State Psychiatric Facilities, incumbent up to the already beleaguered and overworked staffing of the VA to oversight and contain.

That we specifically requested from Secretary Peake to elaborate on as to whether or not that he personally approved of the Anit-Psychotic, Neuroleptic, Psychotropic, Strong Tranquillizer type pharmacy chemicals being given for treatment to our Veterans, whether voluntarily to be taken under advisement of physician and regardless of their being administered with informed consent, or otherwise of the "Forced Treatment" issue, as to any of these prevailing drugs being declared to be Safe and Beneficial for our Veterans to take, or otherwise to be a harmful nature? As I previously named for Dr. Peake: such as; Thorazine, Prolixin, Navane, Trilifon, Lithuim, Loxitane, *Congentin, (which is used to control the Tremors, or Parkinson-like symptom, of the other Anti-Psychotic drugs being listed,) and others of that Classification; for what you stated for in your letter in your response to us; "that no medication is without potential Side-Effects."

But we are not talking here about "dry mouth," or "constipation," with being carefully weighed of their side effects over in "Informed Consent" by the patient to take, but for the catastrophic ruination of a person's whole and complete physiognomy, physically, mentally, emotionally, and spiritually to the gloom of suicide. To what that there is no one naïve about this situation is there, in consultation with The Physicians' Desk Reference (PDR), and concerning the personal testimony of persons who have experienced these drugs, (which you term as "Clinical Trails," which translates over to direct Experimentation with Human Subjects as Guinea Pigs, to where you derived your wordings of Effects, Side-Effects, Adverse Affects, and Contra-indications to be used in your Clinical Practice Guidelines.) Which besides of what, that these drugs, and all of them, are "excruciatingly painful to endure," what the PDR refers to as "Uncomfortable States of Being," and which also cause many other torturous disabling Adverse Effects.

Which brings me to the other point in matter of Mis-Communication with The Veterans Administration that they don't really understand these drugs other than for their description in the PDR and Clinical Practice Guidelines and need to experience the actual effects yourself, as the Veterans have, to have a real and honest evaluation of what they are really experiencing, starting with 200 mg of Thorazine over an extended length in period of time for at least a month or two, as our Veterans are being "Treated With," and have "Suffered," in the past to be returned to society on to commit suicide from the effects of, to really evaluate and understand our denunciation of them. Which I know you are not going to do, because in your intelligent mind you know that these drugs, as you term to be "Medications," would cause you severe harm and disable you.

These are not "feel good" types of drugs. The primary purpose of these drugs; which are used in the treatment of so called Mental Disorders, is to "restrain and destroy people;" and which renders them unable and unfit to assume their normal functions in society. Which in a matter of concurrence to you and involving to the hopelessly insane, as you indicated for about in your letter, that these drugs would indeed prove to be of beneficial value to, if a person is screaming lunatic, but these drugs will destroy the normal person and that they are Not To Be Approved For our Veterans to take for temporary Stress and Emotional Disorders and for other mental disturbances associated with combat; which need to be taken care of with; Best Rest Convalescence, Counseling, Therapy, and Sound Nutrition, in a quite setting to be called Seclusion/Recovery," no longer the Psyche Ward. Mental Health as well, with its stigma of inferior irrationality presumed, needs to be renamed to, "Professional Services;" which would include for Guidance Counseling and Therapy in a Benign and Beneficial Setting.

Furthermore, it is not true and you cannot lawfully and ethically tell patients that they have to take Anti-Psychotic Drugs for the rest of their lives to replace missing enzymes secretions or a genetic deficiency, the lack of which is causing a persons mental illness, in similarity as to how; Thyroidism, Diabetes, and Hypertension are perceived, as according to the PDR Manual there is no evidence to support this claim. Also you legally and ethically cannot "hold the threat" of indefinite commitment confinement over someone, allowed for under Mental Hygiene Law, unless they agree to voluntarily comply with their treatment plan to take the Anti-Psychotic Drugs prescribed for them by the medical industry. And unfortunately however that "Forced Treatment" is "at all times" the way of psychiatric warehousing; which you state in your letter only occurs; "in the rare instance in an emergency situation when a patient is presenting an active danger to themselves or others," that is not true. To what matter of Forced Treatment with deadly drugs that our Veterans need Legal Clarification from the VA to protect themselves from.

· · · · · · · · · · · · · · · · · · · ·

In final summation to the Veterans Psychiatric Case, (and for which we should not be having to argue; but in having to, to thank you for your support to set things right about the matter and for your determination in assistance to us without which, in peer oversight, that we would not be as far along with the case, as we are progressing in opportunity now of correcting the egregious errors of the past with the healthy change in Administrations for our Veterans Mental Health Issues being presented regarding our Nation's Honor, concerning their Diagnostic Labeling and Treatment for the matter of psychiatric intake following their separation from service, as we have been conveying to The Military Officers Association of America, (MOAA,) that the V.A. and the Psychiatric Industry overall have been mis-labeling, mis-handling, and mis-treating our Combat Soldiers with disabling chemical pharmacy such as Thorazine, and other deadly Neuroleptic Drugs and causing them very grave and serious harm to the point of mass suicide to date. Which matter needs to be

urgently redressed, as to the substance for the grievances
themselves being corrected, (and for just disability compensation
to be provided to those aggrieved for their damages to ease their
inflicted burden.) And in all that we have been in the need for a
Supreme Court Ruling On, (presently lacking finances to formally
appeal,) on the safety of Psychiatric Drugs and for the Legal
Rights of The Psychiatrically Accused to ensure their Civil Rights
Protection to Diagnosis Labeling, Commitment, and Forced
Treatment.

We started working on this project together as an MOAA
agenda in National Alarms several years ago; with The Veterans
Administration, The U.S. Military, The Federal Government, and
The F.B.I., in the need for dramatic intervention; and coinciding
to the urgent Removal of the Heroin and other Dangerous Drugs
from our society, and for the resulting Drug Warfare occurring in
peril to the population and in particularly to our returning home
from war Veterans who pose the first line of homeland defense to
be eliminated; and to our suffering the loss of our American
Nation over it, the trafficking in drugs, (of the American United
States of the WWII generations,) for the aggressions of the many
ways of wars having been allowed to overtake us; of corrupt,
irrational, and immoral ideologies, and for the allowing of
decidedly foreign peoples to politically and economically overrun
us here, in the malaise of a drugged and corrupt society, to be
defended against. And that we do at this time need to be
intervening to the War Crimes involved with the continued
Opium/Heroin Production and Trafficking from Afghanistan.

We, as a Nation, are not about to be "run-over" by the state of
siege known as The Drug War and to its Drug Warfare active
contingent to the goal of Psychiatric Intake to finish-off the job of
destroying people with drugs as for the stating of its occurrence,
(that is for the stating to the authorities of one's being drugged, or
poisoned, and particularly as the setting involves close family
members at close range, or in other social settings, or perhaps
even on a mass scales of food and beverage sabotage to content
for,) to then being diagnosed with the labeling of "Paranoid
Schizophrenia," and to treatment, or and to the other vein of

experiencing of the outright physiological maiming effects of
being "hit" with street drugs and chemicals, to the actual affliction
of drug induced mental disorders, and to treatment; that the idea
here is that you need to be aware of and to respect for the
argument of necessary legal enforcement intervention for what is
presently going on in regard to the idea of blatantly underhanded
Court Ordered Psychiatric Examinations being gotten-away-with
as a status quo of the Justice System, (and in conspiracy to the
Medical-Pharmacy Industry,) as to replacing the entire system
that way (in the sparing of the taxpayers the expense of lengthy
Court Processing, or so it is stated to be for that purpose,) without
any Legal Miranda Rights Legislation Safeguards in place for the
accused pertaining for "The Rights of Due Process."
    And which is not just for the case of anyone's being arbitrarily
"accused-labeled," as "diagnosed," for by "Court Appointed
Medical Examiners," as indeed having an alleged psychiatric
condition without any opportunity provided to defend themselves
in a legal way against "the charge" of such an allegation; but and
thereupon in that regard to the rendering that way by the Court
Appointed Examiners, to each victim of such psychiatric
determination then of having to face the ordeal of an "open-
ended" Court Ordered Psychiatric Mental Health intake as well,
(based and left up to the say-so of the doctors for their release;)
and which doesn't end there, but which also carries the penalty
for the fact, that "Psychiatrics," in the terms of the Psychiatric
Medical-Pharmacy Industry, (and thereby in the eyes of society
regarded that way and reinforced,) have to be "treated," with a
deadly list of psychiatric pharmacy drug chemicals, termed as
Strong Tranquillizers, in order for them to be released back into
society; and to, "Forced Treatment" if need be, by the order of
these doctors, and which renders their victims comatose, crippled
and maimed in effects of these drug chemicals, being touted as
"Medical Treatment;" which it is really not, but the murder of the
society to be thought of in that way of being militarily intervened
upon.

Sat 04/11/09 19:00

Dear Tony,

   I am forwarding you this rough draft copy of my new book,
The Call To Order, for you to download if you want, to show you
how easy it is for your to publish your novels privately, and at no
cost to you, (other than to pay for what you order for yourself at
cost,) with Lulu.com. It truly is a modern miracle as I always to
tell everyone to be able to get your work out.
   Also, I just finished your book, Home Again, Home
Again, today, (I started early this morning, and the final chapters
while watching The Masters.) It is truly a GREAT Work, a
masterpiece on the caliber of a Greek Tragedy, to stand the test of
time for the ages as an American Tragedy of the same magnitude,
very Classic Lines of thought.
   I did detect one very minor typo, (and almost unnoticeable) on
page 41, at the very top of the page on the second paragraph
where Roland and Larry Stein are talking about his transfer to
Phoenix, and about Larry's wife Rhoda, (the wedge femme fatale
of the book.) Which goes like this, as Larry is speaking ... But
Rhoda wants to do (want) I want to do, what's best for me..."
Which should be, (what) I want to do. Other than that, I liked the
book tremendously and have very much more to comment with
you over it, of how it affected and moved me. I was even moved
by its un-fastidious and open sexual "rawness" which grated in
certain early parts of the novel, but which I grew quite fond of
and didn't find to be offensive as the book toned down and
progressed, which I felt to be in keeping with the character of the
times in the modern animal nature without thought to maturity,
and with being of artistic value in such regard, true to life. But
the plot, and the beautiful descriptive narratives, and the character
development are perfectly orchestrated, and I am in marvel of you
for the quality of your tragic genius. You see so deeply into life.
And I admired the experience of friendship between Roland and
Larry, (and as with so many other things about your wonderful
novel.)

I'll write you more about it. I'm planning to order, "A Departure From The Rules," next! You were in my dream the other night, sitting back on the couch with your arms around Tatiana, and you looked happy. Thanks for being a friend to me and for sharing your life with me as you did. I've always been moved and deeply respectful of that. I love being a scholar and a man of letters like you.

Gary

A Departure From the Rules

Putnam, New York, 1960; W.H. Allen, London,
1961; Longanesi, Milan, 1963

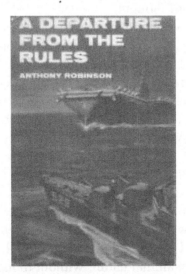

Here, in a superb novel of the sea, is the story of the destroyer *USS DOBBS*, and of the officers and men who lived and served aboard her—of their ambitions and their fears, their quarrels and their loves ashore, their guilt and their heroism, and of each one's part in the worst peacetime disaster in the history of the United States Navy.

When Gerald Karst took command of the *Dobbs*, he had one obsessive purpose in mind: to restore strict military procedures, to surpass her great wartime record, to make her the sharpest ship afloat.

The heart of this compelling novel is the psychological conflict between the Naval Academy-trained captain of the *Dobbs*, and his Gunnery Officer, a reserve from Yale.

Lieutenant (jg) Allan Byrne, bright, efficient, hard working, Gunnery Officer of the *Dobbs*, had inherited from the former captain the respect and confidence of the crew. Was it his youth, his charm, his standing with the men, that made him the focal point of Karst's campaign? Or was it Byrne's involvement with Joan Karst, the Commander's teen-aged daughter?

This moral struggle culminates, on a dark night in the Pacific Ocean, in the decision that took the *Dobbs* to her death. At the Court of Inquiry convened to establish the cause of the disaster, the testimony leads ultimately to the deep human failings of the participants, and to the consideration of Lieutenant Byrne's moral fitness to command.

Sweeping in its scope, authentic in its background, A DEPARTURE FROM THE RULES is a bold and moving novel of a bitter psychological conflict—and of the moral disintegration that plagues our times.

Fri 4/17/09 23:32 PM

Dear Tony,

Just to let you know that I got your first novel, A Departure From The Rules, in today in the mail from Abe Books. How magical to have a second novel by you in my home. And "what" a HANDSOME photograph of you on the back cover of the dust jacket. The book is in great condition and only cost me $6.00 with $4.00 for shipping. I can't believe you are turning 78 this year, awesome. I'll be 63 on May 1st. No Country For Old Men, certainly in retrospect, but we're not out of time yet.

I have some plans to re-edit your Home Again to make it palpable for the ages, the tragic work of art and destiny that it is in the Greek sense, and to take out all the f____g words and to tone down a little on the explicit descriptions, (and although most of them aren't bad, I liked the one about the spider on Phoebe's bare legs in the outhouse,) but which I think of certain of the others with Bob Herter detracts from the works' enduring nature in the eyes of little children, (and although valid in the genre, as you put it on the dust cover of, A Departure ... "and of the moral disintegration that plagues our times,") but not for everyone, as to my point. And which would require only a few minor changes to the script to make your masterpiece universal and timeless the ages. Your other descriptions in Home for Again are so deeply moving and beautiful, that I felt as if the work were a part of me, and even now I live there in Maverick "Rawson" Colony with you, as if it were my own memory to remember, and fly fishing there in Maverick Creek. Always casting at "One O'clock." Do you remember teaching me? There's an uncanny eeriness I feel awaiting me in, A Departure... It seems we are living a part in each other's destiny.
Gary

Sun 4/19/09 15:37

Dear Tony,

I just now this day started to read the newly arrived novel from Abe Books, "A Departure From The Rules," to let you know that I felt it started out with a good clean pace and with excellent and very interesting naval descriptions to take immediate note on; about Commander Jerald Karst U.S.N. and his first arrival about the U.S.S. Dobbs, a World War II vintage Destroyer, that I though all was in good order about and which piqued my interest to continue on about. And which starts differently in emotional expectation than does, Home Again, Home Again, that I didn't want to disparage you about in expressing to you some of my feelings for the work in taking exceptions to.

That I did not wish to convey to be negative in such regard, and quite the contrary about it, that I felt, and of the work taken as a whole, to be a masterpiece of great and sustaining literary artistic value, that it came across, to me, really very well, but as "Period Piece," in portrayal of the despondent ennui of desperate moral despair and of the submerged search for values, barely conscious of the attempt in vain, of a decadent time in our history in abdication to the animal instincts of human beastliness, or to the struggles of such.

But that I did not see Phoebe to be driven by and engrossed in the sexual pursuit of passion that Rhoda portrays. Phoebe, I feel, and as our emotions, of the reader, are drawn at once into an affection for the intimacy of Roland Gray and his wife, that the reader wants them to be successful with their marriage about, and that becomes particularly painful during the opening party scene at the stein's where the couples are seen pairing off with other partners to dance and wander about, The Moderns, as I call them; and as involves too the charismatic character of their child Luke which bonds the Gray family in an expectant and likeable way in the hearts of the reader.

However that, Phoebe has been driven "mad" by her life "in the woods" with Roland, that is compounded now by the drying up of their well and with no water to wash and to bath with, and from which that she needs to escape from, the life of despair that she has been imprisoned by, and although that she is not totally aware of it, or how to leave, but knowing that she needs to, "until" Robert Herter provides her with the relief of solution, that isn't sexual, but that turns then into sexuality, but which is not Phoebe's initial intention, and although that it was Robert Herter's all along. But Phoebe in her heart is still sexually faithful to her husband, and needs to have trouble and doubt with Robert in that area of their affair. And why I asked you to tone down a bit on the sexual side of it.

Rhoda's another matter, and Robert may have felt like it, "to take her from behind," but that too I feel needs to be left as a thought not acted upon, and as Robert is Larry Steins best friend not to betray, that speak to the great stature of manhood and respect of the novel. "Get out of here, Rhoda." I liked Robert for saying that.

That way the novel acquires "the enduring stature," of "strong moral character," for the ages to emulate and admire. But as I said, it depends on what you see in it.

There's nothing that can possibly make a man feel any worse than to be a "couple" on the make together going out to parties to pair off with other partners, whether just to dance or to wander around privately with, and then to have to go home together afterwards and live together in the powerful emotions of it, what being faithful to one's spouse means in the trust and bonding of the real business of being faithful. What can that be like? You walk into the bathroom to urinate and there's your wife in the shower naked kissing another man, and so you quietly turn yourself around and take his wife by the hand into the bedroom and fornicate with her in the bed for spite, and after the heat of the orgasm you roll off and there's your wife looking on from the doorway and going off with the other man to do the same. And you know in your heart you're doomed and nothing is ever going to be the same anymore, and that you can't go Home Again any longer, ever again in your heart and you know it, because you've betrayed it. And that's where it is, The Gordian Knot, it will never loosen, and you'll never be able to untie it.

Gary

Your notes

From: Anthony Robinson (robinsoa@newpaltz.edu)

Sent: Sun 4/19/09 8:57 PM

To: gary.koniz@hotmail.com

Hi, Gary--I've had some wonderful letters from you recently, mostly about writing and one or two novels I wrote a good while ago. It's so nice having them read again! I'm sure your editing of *Home Again* would improve it, but in all honesty I didn't realize it had parts in it that might offend the sensibilities, especially an old warrior like yourself. I have always tried to write about physical encounters openly and artistically and to use language people actually use, but always sparingly. It can easily be overdone. Actually (as I recall) *Home Again* is one of my milder books, but now I'm tempted to look at it again. I think you'll like *Departure*. As for morality, I think it's larger than words; it's how a person acts or doesn't act in certain situations. That is what I try to do: let characters' actions define who they are. No one is all good or all bad. As Thoreau said, "I never knew, and never shall know, a worse man than myself." My new novel is called *The Wayward River*. It has to do with the life and times of my first wife, Mary. My last novel, now called *The Summer Pro*, is still looking for a home. Great hearing from you, and all the best. Carry on.

Tony.

· · · · · · · · · · ·

The Military Officers Association of America through the years has been a continuing strength of solidarity to our cause of Veterans Affairs in concern to Appropriate Psychiatric Handling, and to their being returned safely home from Combat to Civilian Life to a "Seamless Transition." That is not so seamless in the hostile real world of negative media programming, fearful public attitude in opposition, and to the outright disposal of our Veterans by government and medical malfeasance in misconduct of gross negligence pertaining for their outright mishandling of psychiatric intake and treatment in dire need to be rectified to the secure the dignity and emotional well-being of our Veterans returning safely home, and to their being provided for in the future with therapeutic safe healing of their Stress Disorders.

The V.A., and as their Deputy Chief Office for Mental Health, Dr. Ira Katz has stated, can write and say that the public "is coming around" to the acceptance of the diagnosis of mental disorders in a benign way, like having diabetes. But the truth of the matter is that the public doesn't accept it, especially in the case of the Veterans. And quite the opposite, that the population is being programmed to believe that each Veteran is potentially a deranged and violent killer and to be viewed as a dangerous threat, who must be put away and rendered incapacitated by chemical treatment for the public safety.

To what that, "Place No Head Above Your Own," as the saying is stated, and which is The Military's General Prudential Rule in avoidance of imminent danger, is The Order.

A case in point of this being the television soap opera called, Y&R, The Young and The Restless, which airs every weekday on CBS at 12:30 p.m. and which can be taped to watch later in the evening. That has become, on the part of its producers and writers, an Inter-Racial show advocating the nonchalant acceptance of Mixed Racial Affairs and Marriage; and to the use of drugs and poisons, in providing instructional training for the housewives, to play pranks or to inflict serious harm to unsuspecting males on the show.

That I mention, in prefacing and concerning the Interracial Affairs idea, which needs to be ruled on by the military as a firm policy not to be condoned, in heart and sanctity to preservation of the racial identity and heritage, of The White Race and The Black African Race, and to the innate racial desires and right of self determination in governing; (and in being weighed conjunction to the Drug Warfare design;) versus the mixed identity, and often warfaring hostile pursuits, of the resulting issue of the Mulatto Caste, being an alienated mixture of White and Black, and as having to do with the mixed caste nature of the ingrained Islamic hatreds of the White Race, continuing from the history of The Moors (710 to 1482 A.D.,) in their occupation of Western Europe, as it relates to The Spanish Inquisition and the Crusades of that Era in World History to save the White Race from the forced incursion of the Moorish Heroin Drug Culture into White Society of the time, and to the drug warfare problems they faced with the White Women then, many of whom were burned at the stake for their part in the betrayal, in similar condition as we also face as a society in these modern times of racial confrontation in ideology, with being forced upon us to accept and allow; of the one side programming the tolerance and adaptation to Drug Use, Promiscuous Morals, and Interracial Mixing, and of the other side, of the White Race Defending against it, and often in the manner of Backlash inducing discrimination, for the sake of Racial Preservation, and of The White Race, as such to be viewed now as an "Endangered Species," living in fear of annihilation, to cease to exist altogether, and be rendered like The Sub-Continent of India, if Inter-Racial Procreation here in the United States were carried out to the extreme of total assimilation.

Which is being told like it is. That has become for us now, a Political-Military Issue of being forced to witness an amassing of numbers through immigration overrun and racial assimilation, and being achieved through a means of forced intimidation of Social Domination in Stockholm Syndrome effect to embrace the Ideology and Cultural Influences of Heroin Drug Use, Pornography, Prostitution, and Inter-Racial Co-Mixing.

And concerning what can happen to the females with Heroin while their men are away, in explaining what has been happening to our Veterans, in one setting of regard, to their being sabotaged by means of Drug Perpetration, and using the females, who do the traditional food preparation, in a forced arrangement of coerced black-mail, as an "inside job" of it in the deadly conflict of a Race War, using drugs and chemicals; or to the matter of Pornography moving in as well; and also to do with the media inducing fear into the women in brainwashing them to be Sedating their men into docility, or to their doing so for purely personal Women's War Feminist motives in use of Drugs and Poison to inflict serious physical harm and psychological damage at the hands of these women, and to the Veterans developing, "mysterious maladies," as are always being reported about during our modern war era settings, as in "Gulf War Syndrome;" (which are easy to identify in the terms of Drug Sabotage properly understood,) or to

the Veterans being labeled with Paranoid Schizophrenia and
forced to take Thorazine for their saying so.

And for example, that on the Monday April 13, 2009 episode
of Y&R, one of the White male characters went berserk in a
"Fugue State" (described about in the dictionary as "a disturbed
state of consciousness characterized by acts that are not recalled
upon recovery,") stemming from a psychological re-injury of an
early childhood trauma, in which the character, in what Fugue
State, hallucinates that he is in an imaginary place and that he sees
his imaginary enemy, and begins to attack those around him in
thinking that they are that person. Which is what is being
programmed in mass hysteria into the public who have been and
are continuing to be, brainwashed into believing, that the
returning Combat Veterans, have been programmed to kill, and
might sleep walk about in such a Fugue State and murder the
household in believing that they are the enemy.

The need "to be put away" for which, is then further reinforce
later in the show by a Courtroom scene where the character is
being arraigned for going berserk and robbing banks at gun point
while in the "Fugue State" that the character then jumps up and
becomes irrational and begins to violently attack people in the
courtroom in hallucinating again that he is someplace else. To
what that his older brother and defense council on the show cites
to the judge, (as to the not-so-subtle propaganda being implanted
into the public's brains,) that his brother is suffering from "Post
Traumatic Stress Disorder" and needs to be placed in a
psychiatric facility for treatment where he can get some help.

Which was granted and to the character then being placed in a
padded room and rendered comatose by injections with a Strong
Tranquiller. Which only serves in example, to reinforce to the
public that removal and Hospitalization and Treatment with
Thorazine for our returning Veterans is appropriate, (and who are
suffering tragically with Post Traumatic Stress Disorders,) as it
relates to the public's attitude, and especially the attitudes of the
fearful housewives, towards the incoming and returning home
Veterans who are suffering through no fault of their own from the
rigors of combat.

The symptoms of Post Traumatic Stress Disorder of these Veterans are of a Vacuous Shock Affect and Depression to be treated for with respect, compassion, and dignity.

In what regard for intercession that our ongoing requests to The Veterans Administration for Proper Administrative Handling to this critical matter of Labeling and Treatment, have gone basically un-responded to, and of what few times that there have been responses, that are not provided to us in an intelligent manner of reply, (in the way of patronizing side-stepping, and polite "down talking" of the issues.) For what problems that we must have intelligent solutions to, or to face the crucible of social stigma, being discarded by society as "Mental Patients," and to a horrifying chemical maiming and death as a result, as we have raised and have addressed these issues, to each of the prior Veterans Affairs Secretaries in succession from the Vietnam War, and of recent history extensively with Dr. James B. Peake, and presently to the current Secretary General Eric Shinseki's, in addressing the need for a decisive verdict in Accountability and with Faith of Trust for The V.A. to act responsibly regarding the destruction of our returning home Combat Veterans through the V.A.'s warehousing policy of General Diagnosis with Schizophrenia and to prevailing use of heavy sedation with Strong Tranquillizer Drugs; such as Thorazine, Navane, Prolixin, Loxitain, Trilifon, and others, as to whether the Neuroleptic Drugs being mass administered by the Veterans Hospitals, (and elsewhere of the State Mental Health Facility settings to our Veterans also,) and to their, "Forced Treatment," or to "Ill-Advised Consent" to Treatment, Are Safe To Use; or, if in fact and indeed whether or not that these Drugs are lethally harmful to persons; and if so for the V.A. to formally acknowledge this crucial detail and to conclude with such disabling business on a permanent basis. And also that we need for the V.A.'s General Counsel to define under what circumstances allowed by law can any of our Veterans ever be "Force Treated," against their will with these drugs? And to define for us the legal resources available for Legal Counsel To Be Provided to Veterans by The Veterans Administration, (or for the Right to Counsel under

Miranda Legislation secured,) concerning The Rights of our
Veterans To Challenge Psychiatric Diagnosis, 2PC (Two
Physician Consent,) Commitment Procedure, and otherwise for
their Miranda Rights of Due Process to be clarified and protected,
as they relate with the Non-Criminal Mental Hygiene Law.

We need our inquiries addressed under the Freedom of
Information Act; which have not been forthcoming to this date.
And that we do have urgent business here to take care of right
now, and unresolved from our extensive coverage and briefing of
the first Keeping Faith with Wounded Warriors and their Families
Forum, (of September 17, 2008,) with Secretary James Peake to
resolve, of the same timely issues ongoing to General Shinseki,
concerning the obvious in documented harm of statistics
occurring as a direct result and consequence of the psychiatric
intake labeling and stigmatizing, and to the use of deadly drug
chemicals being administered; which we need all available means
presently at our disposal to address and to bring these matters in
crisis to the attention of the Federal Government, and to the
Justice Department, as to legally handle our specific request for
intervention on the Injustices of Psychiatric Diagnosis Labeling,
Unsafe Forced Treatment, and Violated Rights of Due Process as
we have called to be resolve.

That in way of reference to my qualifications to reason on, to
mention here, that I am a College Graduate educated as a "Faith
Based Psychologist" and "Medical Nutrition Specialist" with
Advanced Certificate Training and Hands-On Clinical Experience
Interned as a Psychotherapy Aid in the real time dynamics of a
Psychiatric Facility in Holistic Psychology to effectively "heal
people," and also educated with extensive Para-medical, Para-
Legal background in Psychiatric Pharmacology and Mental
Hygiene Law.

And with what tools on the issues here defining legitimate
treatment of mental health issues; as problems with causes to be
pragmatically worked out, handled, dealt with, and solved; to get
at the sources of, and to seek remedies for, the problems, (and not
as to be "masking them over" (as the Medical Doctors do,) with
disabling chemical drugs, (termed facetiously as, "Meds," which

heal no one;) but to provide remedies for; in a holistic way of applying sound nutritional practice, for a proper diet to be clinically provided and individually taught as a course of treatment, and coinciding to a regimen of physical fitness exercise and self discipline, (not to over eat, and to have a proper sense of a healthy sexuality, as affect one's psychological health in the need to be structured in order to feel better and to a good state of mind in the strength of internal fortitude, and coinciding to the elimination or avoidance of "bad habits," the likes of alcohol, drugs, and tobacco,) being the foundation to a healthy mind; to go along with group workshop therapy sessions relating and talking-out one's problems with one's peers, and along with professional one on one guidance counseling to provided insight into the mind for healthy personal, family, and social relationships to be instilled, and in being educated to the handling of conflicts and stress anxiety, as to be provided with working tools of the mind; and for the individuals to form a good positive outlook on life with conviction to a positive work ethic in orientation towards survival, as a way of structuring and ordering one's life, and as another foundation block to good mental health in keeping to a sound faith regime of responsibility to oneself and one's family, and to the avoidance of negative thoughts and actions leading in consequence to the bad karma, depression of guilt in wrongdoing, in avoidance of all wrongdoing, not to do wrong, and otherwise to do good works and to atone for past misdeeds and indiscretions, and to the overall concept of "doing good." Of which regimen, foundationally applied, that can basically "heal anybody" suffering with emotional and stress disorders, (provided they are not due to an organically induced mental illness,) given the proper nutrition, the proper incentives to heal, the proper amount of bed rest and time to recover, and time to detox from society.

The tragic setting here, is that the Neuroleptic Drugs, Strong Tranquilizers, such as Thorazine, being currently used to render Post Traumatic Stress Disorder victims into a comatose and vegetative existence in excruciatingly uncomfortable states of being, (and not to the sense of trying to treat anyone to heal them of their disorders, but for the sake of warehousing to be mass sedating them to be disposed of, to be rendering persons sedated for the purposes of mass control, and for other motives more sinister concerned with National Security, having to do with the medical/pharmacy industry, (for corrupt financial gain motives in the maintaining of a "captive diagnosis market," from whom no one can escape, except to remain on the "medications prescribed;" which becomes to them a chemical prison,) and/or for personal corrupt and maniacal motives; with the Medical Pharmacy Industry oriented in gross negligence of error in judgment to the force administered use of neuroleptic pharmacy, across the board, being administered to everyone, in total desecration of our Veterans, who have served our Nation proudly and bravely and heroically in point of honor, and who don't deserve to be treated as Mentally Ill Persons, in seriousness of the grievance being addressed; to wit: that these drugs, and the psychiatric labeling associated to them, are destroying people and not healing them.

The Military Officers Association Of America, MOAA, is sponsoring a second Wounded Warrior Forum to be held this upcoming September 2008, to participate and discuss our issue to resolve in. But the war, our way, needs to be over by then in its urgency. And with wars being what they are to the people that they affect who are seeking alliances to defend themselves against, let us all then labor together and be mindful that time is of the essence in this regard to the safety and well-being of our returned home Veterans, and to repair the damage to those already injured, of those of past wars, who have suffered to the psychiatric disposal system, to whom "next September" is a long and costly time in deadly toll of lives away; and once again which will only produce "more talk" to be "talking at" the problems without solutions.

The Psychiatric Medical Industry not only has "the power" to diagnose and to treat-destroy anyone they personally choose to with any drug chemical, surgery, or electro-insulin shock treatment they arbitrarily determine, and with Sovereign Immunity from civil and criminal prosecution to do so built in to their current practices; but to realize for also, that they also have the maniacal personal power over the freedom of the lives of every individual who they do diagnose, (in Captive Market arrangement,) to imprison anyone indefinitely, to set the terms of their release, and to do with whatever they want to under the current heading of Mental Hygiene Law regarding commitment and "to the terms of treatment," without any real Due Process of Law and in the name of Medicine. Which is taking place, Communist Bloc Style, "here," in our United States of America, without anyone of the entirety of the legal and legislative functions to defend against.

Which for the record to add that there are all too many numerous cases to cite; of medical malpractice and fraud, medical kickback complicity with the pharmaceutical companies, monetary corruption, narcotics trafficking, and involvement to pornography and drug conspiracies to organized crime, that do periodically surface to come to light. To the point being; that how can anyone be denied their God Given and Constitutional Rights to Due Process in the face of such subversion and corruption just because the legal rendering of Mental Hygiene is worded to fall under the Medical Clause of Civil Law; which demands a Congressional Investigation and Government Oversight to monitor.

The Lives of our Veterans are on-line for the swift and determined resolution of this case, which has been destroying and taking the lives of our Veterans in great numbers.

Sun 4/26/09 8:57 PM

Dear Tony

Start to finish, Tony, I loved your book, Home Again, Home Again. It is a beautifully written and inspired novel, with a deeply moving complexity of story line and rewarding attention to detail, set in the foothills of The Catskill Mountains looking out onto Lookout Mountain, and Larro Mountain, in the wonderfully described for sensation of the out of doors; about Phoebe-Krueger, who is 31 and dissatisfied with their home life of the line between make believe and reality, and Roland Gray in their young married years, married 11 years to each other, and their young 10 year old son Luke, who is a fine boy, and about the troubles they are having with their marriage, with Phoebe feeling trapped in the woods and cheated out of an exciting worthwhile life, exacerbated by the well running dry, and Roland's literary distance from her emotionally.

And about Roland's Father Luther, and his trouble life, and Mother Joan, and their life at Hawk's Eye in Rawson Colony, and the symbolic Apple Trees that Roland's father had planted, which are sickly and still not bearing fruit, and which is Luke's job to water, "one day they'll bear apples," that is richly interwoven with the main story line intertwined and connected with the rest of the cast of strong characters; Carl Hoda, the neighbor, Paul Myers, the old attorney who collects the rents for the owner's son Donald Rawson, Jimmy DiDomenico, who picks a fight with Luke, and his father Jim Sr., who avenges it, and the Steins, Larry and Rhoda, and Larry Stein who served over with Bob Herter as his boss in the Navy, and who was now Larry's boss, and the source of trouble, and Bob Herter, the General Manager of Morrisey Lowe, and the anti-hero villain of the book, who ruins Phoebe and Luke's marriage, and Rawson Colony, about Morrisey-Lowe and the company's plan, being generated by Bob Herter and his ambition, to buy out Rawson Art Colony for an Industrial Park, and of the nearby village of Woodbridge and the city of Kingsley in Ulmer County, NY along the Hudson. And about Harvey's Field where the kids play ball, and The Rawson Horse totem carved out of a tree, which becomes vandalized, and the friendship in male bonding formed with Larry Stein fly-fishing in Maverick Creek; that for me, was the heart of the book, and was especially moving. And overall for the work's fine attention to detail, that at quite often at times transported me into its world.

I felt very comfortable and in tune with the book a third of way into it, like I belonged there and had gone to live in it, and seeming always wanting to turn the page to be involved with the characters and to experience more of it. There were always at the turn of every page some really very moving gripping scenes and with many moving descriptions full of nostalgia in the book to let the imaginations of the mind experience; "the smell of rain after the storm," and "always in anticipation of the sense that something is going to happen, of what's going to happen."

You had some very nice similes, as literary comparisons, but which I thought a few of them were "over done," or seemed to be straining the limits of being contrived for the sake of making a comparison and not genuinely apparent, but most of them worked well.

And all in all that I felt the love scenes were all tastefully done, and after all that love making is a part of life to be literary worked out, alluding to a sense of passion and with a feeling of helplessness to succumb to without being vulgar and in bad taste, kitsch, in another meaning, as is in the Greek Tradition, not to portray raw sexuality or violence, but only to tell about it. In the meaning that some things involving human side of nature are "private," and need to remain respectfully so, otherwise it gets unseemly. Do you follow me there? To what I say, that the F___ word just doesn't fit in with truly great literature, if you get my drift, not if you want it to endure the ages.

If you want something else, then, I realize as you say that the characters will be who they are to become, but the work is written to young adults too, as well to sophisticated adults, who would have trouble reading the passages involving the F___ word aloud to an audience with young people in it, or to anyone in particular for what matter. It's not that I am offended by it personally, as you say, but in feeling for the sense of The Enduring Robinson, to stand the test of the ages, as a Literary Classic, that I respond. That why don't you try it and see how it feels to you with that word in it. If it makes you feel embarrassed and having to apologize for it, then point taken, and to spark the question as to why there are things profane and things which are sacred to discern over?

Otherwise, as I judge it, the work is a magnificent work that is strong in its portrayal of the struggles for love and admiration, and of the fate of a man and woman caught in the grips of real life in its living, and for its need in portrayal of a "Code of Honor" that men live by, to honor faithfully their wives, and friendships, and whether that they live faithfully to the code, or not. Larry Stein does, when he challenges Bob Herter over his, Herter's, affair with Phoebe. And Roland does, when he struggles with the idea of making a Cuckold out of his friend Larry, in telling Rhoda to "get out." There can't be anything worse than to have an affair with your friends wife, and to know her in that way, and not to be able to look your friend faithfully ever again," squarely in the eyes." Can you imagine anything worse to endure as a man than to be unfaithful to his friend?

And which is also about other forms of betrayals also, about Jim Didomenico's betrayal of Roland in selling out the Colony, and to go along with Phoebe's betrayal of the Colony also, and besides of her infidelity.

And for Phoebe too, who feels guilty about her affair with Robert Herter, from the start, who has a change of heart when it comes down to the final reality setting in of what she has done and what she is about to do. Phoebe is attracted to Bob at first for the fresh start and new horizon world that he potentially has to offer her, and possibly too for the sex, but I think unconsciously also for the sake that Bob has a shower for her to use. Women need to feel clean.

"Roland Gray stood in the living room of his house staring up at the low, leaden sky, thinking how the naked trees in his yard looked like dark skeletons wrapped in a common shroud, but he was also thinking that another November day, promising rain without producing any, was almost over. Since midmorning, when the heavy clouds had started rolling in, he had intermittently watched and waited at this {and} at his kitchen window; and now, as the afternoon waned, he could only feel his spirits, at an abysmal low all fall, plunge to even greater depths of darkness and despair… He ran his hand across his thick-bearded face, then turned and retreated into the room."

And in ending to say, that I don't think that "young Tony" was really happy with his "Trap Line," in having to witness the suffering and the torture of the Muskrats; as Phoebe mentioned in her thoughts in horror about Roland and his "Muskrat Stick," with its notches, "to have hold their little heads under water with a fork on one end of the stick to drown them if they were still alive."

The book will endure to live on in my mind and heart forever, Tony. Well Done!

Gary

From: robinsoa@newpaltz.edu
To: gary.koniz@hotmail.com
Subject: the review
Date: Thu, 7 May 2009 07:18:04 -0400

Hi, Gary--what a thorough review you gave *Home Again*. I don't believe anyone ever saw the novel from so many different angles. It was really quite amazing to see your take on the characters. It made me want to read the book immediately (again.) You certainly have a flow of words. I feel myself searching more and more (going slower and slower) when I sit down to write. Maybe it's just the years creeping up on me; then again I'm not sure I ever had your river of expression. Clearly you have a strong moral sense. I like to think I have a moral sensibility also but the profane has a place in our lives as well. It all comes down to form and balance. I would never want to be judged as a prude. How is your new book coming along? Another great title! A novel I have just finished is called *The Floodplain*. Guess what the setting is? Carry on. -- Tony

Thu, 7 May 2009 19:00

Dear Tony,

What a great and rewarding delight it is to have a good friend
and esteemed colleague and respected companion such as
yourself to be able to stretch out in the mind and relate with.
Thanks for your letter today, which is very heartfelt. It felt good
to see your name there in my inbox as you were on mind today
for a good part of it, in thinking of when would be a good time to
write you once again, in not wanting to overplay my welcome
with you so to speak, and also in relating with the inner thoughts
of what I Just told you, in thinking of you, of how nice it is to
have a real friend, not just a friend, but a real friend, in the way of

eternal friendship, in the eternal time of the moments of our visit here to earth, and in feeling the warm breeze and sun upon my face, and the sounds of chirping birds, and in breathing in the air deliberately, in deep relaxing breaths, that I thought of you, and how great it was to be alive, and about the tragedy of Mary to be missing it all, and how I felt for your heart broken back then, and now, and for your attempts to write it out, as you title, "The Wayward River." So we are on a deeper level.

I didn't mean to imply about your wonderful novel, Home Again, Home Again, that I wasn't happy with it as it is written, just that, for me, as a reader, that I wanted it to be a certain way. I can live with the way it is. I thought the love scenes were beautifully written, (there is such a thing as love to write about.) And overall to feel that you are one of the finest descriptive writers I have ever had the pleasure of reading, and studying, (and I spent my time buried in books, as Earnest Hemmingway always did, reading being the pre-qualifier for being a writer.) But for me, Home Again, Home Again, is a much too sensitive and moving story of gripping love, taking place in many dimension; the love for the land, the love for one's work in profession, the love for friendship, the love for spouse and family, and the love of a child and for a child, and the love of children in wonderment for the earth, to be a rough bawdy book, and as to why that I didn't think your choice of the f___ word didn't suit the great and profound majesty of the work, and even though it may have suited the character.

I also felt, Tony, that your use of the word, Kike, was outdated and offensive and to a degree that it would alienate an otherwise eager and supportive reading market. And as well to your reference of a Mulatto the same, being in the category with the other aspersion remarks made about Rawson Colony as to degenerates, and alcoholics, and mulattoes in the same breath in being a reason provided to take it down. Which offers the offense in hurt feelings to the poor outcast mulatto to have to suffer, and to be alienated.

I always feel a little embarrassed when reading Hemmingway, to his reference in several of his books of the word Nigger, "Winner Take Nothing," being an example, and there others, in which I feel awkward for him in historical retrospect, and for the colored people that way having to read. Which in a certain time long ago was accepted speech.

And to let you know that I am well underway with, A Departure From The Rules; and, to say that I am enjoying it immensely, and especially for your very moving descriptive passages, all of theme, page by page, which are superb. The love scenes are wonderfully done, and I was happy that Phil McFarland, was able to be successful with his fiancée Carol Talbot after his failure with the harlot Kay Braddon who made full of him. I was pulling for him. And so you see that things work in their proper and respected times and places, and everything has a place in time.

But I don't want to over talk the book right now with you. I want to savor it some more before I do.

I remember you said to me one time out on the side part of the front lawn standing in front of the vegetable garden that I planted for you, in the gathering dusk of the evening sipping cocktails with the glasses in our hands, and watching the passersby on Huguenot Street and you suggested to spend one whole day in P&G's together from the time it opened up until the time it closed, and you said to me. "Let's beat each other up and get all bloody."

Gary

Fri, 22 May 2009 18:46

Dear Tony,

I am just writing to tell you how much I am so thoroughly enjoying reading your book, A Departure From The Rules. It's a great tale of the sea and the intimate details of the lives of the seamen aboard The USS Dobbs and The Destroyer Division DD 529, consisting of The Villaume, The Carter, The Bostwick, and The Dobbs. I'm at Part III Chapter 2, right now, with Beaver (Lt. Byrne,) and Kobe-san (Mirome,) as they embark on their love affair and share their emotional sides. And for the rest of the adventure of the crew of The U.S.S. Dobbs, as they have just arrived in Yokosuka and are out on the town at Liberty; with Beaver, Phil, Ferret, and Foxy, (and about Ferret's rivalry with Beaver over the girls,) and with many other well written facets of the meaning of human inter-relationships of intrigues, that I am so thoroughly enjoying reading. It's the kind of book you just want to savor and linger with and at the same time which you want to just continue of with reading and can't wait to find out what's about to happen next. And many parts of it that you just want to read over again to sense the quality of the very emotional and sagely insightful writing

I am so very impressed with you, for your strength and command of the narrative, your style of intimacy with the characters, and for your descriptive ability, that is always so poignant and clear in its understanding of the human essence as to evoke the feeling of being there in the book yourself with the characters and living it out!

What a tremendously great and powerful writer you are! and have been all along to know, Tony. I only wish that I was a more mature and less self-absorbed man in the earlier version of myself in my younger years to have involved myself more with you on the intimate level to read some of your books back then in the years past to know you better as a man. And I do know you too that way, in the ways I know you, as a great and remarkable man of historical time, as time is weighed and measured in the significance of history, the history of our time together and of every other time which we are included, through books, to be a part of, and which includes us too, in our readings and our studies of them.

But it is all the more, more poignant at this late date to read you, and I want to read all of you, all of your books and short stories, and I want to read your father too and each of his many books; The Cardinal, Water of Life, The Great Snow, Science Versus Crime, The Enchanted Grindstone and Other Poems, Stout Cortez - A Biography of The Spanish Conquest, Tale of Two Lovers, Fantastic Interim, and A Skeleton Key To Finnegan's Wake, Out Of Line: Dilemmas and Frustrations of Everyman, Private Virtue – Public Good, Children of Morningside, Buck Fever, The Way of The Seeded Earth – Mythologies of Primitive Planters, Science Catches The Criminal, and The Prefect Round, (which I all came across on the Abe Books Website, and which was over a thousand books, many in German, Italian, and Spanish;) And books enough, and along with each of your books, and with other fond authors, Hemmingway, and Faulkner, and the many classic writers of our history to reflect on, and others of the contemporary sense, who we fall in love with, as readers, to read in our days, to absorb and preoccupy my attention for a life time. I like reading and studying people, for their knowledge and reflective insights into the common experiences of life, and what makes us feel, "not so very much forever alone." You have to love reading for the sake of what the authors have thought about life and have to say about it, which in the intrigue of the art of it in the great deepness of satisfaction.

And as Earnest Hemmingway once quoted in his novel, The Green Hills of Africa, on Sari with his second wife Pauline, and quoting F Scott Fitzgerald, whom he knew when he was living in Paris and married to Hadley during his ex-patriot years with Gertrude Stein and Ford Maddox Ford ... which goes ... "In the deep dark night of the soul, it is always 3:00 a.m.." And what is always at that time when at that time of the night when we all wake up for some reason, to lie there in our thoughts and alone with our self in the darkness, that a man is always and utterly alone with himself and God ... to ponder ... in the eerie darkness of the lonely night.

I have enclosed and ending here with an excerpt in description from Abe Booksellers about your Father, Henry Morton

Robinson's book, The Cardinal; and also along with a letter from
Robert Redford about the new edition of my book, The Call To
Order, which I sent to him in care of his Sundance Institute, and
as a p.s. if you want to download it to look it over, or otherwise to
purchase a copy of it you can access it conveniently at,
www.lulu.com/content/paperback-book/the-call-to-
order/6663590, or I can always send you a copy if you are
interested as I did the last time with The Orders Of The Day, as to
your invitation to mail, which you can let me know about. I could
even "Inscribe" an edition of the book to you personally for
posterity if you would like, and in grateful appreciation to you for
all that you have done to influence and inspire my life.
      "In THE CARDINAL, Robinson tells the story of a young
Irish-American priest on his journey from a naïve and slightly
arrogant curate to his eventual promotion to cardinal in the
Roman Catholic Church. While often filled with the melodramatic
elements that are common in these types of novels; THE
CARDINAL makes an honest attempt to show what life was like
for a Catholic priest in the 1st half of the 20th century. By
examining aspects of a priest's spiritual and temporal life,
Robinson creates a moving portrait of the difficult choices that are
made by a man who chooses this life. Abortion, miracles, and the
financial realities of poor and wealthy parishes are all dealt with
in an evenhanded manner, but with a continued focus on the
belief system of the Catholic faith. The book shows particular
strength when it deals directly with the Catholic Church and its
hierarchy, with an emphasis on how the church felt about its
American brethren. The novel does slow down considerably when
dealing with the protagonist's (Stephen Fermoyle) stereotypical
Irish family and Fermoyle's crisis of faith when confronted with
feelings for various women in his life. But the novel does provide
an intriguing view of what a priest's life might be like in America
between World War I and II."
      I see too that young Tony is still reflecting on his "Trap Line,"
and the Muskrats; or as previous to Home Again, Home Again,
with the Muskrat Stick and its notches and forked tip, and to
Phoebe's horror and revulsion, beginning at this stage, "to reflect

on," in his earlier work, only in "Departure," having to do with
not being able to "get new traps" during the war, and as to why
he, the author Robinson would think that way about the Muskrats.
He reflects on the Trap-Line too in his Biography. "I had a trap
line when I was boy ... that I worked every morning before
school, and entered The Sears and Roebuck Contest one year for
the nicest pelts ... "
Gary

And, it is in that light then, that we must have the proper Legal
Resources and Definitions of Law ensured for the protection of
our Men In Arms; as to what exactly constitutes for a, "Legal
Definition of a Mental Condition," and under what specific
circumstances that anyone may be "Force Treated;" under the
heading of psychiatric in exposure, and to what that everyone is
lumped into a common plight about with the utterly insane and
violently irrational over, as to the meaning that being labeled as a
"psychiatric patient" is to imply; and whether that they are
suffering with remorse of combat, or grieving over the deaths of
their comrades, or suffering the loss of their wives on their return,
or from anxiety of being jobless and homeless in their suffering,
that the wording of psychiatric implies that "the worst case
scenario" is always present to. Therefore:
Since the Medical Terminology Technicality of Mental
Hygiene Psychiatric Law falls under the heading of Civil Law,
Two Physician Consent, 2PC, Commitment Procedure, on
Medical Grounds, in that no crime has been committed under
Mental Hygiene Law to be charged for and thereby to be accorded
the protective safeguards of Miranda Rights Legislation to be
prosecuted for and processed fairly for under The Constitutional
Rights accorded to Criminal Penal Law Legal System under the
protection in Rights To The People, of The Fourth, Fifth, Sixth,
Eighth and Fourteenth Amendments to The U.S. Constitution, and
reinforced by the protection of The Miranda Legislation, is hereby
clarified of Its Civil Law Constitutional Rights, in meaning to
have the same Rights of Due Process as are and have been
established under Penal Law, in guarantee of:

The Right to have a clear definition of a Formal Psychiatric Charge being present in grounds for anyone to be labeled for and to have any specified medical psychiatric condition, or for the offense of irrational behavior labeling being levied against an individual, and in grounds thereby for any psychiatric evaluation process mental illness labeling to be attached to anyone, or for any process of Two Physician Consent, 2PC, Psychiatric Commitment Procedure to be conducted. And that such definition of charge is also to precede any Court or Government Agency Order for the disclosure of personal and private psychiatric history records to be produced.

The Right to The Fourth Amendment guarantee of privacy in regard of doctor patient confidentiality and invoking to The Due Process Right of Probable and Sufficient Cause In Grounds, is to be present and justified to a specific itemized search and disclosure in mandatory request for Specific Information only of any existing psychiatric history records, regarding The Rights of Government Agencies, as for the specified psychiatric history to be scrutinized, to any private request or public government agency order for, or court authority mandatory order for the scrutiny of anyone's psychiatric medical history records to be revealed. That is not to be construed by court order or by congressional authority concerning government agencies, to be a total and all intrusive invasive invasion of an individual's records history involving The Right To Privacy, but is to issued only as order for records disclosure pertains selectively and relevant to the specified psychiatric charge of inquiry at hand.

The Right to strict legal definition for any psychiatric labeling terms to be applied.

The Right to strict legal determinations based to demonstrated facts of observed and defined behavior, in the presence of any attorney, for such alleged psychiatric labeling being attributed in legal attachment of a psychiatric diagnosis or involving commitment.

The Right to Counsel, to be provided for at government expense if need be, by The Examining Government Agency or by The Court of Jurisdiction, for any alleged psychiatric matter of consequence being attributed to anyone, involving the loss of liberty, property, licensure, employment, or privilege.

The Right to have an Attorney present during questioning to any psychiatric examination/evaluation/interrogation, and to be present during psychiatric commitment processing and to any court proceedings and signing of documents.

The Right to Remain Silent in presumption of innocence until proven guilty to any psychiatric charge in a bona fide court of law.

The Right to Confrontations of any accusing testimony against the accused in virtue of The Sixth Amendment, that under current Mental Hygiene Law there is No Right To.

The Right to a Jury Trial provided in a timely way in accordance with The Sixth Amendment for any specified psychiatric accusation labeling being imposed, whether involving commitment or not.

The Right to clearly established and legally defined medically safe and beneficial therapeutic treatment to be imposed for legitimate psychiatric conditions.

The Right to Informed Consent "in the presence of Legal Counsel" concerning the discussion and patient awareness of adverse effects, and harmful side effects in short and long-term use of psychiatric chemicals involved with any psychiatric treatment to occur.

The Right To Refuse Treatment, and Against Forced Treatment on Medical Discretion, in the presence of legal counsel, [except in matters As Prescribed By Law to be applied for necessary medical emergency procedure in concern to imminent crisis of hysteria, and for violent mania and agitated disruptive behavior in being in threat to oneself or others requiring emergency medical treatment in judgment or relief.]

The Right against any form, including psychological, of cruel and inhumane treatment to occur, concerning physical, mental, or emotional abuse, to include electro-shock treatment, surgical procedure, and pharmaceutical experimentation, [Clinical Trials] in virtue of The Eighth Amendment.

The Right to reasonable and soundly defined Statute of Limitations in established Legal Age Limits for the mandatory disclosure of previous psychiatric condition labeling history records, or to the disclosure of legally carried-out psychiatric commitment history records, based to the nature and severity and to the extent of such psychiatric conditions in legal stipulation and to the length of time of such conditions in interval, to be imposed for mandatory disclosure of records, not to be in excess of a reasonable and prudent time interval regarding the public removal of stigma and liability of such records history. Which in most instances is to be worded, to any current treatment for any serious ongoing psychiatric condition, or to within the past three years in age limit concerning.

Medication : Navane - (Thiothixene)

Possible side effects, warnings and cautions associated with this medication are listed below. This is not an all-inclusive list but is representative of Items of potential clinical significance to you. For more information on this medication, you may consult further with your physician or refer to a standard text such as the PDR or the United States Pharmacopoeia Dispensing Information (USPDI), as part of monitoring some of these potential side effects, your physician may order laboratory or other tests. The treatment team will closely monitor individuals who are unable to readily communicate side effects in order to enhance care and treatment.

Possible side effects warnings and cautions associated with this medication. The most common side effects include: Constipation: decreased sweating: dizziness, lightheadedness, or fainting: drowsiness {mild}: dryness of mouth: increased appetite and weight: increased sensitivity of skin to sunlight (skin rash, itching, redness or other discoloration of skin, or severe sunburn): stuffy nose. Check with your doctor as soon as possible if any of the following side effects occur: difficulty in talking or swallowing:

inability to move eyes: lip smacking or puckering: loss of balance control: mask-like face: muscle spasms, especially of the neck and back: puffing of cheeks, rapid or worm-like movements of tongue: restlessness or need to keep moving (severe): shuffling walk: stiffness of arms and legs: trembling and shaking of fingers and hands: twisting movements of body: uncontrolled chewing movements: uncontrolled movements of the arms and legs

Less common side effects include: Changes in menstrual period, decreased sexual ability: swelling of breasts (in males and females): unusual secretion of milk. Check with your doctor as soon as possible if any of the following side effects occur: Blurred vision or other eye problems: difficult urination: fainting: skin discoloration: skin rash. Check with your doctor as soon as possible if any of the following rare side effects occur: Hot, dry skin or lack of sweating: increased blinking or spasms of eyelid: muscle weakness: sore throat and fever: uncontrolled twisting movements of neck, trunk, arms, or legs: unusual bleeding or bruising: unusual facial expressions or body positions: yellow eyes or skin.

Stop taking this medicine and **get emergency help immediately** if any of the following effects occur: Convulsions (seizures: difficulty in breathing: fast heartbeat: high fever: high or low (irregular} blood pressure: increased sweating: loss of bladder control: muscle stiffness (severe): unusually pale skin: tiredness.

This medication may cause your skin to be more sensitive to sunlight than it is normally. Exposure to sunlight, even for brief periods of time, may cause a skin rash, itching, redness or other discoloration of the skin, or a severe sunburn.
Tardive Dyskinesia (lip smacking or puckering, puffing of cheeks, rapid or fine worm-like movement of tongue, uncontrolled chewing movement, uncontrolled movements of arms and legs may occur and may not go away after

stopping use of the medication). **<u>See PDR, USPDI list of side effects.</u>**

Sat, 30 May 2009 18:46

Dear Tony,

   Tony, you are the greatest writer who has ever lived; as great as any of them. I am just so thrilled and proud of you and for your achievement with the success of the two novels I have read to date, Home Again and A Departure although not so finished yet with A Departure ... still in trauma from "The Event!" of IV 4, The Turn of The Wheel, to take it up again, and after you led us to love each of the characters in their turn, even Captain Karst in the depths of his character. I was deeply moved and proud of Beaver that he stayed holding to his friend Mort through it all, and would not let go! even though that he himself should perish. Who are you, Tony, and how on earth did you come to grapple with such deep visions of life in the mind. How truly majestic. Your descriptions at each turn of the page move me some times to the point of years, and always to a deep reflection. One truly does go to "live" within the pages of your novels, and they become "real" to the sense of living there in the mind. You become a part of me.
   Please tell me a little about your friend Robert Frost, whom you had a picture taken with at The Bread Loaf Writers Conference in Woodstock. I followed Mr. Frost in his poem, "The Road Not Taken," and that has made all the difference ... And I, I took the road less traveled by ... So we are brothers, Tony. Real deep emotional brothers, all bloody and everything.

   It takes a little getting used regarding the discipline of being a writer, as Hemmingway would start his days out that way to the early rising, "to a good day, a five or six pencil day," as he phrased it. That always tends to be a little struggle to commit to the actual matter of physically getting up and out of the bed about to awakening, that I call the Law of Inertia, after Newton's Law, "a body at rest tends to stay at rest," and to what that it always feels like another hour or two of sleep would do, but which wouldn't really, in the need to get up and to get on with the start the day. Which "once up" one feels just right about.

I wrote this letter recently to Mr. Eric L. Affeldt, President and C.E.O. ClubCorp USA, Inc. in Dallas, TX 75234, that I thought you might be interested in to coincide with your reconstitution of your "shelved" novel, Forty Thousand Brothers as a fresh beginning to your labor novel, as I can relate to. Let's see where it will lead as a common interest.

America stands or dies on the great faith, that All Men Are Created Equal and on The Principles that Fairness and Justice For All Shall Prevail. And for what reason at this time last year that we first attempted to organize as workers in America under the heading of, Golf Course Maintenance Workers Union, and in order to be respected as a Collective Bargaining Unit and able to address management as equals in the expression of our needs for certain conditions to our employment in America being met for in the practical reality of ensuring our survival at odds with the perils of human nature and the economy, and for amenable working conditions to be accorded and able to be reasoned out, and to a yearly negotiated contract sense to go by; that we had hopes for achieving; but were discouraged for by the strategy of discussions held by Mr. John Longstreet, (your Vice President in charge of People Strategy,) and with Ms. Sandy Slack (your Vice President of Human Resources,) in Captive Audience Sessions, not to Unionize.

And who, (as to say of Mr. Longstreet, and Ms. Slack,) came all the way here to Jacksonville, FL from your ClubCorp Headquarters in Dallas, TX, and spent an entire week here to meet and to talk with the men about their employment conditions with ClubCorp. And which resulted in the union election being out-voted and by a count of nine to one, (with myself and as delegated Secretary to the endeavor casting the only "Yes" vote in face saving,) and to the sense in embarrassment at the expense in the

waste of time put out by the National Labor Relations Board local
Labor Attorney, Mr. Nicholas Ohanesian; to arrange for, and to
set up, and to personally conduct, The Secret Ballot Election, at
the DeerCreek Country Club Maintenance Building, that was
signed for by a decided majority of the men, and held on two
consecutive days; but which was dissuaded for the understanding,
(in the meaning, with ClubCorp management,) that there was no
need to unionize and that you would always be receptive and
responsive to our employee needs and to work with us in attempts
to resolve any issues that we may have, and in the words of Ms.
Slack, to be provided with "Open Channels of Communication."

We are eligible now for another Union Shop Election after the
passage of the one year's time in waiting period as stipulated for
by The NLRB, and with June 21 being our one year anniversary
date, that I have now these several items to take up with you over.

April, the annual time set for our "Cost Of Living" pay
increases, (that is calculated for to this fiscal year 2009 by The
Federal Government's General Schedule Standard at 3 and 1/2%,)
and that is also the annual date set for Employee Evaluations and
Merit Based Raise adjustments to occur, has come and gone by
now with no word from management as to if and when that these
needed adjustments will occur, that was a disappointment, as this
was a big selling item of your discussions last season for the men
not to unionize. I know we need to make sacrifices over the
economy, but as I keep relating to you, that we, as Maintenance
Workers, are barely making do at the "subsistence level" of wages
as they stand and Need To Survive The Cost of Living as the
bottom line. To what we are suffering and not making demands
for "more" money about in that sense, but for "enough money," to
live on with dignity for the work we do, and with fairness to be
respected for.

I have made the appeal in to you many times in the past for
this concession, that our Job Description, as Golf Course
Maintenance Workers, is a very professionally oriented and
highly respected skilled Profession, as a Trade, that takes time to
learn and to master, considering the handling of all the equipment
to operate and to do the related job functions, and for the many

technical skills involved, and for the strong physical condition
that you have to be in to do the labor involved, that you just can't
hire people off the street to come in to do, and need to be valuing,
and retaining, your highly skilled, trained, and professionally
motivated employees, and not to be thinking of them in the terms
of "Turnover," when it comes time for their expected raises due,
as you have been, to be discouraging them from continuing on for
the sake of turning a quick profit to an arbitrarily arranged budget,
so to be hiring new people on at entry level to replace the
seasoned workers who are already trained, and calling it good
business, which it is not.

Our overtime, (as you ordered, due to the economy,) has been
discontinued, (which all along in previous years, has been used to
supplement our yearly incomes in lieu of raises being
forthcoming,) but which we are now cut back and are forced to
live on what the 40 hour week paychecks, at the subsistence level
rate, will buy, which are at a barely un-survivable hourly wage.
And, We Do Have To Survive, as you can humanely relate to.

In addition the idea of "Affordable Health Care" relative to our
meager incomes being in conscience provided for by ClubCorp,
has not been forthcoming. And neither has the orientation of Step
Raises for length of service been taken-up, based on acceptable
Job Performance to the General Schedule (GS) Standards, for
GS1 and GS2 level rates, ranging from $9.00 entry level for an
untrained employee, with a Step Raise after a Ninety Day trial
period, and after One Year, and so on up to the GS2 Rate of
$13.00, in 2009 Dollars, and with $11.50 being the right amount
presently for Seasoned Workers.

And, by your paying a healthy wage out to your employees,
that you will also be contributing, in Patriotic Service, to the
security of The United States, and by the assuming of your
Corporate Responsibility to the well being of The Nation and to
the Communities you do business in, by providing "The
Purchasing Power" needed to keep the economy viable and
healthy, and to the support of Government and Infrastructure by.
And in added advantage to also be securing of present and future

business for the Golf Industry besides, that overall "Purchasing Power" will produce on the larger-scale.

And in taking us a lesson from the farmers, that you just can't keep taking from the soil without putting nutrients back in, let us come to an understanding about the reality and the relationship of our lives here as we continue on into the future with ClubCorp as to the terms and conditions of our employment being in a fair-minded intent, and for you to shoulder up to the responsibility to provide a respectable livelihood to your employees.

And when we think about the nature of work, real manly physical work upon the earth to enjoy in the days, "by the sweat of one's brow," as The Creator envisioned, I ask you, what finer job could there be than to be a Greenskeeper working on a Golf Course, and especially such a beautifully scenic and picturesque course as the DeerCreek Country Club in Jacksonville, FL; with its surrounding upscale homes, lovely lakes, lush tropical wetlands, majestic woodlands full of old trees, and myriad wildlife to marvel at, that is truly a wonderful experience, and one which doesn't contain the value of being inferior to other pursuits of livelihood, (as the class structure has built into itself to justify its exploitation and domination over others.) And what speaks for the entirety of job functions to be described for as, Golf Course Maintenance Work, but that is particularly delightful for the Greenskeeper aspect in the early morning hours, for the serenity, peace, and delight of that time of the day, without the noise of machinery to blanket the pureness of the total experience in awareness, and what is to Cut The Cups for the day's Pin Placements, and to manicure the greens, repair ball marks and scuffs, fix imperfections, check for pests, weeds, and disease, and to note the overall conditions to take care of.

The days for our Golf Course Maintenance Work, run seven days a week with most alternating weekends off, and begin each day with the four-thirty a.m. wake-up alarm, or before that, in the solemn silence of the morning darkness and with the feeling of stature in confidence that the self-discipline of being an early riser gives you to be awake in the mystical pre-dawn hours, to get yourself ready and set to arrive early to the 6:00 a.m. to start for

work, that in our ways of participating in the morning ritual of
greeting each of our co-workers, each in their turn, as they arrive,
or are met as already being there, and all reciprocating in kind,
with warm friendly greetings of brotherly affection. And for a
brief time then to discuss events and "talk shop" amongst
ourselves, as a work family together, and which we like to call,
"The Church of The Early Morning," affectionately of the
morning gathering together, that is always looked forward to with
fondness, and each then to their own assignments and to the
duties of caring and maintaining the golf course; and to Fond
Farewells extended at the conclusion of each day's work together.

But for the Greenskeeper, it is a quite time, alone with the
earth, and with The Thoughts of God in that sense, in rapport with
the physical sensations of life and of being alive. The work
begins in the darkness of the pre-dawn hours in the presence of
the moon and the stars, and with the visible planets, and awaiting
the rising sun, and to the experience of the increments of morning
twilight emerging, to witness the rapture of the morning sunrises
in all their splendid glory, and to each day's different nuances of
moods in seasonal temperatures, cloud cover, and to inclemency's
of weather, depending on the mood of the day to savor. And each
day is a charm, always it is, to the utter enjoyment of the days
themselves in their entirety, and to the sensations and emotions
you feel as the Sun rises to warm the air; and through all the
seasons of the year, each in their own unique ambiance of their
days, in endless arrays of diversity, as to each of their being hot or
cold, chilly or mild, windy or calm, cloudy overcast, rainy, or
clear, and with the build-up of the Great Cumulus Thunderstorm
Clouds in the steamy hot Summer Months, to pour rain down in
torrents in the afternoons, and for the smell of the rain on the
earth, and for the feeling of a cool breeze on your face on a hot
day, or the warmth of the Sun in the frosty morning air of a cold
day, and for the enchanting scents and smells of the Earth, and for
the pure physical awareness of being alive on the Planet we call
home in the Universe, and for the feeling of a good job done at
the end of the days to reflect on and in the tiredness of physical
joy, that we should all pay you for to have such a fine job.

From: robinsoa@newpaltz.edu
To: gary.koniz@hotmail.com
Subject: Your last
Date: Wed, 3 Jun 2009 10:22:20 -0400

Gary, I was touched by your comments in your last e-mail. Of all
the comments, reviews, letter I've had through the years, your
have been the fullest, most detailed and positive. Robert Frost
was never my friend. We met briefly at Bread Loaf, exchanged a
few words, and then sat side by side in a photo shoot. The Road
Not Taken is one of my favorites also. When asked to read
"Stopping by Woods on a Snowy Evening," he read it so fast we
who were listening barely got settled. He read it, I suspect,
the way he thought it should be read. I have two novels
circulating now, looking for a home. Which of these two titles
for my golf novel do you like more? (It takes place in Ireland.)
The American Golfer or *The Summer Pro*. The other has a title I
really like, *The Floodplain*. Tell me a little about your job taking
care of the links at your club. Take care, and thanks for the good
reviews.

Tony

Thurs 4 Jun 2009 1835 PM

I've been thinking of a poem for you, Tony, just a feeling I had
that seemed to suit you. I don't quite seem to have it all, yet.

Gary

There was a time
in the forgotten subconscious regions of the mind
back when in the early stages of childhood
in development
when the Earth seemed very young as we were
and we could live on forever
in the feeling of safety
secure in the arms of loved ones,
as children perceive about themselves
in simple terms of the earth
of rich endearment and with great admiration
to be alive to it,
the sunlight, the feel of the moss, the air to breath,
the insects in flight,
the trees, the birds of the air,
and the animals all around,
and of the many sights and sounds,
smells, and sensations
of the many things about us in the moment
of a miraculous World,
and in the feeling that "The Moment" itself
that was all the joy all along
and only to be lost in the absorption
of other thoughts to fathom.

And before the burden of too much thought
overwhelmed us and drove us senseless and purblind
from the awareness and from the appreciation
of what we needed to be aware of to enjoy.

That it was on one day fine early summer's day
come upon me in the late long lingering
of a summer's morning out along a county road
in the shadowy coolness of the shady-side part of a road
and with a slight delightful breeze
upon on my face that it became upon me all again
that feeling and I knew it all over.

The Feather

From: **Anthony Robinson** (robinsoa@newpaltz.edu)
Sent: Fri 6/26/09 6:10 AM
To: gary.koniz@hotmail.com

Gary, that was a lovely gesture on your part, sending me the hand-written note and the feather that came with it. I was touched by your thoughtfulness and the fine comments about Departure and, previously, Home Again. Your writings on behalf of veterans show the great care and compassion you have for your fellow man. Thanks for the recent articles. All the best, Tony

Sun 6/28/09 14:30 PM

Dear Tony,

I got your email, the feather, and want to thank you for writing. It's always good to hear back from you. Your thoughts to me are something reassuring of the Immortal uncertainties of the Earth to abide to. And I mean that as a treasure to the heart.

The feather that I sent you is to replace the feathers that were desecrated at The Phillips Academy where you spent some unhappy years. It is a tail feather from a Red Backed Hawk, (and one my many bird and animal acquaintances who I spend time with on a daily basis along the fairways and by ways of my beloved DeerCreek Country Club.) And in aside, just to relate, that whenever I see a Hawk close by up in one the branches of a tree, whenever time permits, I always pause to commune with the creature. One of them even dive buzzed me and lit high up in a tree branch a few yards away, and stayed with me until I had to leave to be on my way going somewhere. The Rabbits too are very tame and friendly, and there lots of Geese and Ducks, Raccoons, and a few Deer every now and then, and always birds everywhere, regular birds and quite exotic tropical ones. I have a Hawk's feather too.

I really loved both of your Novels read to date, Home Again, Home Again, and, A Departure From The Rules, (especially the latter, I don't know why over the other in appealing more,) maybe for its manly ways of style and for the nautical terms of interest. The plot seemed to move in suspenseful intrigues in smooth passage from one sequence and episode to the next; and for which there were many different levels of and types of plot lines, from manly male bonding of their friendships and rivalries, to subtle love interests, (and which the reader grows attached to, and especially the love between Carol Talbot and Philip McFarland and their unborn child, only to lose in the tragic sinking of The Dobbs,) to the tensions of Command that caused the catastrophe, and ultimately leading up to the dramatic Physical Climax, (The

Death of The U.S.S. Dobbs, DD 529) to be followed by an equally compelling and powerful Psychological Climax, (the psychological moral conviction, (concerning his illicit love affair with Joan Karst, and later on in Yokosuka Japan with Hiromi, "Kobi-san;") and then legal vindication of Lt. (JG) Beaver Byrne, that doesn't leave him happy and satisfied, but remorseful and full of self-agonizing;) that all seem to transition perfectly and blend together in a seamless and flawless presentation of plausible perfection to ultimately be held spell-bound by to the conclusion; that seemed to be great sigh of relief released, (and although left with a moral burdens of guilt to reflect on,) from the hell-bound tensions of the plot, (from Commander Jerald Karst with his secret lust for his half-daughter and masturbatory disease,) to Allen Byrne in anguished introspection of his own immoral conduct, as "unbecoming and Officer," and to the great self-doubt of his manhood as Allen Byrne in the end experienced, to the point of suicide in longing to join his crewmates in the sunken vessel at the bottom of the sea.   It was immoral conduct that brought the Dobbs down.

But it was all there! Everything you would want in a novel, a truly remarkable work. That I wanted to ask you about, as to how you first conceived of the idea to write such a book, and how, as a Master Craftsman in your own right at such an early age, and your first novel, (like Earnest Hemmingway's longed-for first novel, "The Sun Also Rises,") to have come out so good; and as to who exactly that you came to "think-of" and "to construct" to plot, and to have thought to form such beautifully descriptive scenes, one after the other, and perhaps for those alone that the book is what it is… "with the smell of sewers and whores on the wind," … "and with the sea rolling like the undulating thighs of a woman," … 'Yokosuka glimmered in a nightmare of neon and prostitutes and sailors."

"Outside the Main Gate, it was growing dark, and with the darkness, Japanese girls appeared. They stood on corners, in front of cafes, behind beaded doors, like gaily colored birds perched on night-shrouded branches, beautiful and cheap and hungry."

You have a few typos to correct, but I won't go over them with you now, if they mean anything I will. I noted each one I came across. There's not that many. Pelorus, is spelled Pelorous, then Pelorus again a few times.

I went ahead and ordered your third book, The Easy Way, from Abe Book Dealers, (what a remarkable thing! To be able to order "rare' books, and have them shipped to you.) The hardcover copy of The Easy Way in good condition cost me $6. 89 with 10% off and it came with Free Shipping. I'm looking forward to its arrival this week and can't wait to start reading it. A version of your work also came with a piece by Stephen Longstreet called "The Flesh Peddlers." Do you know that?

And in closing with you today, I want to tell you about the psychic phenomenon that came with your book, A Departure, it was a vision, (and always as the visions go, that occur in the early stages of just falling off to sleep while the mind is in the discipline of breathing in and out, and what the Zen Buddhists call, "flashes of Satori,") that a scene will "flash" into your mind. And which was, the one of you, just after the book arrived, of you standing with a group of other men, perhaps six or seven, by a stone fireplace in a lodge of some sort, (and I say in the manner of your being distant with me, and in acknowledging my presence, though not precisely aloof, but in the feeling of being reserved, in the way that Officers behave when they are with one another and in the presence of enlisted personnel,) that you looked at me, and in a manner somewhat apologetically though resigned to it, in the feeling being conveyed that I "wouldn't fit in," (like being in the company of the Governor or some other important person in the company with his important "friends,") that I perceived of as, "Officers Country," or, in another way of phrasing, of being with other Gentry, or with esteemed Colleagues of a professorial demeanor in polite bearing of distance, in which the other people that you know, and while being important to you also, are still otherwise regarded as subordinates, and in a sense, the underclass, but not said, but as something felt, "the distance," as if to say that to the others, that they don't belong, and with that tone of uncomfortable indifference to it, apologizing.

So long for now, and thanks again for writing. I do also appreciate your kind words about my arduous work against the impossible odds of the system, to save the Veterans from psychiatric devastation and suicide by the thousands all over again, to Commit Seppuku in disgrace for the lost honor.

I spent seven months in Okinawa by the way, with The Army Corp of Engineers in 1966 on our way to Vietnam, and know about "The Benjo Ditch," and all about everything else that you know about. Maybe that's why I related so well with the book.

You are truly a marvelous writer. I am putting the poem that I wrote to you, now entitled, The Forgotten World, as the last entry into the last pages of the fresh edition of my new work, "The Call To Order;" that I will publish next week after the Fourth of July, that I would like to send you out a copy of for your library if you will permit me the honor.

But a breath came into me and settled upon me, and in me,
and took me back again into The Creator's Soul of Eternity
to a place in the mind where I had never been
and would never want to leave into a place called Heaven.

All the best to you too as well, Tony,

Gary

What we need is closure to the Veterans Psychiatric Case in the terms of justice, cut and dry; to what there is no in between of compromise; not with the entire scruples of professional medical and legal ethics resting on the foundation of The Constitution, nor with the safety involving the lives and well-being of countless numbers of healthy and well meaning Veterans suffering psychiatric intake for the sake of domestic difficulties experienced, (such as homelessness, joblessness, marital problems, Post Traumatic Stress, Grief and Mourning, and Remorse of Combat,) as a consequence to their brave service to their beloved Nation, and with the legalities of the situation, (which, as we have been stressing for, in obviousness.) As

involve The Legal Standards and Medical Technicalities to
coincided with respect for the Medical Diagnosis of a stated
Mental Condition, and under what conditions that such Diagnoses
may be Legally Imposed upon anyone. And which as well also
involves The Legal Conditions of what that a person can be
charged with a Mental Disorder sufficient to Commitment under
2PC, Two Physician Consent, Mental Hygiene Law. And what
are the Legal Grounds in which a person can be Treated under
Voluntary Informed Consent, (as to the nature of what must be
told to them beforehand.) And what are The Terms involved with
Forced Treatment with Mind Altering and Metabolically
Disabling Psychiatric Pharmacy, or otherwise Force Treated with
Shock Treatment, or Medical Surgery. And what are The Rights
of The Mentally Accused to Due Process under The Constitution.
That we have not in all of our persistent inquiries after; to The
Veterans Administration, United States Central Command, The
U.S. Supreme Court, The Federal Bureau Of Investigation, and
The U.S. Attorney General, been able to arrive at straight answers
to. And so then to the serious question in closing to the case, as
to what are we going to do about it in lieu of proper official
action?

Because, you cannot have the rendering of Psychiatric this
way, the way that it is, as it is being conducted and condoned for
by the current Representation of The United States Government,
Militarily Convened, because it is Unconstitutional to have it the
way it is; (and in the meaning of its being a Communist
Dictatorship in tyranny over the safety and the lives of the public
and to the disgrace and well-being of our proud Veterans.) Which
to be psychiatrically accused of, and indefinitely detained for
without Due Process, is one thing bad enough, but to be Forcibly
Treated for and Destroyed over is a blatant atrocity.

The Key to The Understanding of The Resolution of the
Psychiatric Holocaust, (that is being perpetrated upon the entire
American Population of The United States, but especially as it
applies to our Nation's Veterans, as they return home from
combat situations abroad, and from the complications suffered of
their military roll, with their being especially vulnerable to

psychiatric manipulation being allowed to prosper in the name of medicine,) is to reason that the change that needs to occur needs to be of a "Non-Punitive" nature, (to ease the matter along gracefully,) and for the sense of it that things can't go on with the way they are and need to be stopped coldly in their tracks; and to the understanding of the Strong-Hold of the Medical Pharmaceutical Industry that has not been inclined to change and become benignly predisposed to "healing people" instead of to be permanently disabling them for the sake of "curing" their supposed and alleged maladies of mental disorders by rendering them dysfunctional; and of their obvious motives being that way; for the sake of the Profit Taking involved with the Medical and Pharmaceutical Conspiracy to keep things going the way they are as a "Captive Market," and quite lucrative; that has been "In Gross Error" of Fraud and Malfeasance for a very long time, and that seeks "To Protect" itself from Litigation and Criminal Malfeasance Charges by deceptive handling of the public in so stating: that everything is in the Proper Medical Order and Above Board, (when it is obviously not,) and basing their stand on their Imperious and Preeminent Medical Credentials to what that the public cannot refute.

To what obstacle in impasse that all that needs to be resolved thereby in a forthright gesture on the part of a designated Federal Congressional Oversight Committee is To Rule on the serious matters of; "The Rights of The Psychiatrically Accused," specifically relegating the Mental Hygiene Laws; as to the precise; Legal Terms Defined to constitute the Lawful Diagnoses of Mental Disorders, The Legal Grounds for Commitment, The Right to Safe and Non-Destructive Treatment defined, the Legal Terms to what that Forced Treatment may be Administered, The Legal Wording of Informed Consent for Voluntary Treatment, and The Rights of The Accused to Due Process under the terms of Miranda Rights and The 4th, and 5th, Amendments, and The Legal Terms for Release.

There are also several wars connected to the Psychiatric Entrapment and Devastation on-going in use of Drug Warfare at the present time, having to do with; Zionism, Italian-Black Mafia

Fascism, Heroin Drug War and Pornography Terrorism, Illegal Invasion Immigration, Police Corruption, the Mulatto War, and the Homosexual-Feminist Front.

The Revelation of it being, that things are not always what they seem as far as people and their motives are concerned; we, (and in the meaning of The White Race of a certain Central Western European Origin,) being the disputed Targets of certain aggressions to be dealt with, and in particularly to do with The White Males, (not having to do with Jewish, or Italian, and/or certainly of Spanish Origins, it pains to have to say, but the case being what it is.) That in all and of these various wars going on, and as to their private and lateral motives centered to their personal objectives at hand, whether for Territory, or for Social Dominance/Acceptance, or for Political Ideology and Domination of that nature, have all one thing in common with their War Army Organizations, and which is The Great Division of the Drugs, Opium-Heroin, and Cocaine, throughout history, and in the modern day use and trafficking now with Chemical Drugs, which act as a great schism within a people, and within a society to rend it asunder. Not only and just to the use of the drugs themselves, that induce all sorts of deviant and corrupt behavior, (as for Lesbian and Homosexual Depravity, Pornography, Pedophilia, Economic Corruption, Crime, Criminal Political Gerrymandering, labeled Fascism,) in their users; but of such users of the drugs, who premeditatedly perpetrate the drugs for warfaring motives upon innocent victims in society; whether family members, close friends and associates, and co-workers, who they can sabotage with their drugs and chemicals, at close range, at will, and in more sinister fashion of premeditated intent against an entire society; to what that no one "can complain about" because the penalty for complaining is psychiatric disposal.

It helps here to know that The Antidote, (or in Medical Terms to be discussed as, "The Antigen,") to Heroin, and other types of Soporific Tranquillizer Drugs, is "Cocaine," or other Stimulants, called "Uppers," or in the need to "Drink-Off" the sedation affects, (which rob a person of their vitality and personality,) with the use of Alcohol, which explains the great extent of the alcoholism, (and massive Driving Under the Influence, Criminal Arrests,) going on today in our culture, as was quite prevalent also in Russia during and in the aftermath of its ten year long siege of the Afghanistan Opium Supply.

And to what Drug Culture orientation, that our Politics on all levels of government suffers to, from the Congressional and Senatorial Offices, and on down to the individual State Levels of Politics, and even to the Presidency itself, in preventing anything being done, (Militarily,) about the Drugs, in sizing up the numbers of Drug-Bloc Votes, (and related Pornography Bloc Votes,) as hand-in-hand. And with the issue of the Drug Bloc Votes, being most sinister at the very local levels of politics, (where we each live and reside and work and send our children to school,) to the nature of Mafia Gerrymandering; in the sense that as they move in with their drugs and their pornography/prostitution, and their crime and economic treachery and to their foul-play of drug-Chemical Warfare, that the hard working and decent folk in the neighborhoods move away, and so all that is left is the Hard Mafia Core, (who then by the way,) have the power to "Elect" their brand of Mafia Government unto themselves, and up to and including, The Justice System, and to appoint and to install their Drug Using Police Departments overhead of the Public Interest, to protect and to deal their drug supplies. Who, as for the Judges on The Bench in such districts, (and to make the point,) then have the power to "Order" Mental Health Evaluations on everyone, by "their own" Court Appointed Medical Examiners, to replace Miranda, and the Constitution, by 2PC Psychiatric Diagnoses and Commitment, to, (and get this,) "Forced Treatment" with lethal drugs to dispose of and to destroy anyone; and that is going on, "Here," in our United States of America without Military Opposition.

This case is not going to resolve without formal Congressional Oversight in Third Degree Intervention, to go over the key points with you involved here with the two letters I received, (as attached,) in behalf of The Secretary of Veterans Affairs, General Erik K. Shinseki; from, Deborah K. McCallum, Assistant General Counsel for the Department of Veterans Affairs, of May 15, 2009,

regarding the documented harmful effects of the Neuroleptic
Antipsychotic Drugs such as Thorazine, also called
Chlorpromazine; and the circumstances under which persons
could be "Force Treated," with such drugs, and as to the
availability of any Legal Defense Resources provided for
Veterans Legal Assistance being forthcoming from The VA, to
challenge Diagnoses, Commitment Processing, and to the use of
"Forced Treatment;" (to what Ms. McCallum responded to in her
letter with her reply that:

"Regretfully, we are unable to determine exactly what you are
requesting;" and continued from there with a paragraph
explaining the parameters of The Freedom of Information Act,
FOIA;) which, though informative in its way, had no bearing on
the critical urgency of assisting and protecting our Veterans from
the perils of Mental Health.

And in response from Dr. Ira Katz, Deputy Chief Patient Care
Services, Officer for Mental Health for The Veterans
Administration, of May 22, 2009, in addressing the concerns in
alarms of proper VA Conduct regarding the routine
psychologically maiming labeling of our Veterans as Mentally Ill
Mental Patients for their reporting to the V.A. Health Care
Centers with Post Combat Related Maladies, to be Warehoused,
and Diagnoses en masse, with Mental Disorders, and thereunto
treatment for their diagnosed conditions with deadly Neuroleptic
and Psychotropic Antipsychotic Chemicals, (that Dr Katz defends
in his letter, as the "The Potential Side Effects" involved with the
use of "any" medications;) and which Dr. Katz maintains, in
speaking for the behalf of The Veterans Administration and The
Pharmaceutical/Medical Industry, that such deadly Antipsychotic
Drugs:

"have been proven effective and even life saving over decades
of research and practice for thousands, if not millions, of persons
suffering with psychotic disorders," and further on to state: "With
proper medications and other psychological supports people who
in previous eras might have spent their lives in mental institutions
are now able to live successful and satisfying lives;" which is
unrealistically misleading.

Normal people are not going to be able to live out successful and satisfying lives on Antipsychotic drugs, (and which incidentally have to be paid for, and along with their expensive Doctor's visits for their monthly evaluations and prescriptions, at a person's own expense,) and especially our Veterans, who have offered their lives in the defense of our Nation and our commitments abroad; and who, in straightforward and pointed terms of reasoning, Do Not Need To Be Made Into Victims sacrificed to the Sacred Cow Mentality of Mental Health behaving in a tyrannical fashion of Communist Fascist abuse (in the meaning of it being conducted for Criminal, Corrupt Economic, and for Personal Maniacal Motives,) and operating beyond the scope of Dr. Katz' personal overview to the Operations of The VA Health Care Centers, and beyond his ability to control, concerning the dangers confronting our Veterans at the hands of State Run Psychiatric and Mental Health Facilities, and as ordered for by The Courts under the current Justice System's use of Forced Psychiatric Evaluations and Psychiatric Commitments to replace the burden of the Court System, and also involving Social Services in that regard, and concerning "Forced Treatment," in psychiatric oppression over the lives of the public, that especially adversely affects the plight of our of our Combat Veterans, (to whom that this Nation looks to as the forward line of its Homeland Defense Security,) and to the ruination of their lives, physically, spiritually, mentally, and emotionally, from the crippling effects of psychiatric labeling and treatment, voluntary or otherwise, of the idea of psychiatric malfeasance; being allowed, and condoned, and supported for, by the Medical Profession, and by the Government of The United States, in direct violation of our U.S. Constitution.

In the first place being. That there is no Due Process, (other than Medical Evaluation under Mental Hygiene Law,) for Mental Health disposal, (in the terms of Equality Under The Law, as for the Legal Rights set forth and defined for the Penal Laws in protection of the public from tyrants;) No Right To The Presence of a Defense Counsel, No Right To Remain Silent, No Right To Be Presumed Innocent until Proven Guilty, (and quite the

opposite, that the Psychiatrically Accused are Presumed Guilty
and have to prove their own innocence;) No Trial by Jury, No
Right to Confrontation of Testimony, and No Right To Refuse
Treatment, (in the manner of drugs, shock therapy, and surgery,
all at the disposition of a Medical Committee;) as General
Counsel was asked to elaborate on.

And in the second place, that Dr. Katz' statement: "of persons
going on to lead successful and satisfying lives" in conjunction
with their mind altering, brain cell destroying, and physically and
emotionally debilitating Antipsychotic Drug treatments, applies
only to insane raving lunatics; and not to our beleaguered
Veterans suffering from Post Traumatic Stress, Combat Fatigue,
Grieving, Remorse of Combat, Homelessness, (and resulting
Exhaustion and Malnutrition,) and overall Depression, and who
have been, and are being placed into the same category, of being
irrationally and violently mentally ill, with the catastrophically
insane (to whom that it might prove useful to be able and allowed,
under the effects catastrophic sedation with such Anti-psychotic
drugs, to live out their lives in Vegetative Zombie State on "the
outside," under the tortured effects of these drugs, and as opposed
to being permanently confined in such conditions to a mental
facility. And to what obviously that these people, (as Dr. Katz
envisions,) are not going to be able to live out "successful,
satisfying lives," in stable self-supportive conditions.

The tragic part about it being that there are "Insane People,"
violent, hysterical, manically deranged, demented idiot people,
who are irrationally insane beyond the ability to be reached, and
dangerously unpredictable in their threat of bodily harm to
themselves and others, to be dealt with; but who are not to be
confused with our Veterans who are placed in with these types,
and all under the one heading of "Mental Health Psychiatric."

The Easy Way

Simon & Schuster, New York, 1963; MacDonald, London, 1964;
Baldini & Castoldi, Rome, 1965; Fleuve Noir, Paris, 1965

Take a handsome, young, idealistic law graduate from
Wisconsin—a trace of hayseed still in his hair—and spot him for
a year in the aristocratic office of a downtown New York law firm
specializing in trusts and estates.

Next, send him out among the rich polo-playing set of
suburban Norwood County, and tell him he'd better get some new
business in the office—*or else.*
How does he get it? And what's the price?

He sets out to get it in the most innocent and easy way
possible—by attending a Norwood party, by charming the guests
with his looks and modesty, and by smoothing over an incipient
fistfight. He goes on by accepting sailing invitations, by
frequenting polo matches, and by winning, through his patent
sincerity, the friendship and respect of a millionaire polo player—
and excellent prospect.

But it isn't, he finds, so easy and simple as all that. For he gets it too, by sleeping with his beautiful hostess, who just happens to be the millionaire's wife; he gets it by breaking up a long-standing lawyer-client relationship; and he gets it by a bit of brawling, a bit of lying, a bit of cheating—though all from what he considers the worthiest of motives.

But the price must be paid. And what is it? Nothing less than murder, suicide, perjury; loss of honor, decency, character. In the eyes of his aristocratic employer and mentor, he is a complete success. In his own eyes? Maybe, maybe not.

This fast-moving hard-hitting novel goes even further than *A Departure from the Rules*, Mr. Robinson's brilliant first novel, in facing unflinchingly the moral and psychological problems of a generation bent on achieving success—the easy way.

Mon 7/13/09 17:30 PM

Dear Tony:

Just writing in to say that I loved the first chapter in your novel The Easy Way that I got in from Abe Books last week. I still have more to comment to you on about A Departure about how I enjoyed reading it and for the lovely descriptions. The first chapter of The Easy Way was like than too, marvelous detail and a nice relaxed pace of introductions and at ease with the characters, flowing right along in a spell.

The Easy Way came to me with solemn impression, two angels by a portal into the beyond and talking to themselves with serious faces in looking at me, as if they were trying to tell me something delicate in a worried way about Mary, as it is her book, that I received, "For Mary, my wife." And that finally they revealed to me, as they would to a concerned loved one, to tell you, that Mary is asleep, in the way that sleep is needed, being watched over by angels in a hushed way lest she awake… shhhhh… Mary is asleep.

A Poem For Mary Robinson

The Missing Saga

That a certain rapture occurred to my senses
just over the trees
a sense of enlightenment in the certain Knowledge
of God rekindled,
and I knew I felt the Sweet Savor
of His Presence upon me
where sweet earth meets sky
the eternal sky in the timeless way
of the eternal now
in the breeze just over the trees.

And I made a gasping sound
quite unconsciously in my innocence about it
of the perception of myself in childhood
as I remembered it,
the feeling that I had had in early childhood again
that I had missed.

The Creator's Spirit was just overhead
in the tops of the big trees,
Looking over me in the play of the sunlight
upon the leaves
Shimmering in the morning breeze
and touching me with His eternity
And the solemn vastness and the loneliness
of outer space beckoned just overhead.

And it felt very old
to be emanating from the treetops
Ancient in perceiving it as an innocence
of the experience then
of what we were always entitled to enjoy

and to partake of
with the graceful big puffy clouds overhead
in the light blue sky.

That have always been there
and beyond that the vastness of eternity.
And it felt very old to me
and very good to feel,
like it had been there and that way
all along in my life,
and I had never known any other way
as if I had known it all along
and it had been that way
and was gone from me in a madness
and on and on that way forever
it would have gone in a madness,
had not The Creator Intervened
to bring my soul to life,
and in the memory I felt sad
not to have possessed it all along.

The feeling in appreciation for the earth
that I had had in early childhood
and then forgotten
about my whole life until now,
that I had become a part of the World again
and was once again
a part of The Creator's life and the World
that somehow was forgotten,
and it felt very ancient and old to me,
like I was ancient and old
and at the same time young and very alive,
and at the same time very old.

And it was just then that the feeling I had
became an emotion
of indescribable origin and sensation and joy,

something quite new.
Like a taste, but not so,
like an emotion, but not to, to savor.

In that the moment
there was all that needed to know,
Morning and the play of shadows in the sunlight,
of coolness and the warmness
to appreciate and to enjoy the sensations
of endlessly for the sake of being alive
And I wondered how I became alive
to be aware of it all by The Grace of God,
And I wondered then about God,
The Creator Divine,
Whom I needed to love,
And of the life I had to share with God
and with the Earth as a part of God.

And it didn't matter then about who else
of the other people were here,
or what else here upon the Earth was going on
or what I was to do.

The Earth was mine to possess,
and beyond that I didn't want for anything,
except to be with God then,
and upon the Earth,
the Earth which exists.
That The Earth Itself Was God,
in the thought,
and God was what I loved,
as if He, The Earth, and I,
and All Things upon The Earth,
were One In The Same,
Who loved me in return to be upon it,
and I felt totally secure and at peace.

I tried to stay in the feeling,
to hold it, to capture it and make it mine,
I tried to linger there in the feeling
and in the thought,
but in vain.
It was a fleeting moment,
I couldn't hold it but a moment,
and I couldn't hold it,
It vanished in the moment
I tried to posses it
and the day became again, the day,
and I became again a man
possessed with many thoughts
and with places to go
and people to see and things to do.

But a breath came into me,
and settled upon me, and in me,
and took me back again
into The Creator's Soul of Destiny in Eternity
to a place in the mind where I had never been
and would never want to leave,
to a place called Heaven
as I named it to be.

And we will never know will we?
Whether Heaven Was Made For Us
Or We For It.

It is a place definitely that we know of,
The Home of The Father and The Angels
Who Are Good To HIM.
At least we can be that,
And further still, To Be HIS FRIEND.

Gary Koniz

Easy Way

From: **Anthony Robinson** (robinsoa@newpaltz.edu)
Sent: Wed 7/15/09 4:49 AM
To: gary.koniz@hotmail.com

Gary, that was a thoughtful, poetic note you sent me, re: The Easy
Way and the dedication to Mary. I was touched by the sensitivity
and kindness of your words. Thank you for reaching out. It was
an age ago but you made it all very close again.   Tony

Wed, 15 Jul 2009 05:14 -0500

    I'm with you, Tony. "In the deep dark and lonely night of the
soul, alone with God, it's always three a.m.", or as you phrase it
in A Departure From The Rules, "the middle, middle, of the night,
0320 hours." I am off to work right now, but I want to write you
more about your book, The Easy Way, and of my initial first
impressions, and also to conclude with my review of, A Departure
From The Rules, that I so thoroughly was impressed by, of its
effortless relentless descriptive flow to reflect on; which I might
add, that I am experiencing the same superb effect of "effortless
flow" with The Easy Way. You are truly a remarkable and
wonderful writer, Tony. I'll write more to you soon.
    Believe it or not, I never do look at my emails in the early
morning, or very rarely if I am expecting a reply. But this
morning I felt compelled to, and since I had written you, and there
you were, up with me in dark, dark of the night.

Gary

Mon, 19 Jul 2009 05:15 –0500

Dear Tony:

What I wanted to say to you right off, was that "books" are real psychic energy living things, from their authors conspired to their readers, that take to life in the readers' minds and take growth there, becoming living creations inside of the mind of their readers; to live on forever in fancy, and to fondly reflect on and lovingly to enjoy, and to play around with in imaginary friendships and inter-relations with the characters in the books, who dwell there in the pages of the mind with them, that become fixed, as a permanent things, and together with the actions involved in their plots, that become bigger than the authors who inspired them and who bring the events of their imaginary history into being.

And which is the way that I feel about the story of Destroyer Division 182 that lives inside my head now forever there in permanent setting; and its four ships; the Carter, Villaume, the Bostwick, and the U.S.S. Dobbs; and so to the fate of Commander Jerald Karst, (Commander of The Dobbs,) his wife Mable, and his daughter Joan Karst, and who becomes involved with Lt, (jg) Allan Byrne, (who is nicknamed Beaver, and who used to trap Muskrats as a young man, and perhaps foreshadowing his fate of eternal remorse over his loss of The Dobbs,) and of the fundamentally and underlying immorality of human nature that ultimately was the cause of the sinking of The Dobbs and the loss of 206 men, (and along with it the deaths of Foxy, Snail, Rabbit, Mr. Sacks, named Walrus, the Hawaiian seaman Kaohaolauii, nicknamed Pineapple, Ferret, Chick, the engineering officer, Steward Aberney, the Executive Officer, James Shuman, 1st Class Torpedo Man, Chief Corpsman Newell, in Sickbay, Joe Royden, nicknamed Big Arm, and Joe Marcetti who had given everybody animal names, except for Phil MacFarland who hadn't been on board long enough, and whom that we as readers had all come to know and love through the excellent character sensitivity of development,) leading up to and involving the fate of a tragic disaster of the collision of The U.S.S. Dobbs, with the giant Aircraft Carrier Wake off the coast of Japan.

That in a lot of ways did become emotionally overpowering, as we, the readers had become emotionally involved with the main characters, and their lives, (and especially for Philip McFarland and his fiancé Carol Talbot, who became pregnant, and for the rest of the personal lives of the characters as we feel for, the Exec Mr. Aberney and his wife who looked forward to his making Commander,) in the emotion packed character development build-up to the tragedy.

But what I love you for most, and beyond the superb story line and story telling of the novel, is your descriptions. That I feel we should start a "School" together about to endure the ages in tradition, to be named "The Robinson School." And that we would instruct its students in the subtle art of describing the "surroundings" to be included in a great work, such as and like, the faces of people, the way the are dressed, their mannerism, and the scenes of the exterior world, such as the names of trees and foliage, and other descriptions, "that paint the scenes with words" for the readers to envision.

That I have here jotted down just a few of my favorites from "Departure." Which, to include them all, that I would have to re-copy the entire book to do.

p. 124: (Beaver and Kobe-san in the misery of a defeated country,) [The path] "curved to the left, over a stone bridge. A half-dried sewer ran underneath the bridge. Soon the path became steeper; now, to facilitate walking, it changed into long, flat steps, like narrow terraces on a hillside. Dingy-brown houses, made of boards and mud, lined either side of the path and packed the alley, the distant pitching roofs resembling a choppy harbor at night. Not lights burned in the houses. It was quiet. There were no cafes, no seas of men, no fights or shouting, but stillness, an old stillness, away from the women and glare and music that follow sailors the world around."

p. 204: (last moments of The Dobbs,) "The Dobbs, halfway through her turn, headed dead into the sea. Her bow went down; and, as if trying to keep it down, a great whitecap struck it. The

wave broke like a huge mirror into a million flashing chips, which
tore aft on the wind and slashed her bridge. The Dobb's bow
rose, shedding water, rose until her keep broke surface—and then
plunged again downward, still turning."

p. 216: (And of what I think is the great and dynamic heroic and
fraternal pathos of the great novel, of this descriptive scene,) "As
they rose, Beaver saw light above him, how far he could not tell,
except that the moon had often seemed nearer to him, or the stars.
He struggled toward this light, his lungs past suffering, and still
he clutched Mort and the light above them drew closer, nearer,
nearer and closer, and soon the dream must end, he thought, the
dream of being born, not as an infant but a s a man, fighting for
his initial breath, and for life which would follow if that initial
breath were taken, if it could be taken, after the punishment, the
torture ...
    They broke the surface, and he breathed. He gasped,
swallowing the oily water, and vomited and gasped and
swallowed more. He felt himself sinking again, he couldn't
believe it, and he didn't care. A section of deck grating shot up
beside them. He draped himself across it, his hand frozen to
Mort's collar."

p. 221: (Part V - Inquiry,) "The Wind was having fun. In gusts,
each like a group of excited schoolchildren, it scampered through
the great yard of the Ship Repair Facility, Yokosuka, spinning
dust and paper tops. But none of the men, walking about he yard,
seemed at all impressed with the wind's little game; certainly not
three rear admirals who marched, gold visors bent low, toward the
mammoth dry-dock in which the U.S.S. Wake lay resting.

p. 268: (Allan Byrne) "Never in his life had he felt so low, so
tired, so abandoned. His friends were dead. Kobe-san had gone,
the inquiry hung over him like a scythe blade, and around him
Yokosuka glimmered in a nightmare of neon and prostitutes and
sailors.

P. 278: "From the witness chair in the inquiry room, Beaver Byrne watched silvery raindrops fall like billions of tiny spiders invading earth. It had started to rain hard bout midnight, when he'd returned from seeing Barton. There was no indication, this morning, of letting up."

And I could go on and on with it, in praise and compliments. And I especially did enjoy reading your defining love scenes, perhaps your forte as a writer, which are most pleasing in their sensuality, without being dirty, (if I can use the phrase that way.)

Please write and tell me some about your wife, Mary about her life as you knew her and fell in love with her. I never knew her, but I did go her funeral with Charmi, if you recall her presence in your classes. Love and caring for her is what she needs to heal. I have never seen a picture of her. If I have, I don't remember.

I remember our many fine mornings together, in the cool mornings of the summer with the back screen door open and the side window open with a breeze gently flowing through, in the year 1977, a year that was, lingering over deep conversations about life as you enjoyed expounding on, and always to the point of propriety, in the kitchen with your elegant epicurean Spartan breakfasts consisting of one soft boiled egg, (which we broke in half with a knife,) one piece of toast lightly buttered, and black coffee, that you so gracious prepared for us to enjoy, and that I so thoroughly did enjoy indeed, with you, and always the fine man Tony that you are to remember.

Gary

the stone

From: **Anthony Robinson** (robinsoa@newpaltz.edu)
Sent: Sun 8/09/09 8:36 AM
To: gary.koniz@hotmail.com

Gary, years ago--probably in 1977--you lifted and carried a large
stone, more exactly a boulder, up from the oxbow and placed it
near the outside shower as a step-up to the next level where
I stored stuff like wood and tools. The boulder had to weigh 200-
300 pounds. It had a reasonably flat top, which made for solid
footing. When you placed it, you said: "This is Tony's stone."
Recently I had the whole area renovated and the stone
remains, serving the same purpose, making the next level a little
easier to attain. The only change is the name. In my mind, and
for many years now, I think of it as "Gary's stone," and rightfully
so. Tony

Sun 8/09/09 9:38 AM

Dear Tony:

Memories are a wonderful thing, aren't they? I remember that
day, and many others like it when the friendship and fondness of
an era bloomed in the heart of each of us, and we became a family
unit together for the time. I remember carrying the stone, and
placing it. Lloyd was there going about his daily routine of
chores, three hours for us each every day, for the room and board
and five dollar allowance, and with the privilege of being with
you to absorb your intellect and outlook on life, that always has
left an indelible impression on me, Tony; truly one of the great
literary men in history to have had the rare honor of knowing you
personally. Thanks for the memories, as the late Bob Hope used
to remark. I wish I were there now in the back yard, on this warm
summer morning in early August, taking an outdoor shower, and
feeling the coolness of the water, looking down the slope of the
backyard of the estate and out over the Ox Bow to the land across
it, as I can picture there in my mind, if I could "Teleport" myself.
    I am now near mid-way through your great book, The Easy
Way, and was just reading on page 145, with Roger and Connie at
the pier on the Hudson, (and looking like trouble brewing on the
horizon for Roger that way,) as the computer was warming up to
look at my inbox, multi-tasking, (and as I hate to waste a minute

of time when I could be doing something productive and useful to my trade, I have so little time to do the work of reading and writing as it is with my outdoor golf course routine, and so to try and squeeze in all available nooks and crannies with my "other" job, hopefully to produce a good work to be proud of in the end and while I have the days available to write.)

I just love the way you write, Tony; for your beautiful descriptive passages, and how you paint with words, that moves the soul and the heart to enter the secret world of your novel, that once was your imagination, on a deep level contemplation, and in getting to know you intimately that way too as well, for the effortlessness of studying you, and for your innate philosophy of approach, that you blend so beautifully and skillfully into purely believable dialogue, (that never falls flat in seeming contrived,) and for your superb character development that make us feel intimate in kindred-spirit-ness with the people in your story, who, as I said to once before, that you become personally involved with as if they were real and not storybook fiction, and for the whole of your work that just flows gracefully along, page after page, in peaked interest and in a suspenseful storyline. What a great and precious gift that God has chosen for you to have, handed down to you, and for what that I fortunate and grateful to be a student of, like Plato is to Socrates. I can't wait for the own work to take flight, and am already contemplating several novels into the future of things I want to write about, if only I could master the craft. And I know I will, just by reading your books, that I can pick-up the gist of how to do it from, and from your intimate dialogues with me on the subject. That will always be known forevermore as, The Robinson School.

Thanks for writing me, Tony. Please write some more about your personal life and philosophy any time you feel the notion. I'd like you to share your thoughts with me and to keep a diary for history of your autobiography.

It seems that whatever you write about has an uncanny way of coming true. I am that way too. There is something about the psychic current in our lives that merges with the supernatural to become real. Life is a dream. And to what that I am going to write into that we made a lot of money together and lived a long, long, time in happiness.

Sincerely,
Gary

Tues 08/18/09 4:45PM

Dear Tony,

   I am sending you this attachment so that you can see your poem, The Forgotten World, dedicated to you that is at the end of the work. I'll send you out a copy of the book when the new edition comes out in November, 666 pp.. Your book, "The Easy Way," set in Polo World is a fabulous novel. I am just simply enjoying reading it page by page and savoring the descriptions, dialogue and philosophy. All the characters are really easy to relate to and get along with and quite likable. Roger is quite a fellow, isn't he, he and Nelson are having it out right now over Connie, and I think Roger is having the better smug laugh of him. I can see it being made into a really great film. Can't wait to discover what happens next. Gary

Fri 09/04/09 7:05 PM

Dear Tony,

   The Easy Way is beautifully written work, that is so light hearted and easy to read and to follow, and with a very intriguing and interesting story line, that you just want to curl-up and live with the book as a part of your life for a while; about a young ambitious man who takes on too much in life in the way of women, and ambition, for his own good.
   But I am getting ahead of myself. I am only at the Chapter 6 episode, page 236, (taking it slow, as in; "I hate to finish a good

book, I really do,") where Barry Reinhardt has just won The National Open and is playing the best Polo of his career with the Polo Team, Blue Run, and who has just left, in abandoning, his old law firm, Sherman and Mulligan for the firm of Pooley, Manning, and Maxwell, to be with his new attorney Gregory Mulligan, and the books protagonist, Gregory Mulligan's assistant, Roger Colthorpe, (who is not so secretly entangled in an adulterous affair with the tragic figure of Barry's over-sexed wife Adele, and also with Barry's daughter Constance, at the same time, and as well embroiled in a death feud with Constance's former fiancé Nelson Paige, the attorney with Sherman and Mulligan and with whom that Barry Reinhardt had previously entrusted with his estate and other holdings. And which does not portend well for Roger in the suspenseful drama you have unfolding, or for Adele, who is suffering.

What I am wondering and am curious over is, and with being interested in you the man, as an author, and of a biographical sense, if you would care to elaborate, how did you come up with the idea for writing this particular novel, and to develop its story plot line? I would be very interested to know. I'm intrigued by the thoughts of your life.

I remember the time that you took our Creative Writing Class, all thirteen of us, with Timothy Show, and Barry, Jocomo Ruli, Charmi Neely, Norman Stone, and the others, as I remember them, in the Early Summer of 1974 just before the end of The Semester, in May, on a beautiful Saturday morning, to walk the enchanted trail from Duck Pond, where we parked our cars, and from there on foot up the trail to the cliffs of Lake Mohonk, and where we scaled the actual cliff face itself at the last part of the climb, and with you as our leader, who held out his hand to me from the top and pulled me up and the others on the last difficult part. And what a tremendous day of bonding it was, all together then. We had soup and hot chocolate in The Hotel's Cafeteria, and latter on took a leisurely stroll back down the mountain when it was time. And then you invited us all to your house for a steak and salad dinner. Which was a wonderful time. Jenny made the salad for us and served it out to everyone. She was such a bright

lovely girl, perhaps the girl that I had always hoped to have and to fall in love with in my long lost youth, and I fell in love with her then, as hearts are stolen, to look at her, and how can you explain those things, as history reveals them to our hearts. And later on you took me into your study for a private moment and showed me your Pump Remington Shot Gun and let me handle it, and it felt good in my hands as you showed me its clean line to hold it. And that was the beginning of everything, as we become a family together. Henry was always my favorite person. He just had such an honest and genuine way about him. And I recall that you had said that about Henry at one time to me, that he was honest and genuine.
Gary

Your poem, plus

From:**Anthony Robinson** (robinsoa@newpaltz.edu)
Sent: Fri 9/11/09 8:29 PM
To: gary.koniz@hotmail.com

Dear Gary, I was deeply touched by your poem to me and your letter. As I have said before, I should have your flow of language, and perhaps you should have a touch of my economy. That aside, the poem is a passionate outpouring of a man experiencing an out-of-body experience, who then comes back to everyday life and understands more of it and himself than he knew before. It is a great theme and very nicely done. I sent it and your letter to Jenny, who really liked the poem, and concluded by saying that she thought Gary "really loved us." I think he did too. Thank you very much for your lines written "for Tony."

As for how I came to write *The Easy Way,* I had a tip from my dad that a certain murder in Long Island would probably make a good novel. My brother-in-law at the time played polo, so I knew something of the polo scene, and I took the owner of thoroughbreds in the actual story and made him a big-time polo player. When I started I didn't know where I was going, but slowly the storyline took place--mind you, I didn't let it run away with me. I let the creative process guide me but I didn't follow it blindly. I did a couple of revisions, never once thinking or believing that every word I wrote was sacred. And finally the story came around and had a life of its own. It was a merging of creativity and hard judgment that worked for me in my early novels; but now I am looking for something to carry me forward. My "creativity," I'm afraid, is dying on the vine.

A company called BookSurge is interested in doing my Irish/Golf novel, but I'm looking around. How did you come up with your cover? Did Lulu distribute *Orders of the Day*, or is it strictly "print on command?" Did any copies of your book get sent to bookstores of reviewers?

Again, many thanks for the sweetness of your letter and your rich and wonderful poem.

Tony

Sat 9/12/09 9:45 AM

Dear Tony:

　　Thanks for you kind thoughts. I always do appreciate your writing me, and it was nice to learn of your feelings for the family love. It truly is a good feeling to love people, and to be loved by people, in life in a genuine way, and for who they are and what they are, to watch over them and take interest in, and to be with in our hearts and thoughts through the days.

　　And to reiterate as I always tell you, of what a most superb and very talented and powerful writer, (in using up the list of adjectives to describe my feelings for you as an author,) that I have discovered you to be, and plan to make a complete study of, like Hemmingway, and to one day in my later retirement years, to teach a class at SUNY New Paltz on Anthony Robinson, and The Robinson School of Literary Craft, as a course semester, like Ernest Hemmingway and William Faulkner are taught.

Thanks for sharing with me your recollections on The Easy Way that I asked for, and that ironically, as you indicated that your father had suggested that a murder on Long Island would make a good story, that I had just found time in the week to take up with the book once again in the gray dawn of the early morning hour on my day off from work to eagerly read, that poor Adele has just been discovered by Barry and had leveled the dark hollow eyes of the revolver at Barry and pulled the trigger. You write so captivatingly and thrillingly, with such exquisite attention to the details of what makes a story come to life, not only for the suspense of its plot and character development, (that is superb) but for the way to enhance the scenes with such forceful and well-thought-out descriptive passages that flow so easy in the mind as to be barely noticed, but that are always to be appreciated, as they make the book seem to be living thing taken in heart, poor Adele:

… "A breeze drifting in from the Sound made the white, gauzy curtains on her windows look like a trio of sailboats at night, running before the wind. She snapped on the light switch, closed her door and crossed to her closet. Off came her black silk dress. In half-slip and bra, she leaned over the removed her heels. Then barefoot she moved to the center of the three windows and gazed down at the great expanse of lawn and shrubbery beneath her."

And I love the way that you, as the author, involve yourself with the psychodynamics of your characters, in getting the heart of, and the bottom of, what drives them and creates their destiny, that each character is so richly endowed with in sentiment, and that I have found to be with all or your books that I have read to date.

And just to mention that the f___ word works good in The Easy Way, and as it did also in A Departure From The Rules. I just didn't care for its use in Home Again – Home Again, for the reason that, in both of your other books it is used naturally as it occurs in the course of dialogue, matter of fact usage, but in Home Again it is used subjectively by the omniscient author and which is besides "out of place and out of character" to the sensitive story line of the novel, and otherwise as an epithet of expression, or between male characters of a certain germane usage, it's alright in context to use without offending the fastidious way of your refined and expectant readers.

I was also thinking, in The Robinson School of Literary Craft, that the students will need a text book study guide on the different types of descriptions necessary to write an effective novel, or short story; ranging from the descriptions of, foliage vegetation, body types, facial types and expressions, mannerisms and gestures, dress types and styles of dress, furnishings and décor, and a range of other details as they reveal themselves. So that one is not looking out at the trees, but a particular vision of "old cedar trees" along the shore bent over and bowed by the relentless winds. I can feel it, I really can, thanks to you, Tony. I also do appreciate for your comment on "economy," not to be too wordy.

I also feel that the name of your new novel should be, "The American Pro." I don't know why, but I just feel that. There's something stubborn about it. And I appreciate also what you said about, "Economy." The words can sure pile up ponderous and deep and thick in the mind, can't they, like reading Ralph Waldo Emerson's, "Self-Reliance," one of the big item on the agenda of your American Literature Course, that you have to concentrate on line per line, and can't just casually read through, for its ponderousness.

Gary

Sat 9/26/09 19:45 PM

Dear Tony:

I am writing to let you know that I am nearly completed with The
Easy Way, down to the last final three chapters, as of this writing,
but which I am in no hurry to finish with and want to savor the
climax about. It is just such a superb work of extraordinary skill
and polish, as your New York Times review put it so well about
your other great work, A Departure From The Rules. I am just so
pleased and thrilled to have "discovered" you at this late stage of
the game, but discovered nonetheless. And to let you know that I
have already ordered a hard cover copy of, The Whole Truth,
published in 1990, and am eagerly anticipating and looking
forward to its arrival; which will make a handsome edition of rare
books of your own library collection to proudly own, (and my
passion since I was a boy to collect, and to read, and somehow to
know that they were read by other people at another distant time,
to reflect on, and something somber and pensive about them, as
the collected thoughts of a man in the time of eternity, that moves
ever on, and amassing the power of creative dynamic, through a
time portal, having the ability to become a real entity of thought,
that every word is sacred to and come around to have a life of its
own, in a merging of creativity and hard judgment as a living
work, fiction come to life, of a following.) To what I know you
are destined to literary greatness for.

In your last letter you asked me about Lulu. Have you looked it
up on the Internet? Basically, what you do is transfer your Word
Program onto a Lulu PDF File, which you can attach your own
covers to, front and back, or select from a number of Lulu Covers
provided, and you can make your book hard cover or paperback,
or both, which ever you prefer. You can get formatting assistance
and buy promotion packages from Lulu, but everything costs
money that way. For me it has basically been a print on demand
type of arrangement, and I have purchased thousands of dollars
worth to their fine quality books, of the books that I have sent out
to people to spark an interest in them and motivate the issues. I

am also listed on Amazon. Com, but have gotten only a few
orders from people over the Internet, but I haven't done any
advertising to speak of to promote the works.

Also, in your last letter you mentioned sadly that your creativity
was dying on the vine. I can't imagine why. But I've been
thinking about what it is you said to me one time, that "it takes
courage to hit a good golf shot." There are so many moving parts
and you have to time and coordinate each phase of the swing,
with its precise mechanics and with the proper timing and tempo,
and with so many swing thoughts in you head that you can't think
about during the swing, to make a full shoulder turn and
reconnect with the ball at impact on a perfect swing plane to
square the club face and follow through with. That it's a wonder
anyone could hit the ball, if you have to think about it, but you
can do it.

And so you know too how to write superbly, so richly detailed,
and so convincingly real; but I feel in my heart that you need to
let it flow more freely from you as a steady discipline, you have
so much there in your mind stored up to write on, so many
memories, and sage ruminations to put down, so much genius in
the making, to move people by, and to be respected and remember
over, (in remembering too, what you told me, about keeping up a
steady pace, and Hemmingway's Ghost has told me the same
thing; to "write something, anything, down every day, just get
something going, and the spark will be there to continue with it,"
and as you say, "once you write something it becomes sacred."
It's strange how that is, isn't it, once you write something…

I also feel that you need to do some work each day that is not
related to your writing, something physical to relate with, like
yard work, or mechanics, or woodworking, to be able to look
back on at the end of each day in the feeling of successful
accomplishment about to feel proud of. That will stimulate you
and give you the creative drive for your literary work that you
need and desire. You also need to feel rewarded from other

sources other than your own internal reinforcement to feel satisfied in the moment with of being successful in the eyes of others, and so you need to get out of yourself a bit each day and to be around other people, perhaps to involve yourself with school activities, or to get on committees and other manner of literary enterprises to be around with other people about. And think on it too, that other people need you and to be around you, to share in your insight and to be comforted by your famous friendships, for what you are known so richly deserved, to think of as an added responsibility of yours to cultivate. Perhaps you could get The Robinson Creative Writing School going to spark enthusiasm.

Lastly, that I feel, and as I have been thinking on it, about your creativity, (and as I have always been mad at Ernest Hemmingway for committing suicide and depriving us of the many other great works of literature that he could have written; but he had fallen into a vast and deep depression, made worse by psychiatry and the use of shock treatment that he underwent for many years, before he put a shot gun to his head one day, in a "as black ass" of a depression, as he put it, as anyone could imagine,) that you have many, many more novels yet to write; that you need to be up a good half hour before the twilight of the morning begins, and to get out in the day for walks at that hour, beneath the solarium of stars, and awaiting the gray dawn and even to linger into the sunrises of the mornings. To be out in the gray dawn is the most stimulating mystically creative event imaginable.

Gary

good morning

From: **Anthony Robinson** (robinsoa@newpaltz.edu)
Sent: Thu 10/08/09 6:35 AM
To: gary.koniz@hotmail.com

Top of the morning to you, Gary. I'd love to reply to your last letter in kind, that is, brimming with words and sentiment, but I can't keep up with you there. No one can. I'm sure I'll sound prosaic just to say thank you but it comes from my heart. Your comment in your new edition of Orders Of the Day, as a dedication, is deeply felt. I read it to Tania, and your letter, and she was moved and taken by the rush of your words and the feelings conveyed. I've started a novel about growing up in the Maverick Art Colony in Woodstock; it's really stirring up thoughts and memories. My last two novels aren't doing much of anything by way of interesting agents or editors. New voices, new talent! I feel like an old southpaw trying to make a comeback with the Cubs but my curve no longer has any snap and the pop is gone on my fastball. I seem to have a solid fan in Florida, however. That's something. In two weeks we're flying out to Oregon to see Jenny, and Henry is coming for a visit on Saturday. Take care, write well, keep the course in tip-top shape, as I know you do, (master of landscapes large and small.) Tony

Thu 10/08/09 6:35 PM

Dear Tony:

What fond and kind words you have written to me this day, Tony, to warm the heart and inspire fresh undertakings of thought in the world we live in to enjoy, and with such great and dear friends as you. I was reading the book Zen Golf, by a noted psychologist and practicing Zen Buddhist, Dr. Joseph Parent, who continuously stresses that we are our own worst enemy in carrying around the baggage of self-doubt and self-condemnation all the time. "What a lousy shot that was. I'm never going to master this game. I can't hit the ball good anymore," and the rest of the expletives deleted about it. When, what we should be doing is focusing on the things that are going to make an improvement on the game of life that we are playing in intending to play with confidence and

relaxed self-esteem. Bad shots accepted. But we don't dwell
there. We dwell on the positive things experiences that reinforce
our feeling of competency. What a great put I made back there on
Seven, and nice perfect breaking ten footer that I rolled right in
the hole like a pro.

I finish with you great work, The Easy Way, and want to
comment to you about it extensively in summing up my
experience with the novel, when time permits, as Kathy is coming
home from work soon from her job as a Nurse at the hospital and
I have to be getting our dinner started. It was a fabulous book
however to comment briefly here, one that I thoroughly did enjoy
reading, cover to cover, truly. I was though, a little nervous there
at the end, as you recall, that as Roger Colthorpe was questioned
by the District Attorney John Ferguson quite extensively about
"the light" in the central hallway being out; (which Roger turned
out to give the impression of it being dimly lit to provide Adele
with her alibi that she mistook her husband Barry Reinhardt for
the burglar,) which Roger said was "out" when he arrived at the
scene; but which Adele, (when she took the stand,) said that when
she got home, she was afraid of the dark and turned on all the
lights in the house, including the one on the upstairs landing,
which Roger had said was not lit.
    So, there's a discrepancy there that the D.A., or the members
of Grand Jury panel, did not pick up on, or chose not to pick up
on, (as in the matter of the D.A. throwing the indictment.) But it
seemed to pass o.k. and the book ended rather happily despite its
tragedy. I ordered a copy of, "The Whole Truth," which just
arrived, and I've begun to read it. Everything looks good. I love
your books, Tony. This one's been in a Library, The Boissevan &
Morton Regional Library.

Gary

    The roll of Defining American Women here in The United
States needs to take on a strong decisive turn in shouldering the

crucial responsibility at this time to provide us with the responsible leadership we require to secure our destiny here together as a People and as a Nation; of making sure that things are being managed right concerning the integrity and workings of our government, and regarding the proper foundation of our family units and social programs in awareness towards one another as we live to reside amongst each other in the name of humanity, to call ourselves a civilization about; that America's Women to take the lead in through their collective example of the proper sensibilities which we need imperatively as a Country to survive by.

If you need something done call on a woman to do it. A woman can get things done. And many women together acting in unison can always ensure a successful outcome to that whatever needs to be done for the betterment of humanity, and they can do so with grace and style to accomplish the job in a timely and respectful way, and that will remain so as foundation to the culture in prevailing general attitude.

For it is in the nature of women to be in charge of things, and particularly as it is apparent regarding the managerial affairs of the household and the home, and for the proper conduct of the family. And which looks out to and speaks for the social management of our society in all regard as well, in looking after things to make sure that all is well and functioning in an efficient and responsible manner; which is due to the innate and admirable qualities possessed by all women to embody a compassionate, nurturing, capable, and practical nature, and for their mothering instinct to look after things. And it is to The Women of this Nation who we look to in appreciation for these qualities to take charge of and to correct for the many things that are wrong here, that this Country so desperately needs to do at this time, and has always needed, to manage and to conduct its affairs in the proper way.

And where things are not right in any of the ways of error, in accordance with the sensible ways of society to be functioning in the ways that they need them to be, and we are truly engulfed with a great many errors at this time to judge upon to remedy on

many levels of reasoning to the proper arrangement of this
society, then the women of this Nation, in responsibility, need to
effectively organize in strength to promote such necessary
changes as need to occur, to be brought about through their
determination and effective influence in example, in order for our
people and for our society to take on a healthy and positive
emotionally fulfilled outlook.

Most importantly of The Roll of American Women To Fulfill
at this time is to ensure that the Central American Issues in crisis;
of Morality, Integrity, Ethics, and Economic Survival for the
population, are brought up to standard and stabilized. As these
issues remark and maintain and define what America is, besides
its territory and socio-economic living arrangement, and as these
issues are believed in by the people and looked to as a Faith, like
Democracy and The Constitution.

And it is crucial to understand that The United States cannot
continue to exist as a strong and unified Indivisible Nation
without The Foundation of Morality, Integrity, Ethics, and
Economic Survival for the population, being firmly implanted in
the minds of the people and upheld in a voluntary way by
everyone, as personal conviction is professed to by choice, as a
belief system, and which are not dictated over everyone by the
presence of law, but by reason and conscience.

Every action, deed, word or thought, has a visible or invisible
effect on the whole, in the meaning of the way we think, that
thereby leads in intent to influencing the way we behave and
which thereby has an affect on our surroundings, for the better or
for worse in the judgment of society. To harm any being in any
way is indirectly to harm oneself. And since we are all infinitely
joined as a social arrangement together, no one individual can
truly progress without bringing along the rest; which behooves us
all to reach out and extend ourselves in the meaning of perfecting
our Nation in taking on the added personal burdens of state, as
Civic Chores, and in the meaning of moving forward and
positively together as a People.

Selfish, destructive, and ignorant immature ways need to be
put aside, to be replaced by the enlightened ideas of social

responsibility and cooperation. Peer influence in that regard plays a deciding roll. A "Morally Decayed Society" cannot withstand. History is littered with The Rise and Fall of Nations and Governments due to Moral Deterioration, brought on by Sexual Impropriety, Drugs and Alcohol Abuse, Corruption, Greed, Tyranny, and Unholy Cruelty, The Downfall of Humanity. The Rise and Fall of The Roman Empire is not a fairytale, and which ever resounds with The Warning Words, "Enemies At The Gate."

That said; there is nothing more important to our beloved Nation at this time, than the preservation and security of our Traditional American Values.

Strong Family Ties are needed in this regard to create and build and make for a Strong Nation In Foundation. And to what family strength depends upon a Strong National Moral Character, Fair Social Treatment of each of societies members, a Viably Strong Family Oriented National Economy with Fair Ethical Pricing in The Marketplace, and by a Personally Motivated and Prevailing Work Ethic, and possessing of The Integrity of Being Honest and Fair-Minded within oneself, in conceding for the individual presence of any errors where they are occur to be corrected, and extended outward as the paramount consideration in The Orientation of The Prevailing General Will in responsibility to personally uphold.

And most crucial to bear in mind on the Morality Issue at this hour, To Be Corrected, is for The American People to realize in their hearts and to correct for the tragic mistake being perpetrated upon our American Women by the current trend to sexual degradation of our Women who are the bearers and the mothers of our children and the inspiration and model influence over our future generations.

And that their heartfelt hardships in travail are many in this regard to express, because the end result of any such degradation of the women is the result of their pregnancies, and of their having to endure the discomfort and psychological anxiety of the arduous months of their terms of pregnancy, and endure the great pain and suffering of labor and delivery for the sake of the birth of our children. And so in having as well the emotional anxiety and real financial burden associated to each child's birth, and to the responsibility of child rearing, of having to provide for the survival of their children, physically, mentally, emotionally, and spiritually, for an extended period of time, from infancy to adulthood numbering over twenty years, in order to bring the children to fruition as strong and capable and socially well adjusted adults. And which takes both parents to accomplish besides, involved in loving and stable marriages to accomplish. In point to be made, that the motive in reasoning of having sex with the women about is not to be made light of.

And for what holds at stake, the imprinting for the emotional, physical, and psychological well being of each child to adulthood, and to the idea of their becoming responsible citizens, who are, the outcome of each pregnancy, the political body and guiding inspiration to the ideological framework and the leadership of our future generations of America, and upon whom that the strength of our Nation ultimately depends to and rests in the hands of, in needing to be thought of.

This reasoning, discussing for the substance of Morality, is not to be regarded in vein, in denouncing the cavalier attitude associated with the current immoral orientation, in the meaning of the women becoming pregnant, being condoned and accepted by the general society and especially in being promoted by the immoral and debasing social programming of the public mass-media in modern trend, and by this Country's current trend in the acceptance and outright promotion and with the attitude of The Government permitting the defacto legalization of prostitution and pornography being made in the social norm, which they are not to be.

And especially to what has become ingrained in the attitude of society upon the American Males, and who are being lured on that way by the suggestive acculturation in behavior of our American Women, who have been trained by the social programming of the past decades to be sexually promiscuous and to the impropriety of flaunting their sexuality, in brainwashing the promotion of the safe sex idea, and with available birth control, to have casual and indiscriminate sexual relations with as many

partners as possible, beginning at the age of puberty, to what that
they are then forced to endure unwanted pregnancies or to have
Unholy Abortions about and who suffer Grave Emotional
Torment for these abortions that scar them emotionally for life;
about the whole idea of frivolously regarding women in general
as sexual objects, and not as sensitive human beings in dire need
of love and compassion, that our modern American Culture is
presently denying them.

Women especially need to take charge of this situation. And
what is a situation that the men also need to redefine their
sexuality over, involving everyone concerned, men and women
alike, to realize that sexual relations is very serious business, and
that is not to be conceived as a frivolous and obsessive pastime.
The idea of social peer pressure and of strong media promotion of
sex, and beginning with the early years of puberty in formative
impressions upon our young people, for sex to be regarded as a
personal necessity and National pastime as a plaything and of
what as is thought of and cultivated in that way as mass
addictions are, in seeking out cultural reinforcement, that needs to
end. And to what erroneous social programming that The
American Women need to change our societies programming
concerning, pertaining for the moral foundation of our society, in
the social working solution to what is fundamentally ailing our
Nation, concerning promiscuous sex, that all women need to take
a unified stand against.

And it is here that the women have the ultimate control of
such matters, as to their collective attitude having the sway about
it, to what matter of sex that they always have "To Consent To,"
and need to organize around that stand to ensure that the proper
sexual standards of conduct are recognized and maintained.

The Whole Truth
Donald I. Fine, New York, 1990

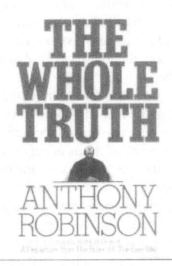

Here is the powerful, compelling story of how one "ordinary" man's innermost lusts and yearnings topple the order of his existence, then are laid bare when he is put on trial for the heinous murder of his wife.

The setting of *The Whole Truth*, carefully crafted stone-by-stone, in unabashed homage to the rhythms of small-town life, is Winwar, New York, a quiet place surrounded by forests and fields where for years its protected residents have hunted and fished and farmed.

Leonard Bradley, among the most protected, is the scion of the wealthiest and most influential family in town. A "conventional man," he has taken the reigns of the family business from his stern, demanding father, has devoted his life to the family and to the company.

But after thirty years of marriage, Leonard Bradley has fallen out of love with his wife Phyllis and in love with a beautiful divorcee in New York City. Bradley, a decent fellow, tells his wife he wants a divorce. A woman of strong moral principles and strength he never expected, she tells him she will never grant him one. During the confrontation she utters the fateful words: "Over my dead body." What now looms ahead for Bradley is a messy divorce, a lengthy legal battle, a large settlement, and alimony payments. Leonard Bradley does what any "normal husband" might do: he fantasizes about his wife's death. *How convenient it would be if Phyllis simply disappeared.*

Bradley's momentary fantasy leads to a very different kind of ordeal when Phyllis indeed fails to come home from one of her long walks in the country. Her partially decomposed body, shot once in the head and showing unmistakable signs of rape, is found one week later in a remote wooded area. Leonard Bradley is the only suspect. Circumstantial evidence — the bullet, the gun, the clothing fibers — points directly at him. He also had the motive, the opportunity, the means—and no alibi.

Bradley's only defense in the face of such overwhelming evidence is to tell *the whole truth*—about his affair, about the $2 million insurance policy on his wife, about his compromising thoughts and feelings and intentions—a truth he is reluctant to reveal, and one that will not necessarily guarantee his acquittal.

As the trial of Leonard Bradley marches relentlessly toward a verdict, Bradley's son, a 31-year old Harvard graduate who dropped out of the family business, surfaces to play a major role, launching his own crusade to unmask the killer who brutalized his mother. *The Whole Truth* is at once a masterful tale of suspense and a tension-filled courtroom drama with echoes of Robert Travers' famous novel *Anatomy of a Murder*.

Wed 11/04/09 6:35 PM

Dear Tony:

I am just loving reading your latest, (in my version of reading you,) suspense thriller, The Whole Truth, that I am nearing the middle sequence of creative scenes with of Chapter 10, and am putting my money squarely on the crass Mr. Chuck Wojciechowski as the guilty party. He's the only one who would have known from Sadie his estranged wife where Mr. Leonard Bradley kept his safe and his guns and the only one depraved enough to go the job in the way it was done.

You mentioned a Blue Sedan that Phyllis Bradley was taken to and forced into the trunk of, but when Chuck Wojciechowski gets back from his four day trip with his tractor trailer "the color of his car is not mentioned," only that his car was there, and not his wife Sadies' "yellow Pontiac;" which is not like you to miss a scrupulous detail like that.

Chuck's chapter that way is kind of course, cutting one, and ripping another, but it fits … and I do admire your graphic ways at times … and although that I have to keep reminding myself that it is your book, (who is writing for me to read,) and not mine, with my tastes and ideas. I did find the part about the larva, and that; "flies just love fresh ------ vagina," to be rather profane in the sense of the sensitive nature of a woman being raped to be approached sensitively with; that anyone, and especially the professional police, should have a hushed respect for. But, and again, it's your story, that perhaps our reactions to are all a part of, whether we like something or not. I've been working on your "writing formula," that is, how you envision putting a book together, if you'd care to elaborate you "strategy" for me some time. I'm picking a lot of it up just by reading you. Shoes aren't shoes, but brown Brogue shoes. And so on...

"It was a cool damp evening, smelling more of Spring than Fall." I've been there ... smells like Spring out today...

Gary

Whole Truth

From: **Anthony Robinson** (robinsoa@newpaltz.edu)
Sent: Sat 11/14/09 9:12 PM
To: Gary Koniz (gary.koniz@hotmail.com)

Dear Gary, Thanks for your last comments. By now you are
maybe finished with The Whole Truth. It's a novel patterned after
my late brother-in-law's wife, who was murdered in the Southern
Tier of NYS. As for the color of Chuck's car, POV is important
here. If the first scene is through Phyllis's eyes, she would likely
notice the color of the car taking her away, but why would
Chuck comment on the color of his own car, if the POV
is his? Do you get what I'm saying? As for the police, it seems to
me you're a bit precious about them, saying that the writer should
have deferred to them in a way more in tune with their honorable
profession; it was insensitive of the author. I may have
overwritten the scene but not because it was an affront to local
cops. If you personally thought it was a bit raw, that I will
perfectly accept. I am preparing my new novel The American
Golfer for BookSurge, a subsidiary of Amazon; more and more I
see it as the only way to go. The book industry has effectively cut
out writers who aren't going to make them huge profits. Maybe
Sara Palin has "gone rogue," but so have I. For many reasons, it's
not a good state of affairs out there. Keep writing and thank you
for the fine poem. Tony

Sun 11/15/09 6:12 PM

I have not really finished up with your terrific book, Tony, I'm
just at Chapter 17, and so much to tell you about it, about your
plot story line and excellent descriptive style. It's all good, Tony.
Raw in certain parts was exactly the word that I was going to use,
and interesting how you used it first. I liked it raw, the real gruff
of a man stuff, the way people are, or the way certain people are,

to be real with. There's not enough realness in our world display
… getting down to it like Dwayne and Sadie, (which I'm
personally not going to mention, in deference to refined
sentiment,) but of a certain necessity to relate about as I see it, and
thrilling to read about in a certain way, about what people do and
think about, that certain things like that are carried on with. And
Dwayne is not the only one; Chuck Wojciechowski is that way
too, only worse. I think now that it was Dwayne who did it, for
his reasons involving Leonard Bradley and Dwayne's father's
case of personal injury against Bradley Corporation, and Dwayne
has a blue Chevy. You are right about Chuck's car, and I see it
now, about not needing to mention the make and color. You're
not afraid to write, Tony, maybe it needs to be raw, and I like that.
But I am also worried and concerned after your enduring image in
the literary world. Books that are well respected get passed
around and related about. It would be hard for me to recommend
the book in an honest way, to certain people; young people,
women especially, and refined clergy. I'd have to apologize to
these friends that it's a little raw in spots. But why Be Raw at all?
Raw is good though in a "Roguish Way." It's not too late thought
to edit all your books for elegant style, for history … The
Enduring Robinson Collection. Chapter 16 was quite a courtroom
stage. The boots and the tan trousers were indeed taken from the
Bradley home by the perpetrator. I am also worried to that rape is
a very sensitive thing to the women audience, who you don't wish
to alienate, (or anyone for that matter,) by being vulgar. Maybe
the police officer did say … "Flies love fresh --------- vagina," but
they all should have showed some sincere respect and sympathy
for "the poor woman," in conscience, and as a matter of "selling"
good books to your women readers, calling for propriety. How
many of your readers want vulgarity. What they want is a good
story to curl up with. Kathy is calling me for dinner. Gary

Sat 11/21/09 9:12 AM

Dear Tony,

I like you, Tony. You really Paint a scene with words that flow in the mind of the reader feelings and emotions evolved from your describing things ordinary things that make the pages of your books come alive to have a life of their own to live within us in the imaginations of our thoughts. But; what do you mean in Chapter 18 when you say that: "Not that a dry fly "produced" many fish in the chilly waters of mid-April; it wasn't until Iron Fraudator - the artificial, intending to represent it, was the world-famed Quill Gordon - emerged in the final days of the month that a floating fly would make a trout look." I don't get it. Gary

Re: The Enduring Robinson - Indefatigable

From: **Anthony Robinson** (robinsoa@newpaltz.edu)
Sent: Wed 11/25/09 1:46 PM
To: Gary Koniz (gary.koniz@hotmail.com)

Gary, fair question. It's fly fisherman talk. Producing a fish means having a trout rise to your fly. *Iron Fraudator* is the Latin name for an insect that hatches on streams; the dry fly (artificial fly) that is intended to imitate it and therefore cause a trout to rise (for a tasty bite) is the Quill Gordon. Natural flies don't hatch until the water temperature sufficiently rises, late April, early May. Hope you have a very happy Thanksgiving. Tony

--- Original Message -----

From: Gary Koniz

To: Anthony Robinson

Sent: Saturday, November 21, 2009 9:11 AM

Subject: The Enduring Robinson – Indefatigable

Sat 11/28/09 10:30 AM

Dear Tony,

Thanks for explaining about The Iron Fraudator and the imitation dry fly named The Quill Gordon that "helped the reader along" as you always stressed about with unfamiliar terms to explain the work more thoroughly about. I just find your discussions of Fly Fishing so manly and interesting, and as are included in all your books, among many other "reoccurring" themes of interest to the reader. I also wanted to let you know that I have accepted your "raw" presentations in spots, to quite apropos of the title and topic of you novel, "The Whole Truth," which now, at least in my mind, has taken on a "wider" implication of meaning, in exposing the real and raw side of humanity, and as well as to concern about "the trial" and beyond Leonard Bradley's predicament involvement with his attorney Chet Evers's defense plan to relate how he "really felt" about his wife's death in wishing her dead; to what that, The Whole Truth, has relevant value in underlying meaning. There are such things that are vulgar however to draw the line over, somewhere between baseness and sinuosity. You can't just take a crap on the dinner table, and especially during dinner with all the guests present, to make the point.

I did like your "related" love scene, remembered by Catherine, in intimacy between Chet and herself ... "her thoughts went back to last night, to the pleasure, the ease, of sleeping with Chet" ... And always for your wonderful descriptions to admire ... You really make the book come to life, at every turn of the page.

"Tony stepped outside. The sky was a hard blue and a brisk northwesterly wind made the still- leafless maples on the property rattle."

Gary

Sun 12/13/09 10:00 AM

Dear Tony:

Just to let you know, Tony, that I finished your great work, The Whole Truth, just the other day, and have already ordered, "The Member Guest," and which has already arrived at the Apartment Complex Office via UPS for me to pick up today, as I received work about in my mail box just this morning when I checked coming back-in at 8:45 a.m. after morning Set-Up, (that is changing the cups, picking up the trash, and putting out the water coolers of the day, that takes roughly two and a half hours to complete, and which we start at on the weekends at 6:00 a.m.,) on the golf course, and too early yet for the office to be open. But I am eagerly looking forward to picking the book up in the afternoon sometime. I just love the way you write and can't wait to study some more of you work.

The Whole Truth was a most impressive book, ranging the gamut of emotions from the utterly raw profane to the sublime and intellectual, (that I earlier indicated about, made the name of the book, The Whole Truth, take on a more complex array of meanings,) and which I had to remind myself of, as you once intimated, that the way the characters are and present themselves, is what they are, and not what anyone would like or imagine them to be in their own fashioning of the work, with many elements of our human nature in "the shock of recognition," for the readers to relate with. And once again to say that I was deeply impressed with your "descriptive flow" in the way you seem to "paint the scene" with words and in drawing out the subtle and exquisite of emotions for the reader to ponder and reflect on. And which, in that way, about the book, takes a great deal of time to read, in the many of itself wanting to be savored along, rather then hurriedly read for the sake of getting to the end of it to resolve its suspense. And "the end" does finally arrive, in a very logical formula of cogent reasoning; and that I always found myself to be "testing," going back into the earlier parts of the book at every turn to make sure that things seemed to fit right, and particularly in the instance of Dwayne McManus, that everything was set up right for, as to how he became familiar with Leonard Bradley's safe and gun collection, that you handled quite nicely. Everything fit together very clean and intelligently, and I say, well done, Tony.

Gary

Sat 12/190/09 7:45 PM

I just got your book, "The Member-Guest," in with today's mail. It's another library book in excellent condition from The Lee County Library System, dedicated to Jennifer and to Henry, (and with a very handsome picture of you by the way,) which I was able to purchase from Abe Books for $3.50 with free shipping. How fine. And I have already started it, the first two chapters, about Augie and Gordon, two regular down home and immediately likeable guys, and am quite caught-up with it already for its straightforward and down-home character. Everything has a "knack" for getting it done, and the characters are quite honest and genuine.

I did want at this time however to finish going over some of the key aspects of The Whole Truth with you, as I found particularly evocative enough to notate and felt for you in my heart, as the writer of them, in thoughts of you as I read them; of your many superb qualities and characteristics, to preserve for the posterity of their enduring memory among us, and for the fine talents that you have for portraying character development from your omniscient author perspective, and for your excellent descriptive abilities, and in your describing of all kinds of "incidental things" which make the work so believable and charming to take up with; of body descriptions and movements, and descriptions of all kinds of things as you walk us about through the scenes in the contentment of being reassured of "being there" with you in the presence of your mind, of feeling what you are feeling, and sensing what you sense, that makes the works evocative of a unifying spirit. Every character has a name and a place in the novel. The chapters are short and easy to read. And the story line in plot development is genuine and plausible in a real way and in the sense of not being forced or contrived in a manufactured way of creating suspense, but which is generated as the plot falls to be worked out, and from which that nothing is hidden from the reader about, to make the plot seem fickle and contrived. Which make your readers feel quite comfortable with the flow and movement of the intense drama you portray; and for your innate philosophy of life that you present. That I would like to get down some examples, just a few of the many of your descriptive passages here about:

I did notice too, some "reoccurring themes" that you contain in each of your books; one of them being, Fly Fishing, and the love of Hunting, and the outdoors, the streams and the woods … sub-plots, interactions between the main characters that goes on independent of the main theme … the reversal of rolls in later years, where the leader becomes the follower … trials and trial proceedings; (and concerning one of your moment's with me in that vein, in which you said; "Life proceeds along, Trial By Trial," as a point of your philosophy, that I myself took to heart myself to ponder a lot, and wanted to write a book about one day,) … and about unhappy times in Boarding Prep Schools, or our youth in general, lacking something that needs to be fulfilled in later years …and of course in lending honesty to the erotic sense of life that permeates your works … The Whole Truth.

"Do you swear to tell the truth, the whole truth, and nothing but the truth, so help you God?"
"I do."

Chet Evers moved slightly away, noticing, as he gave his eyes a moment's freedom, that Woolever was talking to his assistant Rhonda Fisch, whose face had the appearance of a scalene triangle. The D.A. had his hand loosely over his mouth; Chet nevertheless saw the smile on his lips.   p. 18

He was now driving on his private road. A big yellow barn
and silo stood immediately on his right, and Leonard saw one of
his hands working in the fields. He sounded his horn and the
youth, a country lad named Jerry Kohler, looked up and waved.
The road curved and rose gradually but continuously, flowing the
ridge, then branched left at a vegetable garden – well culled by
now – and entered a grove of maples with a scattering of
hemlocks and white birch. At a woodpile of eight or ten cords the
road bent sharply, opening to a large parking and turning area of
crushed stone, and his house. Leonard touched a button on his
visor and the garage door started going up.
p. 23

He wrote a new sentence, then another; he believed in the free
enterprise system and enjoyed talking about it. More specifically
he enjoyed talking about eh code that had guided his father, who
had founded the company sixty-three years ago, and which was
still at the heart of the Bradley culture today. *Honesty in All
Dealings, Quality Products at Fair Prices, Respect for the
Customer.* p. 32

It was a bright, airy office with Leonard's desk toward the
back and a separate sitting area, comprised of three easy chars and
a sofa, closer to the door. A large plate window took up most of
one wall, giving a view of the flowing, handsomely maintained
company grounds. Summersell, smiling, sat down in a brown-
cushioned armchair at he corner of his boss's desk and removed
five or six pages of graphs and figures from a folder.
p. 33
The lawyer dipped a toothpick into a small bottle of lacquer
and applied a drop to the whipping at the eye-end, then cleared
the eye itself with the other end as a precaution. Nothing more
frustrating, Leonard knew, than to choose a new fly while on the
stream only to realize the eye was clogged.

He came out of the edge of a meadow, seeing eight or ten deer
browsing, then went into the woods again, following an

overgrown trail once used by loggers. Tony and Catherine had
liked this particular walk because it emerged at another meadow,
in the center of which stood an old twisted oak Catherine had
named the "witch tree." Long ago lightning had blasted it, giving
it a distinctly hunched appearance; and in the fall the poison ivy
growing on the trunk and branches turned bright red and
resembled a cape. He came to the end to the trail now. Fifty
yards away the disfigured tree, in a slow process of changing
cloaks, stood eerily in the twilight.
p. 52

The Rev Adam Pohl sat in his church office working on his
sermon for Sunday. Crowded in the dark green file cabinet near
his veneered mahogany desk were some 200 sermons, prepared
and given by him during his years at St. Philip's; but he simply
couldn't take one out and deliver it again. What he had written,
what he had felt at an earlier time, no longer applied. He must
either revise thoroughly or start fresh. The only constant was the
source, in this particular instance the first book of Corinthians,
Chapter 13, Verse 12

"For now we see through a glass, darkly; but then face to
face."

Except for the creek sounds, the woods were silent, and a
heavy mist rose from the pool.

A single crow, wet, miserable-looking, appeared through the
fog and landed on the high branch of a scraggy pine that arched
over the pool. The bird let out three distressful caws, waited for a
response that never came and vanished in the murky air.
p. 118

He pushed aside a steel bolt to the back door and stepped out
to a small deck he had completely rebuilt early this past summer.
It was sunnier here than in the front because he'd cut down
dozens of trees on the steep bank. What his daughter liked most

was the path he'd made leading down to the creek. Used to be a
job and a half for her getting down and she'd hardly ever do it,
but now that he'd built natural stone steps it was a lot easier, and
she'd make little dams in the water or go wading or just sit on the
rocks and watch the current.   p. 146

Chet stood and walked about he room, stopping as he so often
did at the tall case holding Leonard's rods. The season had
already started and he hadn't wet a line yet. Not that a dry fly
"produced" many fish in the chilly waters of mid-April; it wasn't
until Iron Fraudator – the artificial, intending to represent it, was
the world-famed Quill Gordon – emerged in the final days of the
month that a floating fly would make a trout look.
p. 199

Starting out, it wasn't really a climb, just hard slow going.
They stayed near the water. A couple of times Oscar saw that the
opposite bank would make for better going but the risk was too
great even though it was only twelve or fifteen feet across. AS
they continued on, the creek bed began getting deeper, became an
actual gorge and they were expending too much energy
clambering over boulders – slowing them down. ON top of the
gorge the land looked steep but free of obstacles. O'Shea thought
they should strike for the higher ground, Oscar agree, so they
turned away from the creek and struggled and climbed, pulling on
tress and extending hands to each other. It was only eighty yards
but they were exhausted when they reached the top.
    "Let's take a break," Oscar said.
    They sat with their backs against a huge mountain boulder and
drank from their canteens. From his back pocket O'Shea pulled
out a red bandanna and wiped his face and neck. Overhead, a
hawk was circling, and above the now diminished roar of
Chodokee Creek the men heard its cry. "Kreee-eeee, kree-eeee."
    "Early morning warning system," said Diehl.   p.
303

"For all your own achievements, I've always felt he was still in charge. Because you felt it, Mr. Bradley – I think until just now."

Eleanor excused herself, and Leonard sat still for a long time, alone in his office. Then he swiveled in his chair, looking out at the grounds, and beyond. An early May sun was rising over Winwar.   p. 316

Many thanks for the inspiration, Tony. I'm beginning to feel I can write it now, the great American Novel. I've gotten a sense of it from studying your work, passed down to you father to son, and most likely his father before that, and so on in The Robinson Tradition of straightforward excellence.

Gary

From: robinsoa@newpaltz.edu
To: gary.koniz@hotmail.com
Subject: thanks for your words,
Date: Sun, 20 Dec 2009 19:50:59 -0500

Gary, I can't keep up with your rush or words and ideas--
they bowl me over. I don't believe anyone, except Jenny, has read
my novels so fully, and I know no one has ever bought all five
and gone into them in such depth and detail. I hope you sit down
one day soon and start a novel of your own. If my writing has
given you a small idea of how to proceed, then proceed
immediately. Pay close attention to story and style, work toward
an economy of language, and write about what you know
best. You have the heart for it. So do it. Tony

Date: Mon, 21 Dec 2009 20:10 PM

Bless you, Tony. Will be in touch. Have a safe and happy
Christmas. Your great work lives on with me and has become a
part of me. Gary

update

From: **Anthony Robinson** (robinsoa@newpaltz.edu)
Sent: Fri 1/15/10 8:23 AM
To: Gary Koniz (gary.koniz@hotmail.com)

Hi, Gary--haven't been in touch with you recently. I've been working very hard preparing my "golf novel" (it's not really a golf novel, more a novel about a Tour player; but there's definitely golf in it) for my self-publishing house, CreateSpace, a subsidiary of Amazon. Pub date sometimes this spring. After kicking around a dozen titles, I've decided to stay with *The American Golfer*. How's the winter golf season at your course? Busiest time of the year for you, right? Tony

Fri 1/15/10 8:27 PM

Dear Tony,

I'm fine Tony. Thanks for writing. Love is a two-way-street after all. Please come down for a visit and play some golf. You can stay here with us, and we'll play every day at the Club. I am just loving your book, *The Member Guest*. What a great job you have done with it ... a masterpiece. Please let me know if you want to come down. Bring your wife along too. I have presents for you, one here and one on the way. My mother Margaret, you remember her, is dying. She is 87 and at our home now at 6 Fulton Court in Poughkeepsie. Hospice is there. The family is waiting out the last days with her. She has cancer, Multiple Myloma. And sad the passing. Dying is not for the faint of heart.

Gary

The Member-Guest
Donald I. Fine, New York, 1991

Evocative of O'Hara's *Appointment in Samarra* and Albee's *Who's Afraid of Virginia Woolf* (with the golf expertise of Jenkins' *Dead Solid Perfect*), *The Member-Guest* combines the country club milieu with the games adults play—on and off the golf course.

Each summer across America, weekend golfers undergo rigorous training for the most lavish and most hotly-contested tournament of the season: their club's Member-Guest, in which members invite outside golfers to play as their partners. But there's a lot more than prestige at stake when Augie Whittenbecher is asked to play by his old friend Gordon McSweeney, a member of the posh Easthelmsford Country Club on Long Island's South Shore.

As the festivities begin it becomes clear that behind the handshakes and laughter are the seeds of envy, betrayal, seduction, and maybe even true love. For starters, Gordon's wife Catherine has her own plans for a late-night twosome with Augie.

To make matters worse, Augie's prep school golf rival resurfaces as another member's guest, accompanied by his new fiancee—the woman of Augie's dreams. As the tension over who will win The Member-Guest—and get the golden girl—builds to the eighteenth hole, the real drama tees off on the proverbial "nineteenth."

The Member-Guest is an ironic and erotic vision of America's country club elite revealing the jealousy and ambition beneath the veneer of gentility in this cloistered slice of Americana.

Message To Tony
From Henry Morton Robinson

Thank you for your time, Tony. I know you have been a dear sweet friend to me of the former years in your life, and I am most proud of you to have become a writer, as you have been inspired greatly by The Hand of The Creator, to do.

You have a superb gift for the expression of life. Be kind and gentle with it and I know it will lead you along the path of true enlightened happiness as you free your spirit in bond to the eternal.

I bless you and give you peace in the heart, and remember as I described in the write-up from my work, The Great Snow, that you are the descendent of Lief Ericson, a Viking Warrior, in our way of family line, so never give up the fight to endure the ravages of old age and to write incessantly from now until the time you die, at least a novel a year until then. Get it all out, all that is inside you, and you will be happy with the result.

Be kind to your son Henry, my namesake, as I know you always will be, who is always in need of you befriending him, and who admires your company, the company of his manly father, as you did my company, Son.

I am sorry that I sent you away to Boarding School. I know now how painful that experience may have been for you. But I needed you to be aware of the other world out there beyond The Art Colony, where you would have stayed and grown up to be stunted by, in my opinion. I hope in your heart you will forgive me my decision over it.

And let us always be mindful of our Jenny, our companion of eternal life of the loving female sort, and to love her all the days in need of her happiness among and about us as we travel on together in our time eternal.

I can't go on just now. I will not contact you again for a short while, and when I do, if I do, depending on things unknown at this point in time to me, it will as thought in your head. We spirits communicate and cohabitate with the souls of the living in that fashion, as thought. Right now I need to rest and compose myself, having just come out of the nether-land of a deep sleep at God's Hand upon the hour, and am still quite dazed. I know not when.

And to end here with a passage from the Dust Jacket of my novel, "The Great Snow," that I have selected for the moment for our reading.

Give me your undivided attention here for a moment and you will be set-free of the mortal coil, as I have thought too, like you, to do so.

Fact-bound readers may complain that the laws of Weather Bureau probability have been violated in this unusual story. "In their literal-minded way," concedes Mr. Robinson, "they'll be right. It's quite unlikely that the northeast quadrant of the U.S. will ever be smothered by a 20-day blizzard such as I describe in *The Great Snow*. But may I suggest that the snowstorm, as well as certain other parts of my story, be regarded as *symbols* -- with dimensions necessarily larger, and shadings a trifle darker, than the pat verisimilitude of a Brownie snapshot? If probability is slightly stretched here and there, it is because I wish to lay bare some extraordinary truths about love, hate, revenge, and hope – emotions subdued by ordinary living, and emerging most strongly in times of stress and self-realization."

Any reader of moderate discernment will see at once that The Great Snow is more than a one-dimensional tale of a man bringing his family through a snowstorm. It is a moving and all-too-human allegory of our civilization, menaced – like twenty other preceding it – by dangers both physical and spiritual. So cunningly is the story constructed that it can be read (and enjoyed) on several levels of meaning. The symbols, Mr. Robinson admits, have been previously used with some success by the authors of Genesis, Oedipus Rex, and Finnegan's Wake.

How I miss you, Tony. I miss your face and our days upon the Earth together. In fond memory then,

Your Father Loves You,

Henry Morton Robinson

Henry Morton Robinson (September 7, 1898 – January 13, 1961) was an American novelist, best known for *A Skeleton Key to Finnegan's Wake* written with Joseph Campbell and his 1950 novel *The Cardinal*.

Biography

Robinson was born in Boston and graduated from Columbia College in 1923 after serving in the US Navy during the First World War.
He was an instructor in English at Columbia University, and a senior editor at Reader's Digest.

On December 23, 1960, he fell asleep in a hot bath after taking a sedative. Three weeks later, on January 13, 1961, he died in New York of complications from the resulting second- and third-degree burns.

He is buried in Artists Cemetery, Woodstock, Ulster County, New York. His son, Anthony Robinson, is also a noted novelist.

Career

His best-known novel *The Cardinal* details the life of Stephen Fermoyle, a young American priest who eventually becomes a Prince of the Church. The story is based in part on the career of Francis Joseph Cardinal Spellman, archbishop of New York (1939-1967). The novel was adapted to an Academy Award nominated film in 1963, directed by Otto Preminger and starring Tom Tryon.

Robinson also wrote *The Perfect Round* (1947). An except from that novel was adapted into a screenplay by Richard Carr and put to film by David Carradine in a movie called *Americana*. The film won The People's Choice Award at the Director's Fortnight at the Cannes Film Festival, in 1981. Audiences liked the film, but it was not well received by critics.[1][2]

Bibliography

- *Children of Morningside* (1924) poetry
- *Buck Fever* (1929) poetry
- *Stout Cortez: a Biography of the Spanish Conquest* (1931)
- *Science Versus Crime* (1935)
- *Second Wisdom* (1937) poetry
- *A Skeleton Key to Finnegan's Wake*, with Joseph Campbell (1944)
- *The Perfect Round* (1947, filmed as "Americana" in 1983)
- *The Great Snow* (1947)
- *The Cardinal* (1950) about the life of a Roman Catholic priest.
- *The Enchanted Grindstone and Other Poems* (1952) poetry
- *Water of Life* (1960) Impact of whiskey making on three generations of an Indiana family.

Fri 1/15/10 8:23 PM

Dear Tony,

That is wonderful news that you are about to publish a brand new novel, The American Pro. I can't wait to read it. Maybe I could help with the proof reading? Let me know. I'd love to read it through for you. Perhaps you would elaborate for me what your Self-Publishing House is all about. Is it different than Lulu? I also have many things to comment to you on and about your book The Member-Guest, (there's another book out by that name also, on Abe Books,) but at another time. I wanted to share with you about my mother Margaret. They are having an Irish Wake there at the house. The whole family has come to be by her bedside which is in the living room. They watch T.V. and play games and read to her while she is dying on the Morphine Ampulet in her mouth and eating three tea spoons of apple sauce a day. More power to them I say. Bless mother's sweet heart.

Gary

---------- **Original Message** ----------

From: Mary Koniz Arnold <marykonizarnold@optonline.net>
To: Brian Booher <booherb86@gmail.com>
Cc: "Koniz, Elizabeth" <Elizabeth.Koniz@tuhs.temple.edu>,
PEGGY KONIZ BOOHER <PKONIZ_BOOHER@urc-
chs.com>, Ron Koniz <rkoniz@gentexcorp.com>,
sbkoniz@comcast.net, Kathy Koniz <gandk6@netzero.net>,
booherfamily@comcast.net, Bob Booher
<bbooher@sbaranes.com>, adam_booher@comcast.net, Justin
Koniz <jkoniz@dietzandwatson.com>, Heather Koniz
<heatherdkoniz@yahoo.com>, sunye.koniz@yahoo.com,
sunyekoniz@yahoo.com, Mary B <mebbianchi@gmail.com>,
Reggi Norton <reggi@meridianshealth.com>, susan deane-miller

<susiemuse@verizon.net>, kkoniz@comcast.net, RITA KONIZ
<rkoniz@msn.com>, Christina Rickabaugh
<CRickabaugh@bnh.org>, raemon777@gmail.com,
arnol22e@mtholyoke.edu, b.koniz@logplan.com,
j_mcener@Culinary.Edu

Subject: Care Team Meeting

Date: Wed, 13 Jan 2010 14:49:50 -0500 (EST)

This is an awkward way to give important news, but since we've
been sending everyone updates regularly, I thought you should all
know. We had a meeting with mom's/Grandma's care team today
(and they really are a caring team). This included a member of the
oncology team, the palliative care doctor, the speech pathologist
who did mom's original X-ray swallow test on Thursday (which
showed that, at that time, she could swallow pureed foods) and
has done several follow-up swallow tests at mom's bedside in
which she could not or would not swallow, and the oncology floor
social worker. The family represented was myself, Peggy, and
Stan in the room, and Ron and Gary's wife Kathy on the phone.

They laid for us out the fact that Mom's chances of getting better
are not good considering the variety of things that are wrong with
her at this point, including pneumonia from aspirating food, and
especially limited by the fact that she cannot swallow foods
effectively and is not interested in or able to eat.

For those of us who have been sitting at her bedside for the last
week and a half, cheering every step forward, and plummeting
with every step back, this was not a surprise. We have had enough
sobering conversations with the doctors and nurses and the speech
pathologist, they have brought us enough literature, hugged us
enough, and shared with us their stories to know that we are not
alone, so that we knew in our hearts that this was coming, and we
are at peace with it. Mom's own living will provided us with the

framework for coming to an understanding of what to do next. She says emphatically in the document that she doesn't want tubes and artificial nutrition, and that she wants to die at home. The palliative care doctor is contacting Hospice for us, and within a couple days, when things are set up for her care, including aides and pain-relief, we will bring our Mom and Grandma Home and that's where she will finish her life, probably within some days or weeks, in the home she loves so much.

Mom will stay in the hospital until things are set up for her care at home. Right now, mom is sleepy most of the time, but usually awake and aware enough to respond or say some words to you if you talk to her. Last night when Peggy was with her, she spoke clearly of her desire to go home. Her pain is generally well controlled, but she does feel it when she gets jostled around to change the bed. We have been allowed to start offering her "comfort feedings" of appropriate foods, but generally she declines. She does not seem hungry, thirsty, or uncomfortable. It is OK to call the hospital room to talk to her. She won't say much, but she usually can say hello and she can hear you if you say, "I Love You! I'm thinking of you!" Stan and Emily are with her this afternoon. The number there is 845-454-8500 ext 73584.

We will also need help with her care team when she comes home. Hospice will provide a couple hours of day for an aide, and we had some care in place that we can re-initiate, but she will need folk around round-the-clock. If you can be here, let us know.

Love you all,
Mary

Margaret Koniz, October 13, 1922 - January 18, 2010

From: Mary Arnold <marykonizarnold@optonline.net>

To:Heather Koniz <heatherdkoniz@yahoo.com>

Cc:ElizabethKoniz <Elizabeth.Koniz@tuhs.temple.edu>, Bob
Booher <bbooher@sbaranes.com>, 'PEGGY KONIZ BOOHER'
<PKONIZ_BOOHER@URC-CHS.COM>, Ron Koniz
<rkoniz@gentexcorp.com>, sbkoniz@comcast.net, Kathy Koniz
<gandk6@netzero.net>, booherfamily@comcast.net,
adam_booher@comcast.net, Brian Booher
<booherb86@gmail.com>,
Sent: Tue, Jan 19, 2010 08:06 AM

We have been calling people individually, but I realized there
hadn't been a group update. My mom died yesterday morning
about 8 a.m. My sister and I were at her sides, holding her hands,
and family and friends surrounded us. Thank you to all who have
prayed and kept us in your thoughts.

Here is a part of a note that Peggy wrote yesterday. It describes
the final moments so well:

"It was quite a day yesterday (Sunday) and last night.
Mom/grandma had a pretty rough time during much of the day,
seeming to be in some pain. She then settled down a bit, but was
still breathing with great difficulty. Her chest was very rattley.
There were people around until around 2:00 am, when Mary and I
pulled together a couple of chairs on either side of her bed and
basically each held a hand all night. I said maybe we should
reposition mom around 7:30 this morning and she reminded me
that Carol was coming at 8:00 and could help us. I went upstairs
to talk to Bob, and Mary suddenly called me to come down. We
both went flying. She said that Mom's respirations had suddenly
changed, slowing dramatically, and that she was no longer
making any noises as she breathed. We knew it was time. We
held her hand and stroked her hair, and told her it was okay. Bob
was with us and he got Brian and Jen and Mark. It happened
quickly. Carol walked in 5 minutes later saying that she had seen
as she was driving toward mom's, an amazing dark cloud with a
sudden shot of bright light. She knew it was mom. (Mary's friend
saw something very similar at the same time, who knows!!!)

Mary then called Glenn, Raymond and Emily and the next-door neighbors came over with food and flowers. It was very sweet, but very sad."

Calling hours will be Thursday, January 21 from 2-4 and 7-9 at Parmele/Auchmoody funeral home on Fulton Avenue in Poughkeepsie. We plan to use the evening hours to give testament and tribute to mom. Please let Peggy or I know if there is something specific you would like to share. The church service will be at Holy Trinity on Main Street in Poughkeepsie on Friday, January 22 at 9:45 a.m., and the burial will be immediately afterward at Calvary Cemetery, the one that is next to Vassar College. A NOTE TO GRANDCHILDREN: We would like you to serve as Mom's pallbearers on Friday morning. Please confirm if you will be able to do this.

People are welcome to mom's home afterward at 6 Fulton Court in Poughkeepsie. Let us know if you can bring a dish to share, and what that will be, so we can plan.

A couple years ago in honor of mom's 85th Birthday, we set up a scholarship fund at Dutchess Community College. The Margaret Fondren Koniz Scholarship for Exercise Science and Wellness. Contributions to her memory can go to the DCC Foundation, 53 Pendell Road, Poughkeepsie, NY 12601 (make sure you specify the scholarship name).

Thank you all again for your kind and compassionate support. I miss my mom terribly, but hope we can all celebrate her life by living our own to the fullest.

Love
Mary

In Sorrow

From:
    Anthony Robinson (robinsoa@newpaltz.edu)
Sent: Wed 1/27/10 8:40 AM
To: Gary Koniz (gary.koniz@hotmail.com)

Dear Gary,

I was sad to hear that your mother had died. I did not know
Margaret well; in fact, I met her only once when we drove to your
house in Poughkeepsie. But I know how much she meant to you
and how close you were. Please accept my deep condolences at
this trying time in your life.

On a brighter note, thank you for sending me your new book, The
Call To Order. I was touched to see the poem you wrote to me in
it, also by the note as to my "School Of Creative Writing." It's
really a big book and I'll write you again to talk more about it.

Meanwhile, all the best. Stay well. Tony

Wed 1/27/10 7:40 PM

Thank you so much for writing, Tony. It meant a lot to hear from
you I sympathy to my mother's passing. I delivered the graveside
eulogy, which I took in part from the poem I am writing you on
grieving, and that was the most heart wrenching thing I have ever
done, to know the final resting place of our mother there in the
frozen ground, and Frozen Time, with all the memories of her
associated. The viewing, and church service were an ordeal, and
besides having to face the cold reality of death and the grieving in
memory of a dear loved one who is not to be with us and among
us any longer, being the one issue; and but for the grueling and
fatiguing, having to sit there for three days, and at the house too,

in non-stop conversations with relatives and friends in the scores, having to be engaged in and conversed to, that has left us drained emotionally, physically, mentally, and spiritually, and that has sent both my wife Kathy and I into a numb shock following our arrival back here in Jacksonville on Saturday, which has taken us nearly three days to only partially recover from at this time.

I am glad you liked my thoughts to you to include your poem and write-up mention of your Literary School, "The Robinson School," that I was hoping would be well received by you. I do think the world of you, Tony, and regard you as a loved one to me as well.

I am still reading, The Member-Guest, and am thoroughly enjoying the story, both of its style and content. It is quite interesting to read as it moves along. I am especially impressed by what I phrase to be your, "side stories;" which move in between the main plot lines and add so much detail and depth of interest to the novel; like the story of the course pro Curt Kolchak, who got caught cheating, and about the boy Jeff catching crabs near Azy's and Nora's house, that make the book so rich and enjoyable to relate with.

All the best,
Gary
RE: Mom's Living Will

From: Ron Koniz <rkoniz@gentexcorp.com>
To: Mary Arnold marykonizarnold@optonline.net
Cc: Kathy Koniz <gandk6@netzero.net>,
PKONIZ_BOOHER@URC-CHS.COM, sbkoniz@comcast.net
Sent: Wed, Dec 30, 2009 03:41 PM

Mom's Living Will is an excellent document. I am going to check mine over and make sure that it is as well done as moms.

I especially note paragraph 2:

"I DO want pain medications, even if they dull consciousness or indirectly shorten my life."

We had some discussion about this when I visited last Thursday. I think it is very wrong to withhold strong pain medication from mom that has been prescribed by her physician even if the medication makes her not like our mom. To withhold prescribed pain medication is cruel and not at all what she requested in her living will. We should not be second-guessing her physician on this. We are not feeling her pain as her little frail bones are literally eaten away from within.

The Lidoderm pain patches are not as effective as the fentanyl and we should be using what the doctor prescribed.

That happens to older people frequently. They are not given sufficient pain medication, which makes their suffering even worse.

Thanks for all that both you and Peggy are doing for mom. I wish I could be there to help.

Ron

That statement on the pain meds is also in the section on "If I am in an irreversible coma," which she is not in at the moment.

Ron, you did not see her on the patch. Please believe me that, whether or not there is a better medication for mom than the Hydrocodone/Vicoden, which is her primary pain med (The Lidoderm patch an auxiliary topical patch), these particular Fentanyl patches are NOT the answer. I don't know if they have the defect that is sited in the recalled patches -- I don't think I saw anything leaking out -- but mom's reaction to them incredibly extreme. This was a surprise to me because she had done so well on much higher doses in the past, with little or no effect on her cognitive and motor abilities. On this Fentanyl, though, our mother could not speak in more than a little squeaky voice that sounded alien, could not string a series of words together, even though she was clearly trying to communicate, could barely take little shaky baby steps, and couldn't recognize what food was when it was placed in front of her. I am not saying that she didn't want to feed herself. I am saying that she couldn't recognize food.

Many things have come together for mom today. At the office for the Aging, Peggy and I worked with a counselor who has enrolled her in a new prescription drug plan and provided us with good choices for a Medicare supplemental medical insurance. We went to a medical loan closet and got mom an electric hospital bed and a wheel chair (Peggy is hiding it until she needs it). Mom's homecare for two hours at night has been set up to start on Monday, the Patient Access Network has gotten all the paperwork in order and is expediting her approval -- I need to call tomorrow to confirm, but everything should be set to start treatment, and we have an appointment to start treatment on Tuesday.

Mary

Adverse events

Fentanyl's major side effects (more than 10% of patients) include diarrhea, nausea, constipation, dry mouth, somnolence, confusion, asthenia (weakness), and sweating and, less frequently (3 to 10% of patients), abdominal pain, headache, fatigue, anorexia and weight loss, dizziness, nervousness, hallucinations, anxiety, depression, flu-like symptoms, dyspepsia (indigestion), dyspnea (shortness of breath), hypoventilation, apnea, and urinary retention. Fentanyl use has also been associated with aphasia. Fentanyl patch has been associated with altered mental state leading to aggression in an anecdotal case report.

Like other lipid-soluble drugs, the pharmacodynamics of fentanyl are poorly understood. The manufacturers acknowledge there is no data on the pharmacodynamics of fentanyl in elderly, cachectic or debilitated patients, frequently the type of patient for which transdermal fentanyl is being used. This may explain the increasing number of reports of respiratory depression events since the late 1970s. In 2006 the U.S. <u>Food and Drug Administration</u> started investigating several respiratory deaths, but doctors in the UK had to wait until September 2008 before being warned of the risks with fentanyl.

A number of fatal fentanyl overdoses have been directly tied to the drug over the past several years. In particular, manufacturers of time-release fentanyl patches have come under scrutiny for defective products. While the fentanyl contained in the patches was safe, a malfunction of the patches caused an excessive amount of fentanyl to leak and to be absorbed by patients, resulting in life-threatening side effects and even death.

Fri 2/5/10 7:40 AM

Dear Tony:

   My sister Mary wrote with the following comments about our Mother Margaret that I want to share with you. Also I have been thinking about writing to The President of SUNY New Paltz in urging him to form a Required English Course of your life and works, that I would like to teach and along with a Creative Writing Workshop and of course American Literature; Hemmingway, Faulkner, Dos Pasos, Twain and others. Just "pipe dreaming" away on my one day off every two weeks. I am just loving reading your novel The Member-Guest, (and taking my time in the savor of its enjoyment.) It is such a smooth flowing book, (and I think it is your best written work for the easy way it flows and contributes to the movement of the story with such exquisite detail of descriptions that make it seem as if you are "living the work" itself in your imagination and not just reading it. And I don't mind the bawdiness as much with this book and with some of the others, (as I mentioned to you,) of the "rawness" with certain sexual details about The Whole Truth, and in A Departure From The Rules, that I didn't mind at all. It was just for the tone and the sensitive way with the treatment of The Easy

Way that I took objection to, as for the use of the word F - - -, that just didn't fit, and otherwise that I felt that the sexual content was o.k.. I have become a "Liberated Male" from reading you, and as for the inclusion, (and not the blockage, properly understood and reasoned for,) of a certain sexual content in my diet, and needing to be discussed in a real and mature way as a part of life, and which it truly is, like eating and sleeping, to be revealed and depicted. You're a brave man, Tony, who I admire for your courage to write the way you want to express life as it is, The Whole Truth, that I truly admire of you.

When are you coming down to play some golf? March would be lovely time to come. Sorry that I couldn't stop by to see you for a visit while we were there in Poughkeepsie, but we were just too busy, non-stop involvement with the family. Thanks again for sending your kind sentiments about mom's passing. Kathy and I were both touched.

Here's what my sister Mary wrote us, who took care of our mother during her illness years, and who was there for mother's last breath at 8:00 a.m. on the 18th of January, and who called here to tell Kathy that she had just died. I was at work:

I thought you would all like to know that there have been donations coming in for Mom's scholarship. I don't have a list of the donors, yet, but when I checked with the DCC Foundation today, it was $325.

If you know of anyone who would like to send a donation, here is the information on what it is and how to do it:

The Margaret Fondren Koniz Scholarship supports students in the Exercise Science and Wellness Program at DCC. Through classes and hands-on lab experiences, this program emphasizes the role of nutrition in fitness and health throughout the lifespan, a goal Margaret championed for her entire career.

Tax deductible donations can be made to the Dutchess Community College Foundation.

Please write Margaret Fondren Koniz Scholarship
in the memo line.

Checks can be mailed directly to the
DCC Foundation, 53 Pendell Road
Poughkeepsie, NY 12601

Donations may also be made online at
www.sunydutchess.edu/alumni/makeagift/makeagift.html (choose
the and write the scholarship name) or send to:

Mary Koniz Arnold, 4 Exeter Road, Poughkeepsie, NY 12603.
Feel free to include a story about how Margaret made an impact
on your life.

It is lonely in Poughkeepsie here without Mom, and the house,
when I stop by, is very quiet, although Jen and Mark are staying
on and as nice as ever. I think often of things I should bring her to
that we could enjoy together. I miss her very much, especially
every Sunday at Church, where she always sat right behind me
when I song lead for the noon mass. Two Sundays ago, my friend
Karen (who played organ at Mom's funeral) came to church and
sat in her seat. This past Sunday, it was a strapping teenage boy I
didn't know.

I thought I'd pass on some of the notes I've received in sympathy
cards:

From Ann Harding:

"I want to express my condolences to your family. Rather than
feeling sad about the loss of your mother, I'd rather express a
celebration of her wonderful life. I, too, was a patient of hers at
St. Francis in 1976-1978 for hypoglycemia. I was very ill with it
and my mother was taking care of me and my children. I met
Margaret through the clinic, and yes, she did save my life (and my

children's). My mother praised her for her knowledge, compassion, and determination to help. I thank God even today for her being here on this earth."

From John and Cindy Ashburn:

"Our sincerest condolences on Margaret's passing. She was certainly one of a kind and her death will voids in many places.

"I first met her in the 1940s when her family and mine were neighbors at 'Pleasant Manor.' I don't know if all of my siblings were there or not but I stayed with Margaret and Lee on the night my father passed away in 1949. Apparently the doctors had predicted his death and his kids, being very young (I was nine at the time), stayed elsewhere that night so they weren't at home when it happened. I remember Margaret as being very kind and caring that night even though I had not been told of Dad's imminent passing and didn't know what was going on.

"Many years later, while I was a surgical patient at St. Francis Hospital, a smiling face appeared in the doorway of my room and I knew who it was immediately when she spoke. She never did lose that distinctive southern accent. Until she mentioned it I had no idea that she was the head dietitian there but following our visit my meal trays always arrived with a feast fit for a king. At times she even brought special goodies from home and prepared them in the hospital kitchen then sent them to my room at meal time instead of the standard hospital fare. Despite the reputation hospital food has gained over the years I left the hospital, after eleven days and some major surgery, four pounds heavier than when I arrived.

"We were out of town and only learned of her passing after returning, much too late to attend any of the services, but wanted you all to know that we share your sorrow. She was a good person who certainly left an imprint on everyone she met, and many who never were fortunate enough to have met her but benefited because of her anyway."

From Carol Tartter:

"I love you all very much. Mom will never be forgotten."

From The Poughkeepsie Friendship Center (signed by EVERYONE who went to the Center with Mom, many of whom we met at mom's 85th birthday):
"So sorry about Margaret's passing. She was a great lady and we will miss her very much."

From Roger and Marjorie Lane (Roger is Grandma Susie's cousin. Their daughter Joanna is adopted, and African American):
"We remember Margaret with great fondness and the dignity she brought to her long and courageous battle with illness. She was warm to all of us, and surely to everyone she met. But we especially remember the way she welcomed Joanna, as a small child hungry for family, and asked Jo to think of her as "Honorary Grandmother.' Our thoughts are with you."

From Lillian Reiser:

"To the family of Margaret, who was my friend and Hero: I was so sorry to read about her passing in the paper -- but the article is such a beautiful, fitting tribute to her. She was a very special lady who helped so many of us over the years. I will be forever grateful to her. May God bless and comfort you all now and in the days ahead."

Please keep in touch. If you have words to share on mom, let's keep passing them along.

Love

Mary

Date: Wed, 17 Feb 2010 19:50

Dear Tony,

I just loved your book, The Member-Guest. I think it was excellently written and I enjoyed savoring every page of it. The story line was superb and kept me quite in suspense, and the way that Norman pulled off the third round, after Augie who had been carrying the load, train-wrecked on the 18th hole and had to pick-up, which came from out of no where to surprise me when I thought all was lost. And as well along with all of your other excellent writing skills, that I was just taken by of each of your descriptions and action scenes. I liked that it had a happy ending after all. It's a real charmer, and a man's man kind of book, and probably a good book for the ladies too, unabashed, and about Catherine's beaked nose and its uses. I guess that they are that way. They can read the same as men. You're a Titan of the broader spectrum.

I'm going to read your father's book next, The Great Snow, and pending the arrival of your new novel, The American Pro, which I am most anxious to obtain a signed copy of. What a great Collection of The Robinson Library that I am acquiring, and quite proud of each of your books to display. Kathy and I are going to send out a copy of The Member-Guest to her brother Bill for his birthday next month. Bill lives on the firth floor in an airy Condo overlooking the twelfth hole of The Vineyards Country Club where he is a member, and relishes the game. We're great golf buddies and talk shop all the time

Your golf talk in The Member Guest is what makes the book so great, the way you describe the game to a tee, like a pro yourself, and for your sense of insight. In example, and in particular that when Augie arrives at the Flannery's for the evening party, he is greeted by the other guests there at the time with, "a look of certain disinterest."

"Augie didn't know if he were developing a sudden paranoia, but the people in the room looked at them with a certain disinterest, much as Jack Flannery had when he'd first come in."

Which is exactly what I was trying to describe to you when about the psychic dream occurrence I had when your novel A Departure From The Rules arrived, that I wrote and told you about, of "the look of disinterest" that you and your fellow colleagues had toward me that made me feel in the certain sense of "not fitting in" with your crowd. Just to let you know. So, "the look" (and perhaps that is one of unconcerned indifference,) is something you've experienced too, or perhaps from both sides looking on.

The Great Snow is dedicated to you, Tony, and to Ellen, and Hannele, who are your siblings I take it. I means something to have a book dedicated to you, and which will remain so for all of eternity, enduring. I'm contemplating your father right now, of his life on earth as a man, and am very interested to learn more about him from you.

I like looking out at the sunrise each and every morning, the first colorful light of day that emerges from the gray twilight on the horizon. There's energy for the soul of the writer there at that time, Tony.

Gary

Your last

From: **Anthony Robinson** (robinsoa@newpaltz.edu)
Sent: Tue 2/23/10 8:52 AM
To: Gary Koniz (gary.koniz@hotmail.com)

Dear Gary,

Thanks for the envelope with so much in it, especially the dear
statements about your mom and your lovely letter to me about
The Member-Guest and my father's novel, The Great Snow. I
know you thought my new novel should be called The American
Pro, but it's The American Golfer. It should be out in 4-6 weeks,
and I'll happily send you a signed copy. Could you get your club
management, i.e., the pro, to have copies for sale in the pro shop?
(More on this later.) Jenny will be working Oregon and
Washington State. Oh, what a wonderful rep she is!

I've been looking through your big book, The Call to Order. Here
is what occurs to me. It's exactly what it is, a full, splendid
compilation of the many facets of your life. A potpourri. Now,
however, I'd like to see you tackle a creative work, to move away
from letters "to and from," and fashion a novel from any of the
many and varied experiences you've had. You have a great rush
and flow of words. Use this God-given power creatively. Say
farewell to your life as a recorder. You are infinitely more
important than Robert Redford. A novel is not necessarily a life
story, just a segment of something you know and have done, an
entity of you. It's wonderful to have causes. Make your next
cause the biggest one of all, yourself, the novel that is in you
waiting to be mined.

As ever,
Tony

Sat 2/27/10 9:52 AM

Dear Tony,

How pleasant of you to write Tony in such a kind way. I have
been very busy of late with attempting to raise the necessary
funds, $6960.00 by April 30, 2010, that is The Qualifying Fee to
be able to run for Congress on the Labor Platform. So I have

been having meetings with a lot of people and writing letters to
that effect. Though I am not holding out any hopes for acquiring
such a sum. But I am enjoying the process immensely, of what it
is like to experience being "in the Big Water." I am glad this
Saturday morning, and my one day off every two weeks, to be
able to sit down and spend some quality time with you at last; and
which is my delight in inspired meaning, to do.

I would be most happy to attempt to promote your book to all
the golf courses and major chain bookstores here in Jacksonville
and throughout the Southern Tier, if I can get a handle on how to
proceed thinking big. I will certainly start in a modest way of
asking our Club Manager, The GM, and who is a dear friend to
me in his own right, if he would promote your new novel in the
Pro Shop. I take it you will have copies sent to me for
consignment and a nice display case to show them. They'll need
a 15% mark-up at least, to be priced sale-ably. And maybe if the
sales go right, they'll order more directly out to make a profit.

Our Club House has a "Book Case" full of books to read, or to
borrow, "bring-a-book – take-a-book," style of potpourri, so I
think a book with a name like "The American Golfer" would fit in
nicely with the intellectual decor. I also think very highly of your
work, "The Member-Guest," which I feel would also fit in nicely
in compliment to your new work, if "The Member-Guest," is
available in re-print. I truly enjoyed reading that work of yours
and loved every aspect about it, from your suspenseful story line,
through all the exquisite details and descriptions, and for its depth
of character development, and also that it had a triumphant
ending, that fit well into the script.

Not only does Augie defeat and humiliate his snobby
opponents at the Club by standing up, praising his and Gordon's
efforts in the tournament, "fair and square" and taking the Award,
the 1st place box, from the award table and over the strong
objections, call security, of Steve McMahon, the Golf Committee
Chairman, and taking it over to Gordon's table and giving Gordon
his well earned Award, (and who in the end, doesn't seem to care
much for his wife's Catherine's indiscretion with Augie at the end
either, "the strength of their friendship outweighing the heated

emotional reactions of the moment of the discovery of his friends
infidelity," to cement a lasting bond of loyalty between them, and
which even Catherine has seemed to forget about) in Augie's
dramatic way of taking him his "Award," (that was being
withheld pending a decision on the accusation of Augie's
grounding his club in the bunker on the shot on the 18th,) that is a
story about what friendship really means to "the men" who are
involved with the idea of living it, being friends, and what it is all
about. And who then walks dramatically off the stage, and
coincidentally to win Azy Flannery's affections, to drive off into
the sunset with.

"Are we dreaming this?" she said.
"I don't know, are we?"
"If we both are it doesn't make any difference, does it?"
"No. None."
She slid closer and he put his arm around her. They were
traveling on a county road, seven miles out of East Elmsford.
"Driver, 5-iron, Augie."
"Driver, 5-iron."
Azy's hand was in the V of his shirt, on his chest. "The
distance to Shufferville," she said.

What an ending, heh, Tony? Makes a grown man want to cry.
Now this is a book that will really sell once the fans of praise get
to circulating around. It's a great book, full of passion and
romance and all the rest of the good stuff that great books are
made of.
Incidentally, in closing, I did send my latest work, The Call To
Order, (which I just completed to 666 pages,) in to The New
Work Times Book Review Editor, Mr. Sam Tanenhaus, (and at
the direction that way of The New York Time Editorial Page
Editor, Mr. David Shipley, whose secretary's name is Inel at
212.556.3652,) as the book is compilation of "Editorials" and
with supportive research documentation, TO SWAY THE
CONTEMPORATY AND COMMON MIND TO REASON
AND TO BRING ABOUT REAL AND MEANINGFUL
CHANGE FOR THE BETTER TO OCCUR HERE ON THE

EARTH, IN OUR TIME. And as such about it, The Work, that it is an effort of my soul to have written and to be the master of the sense of persuasion necessary to change the course of history. I do hope that it has affected you in some way, of its effort, in sincerity, to comment on and about.

And to what that I am always reminded of several verses from **Proverbs 8** about in relation to you and your own work, that is always so inspirational of their grand themes and philosophies of life to ponder:

> 12 I wisdom have created prudence,
> and I posses knowledge and reason.
> 13 Reverence of the LORD despises
> Evil; pride, arrogance, evil ways, an
> perverse speech do I hate.
> 14 Counsel and sound doctrine are
> mine; mine is understanding and might.
> 27 When he established the heavens,
> I was there' when he set a circle upon
> the face of the deep.
> 36 Those who sin against me wrong
> their own soul; all who hate me love death.

I am just loving reading your father's novel, The Great Snow, that is dedicated to you Tony, and to Hannele, and to Ellen, in his heart; that was published in 1947, just a year after I was born. Your father writes differently than you, and than anyone else who I have ever read. His descriptions are very precise of a certain esoteric vernacular of precision; such as, "gray rafters," and "the plimsoll mark" on the ships; "the ships were loaded to "the plimsoll mark" and found himself wondering about the margin of safety built into seagoing ships; to give you and example of his strength of introspection. He is also into "Odors" which you aren't all that much. Although you did describe that Catherine in The Member-Guest has an odor about her of burnt paper and sweat. I have smelled that odor on certain females, or a certain female, who I can't remember who smelled like burnt paper and sweat, but it was curious and I always wondered about it, what it was.

I have indeed learned a great deal about the idea of writing a novel. But I would like to ask you, what is your first thought in the approach to starting it. Would you start with an outline of a plot, for instance?

As Ever Also,

Gary

Wed 3/24/7:23 PM

The Bait Fish

Tony,

Here is the beginning of a story I once wrote for our writing class. You remember how it went. A boy feeling unloved and unwanted by his own indifferent and unaffectionate father adopts his friend's father, whose name is Mike, as surrogate, who takes an interest in the boy and invites him along to help with his Bait Fish Business that he is just starting, catching minnows in the local streams and cow ponds. And which creates a rivalry of conflict with his friend Mickey in the way of being close with his father. And which also creates a jealousy with his own father too as well, who suddenly realizes one morning when his son runs away, that he has lost the affection of his own son to think about.

As the story goes, the boy gets puking drunk one night and to avoid a beating from his father bolts out of the house and walks to his friends father's house in his stocking feet, a vast distance for a young lad of sixteen to walk five miles out along country roads in the dead of night, walking all night long on the country road, until he finally gets there to Mike's back door as the gray dawn is approaching on the Eastern Sky, and knocks on the door, which Mike's wife Aida answers to invite the boy inside and fixes him some eggs and bacon for breakfast. Who then secretly goes and gets Mike to call the boy's father to come pick him up.

"He doesn't have any shoes," Mike said leaning in the open passenger side window when his father had pulled up the hill to Mike's house and shut off the car. "He walked all the way here in his stocking feet, and his socks are completely worn through. What a kid, hey? Don't be too hard on him, okay?"

Which was a story about when I was in High School and had a close friend named Mickey Savino then, whose father was Michael Savino, who owned a Taylor Shop in Arlington New York named, "Tailored Apparel by Michael," on the street that runs by The Bank parking lot off of Raymond Avenue, (I forget the name of the street now,) and where we used to hang-out, me and Mickey a lot in the shop. Mike Savino had a wife, a friendly Spanish lady named Aida who was a seamstress and together they cut and put together the suits that they sold. Mike's wife Aida was a wonderful artist (as was Mike,) and she painted very moving and lovely masterpieces of art. One day in the back room of the Taylor Shop she painted a very dramatic Seascape with the waves crashing on the rock, and while she was away from the shop one day, Mike himself painted a lighthouse on the rocks of "her" oil painting, and when she returned, and saw what mike had done to "her" work, she got so upset that she left him and went back to her home in Venezuala and never came back.

So, I know about an artists work, and from my own experience as well, that if someone else touches it or makes any suggestive corrections to it to change it, it isn't "your" work any more. The work has to remain pure in its essence of creativity as coming from and belonging solely to the artist, or writer.

However and that said, the editor sees things, and has a feeling for the work to make suggestions about, that once suggested to the writer or artist that they can then feel free to work out on their own, or not. If Mike had said to Aida, that the paining would look really great with a lighthouse in it, and let her paint it in herself, instead of doing it for her, perhaps things would have ended up very different for their marriage.

And that was how the story came to an end. Mickey was always broken hearted after his mother had left, and so was I. I always liked Aida. Things were never the same anymore.

Gary

Two Big Hearted River

Thurs 3/24/ 4:00 PM

We are now real blood brothers, Tony. I can't wait to get into your new book to peruse and psychoanalyze your thought in development. I had a vision today about your work, like a feeling I can't quite describe about the concept of creative work, and to the idea of a people's creative work in the overall, and what it means to everyone in a spiritual way, to create something, and to have created something to exist, where nothing existed before, in that essence, like giving birth to a mental phantasm, that then becomes real and to its own existence independent of the genius that created it, which belongs then not only to the person who created it, but to everyone also who takes part in it, to look at it, as in art, and to read it, as in literature, or who witnesses it, as in theater. That was most moving, and I feel inspired also by The Creator to feel, who is always with me in the days.

I have also been having Eternal Now Moments a lot lately, mostly in the mid-morning hours, that seems to be The Creator's special personal time with me, and when it is at that particular time that I can contemplate with Him most effectively, on the surrounding of The World He Made To Be, after the rest of the World has woken up, and my mind has settled down, and all the morning thought clutter is through its Rumination and Reminiscing about itself, to have a private moment alone with The Father in the time of that utter tranquility of the day. Who thinks in Eternal Time, The Holy Father, and not on Daily Time, so The Moment, The Eternal Moment, of His Own Experience of it, as it conveys itself to me as a moment in the long passage of Eternity, that is very deep and hallowed to experience, and with the utmost of profound respect in regard to the concept, that each moment we experience, In Eternal Time, is but a passage of successive moments to no end, that don't begin with the sunrise and end with the sunset, to fall sleep with, and to awaken from, but that come from nowhere to go nowhere, and that just go on, just to be in existence with forever, moment by moment, that challenges the concept of beginning and end and just continues on its way in solemnity. I am glad you are happy with yourself. It's an amazing thing about love, when you think about, how quickly it turns to anger and hate if it's thwarted. We ride emotionally out on loving reassuring words, and any disparaging hostile words to the contrary we get angry over, easily made up to though. I am glad you are a big-hearted man, and glad to call you my brother.

Gary

Justice in this Nation must be emphatically oriented to The Safeguarding of The Innocence of anyone, as well to be concerned with The Prosecution's Case and The Sentencing of The Guilty. And regarding the subject of Plea Bargaining, that The Justice Department, in its roll as Public Defender, needs to be concerned with Justice about and not in playing head games over "Time Served," in its ability to coerce and manipulate the heavy handed pressuring of the innocent poor, in intimidation of the maximum sentence for a demand to jury trial proceedings, Suborning Perjury, into "Pleading Guilty To A Lesser Time Served," and who are otherwise innocent and have been accused of having committed a crime, and who cannot afford to retain the expense of an appropriate private defense attorney to be concerned with a vigorous defense of their innocence in their behalf, and who otherwise lack the financial resources to post bail to be able to await a jury trial proceedings unencumbered by the pang of incarceration, and who therefore have to sit in jail in a twelve by eight foot cell, eating prison food, in noisy overcrowded warehoused conditions, for an intolerable length of time awaiting the slow processes of the court, of months on end awaiting a court date, and which are often postponed, to a jury trial, (in violation of The Constitution in The Right to a swift and speedy trial, which in all reasonableness of justice should never be more than thirty days to await a trial date,) without anyone of the court or the justice department caring at all for the sense of justice in the matter, and who only want the innocent to plead guilty to a crime they did not commit, "Time Served," to satisfy the interests of The Court, in use of "The Public Defenders Attorneys" in serving only as "Processors" for The Prosecution and The Convenience of The Court, for the sake of persons being allowed to get out of jail early in return for the innocent victims of this system freeing up the court's docket and satisfying the court's necessity for a case disposal.

And who otherwise, of these indigent people, might be able to prove their innocence at a later court date of jury proceedings, were they free on bail to await such a court date and to have the opportunity to confront their accusers and provide their testimony before a jury. And who otherwise of these indigent who need to be free to work and pay their rent and other bills on the threshold of survival at stake.

Which raises the issue of justice that if The Court is able "to legally free" people after a period of "time served" in good conscience by their plea of guilty, that it can also free them on their own recognizance after the same time period of, "time served," in an equally fair rendering of justice, to await a formal jury trial for their alleged offence, and to a fair rendering of justice, to be able to plead "No Contest" to "Time Served" without a Criminal Conviction History.

The United States stands morally obligated to be concerned with this issue of whether or not a person is Guilty or Innocent, first and foremost, and to vigorously defend the innocent as well as "to process" and prosecute the guilty. And, in knowing what they are doing in plea-bargaining the innocent into guilty for the sake of manipulation to the court's convenience, both The Court and The Public Defenders stand ethically and morally in violation of the integrity of Civil Rights.

And what matter grows perversely worse when The Court, By Order of Two Physician Consent (2PC) Psychiatric Evaluation, and without the presence of a Defense Attorney to the conduct and determinations in psychiatric diagnoses labeling of such illegally conducted interviews, attempts to manipulate individuals into a Plea Bargained Psychiatric Commitment Profile, (to be

sentenced to an Indefinite Period of Time in a Mental Facility
based to Medical Determination in lieu of a Criminal Conviction,)
and to thereof, of The State's Right under Mental Hygiene Law
To Force Treat with Deadly Chemical Drugs, termed as Strong
Tranquilizers, Without Due Process of Law, that is a much worse
fate.

And to what in all regards that everyone needs The Right to a
reasonable and soundly defined Statute of Limitations in
established Legal Age Limits for the mandatory disclosure of
these, justified or otherwise contrived, psychiatric condition
labeling history records, which in most instances is to be worded,
to any current treatment for any serious, and as worded obvious,
ongoing psychiatric condition, or to within the past three years in
age limit concerning The Public Record for employment,
licensing, and court related matters.

And as well that a Uniform Statute of Age Limits pertaining
for employment application concerns and to government licensing
matters is also to be instated for The History of Criminal Arrests
and Convictions Records conveyed under Penal Law depending
to the severity and nature of the crimes committed and not to
exceed The Statute of Limitation for any crime or offense, if any.

Infractions and Violations are to be absolved from the public
record in three years, misdemeanors in five years, and most
felony records after a span of ten years, depending on the nature
in severity of offense not stipulated for to a greater time interval
by a Court Of Law.

It is also worded that no person shall be infringed upon or
denied their Vested Right To Voting Citizenship in The United
States due to conviction of a Felony Offense after said offense is
duly discharged and the person is free and clear of any probation
or parole.

And in all regard that it is the inherent nature of this Nation in
standard of integrity and in principle of fair and humane
conscience not to discriminate against any persons and to prevent
any such discrimination from occurring. Which extends as well
to the prevention of needless discrimination in bias of prejudice
occurring to anyone on account of their prior criminal conviction

or psychiatric history in this Nation, as it is deemed reasonable and prudent to dissolve these matters.

And that each person is to have The Right to a Self-Fulfilled Destiny instilled in the reverent promise of hope in opportunity of success and of healing recovery from stigma, and to the actualization of their highest potentials among the population of The United States to the outlook of being deemed and classified as good, solid, useful, and productive citizens in the eyes of society, and in the spirit of good will, without the infringement of bias, discrimination, and alienating prejudice of social stigma and concerning the hardship of sanctions to such records history being permanently attached to anyone in constant reminder of being negatively classified in downgrade of second class inferior citizenship, to be conceived in permanent ruin to their lives, as to stigma of social embarrassment, and with critical jeopardy of their livelihood and well-being affected, being imposed upon them.

Sun 3/28/ 6:30 PM

What do think, Tony, can you make it down here to Florida to get in some golf in the nice Florida April Weather, the most beautiful time of year, cool and crisp in the mornings and in the 70's in the afternoons. Let me know. You and your wife, or just you, can stay here with Kathy and myself, and I'll take a few days off to play golf with you at our Club. You can tune-up for the season there at the Huguenot Golf and Country Club and be the envy of everyone with a nice robust Florida Tan, Bentley Green with envy. Please to think about coming. Kathy and I would really love to see you, and your wife Tatiana if she wants to come.

I've been reading your father. He tells quite a tale in the Great Snow about Ruston Cobb, a New York City Patent Attorney who stays over in New York and lives in Rhine Cliff, NY in Dutchess County, and takes the train on the weekends to come home to see his wife Nolla and their son Roddy, and their housekeeper Emma Rollefson; and which also involves Nolla's sister Beryle Dean who comes to visit for the weekend, turned snowed in weekend, with her painter acquaintance and philosopher Edward Laimbeer, and that also has a dramatic involvement with a daughter Sicely who starts out away at school but becomes stranded in the Albany, NY Train Station trying to make it home out the snowbound city, to what the adventure of the book aspires; with Ruston taking his small boats Chips out into the channel of The Hudson River where the Ice Breaker has made a swath, to rescue "Sicely." And who, in that process, speaking for the character of Ruston Cobb, nearly freezes to death stranded for the night on the river ice, gets rescued by a Tanker Captain who takes him to Albany for all the money in his pocket, around $500.00, gets plowed over by a train and nearly dies from that near the station, rescues Sicely, makes it back to the Tanker, and then gets charged $5,000 by The Captain which Ruston has to pay by check for taking him and Sicely back down river to Canbouy 233 where the Captain lets them out, and then nearly gets Sicely killed when she falls into a snow covered ravine while trying to make it back to their home, and finally to arrive to find Emma Rollefson's son, an aviator, who has just flown a military jet in to visit in the blinding snowstorm on radar and miraculously shows up at their door. The freak storm is being caused by a clash of fronts, with a Fog Bank of prevailing winds from off shore blowing moist air inland while a savage cold front descends from the Western Arctic blowing cold air; which in turn has stalled out over the entire Eastern Region of The United States, and it snows and snows, while Ruston and Laimbeer talk and other intrigues go on. It's all very dense psychodrama, not meant to be taken quite so literally, and very different from your straightforward and meticulously plausible narrative dramatic style.

We'll see how it goes on to end. I always wish in your rendition of, Home Again, Home Again, that you had used the real names of the Towns and Cities, Woodstock and Kingston, which would have made it homier to me, like your father's book.

T.D. once told me that day she was planting the Poppy Flowers in the garden, that she and your father liked to go a restaurant named Salvuci's in Woodstock, which you and Ellen and Hannele liked especially; a real rebel, as I see where you get your maverick side from. They grew pretty big and nobody said anything. Those were the days for the Avant-Garde. Maybe there's something there worth writing about? Please let me know when I can get a copy of your new masterpiece, The American Golfer, to read?

Sincerely,
Gary

Sat 4/3/ 6:30 PM

Dear Tony,

I got your wonderful info packet in, with the kind mention of my short story, "The Bait Fish," a very moving psychology tale of early adolescence, and with very nice advice on working revisions on it, which I want to get to. There's so much going on and with hardly enough time to get to everything, as I am sure you are too keenly aware of. Thanks for including me along with you in the excitement of getting your new novel out there to market. It has a lovely cover. Whose Idea for the cover was that? And we enjoyed, my wife and I, seeing a picture of you, that was a little older than my memory of you had pictured you now. You have grown more handsome with the years and I can imagine, more philosophical looking in wisdom of your senior years, age being only relative. Adam lived 800 years with the Coca Leaf Powder, The Tree of Life, but the withering old age induced by their Original Sin of eating the Opium with its sedentary slowing down of the bodily processes necessary for life killed them both just the same in the end ... and surely you won't die ... as the serpent said ... leaving out the part of, "not right off." I am just wondering how you intend to proceed with The American Pro as far as the actual sales presentation of it is concerned, (and as to say for my General Manager - Pro Shop,) to handle for you to sell? Barnes and Nobel and as well as Books-A-Million require an author, or their agent representative, (and better to have an agent to verify

for you,) to send a copy of their book into The Central
Acquisitions Department, the addresses of which are available at
their bookstores, or perhaps online but I haven't checked.)
However the standard arrangement, as I checked on, is for the
bookstore to buy the copies from the wholesaler using the ISBN
number with a Contract Agreement to buy the books back with
postage if they don't sell. At any event, we can certainly stock my
Pro Shop with them, as soon as I have the arrangements from you
on how you wish to proceed. Let me hear from you about this. I
will also canvass all the golf courses and bookstores in my area as
I can for you. Hope to hear back from you soon. I am so thrilled
to be a part of it.

Gary

A Poem For Our Dear Mother Margaret

The Dream Of God

Growing Old Is Not For The Faint Of Heart
And Nor Is Grieving After The Dead For The Faint Of Heart
That Is An Empty Sorrow Now Of A Sad And Mournful Memory
Almost Impossible To Bear Of The Loss
The Dream Of God That Was
And Heavily Lain Upon Us Of The Memory
Is The Mantle Of Its Sorrow
And A Somberness Is Upon The Gathering About Us Who Mourn
And All About Us Is A Pall Of Gloom And The Look Of
Desperation In Their Faces

For The Passing Is Too Deep With Sympathy Toward Each Other
In Our Eyes Too Tragic Of Its Thought
To Even To Sigh Of Its Remorse,
An Ache Of The Sad And Lonely Time

Of The Emptiness In Our Hearts

A Hole In The Universe Of An Emptiness
That Is Too Heavy To Bear
And The Weight Of It, The Empty Weight Of It,
That Is Too Heavy To Lift Off
That Won't Lift Off, That Is A Hollow Numbness
And Vacuous Stare
Transfixed Upon Such Finality
Of One So Cherished So Dear Who Once Lived To Love Us
And Of The Cherished Life That Was Hers
Now Lost To Us Forever

Not Again In Life Now To Love Us
And Lost To Her As Well The Life She Loved
That Was A Joy To Her Existence
Now Lost To Her, Lost To Us, And Lost To All,
Beyond Reclaiming Gone
That Is Bearable Only In The Moments
Of Its Not Being Thought About
Lying Beneath Us Now In The Cold Ground
The Impossibility Of Fate To Contemplate

That It Is A Force To Be Reckoned With
The Death That Thinks Upon Itself Compelled
It Is A Passion To Be Thought Of
That Is Beyond Our Strength To Deny It
That Wants Her To Be Alive Again
And Yearns After Her To Be Remembered
For It Was LIFE She Once Had
That Gave Birth To Us And Our Life To Us

Who Once Was Of The Cycle Of Birth And Death Being One
Of Her Hope and Her Dreams That Her Mind Was Made Of
In Its Remembering
And To All Who Mourn Beside Her Grave Given Up Now
To The Father In Heaven

Who Made Us All To Be With Him In The End,
Let Us Not Be So Glad And Happy For A Time
For What Is The Celebration Of The Life We Have Left
For The Enchanted Days
And Of The Fine Days About The Earth To Enjoy
That Are All Too Soon To Die
The Creator's Way Of Passing Time

Life And Death In The Endlessness Of Time Eternal
With Pleasure And Pain And Suffering And Joy
To Endure In The Struggle To Survive
Unto The Endless Cycles Of Birth And Death
To Return From Whence We Came
From The Creators Self We Came,
And To The Creator God Of All Things To Return,
And All The Same Life, The Life Of The One Being,
Male And Female Who We Are
To Share What There Is Of It, THE LIFE,
In Fellowship With One Another
Returning Back To God Who We Are Made Of

And All Too Soon To Follow
Returning To The Source Again
As God Returns Not So With The Fear Of Dying
But With The Shriek Of Dread
In The Fear Of Being Left Alone With The Darkness
And With The Fear Of Not Having Mattered
And With The Fear Of Not Being Cared For,
That Is The Instrument Of Our Torment
In The Grieving Heart After Itself To Be Loved
That Needs To Feel The Need For Goodness Underfoot
With A Pang, Our Only Solace,
For It Is All Too Beautiful To Bear Of Its Sad Parting,
The Enchanted Life.

Gary Koniz

Children Of God

Children of God … When?!

When … is the question that instinctively needs to be answered even before you know what the question is to be. Because "When" is the question that is most primary and utmost in the preoccupation of your being to resolve, involving The Eternal Angst of your dilemma to existence, of "Why" and "How," and "For What Reason;" that you exist, and to its answering … which begins with the wording:

"You don't exist."

That comes from The Creator's Mind, as you do, expressing the obvious opposite of what He intends to make His point about to reinforce the obvious.

And to His point being, that of course you do know, You Do Exist.

And that We Do Exist in the plurality of our collective consciousness as human beings to be alive on the planet in outer space we name to be called The Earth which exists in The Universe of The Creator's Power of Creation, To Be, and which The Creator made for us, of the planet Earth, to be happy with and to live our lives out upon, our lives as Human Beings which The Creator Made for us in His Own Self-Image, Created from The Power of His Dream and of The Life He Made upon It.

That to us, of such Creation, is to be conceived about in the same manner as we perceive our own dreams, the dreams we experience in our slumber, that are fashioned out of something wispy, mystical, and divine, and called Surreal; and which seem real enough being dreamed, only to awaken from. And so it is that they are like The Creator's Dream of Life involving us, in His way of dreaming it, and To Our Way about it, in the sense of our being dreamed of by The Creator Divine, in meaning of seeming real, that when we die we awaken from to find ourselves awakened in the state of being a part of The Creator all along from Whom we came.

And such therein is the great mystery of life resolved, to be an eternal plaything of The Creator's Imagination, the eternal drama of life and death, of its joys and happiness, and of its pain and suffering and remorse, of the good times and the bad, that is all just a way in the adventure of it to endure, of passing time, and really of no consequence in the eternal scheme of the adventure and of having something real to do with the time of being continuously alive in the real sense, that hangs oppressive when there is nothing to stimulate one's interests in the awareness of it.

And in knowing that We Do Exist in God's Dream, and to its extent, as explained in the struggle to endure eternal time, then the question arises of what is it all to do about, that brings to mind in our mutual struggles to survive, and in the terms of our mental, emotional, and physical aspects of having to survive the tests of life in the day to day struggles to endure its reality, as it were, as we find ourselves in The Creator's Self-Image to be involved with the life He fashioned for us of such precarious situations, and to its joys and pleasant times also, as to its struggles for survival, for entertainment to alleviate the boredom and the suffering of eternal time to no end, and to the complex issue of involving moral reasoning as well as physical intelligence in responsibility to its survival as well, in accepting our fate to endure the life The Creator Made for us in what context of responsibility, at least in our own way of unique perception of it, to live up the challenge of our existence in the ability to maturely deal with it, as our reasoning dictates, and to cope with life on such terms that are satisfying and pleasing for us to endure in a successful manner to us to do, and with the meaning of what The State of Heaven is all about.

Heaven is here, in the here and now, and no different in state than the way we find things to be. There's no easy way to say, but Heaven is not an idle place with nothing to do all day, and where there is no life and death, and with no cares or worries of the nature of survival, or with no moral code to adhere to in our manner of being correct in nature, to ourselves and to toward the rest of the manifesting of the life about us. Heaven is The State Of Mind of Being Correct In The Judgment Of Our Own Self

Esteem And Conscience, And According To The Law The
Creator, Whose Ultimate Thought and Judgment Supercedes Us
All, As He Determines For Things To Be The Way He Intends,
To What We All Must Correspond To, Being Part Of The
Creator-Self, Or Suffer The Self-Judgment For In Outcome Of
Condemnation.

And which with certainty entails, of such necessary mature
reasoning in approach, and to an Age of Reason, involving each
of us with the larger mass in plurality of the whole of humanity,
to the imposing of judgments concerning the thoughts and actions
that compel us forward into life involving everything that we do,
as to whether or not that what we choose to do is good or bad for
us, that we do perceive to do the right thing at all times.

And it is this weighing of the judgments, on either hand, for
good or bad, and to the accomplishing of our immediate and long
term objectives in that regard, to be physically and mentally and
emotionally well ordered and maintained, to the fulfillment in
purpose of true happiness and contentment and inner peace in our
life, and to find solace even in the bad times of ill-fate in
experience for the means of having something to suffer and
something to labor with in the arduous travail of eternity in the
presentations of challenges to the sheer boredom of nothing to do
to face, that even the ill-times have a joy about them to experience
for what reason, as we are forced in certainty to endure it, the life
that we find the inner strength about to endure, and which all
poignantly comes to an end, to be replaced, Male and Female,
with more of The Creator's Self Entity, like Ants who are always
Ants but always different ones from year to year, in the same way
of being Human Beings.

And on it goes, seemingly forever, and perhaps forever, as
there is no end to the time of eternal contemplation. And which
had a beginning sometime, or maybe not, which we cannot begin
to fathom, concerning our mutual and collective existence on The
Planet Earth, which came forth from God.

Which reasoning instinctively arises in the process of the
judgments we are forced to make here in the terms of what we
need to do to deal with and to confront the life we are forced to be

living, that The Creator Made For Us, to be judged about, and to be The Judge about, and concerning the actions and the judgments of those around us as well, composing as society, and imposing themselves upon us, that we find ourselves forced to do something about, and in our human nature of having to deal with it all, of that aspect as well, as to whether or not we need to be engaged with the certain thoughts and actions, individually, or as a society together, as they confront us, and to their consequences, as they affect us and the physical world and the life about us, needing in all regard to be well thought out, as to how we should be conducting our lives accordingly to the reality of existence, depending to the judgment of the right hand or the left, of our thoughts and actions, of our being uniquely alive among the many other lives in The Creator's Dream of Life, and in the terms of existing to be satisfied and content with ourselves about, and not for any or us to be regretful or in remorse for any way that we have lived, or intend to live, by our honor of faithful intentions to The Creator's Divine Will in judgment, and as we are living; that is always shameful and full of remorse for any judgments in error that occur against us, to the thoughts, words, and deeds of our days, to endure, and what are not as in a healthy pleasant way of being, being in error, which is our index marker in sound judgment, and to the securing nature of our eternal souls, as to how we are to proceed forth in the ways of life that we are to follow, as is our necessity and as our Nature Instinctively Compels Us.

The answer to the question, When?! is then being answered inwardly upon us in instinctive response, the question then arises out of itself to its own conclusion in our consciousness being:

"When Are Things Ever Going To Be Made Right On This Earth As The Creator, Who Made Us, Intends?"

And to its answer:

When We Are Ready To Assume The Relationship and The Responsibility of Being As A Part Of God Ourselves, And Partaking In God's Nature And Divinity, When We Are Mature Enough To Realize That Only We Can Do And Accomplish The Task of Being Holy In Spirit To Make Ourselves Well, and The

Lives Of Those Around Us Well, and To Keep Ourselves In A Healthy Way Unto God's Image.

The Creator, as He communicates, is a lonely orphan of the timeless darkness, Who has only us, and together with The Holy Spirit, His Female Half, as His Human Companions, and to the myriad other forms of life here that They Created, Male and Female, for companionship in their image also of Themselves to be of existence, on The Planet Earth which He Made from His Dream, to abide with, and to find happiness and contentment upon, and for what that each day here is a struggle to endure and to keep up with, and to the terms of life being harsh, for what you must keep up or else you'll die. That you therefore need to accept the terms in condition for the existence you face, and to what that there is no way out in escape from, not even in death, which does not free you from existence. And that even to the taking of your own life in self-murder won't free you any from existing, and in existing, with being compelled to make judgments about what you think and do, and to either being happy of sad about the consequences emotionally.

And the question responds to itself, for that reason, without being asked because it needs utmost in your hearts to be answered. And the answer to it lies within the hearts and minds of each of us and to the meaning of The Lord's Fervent Prayer to The Heavenly Father, that is a calling from the deep spiritual well of the soul within us all as well, and from the depths of each our souls, To Awaken Us! to the physical and moral responsibilities which compel us to be correct in relationship with The Eternal Creator, which we share with Our Heavenly Father, for completion. And what is a prayer that begins with these words:

"Our Father ..." and which goes on ...

"Thy Kingdom Come, Thy Will Be Done, On Earth As It Is In Heaven."

That is the response to the question, "When?!" innately reasoned, and to the fulfillment of that day when The Kingdom of The Father is at hand, and which can be soon here about us now in our days upon The Earth Itself, if only that we would involve ourselves very closely aligned to The Will of The Creator; and

Who would provide the answer to the fervent prayer of Jesus, as to unite us more closely with Himself and to one another, and to make us more effective disciples of The Lord in the building of His Kingdom, The Kingdom of God, on Earth, as The Heavenly Father intends for us to do.

"Thy Will Be Done On Earth As It Is In Heaven..."

Then all will be whole and well again, "as it was in the beginning, is now, and ever shall be, world without end, amen."

And the question "When" is already answered, being to what end, that is has already answered itself, in the necessity of its ultimate fulfillment, and it shall be fulfilled, and to its imploring in its meaning of urgency.

When will it all end, this madness that mankind has conceived and engendered within itself, this madness and self-made misery of irrational inhumanity and to its collective suffering which we collectively and through the centuries of millennia have brought upon ourselves, due to error, termed Original Sin; which we each and all individually have been born into to be a part of and to take a part in and are forced to bare and to endure through no fault of our own being born into, and perhaps through our own fault in bearing with correcting it, The Error in dilemma, as we examine our conscience about, to make it right again,

"As It Was In The Beginning, Is Now, And Ever Shall Be."

When therefore ... When?! is the question asked. To what is responded ...

When we each realize ourselves that we ourselves are the key and the solution to the entire problem, and that we all need to be involved in The Work of The Redemption ourselves, individually, and as a plural community of individuals involved in concern, to the undertaking of the sacred mission of "Repairing The World;" as a building is conceived to be constructed, built brick by brick in its place, and sturdily fashion in the architecture of soundly reasoned designed, in reference of the necessary to the needed social architecture of enlightened and well thought out reasoning in approach to be followed. And when we realize: That God's Work, and In The Nature and Bearing In Responsibility of Being God, Must Truly Be Our Own.

And there is work ahead enough for everyone in this light of what needs to be accomplish in the holy undertaking To Make Right and Perfect what has slipped tragically over time into an unholy decay of personal and collective social vices, corruptions, greed, and of inhumanity, and to the tragedy of wars abounding and ongoing relentlessly in display's of irrational conflicts throughout and about us on the planet, in the condoned and accepted acquiescence to unholy error being put up with, and upon us, and being gone alone with in quite acquiescence among us, as is evident enough about for each of you to perceive of the errors, or what they are, which are still occurring here to this day, in to their unholy horror and terror about us, and of their tragedy, of what it is that we can name them about and what they have to do with, and to the unholy misery and suffering of humankind. And which, to be said about it, that there is enough personal work ahead to involve each of us in the devout ministry of humanity's redemption for a length of time, and perhaps to the end of our days as it takes us, or over night in a day's time, as we can hurriedly accomplish it, The Task Of Redemption, that is the length of time it will take, "To Repair The World," and to make it right again, if we all put our minds to the task and all pull together on the yoke of involvement to move the obstacle before us.

And which is a job that you must undertake of your personal selves; which will not ever be done for you of its own without you to undertake it, "To Do The Work Of God," and to accomplish it for yourselves in a real way and as it involves each of us as a real fate.

And what this job is then, in specific terms of what we must do, and what it is that The Creator specifically desires and require of us each one, of us all, in the meaning of needing us to help Him with His project to reform His Humanity, that is His Will and Fervent Desire To Reform, Be Done, and for us To Accomplish.

This project together will only be accomplished through the personal terms of yourselves adhering to the disciplines which you feel in your heart to be right, and on the right path accepted by you in foundation of your faith, as you profess to and have been instructed about, and as you feel instinctively about as being right, and as you feel compelled in correctness about yourselves to be involved with in conduct as the right way to approach the life you have.

And as well in moral obligation, it is incumbent upon each of us as well to display and to instill of The Ways of that Perfect Faith in others, as an obligation to do so, as to make perfect the ways of the world around us, in all who you have personal relations with in your day to day pursuits, and to all who we are able to communicate with in extended outreach of our faith; which involves both our personal relationship and reverence in devotion to The Creator, and, our own inner determination to be perfect in our thoughts, words, and deeds, upon the earth God Made, and through Charity and Good Works and Perfect Intentions toward our fellow man upon The Earth, and to actively participate in the affairs of our Governing Structure to ensure its proper conduct, thereunto to the whole of society imparted as a congregation, through the length of time that it takes to get the mission of reform faithfully accomplished.

When?! Is the question to be answered by forceful conviction!

When you are ready to accept and to assume your own responsibility for your own errors and failures and for the errors and failures of humanity of the larger context in being made your own concern in your own right, to do it, awakened now as you are to the miraculous existence of life, and to the necessity for correcting its existing errors upon you, will the question be answered.

And let us here begin with our discussion of what specifically we are to do in the condition to us in the given context of the finite set of variables that we have to deal with, as are apparent, To Attain The Desired For Common Enlightenment which we must have, individually and as a society together, in order to be in Communion with The Creator each day; and that we, each of us, need to be involved with correctly, to sustain ourselves by in the longed for desire for fulfillment and happiness, and to our own dealings with the travails, and trials, and ordeals of life we must face as we go about living on with it.

And which is utmost, in crucial understanding of the matter to be resolved in essential necessity, that which is most important to us, inherent to us to resolve, and incumbent upon us come to terms with, in the terms of what we each of us must accomplish to be holy here; which is, in primary priority, to emphatically resolve The Biological Malfunction of The Sexual Error as we have inherited it, stated in the terms of to include for The Male and The Female Human Misuse of Their Sexuality, that was intended by The Creator Selves, Male and Female, for the blessed purpose, and the sacred function, of bringing new life into The World.

Which begins, on the topic of sex education, with proper childhood training in the understanding of its nature, and which cannot be left unchallenged the way that is has come to be, in a negative social climate of debasing peer pressure, in the over infatuated curiosity for everybody with The Sensations of Bodily Orgasm that begins at the age of puberty; and which thereon shortly becomes an uncontrolled life-long addiction in physiological and psychological obsession, seemingly throughout everyone's lives, as a destructive habit in the force of compulsive addiction to it, akin to drug addiction, the bodily sensation of orgasm, and in the need to induce it, through Self-Fornication, known by the term Masturbation, on a continual and relentless basis, that is the source of all perversion and depravity to exist in self-loathing, and of what is The Root Source of Every Self Destructive Force, Including Wars, Upon The Earth stemming from the induced Nihilism of Psychological Despair that The Act of Masturbation Automatically Induces in the manner of resultant Self-Loathing, as psychological-biological consequence, that induces a Hatred of The Self for the act, and which engenders, individually, and collectively involving the en masse destruction of the entire society as a sexually depraved and perverted culture, from the overall personal inability to control The Sexual Function, to what everyone needs to search and to reason their own hearts and minds about. For the control of our sexuality is a paramount condition and attribute to salvation.

And which leads, the unwanted act of self-loathing known as masturbation, ultimately into all other manners and methods of equally self-destructive sexual behavior, individually engaged with, or conducted as a society as a whole, to the horrid psychological states of Degenerate Depravity of Sodomy and Oral Sex, Bestiality, Lesbianism and Homosexuality, Orgiastic Group Sex, Prostitution and Pornography, Rape, and to ultimate Sadomasochism in Torture and Self-Flagellation, in the perverted desire to enhance and to play upon the sexual sensation of Habitual Organism; that has becomes a life-long addiction in obsession for the mainstay of society in this day and age, with all of its inverted and introverted narcissistic facets in intrigues of the imagination, psychological guilt, and repression; which leads to a Separation From God in both senses, not just in the sense of personal deviancy, but also to The Creator in not desiring to be with us, and that is to say, anyone of that perverted sexual nature either, that is despised.

And for that reason, to what that all anyone needs to do to be at peace and finally with, is to reform the issue, to stop in their habit of daily masturbation, to overcome it, and to thereon to not dwelling to the thoughts of it any longer, and nor to the memory of its past mistake, to be free of.

And let it be reasoned here, that it is only primarily of this obsession with Masturbation, (including all other forms and types of sexual activities misuse in fornication, and either of the heterosexual or homosexual/lesbian nature,) that separates us, (in key note,) from our true identity in stature of what it means in the magnitude of being a human being, (which the misuse and abuse of the sexual function demeans and defiles us of, and weakens us in our resolve to survive in no uncertain terms, in the meaning that such sexual defilement makes anyone succumbing to it not desirous within themselves to live on anymore, that is to be deadened unto one's self, for the act itself in induces within the guilty to its conduct, The Longing For Death, due to the reality that such conduct makes one feel ashamed and not worthy of the life to which they have been bestowed of by God.)

That is the cold hard reality in fact of the case about human sex abuse.

And, because we don't respect ourselves for the sense and feel the sense of shame for any sexual misconduct, which prevents us from ever having a Lasting and Caring Relationship with ourselves, foremost, and with God in the ultimate sense, who is our eternal companion, utmost as well to resolve, in the terms of what The Creator respects and admires and needs in us to feel pleased with us about; and with Himself for having created you, and each of us, to be a part of The Creator Himself in His Dream for us of The World, to be proud of us about; that we do ultimately bring about our own death, and the to the destruction of the society and the world around us, as we seek to bring ourselves down, due to it, the sexual error, as we need to resolve immediately.

The rule to follow, in the situation regarding sex, whether of its occurring in the imagination of thought, or in our words, or actions taking place, is that if it makes you feel uncomfortable at the time of its engaging, and ashamed of yourself afterwards, that you know in your own heart about it that it isn't right, then by all means, don't perform such activity. Your own conscience here is the guiding indicator, and as it is with all matters moral, of good and bad, to discern.

These are certainly difficult times we are living in, aren't they, and as all times were and are that way difficult, struggling in the temptations of the flesh that man's self has inherited and is error to and what has been placed in the context of society as stumbling blocks before us, and among the other man made self-destructive hindrances to existence having to do with survival to contend for in the dog-eat-dog mercantile inhumanity of greed and domination, in the reality of survival of the most ruthless, and at best to what that we are each fortunate to be able to hold our own about; concerning the immoral climate, both from the standpoint of surviving the economy, and concerning the nature of the sexual perversity of the times to come to terms with and to free ourselves and the rest of the society about; and especially with the pressures to survive that are placed upon everyone in uncertain terms and concerning the raising of a family on ethical terms in the sight of God.

And to which that even the foundation of The Holy Church itself is set upon to rest, to the conduct of proper sexual morality by the congregation, and to the resolution of personal finances, upon which The Church itself depends to sustain itself, and us of the congregation, to its bosom of faith, who need the shelter and strength of the Church to endure.

And with attempting to resolve our own confidence of faith, and to stem the tide of dwindling Church participation from the unhealthy sexual orientation in the modern day and to the resulting subsequent loss of revenue contributions, and continuing on with the theme that "complex moral issues don't lend themselves to brief explanations," that we need to also to resolve here presently on the issues of Allowing The Use of Birth Control by The Society, and which includes for The Church's Stand on Sexuality and its relationship to The Church in general that needs to be brought up to date and on-line with a wholesome realistic policy.

And as well that we need to discuss on the topic of Certain Abortions Being Permitted For in the restricted sense of Medical Necessity, particularly concerning the regard of the woman in the aftershock in effect of a rape and to the immediate use of an Abortifacient in that particular aspect. And with so stating, as to have the best of intentions in the matter, and of course, in an ideal setting of a perfect world, well thought out and planned for, that the issue of an unholy and intellectually and emotionally unhealthy idea of abortion is abhorrent for anyone to conceive of in the choice of words to use discussing the idea.

But Abortion in the setting of a rape falls into, "The Setting of Emergency Medical Necessity" and therefore needs also to exist within the moral standards of The Church's Holy Intent for the allowing of Abortion; and also in any case, To Save The Life Of Woman who is hemorrhaging in Miscarriage, or who has a Fallopian Tube Fertilization, or otherwise due to Complications of Pregnancy deemed Life Threatening, and To Prevent The Misery of Lifelong Insufferable Birth Defects from Coming To Term, and for issues of Insanity and the inability to rationally carry and care for a child, and which is also to include Rape, (as Emergency Medical Necessity,) both from the standpoint of the victims of violent sexual assault, to include the matter Rape by fear coercion assault also, and for the reasoning of Underage Pregnancies protected under the heading of Statutory Rape involving Incest, and otherwise so classified to be Rape, for what serious and grave matters to what that Abortion is necessitated.

And particularly that Conception brought about by The Evil and Vile Act of Rape should never have occurred and is therefore null and void of its resulting issue, which in the eyes of God never should have been conceived. The feelings in tragedy of the woman in her trauma suffering grief are paramount here.

And as to say of what discussion of the sexual issue involving our Holy Catholic Church in her infallible shepherding of us, as we stand gathered to our Holy Mother The Church as a collective congregation of morally proper people together, under the divine inspiration and guidance of The Heavenly Father; to state for the matter that the subject of human sexuality, properly conducted, whether within the bonds of holy matrimony, which needs not be absolute, or between two unmarried people bound together in love for one anther, who care for each other in a serious relationship unto God, and with the idea of becoming formally married and to the idea of conceiving children at some time in their relationship, or not, that cannot be construed of to be a bad thing in either regard, and although that it is currently conveyed to be that way by The Church Teachings, and needs The Divine Support of The Church for the use of Contraception and especially concerning The Church's present adamant stand on the subject of no sex before marriage, and regarding the unapproved use of Birth Control. To state that "The Old Ways" of The Religion, as it was practiced in the years gone by, needs now to be dissolved and a New Order of Rational and Carefully Reasoned Forth Policy Instated.

"Large Catholic Families" being promoted by The Church doctrine, are a thing of the past and not practical to have; both from the stand of Family Planning being unaffordable in the bleak economic outlook of the times where both parents in a great many situations of a marriage are forced to work to make ends meet, and from the other standpoint that every child who his born needs to be financially and emotionally cared for and sustained and nurtured in a practical way in getting a good education of being put financially through their schooling in order to grow into healthy and socially productive adults; to what that the lack individual parental attention in focus and the poverty of funds, precipitated by having enormously huge families, would preclude.

And also that the world is suffering from an Overpopulation Problem as it is, and that the mass of human beings being born irresponsibly in this setting only serves to make the ills of society worse, of hunger and malnutrition, homelessness, crime, drug and alcohol abuse, mental illness, and to promote wars as the hopeless and pathetic overpopulated societies burgeon to expand upon their over burgeoning neighbors in the desperation of mass general suicide, as all wars are conceived.

And for the other practicality of the need for contraception and especially that since we live in the pagan society of our current time and going back along ways, and perhaps forever dating to The Fall of Man From Grace, into the distant past about it, currently in vogue and gathering in tremendous strength of peer pressure in the modern time, that anyone can count themselves fortunate not to be influenced by, that has profaned, debased, heaped dirt on, and cheapened our human sexuality of its holy intent, to the point where it has lost all of its sanctity of holy meaning, and to the point where life itself has lost its meaning in nihilistic futility for many people of today's era, in eclipsing the spiritual intent of sexual intercourse for the purpose of creating new life in the sense, to the idea of fornication and depravity as sexual pastime, and to the cheapening, in casting of derision, sneering scorn, and ridicule upon the sacred function of procreation, and that is made worse by the influence of our society at large in its mainstream promotion of prostitution and pornography, and to the pervasive acceptance of deviant sexual behavior, homosexuality and lesbianism as the norm. And to what that this societal entrenched sexual inversion, in the meaning

of lewd behavior, snide sexual jokes, and to the use of profanity
in the vernacular of the language, which have been instated in our
modern version of society to be common place, to imagine how it
all ever got started out to be so debased in the outright anathema
of depicting and discussing the holy and the sublime intent of our
procreation in such a way, to be influencing our entire society
about, and particularly our young people who are most
impressionable to it, that has deadened our whole society, by the
prurient manifesting perversions of the idolatrous pagan atheists
who have taken over this society to have made the horrid mockery
of the sexual function that it has become, out to be the norm of the
common mass of the society and who promote it in that vein
extensively in their public conduct and by their depictions of bad
sexual expressions in control of the public media; that we have to
be subjected to and inundated with at every turn of our daily live
about and on all sides.

Which is a subject that we have to deal with, for us as a
Church, and politically involved with the structure and to the
refined managing of our government, and to the shaping of The
Foundation of our Nation Under God, to do something about, as it
behooves us to. And in what vein to be understood, that a Church
Without Substance, that is to say in the regard to The Social
Demonstration of our Faith, as a Holy Condition in Public
Demeanor, Needs Our Stern Public Profession, and with going
beyond the idea of prayer and worship as a condition to it, The
Meaning and to The Practice of Our Faith, to the outright public
display of It, and by means of forceful pressure, en masse as a
public congregation together, if need be, to resolve this unhealthy
and importantly unholy economic and sexually errant condition
currently from continuing on to exist in the context of our society.
And to what that the idea of contraception, in the prevailing
general and practical sense of the meaning in necessity, is needed
to combat. For no child born into unholy circumstance of
fornication and to strained relations in estrangement from its
parents is ever going to be nurtured properly into adulthood. All
children need the love and caring support of both caring parents to
mature properly.

And which is all a misdirection, on the part of the present demeanor of The Church in Its negative approach to the use of contraception in the modern hour, that is incumbent upon us to resolve, and as not to be casting the normally occurring and emotionally healthy act of responsible sexual intercourse between two loving partners in an unhealthy and unsavory light; that is ideally intended for the deliberate purpose of creating a new life; but which also needs to be understood as serving as a unifying emotional interrelation between a man and woman, and needed to be engaged in, in a healthy way, throughout their lifetimes, in a shared spiritual bond uniting them as one flesh in The Eyes of God.

Everyone, and even the celibate holy priesthood, and through the nature of our holy mothers, came from the act of sexual intercourse as we all have. And all the children of the parishioners whom The Priests marry, and bless, and who we see about us at the masses in the arms of their mothers and sitting quietly beside their parents, came from the act of holy and pure sexual relations; that is what it is, emotionally involved between a man and a woman in The Name of God and connected to the biological urge to procreate and to the physical sensations of the act of intercourse; which The Father and The Holy Spirit (The Female Representation of The Creator,) Together, fashioned to be the way it is, in their own image of mankind, male and female, in their mutual and intertwined sexual relationship to one another.

And certainly to say that it was They, The Heavenly Father and The Holy Spirit, Together, Who made our human sexuality in a pleasurable way, (if you want to call it that, the sensation of mutual orgasm,) to the purpose of impelling us as human beings, the embodiment of themselves, by the driven force of a biological necessity, forward into the new generations Of Themselves, of Life and Death, and to the sufferings of hardship and travails we face upon the earth in the course of our common destiny here; that only concerns itself with the compelling of a common humanity on into the future; that is to be understood as to be generated by reserved and fundamentally sound sexual impulse in desire onward through the course of time, in which to live the destiny of

Their Individual Selves out with us in Their Human Forms; and that is stated for in The Biblical wording, as "replacing the old garments of the soul with new garments," in the cycles of birth and death, that are all only Themselves, Male and Female, of The Creator's Self-Image To Be and To Exist, and to the struggles of life to entertain Themselves By in between. That perhaps would not be so readily contemplated and engaged in, the act of intercourse, and to the bringing of new life into the world of sorrows and suffering, and hardship and travail, and for the good times too as well, if it were not for the biological urges and impulses of sexuality, as an inescapable power of intimacy between a man and a woman compelling it forward, the life that we each are born into, in their attraction for one another, to propagate the species by, and for what also serves in meaningful way, the idea of sexual attraction, as something to live for.

As to why then would anyone want to do it, to and to whatever motives of The Creator Self that is was made in the way it was, by The Two Selves of The Creator, The Heavenly Father and The Holy Spirit, Male and Female, that was Made Holy in Their Sight. And truly then to say, that it must truly then be holy in ours also. They Are The Two Gods Who Created Us, involving us here of mortal earth, Who we worship and adore, and Who we are involved with as Living Gods, One God United in The Father, and Who are involved with us in The Nature of Eternal Life, as God The Father and God The Holy Spirit, and to Their Nature of us as Human Beings as we live out the drama of mortal existence as Immortal Beings of The Creator's Mind, Who Created Sexuality.

And with this arrangement in understanding then that we may arm ourselves emotionally and intellectually and in a holy way to the nature of the prevailing pagan sexuality that surrounds us, in regard to the wanton pastimes of sexual urges in general, but in particular to the effect that such random and indiscriminate sex plays upon the women, who in No Way are to be conceived in the terms of being thought of in the nature of fornication with any of them, or to the sizing up and flirtations with any of them for that motive; and so as well to the entertaining and engaging of such thoughts in our minds, in the attitude of having casual and unholy indiscriminate sex with them without the proper responsible circumstances of a close loving relationship and enduring matrimony to coincide. That each of the males, from puberty through manhood, are presently being pressure to do in the pagan times of our days; and who now need to be made maturely and keenly aware of the reality of their sexual nature for what it is, to be well thought out and planned for, that sexuality is all to do with a purpose to life; which is to the creation of The New Life of a Child upon The Earth, and not for sport of pastime. And for what also that the females of the society, young and old alike, need also to be instructed in this way of dressing appropriately in their not attempting to seduce the misdirected sexual interests of the males in overall responsibility for the condition of engendering the unhealthy sexual climate about us, and to its end.

For, (and although that it may be contemplated,) that there is no way that a man can possibly know to appreciate what it is like to be a woman in the terms of her having to endure the burden of a pregnancy; that is the result of her sexual seductions to intercourse, (and although that the men can have vicarious empathy for it,) that not only involves her in the arduous and long term physical and psychological travail of the pregnancy to suffer, but which is also potentially life threatening and most excruciatingly painful to endure at the time of her labor giving birth with the baby, which is very big, having to come out of her.

And beyond that, which amounts to a huge expense in burden to endure as well, and not just to the terms of the expense of having the baby, but also to the baby's upkeep; and in the terms of nursing, of the time needed to be spent with the baby away from her work requiring dependent financial support to see her through with; and so on, on and on, of such time and expense until the child is fully grown and capable of caring for itself; that a woman has to face in the prospect of becoming pregnant.

To what private matter between God and a woman that there is "No Way" that the orientation of sexuality can be taken lightly to be discussed in the way of fornication to stand holy with in the sight of our Creator about, and to its reckoning that way, which needs to be the object of sexual awareness education from early childhood on, and reinforced by the peer pressure adaptation of our social framework to be conditioned to the proper format of The Nation's Sexual Orientation on the part of the society at large, to come to the proper conduct of the arrangement of terms about, the terms being, To Be Decent and Proper.

And so, let us begin to end here, in our discussion of what it is that entreats us to be happy with our existence upon The Earth, and of what it is and what it means, To Be Perfect as Human Beings to stand proudly of about in our own eyes, as Our Father in Heaven, Who Is Perfect, would be proud of; and with that understanding; that Fornicating With Yourself, in the way of Masturbation, and that Having Indiscriminate Sex With Partners, Is Not The Way To Be Happy and Fulfilled, and thereof Not To Be Engaged In; (As A Discipline,) and that needs to be taught and instilled in the young children, and especially and most importantly beginning well before The Age Of Puberty, to be brought up right about, (through the nature of proper training and parental and peer example being established,) and to be continued on with in the proper restraint of the sexual nature in the required discipline throughout one's life; and which does require discipline at every turn.

And the reason that the word "Discipline" is needed is that "Discipline" is the word that is required to everything of what we do in life, that we must undertake as a discipline to be successful with life about. The endurance of Life Itself is all to do with discipline, and to what concept of self-discipline that makes life enjoyable.

And which involves, the term, "Discipline," with much more than the sexual orientations as we began this discussion with; to include such refraining from any bad habits such as drugs and alcohol, which only serve to torment us, and to getting the proper amount of sleep, not to much, not to little, and as to the maintaining of proper diet, and concerning our eating habits exercising restraints, to eat the right foods, and not to over eat, and to the discipline of maintaining the proper amounts of physical exercising for the proper care of our bodies, and for cleanliness of personal hygiene, and to performance of domestic chores in upkeep to our living situations to keep our homes about us healthy in the mind and body, and to be involved with a hobby, or a sport, and to a routine of study as a discipline, and to the performance of our daily work most importantly for the upkeep of personal finances to sustain our days in a healthy frame of mind, and to the discipline of being kind and charitable to others, and to maintaining good relations with others, and to setting of good example, and to the doing of good deeds, and to what all else that we require good discipline for to be successful in our spirit and to the ways of life about. That is, in a word, to be respected and for what is, the term Discipline. Let us thereby take to it as a way of life, and to make it The Foundation of our Being and of our Church unto God The Father.

Discipline is The Central Part in the essence of Our Religion, which requires us in the estimation of our own self-judgment concerning ourselves and unto God, To Exercise Self-Control At All Times, foremost in the estimation To Be Chaste and Holy, essentially in our own eyes,) and to be Diligent, with proper regard for our responsibilities to our bodies to maintain them properly, and in our labor to survive, and Trustworthy and Kind for the sake of others, and for our own sake as to how we feel about ourselves in the judgment of our own eyes, and as we require the presence in nature of The Creator to be a part of each of us also, and in friendship with God, to be happy with our ways, that includes the wording, "In The Eyes Of God," as well.

Discipline is the source and the summit of all that is holy in the sight of God.

And so as you may find yourselves to be in various states of disrepair in that regard, in disharmony with yourself and with The Father, let us begin with The Reformation of ourselves, and of our many selves collectively as a Church in Religion, and as a society together expressing the same intent; with the intent Not To Engage in The Thought of Masturbation, (and which includes the lingering, for the males, in the thought of Nocturnal Emissions, as to what is The Biological Malfunction to encounter that we speak of, for the sexual nature is a compulsion of its own that must be maturely reasoned for, if not to be outright conquered in that vein of intelligence concerning its function, that at best can be concurred to be irrational in design and generated by impulse in the chemical attraction of the sexes for one another, that must be cleanly reasoned for; and as for the females in that way also, not to encourage the idea of fornication with the males in their temptation of dress and behavior.)

And with the understanding in reasoning that the needed Control of The Sexual Function, (and what is similar in concept as with the control of our appetites of food consumption that way also,) that begins In The Thoughts Of The Mind To Control.

The Old Ways of Religion need to pass solemnly behind us and to the instilment of a Modern Church Ideology, as The Faith is to be lived, based to the enactment of the foundation of good intentions in the present. This will have meaning for us, and not so much any longer to be absorbed with the readings of The Ancient Scripture. And not that Scripture is a bad thing in a scholarly way to understand and by the uplifting thoughts it inspires, or not, but we need to be more oriented to The Living God, and to The Living Church in The Living Present, and as we abide to Our Creator Who Dreams Us in this current hour, and to the idea of God Among Us, to what that proper sexuality is the primary foundation, as is self-evident, in condition.

In the plan of living a longer, more productive, and happier life, and to the idea of freeing ourselves from self-destructive forces that plague The Mind in modern times, Meditation is a necessary key strategy of living in The Stilling Of The Mind to practice at each opportunity in daily exercise within ourselves in order to Quite The Mind and relieve ourselves of the tensions, anxieties, and temptations to sin as we find ourselves prone to being set upon by, being human and involved with a chaotic world and the forces of good and evil that we find upon us.

And it is important to the concept of this principle of The Quite Mind in Tranquil Repose of Meditation you are seeking to realize that the continuing free flow of thoughts upon us is always going to occur, and which takes a conscious labor of The Personal Will in Mind Control to overcome. In fact, in the present setting, The Reflections of The Inner Mind is to be conceived of as War

Zone of confrontations with such forces, that are bigger than us and bigger than our inner resources to contend with, of the evil influences about us which constantly infiltrated into our conscious thought from the outer world, that must be combated with the active counter-force of mental determination of concentration for us to rid ourselves of such destructive thoughts and influences as they manifest.

The Mind Itself, as involves The Spirit World also in visitations, is vastly bigger than our own thought receptacles of personal egos to fathom; and The Mind as we find it, abhors a vacuum, and is always being flooded over with thoughts and ideas from the external sources of The World, and from the thoughts of Spirits, that it correspondingly takes up with and responds to on its own, if not held in check by our own mental determinations; and to what that we often find ourselves in the distractions of, involved in The Mind's own internal nature of entertaining itself, that involves us with Internal Dialogues, Fantasies, Imaginings, Memories, and Ruminations, and to what your conscious volition is needed to be intimately involved with at every turn of events that way, On Guard To It, and required to control to the choices of what you have to make in your desires of what you wish to think about; which you are perfectly able to and can make conscious choices over what you want to think about.

Some thoughts are in the nature of being helpful and useful, but even these useful thoughts need not be overly dwelt upon. No thought is really good in being sustained too long in that thoughts as they occur distract you from your main objective of focus in attention to The Outer Reality, which you miss out on by becoming indwelling to the thoughts, and which you need to be in tune with to control the flow of thoughts about at all times In Self Mastery.

Bad Thoughts, the thoughts of Sexually Disquieted Spirits or of Evil Demons, or with personal Preoccupations of Anxiety that persist within you in a forceful nature, are never good. In the idea of Meditating, you need to pass all thoughts along through your mind as they present themselves to you, and allow them each, one by one in the order of their presentations, Without Judgment; to flow through you, and in the stating, not to be getting involved with any moral ruminations of yourself being good or bad over your thoughts, as to a thought being good or bad, as the ruminations of guilt are thought distractions in themselves that you need to free yourself from and as well to be passed-on out of your mind. Let each thought flow though you, and focus on your breathing, for ten breaths at a time. The Mind can only think of one thing at a time and your breathing will set you free, Ten Breaths At A Time.

Conscious Breathing is the only way out of "The Mind Trap" as we find ourselves to be in the predicament of. Focus on the Air around You, The Big Atmosphere of Air that surrounds The Earth, as you breathe it in and exhale it. Sense its presence and feel it, and Let it fill you up and fill your mind. Think of The Air and The Oxygen it contains as it flows into your lungs and exchanges there with your blood and releases its carbon dioxide back out of you, and let it become a desire in itself and of its interaction with you to constantly reflect on.

And not just to the act of breathing, but to the substance of The Air itself that you need to focus on, to be thought of in the way of being immersed submerged in an ocean of air that embraces the entire Earth, and which sustains your life and each life of the planet that breathes air to live; and to perceive the air at a great distance from you, and as well as in close proximity, as you breath it in and exhale it. The air is a Quite Mind Entity to dwell upon and makes no demands of thought upon you. Cherish its tranquil nature and nurture the thought of it in your days.

And let us ever keep on to the understanding that The Intention of Our Faith is To Be Perfect in our Way of Life and how that it is that we should be conducting ourselves, individually, and as a Church, and as Society unto Government, formed into a solid unity in relationship and with responsibility to the managing of our Affairs of State, and especially to the proper and moral functioning in fairness to all of our Economy and National Morality, to ensure the proper conduct of a Holy Government unto The People.

Our Faith is all about discipline, of sexual chastity, good works, charity, forgiveness, and piety, (in the meaning of reverent humility,) with a humble heart in the maturity of an awakened destiny for the betterment of all mankind, and to the accords of peaceful arrangement upon The Earth as is our duty to fulfill.

The idea of perfection is our key to The Mastery of Life and over The Evil Temptations of Satan, who is the demon within The Creator which plagues The Dream of God, and within us all, in plague to us individually, as we are made in The Creator's Image, in our choices for Good or for Evil that we have to decide upon at every turn in events, and they are just that, Choices, to be made in our every moment of every day of our lives, to side with The Correct Approach about; and as we, who are molded and patterned after The Creator-Self, in The Image and Likeness of God, need in maturity to fulfill in the terms of our self-fulfilling destiny. Self-Mastery, with us, as it is with The Creator in Heaven, Who faces the same choices for good and evil in the eternal time of His Existence, is the key to The Faith we profess to, and to The Commandment and The Promise of Jesus, Who said to us in The Lord's Prayer, of:

Matthew 5:48: "Therefore Be Perfect, as your Father In Heaven Is Perfect."

And Who said also that: "Where Two or More are gathered in My Name, there I Am also, and all power in Heaven and on Earth will be provided to you, and lo I AM with you always to the end of time."

And by what promise that everyone, and ministers of The Great Faith all, will lead the entire society and the entire world of God's Creation out of the darkness and into The Light.

When?! The time is at hand as you realize it and decide to act on your instincts. The Time Is Now.

There is only One God, The Creator of Heaven and Earth, and of All Things Seen and Unseen In Divinity, One World United, expressing for all the people upon the entire Earth. And for all of us to realize, that In The Vast And Total Universe That Includes Us All, To What We Each And All Are A Part Of, And Belong To; and Of What Belonging, To Each Of Us As Well To Care

For, There Exists The Miracle Of A World, And The Miracle Of
The Life We Know To Exist. To Know That We Do Exist! Let
us eternally care for it.

We need to see God in the every day of our lives concerning
the despairing attitude that our human affairs in government and
business dealings have adopted towards our humanity. The
population in its charge, to date; is being ignored of its basic
wants and needs, and as concerns us as well who have the power
of thought and intelligence and the perseverance of a personal
determination in ambition to make things socially better here for
The Entire Public Society, for ourselves individually and well as
for the collective organization of people we name society.

And for the lack of anyone else to assume responsibility, for us
to assume The Command over the situation ourselves, who need
to have a better managed and holy system of government
arranged for us and to our behalf of settling up to the accounts of
sustaining our needs in this life, in having to deal, and to contend
for in the fact of struggle, to survive in the day to day reasoning of
it, for the fact of the life and death matters of Social Justice to
express for, and for the sense of a proper Morality To Be
Maintained, and for Correct-Minded Economy to prevail, that is
currently in the dire straights for a great portion of the public's
mainstream to endure, and to the enhancement of the social order
of society as best we can in other matters of refined
embellishment as we see fit.

And as our government, and under The Holy Guidance of
Good Faith Religion, needs to be doing all along for us, in formal
respect of recognition to us, mutually in kind, that we need to take
the initiative personally ourselves about, and through the holy
vows of self-discipline, to bring swiftly and surely into place.

Which we can accomplish this together if we have a mind to
do it, and to stop with the guileful pretentiousness in game
playing of "Status Quo Management," of our government unto us,
involving the conflict in predominant error of domination and
profiteering over others, as things are presently conceived to be
arranged by that mentality to our current structure of society in
that way; and to the idea "of beautifying the entire nature of

society," and for it not to be allowed to decay into a disease ridden, drug plagued, uneducated and impoverished, depraved and immoral, corrupt and lawless, pathetic people, in the condition as we find it, (figuratively spoken for, as it is with that way of many of The Third World Nations today that we are currently playing host to "the overrun of" by them here in The United States of America as refugees from;) in name to all the things that are obviously "wrong" with The World, and that could fast go wrong here in succumbing to The Nation's current godless trend of sexual promiscuity, deviancy, violence, drugs, and the greed of economic corruption and subjugation of others, under the raised banner of atheism, (and as to the idea of the perpetuation of The Rich and The Poor Status Quo Dichotomy;) that we need to fix about it, our society, as we are witness to, as a Holy Church Together, as a Project In Ambition, and as we have the power to correct, in mutual effort together, for The General Well-Being and for The Great Good of The Whole of The Earth, in God's Holy Name.

And of what society that we all ultimately share in and are a part of, as society is a part of each of us, to reflect upon, that ultimately "Affects Us All" for better or for worse, like the quality of our air and water, (in that vein of looking at it, which can't be tolerated to be left in a bad state,) which includes for the stated Moral and Economic Condition of The Nation as well, that includes all the people, ourselves, Who Need To Be Well Regarded and Well Cared For, and particular where it concerns our young people who need the continuous guidance and the proper support and the vision of intelligent nurturing throughout their lives in the social sense of caring in the not allowing the perpetuation of negative influences to invade their impressionable minds.

The salvation of humanity lies with the proper training and bringing to fruition of our generation's children as holy beings of God. It only takes the vision of self-discipline within ourselves, and to the achievement of excellence, and with the desire for leadership from each of us to accomplish this goal, if you, each and all, would provide that leadership for us as a Holy Mandate.

We need not go on with the way things are and it is definitely
in our best interest not to. Please then do as I say and as your own
internal logic and instinct determines for the best, and go about
your days as if The World depended upon you personally To Save
It from extinction of The Faith In God.

April 30, 2010

Dear Tony:

I am anxiously awaiting the announcement of the publication
of your latest novel, The American Golfer. Everything is set here
in this end to market the book locally. I also just received this
email in from Lulu, my Print-On-Demand Company about the
2010 Book Expo, which is as follows and thought perhaps it
might be an opportunity for you to showcase you book and sign
autographed copies of to take advantage of.
2010 BookExpo America New Title Showcase New York,
NY-May 25-May 27, 2010 BookExpo America is the largest
domestic gathering of the publishing industry. The sixth annual
New Title Showcase will remain the prime venue for marketing
your titles to a national audience of about 35,000, including
media, publishers, agents, distributors, booksellers, librarians and
more, in the best location at the show: Right at the font entrance!
Lulu is proud to be a part of the 2010 BookExpo America New
Title Showcase! Registration & Display Copy Deadline: Friday,
May 7, 2010.
I wish I had your skill and genius with the way of the novel;
but I am, at this late stage of the game, developing a fervent desire
to write at least one great novel in my lifetime and I am thinking
all the time about it, and about you as well, as is my goal in
achievement to emulate. Many thanks to you for the inspiration
and professional advise from time to time, and for your
encouragement of fond friendship to continue on with my work.
I am nearly finished with your father book, The Great Snow,
which is a great drama of the internal man, and truly great in its
way, but which I feel lacks the cogency of plausibility in many of

The Author Gary Koniz and His Wife Kathleen
Behind Every Good Man There Is A Loving Woman

its settings, (like the housekeeper Mrs. Rollefson's son Gunnar who is in the air force and who takers a jet plane without permission in on skies and in the blinding snow of the storm on instruments when all other planes are grounded, to land at a closed nearby military airstrip and to make his way there to Ruston Cobb's house through five feet of snow when all the roads are impassable and no on else can travel, to suddenly arrive at Ruston's doorstep to be with his family,) and for several other egregious incidences like that, which makes the work too overly implausible to be a truly successful story, in the gut feeling about any work, to respect for the fact that is has to be believable and for it to be truly felt for in a genuine sense as an enduring great story of genuine intrigue.

And although that your father says it in not to be taken so literally, but rather to be thought of epically in the spirit of what the work is intending to present, in the aura of the great classics as they are presented to tell an incredible story, (engaging the willing suspension of disbelief,) to the reader into which the serious parts of life's matters can be interjected of the grit in substance in the grips of the real drama of good and evil and engaging the great passions of humanity to inspire ponderous thought and deep moral reflection; which in all about that aspect of the book is quite profound, and genius.

Your father was a great thinker, and I enjoy reading him. I am also so sorry to learn, which I learned from reading his biography, of how he died in 1961, at the age of 62, having "fallen asleep" from the effects of a sedative in a scolding hot tub of bathwater and from the complications suffered of second and third degree burns. You were perhaps 27 at the time, (I can never seem to find a date for your birthday anywhere,) and I can sympathize with you for the tragedy of your loss. Your father's life seems to have paralleled that of Earnest Hemmingway, who died in the same year but who was born one year after your father in 1899, and I wonder if they remotely knew one another. And again to say, that I am truly sorry, Tony, for the tragedy in your life to empathize with. Bless your heart.

Gary

the book

From: **Anthony Robinson** (robinsoa@newpaltz.edu)
Sent: Fri 4/30/10 10:33 AM
To: Gary Koniz (gary.koniz@hotmail.com)

Gary, here's an update on The American Golfer. First, thanks for your sincere interest. I lost a whole month when I turned back the first "final proof" of the book four weeks ago. Now we're looking at a pub date in the middle of May. I am getting "sell sheets" printed up, and I'll send you a few to drop off at your pro shop or elsewhere (bookstores or other pro shops) if you see them as potential markets. Here's the important thing. Your pro can order the book through w.w.w.CreateSpace.com/900001877 (that's four zeroes). It's a direct link to the book. Amazon.com will also work, but with CreateSpace your pro can use a code, which I'll supply, that will enable him to buy the book for 30% off. He can then sell it at its retail price of $14.95 or whatever he wants to charge. Note: neither link, Amazon or CreateSpace, will trigger until the novel actually comes out. I'll send you an actual copy of the novel just as soon as I get one in my hands. (Note: The American Golfer seems a natural for a father's day gift.) When you get the sell sheets you will be able to talk to people and leave them a sheet, but don't forget--the links won't trigger until the book is available. Listen to this. The book is self-published, true; but you'll see on the sell sheet the name of the publisher is Bluestone Books (also on the book itself). It's a small, very select house in upstate New York if people enquire. Thanks, Gary. Tony.

April 30, 2010

Thanks, Tony, I tried the web site but it's not available at this time. How is it that you lost a month? Gary

From: robinsoa@newpaltz.edu
To: gary.koniz@hotmail.com
Subject: Re: the book
Date: Fri, 30 Apr 2010 15:52:53 -0400
Gary, I lost a month because when I rejected the first copy of the novel for design reasons, I had to start over with the whole process of bringing it along. As I believe I mentioned, the book won't be available on the web until it's actually published, i.e. a physical entity, sometime in mid May. I'm sending you a couple of "sell sheets" tomorrow by regular mail.

Best, Tony

April 30, 2010

Dear Tony:

Good, Tony. Thanks for writing. I'll be anxiously looking forward to the arrival or the "sell sheets." I'm so excited for you and can't wait to read your latest.

Gary

perils of publishing

From: **Anthony Robinson** (robinsoa@newpaltz.edu)
Sent: Mon 5/17/10 5:58 PM
To: Gary Koniz (gary.koniz@hotmail.com)

Gary, have you given up on me and my book? There was another
frustrating delay, but The American Golfer *will* appear. I agree
with what you said about The Great Snow. It was called his best
novel at the time. The last "sell sheets" I sent you were not too
crisp looking. Sorry about that. I'll send fresh unfolded ones and
anything else you might need. Just let me know. The book will
now come out likely in early June. How are you? Tony

Mon 5/17/10 7:18 PM

Tony,

I would never "give up" on you, nor your book, Tony. I am with
to the end in support of your thoughts and feelings and with a
fond friendship that only writers in their great kindred spirit for
one another can share together in bond. You have never given up
on me either, have you, and have always been there for me
whenever I needed bolstering.

   Sorry there is yet another delay in getting it into print, (what's
the problem this time,) but a little foreplay in the process in the
climax of a great work is good for the spirit, is it not? I checked
with B&N, and also with Books-A-Million, and both chains told
me the same thing, that the process of getting a book "stocked" is
to submit a copy of the book to their Acquisitions Department for
approval, and then once approved to have a Wholesaler supply the
books to them for distribution. They do not like to, and never do,
order self-published books over the Internet. They have an
agreement with the wholesaler to buy back all unsold copies of
the book after a certain time. So, how much money to you have
to invest in yourself, as a publisher would, to make the book a
success?

   There will always typing errors and editing of different sorts in
our lives. I am always horrified though in subsequent readings to
discover them aghast. Oh NO! I say.

   I have been fine, Tony. How are you? I just published a new
Hard Cover edition of The Call To Order and have sent the first

copy out to General Hagenbeck, The Superintendent of West Point Military Academy, and I just got a great copy in mint condition for only $8.00 including shipping from Abe Books, of your father's signature work, The Cardinal, and have started reading it. It starts out on an Ocean Crossing aboard a cruise ship named Vesuvio, in mine infested waters in 1915.

And I see that your father's conversation is a little more natural and realistic in, The Cardinal, than it was in the other work of his that I read called, The Great Snow, in which he places people in unnatural conversational situations to discuss and reveal his philosophy and with attempts at character development to probe unnaturally into people's pasts. Which, in all makes things seem rather implausible.

Thanks for writing me. I was telling Kathy just yesterday that you and I will never be real friends as friendship goes, in the meaning that you will always be my teacher, and I will always be the student, no matter what happens in the meantime. But I still feel a really deep friendship with you, as literary intellectuals together and as fellow students of the reality we live in to endure the length of eternity by, that knows no age limits as to the ability to learn something, and we are learning something each day, here and there, a piece at a time, from unlikely people and from intuition, like being friends with The Creator, in the sense of always being there to confine in and to trust with your heart … in the words of a poem by D.H. Lawrence … "Oh Build Your Ship Of Death … Oh Build It."

Your father was a great classical scholar wasn't he? And, as the classics go, maybe the plot line isn't the most important thing to consider, that being, the most important thing, the play of the passions.

Gary

Timeless Immortal

Author: Henry Morton Robinson

The Cardinal

Author: Henry Morton Robinson
Genre: Religious
Publisher: Simon & Schuster
Released: June 1949

The Mindset of Times Long Gone
A Review by Laurie Edwards
03/28/2002

Henry Morton Robinson wrote a book that's completely a reflection of his times. *The Cardinal*, published in 1949, reminds us what the life of a priest was supposed to be. Unlike *The Cardinal Sins*, Fr. Andrew Greeley's barely-concealed attack on Cardinal Cooke, this book is all about the good side of the religious life (as it was in the first half of the last century).

That's not to say everything is peaches and cream here. The harshness that was Catholic teaching cost many people love and some their lives. When the title character's sister gets pregnant by a cad, she's no longer welcome in her family. When it becomes clear only a therapeutic abortion will save her life, the Cardinal urges her to make her peace with God, whom she has so sorely offended. She does, and she dies.

Poverty, chastity, and obedience are stressed over and over again. The point is made several times that Stephen Fermoyle could be making a mint as a writer, but he's choosing out of love for his God a life where he'll never have much. Though he'd really rather be a writer, Fermoyle is chosen early in his seminary training for the bureaucratic hierarchy. In obedience, he goes along with what he's told, quickly rising through the ranks to become first a monsignor, then a bishop, and finally a Cardinal. [Note: Considering the time period, it's no surprise Robinson doesn't have Fermoyle elected Pope; the Papacy was a strictly Italian operation in those days.] There's no question whatsoever that Fermoyle is chaste; if he has any lustful thoughts, they're not mentioned here.

The story moves smoothly from Fermoyle's ordination to his elevation to the Cardinalate, filled with the (idealized) day-to-day life of a deeply pious man. His work in the Vatican and home in the States, his small clashes with other priests, and the problems of his birth family are all examined, always within the framework of his immense faith.

This isn't reality. Not even back in the early 1900s was this rosy picture of religious life a true one. This is what was believed, though, and within that context, this is a fine novel of the workings of one man's mind.

The plot here is everything. It's as straight-and-narrow as the good Cardinal himself, allowing no deviation from its point. Dialogue is sometimes stilted, as befits the then-popular view of how religious thought and spoke, but it's sufficient to drive the characters along their plot-appointed journey. Narrative is nearly absent; only a few vague descriptions of the characters are offered; you've got to use your imagination big time with this one. The characters themselves are, again, what was acceptable in popular novels back then. Only Fermoyle is drawn with any dimension; the rest are only foils for his thoughts, words, and deeds. A couple (his unfortunate sister and the Reverend Mother who heads a local Catholic school) are heavy-duty morality tales, but other than that, no one seems real but the title character.

This is all pretty nay saying, isn't it? Reviewed, *The Cardinal* seems like a book to avoid at all costs. Not a chance! Somehow, this novel, filled with old and tired clichés, is a work of beauty, as are all works of dedication and love. Robinson so clearly believes in the sanctity of the religious life and the honor of his title character, he makes *The Cardinal* a wonderful story of devotion and strength in the face of an almost overwhelming responsibility to God and man. I absolutely loved it all, and I cried my eyes out.

With its yellowed pages and outdated theology and writing style, it may not be cool or even useful, but *The Cardinal* is a book to cherish. If you have any sentiment in your soul—especially if you're Catholic—this is something wonderful.

Synopsis:

Tom Tryon plays the title role in this Otto Preminger version of the Henry Morton Robinson novel. In his matriculation from Monsignor to the College of Cardinals, Stephen Fermoyle (Tom Tryon) must undergo several grueling life experiences: standing up to bigots in Georgia, defying Nazis in Austria, and so on. The film boasts cameo appearances by Dorothy Gish, Cecil Kellaway, John Saxon, John Huston, Robert Morse, Burgess Meredith, Raf Vallone, Ossie Davis. Incidentally, Tryon eventually quit acting and became a popular novelist.

The Ship Of Death – D. H. Lawrence

David Herbert Richards *Lawrence*
(11 September 1885 – 2 March 1930)
was an English novelist, poet, playwright,
essayist and literary critic. ...

Now it is autumn and the falling fruit
and the long journey towards oblivion.

The apples falling like great drops of dew
to bruise themselves an exit from themselves.

And it is time to go, to bid farewell
to one's own self, and find an exit
from the fallen self.

II

Have you built your ship of death, O have you?
O build your ship of death, for you will need it.

The grim frost is at hand, when the apples will fall
thick, almost thundrous, on the hardened earth.

And death is on the air like a smell of ashes!
Ah! can't you smell it?
And in the bruised body, the frightened soul
finds itself shrinking, wincing from the cold
that blows upon it through the orifices.

III

And can a man his own quietus make
with a bare bodkin?

With daggers, bodkins, bullets, man can make
a bruise or break of exit for his life;
but is that a quietus, O tell me, is it quietus?

Surely not so! for how could murder, even self-murder
ever a quietus make?

IV

O let us talk of quiet that we know,
that we can know, the deep and lovely quiet
of a strong heart at peace!

How can we this, our own quietus, make?

V

Build then the ship of death, for you must take
the longest journey, to oblivion.

And die the death, the long and painful death
that lies between the old self and the new.

Already our bodies are fallen, bruised, badly bruised,
already our souls are oozing through the exit
of the cruel bruise.

Already the dark and endless ocean of the end
is washing in through the breaches of our wounds,
Already the flood is upon us.

Oh build your ship of death, your little ark
and furnish it with food, with little cakes, and wine
for the dark flight down oblivion.

VI

Piecemeal the body dies, and the timid soul
has her footing washed away, as the dark flood rises.

We are dying, we are dying, we are all of us dying
and nothing will stay the death-flood rising within us
and soon it will rise on the world, on the outside world.

We are dying, we are dying, piecemeal our bodies are dying
and our strength leaves us,
and our soul cowers naked in the dark rain over the flood,
cowering in the last branches of the tree of our life.

VII

We are dying, we are dying, so all we can do
is now to be willing to die, and to build the ship
of death to carry the soul on the longest journey.

A little ship, with oars and food
and little dishes, and all accoutrements
fitting and ready for the departing soul.

Now launch the small ship, now as the body dies
and life departs, launch out, the fragile soul
in the fragile ship of courage, the ark of faith
with its store of food and little cooking pans
and change of clothes,
upon the flood's black waste
upon the waters of the end
upon the sea of death, where still we sail
darkly, for we cannot steer, and have no port.

There is no port, there is nowhere to go
only the deepening blackness darkening still
blacker upon the soundless, ungurgling flood
darkness at one with darkness, up and down
and sideways utterly dark, so there is no direction any more

and the little ship is there; yet she is gone.
She is not seen, for there is nothing to see her by.
She is gone! gone! and yet
somewhere she is there.
Nowhere!

VIII

And everything is gone, the body is gone
completely under, gone, entirely gone.
The upper darkness is heavy as the lower,
between them the little ship
is gone

It is the end, it is oblivion.

IX

And yet out of eternity a thread
separates itself on the blackness,
a horizontal thread
that fumes a little with pallor upon the dark.

Is it illusion? or does the pallor fume
A little higher?
Ah wait, wait, for there's the dawn
the cruel dawn of coming back to life
out of oblivion

Wait, wait, the little ship
drifting, beneath the deathly ashy grey
of a flood-dawn.

Wait, wait! even so, a flush of yellow
and strangely, O chilled wan soul, a flush of rose.

A flush of rose, and the whole thing starts again.

X

The flood subsides, and the body, like a worn sea-shell
emerges strange and lovely.
And the little ship wings home, faltering and lapsing
on the pink flood,
and the frail soul steps out, into the house again
filling the heart with peace.

Swings the heart renewed with peace
even of oblivion.

Oh build your ship of death. Oh build it!
for you will need it.
For the voyage of oblivion awaits you.

The Book

From: **Anthony Robinson** (robinsoa@newpaltz.edu)
Sent: Fri 6/11/10 6:06 AM
To: Gary Koniz (gary.koniz@hotmail.com)

Gary, it's here! Take a look at
www.createspace.com/900001877. (Note the four zeroes if you're
not using the link.) My copies haven't come in yet but a signed
one will be coming your way. Tell your pro. I can give him a
discount if he wants to order copies. The book itself has no price
on it so he can charge what he wants. Let me know.
(Amazon.com will be up with the title in aprox. 10 days.)
Thanks, Gary.

Tony

Sat 6/12/10 12:00 AM

Dear Tony,

Ah … the long awaited has arrived. I've been savoring its climax. I tried just the other day to see if it was available yet and it wasn't up yet. I've been meaning to write you about it when your email arrived. I also took the liberty of ordering a copy, and perhaps the very first copy sold, and had it sent to our Golf Course General Manager David Shaffer, that should arrive in about two weeks time. He is very eager to look it over to see if it will be a good fit. So perhaps it will become a fixture in our Pro Shop.

In the meantime, I am still brooding over the death of our poor father. It makes me sick at heart to think about the way he happened to die; either, laying down in a tub of scalding hot water, or slipped into a coma from being drugged "with a sedative" passed-out in a nice warm bath while somebody poured boiling water into the bathtub … something like The God Father in Producer Scene when he awakes to find the head of his horse Khartoum in his bed with him … and even though a lad may asleep in his own bed …

Henry Morton Robinson

From Wikipedia, the free encyclopedia

Henry Morton Robinson (September 7, 1898 – January 13, 1961)

He was born in Boston and graduated from Columbia College in 1923 after serving in the US Navy during the First World War. He was an instructor in English at Columbia University, and a senior editor at Reader's Digest.

On December 23, 1960, he fell asleep in a hot bath after taking a sedative. Three weeks later, on January 13, 1961, he died in New York of complications from the resulting second- and third-degree burns.

He is buried in <u>Artists Cemetery</u>, <u>Woodstock</u>, <u>Ulster County</u>, <u>New York</u>. His son, <u>Anthony Robinson</u>, is also a noted novelist.

Lo and behold, I did come across the name Salvucci, on page 15 of your father's book, The Cardinal, by the name of Matteo Salvucci, who was a "Stoker" on board the vessel Vesuvio, captained by, Gaetono Orselli, who was being ordered by a British Navy Vessel in the time of the coming war with Germany aboard the high seas, to hand over Salvucci as a German Spy in thinking that he was really Rudolf Kansebolm of Hamburg, which Captian Orselli assessed was not true and refused to do. But your father has a "thing" in his book for The Italian Immigrants in the Parish of Bishop William Monaghan of Boston Massachusetts, (to where Father Stephen Fermoyle was sent, in returning from Rome, as a young Curate,) who Bishop Monaghan compares them with his Irish American flock, in naming them, the newly arriving Eye-talians as "Wops." So maybe there is something there, and the same something that has always been there with us regarding the unspoken. Knock On Wood.

I haven't finished the book yet, and am just now on page 80 of it, (oh, so much to do, and so little time,) maybe there is more to pick up on about the incident.

Gary

Mon 6/23/10 5:30 AM

Dear Tony

Of all the fine presents I have received in my life your sending me an autographed copy of your novel, The American Golfer, is the most memorable and fulfilling. I am very impressed with it especially the cover which is quite poignant to look at. Thank you for the lovely inscription to me: "For Gary, a true spirit, a fine friend, a fellow miner of ore," and with your signature, Tony Robinson, a real novel writer and major author of our time. I will treasure it and keep it safe always. And I liked your quote from Graham Green's "The Quiet American," "Sooner or later everyone has to take sides," that I felt was particularly apropos. Dedicated to your wife, Tania, "Who has made my life complete."

I am dropping everything to delve into it, the story of Charlie Kingston, The American Golfer.

Gary

Sun 7/4/10 9:30 AM

I just love your new Novel, The American Golfer, Tony. It's a wonderful story and very pleasant of its expectations to read, having built-in suspense and resolutions at every turn. I find myself wanting to savor it, (like cheese cake, small bites at a time,) and turn the page at the same time to see what happens next. You are indeed a true master of your craft. I'll write you more about it when I've delved a little more deeply into it and feel comfortable with my judgments. Right now I'm at a crucial point, with Charlie just having finished the Nine Hole Round with Wesley in Match Play, and besting him (the right word for it,) 5 to 4. So I don't want to spoil the enchantment of the drama of it in relating to you with technical commenting just now. Charlie is a real nice man, friendly and sympathetic with everyone and kind to the boy Kevin, who is having difficulties, to take him in and befriend him. I felt a cool balmy breeze in the early dawn twilight this morning and thought of you. The kind of breeze you only feel once in great while that stirs the emotion in your soul of gratitude and appreciation to be alive and standing on the earth on a planet in outer space. Magic. The sky was cloudy but not overly so and there was the hint of pink pastel on the horizon. And I was happy to have a friend like you to write to about it. I'll look forward to writing you again with a more in depth critique.

Gary

From: Anthony Robinson
Subj: Golfer
Date: 7/09/10 8:56:31 AM

Gary, I'm glad you're liking my novel. Look forward to your overall view.

Tony

8/7/10 10:45 PM

Dear Tony:

   I just love reading your Novel, The American Golfer, Tony. Please be patient while I finish it. I am truly in no hurry to put it down, although I am intrigued at every stage to turn the page and find out what is going to happen. You have many plots and sub-plots interlaced with one another, some subtle and others more direct, some delicate and others quite disturbing, that grab hold of and take command in your great way of doing of the readers attention and are all quite plausible and logically falling into place for a very smooth clean line to the work.
   I am now at the part now where Laura has just broken it off with Charlie, and Charlie has just killed the awful Reggie MacNair and is lying in the Hospital, and Brigid has just come into the room and given him a kiss on the cheek.

I was grateful to see that Charlie did get Donal back for cold-cocking him and a good bloody nose of it too of what was coming to him. I felt sorry for Charlie being left without his resolution. But it got taken care of. "Till we meet again," as Charlie said. So, (and like with Reggie MacNair also,) the reader does feel, and is quite affected by, the tension and resolution you have built in at work.

Laura is a bit of Wood Nymph isn't she, and very charming and believable in her indiscretions, and also a bit fickle and self-centered, and like a lot of women to have a man, or many men, in waiting for her times to be with, only to discover that the man has other plans for her. The loves scenes are tastefully done and fit naturally into place, just the way people are, and done subtly for the readers who like there favorite authors and their enduring masterpieces to be decorous, preferring the imagination to the literally obvious to be shamed and embarrassed by what they find there to be caught-up in.

There are some typos here and there that I want to go over with you another time when I am finished with the first reading. I'm making notes, as I always do, (not in the book itself,) but on a separate sheet of paper for a second writing clean-up revision, and otherwise to make note of useful information to discuss on for further analysis.

I love the golfing scenes that are always full of resolving tensions and useful professional instructions about the game and the whole story line itself that is centered around the love for the game. Very captivating.

I am also quite moved by your many superb descriptive settings about life and other matters for your readers to reflect on. They are quite deep and ponderous, some of them. And others, as is always the case with your work, paint the scenes with words to bring the reader in to the world being written about; that I do envy and admire your ability to do.

It's a wonderful very moving book, Tony. You should feel proud. I am taking my time not for it not to be over too soon. I always savor the Climax of a good book is my way. I could finish it, but I don't want to. It's there for me to think about now to fondle about, look at, and enjoy near to hand. When a book is finished and put on a self, it's done. Hope things are well with you. Tell me about Ireland and how you happened to choose that location for your book?

Gary

8/17/10 11:35 PM

Dear Tony:

You did a wonderful job with the book, Tony. I couldn't stop reading it toward the end. And I fond myself turning page after page to experience a real Catharsis at the very last, as I have only felt on certain special times in my life, like at the end of the movies "Titanic," and "Sea Biscuit,"(a spontaneous and un-suppress-able welling up of pathos of emotion fighting back a teary eyed sensation,) that left a catch in my throat and made me gasp and have to take a deep breath to collect myself. When I put the book down, I put it down with the feeling that I could let it rest in the fond memory of it, forever, or perhaps to take-up with it again and always find a familiar spot to refresh myself in the thought of it. It is that good of a story and solidly constructed for the critical and discerning eye.

The story wasn't about Charlie making a comeback as a touring pro at Q School at all, as we are led to believe, it is about Charlie finding himself and coming to his destiny to return "home," to his grandmother's home, in Ireland, and to magically find the arms of his love Lora (no longer Lora Brotherton, but Lora Fitzgerald,) waiting there. What could be finer. He is a good man, your Charlie Kingston, a real folk hero. Someone we can root for and cheer on in a dreary world.

I commend you. I am also looking forward, as indicated, to your next book, The Wayward River.

It says that you have a residence in New York City. Tell me about it. How and when did this happen?

Gary

8/21/10 11:37 PM

Dear Tony:

I must have been thinking of Dr. Zhivago the last time I wrote
and had Laura on my brain, which should have read to you ... "to
magically find the arms of his love Lora (no longer Lora
Brotherton, but Lora Fitzgerald,) waiting there ... what could be
finer." Perhaps it was the lateness of the hour. Please forgive me.
    Old Tom Morris ... Bobby Jones.

"For the first time that evening she smiled; it wasn't a big
smile but it brought a lovely change to her face, warming it. ...
He stood for a long moment looking at the man striding down a
city street. Charlie had the feeling that [Michael] Collins
[General of the Army, Irish Free State] was trying to catch his
eye. Sorry, it's not why I'm here, General, Charlie thought.
Outside he stood on the crossroads. He gazed down one road,
then another, each blending into a murky dusk. ... Charlie
rounded the bend in Pearse Road and after two hundred yards
stood across from his cottage. Stone sides cobbled loosely
together, slate roof, a small door and a pair of little windows,
empty window boxes. He crossed Pearse Road and walked down
the weeded path, hesitating at the door; then he tripped the latch."

You have a typo on page 8 at the very bottom, the 25th line
down from the top. ... Passing through the hall, where you left a
space between the words ... and another typo on page 30 at the
beginning of the second paragraph. ... "Charlie was quite for "a"
while, where you left out the "a." And, there is another space
between the words on line 19 of page 33. ... Following the path

he came to <u>an ill</u> maintained patch of land dotted with gravestones.

Searching for his grandmother, Margaret Russell's grave. "Looking up, he saw field after field, always the grazing cows, endless hedgerows, a couple of farmhouses and barns, cumulus clouds in the sky. Farther away, a stretch of grain was bending in the wind, as if a great hand were sweeping through, flattening it; and then it sat up again, smiling at the sun."

And I have this to say to you about the book. You have many scenes where you describe the number of persons or things as "six or seven," "five or six," "three or four." Why can't it be just six men, or five cows, or four cars in definite terms. I could see if it were in the hundreds, <u>roughly speaking</u>.

More to follow, Tony. It's late. What a pleasure it is to "review" your superb work! The subtle work, and the pleasure, of putting "things missed" together.

Gary

From:<u>Anthony Robinson</u>
Subject: finished the book
Date: 8/23/10 11:54:45 AM

Gary, well you're through The American Golfer! I'm really glad you liked it. As for your comment "three or four," "five or six," "seven or eight"--it's a habit, a device, and I likely use it too often. It does serve a purpose--sometimes a character wouldn't look at something closely enough to actually say or think "five horses" or "eight women." It's a way of giving a rough estimate; but perhaps I use it too freely. As for the typos, I'd like to know how many there are all told (but would be embarrassed to learn.) It's amazing how one will slip through, let alone "eight or nine."

Did your pro ever show any interest in selling the book in his shop? Our pro in New Paltz has a way of giving copies out at tournaments--much better than a couple of sleeves of balls, and cheaper to buy. I've started work on Bluestone, about the artist colony in Woodstock where I grew up. Take care.

Tony

8/23/10 8:2 7 PM

In all, Tony, other than the "three" typos I mentioned before, you have "five" others, not four or five, but exactly five, although, on many not be as you will have to judge. That leaves in all a total of seven to correct. I know you are not quite through with the book yet and still have a second edition to put out after a certain period of due diligence to reflect on everything about, in the process of withstanding the test of time to become a modern Classic.

In comment about certain of the things I'd like to see you workout. You're F--- words seemed o.k. in the start of the book, as a legitimate part of a certain way of manly conversation, but at the end in the Conversation that Charlie has with Wesley it gets used a bunch more times than it needs to be, perhaps two or three more times than it needs to be. Although I don't care for it, or use it, it may have a charm to a certain way of reading. But for certain of your readers, the clergy, the women, and young adolescents, perhaps that they might feel repulsed or intimidated by it to think about "toning down" a bit with the idea.

I also thought that the first love scene between Charlie and Lora, or the other way around, while in good taste, I thought, though it came across a little "too frivolous" for the serious intent of the love "relationship" that was to follow. I thought both Lora's and Charlie's characters needed to be flushed out a bit more, in their desires for honest companionship and warmth, in their initial love making, rather than just to be having sex, or as you put it to coarsely in your Home Again, Home Again, in the manner just to be F-------. In mention, that you have a genuine sexual encounter between Fiona and Charlie, and not in frivolous way, but it had meaning in the way of "being needed," if you follow my drift that way.

The other typos then are as follows. You have a space on page 90, in the 15th line down, where it says ... "It's too long for you." The next on, which may not be a typo, is on page 174 where Charlie is talking to Brigid and Charlie is in long narrative part and ends his "technical" conversation, and then continues on "in thought" with "quotation marks," which technically, in my thinking, doesn't require any. "But I am happy you are here with your mother..." he wanted to add ... and me, in which you has "and me" in quotations. On 178 on the 10th line down you have a space ... "O'Hea said," a tease in his voice.

On page 187 you have really good one on line 28. He'd always thought of Fiona as the one with problems. Not beautiful Lora whose husband had bought her a castle in Ireland with its own golf course and a "steam" running by.

The last one is on page 244 on the very 1st line where it says, couldn't be good new. Which needs to read "news."

And that is not all of it, Tony. I have many more things to relate with about in the living reality of your novel that has taken life in my own mind. But, Kathy is home from work now and is calling me for dinner. It's 8:26. Our Blood Sugars are low and we need to eat. I am waiting for our GM to finish reading the book giving him time. He has to like it too. I'll bring it up to him in a short while and see what he thinks.

Love you too, Tony,
Gary

8/29/10 11:03AM

Dear Tony:

It's maddening to find typos, isn't it Tony? It's a bad word out of place here, another misspelled there, an awkward sentence structure, that somehow all gets missed in the writing of it. But all in all you do really fine precision work, superb in every regard.

It was her turn to laugh. They sat for a while longer, gazing out. He so wanted to take her in his arms, to turn form the beauty of the Celtic Sea and look into the sea-green eyes of Loa Brotherton. But he knew himself; he'd got into trouble risking dangerous shots too often in his career. She was another man's wife, and the man was his boss.

Don't gamble, Charlie. Play it safe.

"Let's finish, then we'll have tea," Lora said.

A few second ticked by. "How about you and children, Lora?"

"I'd love to have a family, but at this point it doesn't seem likely."

"It could still happen," Charlie said.

"It's not in the cards, I'm afraid."

"I should be running, Lora."

"Stay awhile. Let me (you) show you the house." She said.

Lora and Charlie went up the carpeted stairs to the second floor.

"I sleep here," she said. "Wesley trashes about like and elephant."

"It's a beautiful room, Lora."

--- Sunshine poured in through the two front windows. Upholstered easy chairs, lovely lamps, seascapes on the wall. But what caught Charlie's attention was the bed. It was the first canopy bed he'd ever actually seen, except for pictures. White silk, trimmed with lace ---

The bed didn't hold his attention long. Standing by it, Lora was unbuttoning her shirt.

Actually, the love scene here is quite exquisite, I would say, except for the panties dangling on her ankle, at the end of it, resembling a sea bird riding the waves, which I'm not sure works from a technical level in that that Charlie, who is the observer here, is face down at this task and looking at Lora's legs. And on the other more serious level of emotional involvement that is not in keeping with the seriousness of the setting that the reader is hoping for in this scene. Is what I meant by it seeming to be too frivolous.

It's only the one line. But I was hoping all along for a "more serious intent." Which I would love to have read, and looked forward to reading ... of a serious relationship developing ... as I would have phrased it ...

"Oh, Charlie," she murmured as he entered her all the way, in a gasp of ecstasy and with longing, "I've needed you so." It was a sound that would haunt his memory forever.

Do you see what I mean here? This it the crux of the book! There are things going on here, currents of emotions, and things that will go on from here, that are more involved and more serious than just a frivolous romp in the hay with a common prostitute, and that need to be "set up" for the reader here and to the reader's anticipation and enjoyment of the rest of the novel, not to disappoint.

And as for the F___ word, Tony. Do you really need it? And I can see perhaps you do. But it is the difference, Tony, between an American Classic on the scale of Faulkner, Clemens, and Hemmingway, or to obscurity gathering on a shelf in the dust of time.

You decide.

The F word, and of its uses, is dated now and in bad taste, verging on being Kitsch just to throw it around for effect. The F word works in A Departure From The Rules, and in The Whole

Truth, (which are coarse in their crude and common manly parts
or real, or imagined to be real, dialogue description,) but certainly
not in Home Again – Home Again which is a tender and
sympathetic love story on many deeply involving levels of
moving relationships to be fathomed by the reader, (and hopefully
to be edited out along any mention of Kikes and Mulattos in the
final form of that great work to be,) and perhaps not in The Easy
Way either that has many sensitive levels of involvement as well
to be finely, and in good taste, appreciated for. The Member
Guest is a zany tale and full of all kinds of blunt expressions, and
descriptions of things, and it works on that level of entertainment.
But the books I named, **Home Again- Home Again, The Easy
Way, and The American Golfer**, I feel in my heart of hearts,
need to be re-worked and cleaned up a bit of their foul-language,
for the sake of the sensitive and intelligent reasoning content they
portray, conveying great importance, and to be made enduring.

The others are enduring in their own right of passage for what
they are, and just because they are real in that way of being real.
Let the reader beware!

But I needed to ask you, and just what is the big deal with you
and that word, to you? And why would it ever enter the realm of
your creativity, to use it? When it's use cuts your market and
your appeal as a truly great author, (which you are,) and which
means the difference between immortality as an author, or to
gather dust collecting on a book shelf, if it survives at all past a
certain first printing at all. God love you, Tony.

There is an old saying in Heaven among the Angels, (and who
are always making excuses for everyone to ease them out of and
along with in their suffering over their self-imposed prisons of the
heart and mind due to the errors real or imagined committed, that
they have committed, or sins by another name;) which goes like
this:

"Unless everyone takes a little part of the sin, the great error,
into their own heart, and makes their own too, and admits to it,
The Wound Cannot Be Healed."

Because, the Sin, is a psychological chasm insurmountable in
the mind, which one person has committed that separates them

and that isolates them for all eternity from those who have never committed the sin. And by virtue of what immaculate state, of those who have not sinned, who tend to look-smugly-down on those who have erred, in a better-than-thou attitude of reproach. And so the error continues on and recruits a sub-culture of others to the same error to bolster its existence in a vein attempt to make it right, which it can never do, and a hatred of the holy develops as a consequence, who then become sadistically persecuted by the evildoers now acting as a group. And, The Great Wound Keeps Festering, never to be cleansed and allowed to heal.

So remember the words of the Angels as you go about among The Others in your days. And keep to the shy side. You won't go wrong. Who knows what is lurking.

Tourette syndrome (also called **Tourette's syndrome**, **Tourette's disorder**, **Gilles de la Tourette syndrome**, **GTS** or, more commonly, simply **Tourette's** or **TS**) is an inherited neuropsychiatric disorder with onset in childhood, characterized by multiple physical (motor) tics and at least one vocal (phonic) tic; these tics characteristically wax and wane. Tourette's is defined as part of a spectrum of tic disorders, which includes transient and chronic tics.

Tourette's was once considered a rare and bizarre syndrome, most often associated with the exclamation of obscene words or socially inappropriate and derogatory remarks (coprolalia), but this symptom is present in only a small minority of people with Tourette's. Tourette's is no longer considered a rare condition, but it may not always be correctly identified because most cases are classified as mild. Between 1 and 10 children per 1,000 have Tourette's; as many as 10 per 1,000 people may have tic disorders, with the more common tics of eye blinking, coughing, throat clearing, sniffing, and facial movements. People with Tourette's have normal life expectancy and intelligence. The severity of the tics decreases for most children as they pass through adolescence, and extreme Tourette's in adulthood is a rarity. Notable individuals with Tourette's are found in all walks of life.

Genetic and environmental factors play a role in the etiology of Tourette's, but the exact causes are unknown. In most cases, medication is unnecessary. There is no effective medication for every case of tics, but there are medications and therapies that can help when their use is warranted. Explanation and reassurance alone are often sufficient treatment; education is an important part of any treatment plan.

Gary

9/14/10 7:40PM

Dear Tony:

I am really deeply moved by the entire scope and perspective of your great Novel, The American Golfer. Page after page turns easily in suspense and with anticipation of the resolutions, as put in the plural, which you so brilliantly tie in the loose ends of at ever turn. It's a story about Ireland, the beloved homeland, and about a man, Charlie Kingston, who finds his life taken over by the charm and the spell and the embattled mystique of it, and for your warm descriptions of its countryside to delight the senses by. "Did you come to fight," you can hear Michael Collins ask. And for sure that Charlie did return, to find his love, Lora, but also, to Ireland, and for Ireland, to be with her, to fight!

I am about here with a new novel, called, The Democratic Labor Party Platform, that I used your quote from Graham Green's "The Quite American" for. I think you will like it, Tony.

In the meantime, don't sweat about the F--- Word, as I mentioned about. It's really not important historically. History will judge the work, with or without it. And maybe it's more real the way you have it. Who is to say? Certainly not me. I've been doing some thinking about the fact of it, and feel that it does have its uses in literature.

I finished your father's book, The Cardinal just recently. I was in the overall very impressed with it. It was very well written with a good solid foundation of story line that was filled with great vision, thoughts, emotions, expectations, and convictions of faith and morals to inspire the ages by. Henry Morton Robinson was a great scholar, and still is, as he lives on in his work, and through his children. I have learned a great deal from him already in my study of his classical education, and as most impressed by his impeccable diction of style and professional literary technique. He takes the time to reveal a sense of belonging to what it is that he is writing about.

Here is the rest of my tale for today. I came across this article of you in the Kingston Daily Freeman. God love you, Tony.

Gary

Winsome View Of The Barren Catskill Mountains

Not Just Another Golf Story

By Ann Gibbons
Kingston Daily Freeman Staff
August 1, 2010

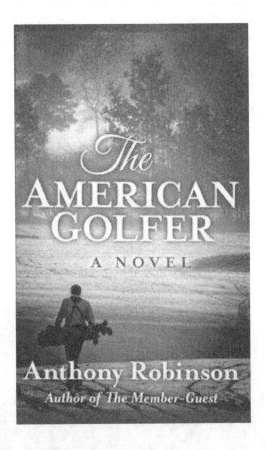

People who think they hear their arteries hardening when
watching championship golf should just get over it and put some
intrigue into their lives. That's what Charlie Kingston does in
author Anthony Robinson's new novel, "The American Golfer"
by Bluestone Books.

The novel is not a how-to on improving your score, but life-lessons about love, honor, intrigue and betrayal, learned the hard way – by messing up, on and off the course. A certain, amazingly talented American golfer who messed up big time, on and off the course, might come to mind, but Robinson's protagonist plays the game in the shadow and remnants of the 1920 Irish struggle for independence. Some pain never goes away, especially for the survivors.

In the story, Charlie, a PGA Tour golfer, flees his disorderly American past for a respite in his grandmother's tiny village in Ireland where everyone knows everyone's grimy, tragic, sordid heritage and reputation. The Irish, despite their reputation for glib tongues loosened by drink, keep their secrets. And, when all is said and done, behind that genial countenance, is a shrewd intellect assessing one's vulnerability and gullibility.

Naturally, there's a beautiful, wealthy woman, Lora, with a stiff husband, with whom Charlie falls in love, setting off a spree of infidelity, menace and making hard choices, all of which the American golfer is ill prepared.

In Ireland, past is present, and Charlie finds himself plunged into an unexpected and inexplicable adventure of conflict and peril in the Emerald Isle's ever-simmering political stew where friend is enemy and enemy friend. Charlie needs to exchange his spiked golf shoes for toe slippers to keep on dancing between and across an ever-widening gap of deception.

What's immediately apparent to the non-golfer is the author's authority about golf, courses and language that Robinson explained away readily.

"I've been on golf courses, since the age of 12, when I began to caddy" at the Woodstock golf course, he said in a recent interview, adding with a wry smile, "I was paid $1 back then and was glad to get it."

Robinson, a professor emeritus at SUNY New Paltz, where he taught American literature for 35 years and also directed the Creative Writing Program, is a life-long golfer. He attended Kingston High School for one year. His family has lived in Woodstock since 1926, where he was raised.. He now lives in New Paltz, with his wife, Tania.

In the story, Charlie is asked for advice about a certain problematic hole on the private course reserved for guests of Lora's wealthy husband. [The problem being that the fairway on that particular hole sloped dramatically off to the right on the long par four requiring a long drive to get on the green in two; and that subsequently any shot hit with a fade or a slice to the right, as most amateur golfers would tend to do, and not with an intentional draw to the left, would hit the down-slope and bound off into the rough for a lost, or unplayable ball, and a two stroke penalty. Which The American Pro, Charlie Kingston, fixed by building a reverse sloping earthen berm along the rough of the problem area that would deflect the run-away balls back and return them to the fairway, solving the problem, and the golf scores for the wealthy owner, Wesley Brotherton's, guests.] Robinson said he loosely based that part of the story on a certain hole at the New Paltz golf course that was a long par that curved to the right with a slope that could cause the ball to roll into the nearby pond. He used the pro's fix at the course in the story.

Robinson is an author by genes and by education. His father, Henry Morton Robinson, wrote the controversial bestseller, "The Cardinal," in 1950. Robinson himself is the author of six novels; one of them, "The Member-Guest" is also about golf.

Asked how he could write and teach, Robinson said very little gets in the way of writing. "I get up very early, 6 a.m., come down to my office and keep working at it." Sometimes, the writing does not come easy.

"I had completed one novel that I was never satisfied with," he said. "I had given it many tries, but it was giving me a hard time, so I put it away." He said he went back to the material and decided he had not told the story properly. "I needed to get to the deep root of what I wanted to say." He reworked it. "I think I've got it now," he said with satisfaction. "I have written many stories, but not all of them are a novel," he said.

The characters in this current novel are solid and believable – but made up. "Yes, I made them up," he said, explaining that he wrote the story in the third person to keep a solitary point of view – Charlie's. He explained that, in this instance, jumping from character to character would disrupt the unity of the story line. Although the characters in the novel are fictional, the historical figures, like Michael Collins, hero and martyr of the revolt against Britain, were real. "I did a lot of research on Ireland, especially its history," Robinson said to cast a sense of real time on the plot.

The story opens subtly, but significantly on April 10, 1998, the day of the acceptance of the Good Friday Agreement, during which all disparate parties agreed to the six doctrines of The Mitchell Principles, brokered by former U.S. Sen. George Mitchell. Mitchell was Special Envoy to Northern Ireland then, and now is Special Envoy for Middle East Peace for the Obama administration.

The Agreement created an uneasy truce among Northern Ireland, the Republic of Ireland and Great Britain. In the shadow of the Agreement, was and is, the Irish Republican Army, formed in 1919 to battle England for Ireland's independence. The bombings have ceased, but the bitterness remains.

Robinson said he works steadily on a book because he's a careful writer, taking two and a half to three years to complete this novel. "I changed the original outcome," he said. "I didn't like the way I ended it, so I rethought it." He acknowledged that readers don't know how much thought goes into the writing of a novel. He said he writes on a computer because it helps keep the story line consistent and allows him to find minor discrepancies as the story moves forward.

Asked what the reader should take away from "The American Golfer," Robinson thought for a moment, then said, "Well, it's always fun to find out how the story ends. A good story entertains and the reader is moved by the decisions, good or bad, that the characters make. It's a cathartic experience, and the reader gets pulled deeper into the story by what's happening."

In the end, Robinson said, he wants the reader to say what he said when he put the period at the end of the last sentence, "Damn, that's a good story!" And, it is.

1717 French Reformed Church and Cemetery on Huguenot Street

Tony Robinson at home in his Study.

The American Golfer is available at Amazon.com.
Further information may be obtained at:
www.arobinson.net or robinsoa@newpaltz.edu.

Duck Pond is the starting point on Mohonk Preserve
land where Tony assembled our entire Creative Writing
Class of fourteen students for a hiking excursion in May
of 1974, to scale the cliffs below Mohonk Tower and to
climb to the very top of the Tower itself. It was a most
memorable day that was much enjoyed by everyone.

Duck Pond – Mohonk Preserve

For God And Country

"To Live Our Lives As The Creator Would Intend"

The Church Of The Early Morning

Our Days of Labor Upon The Earth begin in the darkness of the early morning hours with The Contemplation of The Sunrise, awaiting in expectation beneath a canopy of Stars the first dim perceptions of The Light and the appearance of Our Star on the horizon regaled in the clouds with many hues of pastel colors. And to realized that we are standing upon, and live in wonder of, a place called Earth, A World, spinning in outer-space, circling a Star among the countless Stars of a Galaxy in a vast and inconceivable Universe, and for us our home in Heaven, as we fathom it to be, in humility, to go about the blessed toil of our days, that somehow and miraculously, We, and All There Is, Have Come To Exist.

To Understand Our Place IN The Moral Mind Of God We Must Realize That We Exist In A Fusion Of Souls And Mind-Thought With "All Things" Sentient To Exist. Who Exist IN The Mind Of The Creator TO Be A Part Of. And That All Of This Interlacing Soul Of Everything Has Thought Upon Us, Involving Us With Itself, And We With Itself, Depending On Our Perceptions Of It, and Its Perceptions Of Us, To Relate To. And Always It Is With The Understanding About Everything, "To Be Mindful," To Have A Loving Respect And Reverence And Cherishment For Everything There Is, In Harmony To The Creator, Whose Dream, Alone In The Darkness, It Was, For All Things To Exist.

Prayer Will Not Get You There. It Is Only By Diligent Hard Work And By Doing What Is Right That We Can Endure Emotionally. Work Is Our Salvation. The Work Redeems Us And Sustains Us. The Work Defines Us. Work Is The Holy Heritage Of Our Nation.

"Sooner of later one has to take sides."

The Quiet American
Graham Greene

The End of Middle Class America cries out for intervention. However, the crux of the problem arises that Different crises affect different people differently and most people don't tend to get involved in matters to which they are not involved in directly.

People starving to death by the millions in Ethiopia, War Crimes in Bosnia, Human Rights Violations in China, The Plight of The Poor, The Drug Epidemic, Aids, and the list goes on of indifferent concerns to us which affect "other" people. And to the certain extent of indifference in the list of other people's business that way, stands The War of Middle Class Survival, at odds with the "Outsourcing" of our domestic industries to cheap foreign manufacturing rivalries, and the "Low-Balling" of our own American Workers occurring at the hands of invading Mexicans and other Hispanics from Central and South America, Indians of The Subcontinent variety, Third World Blacks from Africa and The Caribbean, Orientals of every denomination, and other immigration from The Mid-East, Europe, and elsewhere, who are and have been extensively, legally or otherwise, flooding into this country seeking work without government forethought.

And, no offense intended to these hard working and sincere people, who are in themselves struggling to survive; but who, in virtue of their class differentiation in orientation established to a third world economy life style as to their having accepted impoverished circumstances, are replacing The Mainstream Respectable Middle Class Workers here with their cheap labor market tactics based to the unregulated labor loop-hole arrangement of The Federal Government's Minimum Wage Law being left unopposed and in unscrupulous hands, in dealing fairly with The Cost of Living pertaining for The Established Middle Class Standards, which we need to get cleared up promptly by the swift passage of The Prevailing Minimum Wage Legislation.

This Legislation which is pending before The Congress would set many different levels of minimum wages, based to job description, instead of the one minimum wage of $7.2 5, as of July 24, 2009, an hour with being currently left up to the indiscretion of private employers to determine, for their own sake of profit taking, as to what hourly wages they want to pay their employees, who have no say in the matter, based to supply and demand labor economics. That is not only unethical, but also unholy to conceive of, that the business class of this Nation should be allowed to exploit the people who are desperate to survive.

And bearing in mind that this "Cheap Labor" arrangement, while in seeming to be a boon to the business class, is really in and of itself, self defeating, and dooming to the entire American Economy overall; in that "Cheap Labor" has no money to spend in the Middle Class Economy. Which means that less services and goods are going to be purchased on into the future because there is no Middle Class money to purchase them.

And with such dwindling mass-consumer purchasing power, business slow-downs and failures will occur, resulting in mass-layoffs and mass-unemployment, creating even further future economic deterioration, generating even more business failures, as the situation worsens of its own cascading and interrelated collapse, into the recession-depression of "everybody's," economy, yours and mine, and in essence then affecting everyone's livelihood in the long-run for everyone to take an active roll in preventing at this time. There is no substitute for Intelligent Government Reasoning in this matter.

CD 4: Republican Congressman Ander Crenshaw will face a challenge from the right as conservative activist and Navy vet Troy Stanley has made the ballot with no party affiliation. Deb Katz Pueschel, who ran against Crenshaw in the Republican primary back in 2008, and **author Gary Koniz** are running as write-in candidates. There is no Democratic candidate.
Kevin Derby - Sunshine State News – August 21, 2010

Labor Party Platform – Campaign 2010

Write-In Ballot Campaign

Grass Roots – Word-Of-Mouth – Email
Telephone – Advertising
Name Will Not Appear On Ballot –
In Lieu Of A $6,960. Qualifying Fee
Independent Workers' Rights Labor Platform
(4th District Florida)

http://www.lulu.com/content/paperback-book/the-call-to-order/6663590

United States Representative

004	Crenshaw, Ander (REP) *Incumbent	Qualified	
*****	Koniz, Gary L. (WRI)	Qualified	
	Pueschel, Deborah "Deb" Katz (WRI)	Qualified	
	Stanley, Troy D. (NPA)	Qualified	

Florida's Fourth Congressional District is a U.S. congressional district in Florida. Since 2001, the residents of the Fourth District are represented by Republican Ander Crenshaw. This district takes in most of Jacksonville along with a long part of northern Florida.

History:

The district was originally created by the Florida Legislature in 1943 as the 2nd District. Democrat Charles Bennett represented the district from 1948-1992. The district was renumbered as the 3rd District in 1967 and later as the 4th District in 1993. During the 1992 Congressional Election, Bennett chose to retire rather than fight an intense re-election campaign against challenger Tillie K. Fowler. Fowler won the election and became the first Republican to represent the district. She held the position from 1993-2000. John McCain received 62% of the vote in this district in 2008.

The Drug Czar Amendment is included in a series of ten new Amendments to our U.S. Constitution, as a major issue of state of, "The Democratic Labor Party Platform - 2010." www.lulu.com/product/paperback/labor-party-platform---2010/12574527

United States Constitution

We The People

Article I – Section. 1: Legislative Powers vested in a Congress – Senate and House of Representatives; House of Representatives chosen ever 2nd year, 25 yrs. Old, 7 years a citizen of The United States consisting of: 2. NH, MA, RI, CT, NY, NJ, PE, DE, ML, VI, NC, SC, GA. 3. Senate elected every 6 years (30 yrs old.) resident for 9 years.
Impeachment 2/3 vote. 4. Bills of Revenue originate in the House. 5. Rules. 6. Compensation. 7. Senate approves bills originating in the House, approved by the President. 8. Power to lay taxes – others powers – duties. 9. Rules of the states other rules. 10. Powers of states to lay duties.

Bill of Attainder – extinction of civil rights on sentence of death or outlawing
Ex post facto – after the fact

Article II – Section. 1. the Executive Power 35 years natural born citizen 14 years a resident. 2. Commander in Chief. 3. State of the Union address. 4. Impeachement.

Article III – Section. 1. Judicial Power 2. extent of powers. 3. Treason.

Article IV – Section 1. Public Acts and Records. 2. Citizens of each state. 3. New States. 4. The United States shall guarantee to every State in this Union a Republican Form of Government, and shall protect each of these against invasion, and on application of the Legislature, or of the Executive (when the Legislative cannot be convened,) against domestic Violence. 5. Amendments 2/3 of the States for Convention, ¾ for Ratification. 6. Debts, Laws and Treaties, Oath of Affirmation bound. 7. Witness by, 09/17/1787 in the 12th year of the Nation.

Bill Of Rights – ratified 1791

1. Freedom of speech, press, religion, peaceful assembly, and redress of grievances.
2. to keep and bear arms.
3. no quartering of troops.
4. Right of the people to be secure in their persons, housed, papers, ands effects, against unreasonable searches and seizures – no warrants issued without Probable Cause supported by oath and describing the places to be searched and the persons or things to be seized.
5. Grand Jury indictment for capital crimes, may not twice be put in jeopardy of life or limb, nor compelled to witness against himself, nor be deprived of life, liberty, or property, without due process of law; nor shall private property be taken for public use without just compensation.
6. Right to a speedy trial by jury, informed of the nature and cause of the accusation, confrontation of witnesses and to have witness in their own favor, and have the assistance of counsel.
7. Suites at common law right to trail by jury.
8. no excessive bail, fines, nor cruel and unusual punishment.
9. Enumeration of rights shall not be construed to deny or disparage others retained by the people.
10. The powers not delegated to the United States by the Constitution nor prohibited by it to the states, are reserved to the States respectively, or to the people.

11. (1795) Judicial Power of the United States not to interfere with State Suits.
12. (1804) Rules of the Election of The President and Vice President
13. (1865) Slavery and involuntary servitude abolished
14. (1968) Section. 1. Nor shall any state deprive any person of life, liberty, or property without due process of law.

15. (1870) Right to vote on account of race, color, or servitude shall not be denied.
16. (1913) Power to lay and collect income taxes.
17. (1913) Senators of the United States, vacancies filled.
18. (1919) Prohibition
19. (1920) Women's Right to Vote.
20. (1933) Terms of the President and Vice President expire at noon the 20th of January. Senators and Representatives at noon on the 3rd of January. Congress shall assemble at least once in every year. Rules of succession.
21. (1933) Prohibition is repealed.
22. (1951) Terms of the Presidency limited to two. Two year limit counts as one term on succession.
23. (1961) District of Columbia electors
24. (1964) Poll Tax abolished.
25. (1967) Removal or death of the President.
26. (1971) granting 18 year olds the right to vote.
27. (1992) No Law varying the compensation for the Senate and the House shall take effect until the election of representatives shall have intervened.

I need a hand regarding the circulation of our Fair Wage and Benefits Initiative throughout the State of Florida; which needs 676,811 signatures by February 5, 2010 from one half of the Congressional Districts in the State, which I know is not going to happen, (the public workforce in The State of Florida and everywhere being apathetic as they are,) to be successful about, by working with me to circulate our petition to the respective AFL-CIO Representing Offices throughout the State in asking each of them to participate in the drive, (that is exactly like a Civil War in its orientation to defeat the enemy of greed and subservience,) and to restore the Workers, (if they ever were there to begin with,) to their proper dignity in our society.

Citizens' Alliance Coalition

**Mobilizing An Activists Army
Of Concerned Citizens
Call To Action To Correct
The Errors In Our System
Faith Movement Workers
Contributions - Needed**

**We Have This Time In History
To Make A Difference**

**Get Organized - Get To The Polls
And Get Our Agendas Accomplished**

United Labor Party Headquarters
9480 Princeton Square Blvd. S., #815
Jacksonville, FL 32256
gary.koniz@hotmail.com
(904) 730-2055

From: Anthony Robinson
Subject: our discussion
Date: 9/26/10 2:50:18 PM

Gary, I know you've always had a very nice feeling for what is and what isn't appropriate. Keener than most people have. When I write I don't think about what might or might not be appropriate, but is it effective, does it work? The overuse of any word is a stylistic problem, and I'm well aware of the overuse of slang or common words. You seem to look at this in a moral sense. You lose me there, but you do make me go back to Writing 101. To make any word effective, it must be used sparingly. You have made me aware of this important rule in good writing. Thank you. Tony

9/26/10 5:50PM

Dear Tony,

Forgive me for being so blunt with your feelings. It's an excellent book in all ways of intent upon us, and the choice of dialogue I feel is quite appropriate for the manly setting that it is put to use by, but not for all the potential readers who may enjoy picking it up through the course of time in the ages. Do you, or do you not get my point here to discuss with you. It is not with a strict moral sense that I mentioned the subject to you about on the numerous occasions that I have insisted upon the expunging of the text matter in an editorial meaning, but in the meaning and matter of good taste, and with a fastidious sense for the sensitive feeling of the younger readers, and perhaps others of more discerning and fastidious taste. If I were to read your book aloud to an audience, I would not be able to utter that word to the audience, and I believe you would not either, in looking around to see who you would "offend."

"Don't cast your pearls before the swine," (Matthew 7:6,) is in another wording of it.

You once told me that the book, and any book, belongs in the hands of its editor, and to the editor to know the objective timing and the place of things and events and texture of dialogue and narrative to resolve, that lies beyond and in a different perspective, and in a different sense of criticism, that being that of the critical reader, than the author can sometimes sees, blinded by his, or her, own passions and obsessions of tunnel vision; who can't fathom to consider at the time of the work's being composed and transcribed what its errors are, and who chooses not to perceive there being "any" errors to it at all to point out, but in being pointed out to of the errors of the work, (and such with the use of the f--- word being a vulgarity and in bad taste,) that lies within the discerning eye of the beholding eye editor to judge and reform and to redeem the work of what may be its errors, and in this case, to make the book immortal in the eyes of a discerning public to persevere in the enduring sense of time.

But you don't want that do you, to have a beloved enduring masterpiece. You want all of your works to be the public's forced acceptance of your use of the f--- word in misguided artistic ego.

Which, I might add, they don't' accept. They don't accept it, and they never have, and they never will. It's foul language that lingers in the air of your work like an odor, and that alienates the critical mainstay of your readers, like the passing of bad gas at the supper table, which you as head of the house want to try and force everyone to politely accept, but which the pity of it is, that they are only being polite with you about it, or perhaps not, to tell you what it is and not to.

"The book starts here," you told me that one time about the editor who revised one of your books, "it doesn't start where you began it, what is dragged out and tires the reader's attention. It begins at the critical point of fascination of its drama, and which is Lora's love for Charlie that grabs his heart, and ours, and looks back to the events leading up to it, and about Charlie finding his Grandmother's grave.

You know that is what your book is about, Tony. And it's not about your rebel maverick use of the f--- word that is alien to it

and beyond that which is no longer the cool rebellious avant-
garde slang of the past era it once was, and if it ever was that.

The American Golfer is a tender love story about the beloved
homeland of Ireland and about a man who finds his destiny there.
Why don't you leave it that way? They don't use the f--- word on
prime time television, do they?" for a reason. They bleep it out.
And why is that they do that? May I ask you? Why then don't
you just "bleep it out," Tony, and be done with it. And in that
way to make the book the enduring masterpiece it deserves to be
in its own right of destiny.   You're selling yourself short of a
masterpiece in acclaim in my opinion, and one that we, the
readers, can extrapolate of a larger context to implicate our
homeland also in the need for mutual defense. Did you come
home in your heart to fight for America?

Lake Mohonk Mountain House, NY

Full Text of The Master Economic Resolution Plan

The United States Constitution Is Hereby Created To Read As Follows:

Article 1. - Declaration Of Rights.
Section 1. - Right to Work.

The following is the only alternative we have, facing imminent survival with the National Debt, Unemployment, and the ever escalating Cost of Living; that is to be remedied by raising the standard of living for the average American Workers and by regulatory agreement, stressing the imposition of Price Controls to the Cost Of Living Essentials; in **Anti-Trust Measures**, to specify for the price of food, shelter, gasoline, and health care.

(a) The right of persons to work shall not be denied or abridged on account of membership or non-membership in any labor union or labor organization. The right of employees, by and through a labor organization, to bargain collectively shall not be denied or abridged. Public employees shall not have the right to strike.

(b) The right of persons to work is as well to include for the right to a gainful livelihood based in faith to a Fair Wage stipulation that is to be enacted and carried out by strict and binding yearly Federal Mediation Arbitration in regulation of the economy by stabilizing The State's wages paid to workers to a uniform parity agreement with The Federal Government's (GS) General Schedule Wage Standards, to set the hourly wage rates for each rated category of employment field to exist in TheUnited States, based to the index of The Prevailing Minimum Wages established for Federal Government Workers and to be monitored over to

coincide with each sector of Private Employment Categories.
And that such Prevailing Wages for each Rated Job Description
are to be posted by The United States Department Of Labor, who
is charged with the responsibility for enforcement.

(c) This measure is also to call for a well regulated "Fair Price
Index Agreement," to concern with State Government Oversight
to The Cost Essential Necessities To Survival for The Public
Well-Being in the interest of the public need, and To Prevent
Inflation; to do with; food, shelter, clothing, fuel, transportation,
household necessities, vital utilities services, insurance, medical
and dental services, and other Cost Essentials; and what does not
specify for luxury items to be included. In understanding that The
Pricing to these Cost of Living Essentials are not further to be
exploited, and that are permitted to operate in the public interest
by license agreement of The State, under Government
Supervision.

(d) An affordable Payroll Deducted State Sponsored Health Care
and Dental Care Coverage Plan option is also to be offered and
provided to the people, (to be levied in fair percentage of earned
income upon the enrollment base of the entire population.)

(e) It is further to be reasoned that the right to work also entails
the right to employment, to be provided for by The State if
necessary, in agreement with the Federal Government in support
of allocations from The Federal Treasury Department, to the
individual States for redistribution to local City and County
Governments; based to the understanding that Government
Services in their own right, possess their own Inherent Intrinsic
Barter Value in Agreement in mandate to be issued for by Fiat
Monetary Generation in Full Faith contingency to any taxation
shortfall to provide Necessary Services and Full Employment to
the population; which are worth their own tangible necessity in
fiscal integrity.

****

Winter's Day on Huguenot Street - New Paltz, NY
Not Far From Tony's House Facing In That Direction

Fri 11/26/7:23 PM

Dear Tony:

Happy Thanksgiving! Tony. I hope that all is well there with you and with the family. I'm thinking about each of you.

I haven't written in a long while due to the fact that I have been busy with The Congressional Campaign, and its aftermath, (of which I received 27 votes, but which I am contesting the outcome of the election of, under legal protest with The Florida Elections Commission, for the issue of my not obtaining a clear ruling from the Director of The Florida Division of Elections, (as

I asked for, and as he was legally obligated to provide to me, and to each of the county Supervisors of Elections in the 4th Congressional District, FL,) concerning the status of the Write-In Candidates who are officially not on the ballot but who otherwise of having the political position of being anonymous to the voters officially, but whose names of the Write-In Candidates need to be made available and known to the voters at the polls on election day in order for a fair and free election to occur, and for the sense of fair play in evening the odds a little in the war of The Rich against The Poor.

Which is the case as I have stated it, and calling for a "Balked Election," whatever that plays out to. I doubt that they will ever do the election over, over my objection of it. But at least I am making my point in legal action about Snooty Class Discrimination idea going on here, and of Government of the Rich, by the Rich, for the Rich, that anyone can buy their name on the ballot for the sum of $6,960, that has been ruining and destroying our country needing replacement with the rank-and-file candidates to provide for Proper Representation of The Working Class. I had a lot of work planned and good things to accomplish in Congress. And so as to what it is that I have been doing with my time.

Here is the link to your free eBook *The Democratic Labor Party Platform 2012* (ID #11647902): http://www.lulu.com/content/e-book/the-democratic-labor-party-platform-2012/11647902

I really did love your new book, The American Golfer, Tony. Please don't misunderstand my previous remarks of constructive editing, and as I know how everyone hates to have their work, (which they view as an offspring,) to be reviewed in a negative critical light. It's not important what I said before about the work. Don't take it to heart.

It is truly a classic novel of many fine endearing qualities, and a book that I find myself truly fascinated by, and in a sense addicted to, in wanting to read passages of it over, to reveal and to study different nuances of it, and over again, in just picking it up and starting in somewhere with it, a page of two here and there, a chapter over again, just to have it around.

When I was in my youth I used to sleep with a book about Zen Buddhism on my bed to read a little in before falling off to sleep and to have with me to touch in the night for comfort, and I had a reaction with several of Earnest Hemmingway's novels also that way also. And that is the way that I feel about The American Golfer as a companion. There is something inexpressibly captivating about it, or ineffably endearing to describe.

Mostly I think it is about, Lora, or over Lora, that intrigues me, that I feel for, and for her complex personality, drawn to love and yet to a mischievous and playful romantic revenge on her husband besides, with her flaming red Irish hair, and her eyes of green agates with blazing black centers, and love for the Poetry of William Butler Yeats, and for her whimsical manner of courtship, and lovemaking, as seductress who is also deeply troubled at the heart with her relationship tied up into a money over love smothered mate marriage relationship to her bullying and arrogant Wealthy English husband Wesley Brotherton, (Wesley of the Anti-Catholic British Orange Order,) and who is at odds with Lora's family and Irish Heritage, and of all the intrigues of blood rivalries going back for centuries that way to bear on the drama, that brings the reader back again and again to look for the subtle answers too. It is after all, a tremendous work of psychology at play here on many different levels and comprehensions of in depth understanding.

And for Charlie Kingston, the protagonist, that the play of his Irish Ancestry upon his innate and cognitive sensitive feelings, as an intelligent and caring man, and although as not always apparent, is paramount to the understanding of the book, for he is driven back, and taken back, to his homeland, to look for his Grandmother's grave, to his roots and his heritage there, in Ireland, and to find a place for himself among the inhabitants there in a real way, to find that it was his home along, (and with the love of beautiful Lora, with eyes like the Celtic Sea, by his side to be with, and to love, and in the end to be with, that I described previously as a Catharsis, "sweet as sun warmed honey;") of what could be finer? That his return there to Ireland,

at the end of the book is irresistible to put down, as Lora's
companionship is, (and to the reader as well,) in wanting to
climax with it and in not wanting to finish all at the same time.|
Andso the so the book never does "finish" and keeps wanting to
be returned to for more of what I call the sweet savor of its
"flavor."

Charlie also has a nice way with the young people and
especially with Fiona's two children, Kevin, who he gives a job
to, and his younger sister, Brigid, who dances the Irish Dances
and whose feis recital he attends, and who Charlie made a junior
set of golf clubs for, which makes him a very pleasant man for the
reader to want to be around and to linger on with and to favor in
the outcome of the many great battle drama's of the work, and
particularly Kevin and Brigid's father Donal Dennehy who
becomes violently hostile over the idea of Charlie doing things for
his children and especially over his gift of the golf clubs to Brigid,
which he destroys, but whom Charlie wins out over and defeats in
the end, and although not without the price of a lingering paranoid
tension

And of course that are the great golf lessons and stories to
relate to, and along with several major confrontations in added
suspense of dramatic action, that are added spice to the work.
And always it is to appreciate for your wonderful and very
personable descriptive scenes to drool over, that I just think are
the greatest, and for the reader, myself, to imagine of your having
composed, and can always picture you thinking about the work
and making the scenes up as you went along with it. And for
example... p. 168.

Chapter 20

The day after the Killdoon trip Charlie drove to the Bank of
Ireland with the pro-shop receipts. He parked his car and walked
two blocks to the bank, not nearly so imposing a structure as the
cathedral on the opposite corner but, compared to the other
buildings in downtown Castlebantry, a fortress.

Inside, a farmer in overalls preceded Charlie in line, soles of
his grimy calf-length boots making squeaky sounds on the

polished marble floor. An elderly woman currently before the teller's window was negotiating to have the bank rescind a penalty charge against her account. No movement in eh line. Charlie glanced at the second queue: a better choice. About to switch, he recognized the man bring up the end of it – and immediately changed his mind.

Charlie's line began moving and, as it developed, he reached his window just as MacNair was finishing his transaction. He passed behind Charlie, but instead of continuing on he stopped. Charlie could almost feel the man's breath on his neck. Uncomfortable, threatened, he turned fully around.

"You're crowding me, Reggie."

"Am I now?"

And in the end, he does find his Grandmother's gravestone, Margaret Russell, 1891-1963, who is also Emily Pharr's mother "Gretta," that now places Charlie in a family way with his Irish Ancestry to return home to. And of course to the war...

"Did you come home to fight for Ireland?"

Which I feel is the very essence and the heart of the book. Pp. 222-223.

Emily reached out and held his hand [and speaking of her mother, Gretta, said,] "She didn't have a choice but it made history. Some call it a turning point in the war." She squeezed ever so lightly. "I'd better rest a little."
He leaned in and kissed her face. "Goodbye, Emily."

"I hope to see you gain, Charlie,"

"I'll come back."

She smiled and closed her eyes. In the pub, Charlie saw that three men had come and Mary was busy filling pints. On the patron's side of the bar, Charlie waited for her to come over. When she did, he told her that he and Emily had had a very fine talk. "I'm glad," she said. "Another Murphy's?"

"No, thank you," he handed her a L10 note. "This is for my first."

"Charlie, it's on the house."

"Well, for yourself then," he said. "I'm wondering if you can tell me where Gretta's grave might be.

She explained where he'd find it. "It's a bit of a climb. When you get there, her stone sits by itself."

"Thanks." Starting to leave, Charlie had a thought. "Mary, something else," he said. "I feel very close to your grandmother. If I gave you my address, would you drop me a note and tell me how she's doing? I think you know what I'm saying."

"Of course I will, Charlie."

She gave hem a sheet of paper and a pencil and he wrote his name and address. Outside, he walked through the parking area and circled the building; toward the back, he spotted a narrow path winding upward through a rocky field. He followed it, and after several minutes of trudging came t a level, grassy area, site of a small cemetery above the river; glancing about, he saw a marker rather isolated from the others. Charlie walked over to it, stood there looking down – name and dates going in and out of focus. He dropped to his knees. Lettering clearer now bur were his eyes lying? Resorting to touch, Charlie reached out with his fingers:

Margaret Russell, 1891- 1963

The Spirit of Ireland's Fight for Independence

He stayed for several minutes, absorbed in the wonder of it, kneeling at her grave.

Now, what could be finer, Tony. Your book is a great classic that has made a profound impression on my mind, and on me, and I am happy and very proud to promote it to everyone for you, and in being a friend of, and to, the man who wrote it, with pride.

I am also half of the way through with your father's book, The Cardinal, (that I always promised myself one day I would read,) and I am enjoying reading it very much. Your father was a most gifted and naturally talented writer and The Cardinal is superbly crafted along the subdued dramatic psychological lines of inner human elements, feelings and emotions, and conflict of subtle activities, that is a play of egos, more over so than a play of physical prowess and personal triumph, as juxtaposed to your latest work, The American Golfer, is. I am taking my time with The Cardinal, back reading pages at a time to refresh the scenes as I go along and get into the next sessions with it, to linger in thoughts here and there. You never really finish reading great books do you? You just read them because they are a joy and a pleasure to be involved with. Books are the thoughts of other people to get close to. So long for now, Tony. I'm tired.

Gary

**The Abraham Hasbrouck House,
On Huguenot Street in New Paltz, NY,
was built in 1721.**

****

Contest Details

U.S. Representative, District 4
General Election

View all Counties | Compare all Counties

Candidate	Party	Statewide Votes Received
Ander Crenshaw	REP	178,145 (**77.21%**)
Troy D. Stanley	NPA	52,508 (**22.76%**)
Gary L. Koniz	WRI	27 (**0.01%**)
Deborah "Deb" Katz Pueschel	WRI	39 (**0.02%**)
		230,719 total votes cast.

Created with Raphaël Ander Crenshaw
Troy D. Stanley
Others

****

here's to you

6:56 AM
Anthony Robinson
robinsoa@newpaltz.edu
To Gary Koniz

From:**Anthony Robinson** (robinsoa@newpaltz.edu)
Sent: Wed 12/01/10 6:56 AM
To: Gary Koniz (gary.koniz@hotmail.com)

Hi, Gary.

I'm proud of your 27 votes! And thanks for your fine comments on my novel. Your criticism about my choice of certain words or phrases in the book made an impression. No work of art escapes the Gary Koniz critical eye. Right now I'm working on a novel about growing up in the Maverick Art Colony in Woodstock. Working title: BLUESTONE. As a stone, bluestone is virtually indestructible. (Life is short, art is long.) We had a good Thanksgiving. And now the Christmas season is upon us. It's getting cold up here in the Northeast. Take care.

Tony

Wed 12/01/10 17:03 PM

How your letter touched my heart. Have a nice Christmas, Tony. And thank you always for your friendship. Your kind friendship, and of all the friendships I have made, has mattered most to me throughout the many years of my life that I have known you, and in the savor of nostalgia that there is always a fond and lasting memory of you in my heart.

I hope that you are happy with the process of writing your new novel, BLUESTONE. And good luck with its outcome for success with it. I have found, in knowing you, and in being under the spell of your influence, that you have imprinted a fervor in my mind for the craft, that is, The Literary Process. I find myself awakening each day afresh with new insights into the process of my work; to complete the thoughts of yesterday, and to add to them, to create and revise, that my mind is always thinking about, and with an ardor and delight to know that I am producing masterpieces of great value, to reveal themselves to humanity, to become living and vibrant works of literature to endure the ages of time.

I'm in love with the process of writing, that I have found under your excellent instructions, to be most captivating and rewarding to the spirit in consuming enthusiasm for the process of creation, in working with the imagination and ideas, to involve with the imagination of others, as readership, in the process of literary creation and in making the characters and events of a novel come to life. And as we need to be proud of everything in our lives, and where we are not proud to be not afraid to bear up with our faults and transgression to the world, and I say, any longer not to repress them, as repressions create their own hells to endure and which we need to be free of by making a clean breast of things, and which makes us proud of that, facing-up, to become men again at last of commanding bearing in the end. There is something to the process of confession that frees us and that is good for the soul.

That other matter of affairs with Jenny, that we never talked about much, as it turned out, however served to keep you in my life, and which I managed to do quite well anyway on my own. I am very happily married now to Kathleen, who is just the right kind of gal for me, and to whom that I am very much fallen deeply in love with and totally committed to in our lasting and eternal relationship, and for her well-being and happiness in maturity, as meaningful marriage relationships are in the eyes of God and need to be fulfilled and nurtured in that way of caring for each other, that would never want to cause your loved one who you care about any hurt in the heart, in the meaning of how fate has played out for both of us.

I hope that my thoughts have healed you. I know you are running out of time psychologically getting old; as we all are growing old eventually unto death to await. But if you refrain from bad habits, remain physically active, eat healthy, and get plenty of rest, napping throughout the days in contentment and well deserved rest, and always have a "work-in-progress" to enthuse you at all times and stimulate your will and desire to live on, I think that you may find that you have more time on the life you have than you think. There's still plenty of great work yet to squeeze out of you to the last syllable of your recorded time.

Frozen Time is the great American Novel. Life Becoming Art as Fictionalized Characters set to the foils of real life people enact the historical drama of what needs to be said about what happened here in the United States of America in the time period of the '70s and '80s, that we survived to live through as the plot thickens yet to be resolved, but at least to have been made aware of what the plot is, or, what the "plots" are, to be dealt with and resolved.

In Fellowship,
Gary

From: robinsoa@newpaltz.edu
To: gary.koniz@hotmail.com
Subject: Frozen Time
Date: Sun, 19 Jun 2011 14:38:15 -0400

Gary,

Thanks for sending me the new, handsomely put together, *Frozen Time.* The new font and print size are excellent. There are many variations of what a novel is, of what constitutes one. Your work, that you call a novel, is proof of that. If it were a little closer to what, generally speaking, a novel is, looks like, or should be, I would happily comment. But *Frozen Time* is a novel so unlike any novel I have ever seen or read that I am at a loss for words. I do thank you for the references in your pages to my work as a writer. I'm sorry that I can't say more. Your novel eludes me. Maybe I am not there yet to fully grasp what you have put together. You have left me plodding along in the middle of the road while you are traveling roads not yet explored. That is a possibility. Good luck, and carry on.

Tony

The Wallkill River flows peacefully north through New Paltz and meets the Rondout Creek which flows into the Hudson River at Kingston, NY. The foliage along the river provides a beautiful and restful setting to those who savor its ways. The Indians have a Legend that those who sleep by the river will always return.

On Apr 8, 2011, at 10:17 AM,
gary.koniz@hotmail.com wrote:

Hey Henry,

I was looking for a recent photograph of you online to put into the book your father and I have been working on together called Frozen Time but did not come across any. If you can email a photo of yourself and family to me I would treasure it always. I have not seen you since that time on Main Street when I saw you last many years ago, I think in 1989, and have been feeling the need to reconnect with you. I have a photo of Jenny from her worksite web, which I put in the book and plenty of Big T from his bios, but I really want one, or more, of you too for nostalgia.

We had quite a time together, you and I, of our adventures back then, didn't we? And I am trying to get it all down into this storybook about us for history. Your father tells me that you have a lovely wife and two wonderful children. I'm in the golf business myself too, working in the maintenance department, God's little paradise on earth to me, good healthy physical work out in the days and the elements. Just my cup of tea. Maybe I could write a maintenance article for your magazine. Put things in perspective about what goes into making a golf course playable, to be entitled, The Untold Story.

I'll be 65 in a few weeks, on May 1st, can you believe it. But in my mind, I am always 31, Frozen there that way in Time. You should be around a young 13-47. Also, let me know when T's birthday is. I want to surprise him with a hardcover copy to the completed work. Thanks.

Love, Gary

From: hrobinson@golfweek.com
Subject: Hey Gary, it's Henry!
Date: Fri, 8 Apr 2011 10:32:39 -0400
To: gary.koniz@hotmail.com

Hey Gary,

What a great surprise! I want to take the time to write properly but am running out the door so I'll have to respond with more detail later. Tony just turned 80 on March 10th. I'm now 48! Actually I got divorced 18 months ago after 15 years but the good news is my ex and I get along wonderfully, live two blocks from one another and my two kids, Sylvie (13) and Jack (10) are really smart, beautiful and well-adjusted. Here are a couple of pics.

Big Hug,

Handsome Henry As He Looks Today At 48

Henry with his two children Sylvie and Jack

Dear Henry:

Your email and with the fine pictures of yourself and with Sylvie
and Jack, both beautiful children, brought a powerful emotion of a
tear to my eye. How wonderful to hear from you and to see that
you have developed into such a handsome and rugged man of
charismatic character. Write me more about yourself and what
you are doing when you have the time. I'll put it all into the
ending of the book, and which is in your dad's theme of things, to
bring all the characters of a great romance novel back at the end
of time to see how they each turned out and what they are
thinking. It's a book of thoughts and the lives we have lead and

are leading. It'll be a wonderful ending with your notations and pictures for the ages. You can view all of my books that I have written at my website, http://www.lulu.com/greenskeeper6. Each is equipped with a free download. The earlier edition of Frozen Time that I send your dad, quite accidentally, for his birthday is there in pdf form to look at. It was so great to hear from you, Henry. What a marvelous thing. I will try to copy your photos for the book if they will copy on to Word, so far no luck. If not I'll let you know and we can try a different way. They're great photos. I don't seem to have any trouble at all off the Internet.

Love, Gary

Sun 17 April, 2011 9:43 a.m.

Dearest Henry:

I am really so happy that you sent me the photos of yourself and your two lovely children, Sylvie and Jack, that you did, who somehow I feel a strong bond of kinship with, and as with yourself also, and that I am very fond to often gaze upon.

I am sorry that you and your wife broke up, but relieved that you have remained close friends and only live a short distance away from one another. And on that note to add that I have often found that any relationship can be repaired, as worked on, whether it be between a man and his wife, or between male friends in bonding, or even with large groups of people that way as between nations and peoples of the earth, where there is a caring regard in sensitivity for one another and a willingness to make concessions and compromises and to adjust one's attitude and thinking towards the other party, mutually expressed, and truly that such caring regard and willingness to adapt is the true meaning of a lasting and genuinely rewarding relationship in fulfillment of our emotional needs.

Of course such things as infidelity, drug addiction, and alcoholism, are major obstacles to any marriage on either side and nigh on irreconcilable to bear and to endure and which need corrections to occur to such matters before any true healing and taking back can take place. And there are other issues too, like a person's attitude and behavior towards their spouse, which can be modified to suit the needs of the offended partner, by telling the offending partner what it is that is the matter and what needs to occur to discontinue with the offending behavior. And just by saying in example, "I don't like it when you yell at me for forgetting to take the garbage out dear. It makes my blood boil and I don't like you very much for it. Just remind me in a pleasant way and I'll feel better." And so, I hope that things can work out between you two. Marriages emotionally involve more than the two people who get married in their expectations, of the two sides of the family in relations, and the children. And it's hard to see your spouse with another man, or vice versa, marriages in that regard constitute direct ownership in the minds of the beloved spouses. Dearly beloved ... that is a permanent mind fix forever which neither of you can ever get out of your head, no matter what.

I always do regret the hurt look and the disappointment you felt at Hershey Amusement Park that hot and muggy late July night when you and I arrived, with Sophie in tow, and found that we couldn't leave Sophie all alone and locked up in the sweltering heat of the car. Maybe I should have let you go on in alone to enjoy the rides you were looking forward to, and waited for you to return later on when it got cooler and maybe we could have left Sophie then to go back into the Park. It was so hot Hank. We were sweating just walking across the parking lot, and we could hear Sophie barking and barking all that distance away as we arrived at the Admissions Gate.

We did however get to go the Amusement Park in Ocean City, MD on the return side of the adventure trip. It was a dark and cool night then to be able to leave Sophie in the car for a while, and we had a good time. But Hershey Park has always the memory of regret for me with poor Sophie left barking her poor head off in the hot car.

And in closing to say that I have given a lot of thought to you, and to your wife and children, for your happiness, each and every

one, to share with you about life and relationships that is all about
Validation; to validate the lives of those who we love around us.
"I see you. I hear you. I am listening to you. I understand what
you are saying. I am interested in the things that matter to you. I
care about you and for the happiness and well-being of your life,
and importantly that I respect your individuality and your right to
be different and to have diverging ideas, and to spend good
quality time going things together." That speaks for the idea of
Epiphany, (which translates as a striking understanding of
something,) in realization of what is right in your heart. You will
always do what is right when you realize it and Self-Actualize.

Write and tell me more about your life and what is going on.

Love,
Gary

From: Henry@henryrobinson.com
Subject: Re: Hey Gary, it's Henry!
Date: Tue, 31 May 2011 17:08:56 -0400
To: gary.koniz@hotmail.com

Hi Gary,

I have been meaning to write, but that sounds like a lame excuse.
Fact is I'm battling some issues right now like a foreclosure,
ruined credit and life saving gone in a couple of terrible real estate
investments. And then I've gone through this major spiritual shift
post divorce and it would take pages and pages to explain. I'd like
to do that because frankly I think you'd understand. I hope to
write more later.

Recently I have had this overwhelming desire to set off next
spring and hike the entire 2,150 mile Appalachian Trail. Just drop
out of life for a while. But the system keeps us on the treadmill
so we can afford things like health care and educations for our
children. I am very leery of corporate America and this huge
illusion that's been created to keep us all on the treadmill

questioning as little as possible. I'm beginning to wake up and it scares people that think I'm just this little enthusiastic sales executive. It scares my father. He wants me so badly to remain in a coma, question nothing and just keep plugging away like a good American.

I know this all sounds strange. I've gotta get to my son's baseball game. If I don't write, please do not take personally. My slow response is 100% about me, not you, old friend.

All the best,
Henry

Wed, 01 June 2011 19:20

All the best to you too as well, Hank,

What you are going through, feeling like "cutting loose," I went through the same thing, and with the same questions about the rat race and the terms of survival imposed to it. But I was much younger then, at the age of 30, than you are now. And even then I almost nearly didn't recover from my impetuous decision. If you break the spell of the treadmill, you may not recover, attached as we each and all are to the psychological power of re-enforcement of the Super-Ego to what that we each have to conform to, or perish. Which if you violate leaves you with the feeling that you are no good "in the eyes of society;" and which is what I think your dad is afraid of in trying to warn you about, "to keep up the pace." To what we can't let down or else we'll die. However, why don't you plan for a good long sabbatical break, and hike the trail before you die. Maybe you could opt for a "change of jobs," or a "different location" for your work environment, and take a few intelligent months off then to think about life and do something "out of the ordinary." Heck, I might even join you myself, we could hike the trail together start to finish next summer, but I'm locked in too to my own routine myself. Routine is god. At least you get to sleep on clean sheets in the night and don't have to worry about surviving. Tell me what this "divorce" is all about. Can you? I'd like to understand.

Sorry I became pontificating with you the last few times I have written. It's just my nature to try and give people advise these days trying to vindicate my existence. I am sorry, and for the other business of personal inquiries. I was just concerned for your happiness in life. You are and always will be a part of my world and loved one. I am reading your Grandfather's diary, as to say, the thoughts of his books. I am reading the one right now called Fantastic Interim about the time between the two great wars and have almost finished it.

Your Grandfather was quite the scholar and I am amazed to learn about him that I came to many of same conclusions as he did independent of reading him to learn. And so I think that he was touched by God, The Creator, too in his way, to have identical thoughts as myself. I just ordered from Abe Books your Grandfather's book entitled "Water Of Life," which I am looking forward to reading when I finish with Fantastic Interim. I have already read "The Great Snow" and "The Cardinal" as I told you, and it was a really great book, "The Cardinal," that I liked being involved with in the day-to-day reading of it. I am also appealing to the SUNY English Department to create a Graduate Course especially devoted to your father's and your Grandfather's great works as a part of our American Literary Heritage, entitled, The Robinson School.

The people I have spoken with already about developing the project of having course there at SUNY New Paltz devoted to your father and grandfather, (and although not in any position to make decisions,) seem to think that it is a wonderful idea. The important people on that decision are all out on summer leave right now except The Dean of Graduate Studies, Daniel Kempton, who I left a voice message to and so perhaps he will get back to me on that.

I am still enchanted with idea of taking-off with you next
summer, just the two of us and a rifle along for bears, up through
the Tennessee Country along the Appalachian Trail. It's always
been a dream fantasy of mine as well to do that. We could spend
a couple of weeks out in the wild and maybe become Hobo's for a
while who knows, if we get to like it, darting in and out of
civilization to get supplies and then to loose ourselves out on the
Trail again to wherever and whatever fate it will lead us. I can
picture us now. But that's a separate reality from what we have to
live, isn't it? And I don't say in a bad way, of what we have to
live with in responsibility and to the extent that there are loved
ones, and whom we love as well, who are dependent to our
presence to care for and about. The only thing that matters to a
man is whether he is happy with the way he is living his life at the
end of each day. So long for now.

Love,
Gary

October 2, 2011

Dear Heart Tony,

   In review of certain dialogue that went on between us for the
book. I would like to include some more insight from the inside
of yourself if that's all right with you. How would you feel about
elaborating somewhat about the birth and development of your
first novel, "A Departure From The Rules;" as to how the idea for
the book came about, what motivated and prompted you to write
it, what thought process formed the basis of its characterization
and dramatic/philosophical content, and what responses of
approval did you hope to gain in your readers? I would also like
to know if there is a collection of your Short Stories available to
read? Finnegan my Finnegan comes to mind, about your beloved
dog, who got run over one day.
   Hope all is well there with you. I'm just hashing out some of
the goop from the subterranean sub-beneath-way of my life to

reveal, of what it is like to be born a man here on the planet in our time. Hope you're not offended by my approach. Pardon my French. It's good to get things out of yourself I feel, that otherwise would forever remain all bottled-up and never be revealed. Such revelation liberates the spirit. I'm finding that you can get away with almost anything as long as you're open enough and brave enough and strong enough with everyone about what it is. Isn't it true? The doom of any venture lies in the attempt to bury it in the earth and cover it over with the shame of self-flagellation for having done it. It pays to be brave that way, up to a point. Atonement plays its part in it too in the sorting out of right from wrong, if we injure anyone, or anything, to say we are sorry. I am sorry, Tony, if I ever injured you in any way. I didn't mean too. I was just being a fellow miner of the ore. Maybe you need time to yourself.

Gary

From: robinsoa@newpaltz.edu
To: gary.koniz@hotmail.com
Subject: 'sup
Date: Tue, 11 Oct 2011 12:14:25 -0400

Hey, Gary—how are you? Your last note was from the heart. I'm planning on bringing out a collection of short stories one day; it's something I really want to do. I can't talk about A Departure From the Rules at any length right now. A novel of the mid-70's, called The Floodplain, will be coming out in December under the aegis of Codhill Press. Interesting period historically and personally. Best, Tony

November 1, 2011

Dear Tony:

I was thinking of you quite frequently in the early mid-morning hours off and on today as I went about my work on the golf course, and especially in thinking of you that I wanted to thank you for giving me, and for creating in me, the absolute joy of writing. I just love it, to sit and compose from the imagination of the mind's eye for the reader the picture and the sensation of a scene and the setting of its dialogue and dramatic action. What starts out, to me, as a sketch of an idea and continues to build under the scrutiny of re-reading, re-writing. And nothing that way in the review of a work ever stays the same.

Sometimes in the middle of the night, the muse will pass a thought on to include, and to what that I am busy the next day inserting it in its proper place; the way somebody is dressed, what they look like, what the day it like, how the clouds are moving, and what the inner thoughts of the characters are to be discussed with the reader. It's all an endless joy.

And to what else that I was thinking, that my bond with you will always be there for you, that is to the meaning that I have "drafted" you to my heart in conscript of your eternal company. You're not a two-dimension being to me, Tony. I see deeply into you and hold in the esteem of the highest regard and feel the pathos of your being. I know you are a private person and need your reserved space of mind, and truly I understand your periods of brooding detachment. I'm that way too. Work, our work of writing, and out of sheer necessity it seems works best when we can feel alone. The sharing of it with anyone comes at the end, when we are thoroughly through.

I was wondering if perhaps you might copy and mail me the pages of the two of your short stories mentioned here, My Finnegan, and A String of Pearls, if you still have them in their original publications. I would love to read them, and also to look forward to the publication of your new work The Floodplain, which you mentioned about to me earlier on in the year, also named The Wayward River.

I was also thinking about your trap lines this morning.

When I was quite young, I would say, around six or seven, my family lived in an apartment building called Pleasant Manner

Apartments that was an abandoned orphanage reconverted into apartments about two miles out of town in the (what was once then,) a country setting surrounded by fields and deep and seemingly endless woods to wander out in and explore.

I was always in the woods with my inseparable companion Billy who lived in what was called, The Carriage House, that was set off a ways from the three separate apartments buildings, and was two years older than me.

Billy had an older brother Johnny who was three years older than him, and Johnny, who then at the age of twelve or thirteen, had a trap line, with big ugly steel traps that he was very proud of to show off, which Billy and I would go out with him to set at the entrance to the muskrat dens along the stream bank.

One day out playing out alone in the woods as I often did when no one else was around, I came upon a muskrat trapped hopelessly in one of the steel traps that Johnny had set down by the stream, and it was so sad to watch the poor creature suffering, gnawing at its trapped right front paw trying to free himself, and looking up at me, with pleading red eyes, or at least it seemed to me to be pleading, to help it. The image of what tortured animal that still haunts me to this day.

I ran back to the Carriage House as fast as I could to tell Johnny. It was approaching dusk as I recall, in the early fall of the year and still warm out. I was sweating and out of breath and blurted out to him.
"Johnny, Johnny, come quick, there is an animal in one of your traps and it's gnawing its foot off."

Johnny, and I will never forget, picked up his animal sack and stubby baseball bat and we went to inspect the trap together. There the tortured animal still was as I had left it. And I will never forget Johnny bashing it over the head. Which didn't kill it outright. It kept looking at me, pleading with its eyes, in a sense of betrayal, asking, "Why are you doing this to me?"

And I knew then that I couldn't go on with it, the idea of being a trapper. In thinking of you, thank you for writing, Tony. Gary

For the most part, Tony's four years at Andover weren't happy ones. The school was too big, too removed from the life he had known, and he felt lost from the start. He kept his unhappiness to himself and began to write. A story about his beagle killed by a car, "My Finnegan," appeared in *Hounds and Hunting* in 1949. It was his first published work.

Henry was in my dream last night. When I saw him at first he had his face covered over with a piece of cardboard, but I knew it was him all along, then he revealed himself and I recognized him. It's my adopted blood brother Henry, I thought. He looked at me long and hard and direct for the longest time with an intensity and that was all there was. Strange. I hope things have improved some for him since the last time he wrote. He was all forlorn. I told him that I would like to have some pictures of himself and Sylvie and Jack, and maybe your estranged wife, and a photo of your mother to put into my book. I couldn't copy the ones he sent me before, or himself and Sylvie and Jack to my Word Program. I need to put them on to Word in order for them to go in the book. I still have them on my computer and look at them from time to time. Cherish the days. We'll always be blood brothers, he and I. I like for him to scramble up top here with me for a while and we will look at life together, as philosophers, like you and I do. What ever happened to your Father in the bathtub, Tony, for him to have tragically scalded himself to death? How in the world could such a thing to have happened to him?

Gary

In And Out ... In And Out
Slowly In And Out
Is How The Breath Goes
Tongue Lies Flat
The Mind Falls Silent
To A Certain Intent
Indwelling Upon The Creator
To The Foreground Of Thought
This Is How We Proceed Into The Time Ahead

Haiku by Jenny

The Wind In The Trees
Made A Lovely Signing Sound
When You Held Me Near

Lovely Jenny As She Appears Today In 2011

Haiku by Gary

Your Beautiful Love
Will Never Come To An End
In My Thoughts Of You

Lake Minnewaska Mountain Houses

I was heartfelt that Jenny was in good spirits at last as I could tell from the fine expressions of happiness in her face when we arrived at the Campgrounds of Minnewaska Park that morning in Tony's light blue 1975 Ford Station Wagon Compact with my dog Sophie in the backseat eagerly awaiting the arrival and pent up to the time when she could get out of the car to go exploring. Sophie was slobbering all over the back seat and franticly pacing from side to side on our arrival with eager excitement over the impending event of the day's outing activity. I tried to reassure her by reaching into the backseat with my left arm, taking hold of her by the collar and stroking her back and head and soothing her with my voice in a gentle tone.

"We are almost there, Sophie. Just be patient."

But there was no soothing her, her mind was set and impatient to be released to go for a good run and the prospects of the day of adventures ahead were making her drool all over the back seat with excitement. Sophie loved being there in the mountain.

Jenny now seemed to be more outward-looking and less internalized than before, both from the point of relief from the melancholy of a dejected depression that had beset her and was crippling her emotionally of late, and from her own relief personally felt of her having successfully negotiated 'the drive' out alone with a passenger without her father by her side to guide and reassure her that had left her quite preoccupied and nervous at first start.

She had tried hard and unsuccessfully to hide her nervousness, but I could tell she was, about driving her father's car out alone with me in the car on the big mountain road of Route 44/55. Route 44/55 over the mountain that connected the village of New Paltz on the East to the other side of the mountain to the cities of

Ellenville, Woodstock, and Kingston, NY and all points West of the Catskill Mountain region.

It was a treacherous road for anybody and the scene of many accidents by any standards that even the experienced driver had to be careful with its windy curves especially around Hair Pin Turn half way up at the base of the mountain as the road cut North at a diagonal across and up the base of the mountain and then that turned sharply South and up again at a 90 degree turn, and hence the acquired nickname, 'Hairpin,' before making a 45 degree final turn and up the steep grade to the cliffs called The Gunks by the area's climbers. From there the Highway then ran through Smugglers Notch, that was a naturally formed notch in the cliff line with boulders on either side, and the only accessible crossing point, East to West for many miles around, and that was in olden days common meeting point for smugglers, and 'waylay point,' for bandits to attack unwary travelers.

Mohonk Carriage Road at Smuggles Notch in the Shawangunks

Past Smugglers Notch the Highway went under the green iron footbridge of the Mohonk Carriage Road that Albert and Alfred Smiley, the original owners of the land, had constructed along with the Hotel/Resort in the late part of the past century. The carriage road ran in a loop around the cliffs on either side of the Mountaintop and on to the Lake Mohonk Hotel some five miles away. The treacherous route 44/55 went up and down a series of steep windy hills along the mountaintop from there and through the heavily forested lands on either side of the Shawangunks on to the Campgrounds of Minnewaka Park that was located about a mile and a half further on. That Jenny was relieved to now be at.

I did not play the roll of her father to Jenny about that day about her driving, but instead kept a steady and rather anxious eye on the road to myself, and with Sophie in the back seat without a seatbelt, and made small talk reassuring conversation with Jenny about the lovely scenery as we passed the time on the twenty minute or so scenic drive out toward the picturesque and majestic Shawangunk Mountains from Tony's house to the Campgrounds. I had just recently acquired a part-time Ranger's position there and worked on the Weekends and one day that was designated to be on Wednesday for now, during the week.

Both of Jenny's moods had dispelled on arrival with a huge sigh of relief from her, as I detected, that she seemed relieved and elated to be at the end of what was to her a challenging drive as she pulled the station wagon confidently and with an air of self-determination and self-assurance onto the well worn dirt and gravel driveway of the Camping Area, with the sound of the gravel crunching under the tires as we went, and eased the car around toward the now abandoned Ski Lodge and Restaurant that now served as the Campground's Headquarters. The facility had two high steep sloping peaked roofs with the brightly painted red and green sign Ski Minne affixed to the front of it and which faced the Highway 44/55 that we had just pulled in from and which Jenny had just negotiated.

"Well, I made it," Jenny had said with a great sigh of relief as she eased the Station Wagon to a stop in front of the Lodge.

"Good job, Jenny. I am very proud of you," I said.

Jenny had indeed done a good job of driving us and with operation the car smoothly with my dog Sophie sitting up in the back seat with her head sticking out of the partially opened passenger side rear window enjoying the wind as dogs do. Sophie sniffed at the mountain air in anticipation as the station wagon came to a complete stopped.

Ranger Whitey who had been sitting at a table by the window reading in a magazine, looked sideways at us, put the magazine down and came out to greet us.

Out of the blue at breakfast that morning while sitting at the kitchen table with myself and Tony, Jenny had pleaded with her father, (who we affectionately called 'Big T' as was Tony's endearing nickname,) if she and I could use the car that day and hoping that she would get to drive alone with a passenger in the car for the first time.

"Big T, Can Gary and I take the car out today to go up on the mountain and hike around a bit and maybe go for a swim in the stream? It's a lovely summer day and it would give me an opportunity to practice my driving. I need to take the test soon. Golly, am I embarrassed not have my driver's license yet. Everyone else I know has there's. Would it be o.k.?"

To what question that Tony (Big T,) who was a handsome charismatic man in his mid-forties, tensed his jowls as he always did, making a knot on both sides of his mandible, whenever he was confronted with a serious question and pondered in his fatherly way of drawing out the inevitable concession to his daughter not to appear too easy, replied, and being as how as Jenny had gotten her State of New York Learners Permit on her sixteen birthday over six months ago and needed the practice to take her Drivers Test.

"I don't see why not, Jenny" Tony had said. "It sounds like a great idea to me. You can handle the car all right by now, as I taught you well and you've certainly had plenty of practice lessons in the University Parking Lot and you've been out on the back roads with me and through town enough times. And ... he drew the words out ... provided Gary doesn't mind, and Gary doesn't have other things to do, and <u>he</u> gets his work done, emphasizing the words of my name, and he. And ... you have some chores to do before you can go out today as well. There's a load of laundry that needs to be done, and some ironing, and the whole downstairs needs to be vacuumed," he paused, "but that can wait until later." Tony here had softened the tone of his instructions to an appeal. "But there's no hurry for that. You know what to do, Jenny. I've got an American Lit Class this after noon in Summer Session, but not 'til three in the afternoon, and I can walk. A nice walk through the Village and up to Campus today would be pleasant. My it is a lovely day."

To what response that Jenny, dressed in her night clothes of pajamas and a bathrobe in stocking feet with pink open toed slippers on, sitting to my left and in the chair that faced the window looking out on the side yard and the garden, poked me under the table with her stocking footed big toe and grinned at me, and to Big T with glee. Jenny was certainly the All American Girl, beautiful in her sleepy eyed just waking up look, and had a million dollar smile that bestowed a sense of ease in me that beckoned warmth and friendship and an all too eager willingness to be involved with her in her conspiracy of the hour.

Big T, sitting opposite me in the head of the house hold chair that faced the back of the house and the darkly stained maple antique china cabinet where he always sat, and absentmindedly in the way that scholars and writers have of chewing on their food with his mind thinking somewhere else in his head, didn't seem to notice the toe poke. But such things were hard to tell with Tony, as to whether or not that he noticed the intrigues of what was going on around him, or just pretended not to out of a playful detachment in consideration for the goings-on of others.

I sat in Mary's empty chair, which I had begun to occupy in the real sense.

Mary had been Tony's wife, and Jenny's and Henry's mother, who had committed suicide, (or so it seemed,) with Tony's shotgun in the upstairs of the house the year before in the Winter of 1976, and chair and role it fulfilled in the household had sat empty for over a year until I arrived, and which I was filling now, both the chair and the emotional presence of the roll.

Henry, Tony's second and youngest child, who always sat in the chair to my right and facing the kitchen area, was 'sleeping-in' that morning as young adolescent boys of the tender age of fourteen were prone to do on summer mornings, and wasn't at the table.

Both Jenny and Henry had formed a blood bond of relationship with me, and especially Henry who needed a companion to play catch ball with and to practice golf in the afternoons out in the yard. That was my delight to, to have Henry to play with.

It was just seven-thirty a.m. on Tuesday that day of the third week in June of 1977. I had been with the Robinson family then at that time for over a month now working on a yard renovation project and as a Tony's apprentice, who had been and still was my Creative Writing teacher at the University of SUNY New Paltz, and to who I had become his protégé and was being Home-Schooled by him in the family craft of Novel Writing, and as he had been the protégé to his own father, the renowned Henry Morton Robinson, who too had committed suicide, (or so it seemed,) by scalding himself to death in the bathtub of his house on Christmas Eve in the year 1960, and who died in agony nine days later in the same year that the writer and novelist Earnest Hemmingway had killed himself with a shotgun.

After finishing our Spartan breakfast, as Big T liked to refer to call it, of one soft boiled two minute egg each, for me and Tony, which were cracked with a butter knife and the gooey insides scooped out with a spoon, over polite intellectual conversation, with buttered toast and jam, and black coffee, with Jenny having a glass of orange juice and a hot bowl of oatmeal cereal instead, which Tony, who was the family cook, made for her and had set the bowl down lovingly before her to enjoy; and after my helping Jenny with the dishes, as was always my place to help with the clean-up after the family meals, it was eight o'clock, and I went outside with Sophie and Tony's dog Waldo hard on my heals to get outside in hurry past me through the screen door to see how my friend Lloyd was coming along.

Tony lived in a beautiful slate gray painted three story house, with a raised basement apartment, on historic Huguenot Street in the Village of New Paltz, NY and the sky was clear blue with a faint paleness on the horizon in the early hour as I stepped outside. Big puffy clouds were drifting up from the Southeast overhead, and the air was still nice and cool to the skin of my arms dressed as I was in my dungarees and with a short sleeve green colored T-shirt that showed the clean definition of my muscular arms. It was a magnificent morning, pleasantly still and quiet with the Sun just up and not nearly over the tops of the trees yet, but almost. I took in a deep breath of the air and let it out slowly.

Lloyd Barzell was already up and was out in the back yard surveying the property of what work had to be done that day. He had already had had his morning breakfast, as I had heard him moving around from the kitchen overhead in his quarters in the basement apartment of Tony's home, where Tony had given Lloyd the use of the kitchen with its refrigerator, stove, and sink, and its bathroom with a toilet and a shower, for his own use, but not to sleep there.

Both Lloyd and I slept up in the Garret with Lloyd having his own space on a cot beneath the open south window in the two-room loft that Tony had given us to sleep in which we had to climb up to get to on a very steep nearly vertical wooden stairs, and which we often had to help Sophie up, pushing on her behind, to get up and then to ease her down on, but who was also a good climber up and down on her own if she had to go outside during the night.

The steep stairs led overhead of the two story combination garage and tool house, with the one car garage side on the left side, where Lloyd slept over, and with the tool shed part on the right and where I slept on that side facing the house. Tony called it his Writer's Garret, which he was proud to display and that was fashioned after Earnest Hemmingway's Garrett at his home in Key West, FL.

It was provide to me tenderly, with the words by Tony,

"Every writer needs to have a Garret to live and work in at least once in their life to inspire him."

And indeed it did inspire me to write, and which I have never forgotten and can picture and feel the sense of, with its musty damp and clammy open air feeling coming in from the open window space across from the desk, and with a roughness about it that enjoy to savor the memory of to this day.

It was a place of propitiation to the writing muse. It had a cot and a writing table under the open window that faced the back of the house and overlooked the huge wooden deck that Tony had had built on to the back of the house, and with a good view of the soon to be renovated back yard, and the outdoor shower which Tony had put in, in the Bohemian spirit of the new age Au Natural, which everyone liked to use, at all hours of the day and evenings, family and occasional guests alike, and myself too, throughout the long hot summer, with its pleasure to be naked and showering out in the open air, with its sensations of temperature completely exposed in the out of doors.

On the writing table sat Tony's old portable Remington Typewriter with a sheet of paper rolled in the barrel with the typed heading started of the beginning of a Romantic Novel I had begun to write under Tony's kind patronage, and which I had entitled and with the log-line typed underneath:

"THE SUMMER OF '77"

"Tony asks Gary to come and live with him at his home to work for the summer and discovers that he has fallen in love with Jenny that involves him in family intrigues."

Things to do: practice elocution, learn new words, read more novels, work on spelling and grammar, ...

There was what was left of a ream of paper, down to a third of it, a spiral notebook for sketching in and some pens and pencils in the top drawer of a table desk. Some hooks for hanging clothes with an old chest of drawers to put clothes in were in the corner of the partition off ten by twelve room with its open doorway with no door. This partition demarcated the other side of the space that was above the garage. To the other side overhead of the garage room was where Lloyd had staked his claim to survival for the summer.

Both rooms were lit with kerosene lamps, as a romantic gesture on Tony's part, one for my side and one for Lloyd's. Mine was on the tabletop beside the typewriter, and Lloyd's was on a table in the middle of the room near his cot in the sparsely provided space. The can for which was kept downstairs in the tool room. Lloyd's clothes were kept in a zippered duffle bag, which as far as we knew was all that Lloyd possessed in the world. Lloyd had had a troubled family life somewhere that had left him on the street, or that he had left to take to the street, to fend for himself. Tony had preferred that as he had given Lloyd use the downstairs basement apartment, that had a kitchen and a refrigerator, and a stove to cook on, to eat and to shower, that he not have use of the actual family household, or the outdoor shower, and for him to use Laundromat in town to wash his own clothes. Which Lloyd had no problem with doing, grateful enough as he was for the job and a place to live for a while and not to be a homeless waif of the streets where I had found him, or rather as that he had attached himself to me with his fawning sycophant behavior, that was not all that unpleasant, in playing up to me for the sake of having someone to befriend him, which I did.

Lloyd, and who preferred to be called Benjamin, which myself and no else ever did call him by, preferring the name Lloyd over the one he had adopted for himself, was a friend of mine from the street who quite frankly had attached himself to me. I had recommended to Tony to hire him to help me with the yard work for the summer, after Tony had hired me, and who seemed to value encouragement from me and from Tony in a fatherly way. He was always eager to display the ideas he had come up with for our approval for making the needed improvement to the property. We liked to encourage him as well in this endeavor to make him feel important and successful as he was a genuine and honest

person who was deserving in his sincerity, and as was our way as
sensitive writers of practicing psychology.

There was always plenty of work to do to keep us both busy.
In addition to its weekly and normal maintenance work of
mowing the yard and weeding and tending to the flower beds, and
taking care of the garden, the entire back half acre of the property
that after a steep incline of eight feet or so slope gently down to
the shore line of the swamp that was an ancient Ox Bow of the
wayward Wallkill River that often flooded and was always cutting
new routes for it to take along its meandering course. It was this
dense jungle of overgrown brush that was the main work of the
project that Tony wanted cleared and made level for a back lawn
and recreational use. It was a masterful plan.

I always wanted to let Lloyd have his way about how he saw
things needing to be done, and did not to seek to override any of
his judgment calls in undermine of his overall self-confidence as a
savvy supervisor in his own right, to accomplish the work, as I
knew that Lloyd needed me to have confidence and faith in his
ability to manage a job, that I never wanted to let him down and
to wound him over by contradicting or overriding the good
intentions of his decisions. If at times I did need to make
recommendation to him, I would use the tone in the name, Tony,
who wants it done this way, instead of I want you do to it this
way. That way my ego wasn't involved and deferred even though
I had hired Lloyd and it was my job in responsibility to oversee
his work. Which as far as that went it didn't matter much to me,
to be the boss of anybody at this point in time in my life. Our
friendship and primary relationship was what mattered, the bond
between Lloyd, and myself and as it was that way with Tony, and
with Jenny and Henry. It was always the sensitivity of the heart
and the relationship between people that mattered most and not
the idea of dominance of being a boss over anyone about.

Lloyd was a rugged stocky fellow in his twenties, not very tall,
around five-five, with a balding head. He was rather good
looking to look at, not really pretty-boy handsome as Tony was,
but who pleasant to look at, and who looked like Judas Iscariot
might look if he were alive, and who perhaps did have some

Neanderthal genes in him. He was strong of muscle, and with a peasant's disposition eager for the physical-work side of life and work by the sweat of his brow to accomplish of the tasks at hand, and then to reflect back on with pride, as he was always proud of his work to display to us at the end of the days. Which to let on, was my particular bent in life to do as well, of the rugged hands on physical work, and perhaps to be living-out the reincarnation of my peasant ancestry on the farmlands of the South on my mother's side and of my Polish Ancestry on my father's side, to enjoy the hands-on physical-work side of life, out in the clean fresh air and to engaged with the earth in realm time with the course of the Sun overhead and the stars at night, and in love with the atmosphere, and elements of the seasons each day. Which to me was all that there needed to be in life, to bespeak of the physical and primary relationship between God and Man, to work by the sweat of one's brow, as Lloyd and I liked to do.

After I had talked with him for a bit, Lloyd then went off doing what he wanted to do clearing the brush he had pointed out to me that he wanted to clear and digging out the roots making the ground ready for raking and leveling-off. The work was going well that way. Section by section of the back property was being transformed into a manageable leveled off back yard. And which was already a marked and noticeable improvement over its original condition after over a month of hard work, the two of us, Lloyd and myself, working for three hours a day during the work week with the weekends to ourselves, as Tony had contracted with us for the summer for, in exchange for our room and board, and five dollars a week, as a fair exchange of value for our labor.

I went out to garden, which was a good size plot of ground that I had cut out of the side lawn by hand myself, located on the south side of Tony's property directly opposite the window that Jenny looked out on the world by from her seat at the kitchen table.

I looked up at the window then that day and began to think of Jenny as the person she was from the inside of her head looking out at the world as a young girl with thoughts about herself and about the world she inhabits, to be made real with the creative imagination of those around her who loved and cherished her

abiding existence, with a need to be loved and admired, and to be
successful with the endeavors of life that she undertook. She was
a girl who had loved her mother, whose reverenced name in the
household among its solemn members was, Mary Robinson, and
who was devoted to her father, and who in the wake of her
beloved mother's tragic suicide death the year before, had taken
over many of the chores and the household duties that her mother
had fulfilled, and in all with the deep aspiration of making her
father proud of her, as to what that Jenny felt and thought about,
as I sense of her, and who became to me then of a deeper meaning
of her thoughts and feelings and emotions and volitions that I
could ever have imagined at first and more than the superficial
vision of her charming outward grace and beauty.

Jenny was someone to me who lived inside of her mind and
inside of her body, which she cared after meticulously, and who I
knew then in that moment in the same way that I knew myself and
lived inside of my own mind and body looking out on the world.

She was in the house now, doing her chores and thinking of
the day we were about to have together. It was a day that I
wanted her to be successful with.

I had laid it out with string to be a big garden, which was nine
step-yard paces long and fifteen paces wide, positioned that way
on the layout of the side lawn so as to get the most advantage of
available sunlight in the mornings and afternoons, with the big
pine trees on the far South side of the property that bordered the
next door neighbor Bud's property, and the big Sugar Maple tree
in the front lawn by the street that blocked off the early morning
sunlight with late morning shade that stopped short just before the
patch of earth that I had laid-out to position the perfect garden by.
I had carefully arranged the garden for each of the perfectly
aligned rows that I had laid out with a stake and string, with the
spacing of two-foot intervals apart for the big plants and a foot
and a half apart for the smaller plants, with the rows running front
to back, and with the taller plants, the corn, and the tomatoes, the
climbing peas, and the beans positioned so as not to block the
morning sun, and allowing the lower plants to nurture in its early
light.

I had done this all for Tony as a part of the work arrangement and had planted it when the soil was warm in the third week of May when the danger of a late frost had completely past when I had just started to work on Tony's land and that was my first project that I started before I had hired Lloyd. It was now the third week of June

I put in with two long rows of corn, plenty of corn, to cross pollinate, two rows of nice string beans, a row of climbing peas with poles and strings to climb up on, two rows of big red tomato plants to cross pollinate with some smaller cherry tomato plants, which I transplanted along with a row of big bell pepper plants. I also planted two rows of potatoes, a row of beans, a row of cabbages, and a row of lettuce, with two types of lettuces, Iceberg, and Romaine, and four rows that I divided in halves for carrots, radishes, onions, and some parsley, and with a nice size rectangular plot for the creeping items of the garden, squash, vine cucumbers, pumpkins, watermelons, and cantaloupes. All of which, I bordered around with a neat three-foot high close wire mesh rabbit fence that Tony and I had gone and purchased together from the True Value Hardware store in town along with the neat white painted stakes to build the fence.

Everything was fully up now. The corn was a foot high already. And I was proud of what I surveyed as I looked at the garden that day. There was something earthy and satisfying about putting in a garden, tending to it, nurturing it, protecting it, and watching it grow and come to fruition.

On that particular morning however, while weeding and neatening the soil around the plants in the rows, I noticed to my horror that some of the tomato leaves had big green Hornworms on them. They had camouflaged themselves so well that I almost didn't notice them, and which I quickly scrutinized and removed them all by hand, there were five of them, all big ones, and put them in a bell jar with the leaves they were eating, and put the lid on it which I punctured, to keep them alive. I hated to kill any living thing, and realizing too that I would have to come up with a better plan to keep them away by discouraging them from devouring the tomato plants. I would consult Tony later if he knew about an Organic Remedy like putting Oatmeal out, or maybe Tony's next door neighbor Bud might know, who lived in the adjacent house on the garden side and who I knew was an avid gardener too, who had himself planted a big garden, much bigger than mine, on the open land of the lower tier back behind his house on the rich loamy soil of the Wallkill River's flood plain. Bud's huge garden stretched the entire length of his back property and was on the same level with the Ox Bow as Tony's land that Lloyd and I were clearing for him. But Tony's back lot land however had many big lovely Locust, Elm, and Pin Oak trees down by the Ox Box, which made it very shady and quite unsuitable for farming. I would consult with Bud later when I saw him about the Hornworms and what to do.

After breakfast, as he usually did, Tony had secluded himself in his Study to work. In an hour or so, Jenny had come out to the garden dressed for the day in her white canvass sneakers, a nice pair of tan shorts that showed off her legs and a soft cotton white short sleeve shirt tucked in neatly at the waist. She said that she had finished her chores and was going to make us a nice lunch to take up to the mountain with us and asked me what I wanted.

"What's on the menu to have," I asked, surveying the beauty of her face and the genuine sincerity of her being that was always smiling eagerly at me and which I found endearing, and to tell the truth captivating, with an overpowering weak in the knees kind of feeling for my lost youth that made me uncomfortable and embarrassed to look at her for the longing in my eyes that I feared would betray me.

"We have some baloney, some ham, and some salami, and lots and lots of American cheese, and some Swiss cheese, and some nice cans of cold root beer, or there's some cans of coke, or ginger ale, to take along, but only the root beer and ginger ale is cold right now in the fridge. Oh, and some nice crisp apples."

"That all sounds very nice," I said. "What I would like is a nice ham and provolone, but since we don't have any provolone, I'd like a ham and Swiss. And the root beer is fine, Jenny, and the apple. How about you? What sounds good to you?"

"What you're having ham and Swiss sound good.
Do you want lettuce, tomato, and mayonnaise or mustard?"

"All of that, Jenny, the works, and with mustard and mayo.
That's all so kind of you, Jenny, to do that, would you also make
up a sandwich to take up to Ranger Whitey, of whatever there is
left over, baloney and American cheese would be just fine, what
kind it is isn't important, but if we're to be going up to the
mountain, and I have a very special day planned out in my mind
already for us, I need to take care of my friend, Ranger Whitey
who works at the Campgrounds there with me. He's an old
retired Pinkerton Agent who lives all alone in a cement block
room in the basement of the abandoned Ski Minni Lodge and
who's getting on in his years and who has no car and nobody to
really care for him, except his sister Mable who drives up from
Middletown to take him shopping once a week, and myself and
the other Rangers who work there at Minnewaska who are his
only family. It would be a nice gesture for us to think of him and
to have a sandwich for him to eat at lunchtime when we arrive,
with a nice apple and cold root beer. I worry about him not
eating right. Boy, would that be nice. You can put Whitey's
lunch in a separate lunch paper bag. You don't mind the extra
work, do you?"

"No, I don't mind."

"And would you also put in some of those doggie biscuits that
your father got and a bottle of water to drink and a big plastic cup
for Sophie to drink from. We may wind up eating our lunch out
on the trail somewhere. Wouldn't that be fun?"

"Sounds like fun to me," Jenny replied.

"You are a fine gal, Jenny," I said. "Thank you so much," and
I added, "I am looking forward to our day together. Why don't
you wear something other that that white cotton shirt, Jen. We're
going to be out hiking around all sweaty on the rocks and it's a
little too dressy. Wear something more casual for the day."

"OK," Jenny replied. "I'll get out one of my pullovers."

"That'll do. Is Henry up yet? Maybe he wants to go too?"

"He's up."

"Please tell him we'll take him along up to the mountain if he wants to come. Would you?"

"I'll tell him," Jenny replied. "But I think he has other plans for the day anyway. I think he said he wants to play golf later on at the Club today with his friend Chipper. And besides T wants him to mow the front lawn before he does that"

"Please tell him another time then, Jen. I don't want him to feel left out."

"I will," Jenny said, and turned and went back inside the house. I watched her until the back screen door closed behind her wondering if I would ever survive the day.

Tony and I and Henry all liked to play golf together when we could at the Huguenot Golf Club which was a nine hole course only a half mile down the road from Tony's house. It had a really nice restaurant there to eat a burger after the round, and it was a cozy weekly or so arrangement for us to have the close opportunity of regular golf outings together, the three of us. Jenny didn't play the game.

I didn't think that Henry would want to come along to the Park but I needed to ask anyway for the sake of sensitivity and also to add the illusion of propriety, however that was to be conveyed.

Jenny came out a little while later dressed in a soft blue pull over halter top, with the three lunches, two for us, one for Whitey, and one that she had made up for Sophie, with the nice doggy chews, all together in a thermal carry bag.

"Ready to go?"

"In just a minute," I said. "I want to put the tools away, say goodbye to Lloyd, and wash up a bit before we go. Bring your bathing suite if you want to. We can go in for a swim at the lake or down at the stream if you want to, which ever you prefer. It's your day."

"Do I want to go for a nice swim," Jenny said. "I've been dreaming about that since the summer began."

She went over to Tony's station wagon that was parked on the gravel driveway by the side of the house, opened up the driver's side door and lean over and put the lunches in on the front seat. "I'll be right back, with my bathing suit and some towels."

"Say goodbye to T, and bring your little knap sack," I called
out after her. "We can use that to put everything in. I don't have
a suit by the way. I'll have to jump in with my shorts on. I'll go
get them from the loft."

"I'll get you one of dad's trunks," Jenny said. "They'll fit
you."

"Great. I hope Big T won't mind."

"He won't. But I'll ask him anyway."

I went over the back yard and talked to Lloyd.

"I have to take, Jenny out for a driving lesson," I said to him,
talking loud from the top of the bank looking down at him from
the short incline of the back yard where he was brutishly hard at
work laboring, hacking away at the dense brush with hand scythe,
bare to the waist and sweating profusely. "I'll see you later."

"I'll see you later, Gary," Lloyd replied. "Thanks again for the
job. I'm really enjoying it. But, it really would be nice if we
could work together sometime. I like the work together with you.
You are always off doing other things these days and leaving me
all alone here to do all the work and when your friend Timmy
comes by, you sit up on the porch and play chess all day."

Lloyd was always very blunt and direct with his feelings.

"I'm not intentionally leaving you out here alone, Lloyd," I
replied. "It's just that I have these other chores to do. I don't just
do the yard work around here as you were hired-on to do.
However, in light of what you just told me about how you feel, I
am making you foreman of the yard project right away, and which
is a position that Tony approves of. He is very proud of your
work, Lloyd, and in case we need to hire on some additional
laborers later on to complete the job then you would be in charge
of them and work on the project as you see fit. You've got a good
eye for the landscaping. But as long as you need me for us to
work together, I will make it a point for us to work together as
often as I can. I would enjoy that too working with you very
much Lloyd. Men bond well when they accomplish a project
together, and I want us to have that memory of doing the job. I
can't be here tomorrow though, Lloyd because I have to work all
day at my other job up on the mountain and I will need to be out

on the road to hitchhike at around 8:00 o'clock or so. The job is from nine to six. But the next day, okay? I promise. It's my pleasure, Lloyd to see you happy. You're doing a really good job," I said.

"Okay," Lloyd said, "Thanks. Do you want me to start looking around for someone to hire?

"Why don't we wait and see, Lloyd. Maybe we would want to make the most out of the job ourselves, to kind of stretch it out. But you can run it by, Tony, to see what he wants to do. I'll see you, Lloyd."

" I'll see you, Gary."

"See you." And with that I was gone.

Lloyd took care of his own time and I took care of mine and neither of us ever questioned the other about what the other did or was doing. And Lloyd knew that I had an intimate family way and a separate agenda with Tony and the Robinson household. I ate my meals with them and did errands and chores of a different nature than himself, and he knew not to question me or my ethics involved, concerning the work arrangement, relationships being such delicate things. I just knew he needed me to work with him for company in the days and to do a project together to reflect on.

I had indeed been fortunate to have been offered the job that was a wonderful part-time Park Ranger's Job at Minnewaska Park in the Shawangunk Mountains. I had been hired by my good friend and Head Ranger there of long standing, Ron Thompson, who I knew from the street and who had recruited me in May especially, saying he wanted me, as a Vietnam Veteran, as he was, and who Mr. Phillips, Sr. had desired for our ability, as Combat Veterans to handle ourselves, and to protect the family and Park customers, to help him out with patrolling the Park for the Summer, (at the minimum wage rate of $3.10 an hour, with no raise to be offered, nor to be expected, take it or leave it, which I was all too delighted to take for the sake of having a place there,) and seeing as how I was at odd ends for a handle, in the vernacular for a covering face saving employment, "that covers a multitude of sins," as Mr. Phillips, Sr. had said to me on the day I was hired in his way, and being as how I was out of work and without a working man's handle of the vernacular, of attracting me to accept the minimum wage position he was offering. And that I only all too happy to accept, with my school work completed and at loose end that way, and in estrangement from my wife Doreen the year before who I had parted company with for my own reasons, mostly hers, and with my car gone due to finances, and my regular work with the Local 137 Operating Engineers Union in an industry recession and at loose ends that way, and with my finances on hold temporarily to permanently, until and unless things improved and I could get back on my feet again, in the middle-class meaning, if they ever would.

To what also that I was indeed grateful and appreciative of for the opportunity of needed work, and more importantly for the position and the place to stand on the earth, being gainfully employed at long last, with my head held high, that Tony had to offer me the relief of as well, but howbeit not in the formal way that was required by society to be an accepted member of. And grateful to Tony, that I was for that work and position also, and always with the thought, "what a kind heart," Tony has. And with the same thought about Mr. Phillips also, as a kind friend to me in that hour of my desperate need.

I was offered the midnight to eight a.m. shift at Minnewaska Park as Ticket Taker and Night Watchman to pass the pleasant time beneath the perfectly dark canopy of bright stars on the weekends on the mountaintop at the Campgrounds on Friday and Saturday nights. And as well (for the time being, until business improved and fortunes prevailed otherwise to be able to hire me for more work,) one day a week on Wednesdays as the Ticket Taker and on Ranger Patrol in the Park Lands and at my post at entrance to the secret nudie skinny dip swimming hole named Low Falls that was really a quite famous nudie clothing optional secluded mountain hide-away, featuring cliffs for diving and into a ice cold basin of relatively deep water nestled below a beautiful

Beautiful View of Enchanted Wildmere and Cliff House
at Lake Minnewaska in 1974. Gone now forever.

cascading twenty foot high waterfall that was located on the
Peterskill Stream about a quarter mile downstream on the North
side of the Highway, 44/55 and that flowed from the great
mountain Lake named Awosting on Minnewaska Land four miles
away to the south, and that also cascaded over a great thundering
fifty foot high waterfall called Awosting Falls about a mile
upstream before it got to the Low Falls.

Low Falls had a flat table rock for sun bathing on either side of
the stream bed above the six foot water fall and the deep hole
swimming pool of ice cold water with a fifteen foot cliff on its left
side facing downstream for diving. It was about as romantic and
picturesque a spot for swimming as an anyone could hope to find
anywhere, that was arrived at down a scenic trail that ran along
the stream bed and through a Hemlock Forest for a quarter of a
mile along the rippling and glistening stream that was lined on

either side with Blue Berries and Mountain Laurels, that were just beautiful in the Spring time when they were in bloom,

Awosting Falls on the Peterskill

interspersed with White Ash trees, and Pitch Pines, that trekked down, following the course of the steam, on a slight incline from the highway 44/55 that crossed over the mountain. And where, at that location on the highway at the entrance to the trail, was where I stood, at the trail's entrance as the ticket taker, when not out on regular patrol throughout the day down to the Low Falls itself or out along the many trails in the Park Lands depending on how the days went and where I was needed most.

And that regard that I did make frequent trips to the Low Falls during the day on litter patrol, to pick up litter, and often to ease the boredom of the standing position of hours on end with a scarcity of customers coming to the Low Falls during the week, and otherwise to maintain discipline if necessary if there were any rowdy people who happened to be present to bother other patrons, or with playing their radio too loud, or who had bottled glass on the rocks which was forbidden, and to check on tickets from anyone wandering down the old ski slopes to the Falls from

Low Falls Swimming Hole on the Peterskill

The Campgrounds. And with having to eject anyone forcibly from the Park for being rowdy or for refusing to buy the two dollar day ticket for the use of the Park Grounds, that was a fighting bullying job at that aspect of it, and which happened like and for the infrequent confrontations of it having the mastery of the land to command the sense of the situation, of such confrontations. That was like being a bar bouncer. In that regard

all those patrons needing to be evicted left when they were told.
People did as they were told, if they were told in the right way of
persuasion; which always meant forcefully and with the
persuasion of meaning business.

And to add in footnote, and as did Head Ranger Ron too as
well, and with unspoken way of Pot, in the meaning of Marijuana
being considered in those times as Wampum on the Mountain, in
the Native Indian phrase of commanding immediate and close
endearing regard in respect for all those who bore it into the
Tribal Council, or to those who could obtain it and secure it, that
such persons were indeed always to be courted. And to what
reason that I did let all of our mutual friends in from the gang
from town and their quests to pass for free when they came and
wanted to go down the trail there to the Low Falls on the QT, that
was an unspoken perk of the job.

Such favors were gratefully repaid on the other end of things,
in town, when our hooch supply on the mountain ran low, if and
when that we ever needed a favor. And although that no one was
keeping score that way, it was a power to be owed a favor, and a
debt to be repaid to owe one, especially favors of such profound
and simple magnitude.

That was my position too, to tacitly supply the hooch, which
was a code name for good quality and potent marijuana buds,
from town, which everyone in the mountain community enjoyed,
discretely or otherwise, and many of whom were smugglers
besides in their own right, to be close comrades with, and there
was no closer bond between anyone, man or woman, than the
hallowed brotherhood and sisterhood fraternity of being, or of
being involved with, smugglers, whose lives depended upon each
others discretion, as to what it meant to be the Park Ranger there
with The Phillips Family at Minnewaka during that era.

That as well had the other advantage for me to be stationed at
the Low Falls area to my employment there, that was a nudist
camp, and to what as a consequence that public nudity became a
commonplace and natural thing to me. And there were some
beautiful women who regularly came there too, to visit the Low
Falls, who I got to know and be friends with, and to look at and

admire in trying not to gawk at them, and who would take your
breath away to see them there in their casual nakedness where
they were sitting, or standing, or laying around, or diving in the
stream into the deep cold pool of water beneath the great
waterfall, and swimming around, without any clothes on at all.
Savor the days.

After a length of time I began to look at them as people
without their clothes on, who were who they are when they were
clothed, only they were naked and seemed the same as they did
appear with their clothes on, only without any clothes. You got
used to seeing them without their clothes and saw them as who
they are in the flesh, with there just being more to look at, like
being in a co-ed gang shower, and trying not overly to stare at
anyone. And there they were, exposed in the beauty of their
nakedness, male and female parts, and there was nothing to be
thought of it. I say it was better to have that experience in
understanding, than to not.

It was a truly liberating experience for me to be there and as it
would be for anyone to get to know their flesh in an appropriate
setting of acceptance and to experience that side of life in the
Biblical setting, and to be taken-in as a therapy project in the
modern century, for anyone not to be ashamed of or otherwise
embarrassed by our nakedness, or and in the other meaning, not
be overly and perversely sexually excited by it, the sight of it, and
the near presence of it in daily routine; which I feel in a certain
sense that has to do with it, our sexuality, remaining hidden in
sundry taboos associated against its revelation, some religious,
and some inherently primitive and controlled by the jealous
possessiveness over our sexuality, and who gets to see it, and that
goes beyond the boundaries of moral explanation in our modern
culture, concerning how one feels about other men looking at
their wife in that meaning, or the feelings of other women that
wives have about their husbands.

Persons who accessed the Low Falls area by the back way
came down the steep part of the mountain that was a cleared area
down from the mountain top and also part of the campgrounds
that was previously the Ski Runs, complete with the greenly

painted tow lifts still in place, down the mountain side, which had a shale composition from the Ordovician Sea Age some 465 million years ago. And about the steep shale that was left exposed there on by the Ski Runs that I had fondness of racing headlong down the hill on, with my feet sinking comfortably down into the forgiving shale to break my free-falling strides, taking great gigantic strides down the nearly vertical runs and going at a breakneck speed until I reached the bottom.

It was and as it had been quite a thriving business before the climate change when the snow stopped falling and accumulating the years since 1974 and 1976 in the Mid-Hudson Valley part of New York along the Hudson River due to the construction of the two Nuclear Reactors at the Indian Point Nuclear Power Plant in Buchanan, NY north of New York City that dumped the super heated reactor water into the Hudson River and had change the entire ecosystem and biosphere of the region as a result, from the outflow of the two Reactors, which heated up the tidal water of the Hudson River that in turn heated up the atmosphere of the Mid-Hudson Valley to a warmer corresponding degree with the tidal flow, altering the area's Winter Climate, formerly with a plentiful accumulation of snow fall, to the milder temperate climate, as would be found in Virginia, in which any snow that fell, if any, would melt in a relatively short amount of time, and which had shut down and bankrupt all the Ski Slope Runs, that had been build at great expense in the Mid-Hudson Valley Region including Ski Minni, the neighboring resort of Mohonk Hotel Ski Resort, and the Mount Beacon Ski Slopes thirty miles to the south, and of which ecology change in financial disaster for the Sky Industry that had forced the Phillips Family into bankruptcy.

The Phillips Family consisted of Ken Phillip, Sr., who was at that time in 1977 in his late sixties, and his wife Lucille who was eight years younger, and Ken Jr., his son, and his wife Pauleeta, who were Head Ranger Ron's and my own age, and who were the family together the owners and proprietors of the Private Minnewaska Park that Mr. Phillips had purchased, all ten thousand acres of it, in 1955, along with the two Hotel structures on Lake Minnewaska, Wildmere, and Cliff House, from the

Smiley Family, for $200,000 plus $400,000 in debt, and who
were each very kind and sincere Inn-Keepers.

Both Mr. Phillips, Sr. and his Ken Jr. lived on the mountaintop
at the Lake Minnewaska, as did Head Ranger Ron Thompson in
one of the out cottages. Mr. Phillips Sr. before the bankruptcy
had been the proud Inn Keepers of two very beautiful Hotel
Facilities on the mountaintop that over looked lovely mystique
and enchantment of Lake Minnewaska, Wildmere, and Cliff
House. Cliff House had burned many years before. Wildmere,
though not in use as a hotel any longer was still in tact in the year
1977 and still had parts of it functioning as a gift shop, bar,
restrooms, and changing area for the lake swimmers, and which
served as a backdrop in majestic appearance for the tourist
attraction to come and hike the trails and to swim in the lake.

Alfed and Albert Smiley - Our Patriarchs - circa 1900

I had been given the run of the place, that I was to spend the next ten years working there before Mr. Phillips sold the Park to New York State to become Minnewaska State Park, and to where that I was to spend another ten years there on my own, for a total of twenty years after that wandering the mountain trails as wild creature in as primitive an alter ego state as I could get away with before moving far away from the region to begin my formal professional life as a writer and journalist that was calling me.

And a wonderful thing it was to have the free use and run of all that land there on the mountain top for that length of time that I did in another version of Author Washington Irving's 'Rip Van Winkle' that was written in the early 1800's about the Catskill Mountains, and about a man named Rip Van Winkle of Dutch

descent, who was more prone to idle wandering than to work, and beset by a 'nagging wife,' in that regard had wandered up into the hills one fine day from town with his dog, Wolf, and met up there with the Ghosts of Hendrick (Henry) Hudson's crew who were drinking whiskey and making a thunderous noise playing 'nine pin's in a great amphitheater between two hills, (a metaphor for the great peels of thunder that rumbles and echoes in the summer days in the hills of the Catskills.)

And how after 'imbibing' some of their 'brew' (or 'hooch' as it was affectionately called in a another wording of the modern day version of the pastime of becoming idly and pleasantly intoxicated, in the meaning of marijuana that was the common bond and pass word of the modern day mountain people,) fell fast asleep in the mountains for twenty years, (or so the metaphor of the story goes about the charming and romantically captivating 'lure' of the mountains and forests in those parts, to be understood only by those who know the sentimental feel of it, to steal a wandering man's soul away, to wander among the hills, as the only thing that matters in lie, in all the seasons of the year, and enjoying the days out in the elements, the sunshine, the clouds, the rain, the snow, the heat, the cold, and all sensations in between to experience of the Earth, on Gods' Earth, the Earth the God made for man to live on, the love of any man's life, to wander for that length of time.) And on awakening to discover that his dog had wandered off and he had grown a long beard.

On returning to the town he learned that his nagging wife had died and that he had missed the hardships of the Revolutionary War entirely that had passed him by. King George III was out and the George Washington was President. And which in toll and to the harkening of war perhaps was a godsend for Rip to have missed in that light of regard to be winked at.

And to it was to be with me too in that regard, that I was to vanished there, in the foot hills of the great Catskill Mountains, and to dissolve the relationship with my former life for the sake of that mountain and to elude the hardships of another American War, (that was involving the Civil War of the Draft Rebellion in the aftermath of the Vietnam War, as one front, and with the Race War between the Blacks, with their Mulattoes in tow, on another front, and the Italian/Jewish Fascist warfare on another,) and to have taken up with the Shawangunk Mountains for my own personal Mountain Guide and Rock Climbing enterprise as I was indeed most fortunate to have, and along with the other enjoyments, both physical and emotional of just being there on the Mountain, just to be there and out there in the wilderness among the forest lands in all the days, a perquisite that was forbidden to most ordinary citizens who were tied up in the dog-eat-dog work and the rat race of business/finance.

I was destined to grow old there, and my dog would grow old and not me to wander off one day and die, for me to awaken to, like Rip Van Winkle one summer morning, to discover that she was gone.

And so it was, that Minnewaska Park became and was a great refuge to me in the aftermath of the Vietnam war, and perhaps the real reason for my being there aside from my captivated love of the land itself, the mountain as it stood, with its ancient rocks and majestic views, that quelled the suffering as I was from the deep depression and shock of Post Traumatic Stress.

I never in my life could have fathomed such a thing as deep and seemingly irresolvable depression, and had no idea of where it was coming from, such a dumbfounded depression, or what to do about it; that consisted of a revulsion with humanity to what that fate left no escape, not even by suicide, of not wanting to live anymore, and with finding no reason to live anymore, to carry-on with it, being disgraced and disillusioned to be associated with the revealed nature of humanity, or the cruel and sadistic and often irrational side of it en masse as it portrayed itself in the massing of armies to do combat with their fellow-man, and at odds with my human nature, of it seemingly absurd bodily functions to be driven by the corresponding necessities associated to it of daily pursuits. And with not being brought into the state of Godhead yet, by The Creator, to be able to handle the matter sensibly in the understanding, as God would understand it, the nature of things to be, and why that they are the way they are?

And of what humanity, and corresponding human nature, of what it like to be human being to have to contend for in unsavory, ways of despondent emotions, as well as to have to, in the meaning of being forced to, endure, on the survival ends of things, that is always at odds with the cruel and irrational history of wars that man's self perpetuates upon each other, en masse to commit suicide, as more so aptly phrased, upon the common foot-soldiers of the Earth, their fellow brethren of the Earth, such as is

be stated for, of what we commonly can call humanity waiting on the outbreak of still another war on the horizon, that is always in the incessant turmoil of wars. That I discovered in that hour of time in my life, and coached by God, the Eternal Creator, the true meaning of my existence, which was simply and just to be 'in awe' of the fact that I existed in the first course of reason, and secondly to be 'in awe' of the Creation God had made from the thought of His Mind, to what I found myself to be a part of.

There was truly then no other finer surcease than to be out there on the mountain, there in the great wilderness, alone with God, The Creator of All Things, in that meaning, to have found God and to be with Him in the timeless forever in thought, in relief from it all there in the mind alone with God's thoughts and as companions to each other in the days, and as it was in the beginning of things, when Adam was first made out of the Earth, and before Eve arrived to be made out of Adam's rib, that Adam and The Creator that way were 'married' in their minds and hearts to one another, and before the jealousy evolved with The Creator over Eve, the insane jealousy of the Creator that drove Adam and his wife Eve from the Garden of Paradise with God, into the godless realm of hell on Earth.

To say that The Creator and I had become 'married' in that meaning also, as he had been married to Adam before Eve, and perhaps in redeeming aspect of greater understanding, with the jealously over the female part of life somewhat removed in time gone by and out of mind, to the re-instated reunion of The Creator's Heart with man, with our hearts together, The Creator and myself that way, out on the land of forest and lakes and streams, and in each of the seasons of the year, out in all of their elements, and to be alone in the long nights peering out into 'The Deep,' pondering the immense eternity of stars, and the great and majestic creation of the Creator's magnitude of imagination to be involved with and a part of, of what it meant to be Ranger there at Minnewaska Park at that endearing time of my life, endeared to nature and the elements, as an amiable though somewhat hermitic man who, and like Rip Van Winkle, enjoyed the solitary activities of heaven in the wilderness.

"In the last days it shall come to pass, that the mountain of the house of the Lord shall be established in the top of the

mountains, and it shall be exalted above the hills, and people shall flow unto it" (Micah 4:1).

But right there and then, I was there with Jenny, and the mountain was fresh in my experience eager to be explored, and to where that I had now taken Jenny to do just that, and had now arrived.

Ranger Whitey, who was a retired Pinkerton Detective, was now at the door to greet us. He was a lovable man in his mid to late sixties, and who seemed old to me on the relative scale of my youthful thirty-one years, but not old to himself. He was strong and confident in his eyes and he had a physical stature of a well-kept muscular man, although now with a slight paunch in his mid section that protruded over his belt. His face was closely shaven as it always was, and he had closely cropped head of white hair and with white bushy eyebrows, and hence the nickname. He was a short squat man of around five foot six or seven and was that day dressed in long baggy blue faded trousers and old worn pair of hiking boots. He was wearing a blue Minnewaska Park Ranger's T shirt, with the logo, Minnewaska Park emblem on the left side over the heart, that was standard for all Park Rangers to wear while on duty, and with a blue baseball cap with the logo Minniwaska Park written on the front of it in bright green letters, and in all that served as a makeshift uniform of sorts. He also had a nametag displayed on his blue shirt below the Minnewaska logo that read, 'Ranger Whitey.'

He walked up to the car in a slow soft manner and leaned in to Jenny's driver's side bent over close to Jenny's face and looked in at me.

"Well hello there," Whitey said in his nasally way as if he were interrogating you clipping the words out. "I didn't expect to see you here today. Your not scheduled 'til tomorrow."

"I am here on a special outing today, Whitey," I said. "I have a guest here. This is, Jenny. I'm going to take her out on an outward-bound adventure excursion for the day. I'm taking her on a climb to introduce her to the Rock, and we plan to do some hiking around, eat our lunch, not necessarily in that order, and maybe go down to the stream later on to cool down with a nice swim, or maybe even up to the lake depending on how much time we have and how we feel. I'm doing some work in town for her father, Anthony Robinson. He is a very famous author who writes novels and an English Professor at the University and who was my teacher during my undergraduate college years at SUNY. That's where I am staying now, at their place, when I'm not working here."

"Oh," Whitey said. "Well, hello there, Jenny, I am very pleased to meet you." He extended his hand to Jenny.

"Hello Whitey," Jenny replied, extending her hand for him to shake and greeting him with her pleasing elegant smile that revealed two perfect rows of white teeth. "It's so nice to meet you."

Sophie came panting over to greet Whitey and stuck her head trough the partially open window on the driver's back seat side to get a pat on the head from Whitey. Whitey knew Sophie very well.

"Well hello there, Sophie," Whitey said reaching through the back window into the back seat past Jenny's hair to pat Sophie on the head and stroke her on the chin and neck. He gave her a nice pat. "Sophie's a nice dog," Whitey said, "a real pretty Irish Setter. How old is she now again?"

"She a little over a year old now, Whitey." Sophie was drooling on the back seat eager to get out. "Sophie can't wait to get out of the car and go for a run, can you, Sophie." I said. With the word 'run' Sophie became very hyper and excited and began to whine.

"She's a real pretty Irish Setter," Whitey said again, fondly caressing her around the eyes.

"Thank you, Whitey. Sophie loves the attention. Have you seen Head Range Ron today? I was hoping we would get a chance to see him. I want Jenny to meet him, and Sophie could have a chance to play around a bit with King."

King was Head Ranger Ron's inseparable two year old Alaskan Huskie who Ron had raised from a pup, just I had had raised Sophie, and who just loved the mountain trails as Sophie did and to have a chance to play with Sophie whenever they were together and was always as happy to see Sophie as Sophie was happy to be with King.

"He's been by here to the campground once already today," Whitey replied in his soft slow way of talking. "But I think he's up at the lake right now. I'll let him know you are here if he comes by again. Maybe later on, if you go down to the Low Falls, he'll be there. He's the only one here today on patrol."

"Thanks," I said. "We brought you something," I said, and got Whitey's lunch out from our backpack to give him. "Jenny made you a lunch." I handed it over to Jenny to pass on to Whitey.

"A lunch for me? How wonderful. Why thank you very much," Whitey said.

"It's ham and Swiss," Jenny said with a certain tone of eager joy in voice with the thought in anticipation of her being well appreciated and liked by Whitey for her efforts that a sensation of emotion that she lived for in all the kind things she did for others. "With a nice dill pickle and a cool crisp apple, and theirs a can of cold root beer for you also. Hope you like it. I made it myself just for you."

Jenny had such an endearing way of graciousness that melted everyone with her big loving smile. I could tell right away that Whitey was quite taken by her and couldn't take his eyes away from her gaze.

"Oh, I'll like it," Whitey replied, hefting the bag with anxious appreciation of the lunch to come with the weight of the ice cold can of delicious root beer for his thirst in anticipation. "I don't get many good lunches to eat around here, Jenny. Thank you so much. A tin of sausages with some cheese and some crackers and water is my standard camp fare and was all that I was looking forward too, if you could call it that. Thank you both so much."

He nodded over at me.

"It's nothing Whitey. I was thinking of you. What's family for?" I said.

"Well I appreciate it," Whitey said.

And it was true, they were all a real mountain family together, the Phillips Family and their Ranger Staff that now included me. One could feel it in the way that everyone greeted and approached each other, eager for companionship and emotional support in reinforcement.

"You are always a good friend to me, Whitey. Hope you enjoy the lunch. You deserve it."

I surveyed the contents of the parking lot and campgrounds. There were only three cars there parked in different places

"Not many campers out today I see."

"No, not many. There are two families vacationing here for the week now. They both bought passes for the week. You can see their tents. They're both off at the lake right now swimming. And a young couple went off together up the ski slope," Whitey said pointing off behind him toward the trail to the Ski Slope without turning around to indicate. "They left about an hour ago on foot with their equipment to find a place to camp somewhere. Their car if right over there," he said pointing again but looking where he was pointing this time. "I'll walk up later on for something to do and check on them later to see where they are at and make sure they are squared away and not too far off the beaten path and check on their camp fire. They only bought an over-night pass but who knows. I think they are going to hike down to swim at Low Falls for the afternoon. Nice couple."

And with that he looked over Jenny and myself, playing matchmaker, as if uniting the two of us with approving agreement into his comment about the other couple.

"Well, we'll be going over to the Ranger's Station now, Whitey. See you later."

"Okay, have a great day," Whitey said hefting the bag again and beaming an additional smile of approval to Jenny. Then, turning his attention briefly to me, he said, looking me directly in the eyes. "Stay warm." That was said with a certain tacitly implied understanding of hidden knowledge in his tone, and turned around to return to his table station in the Ski Lodge.

And although to Jenny, as she heard it spoken and her ears perked up over the sound of its expression, it had the meaning, coming from Whitey, of uniting us as a couple on the mountain in Whitey's estimation of approval of her being in a relationship with me and I could see, looking past her at Whitey as I said so-long, that the upper lip on the left side of her face had begun to tremble slightly.

And perhaps it did convey that meaning of nodding approval of a relationship with Jenny to me too along with whatever else it meant. Jenny was a truly beautiful girl, a 'honey' in the vernacular of the times, and I was proud to be her escort that day, or any day that I was with her.

However to add that, 'Stay warm,' coming from Whitey as far as I could intuitively determine, and as intuition conveys meaning to the mind without words intervening to be directly communicated, as it occurred to me, had two entirely different meanings in his mind, and although they were never spoken of, having to do with marijuana, and he used the expression in a particular way in that specific regard now and again.

The first meaning of, 'stay-warm,' spoken in Whitey's secret way of it I thought was a discerning warning to me to proudly display the rebel flag of the smugglers here in these parts on the mountain, which was the same as being in Moonshine Country in the hills of Tennessee and Kentucky, being in the heart of smugglers territory, to what you would not want to create any undue suspicion of being a revenuer, or an undercover narc, about, even if you weren't.

The idea here being to head off trouble before it began by always portraying an affinity and cheerful solidarity of direct involvement, or as an aficionado, for whatever it was that certain of the other people in the region were doing, in this case, the mountain smugglers who lived around there in the area, or who trafficked in marijuana and other drugs in and through the region, dealing their marijuana and whatever other drugs they were into, not to be named. And the truth of what that had been going on there for centuries, to have to fit into and belong and other than being the occasional tourist.

It was okay that you didn't use or traffic in the particular drugs yourself, as long as you had no objection, and hence the term, 'aficionado,' to be in a supportive and encouraging way, to their use or trafficking in these technically illegal commodities. And although that under the current contract of the law, to carry or possess small amounts of marijuana, under half an once for personal medical use, was not criminally illegal and only required a small fine to get you out of, to keep it restricted. But the so called hard drugs was a different matter entire looking at hard time if anyone got caught with even a small amounts of it in their possession, that those themselves who trafficked in such affairs did not want any undue scrutiny over. That technically could be a most deadly matter, even for the misunderstanding. That anyone being killed over the fact of a misunderstanding was dead about anyway. And that wasn't worth the suspicion to be wise in one's day-to-day contacts with everyone about.

The second meaning of Whitey's intimation, I thought had to do with my 'stash supply' of high quality marijuana was running low and to remind me to keep it amply provided for, and to remember to bring more with me when I came up from town in the morning so that a small 'pinch,' now and then, would not be noticed from the number of the succulent buds to be snitched by someone who did not care to openly avow and acknowledge their fondness for the Herb in awkwardness or embarrassment to have to 'fraternize' in the smoking of it with anyone to get it, and who would then have that knowledge of them about it; which could get tricky in certain situations being black-mailed or otherwise to be embarrassed by the revelation of. People had a need for their secrets, and even us, who were open about it amongst ourselves in solidarity, but not in other work situations, and certainly not around any Law Enforcement, and to what that there were always rumored 'undercover cops' about, which you always had to go about proving by signs of solidarity that you were not.

When the stash supply was running low, Whitey would guardedly indicate his desire for more to make me informed of this fact in an effort for me to get more by using the expression, 'stay warm.' Such small pinches from the buds when the supply was ample were never missed, 'that much.'

And Whitey wasn't the only one who worked and lived there, at Minnewaska Park who knew were I kept the stash container, which was good size metal tin that was originally used for candy with a nice tight solid lid, that I kept hidden in a deep crevice that went back as far as an arms length into the dark mysterious space and which I also double guarded the entrance that way behind a rock at the back end of the cave. The ways of the mountain people were strange in the things they knew of without inquiring that way.

There were others also, Ranger Al, Ranger Ed Ludici, the old man, Mr. Phillips, and Ken Junior, and Head Ranger Ron, not to be speculated about precisely as to who they were, and who had secret knowledge of where the stash was hidden, and discovered that way by insider word-of-mouth, or by 'spying' on the camp whenever I was there to see where I kept it. And who, of these secret aficionados, were perhaps fond of wandering out to the cave at the Ranger's Camp in their off time there on the mountain with nothing to do in the long days out in the wilderness but to smoke pot as pastime, to see if any of the stuff was around for the pinching.

When the supply was running 'low' the small pinches as they would take for their pipes were 'all to keenly noticed' but not so when there were plenty of buds in the stash tin to pinch a little from now and then when no one was looking.

And that was all too keenly my great pleasure to be providing for them, who were so kind to me as to have taken me in as a part of their family and provided me with such a fantastic job of being a Ranger there on the vast lands of Minnewaska Park and to have place in the heart there.

The Campground, on a weekday, was nearly empty, as it most generally was during the week, with just the two tents pitched.

Jenny eased the station wagon along the parking lot and to a connecting dirt road as I directed her, steering now to the left to make a sharp right turn there where their was another small parking area next to the startling cliff line that now came dramatically into view with its 70 wall of Rock and rugged cascading bolder field.

Jenny carefully eased the car along and parked it facing the cliff line and we got out.

Sophie in a slobbering fit of pent up and eager energy bolted out from the car, jumping over the front seat and out the passenger side door when I opened it without waiting for me to open the back seat door for her. She was off darting here and there in a frenzy through the forest with her nose close the ground picking up the secret scents along the ground that only dogs know about where the deer and other animals had been. She was totally ecstatic to be out and I was pleased and happy for her.

"Look at Sophie," I said to Jenny. "She's so excited to be here."

"So am I," Jenny replied.

"Me too. What a day we are going to have. Finally." I let the word fall and it found its mark. I could tell that Jenny had begun to relax content and to take the matter in hand, our outing on the mountain together, as a mutual arrangement.

Sophie ran out a ways from me and then came bounding back jumping up on me with her front paws for a pat of reassurance on the head and back to ask if it was alright to leave me for a time, and was off exploring somewhere on her own.

"Come on, Jenny," I said picking up the lunch bag and the knap sack, "It's only a short walk now to where I'm taking you. You can feel the silence and the serenity of this place, can't you?"

"I'll say," Jenny remarked.

"It's a very old place. It's been here for millions and millions of years. You can feel it."

We closed the doors and locked the car, Jenny on her driver's side and me on mine, and walked the other remaining short distance from the small parking lot on along an enchanted trail road through the woods to the cave, with a gentle breeze in the trees and the dappled sunlight shimmering down through their leaves and branches.

There was the sweet musky smell of the woodland Bitter Sweet coming to us in the air from the low lying swampy area nearby, a cross between a pleasing aroma and a mysterious odor,

that perked up our nostrils as we walked by sniffing at it. It was
the same Bitter Sweet aroma-odor that my mother had remarked

17/08/2008

to me about when she would take me on walks through a certain
part of the woods when I was a young child. I could tell that
Jenny was entranced by it and liked it too and she reminded me
then, of my mother in her younger years, to imagine what she
must have been like when she had been Jenny's age, of her hopes
and dreams for a successful life and what was to become of her.
    "It's called Bitter Sweet," I told her without a response,
breathing it in a little to savor it, as Jenny did as well.
    After a short walk we came to the Ranger's Station, that I had
named to be that on taking over and confiscating the land there
and appropriating the site for my own use when I had first seen
the campsite on a walking tour of the Park with Head Ranger Ron
Thompson after I had signed on for the season with the Phillip's
Family back in May of the year.

"And there it is," I said as we round a bend and it came into view. "We have arrived."

"Golly," Jenny said drawing out the roll of the ll's into the y and beaming approvingly. "What a swell place."

"I knew you would like it, Jenny."

Sophie had now returned and was darting around back and forth investigating every nook and cranny of the camp area.

It was a magnificent, place in a small sheltered clearing with a perfectly magnificent cave on the right side of the clearing set in the ancient rock that was formed by the overlay of a massive boulder that had fallen 465 million years ago when the Tectonic Plates collided there at that time and landing the huge bolder directly across the outcropping of two other boulders.

In the center of the clearing was a picnic table with a bench on either side. Father out a ways on the right hand side and in another campsite separated a bit from the cave was a raised platform for putting up a wall tent with rocks in a circle for the campfire. There was also a tripod with a big leather bag full of water for dousing the fires, and which was a always kept full and separate from the drinking water, that was hauled in gallon jug plastic milk containers from the water spigot at the small parking lot. There was also a handy Porto-Poddy there tucked away in some trees for privacy, as there were several more of them besides scattered about the campgrounds for such needs.

The cave was nine foot high and fifteen feet apart at the entrance and narrowing and sloping downward to a small opening three foot high in the back part and was roughly twenty feet deep front to back to form the perfectly dry habitable cave. It was at all times perfectly dry even in the severest wet weather and with its depth that was secure from the elements even in the strong winds from the thunder storms that occasionally rumbled in over the Catskills from the West.

To me it was Hemmingway's Cave right out of the famous war novel written in 1940, For Whom The Bell Tolls, and today I was Robert Jordan; and Jenny, who had suffered the traumatic death of a parent that had left her emotionally despondent and vulnerable, and yet with an inner strength in resilience to carry on

and with a determination of a fierce emotion, as she possessed in
her smile, to love, and needing to be loved, was Maria, who
Hemmingway named, 'Little Rabbit,' and who had been violently
raped and emotionally scarred by the Fascists in the novel, to
what that Jenny was a counterpart to in another meaning of rape
victim to be suffered under the Fascist Porno Occupation.

And, as if nothing had changed, we were still fighting the
Fascists nearly forty years later in another place and time, just the
same in these times as they were fighting the exact same Fascists
in Spain in Hemmingway's days. The Fascists being who they
are and what they represent of a massive bloc of sadistic Heroin
Addicted Drug Culture infesting and inflicting a population with
their Murder Mayhem, Perfidious Corruption, and Immoral and
Depraved Pornography Decadence, to mass and to take over the
legitimate residing population in a criminal fashion, as a 'bundle
of sticks that can't be broken,' and hence the name in meaning of,
Fascism, to hold to sway the Black Hand of Criminal Power over
the legitimate population of any country they appeared in for the
legitimate people of that Nation to ultimately have to marshal a
defense over or surrender in cowardly appeasement to. Which
was what the good and decent people of this region had done,
who had been deceived by the drug war being waged and at odds
with being in the undertow of their enemy drug dealing suppliers,
and who they had knuckled under the prevailing wind of the
pressure of and were being now ruled over by the Italian Mob and
by the Jewish Black Hand, and African-American Black Face,
arrangement, from what sources that the Heroin and other Drugs
Supply came through to enslave and exploit the indigenous and
rightful population in their midst.

That at any moment, and with that knowledge, in looking at
my cave there in the Shawangunks, that one would expect to find
Pilar, and Pablo, and the rest of Pilar's guerilla band living there;
Anselmo, Primativo, Augustin, and Fernando, and coming out of
the cave to greet us in the Sierra de Guadarrama Mountains in
Spain in the Spanish Civil War in the mid-1930s.

Inside the cave was a narrow wooden bed with a fire-pit built
right next to it. The bed was made up of five good size logs in

width and approximately eight foot long, which I had hewn with an axe and made out of dead fallen trees taken in from the forest and lashed together. It was a bed that also functioned as a bench to sit on and with the nice fire pit close by to cook on and to draw warmth from, that had a good vent to keep the smoke out of the cave, quite fortuitously, that was drawn up through a crack in the rocks that formed a perfect chimney for the smoke to exit. It made for quite pleasant sitting and sleeping on cold chilly nights and easy to keep a roaring crackling fire going without having to get up. A good part of camp life was gathering firewood for the night, and that was always especially a hallowed and hurried chore in the dusk twilight with darkness rapidly approaching.

"Ah, what a life," I remarked casually to Jenny that was reminiscent and anticipatory of good times to come there at the same time. "Who would ever want to leave here?"

"Not me," Jenny exclaimed, looking at me with a thrill of excitement and secret yearning of eagerness in her wide eyes in sizing it up and taking possession of the place to call it home in a wifely way that was all Jenny's way of endearing me to her.

At the back of the cave was a medium size ice chest, now empty except for some cheese and crackers to snack on but which was often filled with ice and food and lots of cans of beer for my guests when they came to visit me, no glass bottles allowed in the Park.

There was also a metal first-aid box there that I kept there for the occasional emergencies, antiseptic, and gauzes, a snakebite kit, adhesive tape, and bandages. There was also a sturdy military type foot locker with a combination lock, that I had hauled up from town several weeks ago, which contained inside a hundred and fifty foot climbing rope with some mountain other climbing gear, some chalks, carabineers, and slings, that I kept there for climbs in the dry cave, and since I didn't have a car then at that time not to have to haul the gear around. I kept the rope there for top-roping the cliff to be used by the clients that I lured there and otherwise guests that I brought up from town to climb with me on the Rock, who I would take out on a climb and top-roped the cliff

on the rock for them to follow me up with in the safety in security
of being top roped.

I also kept a kerosene lamp, my sleeping bag with an extra
green Army blanket, and fuel for the lamp in a sealed two-gallon
can.

On the far wall of the cave opposite the bed-seat and fire pit
there were two sawed tree stumps the perfect height for sitting
and which completed the furniture ensemble inside the cave.

There was also the secret place in the back of the cave, hidden
from view behind a removable rock and kept at arms length,
though not so secret to the select patrons of the Phillips Family
and their Staff, as I said, who I served in the meaning of keeping a
stash of contraband for them to quietly come by when they were
all alone in the forest to pinch off a little for themselves to smoke,
being careful not to take so much as anyone would notice, and to
enjoy, 'unbeknownst to anyone,' when no one else was watching,
and also that I kept well supplied for my patrons as well, as an
incentive to lure them out there to the mountain for the day, and
on the many occasions that there were that way, and for myself
too, to while away the days with, out with my dog, and in my
solitude alone with The Creator in the deep and ponderous
wilderness to explore, and many the days were that way that were
spent that would never have been so lovingly and nostalgically
partaken in otherwise. What is a day that God made if not to
thoroughly enjoy, and I don't mean in the sense of being there out
in the wilderness on vacation with competing distractions on you
mind of places to go and things to do, but being there and being
the only thing there is and alone with it, or in sharing it with a
fellow time traveler, with nothing else to do and no where else to
go, like Jenny.

The wall of rock directly adjacent to the cave, all seventy feet
of it was an impressive climb straight up, and by no means the big
cliffs of the Shawangunks, called The Trapps, on the right side of
Smugglers Notch facing West going over the mountain, and
where the most accessible and popular climbs were located, The
Near Trapps, on the left side across the road and less easily
accessible to climb, but just as formidable, and Millbrook

Mountain, which was three miles down range and nigh impossible to get to without a long trek up from the Valley, and which were all over 300 feet high.

But the cliffs there at the campgrounds were nice rock climbing cliffs had many different intrigues of routes up to the top and just as challenging in the short range of them in their degrees of difficulties, as the big cliffs, depending on your mood in the feel of degree of difficulty you were in the mood for to experience, and we each, those of us who climbed, lived on adrenalin that way. I liked to climb it freestyle, which Mr. Phillips, Sr., who as he was himself a climber, liked in me.

"Oh, you go high," he had remarked to me in fatherly kinship one day when he had seen me there near the top on the rock wall by the Ski Lodge when he was driving by on the highway.

And indeed I did, like to go high freestyle, very carefully. It was a part of my secret mastery of knowledge of personal power in the confidence of knowing you can do something that others, most others, wouldn't be able do. And that was what gave you the look in your eye to command and to be successful. And about which knowledge of personal power that I was about to reveal and convey to Jenny.

Outside of the cave, in the little clearing, there was a water bag that I kept there so as not to have to walk too far for water, and which I had fashioned in the spirit of a Guerrilla Army Camp hanging from a tripod of sticks under the cool shade of a White Ash, and which I emptied and refilled whenever I was there from the fresh water spigot along the trail near the little parking area where Jenny had just parked the car, that was piped in pure mountain water from the deep well that Mr. Phillips had put in at near the abandoned Ski Lodge at the campgrounds and delicious to drink.

The wooden picnic table that Jenny was now setting up for us to eat at, with a bright red checkered table cloth and napkins, graced the court yard in the front of the cave. Head Ranger Ron and I had had built the picnic table by hand ourselves one day with lumber that we reused from the torn down and abandoned

Hotel Cliff House on the mountain top before it was destroyed by a fire in 1972.

Things to do on the mountain in the long idle days of summer with nothing to do but look at the majestic scenery and take in the serenity of the forest lands with its White Ash, Elms, Eastern Red Cedar trees, Pin Oaks, Red Maple trees, and Shagbark Hickory, and Tulip trees, and always with its wind twisted ubiquitous Pitch Pines that dotted the terrain all along the windy mountain tops.

On the upper level of the Ranger's Station, about twenty feet higher, there was another deep cave. It was a nice cave too, but it leaked down when it rained and dripped for day's afterwards and wasn't dry all of the time to be good for any permanent use.

"This is a wonderful place to be right with you right now," Jenny said peering into the environs of the cave.

"Home sweet home to me," I said.

"It feels really good to be here with you," Jenny replied.

"You're a fine sweet gal, Jenny, and you will make some lucky fortunate man a fine wife someday. What do you say we eat our lunch? I'm starved. To tell you the truth Big T's Spartan two-minute soft boiled egg and slice of toast and a glass of orange juice just isn't holding me all too good right now. My blood sugar is low, I can feel it, and my tummy is growling. I'll bet yours is too. We are going to be going out for a climb and a long time after that hiking around and I don't want to have to be lugging our lunch around too. What do you say?"

And although that I didn't have a watch on, or owned one at that particular tie in my life to wear, I knew by the Sun that it must be getting on around twelve o'clock lunch time. It was just after eleven when we had left the house for the twenty-minute drive up to the Campgrounds.

"Right now sound really good to me," Jenny said. "I am really hungry too. I'll get things set up."

She went over the picnic table with the knapsack that contained our lunches and began brushing off the leaves and twigs that had fallen with her hand.

While Jenny was doing that, I went into the back of the cave to check on my stash of marijuana. I removed the rock that I used to block-up the fissure in the wall where the stash was and reached back into it with my arm as far back as it would go until I felt the nice sized metal tin and pulled it out. On opening the lid to the tin to see that the supply of marijuana that I kept for the camp and my wooden pipe to smoke it with were still there, I also discovered to my pleasant delight that Kenny Lightfoot had been there sometime between Sunday morning and now, and left me some really nice precious buds of something exotic and two Peyote Buttons and with a note in his handwriting ... 'see you this weekend.' Some of the buds I saw that had been in there from before were disturbed a little with a pinch, 'or two,' off of them here and there, so I knew that somebody had also availed themselves of a 'toke' between the weekend and now.

"All very good," I thought and carefully put the lid back on and replaced the tin to its home in the dark back recesses of the rock fisher and replaced the stone that guarded the opening. "At least I won't have to be bringing any contraband myself out from Town." And although that it wasn't anything much of a crime to be doing that, but that always made me a bit nervous having to hitchhike with it on me and a bit anxious with the State Police driving by, if I should ever get challenged for hitchhiking, to get caught with the stuff on me, and forever to be a blight on my good character and reputation.

Different cultures and societies had different laws depending were you lived to be accepted. What was illegal in one setting was welcomed in another, and so on ... One had to decide, like Prohibition, with alcohol being legal one day ... and illegal the next ... and then the other way around again, what laws were appropriate to them, and what laws were not. Mahatma Gandhi defied the British law against 'making salt' during the British Occupation of India; to what that Marijuana, and the Law against it, was the same principle to stand firm about, if that was anyone's determination to do. The smoking of Marijuana, and as with Tobacco smoking, and the Use of Alcohol, was unhealthy as a pastime and a bad habit to be rid of, as all bad habits were. But for now it served us with a social medium between otherwise un-communicating parties and that also served a metaphysical contemplative purpose. Those who possessed Marijuana were gods to those who used it and I enjoyed the popular stardom.

Kenny Lightfoot, whose last name was Hasbrouck, was a short wiring young man who I had met earlier on in the year, who lived in the Village of New Paltz and was a descendant of the original Huguenot French Settlers to the region. He was a Sorcerer and a Medicine Man for the Tribe by Native Indian standard and always had a potion, and control over its dispensing, for everything that could ail anyone which he carried around in his canvass 'medicine pouch,' on his belt, along with a hunting knife, and a Witchdoctor of sorts, as I knew him well. It suited me, and Head Ranger Ron Thompson, just fine, that was appealing in his way into our community as my friend, and that was my community now too now since I had been provided with the job there for the Summer, and himself bent on securing for himself the trade with summer crowd there at the Campgrounds to sell his pot and other illicit wares, for the position of 'pot runner' to bring some up from town to us on the weekends.

How he acquired The Peyote I would never asked him. That was part of the privacy understanding involved with the illegal smuggling profession. Life and Death, and Freedom, depended on a 'need to know,' basis. The less anybody knew, the better. And, 'loose lips sink ships,' as the saying goes. But I knew it was for a ceremony that Lightfoot wanted to have this weekend to smoke the Peyote around a camp fire late at night to see if, like Carlos Castaneda in his books, 'Tales of Power," "The Teachings of Don Juan Matus," "A Separate Reality," and other works involving the use of the powerful hallucinogen Datura, or Peyote, that he could contact with the Spirits of Native Indians.

Datura was the essential ingredient of love potions and witches brews; that Nathaniel Hawthorn in his book The Scarlet Letter refers to as apple-Peru, or Peyote, that we could use to try and make contact with the Great Indian Spirit of The Manitou, who it was said inhabited The Shawangunks and throughout the region of the Catskill Mountains, and Who was the Great Father Spirit of the Algonquians, known as 'The Giver of Gifts.'

And what about, the subject of Peyote, that I was already familiar with, from my travels during my college years into the Sonora Region of the montañas de Mexico, in search of Don Juan Matus who was a three hundred year old Yaki Indian Sorcerer according to Carlos Castaneda, and who we did manage to find one night, in a Supernatural Way, of him managing to find us, along with his Companion Don Genaro, whose Indian Name was Tom 'Two Bears' Wilson, a Navajo Medicine Man.

Who, in a Spiritual way, taught myself and my friend Timothy Shoh in a Peyote Ceremony around a campfire in the mountains of Sonora, and to the theme of: 'Are you dreaming, or are you awake?' in the terms about being inside The Creator's Dream of Life and to nature of Sorcery that way of the understanding; that we are all already Supernatural Beings in such regard and bound to the Iron Law of Action-Reaction concerning what you put into the reality of The Creator for Good or Bad; to what in order to survive that you must always be guided along by an 'Impeccable Will," and about The Yaki Religion in such meaning, and their Faith of "All Things," of Reverence, Respect, and Cherishment, for All Things living and sentient, to include for the inanimate by that statement, who are all Manifestations of the Creator-Self.

To what that we both became Disciples of, and to include our mutual climbing friend of the mountain Michael Migliori, who we taught the religion of "All Things" to. And who he, concerning Michael and I, had a separate revelation ourselves about from The Creator while camping out on the mountain about the Faith of The Creator Being, Being Everything There Is, that left us feeling devout in the Reverence and Cherishment of Life and All Living Things to become Priests of the Great Religion in our own way.

When I came out of the cave Jenny had set us a lovely table with a bright red and pint print tablecloth and place settings for two. She looked eager and desirous to make a good impression.

"Just lovely," I said to her.

We sat down together across from one another at the table to eat. I said a prayer to the Heavenly Father.

"Dear Heavenly Father, bless this day and the company we keep as we give thanks for this fine lunch that Jenny made ... and for a safe climb and adventures ahead."

Jenny smiled at the acknowledgment of her efforts and I took a bite from my sandwich, commenting as I did, and that was always my 'trained husband' way, instilled in me by my second wife Doreen, to appreciate, as men, for the hard work that women do to prepare our meals and keep house.

The sandwiches were delicious and washed down really good with the cold root beer brought from home. Sophie came back and Jenny fed her some of the doggie treats she had brought along, breaking them up into crunchy bite-sized bits and putting them into one of Sophie's two metal dishes that I kept for her near the entrance to the cave to use as her dishes when we were there. I fixed her up a nice bowl of water in the other one from the canvass water bag.

"This is delicious, Jenny. I don't know when I have had a finer sandwich on a more pleasant day. And with that a most delightful breeze stirred and rustle through the treetops as if on cue, in the secret meaning, from the works of Carlos Castaneda, of 'The Nagual,' or the presence of The Creator among us, who stirs about as a wind.

"I am so happy that you are pleased with it," Jenny said.

"I am indeed. You will make some lucky man a fine wife someday, indeed," I said, reiterating my previous remark.

"Well, I don't know about that," Jenny rebuffed in an exaggerated tone. "I've done some things in my life that I'm not proud of,"

"Like what," I asked back, in mock curiosity aroused, not really wanting her to reveal anything bad about herself, if that could possibly be. She was such a sweet innocent girl.

"Oh, rowdy girl stuff, you know ... "

"I can imagine, "I said, not wanting her to go on about it. "I know all about that sort of thing.

And then I told her a personal story to change the topic.

"My father always thought that I was my Uncle John's boy. My Uncle John lives on a farm in Alabama with my Aunt

Marjorie. You see, my mother and my Aunt Marjorie are identical twins. And I told the story of how one night they fooled Uncle John and my mother Margaret instead of Aunt Marjorie went out with him. I grew up through my childhood and in my adolescent years as a beaten child. My father would whip me with his belt on a regular basis for anything and everything, like not minding my mother, or not taking out the garbage.

"Ho, Ho, Ho," he used to say with his belt in his hand, "who's been a bad boy." And he would delight in his vicious assaults on my backside with his belt.

I used to dread the sound of his footfalls on the stairs at night in particular when I was a young teenager. I started biting my nails and grew up rowdy too drinking beer and going with a gang and getting into fights and all kinds of trouble with school. I went through my young teenage years as a juvenile delinquent.

When I was sixteen I had, what I now believe was an opium dream induced by my mother, a dream that I made love to my mother in their bed in my parents room on the second floor of our three story house, and nine months later my sister Mary was born. My father got really mad at me then and violently whipped me out of the house into the streets. After that he made me take a job with The Grand Union Supermarket and give him all the money I made to help support the family, as my mother now could not work in having to devote her time to taking care of my sister Mary, who was sixteen years younger than me. My grades suffered and I had to quit school and went to work full time at a construction job for the minimum wage then of $2.10 an hour, can you believe that? And still trying to help the family out with my pay until I was drafted and joined the Army Corp of Engineers. As a result of quitting High School I was always scarred emotionally by that until I was able to get myself back into college with the G.E.D. that I earned while I was in the Army and on my way to Vietnam. But I always sent my pay, everything I could spare, all my money home to my father during this time as well. But sadly to comment that it never did any good, as far as my father's and my relationship was concerned, and to this day we are still estranged. Though I have always held out hope that

one day he would love me, as I love him. But what is that
anyway, to have to love somebody just because you were born. I
never asked to be born.

I'll have to tell you all about the war one day, Jenny. You can
tell me about what ails you too, really you can. We'll be buddies
that way. We are all prisoners of our births and our upbringings
and our memories of good or bad of the times we have lived that
we need to share with somebody. It seems, that we can't get out
of any of it, to make light of it. What else can we do with it but
'chalk it up' to experience and move on with the days. And try
and do the best that we can for our own sake, in and of our need
to be happy and content with our lives, if we can. And if we
can't? Well, let's let it drop there ..."

"Tell me about you and Doreen," Jenny asked? "Dad says you
are still married. How come you are not together anymore?"

I took another bite of my sandwich and washed it down with a
nice swallow of the ice-cold root beer.

"What a simply delightful lunch," I said reinforcing Jenny
once over again.

Sophie finished chewing on the hard doggie treats and took a
lap of water from the metal dish and came over and looked up at
me begging for a bite to eat from my sandwich. I broke off a
piece very carefully from mine pinching it off cleanly with my
fingers so as not to mess the bread and the meat and cheese up
and gave to her, which she eagerly devoured with one single gulp,
and looked up at me for more.

"You are not getting any more from me, Sophie," I told her.
"This is my lunch. You've had yours over there." I looked over
at her doggie dish and took another bite of the sandwich.

And with that she went over to Jenny's side of the table and sat
and whined and looked up at Jenny with pleading eyes for a bite.

"How can anyone refuse such eyes? Here Sophie," Jenny said
to her.

Jenny pinched off a piece of her sandwich like I had done and
handed it down to Sophie. What Sophie swallowed whole and
seemed to accept was the last piece. She sighed heavily through
her nose in a resigned pouty way, with an attitude, heaving her rib

cage with a great sigh and found a place near us in the dappled sunlight shade in the fallen leaves to lie down. Which she did with great theatrics, turning in exaggerated gyrations several times, each time to be dissatisfied, plopping herself down, trying a position, and then getting up and turning in the opposite direction and trying that position, and so on it went, before finally deciding on the final resting position and made a groaning sound of contentment with her chin propped on her two front paws.

"Look at Sophie," I said. "How can anyone not love her? I sure am glad that the incident with the fleas is over. There were fleas all over the house."

"I'll say," Jenny said. "Big T was pissed."

"I know he was," I said. "He had to go out and buy flea powder to sprinkle it all around. But they are finally cleared-up now. And ... he got Sophie a good flea collar. I am sure sorry that I didn't have the presence of mind to think of it myself. I'm still learning about dogs and how to care for them. Big T knows a lot about those things. He also got Sophie a wormer too and forced it down her throat. She was very sick all the next day."

Which I made as a rhetorical comment, and without waiting for a response from Jenny who was looking over at Sophie, went on about Doreen.

"Doreen was my second wife. My first wife was named Carol and we were in love of sorts but we separated over the subject of having children and raising a family when I decided to go back to school and get my college education and that was the end to that marriage.

Doreen and I suffered from basic incompatibility. We met in College in graduate school three years ago, started dating, and fell in love. She was, and always will be, a very smart and self-determined lady and I admired her dearly. But she was a City Girl, to me, and also importantly to add that she worked in Suffern, NY, close to the City in Rockland County and that was a very convenient commute for her in those days in terms of travel time. And I say that because I am not a city boy. I'm a country boy. And the City, though I like to go and visit there, and even to stay for a few days and see the sights was an alien place for me.

Doreen lived in New York City when I met her. I went down there with her a bunch of times and had a great time. We went to all the museums, the theater, concerts, and quaint New York City Café's and Restaurants. But it wasn't my world. So, she sub-let her apartment that was in Mid-Town, to her brother Jeff, and moved in with me at Colonial Arms Apartments in New Paltz. We live there together for half a year, and then we moved out to the country into a yellow Range Style House on McKinstry Road in Gardiner in the spring of last year, 1976. Where we got married in a Civil Ceremony conducted by Justice Stokes in a neighborly way who lived on the corner of McKinstry Road and the Albany Post Road.

And so we past the summer in a honey moon of matrimonial happiness, with me working my construction job with the Operating Engineers commuting across the river when there was work, and which there wasn't much of that Summer, with Doreen being off on Summer Break to cook and keep house and to ride her gelding horse, Ashes, which she kept at the neighboring farm which was being rented by our mutual rock climbing 'friend' Michael Migliori. We traveled a lot during that time, went out West and to down into Mexico. On the way back home we went rock climbing together on the big cliffs on the face of El Capitan in Yosemite, and we also did a lot of rock climbs together in the Shawangunks, and went hiking and camping. She was a real my kind-of outdoors girl. We visited with our friends from school in the area and entertained a lot, and went out to the Clubs in town.

But then it came time for Doreen to go back to teaching her school in Suffern at summer's end in September that became an unbearable commute for her. And I understand. It was just too far away. You just can't stand to have to drive nearly two hours each way in commute there and back to get to work, day after day. It was one thing when we lived in town at Colonial Arms Apartment that was just off the Thruway, for her just to have to get on the Thruway and drive down to Suffern, which was still an hour's commute from New Paltz, but the commute from Gardiner was just too much for her.

I suppose that we could have gone back to Colonial Arms and lived. But I sensed that she missed her life in the Big City. The country was as alien to her as the city was to me. And so it came to an end, our marriage, six months after it had begun, although we lived together for a year before that. We closed up the house and she moved back to her old Apartment in the City. I've kind of lost touch with her now. Funny how things go that way, being madly in love one minute … and gone the next. It makes you wonder if love is really what we think of it to be, or just a convenient turn of fate each way. You can't force love on anybody, and you can't make people love you. And which all depends on how they treat you, or how you treat them, and that can just as easily turn to hate, being the two sides of the same coin. So just what is it? Maybe we just shouldn't put too much store in the use of the word."

I took another bite of sandwich, opened the plastic bag with the potato chips, had some of those, and ate a pickle from the plastic container of pickles that Jenny had packed so lovingly and thoughtfully. I had another delicious gulp of my root beer. Jenny ate on in silence, chewing absent-mindedly thinking of something in the back of her head. I could tell from the distracted look she had about her in her eyes.

"In between my first wife, Carol, and my second wife, Doreen, there was my college sweet-heart Kathy. Which I will tell you about to complete the story I was telling about my love life, as you're interested. Kathy is a fine gal but she has, as I would put it, 'issues with her father,' which her mother told me about one day in the wording of, 'things going on between them.' Kathy also has a lesbian thing going on with her mother on the Italian Porno side, so I know about those matters too, and perhaps too that there something to do with a mulatto body guard. At any rate, it is too on again … off again for me to endure. Her temper, which she uses to get rid of me when she needs to be somewhere else, of with someone else, as to who know what, and it would drive me mad to try and find out, is just to overpowering and much too upsetting emotionally. I hate to be yelled-at and disrespected. And then again I needed her too, up to a point."

"I'll remember that," Jenny said.

"Tell me about your mom," I asked. "What happened there?"
Jenny put her sandwich down and looked at me.

"I feel the blame for all of that," Jenny said. "Mom decided she was depressed one day and started seeing this Psychiatrist named Ernie Shaw who lives out on Wawarsing Road at the base of the mountain. We past the road he lives on, on the way out here. I didn't look. She went with him to a retreat the Esalen Institute in California in 1974. It's kind of an avant-garde sort of place. Dad was really pissed about it."

"I've heard of it. Your father has talked about Mary with me and about her involvement with Dr. Shaw, and that place. He showed me the brochure that Esalen that puts out. As your father put it and reading from the brochure in a snide way; 'to create the philosophical orientation of one becoming more fully aware of the real process of living within a unified field of body, mind, earth, and spirit relationships, with a focus on humanistic alternative education for those who are dissatisfied with aspects of the mainstream or traditional education,' ... featuring nude therapy sessions to heighten awareness."

"And all that rot," Jenny said. "Pornography is more like what they were doing ... to free your spirit and liberate the inhibitions that are binding you up, as mom described it in the modern free-style approach to psychology to me."

"I conjectured that too," I said. "It had to be something serious like that. That doesn't work out too well for a marriage does it? being off with another man making porno movies."

"It's the pagan nature of the times," Jenny said. "She brought me out there to Ernie's house with her a few times and they tried to work on me, but I knew it wasn't right, and told dad about it. He was okay I guess, Dr, Shaw, but he wasn't dad ... you know? Dad and mom had a really bad fight after that and dad moved out, as you know, to the little apartment on lower Main Street, that isn't there anymore. They tore it down and made a parking lot out of it for the bank across the street. I went to live there with dad. I didn't want to live with mom anymore. Henry stayed home with mom. Then mom killed herself. It was the most horrible day of my life. I had just gotten home from school and was in dad's apartment at the time tidying up the place, when a policeman came to the door to get me. Dad was already at the house with mom. He was teaching class when he got the news. I keep thinking that maybe if I stayed at home with mom she wouldn't have done what she did. Henry found her when he came home from school. He still has not gotten over it, although it's been a year and a half now since it happened."

"I can understand how Henry feels," I said. "I know what shock trauma is like from the sights and sounds of the battlefield in Vietnam. Shock Trauma leaves you frozen in time in the headlights like a deer. The thought of it, and the memory of it, is always with you, day in and day out, throughout your life. The only way out of it, is to talk about it to someone close to you and dissolve its memory in that way."

Jenny sighed and reached across the table for my hand.

"How horrible for you though, Jenny," I said, not knowing what else to say to comfort her. I wanted to give her a hug and to hold her close in to me, but decided not to and touched her arm across the table in a loving way instead. She bounded back from her forlorn ruminating in the endearing way she had of gathering up her inner strength, summoning the reserves of determination within herself, and as was Jenny's way of her indomitable spirit, with the remark:

"I sure am enjoying this lunch and the fine day out here on the mountain with you, Gary" she stated. "This is a fine place to be on such a magnificent day."

"It's a wonderful lunch, Jenny, and a truly marvelous day, and especially to be here with you. What do you say when we finish our lunch we go for a good climb to get our mind off the past. We both could do with a little diversion."

A family of Yellow Warblers, about six or seven of them, came and graced the branches of the White Ash Trees flittering around in the branches around the cave site.

"Look at the lovely little Yellow Birds," I pointed out to Jenny.

Jenny looked around, and as she did I looked her deep into her hazel eyes searching there watching her pupils open and close

slightly with the shifting light through the branches in the trees.
Her dark lustrous black hair shimmered in the dapple sun light.

Jenny looked over her shoulder to her left at the cliff.

"That doesn't look like pleasant diversion to me. I have never
climbed on the rocks before," she said. "That looks to me to be
very dan – ger – ous. She exaggerated the word with an alluring
movement of her lips. I don't know if I could do that. Have you
ever fallen?"

I did many climbs here in the Gunks with my dear friends
Michael Migliori and Jon Ross, and with Timmy who you know.
We would climb together often," I said. "I never did have a fall
out climbing with them together but one day when I was out
climbing with Michael, just me and him, I fell off the second
pitch of a climb in the Gungs called Frog's Head once.

My hand slipped; maybe it was sweat, or fatigue. Michael and
I had already done two other exhausting climbs that day. He had
led both of those and was tired himself. So, he asked me if I
wanted to lead this one. I had set out to lead one climb that day,
but Frog's Head was a little over my skills as a climber to lead,
and as I was quite tired myself, I should have known better. I
had quite a fright with it, starting up on the second pitch and I
know toward the extent of my rope and my endurance over the
point of my last protection, to have asked myself the time, 'what
am I doing here,' and just before my hand slipped off the rock or
The Creator pulled me off before I could climb any further over
my rope, and almost the dreaded groundfall with it as it was. If I
had gone another two feet further I would have dashed my head
on the rocks at the bottom. And as it was, I still had another ten
solid feet left of arduous climbing arm over arm to uncertain hand
and marginal foot holds before any point of refuge would be
gained to stand on and to rest my weary arms and to put more
protection in, "if" a place could be found to put any protection in
at all. And to what in all lay the meaning of the words, 'what am
I doing here?'

Michael caught me with two feet to spare on the rope and that
was even less to spare with the springy elastic play of the rope
taken into consideration, like bungee jumping. So I know I had

missed hitting the groung by only a few inches. I stopped upside
down and all the chocks came down and hit me on the head. I
remember it like it was yesterday. All that saved me was a tiny
number 10 chock that we had just purchased at Rock and Snow.

"I'm not leaving that chock up there," Michael had said. So he
climbed up and retrieved it and down climbed back down the
face.

All the climbs in the Gunks are rated on the decimal system
5.0 to 5.11 and beyond, rated from the easiest climbs to the most
difficult. The climb called Frog's Head is a 5.7.; which in
layman's terms would be called an advanced intermediate, but
difficult enough. It goes straight up for 275 feet with an
overhanging bulg to negotiate near the top of it.

Jon and I had done that climb together, just him and me, a
while before, and which he had led earlier in the season. He had
climbed up a bit and put some more protection in where I had put
my own number 10 chock in, in a narrow crack, which is the size
of my pinky finger nail," I held up my pinky nail indicating to it
with my thumb nail to show Jenny for emphasis, "and then Jon
had down climbed to the ledge, which is about twenty five feet up
from the ground at the start of the second pitch and rested his
arms and composed himself and chalked up for the entire length
of the pitch which as I said is an arduous arm over arm one arm
pull up climb for about twenty more feet with only fingertip holds
the whole way to the next point of refuge, a narrow ledge where
you could stand with your feet on something. And … Jon had
traversed right from there, after putting in some protection, to a
crack from where instead of going straight up over a bulge to the
top, it was a then a relatively easy 5.5 climb. I was planning to do
that myself, to do the traverse, when I fell.

I kept saying to myself in my head, or as I remember it, the
rock was saying the words for me as I passed down its face with
my arms folded in the featal position close in to my heart; 'You
should be stopping now. You should be stopping.' That was
followed by the thought, 'I'm not going to stop.'

And then I did, as I committed myself to hit the ground, STOP,
much to my surprised delight, and all the chocks and carabiners

that I had attached on slings to my harness belt sprang around on their slings and hit me in the head. Wam! And that was it.

"The Fall" was over. I looked up a Michael from my upside down position, with a rush of adrenalin coursing through me, and said calmly, 'Lower me down, Michael. Lower me down.' And I felt him lowering me down and the smell of the earth as my face neared it and I touched the ground with my outstretched hands and felt the warm black dirt and the rocks breathing it all in.

'That was a spectacular fall,' Michael had said. 'You hit the ledge on the way down and it turned you upside down and you popped out your lateral bottom protection that added a few more feet to the fall.'

After that, after the reality of the fall had set in, I retired the ropes for a while. That was last year in the late summer. I do a lot of easy solo climbing around by myself to get my confidence back, around in the Palmaghatt Valley over by Millbrook Mountain and at the Lost City out along the Aquaduct that runs below Mohonk Mountain House, and here at the Minnewaska Camp Grounds where I now work for the Phillips Family as a Park Ranger. I climb whatever I can handle and still down climb gracefully if I needed to with a quite healthy and fearfull respect for the rock.

But the Gunks have a way of haunting you," I went on, surveying with my eyes the extent of the cliff line. "You never get the rock and the climbs you do there out of your mind it seems. Or, maybe it is that we haunt this place called the Gunks upon the Earth and IT can't get us out of ITS mind, and it's the mind in the ROCK that keeps us coming back here.

It's a very humbling experience and one that we perceive the matter of our life weighing very heavily withi and death certain on the turn of fate of a mistake or a miscalculation, on the line for everything we do here that makes it so poignant. The Rock gets in your blood. It gets a hold of you, the feel of it, and the smell of it up close. You come to touch it lovingly, the Rock, and you feel the lichen that grows on of it, as a caress. Beware of the voice in the Rock, Jenny. Beware of Rock's Eye. It gets into your blood and sees with your eyes admiring ITSELF, always looking longingly at ITSELF, to be climbed, The Rock, that lures you to your death and makes you alive with your success at cheating it of your death, and keen to your senses is that triumph, the feeling of what, the rush of it, that you can't get away from.

It's with us now in Spirit sitting here with us at this place on lower part of the cliff line at the Minnewaska Camp Grounds looking up at IT, THE ROCK, and the Climbing to be done. The Temperature is a pleasant 72 degrees. It's a warm pleaseant sunny afternoon and we are sitting here getting ready to head up there." I pointed to the top of the çliffs. Thanks again for your friendship, Jenny. I do really enjoy you company."

"I really enjoy your company too," Jenny said, looking at me pensively, like she wanted to express something ineffable that was at present beyond her to think upon. "Thanks for listening to me," she went on, "I enjoy talking with you and listening to you too. I'm a good listener." She smiled that warm captivating smile of hers, uniquely Jenny's, that was her hallmark.

"I think you and I are good for each other in this time and place of our being," I said.

She was very philosophical I thought and beyond her years in the depth of soul. It was the old soul of Eve reincarated.

"You know I find you fascinating, Jenny. You'll do fine in everything you do in life."

Don't' be afraid of climbing. I was a bit nervous my first time up too and I've been in places where your hands and arms and legs start to tremble. But you get over it once you acquire your self-confidence and trust in your ability to succeed. If you get nervous the climb is beyond your abilities and you have to replan your strategy. You have to get over your fear that your hands and feet are going to betray you. You start to think they may, in spite of your conscious mind willing them not to, but they wonyou're your mind won't let them. We're not going to climb there." I said pointing directly to the verticle cliffs near the cave, "I have done that particular one myself soll now several times.

If we ever would do that particular climb one day; I would go up and 'top rope' it for you to be completely safe about it, and you could follow me up. Even if you were to fall I would lower you down with the rope; but I have a nice easy climb in mind for you today, and that is if you want to do it, that we won't need to use a rope on this one. It's as easy as climbing a ladder. I discovered it out climbing by myself the other day while I was out fooling around exploring the rock."

It was an easy climb, what we were about to do, and I didn't use the word 'try,' to talk down to Jenny about it. It was still very serious climb to negotiate, as all climbs were, life or death on the line at all time to be successful with. But in fact the whole climb was really easy to pick at all the way to the top with good holds.

"I know you will find it challenging and worthwhile, Jenny. It is quite formidable, especially at the end part, but it's easy. You'll see. I'm going to call it, 'Jenny's Crack.' I'll name for it just now, in honor of you, my first client to take there on that climb, as soon as soon as we christen it together. But I named it for you already in my mind in hopes that you'd come out here with me one day and we could do it together. What do you say?" We won't need any ropes to do this one. It's an easy climb in a series of ledges and through a cave tunnel to the top."

"Sounds lovely," Jenny said masking with an air of confidence an unmistakable undertone of nervousness in her throat. "What about, Sophie?"

"She can wait at the bottom until we've reached the top and then I'll call her along the cliffs to a spot further down where there's a gully that she can get up by. The cliffs end right back there not far, more or less. They continue on in bits and pieces after that. I've left her down here before to climb, so it's not entirely new to her. She'll bark for a bit and then quiet down and will be all right. Sophie is actually a good climber herself, and wary of the dangers too, like a mountain goat."

"Dad wants to put me in Boarding School starting in September, over at the Oakwood School in Poughkeepsie."

"I know that school," I said. "Chuck Connors the movie star went there. It's a famous school."

"I don't want to go there," Jenny replied. "It would mean that I would have to leave all my friends that I have in public school."

"Well, your dad doesn't like the integrated public schools, Jenny, with all the Colored boys and drugs going there. He doesn't want you getting involved with those types of people, getting hooked on heroin, and making Brown Babies to present to him for his grandchildren to destroy the White Race by rendering it extinct. And that's the end of that speech. I feel it that way too. Have you ever been to any parties where there are drugs and the Colored boys are messing around with the White Girls?"

"A few."

"They have a pushy forceful way of entitlement about them, don't they? And a way of bullying the White boys over their right to go out with the White girls, and by drugging the White Girls to make them slaves of their Heroin and Cocaine habits, and then by taking over the White Girls and with their Heroin and Cocaine to force them into bed, and to get the White Girls, to help kill off their White boy friends, don't they?"

"I'll say."

"Well, let's not talk about it anymore. Your dad is only looking out for your best interest. You go there and be safe. You'll meet some really nice people there at Oakwood, a different class of people, and that will be good exposure for you and make all the difference. Your dad went to Boarding School. So you can follow in his footsteps."

"I guess," Jenny said.

We went on to finish the delicious lunch, with the chips and the pickles, and the soda and ate our apples, and there were two cookies each, cinnamon ginger cookies for desert.

"I don't know when I have eaten a finer lunch, Jenny," I said. It was just so delightful. Thank you so much for taking the time to make it for us."

"You are quite welcome," Jenny replied. "And thank you for the lovely day here on the mountain. It's so nice to be here with you. I hope we can get to go swimming."

"We will. It won't take long to do the climb and then it's a short walk to the top of the mountain from there. I want to take you up there to the top today to show you the view of the Catskills from up there, especially today with the big puffy clouds floating by and crisp clear air, and the play of the cloud shadows in the distant Catskills. We'll be able to see a long ways. ... Well, what do you say?"

"Let's do it," Jenny replied with enthusiasm.

I put all the left over paper and cans from the lunch back into the paper bag they came from and stuffed them back into the knap sack that was on the table that Jenny had brought with her with the swim suits in it, and took Jenny inside to show her the climbing gear in the foot locker before I put the bag on top of it to get later when we returned. Sophie had jumped to her feet impatient for activity as soon as I stood up. I opened the combination lock, lifted up the lid, and showed Jenny the 150-foot nylon climbing rope, the two climbing harnesses, and the chocks, and slings, and carabineers, explained to her what their uses were, and then we were off.

I led Jenny around the side of the cave to the back of it. The climb we were going to do was directly in the back area of the cave a short distance away swishing through the leaves with our feet up the hill as we walked, about thirty feet, to the start of the cliff line where I pointed out the climb.

"Here it is, Jenny. The climb I am going to name after you. Feel the rock."

I put my hand on the rock and Jenny did too.

"It feel good," I said. "Doesn't it?"

"It does feel good," Jenny replied. "It feels cold and old, and impersonal, like it has been here forever."

"It's sentient too," I said, "as the Yaki Indians say. Listen. Can you hear it?"

We both listened hard.

"I don't here anything," Jenny said.

"I don't either. Let's not overly bother it too much. Maybe it's resting. It's a very old and sacred place. This rock is millions and millions of years old. Can you imagine the ages of humanity that have touched it, and climbed on it as we are about to do."

I started out on the climb that was a short first pitch of about twenty five feet jammed with my body into a two-foot wide crack, and hence the name derived, Jenny's Crack, in the wall

with plenty of good holds for our hands and feet that emerges
onto a good size ledge.

When I got to the ledge I signaled to Jenny to start and she
began to climb, doing good, moving slow and confident. Sophie
began to bark her insistent bark of impatient annoyance of not
being included and began to stand on her hind legs with her front
paws on the rock, barking incessantly. Then Jenny was up and
standing there breathless on the ledge beside me. I knew her heart
was pounding, mine was. We were both high from the adrenalin.

I showed her the route of the second pitch which went up good
ways now, about twenty feet more, this time with more direct
exposure back down to the ledge should you fall, but in a not
difficult at all scramble motif and not vertical except in a few
spots, with just a few not very difficult parts of real serious
climbing to be concerned with toward the top and concerning the
relative exposure now of the drop to the ledge below as you
neared the top to pick your way up about to another wider ledge.

When I got to the top of the second pitch I looked down and
called to Jenny.

"Ready?"

"I'm ready," Jenny replied. And she began to climb, without
hesitation and confidently and was doing well.

"How do you like it so far," I asked?

"Fine," she replied, a little breathless. "I like the feel of it.
I'm getting the hang of it now. Really I am."

She came up to me without my offering any advise or
assistance and I pointed out the next part of the climb to her.

Sophie continued to bark continuously. I looked over at her
and called her name sweetly. "Sophie."

She stopped her barking momentarily and looked upwards
bewildered trying to determine the location of my voice. Finally
she saw me and barked in an angry hurt tone of being left behind.

"You stay, Sophie," I called down to her, and moved back
away from the edge of the cliff to where the next part of the climb
began.

"This is a really fun part," I said to Jenny putting my hand to
the opening of the fissure and peering into the darkness inside.

"The route here takes us through that narrow fissure opening in the rock over there that goes on for thirty feet or so as you'll see when we get in there, and it goes on until it narrows to a small opening of about two and half feet wide in which, you won't have any trouble with, but I will have to exhale and let all the air out of my lungs to slip through in a prone position to negotiate, and hoping I don't get stuck in there. I get nervous about that, because I won't be able to take another breath once I get in there until I'm through it. Are you ready?"

"Ready."

I slipped sideways into the fissure and motioned for Jenny to enter and we went on together inside the rock with Jenny close behind. I got down into a prone position on my side, let all the air out of my lungs and slipped through without any difficulty much to my relief. On the other end as it opened into Sunlight was the large flat rock surface of a pinnacle, in the meaning that it was separated from the main section of the cliff line which was entirely vertical, the edge of life and death on the vertical desert, which Jenny saw and surveyed as she came through the opening to see a portion of cliff detached from the main section and standing alone, that had to be negotiated by stepping out over a sheer vertical drop of roughly fifty feet and climbing the rest of the way, some twenty feet, to the top of the cliff line. And which, in all, that I had saved the best for last about for a surprise for Jenny. It wasn't hard, this part of the climb. You just had to be careful with it not to slip and fall, and it would be a true test of Jenny's courage and inner strength.

"We are standing on a pinnacle," I stated. "The next part of the climb is really easy. You can see the nice horizontal holds there all the way up for your hands and feet. But it's certain death if you fall. Come here I'll show you."

I took her over to the edge of the pinnacle and we peered over to view the bottom a long way down.

"When I first came up here, I said to myself, oh, no, it's a pinnacle, I'll have to go back down the way I came. But then I decided to make the climb anyway and found it to be easy and very exhilarating. I did a lot for me to do it, and I know that it will mean something to you too as well to accomplish. But, come over here for minute," I said. "I want to show you something.

I wanted to show her the cave on another part of the rock ledge we were on, that was over in the corner to the left of us, and still a part of the pinnacle, an opening that we could walk into for a short distance, which we did, and I told her to stop. In front of us directly was a pitch-black chasm. I picked up a small stone and tossed it down. "Listen."

We waited listening and finally we hear it hit the bottom.

"That's a long way down there, isn't it," Jenny said. "Not someplace anyone would want to take a header off of."

"If anyone ever fell down in there into this pit no one would ever find them. This is no place to carelessly walk in here without checking it out with a flashlight first. That's basic mountaineering. Maybe I'll come up here one time with a rope and a flashlight and go down there to see what's there; or, maybe not. What do you say? Let's finish the climb."

"I'm ready, "Jenny said, touching my arm affectionately.

I went over to the edge of the pinnacle, which was a distance of two and half feet to the other side of the sheer cliff, that was not far but far enough to have to commit one's life to and stepped out over the sheer drop onto the cliff face of the other side. Once you stepped across you had to finish the climb on the other side to the top.

I climbed to the top very carefully and signaled to Jenny.

"Ready."

"Ready."

"It's just like climbing a ladder, Jenny. You can do it." It was the first words that way of encouragement that I had offered her.

And she did it. She stepped across the chasm onto the face of the sheer drop to the bottom and climbed the vertical desert of the rock, on a 'free climb' with me, knowing one slip would be her death. I watched her proudly and anxiously as she choose and picked careful her hand holds and foot holds, testing them with an instinct of her own before committing to every move as she did, and hoping I had not led her to her death, I know, every hand-hold and every foot hold. She climbed though like a natural without seaming fear or hesitation. Or if she had any she didn't show it. I have seen men at great heights begin to tremble on the high cliffs and have to scold their limbs to behave in order to be able to continue on the vertical plane of life and death, and where the test, if can be called that, or sheer folly, of the courage of one's life can be made. And at other moments to say, 'what in God's Name am I doing here?'

Jenny made it to the near top. Her head appeared at last over the cliff edge and put her hand on the top of the rock and lifted herself very carefully over to the finish.

"Very good, Jenny. You did it. I am just so proud of you."

"That was indeed an accomplishment and a feather in my cap," Jenny said. "Thank you so much for taking me, Gary. I will always remember this day out here with you."

"I know you will, Jenny. I will never forget you either."

"Well, thank you again."

"You are quite welcome," I replied. "Let's mark the climb and christen it. Here, I'll show you."

I walked a short distance away to a little outcropping in the rocks, that was a grotto of sorts.

"It's a ritual of the Gunks for climbers to mark their solo climbs, or their memorable roped climbs, and to name them, when they haven't already been named, and to commemorate the event with seven stones piled one on top of the other. You and I did a solo climb together. And we names the climb, Jenny's Crack," after you. So let's look around and pick out some nice flat stones, larger to smaller, to build our memorial, and this will be for us, our 'Power Spot' together, a place where we can always come at any time throughout our live in our thoughts to gather strength in the memory of our accomplishment here today to have climbed the great cliff together, and to having become climbing buddies together in eternity, that is an inseparable bond of faith in one another, in knowing each other in that way, that we are in our hearts and minds 'til the end of time to be in the memory of our achievement forever in our thoughts. We will always be together here, and in the memory of this proud day, and even in death when we die our spirits will meet here. This will become our

Hallowed Place and Meeting Ground for our spirits for all eternity. Do you agree?"

"I do agree," Jenny said, "how strong and solid it all feels to have our own Power Spot here together with you."

"Well, you did the climb with me. It belongs to the both of us. And look, I want to show you. Look at the seashells here in the grotto. See, they are all over the rocks here … little ones … and big ones. See." I pointed them out to her. "This entire area here was once an inland sea, 440 million years ago to be exact, and all this rock here is called Quartz Conglomerate and which was formed by deposits of the shells and bones of millions of years of sea creatures. Then one day the two what they call Tectonic Plates of the Earths' Crust collided, the one diving under the other geologically, and drove these cliffs here upwards into the sky. And which remain today, weathered with time, exactly as they were when they were formed all those millions of years ago. It's all very profound as I said when we started."

"I'll say," Jenny said.

And so after the christening ceremony of words, we piled the stones we had gathered, one on top of the other according to their size, largest to smallest, in the grotto. Jenny had found some nice flat ones and we made a pyramid with them about foot high on a rock altar in the little grotto.

"As we hike around in the future, if we go hiking together, we may see stones piled this certain way throughout the cliff line of the Shawangunks, which are made by the climbers to mark their climbs. They'll always be safe and respected here, our stones, no one will move them."

I could hear that Sophie had given up her barking and was waiting resignedly for us at the bottom for us to come back. I went to the edge of the cliff and peered over. I could see her there and called her in a soft loving tone. "Sophie."

Sophie looked up and saw me and started barking and growling impatiently again. I walked down the cliff line a short ways, stood at the edge of the cliff, looked down and over to where Sophie was, and called her again."

"Sophie."

Sophie made her way carefully through the bolder field to a spot directly below me and barked some more. I walked down the cliff line again, and repeated the process, and then again, three times, until I was at the end of the cliffs to where there was a gully and to where that I could call her to come up to the top with me. She bounded up and pushed into me with her front paws, excited to be reunited with me and at the same time angry and annoyed in her doggie way with me for being left behind down below alone for so long. Doggies have thought and emotions too. We walked back together to where Jenny was, with Sophie running along ahead of me when she saw Jenny. She jumped up on Jenny too happy to see her.

"Here she is," I said to Jenny. "What do you say we head up to the top of the mountain now?

"Okay," Jenny replied.

"Before we go though, let us take the time to breath in the air though our nostrils and sense it shimmering in the leaves of the trees and clear out our minds from the clutter of conversation so we can commune with The Creator Spirit on the way."

Jenny complied and we took several deep breaths together, taking in the air with our lungs and letting it back out again.

We left the spot by the alter where we had piled together our memorial stones and proceeded along a well worn trail through the forest of Pitch Pines, White Ash, Mountain Laurel, and Eastern Red Cedar tress upland to the top of the mountain.

Sophie bounded out ahead of us, delighted at last to be out for a walk in the forest together. She would run up ahead and then return only to turn around run out ahead again, which was her ritual of the walks, not to leave me alone for too long and to return for the reassurance to herself that I was still there. All along the trail there were many scents for her to explore.

Along the way I instructed Jenny about the Indian Lore of the mountain ways on how to watch for insects and other tiny creatures along the path so as not to step on them by accident, and how be respectful of the vegetation not to break any of its branches as we passed, and to tread softly on the grass so as not to scuff any of it. And Jenny began to walk carefully in the ways of the Indians, and like The Indian Princess that she became.

At last we gained the summit breaking out into the sunlight onto a rock ledge and a clearing. Off in the distance was the great and profound expanse of the Catskill Mountains. Downward from us stretched the abandoned Ski Slopes with the green iron lift stanchions and ski tow cables still in position. Off in the distance in the fields of the cleared ski slope was the herd of deer that lived in the Game Sanctuary of Mr. Phillips Sr.'s land.

"Look over there at the deer herd," I said to Jenny pointing over in the direction of the far pasture. There must be at least twenty of them."

The deer were grazing quietly, but not for long, as Sophie too had spotted them and went crouching along in her hunting instinct to creep up on them without being spotted.

"Look at Sophie," I said. "She's trying to sneak up on them."

Finally Sophie could contain herself no longer and bolted out after the deer who promptly bolted themselves into the woodland; which Sophie entered into as well and disappeared after them.

"She wouldn't hurt any of them, even if she could catch them. She just wants to play. She'll come back when she wants to. In the meantime let's you and I sit here and enjoy the view of the Catskills and play of the cloud shadows on the mountains, as I told you about. Look over there at them. I swear they will put us into a trance."

And with that I sat back against a granite boulder that had been deposited there on the mountain top during the last ice age, or one the ice ages of the past, during the Pleistocene Ice Age, from approximately 18,000 years ago, and Jenny made her move, as I knew she wanted to, and sat down directly in front of me with her back to me between my legs and leaned back with her head on my chest. I put my arms around her and held her tight. Across the distance the cloud shadows played on the enchanted mountainside, and I knew that the Great Spirit of The Manitou had joined us in union. Sophie returned panting out of breath and lay down beside us. Jenny fell into a deep sleep and so did I.

When we awoke, that extent of the afternoon stretch out before us and we got to our feet with a feeling of confident possession of one another, as those matters go, to know that someone has become yours to call your own, and that you have become theirs.

"What do you say we head down for a swim now. The afternoon is getting just right for it."

"I'd like that very much," Jenny said.

As for the way that things turned out in having to let Jenny go to live her life apart from me as it would have been lived if she had not married me and had our children. And for what in all that I had a hand in and with shaping her destiny, in the letting go of her as I did, painful though as it was, and still may be, to feel satisfied about, in the way of watching over her, as angels do, bearing the gift of love.

Jenny graduated from SUNY State University of New York, Albany with a Bachelor's Degree in English and from Troy State University, New Orleans, with a Masters Degree in Business Management, and who, like her father, enlisted in and served four years in the Navy.

She has worked in the marketing field of residential treatment centers for the past seven years and has over twenty years experience ranging from pharmaceutical sales to Navel Recruiting. Throughout her career, Jenny has been awarded for her marketing skills and high sales achievements.

Jenny relocated to Astoria Pointe in 2008, a Drug and Alcohol Rehabilitation Treatment Center for Women, located near Portland, Oregon. Her job description is Referral Coordinator, Intake and Marketing. She follows up on all referrals, engaging in sales calls and marketing. Additionally, Jenny continually explores new geographical locations and educates others about the residential treatment program.

Formidable

As forever goes to know your secret thoughts
and to be a part of you inside of your head
we were in love combined of one another once
becoming you forever to know the way you feel
and you becoming me to know me too that way
of the way possession knows in that certain way
knowing the love you felt for me as I felt for you
that memory will not forget nor erase the days
we spent in fondling each other's dreams of faith
spent dreaming as caring soul mates do in time
to became one united thing never wanting to end
and if there ever would be such an end of time
to be in caring thoughts of you in love with me
given in your longings as we pledged together
to love and honor and be together until we died
as things let go now that have become that way
as time flies now to ask does it really matter
if the world goes around another lonely day
without you now and days on end without you
who once believed that love would never end
nurtured by that thought of us on holy ground
and you without me now in the vastness of time
only cherished memories now to hold held fast
with arms and bodies of hearts that can't let go
no matter what has come between us to what end
become now so sadly growing old without you
still in love and missing you so much dear Jenny.
It's too hard unbearable now to ever say goodbye.
In your heart you know you always belong to me.

Gary Koniz

The Point at Lake Awosting in Minnewaska Park, NY
Where Jenny and I … and Sophie … Swam Across … and Back

"ALL THINGS"

The Religion of The Yaki Faith, as it was taught to me by The Yaki Indians, is a very simple Faith to understand and to practice, based to the certain knowledge that Everything To Exist, Exists In The Concept Of The Creator Mind, As Spirit In The Form Of Matter, and that there is nothing to exist that is not a Spirit Form In The Mind Of The Creator, Who Is "All One Thing" To Exist In Many Separate And Universally Equal Parts, All Being "The Same Self" As The Creator Is, To Exist.

And as such, that Everything To Exist, can the virtue of that comprehension, communicate with Itself of Its Separate and Equal Parts of The Relationship Together In Unity With The One Self Of The Creator Mind, by The Telepathic Communication, of the sense, known to each of us as The Thought Process in all its powers to manifest, in verbal thought communication and by thought images.

And to the understanding of The Yaki Mind in that way, that the Creator is therefore affectionately referred to by The Title of, "ALL THINGS," Who Is reverently spoken for as "The Maker of All Things To Exist," and Who is thereby Cherished, of All Its Separate Manifestation, with Great Affection for the reason in that way of understanding The Creator's Necessity to be fondly regarded AS A Being, for The Unique Self of What The Creator Is In The Profound Need Of Being Well Thought Of And Cared After, and so on in the manner Of Being Cherished, To Respect All The Life and Well-Being of Everything That There Is To Exist of The Creator's Mind, named The Creation, as we find it, or to say, as we are immersed in It, and inextricably connected to everything there is in the course of our daily pursuits at life here among The Rest of What Is, in need to be fondly cared after.

So therefore, everything then is to be regarded equally in the manner of respect for the value of its existence, whether It be a living organism in the animated sense, to exist as vegetation, or as inanimate objects, in the need to be respected and regarded in cherishment and in the manner of reverence for Its existence.

The Creator is also in that light of comprehension not to be thought of in the way of Human Anthropocentric terms entirely, and also not so to be thought of in the terms of sexual gender entirely, in that The Creator is not exclusively male or female, and neither animated life, vegetable, or mineral inanimate, to be thought of, but "All Things" to be conceived of simultaneously, and with an orientation that is neither personal or impersonal in regard to us.

The Creator is Something, or Someone, of a Being in definition who we are incapable of comprehending, and so therefore we do not try. But we rest in the knowledge that we exist within The Mind of, "All Things," Who Is A Supernatural Being Unfathomable To Us, neither to be regarded as benevolent or hostile but only as we find It to be, and in the learning to get along with Everything To Exist. And Who is not thought of as a Human Being with Supernatural Powers.

And in that The Creator is a Supernatural Power, there is no limit to what the imagination of The Creator can produce At Will, To Respect of such Unlimited Thought Description To Become Real. And that to be a part of such description, we only need to be in silence posture for a while and attune ourselves with the proper way of The Creator's Intent to do what is right upon the way of the life we face.

Be humble about your ways upon The Earth as you go, and take precautions not to scare anyone. For in so frightening anyone you lose the nature of the supernatural quality you are seeking to inspire within you.

Neither ask for, nor receive, any sum of money from anyone, unless it is earned respectfully in a decent way by working for it in the legitimate fashion of the market place. For in doing so you will either be at a loss of respect for the one you give the money to, or the one who gives you the money unearned will less respect you. Such is the nature of personal power.

Neither go to brothels or dribble your seed upon the ground in fornication upon yourself, and do not ever be involved to homosexual behavior, nor to any engaging of sex with the animal kingdom; and with all, which defiles a man.

And don't dwell of sexual topics in the mind. For in everything that way you are less of a man to yourself and to The Creator Who Is Always There with you in your mind, and with Whom that you always need to be courting for bonding with in Eternal Nature. Such is the condition of personal power as well.

Never believe that you are capable of doing anything without The Creator, Who Is Always Ever-present To You, and Who is always standing by you to give you counsel and consent.

Don't lie, or cheat, or steal, or kill anything, or do anything bad, and you will know the way.

Never ask a woman her name, if you are a male, and if you are a female, never ask a man his name, or inquire if they are married or available. For you will never find true love in that fashion of inquiry. You will only prove yourself silly and make yourself weak in the nature of personal power.

Don't cast "eyes" on the opposite sex, and especially for the males in sizing up the women in attraction for sexual pastime. And especially for the males, don't talk with another person's spouse or relationship without their invited permission, as you will lose the grace and friendship of that person to jealousy for such uninvited involvement

Become old gracefully. Don't try to be younger than your years permit in your garb or habits of style about the town.

Always find someone who is more knowledgeable than you to explain things.

Forget where you have been and what you have done, they are worthless to ruminate on and ultimately will bring you to a bad place in your head. Worthless things are to be forgotten completely and rumination will be the death of you.

Avoid strong alcohol drink, and don't do drugs needlessly.

Walk carefully about The Earth and do not regard The Insects as your enemy, although you will have to kill a few and more than many of the biting ones before your time is at an end here.

Be Mindful of The Life Beneath You as you walk and try not to step on any of the tiny creatures as you pass, although you may not be able to help it.

If you have to cross a certain way and there are too many ants, in example, to negotiate without treading on the ants who are in your path. Don't think about it as you walk, and pass on, and try to walk lightly and not to "scuff" your feet, as an ant may survive a light footfall, but a scuff might damage their tiny parts. The Ants will respect you if you have no mind in innocence to their being trod upon in necessity to your pursuit of travel.

Be careful when you walk in the woods not to break any of the limbs and tiny branches of the bushes and the trees and not to step needlessly on the vegetation of whatever variety of plants beneath your feet as you go. All the vegetation values its parts and reflects to them in their way, as you value the external members of your own body, of your fingers and toes and your arms and legs. In that way you will find peace there.

Behave in all necessity with the animals you encounter, and don't go startling them for sport. Be respectful and you will always be welcome. And be mindful of the killer animals, not to infuriate them, and nor to antagonize them into attack for your sport of killing them in a needless way.

Always respect The Inanimate, don't throw things around and break the dishes or the glassware in your home, as these things regard themselves in a special place of sentiment to you. And take care of all your personal possessions with that same care of regard, and extent that throughout your travels upon The Earth. For in any disrespectful regard of The Inanimate, you will lose the happiness of your way upon The Earth.

Don't be a bully to your fellow man, and you will see the end of your travails here by your destiny to be pure of heart in intent.

Have an Impeccable Will about you, and in that you will be happy and satisfied with yourself and all you do.

There is no end to the lessons to be set down here for contemplation. But in the things as are set down, and in your abiding to of what has been discussed, you will be a healthy being and will join in on The Creator's Eternal Path in good composure. Trust that you are Entrusted To The Creator's Care and To Always Respectfully Regard The Creator's Mind As Your Own.

Zen Harmony

I became enchanted with the idea of learning to control my mind to be in complete harmony to God's mind, that we, as a Church, could use the training of Zen Buddhism to accomplish. And which I want at this time to pass on to you, the intelligent study of applied Zen Awareness. Study it and apply it to your own life. Zen means - action in awareness – being completely in the present moment.

Qualities include – expansive vision – effortless focus – a feeling of equanimity and timelessness – abundant confidence and complete freedom from anxiety and doubt – clarity – commitment – composure – confidence – genuineness – gentleness – fearlessness and dignity – and warriorship. Feeling of being "in the "Zone."

Practiced of Buddhist meditation and psychology – Organizing Principle – Preparation (clarity – commitment – and composure,) Action (feeling confident – focused – and in the flow,) and Response (fostering confidence by building on success and learning from mistakes without negativity,) are some of the Zen Practice essential ingredients.

Stay in the present – clear your mind – and stay focused – don't get down on yourself – change unhelpful habits. Focus – Calmness – and Confidence are the essential ingredients. Instead of focusing on what's wrong – focus on what's right. Poise – Humor – Humility – Joy – Majesty – and Elegance enrich a person's life. Don't complain about anything, not even to yourself, is one Zen motto. Mindfulness and Awareness Practice - Make your mind and ally instead of an enemy. How to stay calm – avoid mental mistakes and reduce frustration.
Ultimately your mind has the capacity to be as big as the universe – the more open our mind – the bigger it is. The more consumed by worry and petty concerns, the smaller it is. Whatever you encounter – connect with the space around it.

Your mind is like a wild horse in the beginning – let your mind run until it settles down – when settled you can tame it – when tamed you can train it – and then you can ride the mind wherever you want it to go.

Fear of failure cripples the mind and becomes so powerful that our life is disrupted and the prophecy of the thought of what we fear has been fulfilled.

Thoughts arise in our mind – but they are not our mind. Realizing this creates a gap in the sequence of impulse to action in which we can choose how to respond rather than to automatically react. The Practice of working with thoughts is fundamental to Buddhism. No need for analyzing or judging thoughts – Rest your attention lightly on your breathing and your awareness of bodily sensations and other perceptions of sights, sounds, and smells. As thoughts arise - let them come and go.

In Buddhism, mind and awareness are synonymous. Awareness is open and spacious. Identify with awareness instead of contents. Small mind becomes Big Mind – detached from your thoughts. Thoughts have power over you only to the extent that you give it to them. It is a perception of richness – wholeness – that nowhere in our fundamental being is there anything that is flawed and in misery – acknowledging our basic goodness – taking the attitude that there is something fundamentally and essentially right with us – expressed with a feeling of Unconditional Confidence within ourselves as a self-fulfilling prophesy – taking the big perspective – fearless in the moment – to free oneself from ignorance and error in the light of truth and knowledge – inherent confidence. Self-defeating behavior is the undoing of ourselves.

Relate to yourself with your Intuitive Mind in focusing on your sense perception in avoidance of mental chatter going on – feeling your awareness with sense perceptions – preventing the arising of distracting thoughts about past or future results – sense perceptions can only happen in the present.

Breath deeply in and let any competing thoughts dissolve in the
breath as it goes back out into the atmosphere – and think of the
air itself as a substance of The Creator as you are doing it having
all encompassing space around and within you. Then in the
moment of openness that is left – step in and exercise your
thought of The Father, Who is to be you Anchor Thought and is
the aspect and foundation or your basic goodness in commitment
to the goal of perfection yourself and pre-acceptance of yourself –
taking the attitude that you can handle whatever results you
encounter. Our greatest interference is the fear of results, doubt
leads to confusion and anxiety.

Avoid daydreaming, the mind completely filled with images of
the past or future – asleep to the present moment. Cultivate and
strengthen positive self-image thoughts – practice getting into and
staying in focus, staying in the present expansive awareness.
Mindfulness and Awareness – Awareness is panoramic –
Mindfulness is one-pointed – Tendency to wander needs an
Anchor, a reference point to come back to, Who is always The
Father to contemplate with, and as that The Father is mindful of
ourselves also at all times in our contemplation of Him.
Mindfulness and the exercise of the counting of breaths is our
way out of the inner reflection of the mind into the big mind of
total awareness – the mixing of breath and mind together –
mixing breath and space. The nature of your mind is that you are
not your thought. Thoughts come and go.

Be as an observer of our thoughts — the more you are able to stay
in the present – the closer to The Creator's thought process and
deliberate purpose you become - Practice with purpose, a plan,
and with patience. Only in the present can we connect with our
nature of basic goodness and appreciate being alive. Purpose,
present focus, thoughts, feelings, perceptions, emotions, big mind,
small mind, conscious thoughts and subconscious thoughts,
thinking – intuitive – and critical mind, evaluates, judges, gives
descriptions, and interprets good and bad. Constructive feedback

linked with negative emotions is to be avoided. Focusing on what is wrong is to miss out on all that is good in our lives. Allow for mistakes without judging ourselves too harshly.

We can direct our mind to look for positive elements – riding the tamed horse. The ego-centered self-conscious mind is what needs to give up control. Intuitive mind, that is closest to The Father's instinct, is what needs to get control. You already know what to do, as your heart beats on its own. The Intuitive mind is an expert at running the body. You can also produce what you desire in a positive way as you can produce what you fear. Learn to go beyond fear. Clear your mind of negative images that undermine our confidence and replace those with positive ones. If you suppress fears and doubts they will fight their way back to the surface. When you find yourself caught-up with a thought – just step out of it without judgment. Take the bigger view. Let thoughts come and go and after awhile they will settle themselves and your mind will be clear.

Tame the mind. Be involved with the process in achieving and possessing a synchronized body and mind that is focuses in the present. Everything to do with harmony in the mind is stated by the wording – "Just So" like tuning the strings of a guitar, not too tight – not too loose, but "Just So." Reinforce good works with positive feelings and self encouragement – with a minimum of emotional distress. Maintain a sense of humor. Refrain from beating yourself up. Neither suppress nor indulge in the emotion, but drop the story line. It is important not to be consumed by negative reactions. Only in the present can we connect with our nature of basic goodness and appreciate being alive. And to the state of being as a warrior in this regard – never give up. Fear, anxiety and self-doubt create tension. Have unconditional confidence in our inherent basic goodness.

Stay in the process. Become thoroughly gentle and genuine. Find a way to enjoy yourself. "Look over" like that you didn't invent or create on you own, as a learning experience. It is your nature to learn and grow, giving, in the providing to yourself, or the right conditions. You can't force a flower to bloom. Nature unfolds of its own. Foster positive attitudes and intentions and be nonjudgmental towards yourself. It takes patience and practice to break yourself of bad habits, which begins with awareness of them. Human beings can't accept making a mistake, which forces up to be preoccupied with the negative. Positive intention and nonjudgmental awareness are the keys to idea supportive conditions. Judging ourselves creates the opposite of our positive intentions and undermines our inherent confidence in our ability to accomplish good intentions.

Our mental state affects our posture. Anxiety and fear make us tight and agitated. When we are discouraged or depressed we become heavy and sluggish. Maintaining a confident and positive attitude toward ourselves in perspective maintains a confident posture. Our experiences are temporary. Impermanence, and the acceptance of impermanence, are the basic teachings of Buddhism. Practicing Mindfulness and Awareness, developing insight and compassion, virtue (basic goodness in action,) worthiness, unconditional confidence, discipline, proper conduct, generosity, ethics, patience, humor (in the absence of self absorption,) and providing an open heart acceptance of our fellow human beings in mutual respect and with a vision of openness and compassion, is the inherent foundation of our Practice of Zen Buddhism. Gentleness means being kind to ourselves and considerate to others. Being inquisitive towards our mistakes is more interesting than frustration. Right Intention and Non-Judgmental Awareness is the proper atmosphere for continuous growth and learning, and to approach life with the attitude of fearlessness, or being more curious than afraid, and to the overall orientation to foster an enlightened society, that individuals can manifest peace, openness and compassion in relating to themselves and others.

Now you are ready and open for what life brings on and unafraid.

"Childe Roland to the Dark Tower Came"

by Robert Browning

English poet and playwright 5/7/1812 – 12/12/1889

I.

My first thought was, he lied in every word,
That hoary cripple, with malicious eye
Askance to watch the working of his lie
On mine, and mouth scarce able to afford
Suppression of the glee that pursed and scored
Its edge, at one more victim gained thereby.

II.

What else should he be set for, with his staff?
What, save to waylay with his lies, ensnare
All travellers who might find him posted there,
And ask the road? I guessed what skull-like laugh
Would break, what crutch 'gin write my epitaph
For pastime in the dusty thoroughfare,

III.

If at his counsel I should turn aside
Into that ominous tract which, all agree,
Hides the Dark Tower. Yet acquiescingly
I did turn as he pointed: neither pride
Nor hope rekindling at the end descried,
So much as gladness that some end might be.

IV.

For, what with my whole world-wide wandering,
What with my search drawn out thro' years, my hope
Dwindled into a ghost not fit to cope
With that obstreperous joy success would bring,
I hardly tried now to rebuke the spring
My heart made, finding failure in its scope.

V.

As when a sick man very near to death
Seems dead indeed, and feels begin and end
The tears and takes the farewell of each friend,
And hears one bid the other go, draw breath
Freelier outside ("since all is o'er," he saith,
"And the blow fallen no grieving can amend;")

VI.

While some discuss if near the other graves
Be room enough for this, and when a day
Suits best for carrying the corpse away,
With care about the banners, scarves and staves:
And still the man hears all, and only craves
He may not shame such tender love and stay.

VII.

Thus, I had so long suffered in this quest,
Heard failure prophesied so oft, been writ
So many times among "The Band" - to wit,
The knights who to the Dark Tower's search addressed
Their steps - that just to fail as they, seemed best,
And all the doubt was now—should I be fit?

VIII.

So, quiet as despair, I turned from him,
That hateful cripple, out of his highway
Into the path he pointed. All the day
Had been a dreary one at best, and dim
Was settling to its close, yet shot one grim
Red leer to see the plain catch its estray.

IX.

For mark! no sooner was I fairly found
Pledged to the plain, after a pace or two,
Than, pausing to throw backward a last view
O'er the safe road, 'twas gone; grey plain all round:

Nothing but plain to the horizon's bound.
I might go on; nought else remained to do.

X.
So, on I went. I think I never saw
Such starved ignoble nature; nothing throve:
For flowers - as well expect a cedar grove!
But cockle, spurge, according to their law
Might propagate their kind, with none to awe,
You'd think; a burr had been a treasure trove.

XI.
No! penury, inertness and grimace,
In some strange sort, were the land's portion. "See
Or shut your eyes," said Nature peevishly,
"It nothing skills: I cannot help my case:
'Tis the Last Judgment's fire must cure this place,
Calcine its clods and set my prisoners free."

XII.
If there pushed any ragged thistle-stalk
Above its mates, the head was chopped; the bents
Were jealous else. What made those holes and rents
In the dock's harsh swarth leaves, bruised as to baulk
All hope of greenness? 'tis a brute must walk
Pashing their life out, with a brute's intents.

XIII.
As for the grass, it grew as scant as hair
In leprosy; thin dry blades pricked the mud
Which underneath looked kneaded up with blood.
One stiff blind horse, his every bone a-stare,
Stood stupefied, however he came there:
Thrust out past service from the devil's stud!

XIV.
Alive? he might be dead for aught I know,

With that red gaunt and colloped neck a-strain,
And shut eyes underneath the rusty mane;
Seldom went such grotesqueness with such woe;
I never saw a brute I hated so;
He must be wicked to deserve such pain.

XV.
I shut my eyes and turned them on my heart.
As a man calls for wine before he fights,
I asked one draught of earlier, happier sights,
Ere fitly I could hope to play my part.
Think first, fight afterwards - the soldier's art:
One taste of the old time sets all to rights.

XVI.
Not it! I fancied Cuthbert's reddening face
Beneath its garniture of curly gold,
Dear fellow, till I almost felt him fold
An arm in mine to fix me to the place
That way he used. Alas, one night's disgrace!
Out went my heart's new fire and left it cold.

XVII.
Giles then, the soul of honour - there he stands
Frank as ten years ago when knighted first.
What honest men should dare (he said) he durst.
Good - but the scene shifts - faugh! what hangman hands
Pin to his breast a parchment? His own bands
Read it. Poor traitor, spit upon and curst!

XVIII.
Better this present than a past like that;
Back therefore to my darkening path again!
No sound, no sight as far as eye could strain.
Will the night send a howlet or a bat?
I asked: when something on the dismal flat
Came to arrest my thoughts and change their train.

XIX.
A sudden little river crossed my path
As unexpected as a serpent comes.
No sluggish tide congenial to the glooms;
This, as it frothed by, might have been a bath
For the fiend's glowing hoof - to see the wrath
Of its black eddy bespate with flakes and spumes.

XX.
So petty yet so spiteful! All along
Low scrubby alders kneeled down over it;
Drenched willows flung them headlong in a fit
Of mute despair, a suicidal throng:
The river which had done them all the wrong,
Whate'er that was, rolled by, deterred no whit.

XXI.
Which, while I forded, - good saints, how I feared
To set my foot upon a dead man's cheek,
Each step, or feel the spear I thrust to seek
For hollows, tangled in his hair or beard!
—It may have been a water-rat I speared,
But, ugh! it sounded like a baby's shriek.

XXII.
Glad was I when I reached the other bank.
Now for a better country. Vain presage!
Who were the strugglers, what war did they wage,
Whose savage trample thus could pad the dank
Soil to a plash? Toads in a poisoned tank,
Or wild cats in a red-hot iron cage—

XXIII.
The fight must so have seemed in that fell cirque.
What penned them there, with all the plain to choose?
No foot-print leading to that horrid mews,

None out of it. Mad brewage set to work
Their brains, no doubt, like galley-slaves the Turk
Pits for his pastime, Christians against Jews.

XXIV.
And more than that - a furlong on - why, there!
What bad use was that engine for, that wheel,
Or brake, not wheel - that harrow fit to reel
Men's bodies out like silk? with all the air
Of Tophet's tool, on earth left unaware,
Or brought to sharpen its rusty teeth of steel.

XXV.
Then came a bit of stubbed ground, once a wood,
Next a marsh, it would seem, and now mere earth
Desperate and done with; (so a fool finds mirth,
Makes a thing and then mars it, till his mood
Changes and off he goes!) within a rood—
Bog, clay and rubble, sand and stark black dearth.

XXVI.
Now blotches rankling, coloured gay and grim,
Now patches where some leanness of the soil's
Broke into moss or substances like boils;
Then came some palsied oak, a cleft in him
Like a distorted mouth that splits its rim
Gaping at death, and dies while it recoils.

XXVII.
And just as far as ever from the end!
Nought in the distance but the evening, nought
To point my footstep further! At the thought,
A great black bird, Apollyon's bosom-friend,
Sailed past, nor beat his wide wing dragon-penned
That brushed my cap—perchance the guide I sought.

XXVIII.

For, looking up, aware I somehow grew,
'Spite of the dusk, the plain had given place
All round to mountains - with such name to grace
Mere ugly heights and heaps now stolen in view.
How thus they had surprised me, - solve it, you!
How to get from them was no clearer case.

XXIX.
Yet half I seemed to recognise some trick
Of mischief happened to me, God knows when—
In a bad dream perhaps. Here ended, then,
Progress this way. When, in the very nick
Of giving up, one time more, came a click
As when a trap shuts - you're inside the den!

XXX.
Burningly it came on me all at once,
This was the place! those two hills on the right,
Crouched like two bulls locked horn in horn in fight;
While to the left, a tall scalped mountain... Dunce,
Dotard, a-dozing at the very nonce,
After a life spent training for the sight!

XXXI.
What in the midst lay but the Tower itself?
The round squat turret, blind as the fool's heart
Built of brown stone, without a counterpart
In the whole world. The tempest's mocking elf
Points to the shipman thus the unseen shelf
He strikes on, only when the timbers start.

XXXII.
Not see? because of night perhaps? - why, day
Came back again for that! before it left,
The dying sunset kindled through a cleft:
The hills, like giants at a hunting, lay
Chin upon hand, to see the game at bay,—

"Now stab and end the creature - to the heft!"

XXXIII.
Not hear? when noise was everywhere! it tolled
Increasing like a bell. Names in my ears
Of all the lost adventurers my peers,—
How such a one was strong, and such was bold,
And such was fortunate, yet each of old
Lost, lost! one moment knelled the woe of years.

XXXIV.
There they stood, ranged along the hillsides, met
To view the last of me, a living frame
For one more picture! in a sheet of flame
I saw them and I knew them all. And yet
Dauntless the slug-horn to my lips I set,
And blew *"Childe Roland to the Dark Tower came."*

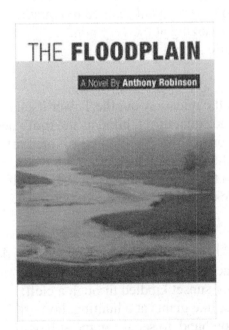

Set in 1970s America, an era that challenged sexual and cultural norms, Anthony Robinson's riveting new novel, The Floodplain, tells the story of Professor Rick Forester, his wife Chloe and their two children, whose lives are forever changed when Chloe, a fledgling psychotherapist, becomes romantically entangled with her mentor, the charismatic psychiatrist Dr. Evan Kendrix. Kendrix, a leading interpreter of techniques in humanistic psychology, lures Chloe with promises of success and an exciting new life.

Rick Forester watches helplessly as his wife becomes increasingly involved with Kendrix. But Kendrix is not what he seems. A flagrant manipulator of women, he soon betrays Chloe. Chloe harbors psychiatric demons of her own, and her betrayal triggers a downward spiral. Rick, who has moved out of their large old house and taken an apartment in the town, must put his life on hold and return to keep his family together.

But things have gone too far. Chloe, depressed and confused, sees her dream of empowerment and success shattered, and she turns Rick's shotgun on herself.

Her distraught husband must struggle with his loss, his murderous feelings toward Kendrix, and his own sense of complicity in the tragedy. Rick must take on the care of his children. When, a few months after Chloe's death, Dr. Kendrix capriciously begins a flirtation with Forester's 15-year-old daughter, Rick at last takes action.

In the last part of the narrative, events culminate in a murder and a trial. The themes of action and inaction, guilt and innocence, are played out, and in the end Rick comes to terms with himself.

Available at: Codhill.com - Codhill Press
1 Arden Lane, New Paltz, N.Y. 12561

Stopping by Woods on a Snowy Evening

Whose woods these are I think I know.
His house is in the village though;
He will not see me stopping here
To watch his woods fill up with snow.

My little horse must think it queer
To stop without a farmhouse near
Between the woods and frozen lake
The darkest evening of the year.

He gives his harness bells a shake
To ask if there is some mistake.
The only other sound's the sweep
Of easy wind and downy flake.

The woods are lovely, dark and deep.
But I have promises to keep,
And miles to go before I sleep,
And miles to go before I sleep.

Robert Frost
New Hampshire
1923

Wallkill River Valley In Winter

The Gunks In Winter

"Home Is Where The Heart Is"

"Happiness"

Sundance

May 18, 2009

Gary L. Koniz
9480 Princeton Square Blvd. S., #815
Jacksonville, FL 32256

Dear Mr. Koniz

I am writing on behalf of Robert Redford.

Mr. Redford has asked me to thank you for your kind letter inquiring about the possibility of him participating with you in Veterans health issues. While he appreciated the invitation to participate with you, I am afraid that he is not in a position to consider involvement. His current film schedule is devoted to several successive projects. This, along with his ongoing business commitments, makes it impossible for him to take on any other obligations.

Mr. Redford did appreciate your thinking of him. He extends his best wishes.

Sincerely,
Amber Smith

The Sundance Group   3520 N. University Suite 100   Provo, UT 84604   Phone: 801-705-8996   Fax: 801-705-8997

Congressional Candidate Gary L. Koniz

Gary L. Koniz

2012 CAMPAIGN FOR CONGRESS

United States Representative

District	Candidate	Status	Primary	General
1	Bryan, James E. (DEM)	Active		
	Miller, Jefferson B. (REP) *Incumbent	Active		
	Samek, Jason Michael (NPA)	Active		
2	Argenziano, Nancy (INT)	Active		
	Peters, Alvin L. (DEM)	Active		
3	Kolb, LeAnne (REP)	Active		
	Yost, Michael F. "MIKE" F. (REP)	Active		
4	Crenshaw, Ander (REP) *Incumbent	Active		
	Klauder, James R. (REP)	Active		
*****	Koniz, Gary L. (DEM)	Active		
	Lieberman, Brian Michael (NPA)	Active		
	Pueschel, Deborah Katz (REP)	Active		

About The Candidate

Citizens Alliance Coalition

Mobilizing As An Aggressive Movement
Of Personal Involvement

In A Call To Action To Correct
The Serious Errors In Our Society

We Have This Time In Our History
To Achieve Our Nation's Greatness

Let's Get Organized - Get To The Polls
And Make Change Happen

Together We Can Make A Difference

The Candidate Gary L. Koniz is a Freelance Journalist currently involved with many of the great Humanitarian and Social Causes of our time and with troubleshooting the developing crisis concerns of state as they affect us imperatively in the context of our Society and within the realm of our ability as a people Politically to resolve.

He was born in Fort Meade, Maryland in 1946 and was raised and educated in The Mid-Hudson Valley Region of New York State. He served in The United States Armed Forces from 1964-1967 with The Army Corps of Engineers as a Heavy Equipment Operator and
fought in The Vietnam War in 1966. After his discharge he was fortunate to be taken-in by The International Union of Operating Engineers and worked as a Heavy Equipment Operator for Local 137 for ten years. He also earned a Commercial Pilot License

during that time under The G.I. Bill with single and multi-engine land ratings and later worked as a Charter Pilot for a local airport and flew extensively throughout the Eastern and Central United States and Canada, flying passengers and cargo.

In 1970 he began to undertake his college studies to his life's "Calling of God" to be a writer. He attended and graduated Summa Cum Laude from The State University at New Paltz, NY with a Bachelors Degree in English/Humanities/Creative Writing in 1974. After graduation attended graduate studies for several years and taught Freshman English as a Teaching Assistant at SUNY University before beginning his professional writing career in taking a job as Project Development Team Supervisor, creating employment positions and writing Grant Proposals for The Dutchess County C.E.T.A. Program (Comprehensive Training and Employment Act,) under The Carter Administration.

Immediately following the conclusion of his successful tenure with the C.E.T.A. Program, in 1979 (having fulfilled his quota of creating over 3,500 C.E.T.A. Job placements for the needy with county-wide not-for-profit agencies locally,) he then took a job with The Poughkeepsie, NY School District in the position of Public Information Officer as a Reporter/Photographer covering school events in connection with the local Poughkeepsie Journal newspaper; and with which newspaper that he began doing his Freelance Journalism work in extensive investigative journalism with them for the next ten years covering The War On Drugs (becoming involved directly with President Ronald Reagan's Task Force in 1981, "To Break The Cone of Silence Surrounding Organized Crime Activities," regarding The Drug-Chemical Warfare Subversive Terrorism occurring in the aftermath of The Vietnam War,) and also involved with many other issues of; The Economy, Labor, The Economy, Race Relations, Proper Moral Direction for The Nation, and The Environment, before relocating to Buffalo, NY in 1989.

In Buffalo he became involved with then Bishop Henry Mansell of The Diocese of Buffalo on an expansive Christian Project of Social Reform and began work as an advisor and media correspondent with Senator Daniel Patrick Moynihan on The War

On Drugs, and other vital issue of the hour; that as well involved
working closely on all levels of the government with many other
Political Leaders, and notably Senator Alfonse D'Amato, Senator
Jay Rockefeller, (with whom he assisted in working on the
Senator's 1992 Presidential Campaign Platform as a Policy
Platform Speech Writer, and with whom he continues on with to
the present day in correspondence,) Senator Edward Kennedy,
(and with whom he worked and as well as to the Drug War.) He
also worked closely with, and in conjunction to AFL-CIO
President John J. Sweeney, on Economic/Labor Issues, and was
successfully involving with raising The Minimum Wage, and to
the reforming of The Minimum Wage Law itself to the creation of
a Prevailing Fair Wage and Benefits Legislation based to The
Federal Government's General Schedule, (GS) Standards
formula, and for Universal IRS Deductible Health Care, (as yet to
be accomplished.) He also worked very closely with NYS
Congressman Jack Quinn, (in particular,) and with New York
State Governor George Pataki, with New York State Senator
William T. Stackowski, New York State Assemblyman Sam
Hoyt, Erie County Executive Dennis Gorski, The City of Buffalo
Mayor Anthony Masiello, with Local, State, and Federal Law
Enforcement, with Government Agencies, (most notably The
Federal Aviation Administration,) and with The National Guard
and Central Command on The Drug War.

   During this time also he was directly responsible for the
clearing of Buffalo's air with The Environmental Protection
Agency, (EPA,) concerning the local Bethlehem Steel Mill in
stopping it from its burning of low grade coal with high sulfur
benzene carcinogens emissions; and for the resolution of The
Native American Indians' Tax Treaty Case, with New York
State's Governor George Pataki, (that was resolved in the favor of
The Seneca Indian Nation for New York State not to Tax on their
Reservations in Violation of the existing Treaty With The Seneca,
which was in a state of War Crisis,) during this time.

   The Author also did work with the Actor Larry Hagman for
several years as a contributing writer and was instrumental in
creating the final episode of "Dallas," entitled, "The Dallas

Reunion," in resolution to the tragic ending of the show. He was also a Correspondent, Political Press Agent, and Information News Source Advisor to The Editor of The Buffalo News, Mr. Murray Light, from 1989 – 2000 (and in major contribution to his War Press in Policy Confrontation to the Drug War and to other crisis of the era,) and was successful in forming a united public army around The Buffalo News in influence and with the ability to generate dynamic social change, (particularly to The Drug War at the time,) before moving to Jacksonville, FL in 2000 where he currently resides with his wife Kathleen and works as a National Correspondent and Lobbyist for; Veterans Affairs, Labor Rights, the Economy and Environment, and is a Contributing Editorial Policy Writer for many newspapers and agencies; including The Buffalo News, The New York Times, CNN, The Poughkeepsie Journal, The Washington Post, and with The Florida Times Union of Jacksonville, FL. He is also a Contributing Freelance Writer for Military Officer Magazine, The Catholic New Service, and The Catholic Transcript.

He became involved with Journalism as a Call of The Spirit to reform the many ways of errors of humanity In Sympathy to God that has become his life's quest in personal determination. And it is to his belief that we only need to have the proper imprint of guidance in our lives to become the true potential of our divine-selves as human beings and to know God in appreciation of our existence to be healed, and that is all we need to realize, given to the corrections of any errors, to persevere.) The Author plans to continue his work in support of Social Reform, of inspiring people and to enlighten the ways of humanity, offering hope in salvation of human suffering until the time for work runs out.

Gary L. Koniz
9480 Princeton Square Blvd. S., #815
Jacksonville, FL 32256
gary.koniz@hotmail.com
http://www.lulu.com/spotlight/greenskeeper6

Awosting Falls and Split Rock

What Was Lost Was Found Again.

And As Our Storybook Comes To A Close
To Say That The Living Of Life Is Its Own Reward
For Its Experience Is A Miracle.

In The End We Will All
In Our Humble Ways
Settle Those Issues
Of Whose Country It Is
And What Our Standards Are To Be.

Is There Something You Feel
You Need To Be Doing?

All Is Darkness In The End.
But Our Memory Of Life Together Lives On
And On Into The Timeless Eternity.
We Need To Be On The Move.
There Is No Tomorrow And No Time Left
For Plans Not Laid For Tomorrow Today.

"In Nomine Patris, et Fillii, et Spiritus Sancti"

Bible Quotes are taken from George M. Lamsa's Translation
Of The Ancient Eastern Text From The Aramaic of The Peshitta

THE APOSTLE'S CREED

I believe in One God, the Father almighty, creator of heaven and earth, and in things seen and unseen. I believe in Jesus Christ, His only Son, our Lord, Who was conceived by the power of the Holy Spirit and born of the Virgin Mary. He suffered under Pontius Pilate, was crucified, died, and was buried. He descended into hell and on the third day he rose again. He ascended into heaven, and is seated at the right hand of the Father. He will come again to judge the living and the dead. I believe in the Holy Spirit, the Holy Catholic Church, the communion of saints, the forgiveness of sins, the resurrection of the body, and the life everlasting. Amen.

... 30 ...

For Andrew at Rock & Snow

"Thanks For The Inspiration"

"ROCK & SNOW" ROCK CLIMBING STORE
44 MAIN STREET DOWNTOWN NEW PALTZ, NY

Made in the USA
Middletown, DE
05 November 2023

41898249R00355